Medicinal Resources of the Tropical Forest

Biology and Resource Management Series
Michael J. Balick, Anthony B. Anderson, and Kent H. Redford, Editors

Biology and Resource Management Series
Edited by Michael J. Balick, Anthony B. Anderson, and Kent H. Redford

Medicinal Resources of the Tropical Forest

BIODIVERSITY AND ITS IMPORTANCE TO HUMAN HEALTH

Edited by Michael J. Balick

Elaine Elisabetsky

and Sarah A. Laird

COLUMBIA UNIVERSITY PRESS

New York

Columbia University Press
New York   Chichester, West Sussex
Copyright © 1996 Columbia University Press
All rights reserved

Library of Congress Cataloging-in-Publication Data

Medicinal resources of the tropical forest : biodiversity and its
   importance to human health / edited by Michael J. Balick, Elaine
Elisabetsky, Sarah A. Laird.
      p.   cm. — (Biology and resource management series)
   Includes bibliographical references and index.
   ISBN 0–231–10170–8 (cloth)
   1. Materia medica, Vegetable.   2. Rain forest plants.
3. Ethnobotany.   4. Traditional medicine.   I. Balick, Michael J.,
1952–   .   II. Elisabetsky, Elaine.   III. Laird, Sarah A.
IV. Series.
RS164.M377   1996
615′.32′0913—dc20   95–13809
                                                                                              CIP

Printed in the United States of America

c   10   9   8   7   6   5   4   3   2   1

Contents

Foreword

Norman R. Farnsworth

I N *Medicinal Resources of the Tropical Forest,* Michael J. Balick, Elaine Elisabetsky, and Sarah A. Laird have brought together the most impressive array of topics and distinguished authors covering the areas of biodiversity, conservation, ethnomedicine, ethnobotany, pharmacognosy, drug discovery, and the practical aspects of natural products chemistry that I have had the pleasure of reading.

Only during the past decade, or less, have American pharmaceutical firms developed an intense interest in drug development from plants, particularly those from tropical forests. This interest has naturally brought to the surface a number of potential problems regarding intellectual property rights, conservation, and ecology issues. If these issues are not resolved satisfactorily, the pharmaceutical and herbal industries in the United States and other countries as well will turn their backs on this area of research. If this occurs, not only will new drugs from higher plants be a thing of the past, but also an understanding of the safety and efficacy of herbal remedies—now used by 75 percent of the earth's population, especially in the developing countries—will be set back.

Consequently, several aspects of research on tropical plants need to be addressed, i.e., conservation, drug development for new secondary metabolites, discovery of secondary metabolites that can be used as biochemical or pharmacological tools in research, discovery of "lead" compounds from plants that will serve as templates for synthetic modifications, safety and efficacy issues for extracts of plants used by many as herbal medicines, intellectual property rights, and the continuation of ethnobotanical studies to prevent a loss of useful information before it disappears from the planet.

I believe that *Medicinal Resources of the Tropical Forest,* edited by authorities in the fields of ethnobotany (Michael J. Balick), ethnopharmacology (Elaine Elisabetsky), and conservation (Sarah A. Laird), covers, in a unique way, all the topics mentioned above. This volume is greatly needed, includes most of the world experts in their respective fields of interest, and should be a strong positive voice for the future implementation of rationally designed explorations into tropical forests for substances that will benefit humankind.

Research Professor of Pharmacognosy
and Senior University Scholar

*Program for Collaborative Research
in the Pharmaceutical Sciences*

COLLEGE OF PHARMACY
University of Illinois at Chicago

Preface

TROPICAL biodiversity has figured prominently in the news of the past few years as a potential wonder source of new medicines, which, in turn, might contribute to the conservation of biodiversity. This volume is a compilation of papers that assess the potential for this strategy to yield new medicines, improve health care, and contribute to conservation of the tremendous biological and cultural diversity of the tropics.

Tropical forests contain a significant percentage of the world's species, including those with unique and more varied biochemical modes of defense and survival than their temperate counterparts. Consequently, tropical forests can provide natural product chemists with invaluable compounds or starting points for new drug development. Although relatively few tropical species have been studied for their pharmaceutical potential (generally accepted to be less than 1%), the tropics have yielded numerous invaluable pharmaceutical compounds, including the anticancer agents vincristine and vinblastine from *Catharanthus roseus;* the muscle relaxant d-tubocurarine from *Chondodendron* and *Strychnos* species, which were originally used in the Amazon for arrow poisons; and steroids from *Dioscorea* species. These examples grew out of research programs initiated in the early or middle parts of this century, programs that had largely been abandoned by the late 1970s. After decades of decline, however, natural products research is once again on the rise, and a number of pharmaceutical companies and university and government research institutes are actively pursuing the structurally diverse compounds contained within tropical species for their mechanism-based screening programs. A number of promising compounds have resulted from this recent round of natural products research, including four species having anti-HIV activity under study by the National Cancer Institute; these are found in the genera of *Ancistrocladus* in Cameroon, *Calophyllum* in Malaysia, *Conospermum* in Australia, and *Homolanthus* in western Samoa.

But pharmaceutical products are a small component of the medical history and potential of tropical biodiversity. Traditional, largely plant-based, medical systems continue to provide primary health care to more than 75% of the world's population. These systems, of varying scale and formality, produce effective, affordable medicines stemming from long histories of local use. A number of programs are currently underway to research and record traditional uses of plants as a starting point for pharmaceutical drug discovery. This information can provide an invaluable head start for industry research efforts, and many pharmaceutical companies incorporate ethnobotanical information into their research and development (R&D) programs. The research strategy of Shaman Pharmaceuticals, Inc., for example, is based explicitly on popular, traditional uses of plants.

In many cases throughout the tropics, the erosion of traditional cultures has led to an impoverishment of local medicine. A number of programs, such as IME-PLAM in Mexico, AMETRA in Peru, TRAMIL in the Caribbean, and CURPHA-METRA in Rwanda, have been established to record, scientifically study, and distribute medicines based on traditional uses of medicinal plants. These programs shore up and build upon local knowledge of medicinal plants and existing medical systems to develop more effective health care systems within the context of local health, economic, and social conditions.

Plant-based medicines are also processed and traded extensively in the regional and international herbal medicine markets that serve consumers in both tropical and temperate regions. Commercialized herbal medicine, as distinct from traditional medicine, is marketed and consumed outside the cultures and geographic regions from which the plants and their use originated. A growing recognition of the limits of isolated compounds in treating many chronic conditions and diseases, and of the potential for plant-based medicines to provide a more affordable and often more effective alternative, has led to a rapid growth in the herbal medicine industry over the past decade.

The papers in this volume discuss and detail issues regarding "medicine" as it is manifested in these three systems—the traditional, herbal, and pharmaceutical. It is important to make a distinction among these different types of medicine and to recognize that each has very different cultural, economic, and social implications and tends to involve very different players. One cannot speak of tropical biodiversity and medicine and produce a single image in the minds of readers. For example, a single plant might provide a lead compound for a pharmaceutical product, which then goes through many derivations and might in the end be manufactured by synthesis. The same plant could be cultivated and processed in the Amazon into formulations of herbal medicines sold in Germany or could be mixed with a variety of other species to be consumed as a medicinal tea by members of a community living in the area where the plant species is endemic. Clearly, tropical biodiversity is manifested as medicine in many very different ways. But these medical systems play complementary roles in health care and in no way can substitute for one another. Medicine is not a linear progression; there exists no ideal system into which all others, given the required economic, social, and cultural conditions, will eventually transform.

Traditional, herbal, and pharmaceutical medicines can also play very different but complementary roles in conservation programs in the tropics. The process by which pharmaceutical products are identified and developed has the most tenuous link with local communities and conservation but has the potential to generate revenues well beyond the scale of other medicines. A portion of these revenues can, in turn, be channeled to conservation programs, the bulk of which are chronically underfunded. The sheer scale of pharmaceutical revenues can also support policy arguments for conservation based on the enormous option values held within biologically diverse areas. Because of the small number of products developed per samples collected, however, the chances for this strategy to provide revenues for a wide spectrum of conservation programs are small, and the type of benefits returned to conservation and local communities during the research phase of drug development become of greater importance. At this stage, benefits usually take the form of training, supply of equipment, infrastructure-building, education, health care, and other, more informal services. It is important that relationships between tropical country institutions or communities and commercial collectors be well structured to allow for significant advance benefits, owing to the small likelihood of commercial product development from each collection. Additionally, because the vast majority of pharmaceutical R&D takes place outside the most biologically and culturally diverse regions of the world, these relationships should include steps to increase the capacity for tropical country institutions and communities to better research and utilize their indigenous biological and intellectual resources.

Commercial herbal medicine products generate far less in revenues than a pharmaceutical product but also require far less time and money to develop. As with pharmaceutical products, herbal medicines developed from endemic species or traditional knowledge can provide revenues for conservation programs and local communities in the form of royalties. Generally, however, economic benefits are restricted to the cultivation or harvesting of commercial species and, in some cases, the processing of these species into extracts. These activities have the potential to provide an important source of income for local communities and can make sustainable use of the forest resource a realistic option. Commercialized herbal medicine products can also be sold locally as a more affordable and, in some cases, more effective alternative to pharmaceutical compounds. Similarly, programs to standardize and distribute medicines based on traditional systems can create economic opportunities for local communities and provide a reliable and affordable form of health care in the short and long term. Overharvesting of species in the wild for pharmaceutical, herbal, and traditional medicines has often resulted in the depletion of valuable species, and any program that attempts to promote the use of these species must incorporate strategies for the sustainable sourcing of raw materials.

The relationship among tropical biodiversity, conservation, and human health is clearly a complex one and should not be oversimplified. The most effective way in which health and conservation can be combined to serve the needs of local and international communities is by incorporating this complexity into a package of complementary activities, examples of which are presented in this book.

This volume is an effort to illustrate recent dialogue resulting from community, research, and industry programs working with tropical medical resources. Although a great deal of attention has been paid lately to the medical potential of tropical biodiversity, few references exist for information critical to a proper analysis of its potential and for a demonstration of some of the possibilities this approach has for health care and conservation. Included in this book are examples of the recent expansion of pharmaceutical industry R&D programs for tropical natural products, such as those of Merck, Shaman Pharmaceuticals, and Smith-Kline Beecham. Of great importance, but largely unknown, are the smaller, grass roots programs around the world that attempt, in some cases, to build local research and development expertise for pharmaceutical drug development and, in others, to build affordable, culturally appropriate health care systems from the vast local natural resource and knowledge base. In addition to illustrating the manner in which tropical species are used in health care, this volume provides an overview of the mechanisms by which the use of tropical medicinal species can offer benefits to communities in and around biologically diverse areas and contribute to the conservation of the biodiversity upon which human health largely depends.

Acknowledgments

Th is volume is a compilation of invited papers on the importance of tropical biodiversity, primarily plants, in the provision of primary health care as well as in the development of pharmaceutical products. It was expanded to include a number of papers from the proceedings of the Rainforest Alliance Periwinkle Project and the Institute of Economic Botany symposium "Tropical Forest Medical Resources and the Conservation of Biodiversity" held at Rockefeller University in January 1992. Many individuals contributed their time, expertise, and advice to the production of this volume, and we would like to thank the following:

Helena Albuquerque, Gloria Coruzzi, Gordon Cragg, Douglas Daly, Betty Farrusca, Nicholas Howard, Steven King, Jennifer Laird, Patricia Shanley, Elizabeth Skinner, Terry Sunderland, and Helene Weitzner, as well as the staff and volunteers of the Rainforest Alliance and The New York Botanical Garden, who helped make the symposium a success.

We are also grateful to the following for their sponsorship of the symposium: The Medical Research Division of the American Cyanamid Company, Bristol-Myers Squibb Pharmaceutical Research Institute, Bremer Public Relations, The Earth Environmental Tithing Trust, Glaxo Group Research Limited, Eileen R. Growald, Merck Sharp and Dohme Research Laboratories, Monsanto Company, Mycosearch Inc., SmithKline Beecham Pharmaceuticals Research and Development, Tom's of Maine, and the Underhill Foundation.

For their enthusiastic and meticulous help in typing, organizing, editing, and overall fine-tuning of these proceedings, we would like to thank Elizabeth Pecchia, Connie Barlow, Sandra Guiot, and Zoë Marchal. We appreciate the efforts of Willa Capraro, who, during the final editing stages, served as liaison between the editors and publisher, coordinated the flow of information between authors and editors, and generally tied up loose ends. Thanks also to Columbia University Press—in particular, to Bob Mobley for his careful copyediting, to Anne McCoy for shepherding the book through the production process, and to our series editor, Ed Lugenbeel, for his support and encouragement.

Medicinal Resources of the Tropical Forest

PART ONE

Biodiversity Prospecting, Drug Development, and Conservation

1

Natural Products and Medicine:
An Overview

Varro E. Tyler

SOMETIME in prehistory, in the part of the world that is now the country of Peru, a raging storm felled a giant tree that came to rest in a pool of stagnant water. It lay there for some time, the water leaching the various constituents—tannins, glycosides, sugars, and alkaloids—from the bark of the tree. Eventually, a native passed that way. He was extremely ill, burning with the fever that Hippocrates called intermittent, which during the Middle Ages was known as the ague, and which we today call malaria. His fever had caused intense thirst, and he drank copiously from the pond. Shortly thereafter a miracle occurred, and his fever vanished. The disease that proved fatal to such well-known victims as Alexander the Great had undergone remission.

Whether the native drank repeatedly from the pool as the fever recurred and how it was that he associated his cure with the bark of the immense tree lying in the water, we do not know. We do not really know whether this imagined scenario approaches the truth relative to the discovery of the utility of cinchona bark in treating malaria. But it is possible, because at some time, some place, something like this had to happen so human beings could wrest the secret of the fever bark tree and use it to cure human ailments (Jaramillo-Arango 1950).

In the beginning, all drugs were natural—animal, vegetable, and mineral. Primitive peoples not only discovered that cinchona bark cured intermittent fevers, but they also found that chewing coca leaves numbed the tongue and reduced the appetite, that feeding ergotized grain to pregnant animals caused those animals to abort, that chewing tea leaves or drinking an aqueous preparation made from them kept one awake, and that swallowing the latex from the unripe capsule of the opium poppy allayed pain. The examples could go on and on because early people were intensely curious, and millions of trials complemented by frequent serendipity revealed many plants useful in treating disease.

Extensive lists of these natural drugs have survived from antiquity, and it is of considerable interest to peruse them because of the many well-known products they contain. The *Pen Ts'ao* written by herbalist Shen Nung in 2800 B.C. lists 366 plant drugs, among them the familiar ephedra. The *Ebers Papyrus,* dating from 1550 B.C., mentions opium, aloes, and henbane, among others. Coming down to relatively recent times, Dioscorides describes about 600 plants in his *De Materia Medica* of A.D. 78. Familiar ones include aloe, ergot, and opium (Tyler, Brady, and Robbers 1988).

For more than fourteen centuries the vegetable drugs recorded by Dioscorides reigned supreme in the materia medica, but then a Swiss pharmacist-physician named Theophrastus Bombastus von Hohenheim, better known as Paracelsus (1490–1541), introduced a new dimension to drug therapy. He advocated the use of chemical remedies, including mineral salts and acids as well as substances prepared by chemical processes such as distillation. Paracelsus challenged the alchemists to prepare medicines, not gold or silver. Although the field was slow to develop, medicinal chemistry was born with Paracelsus (Sonnedecker 1976).

Conventional therapy with the plant drugs recommended by Dioscorides continued almost unchanged for three more centuries. Then, in 1803, a small-town pharmacist in Paderborn, Germany, named Friedrich Wilhelm Adam Sertürner, was inspired by the experiments of Scheele in isolating organic acids from plants to attempt the isolation of the active principle of opium. He succeeded but found the chemical alkaline, not acidic, the first of a group of principles known as alkaloids. Because many of them were found to be physiologically active, the search for alkaloids continued well into the twentieth century. Some discovery highlights include quinine in 1819, atropine in 1831, cocaine in 1860, ergotamine in 1918, and tubocurarine in 1935.

The availability of pure active constituents from plant drugs coupled with the synthetic drugs that began to appear on the market toward the end of the nineteenth century began to change the prescribing habits of physicians. It seemed far more sensible to administer an exact dose of quinine for malaria than to use a foul-tasting extract of cinchona bark, which contained somewhere between 3% and 5% of quinine plus two-score related alkaloids, some with very different physiological properties, in addition to about 3% of tannins. True, some crude drugs, even potent ones, were standardized for therapeutic activity and continued to be used. Digitalis is an example. It retains its official status today in the *United States Pharmacopeia (USP),* being standardized by a method involving cardiac arrest in pigeons.

Still, crude vegetable drugs held on tenaciously to their dominant place in therapy until the time of the Second World War. This is illustrated by the drugs discussed in the first edition of Gathercoal and Wirth's *Pharmacognosy* (1936). Approximately 200 of the plant drugs monographed in that volume were then official in the *USP* or *National Formulary (NF)*. And note that, of the 200 listed in 1936, some 38 (19%) of them or their constituents are still official in 1991. For example, although ergot is no longer listed, its active constituents, ergonovine and ergotamine, are.

This speaks for a significant role even today of plant drugs in medicine in the United States. Farnsworth has substantiated this in a survey that reported 25% of all prescriptions dispensed in community pharmacies contained ingredients extracted from higher plants (Farnsworth 1969). I do not believe anyone has ever counted the number of synthetic drugs for which natural drug products have served either as models or as starting points for synthesis, but it is indeed very large. Numerous examples, ranging from aspirin to procaine, come to mind.

If plant drugs play such a significant role in our existing materia medica, why is it that the search for new ones has been so limited, at least in this country? Vinblastine and vincristine, isolated some thirty years ago, remain among the handful of natural products from higher plants recently introduced into commerce (Tyler 1988). We are all hopeful that another one, taxol, will soon be in that position, but first the cell culture specialists or the synthetic chemists have to develop a reliable production method.

With all the research carried out in pharmaceutical industry and in university laboratories during the past thirty years, why have we not seen more natural drug products introduced into commerce? There are several reasons. Without doubt, the organic chemists who dominate industrial research groups are more oriented toward synthesis than they are toward isolation and structure determination. In the university setting, funding for natural product research has been extremely difficult to obtain from industry, for the reason just stated, or from the National Institutes of Health, where review panels are oriented toward projects with novel chemistry. A major stumbling block has been the failure of researchers to assemble groups in which biologists, chemists, and physicians can interact effectively in this effort. Failure to have all these areas of expertise adequately represented has no doubt caused many potentially significant plant drugs to be overlooked and, in consequence, has discouraged further research. Perhaps the most serious obstacle has been the United States Food and Drug Administration (FDA), whose regulations require costly testing even of long-used traditional drugs for which patent protection cannot be assured. That cost has been reported to average $231 million for each new drug, an expense that is possible to recover only if one is dealing with a new chemical compound or some similar entity on which patent protection is a reasonable certainty (Anon. 1990).

There are other countries in the world where research is carried out on plant drugs, and it behooves us to look at some of them briefly. Probably the most effort of any country in the entire world is expended in Germany. The laws of that country permit the marketing of plant drugs, so-called phytomedicinals, provided they have been proven safe and effective (Keller 1991). However, the proof required is very different from the absolute, $231-million-per-item proof required in the United States. I call the German position a doctrine of "reasonable certainty" that involves use of data from the existing literature, anecdotal information supplied by practicing physicians, as well as limited clinical studies.

Because the costs involved are not exorbitant, a large number of relatively small pharmaceutical manufacturers market a wide variety of phytomedicinals there. They also conduct research on them both in house and by sponsoring investigations in university laboratories. The only fear is that when European union is completed, the standards will be relaxed, and it will become possible to market traditional plant drugs in Germany without proving safety and efficacy as is now essentially the case in France and England. In other words, the lowest common denominator of quality will prevail for drugs as has recently been the case with beer. This would destroy the research incentive for German manufacturers and would also deprive pharmacognosy and medicinal chemistry laboratories of research funding. Let us hope this does not occur.

Because the active principles of many phytomedicinals currently marketed in Germany are either complex mixtures or are not yet identified, many such drugs are offered as plant extracts rather than as single chemical entities. Two such preparations are:

1. Ginkgo biloba extract, the best-selling prescription drug in Germany today, is widely used there to stimulate cerebral circulation in the elderly. Because of the FDA regulations in this country, it is sold here as a food supplement without any indications of use on the label.
2. Echinacea preparations are widely used in Germany, particularly as nonspecific stimulants of the immune system. They are commonly employed to moderate the symptoms of colds or influenza. Although echinacea is a native American drug and once had official status in the *NF*, it can be sold here only as a food supplement.

The list could be extended, but I hope, by means of these examples, to have shown how a favorable regulatory climate can facilitate the development of drugs from plants (Hänsel 1991). Existence of such a climate in Germany makes that country a truly exciting place to visit for those of us interested in the field.

Another country where research is carried out on plant drugs is China. Herbs constitute a significant part of the materia medica there, some 5,000 different ones having been used altogether and about 1,000 in current practice (Duke and Ayensu 1985). A prescription for a single illness may include a dozen different herbs, so it becomes difficult to identify the active component. Further, Chinese medicine is not Western medicine but is based on entirely different philosophical principles. The two ginsengs are a good example. American ginseng, the root of *Panax quinquefolius*, and Oriental ginseng, the root of *Panax ginseng,* are very closely related botanically and chemically. As far as can be determined by Western studies, they have similar actions. Yet the Chinese believe they are very different in their properties, the American species being "cold" (*yin*) and the Oriental being "hot" (*yang*).

Pharmacological and clinical studies conducted in China are very difficult to interpret because they often fail to include adequate controls in their experimental designs. Thus, in spite of the large number of plant drugs available, very few of them have entered Western medicine. Probably the best example is ephedrine from *ma huang* (*Ephedra sinica*), and that was in the 1920s. Nevertheless, the Chinese have large numbers of skilled chemists who are busily engaged in isolating new constituents from the old herbs. American pharmaceutical manufacturers have contracted with Chinese laboratories to supply such compounds for physiological testing here. Perhaps this approach will yield new developments from Chinese materia medica.

Thus far I have examined three very different cultures and their attitudes toward plant drugs. These include the United States, where such drugs are neglected by researchers but where they nevertheless continue to play a significant role in medicine; Germany, a country highly oriented toward phytomedicinals, where new drugs are continually being developed from plants; and China, an ancient nation with much unrealized potential in the field. What I have attempted to do by means of these three examples is to demonstrate that plant drugs are important to us all, and we need to do everything possible to further their development.

I hope I have made a convincing case that drugs derived from plants not only form a truly important part of the world's materia medica but also have the potential to become even more significant. However, before that happens, plants as yet uninvestigated must be subjected to detailed chemical and pharmacological analysis. From where will these plants come? Botanists estimate that approximately 500,000 species of plants exist in the world today (Schultes and Raffauf 1990). About 16% of the total, or 35,000 to 50,000 species, are found in the tropical rain forest of the Amazon. Many of them occur in the westernmost part of that region, which is the least studied. If one extrapolates the number of species to the total rain forests of the earth, it is obvious that we are dealing with a very large number. Yet these resources are being destroyed at a rapid rate—approximately 80,000 square miles a year—and it is obvious that the rate of destruction will far outpace efforts to determine the medicinal utility of the species being obliterated.

This destruction of plant species is a relatively new phenomenon in the history of the world. I suppose that almost every schoolchild can name animals that people have rendered extinct, some of them within very recent memory. The dodo bird and the passenger pigeon are two prominent examples. But plants are a different matter. Willy Ley (1967) tells us that until about 1960 only a single species had been rendered extinct by the actions of humans. According to some authorities, 20,000 species are now endangered. The first exterminated species was known as silphion, and it flourished in the Greek colony of Cyrene on the north coast of

Africa in present-day Libya. Silphion was in fact a medicinal plant; its root and leaves were utilized for a variety of purposes ranging from the treatment of hemorrhoids to facilitating uterine contractions. It grew wild and was never cultivated, so eventually it became scarce and then extinct. Before that happened, a concentrated extract of its stem was worth its weight in silver.

I use silphion as a single example of a drug that might have been as useful in the twentieth century A.D. as it was in the sixth century B.C. if it had not been for the avarice of human beings—for people who preferred a pound of silver to a pound of irreplaceable plant material. They gained in the short run, but humankind lost in the long run.

So far, I have presented many of the problems associated with plant drug research. Now, I present some of the solutions. In doing so, I wish to praise the objectives of the Rainforest Alliance. These range from conservation of forest lands, to education of both public and professionals concerning the problem, to the sponsorship of research on forest crops. All these are admirable objectives and worthy of support.

However, an additional area in the United States that urgently needs to be fostered by some appropriate sponsor is the stimulation of chemical, and especially pharmacological and clinical, research in natural products. In other words, we need to place a greater emphasis on finding out what is there and what it is good for, before it is gone forever. I mentioned earlier some of the reasons why natural products research languishes in this country. The high cost of proving safety and efficacy coupled with the difficulty in patenting drugs that have been known for centuries has discouraged pharmaceutical companies from undertaking this kind of research.

I have already mentioned how this situation is circumvented in Germany. Many other possibilities are available, including the kind of procedure used for orphan drugs in this country. The Orphan Drug Act provides incentives such as seven-year market exclusivity to developers of drugs targeted at a rare disease or condition that afflicts fewer than 200,000 patients in the United States (Anderson and Anderson 1987). Something of this sort could well be extended to the marketers of new natural product drugs. But however it is done, I think it is extremely important for us to bring influence to bear on the U.S. Food and Drug Administration to modify their current regulations so as to encourage research on drug plants in this country. There is at present an enormous interest in herbs among laypeople in the United States. They spend half a billion dollars per year on them in health food stores alone (Geslewitz 1991). If we include the sale of herb teas in grocery outlets, that figure would have to be multiplied many times. Yet, the rigid attitude of the FDA with respect to efficacy testing prevents any substantial research from taking place in the field. If this is not changed, the rain forests will, in spite of the Alliance's best efforts, be gone long before any appreciable number of their plants can be investigated. At the same time, the National Institutes of

Health need to be encouraged to support research on natural drug products. At the moment that support is minimal.

H. H. Rusby, Dean Emeritus of the Columbia University College of Pharmacy, who traversed the Brazilian rain forests by way of the Beni, the Madeira, and the Amazon rivers in 1885–87, has written the following concerning his explorations (1933):

> Young people especially are disposed to envision a life of easy progress, irresponsible security, and pleasant adventure, with ready access to a forest abounding with "wild roots and berries," a myth for which fictitious or semi-fictitious literature is chiefly responsible.

He notes that his book *Jungle Memories* deals not with such myths but with "realities."

These words should be given careful attention by those who wish to promote natural product research. Any assumption that such an activity will be easy is a myth. Nevertheless, thanks to modern experimental techniques and instrumentation, we have readily at hand the methodology needed to attack the problem. It makes modern plant research analogous to exploring the Amazon in a helicopter instead of using the primitive boats employed by Rusby before the turn of the century.

Perhaps the most significant development in medicinal plant analysis in the last half of the twentieth century has been the advent of various separation techniques, particularly chromatography. Thin-layer chromatography developed by the German pharmacognosist Egon Stahl has been particularly useful for the identification of plant constituents. To be convinced that mass spectrometry and nuclear magnetic resonance spectroscopy have greatly simplified the determination of structure of complex organic molecules, one should read the papers published by Jacobs and Craig in the mid-1930s dealing with the structure of lysergic acid (Hofmann 1964). Using microquantities, the workers performed dozens of degradations and prepared scores of derivatives before they were able to achieve their goal. Their work, highly sophisticated for that bygone era, now reads like alchemy in comparison with the techniques made available by modern electronic instrumentation.

These developments in analytical techniques have done much to facilitate research in this field. My personal belief is that the most productive period of medicinal plant research lies ahead of us. Somewhere, possibly under our very noses, lies the one plant that will cure AIDS (could it be St. John's wort?) or ameliorate Alzheimer's disease (possibly ginkgo biloba extract?). Perhaps its discovery will be the impetus that is needed not only to stimulate research in natural drug products but also to preserve the germ plasm so vital to its success. The methods are already available, and the materials are, fortunately, still at hand. We need to use them both wisely, but if we persevere, we are certain to succeed.

REFERENCES

Anderson, Kenneth and Lois E. Anderson. 1987. *Orphan Drugs.* Los Angeles: Body Press.

Anon. 1990. ''Drug Development Costs Rise; 104 Biotech Drugs Under Study.'' *American Pharmacy* N.S. 30 (7):10.

Duke, James A. and Edward S. Ayensu. 1985. *Medicinal Plants of China,* vol. 1. Algonac, Mich.: Reference Publications.

Farnsworth, Norman R. 1969. ''Drugs from Higher Plants.'' *Tile and Till* 55:32–46.

Gathercoal, Edmund N. and Elmer H. Wirth. 1936.*Pharmacognosy.* Philadelphia: Lea & Febiger.

Geslewitz, G., ed. 1991. ''15th Annual Survey—1989: A Banner Year.'' *Health Foods Business* 37 (3):43.

Hänsel, Rudolf. 1991. *Phytopharmaka,* 2d ed. Berlin: Springer-Verlag.

Hofmann, Albert. 1964. *Die Mutterkornalkaloide* (cites numerous references to the work of W. A. Jacobs and L. C. Craig). Stuttgart: Ferdinand Enke Verlag.

Jaramillo-Arango, Jaime. 1950. *The Conquest of Malaria.* London: William Heinemann.

Keller, K. 1991. ''Legal Requirements for the Use of Phytopharmaceutical Drugs in the Federal Republic of Germany.'' *Journal of Ethnopharmacology* 32:225–29.

Ley, Willy. 1967. *On Earth and in the Sky.* New York: Ace Books.

Rusby, Henry H. 1933. *Jungle Memories.* New York: Whittlesey House.

Schultes, Richard E. and Robert F. Raffauf. 1990. *The Healing Forest: Medicinal and Toxic Plants of the Northwest Amazonia.* Portland, Ore.: Dioscorides Press.

Sonnedecker, Glenn. 1976. *Kremers and Urdang's History of Pharmacy.* Philadelphia: Lippincott.

Tyler, V. E. 1988. ''Medicinal Plant Research: 1953–1987.'' *Planta Medica* 1988:95–100.

Tyler, Varro E., Lynn R. Brady, and James E. Robbers. 1988. *Pharmacognosy,* 9th ed. Philadelphia: Lea & Febiger.

2

Biological Diversity, Chemical Diversity, and the Search for New Pharmaceuticals

James D. McChesney

BIOLOGICAL diversity is the name we give to the occurrence of the many different kinds of organisms found in the world. It is important to recognize that biological diversity is an outward evidence of chemical diversity. All organisms interact with other organisms and their environment by chemical means. Plants, organisms that are fixed in place and cannot flee injury, have evolved chemical defenses to protect themselves. Many insects find mates by releasing attractant chemicals into the environment to allure mates. Prey and predators interact through chemical scents as well as sight. Even humankind's exploitation of organisms is based largely on our use of specific chemicals produced by those organisms. All our foods are, in reality, chemicals as are our natural fabrics and all our medicines.

Chemicals derived from higher plants have played a central role in the history of humankind. The Age of Discovery was fostered by explorations to find more economic trade routes to the East to bring back plant-derived spices and other products. Indeed, the discovery of the New World, whose 500th anniversary we celebrated, was a direct consequence of that effort. The prototype agent for a majority of our classes of pharmaceuticals was a natural product of plant origin. Numerous other examples could be cited. However, with the discovery and development of fermentation-based natural products beginning in the early forties and the increasing sophistication of synthetic organic chemistry, interest in plant-derived natural products as prototypes for pharmaceuticals and agrochemicals waned greatly during the decades of the sixties, seventies, and eighties. Today a reinterest in the potential of substances found in higher plants to provide prototypes for new pharmaceuticals, agrochemicals, and consumer products is being evidenced. Until recently, efforts to realize the potential of plant-derived natural products have been very modest and largely restricted to discovery programs centered in academic settings. A number of convergent factors are bringing about the renaissance in higher plant-related natural products research and development. Some of those factors are the following: advances in bioassay technology, advances in separation and structure elucidation technology, advances in our understanding of biochemical and physiological pathways, the biotechnology revolution, historical success of the approach, loss of practitioners of traditional medicine, loss of biological diversity, loss of chemical diversity, and worldwide competition. However, I believe an important consideration or nagging concern that is still responsible for the significant reluctance to initiate a higher plant-based natural products research and development program, especially on the part of the private sector, is the issue of natural product chemical supply.

Efforts to develop new, clinically effective pharmaceutical agents have relied primarily on one of five approaches, most of which utilize existing agents in some manner: (1) derivation from existing agents, (2) synthesis of additional analogs of existing agents, (3) use of combination therapy of existing agents with other drugs, (4) improvement of delivery of existing agents to the target site, (5) discovery of new prototype pharmaceutical agents. While approaches 1–4 are important and need to be continued in that they seek to use existing agents and information in the most effective manner, there is an urgent need for the development of totally new prototype agents that do not share the same toxicities, cross-resistance, or mechanism of action as existing agents. Natural products have, in the past, provided a rich source of such prototype bioactive compounds, and it is essential that the search for new drugs pursue this route. The major advantage of this approach is the likelihood of identifying new prototype drugs with quite different chemical structures and mechanisms of action and, hence, lower likelihood of similar toxicities and cross-resistance. Clearly, the higher plants represent a bountiful source of new prototypic bioactive agents that must be examined.

The fundamental element of a drug discovery program is the bioassay(s) utilized to detect preparations with the desired biological activity. The bioassay protocol selected for the discovery of new prototype drugs must meet a variety of criteria. In addition to the expected criteria of ease of operation and low to moderate cost, the assay must show specificity and sensitivity. An important requirement of the assay is its ability to serve as a guide during the bioassay-directed phase of purification of agents showing activity. This is especially so in the discovery of substances from natural sources since these materials are likely to be in very low concentration in very complex mixtures. Only a combination of procedures meets these demanding criteria to serve as primary screens for biological activity. Other important program elements must be coupled to the appropriate bioassay. The probability of selection and procurement of novel sources of potential preparations must be demonstrated as well as evidence of competency to accomplish bioassay-directed purification and structure elucidation. Initially detected activity must be confirmed in suitable secondary and tertiary assays that will help define the potential of the substance for clinical utility. Finally, a "portfolio" of information about the substance must be accumulated upon which to make a judgment about its potential for successful development to a clinically useful agent. For example, something must be known about its general toxicity, pharmacokinetics, mechanism of action, analog development, etc. On the basis of these considerations, The University of Mississippi Research Institute of Pharmaceutical Sciences has developed an innovative program of collaborative multidisciplinary research to discover and develop new prototype pharmaceutical agents from higher plants. An overview of the general strategy is shown in figure 2.1.

I will review very quickly the drug discovery and development process and its attendant costs. We often refer to the "pipeline" when discussing drug discovery and development. Portrayed in figure 2.2 is this pipeline concept. Three basic stages are evident: discovery, development, and marketing. Each of those periods

Natural Product Case

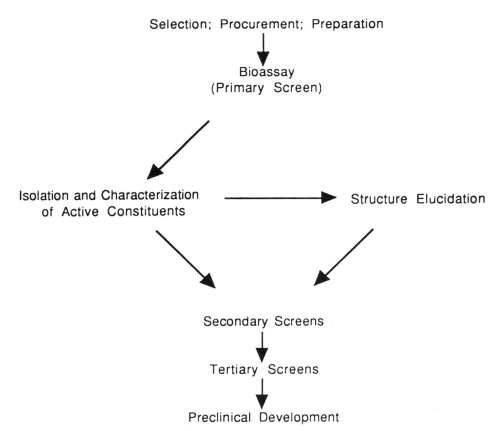

FIGURE 2.1 Strategy for drug discovery.

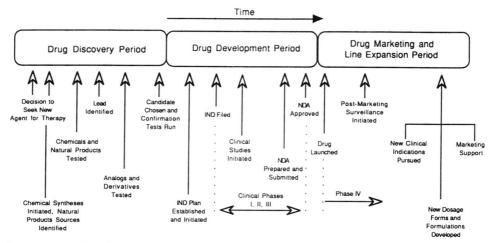

FIGURE 2.2 Pipeline concept of drug development.

is, in turn, subdivided according to recognized discrete activities with their specific attendant costs and time for accomplishment. In table 2.1 are summarized usual and mean times for accomplishment of the various drug discovery and development activities. From these numbers it is clear that pharmaceutical companies must take a long view of product development, in most instances a much longer view than almost any other industry.

Table 2.2 outlines the specific costs associated with each of these drug discovery and development activities. Each new pharmaceutical represents a major cash investment on the part of the company to get it to market.

What is not immediately obvious from these tables are the hidden costs of drug discovery and development. What does it cost to identify that first lead compound? How many of the candidates that enter the development phase fall out before making it to market? How much "lost opportunity" is represented by the necessary investments in drug discovery and development? For example, it is estimated that more than 10,000 chemical substances are ordinarily evaluated before a lead is identified. What does it cost to generate or produce all those substances? A majority of candidates prove to be unsuitable as drugs for one reason or another—too toxic, too costly, not sufficient benefit beyond present therapy, etc. And unfortunately, on occasion, drugs are removed from use even after making it to the market owing to unacceptable side effects or other problems. In summary, although the direct clinical costs for an individual drug might come to 24 million dollars, the average total cost of each successful drug actually runs to between 100 million and 225 million dollars because it must also pay for the failures. Consequently, anything that can make the process more efficient and cost effective is very desirable. Evaluation of new natural products of plant origin holds significant promise of lowering present-day drug discovery and development costs.

With the advances in bioassay, separation, and structure elucidation technologies mentioned above, we are now able to discover and identify substances with potential utility from plant preparations quickly and with very modest amounts of material. The sensitivity of the bioassays routinely in use today and the desired potency for new prototypes of less than 1 µg/ml make it easily possible to detect substances that are present at concentrations of 0.001% or less of the dry weight of the plant.

Ordinarily 50 mg or so of pure chemical substance is sufficient to determine its complete structure including stereochemistry. In order to obtain 50 mg of a chemical that is present at 0.001% of the dry weight of the biomass, one needs at least 5 kilograms (kg) of biomass. Practically, one actually needs as much as 10 kg of biomass since no isolation procedure is 100% efficient.

Herbaceous plants are roughly 75–80% water when fresh, so to obtain 5 to 10 kg of dry plant materials, one must collect 20 to 50 kg of fresh plant material. For woody plants, the situation may be somewhat more complex since we usually process a specific part of the plant—bark, leaves, fruits, roots, wood. For the leaves and fruits the situation is like that for herbaceous plants. In the case of wood, bark, or roots, the dry weight yield from fresh weight is often much higher, sometimes as high as 75%. However, if you have ever had to dig roots or peel bark, I am sure you have greatly appreciated the relatively higher yields of dry weight. So for woody plant parts, one may need 20 to 50 kg of leaves of fruits, 10 to 25 kg of

TABLE 2.1 *Typical Periods of Time Required to Develop New Drugs*

Stage of Development	Usual Range of Time Required (Years)	Approximate Mean Time Required (Years)
1. Project formation to IND[1] filing	0.5 to 2.5	1.5
2. Phase I clinical studies	0.5 to 1.5	1.0
3. Phase II clinical studies	1.0 to 5.0	2.5
4. Phase III clinical studies and preparation of NDA[2]	1.0 to 5.0	2.5
5. FDA[3] review of NDA	1.0 to 5.0	2.5
Total	4.0 to 19.0	10.0

[1]IND = Investigational New Drug Application, [2]NDA = New Drug Application, [3]FDA = U.S. Food and Drug Administration.

TABLE 2.2 *Direct Clinical Costs at Various Stages of Drug Development*

Stage	Cost ($000)
Pre-IND	$ 400
Phase I	2,600
Phase II	11,400
Phase III	7,400
NDA wait	2,200
Total	$24,000

roots or bark, and 8 to 15 kg of wood in order to get sufficient substance to accomplish isolation and chemical characterization of the active principle.

At this stage, we arrive at a decision point—is the structure novel? Does the substance represent a potential new prototype? In order to assess the full potential of the substance so that a valid decision can be made whether to proceed further with development, quantities are needed for an array of evaluations: secondary and confirmatory bioassays, preliminary toxicology, and initial in vivo evaluation. Ordinarily at least 400–500 mg of material are needed for this next phase of evaluation. This represents roughly a tenfold increase needed over the original quantities required for detection of the lead and its chemical characterization. To isolate and purify the required quantities of material may require 100–500 kg of biomass to be processed. Already at this point, concerns about supplies of the natural product are beginning to surface. If one must invest in bulk collection of plant material and its subsequent processing to obtain quantities for these next evaluations, what are you going to do for the larger quantities, perhaps as much as 2 kg, required to take the drug candidate into preclinical evaluation and subsequent clinical trials and ultimately to provide for actual marketing and clinical use of the new drug, maybe tens or hundreds of kilograms?

I take two more or less extreme examples to illustrate the range of quantities of active drug substance that would be required to provide for clinical use of a plant-derived drug. Assume that the condition to be treated is an acute condition; that the agent is relatively potent, i.e., 2 grams are required for therapy; and that only a modest patient population is expected—10,000 patients per year. To provide for this market, roughly 20 kg of drug substance would be required. If again we assume our worst case of 0.001% of active substance isolated from our biomass, then 2 million kg of biomass will be necessary to provide the quantity of drug needed to meet market demand. This may seem like a great deal, but 2 million kg of biomass is the same as 75,000 bushels of wheat, a quantity of wheat produced by even a modest-sized family farm in the United States. Now, if we assume the plant-derived drug would be used to treat a chronic condition in a much larger population, would that make a great difference? For a chronic condition a moderately potent agent might require administration of 50 mg per day per patient, which is equivalent to 20 g per year per patient. If 100,000 patients could benefit from this drug, then 2,000 kg of active drug substance would be needed to meet market demand. This is 100 times the example above; in other words, 200 million kg of biomass would need to be processed to provide the required material. Looked at another way, that is equivalent to 7,500,000 bushels of wheat, a quantity easily produced in an average wheat-producing county of a wheat-producing state such as Kansas. Clearly these are quantities of biomass that can be readily produced and processed if thought and planning for a system for drug plant production is initiated.

Are there any actual examples that might illustrate this point? First I want to comment on two plant-derived drugs that are problems for society, marijuana and cocaine. The best estimates on marijuana production worldwide in 1990 placed the figure at 30,000 tons. The U.S. Drug Enforcement Agency estimated that U.S. production was at least 5,000 tons, more than 4,500,000 kg. At an average price of $1,200 to $2,000 per pound, there is apparently incentive enough for growers to risk even imprisonment to provide for the market demand. Cocaine, a purified drug from the leaves of the coca plant, was produced at a rate of at least 1,000 tons worldwide in 1990. With prices of $6,000 to $18,000 per pound wholesale this was enough incentive to cause illicit producers to grow and process enough drug to meet market demand. These levels of natural product drug production are in place even though governments are making a concerted effort to stop or eradicate the growing of these plants.

Any system for production of a plant-derived natural product must meet certain criteria. It must be economic, sustainable, reliable, and nonenvironmentally impacting. These overarching criteria can be met only if a careful and systematic evaluation of each step of the production system is made. One must discover and develop the following: a superior source of the natural product that contains a consistently high yield of agent, an effective production and harvest system, appropriate technology for processing and storage of biomass, and an economic and efficient extraction and purification system that minimizes waste product generation.

Wild populations of medicinal plants may not be a reliable source of drug entity, and their harvest may be counterproductive to the development of a reliable, cost-effective, long-term production system of a clinically utilized drug. Several unpredictable and uncontrollable phenomena preclude establishment of a stable cost of production of the drug entity harvested from wild populations: forest fires, annual climatic variations, natural variation and presence of chemotypes of wild populations, increasing pressures to protect and regulate harvesting of wild plants, high cost of collection of scattered plants and transportation to processing facility, and lack of assured accessibility of populations that occur on public and privately held lands. Reliance on harvest of wild plants for production may lead to uncontrollable interruption of drug supply.

Even more critical is the fact that wild harvest risks the destruction of germplasm *essential* for the future cultivation of the plant for drug production. This includes genes for disease and pest resistance, hardiness, and tolerance to full sunlight, drought, and flooding, as well as genes for high growth rates and high drug production. The preservation of these wild genes can be critical to development of long-term, cost-effective supplies whether produced by cultivated plants, tissue culture, or genetically modified microorganisms. Because of the critical role wild germplasm will serve in future production strategies, the preservation of wild populations should be considered an essential component of the development strategy for drug production.

Lack of a stable and reliable supply of plant-derived drug at a predictable cost will even more significantly impede clinical use of the agent. Procurement of drug by harvest of limited wild populations may not be appropriate strategy to provide the agent once clinical utility is established. Development of a sustainable, economic, and reliable source is imperative.

The appropriate alternative may be production from a cultivated plant source. Cultivation has the added advantage that it will provide high plant diversities in defined locations that will significantly reduce collection and transportation costs. Two strategies may be taken to accomplish cultivation of the drug source: (1) to bring into cultivation the currently recognized source of drug, (2) to evaluate and select currently cultivated varieties for drug or drug precursor content. Strategy 1 is fraught with all the challenges and uncertainties associated with the introduction of a new plant into cultivation, a process that has been successful in bringing into cultivation only about 3,000 species of the estimated 300,000 plant species known to occur in the world. With our ever-increasing knowledge of plant biology, it is probable that nearly any plant species may be brought into cultivation. However, a period of several years (three to five for annuals and perhaps as long as ten to twelve years for woody perennials) may be required to accomplish the practical cultivation of a new plant species and, thus, to provide a reliable source for drug production. Then the necessity of recovering the investments made during the development period will impact the economics of this approach to yield a source for the drug.

In contrast, strategy 2 presents many advantages. A proven cultural system is in place. An additional advantage is the known genetic origin and uniformity of cultivated plants. The greatest advantage of this strategy is, however, its flexibility and responsiveness to demand. This system can be placed into production for drugs faster and more reliably than any other production system. A diversity of cultivars may be currently available, already in cultivation.

Assume that a cultivated source can be found or developed that will provide drug at an isolated yield of 0.03% of the weight of the biomass. To produce the required 20 kg of drug to meet marketing needs, it will be necessary to collect and process approximately 70,000 kg of biomass. If we were to collect as little as 10 grams of dry biomass per plant we would need to harvest biomass from 7 million plants. If those plants are planted on 3-foot by 12-inch spacings (14,500 plants per acre), then less than 500 acres would provide all the biomass required to meet the clinical need. Even if 100 times this quantity is ultimately needed for clinical use, the biomass can be quickly attainable. This scale of production is easily attainable in a relatively short period of time.

In conclusion, careful and thoughtful analysis of the issue of supply of sufficient quantities of a plant-derived drug to meet development and clinical needs brings one to the realization that this is not an issue that should cause us to preclude the carrying forward of such plant-derived agents through the development process to clinical use. Indeed, it is clear that adequate supplies of most plant-derived drugs can be assured with only modest additional research and investment.

3

Development of Pharmaceutical Companies Based on Plant Products: Suggested Approaches

Douglas Davidson, Peter J. Hylands, William Rod Sharp, and Roy W. Stahlhut

THE aim of this paper is to present evidence that (1) compounds obtained from plants may evoke highly specific responses in humans; (2) many plant products are essential for normal physiological functioning in humans; and (3) plant products induce a range of responses in humans.

In part 1 we show that plant products have pharmacological activity and we consider the history of the discovery of human responses to plant extracts. We also discuss how the historical evidence, taken from folk medicine and herbals, has been explored to provide clues for sources of novel drugs. An alternative approach, concentrating on evaluating as much plant biodiversity as possible, is put forward as a more appropriate system for the present. These approaches, backed by the application of modern biotechnology, should lead to the identification of new therapeutically active compounds.

In part 2 we discuss the steps involved in the commercialization of the processes of identification and application of new compounds. Interactions between academic and commercial entities are considered, together with various ways in which they interface.

1: Plant Products: Foods, Vitamins, and Drugs

ANIMALS AND THEIR PLANT FOODS

Higher animals are heterotrophs. The successful completion of normal development and the maintenance, throughout adult life, of normal body functions are absolutely dependent upon exogenous supplies of many organic compounds. These organic compounds include molecules that are largely, in their contribution to body function, energy sources, e.g., carbohydrates, oils and fats, and proteins. Other required organic molecules include vitamins and various growth factors that are involved in cellular metabolic functions. Over this range of organic compounds, we find considerable variation in the minimum daily requirement for each type of molecule. In humans, for example, compounds that function mainly as calorie sources are required in quantities of tens to hundreds of grams per day. Vitamins and other molecules involved in cellular metabolic functions that are not solely the provision of energy sources are needed in lower amounts: milligrams or nanograms per day are sufficient.

Plants are the major source of energy-rich foods in most societies. They are also the major source of vitamins and related compounds required by humans. Plants provide a major source of calories at the same time as they provide us with the vitamins and growth factors we require. The rich and complex range of organic molecules we ingest as we take in the plant material containing the carbohydrates we need was, until relatively recently, unknown and unappreciated. The discovery of these hidden sources of essential molecules was often accidental. A good example is the prevention of scurvy by the juice of citrus fruits. The active factor was identified long after its therapeutic effect had been established: it is vitamin C. Modern techniques of extracting, isolating, and identifying organic molecules have shown that plants, especially fresh or lightly cooked fruits and vegetables, are excellent sources of vitamins and similar molecules required as nonenergy sources by humans. And just as we now know that in consuming plants as energy sources we are taking in other necessary molecules, it may be that we are also consuming, unknowingly, other plant organic molecules of significant benefit for our normal growth and function.

Nutritional Status of Preindustrial and Industrial Societies

In preindustrial societies with established settlements, i.e., non-nomadic agrarian economies, the principal staples of life were plant products. The food commodities, e.g., cereals, legumes, fruits, and vegetables, were largely perishable and their consumption was mainly directed at achieving adequate amounts of energy-rich foods. As we have shown earlier, however, our agrarian ancestors were simultaneously, if unknowingly, consuming the required supplies of vitamins and other plant organic molecules. It was only with the major increases in population that largely accompanied industrialization and the shift from a rural to a city environment that significant changes in diet occurred for many people. Food had to be bought, not grown, and precooked food—canned or packaged—gradually formed a larger and larger proportion of the total daily food intake in many urban societies.

Techniques for commercial preparation of food often reduce the amounts of vitamins present; to compensate for this loss, vitamin supplements are now added to packaged food to restore nutrient levels to more nearly normal and adequate amounts. These vitamin additions and vitamin supplements are now a common feature of nutrition in many Western societies.

In view of our current dependence on precooked foods, it may be relevant to ask the following question: are there other plant constituents, also necessary for human well being, that are destroyed during food processing but of which we are unaware? Since the evidence for the essential role vitamins play in normal growth and metabolic functions has been fully substantiated only recently, the question concerning other plant products with beneficial, or perhaps essential, functions during human development clearly needs to be addressed. The discovery of vitamin functions in humans has involved not only the application of modern biochemical techniques but also the identification of the effects of vitamin deficiencies. Could it be that some current human disorders result from dietary deficiencies of some plant-derived compounds?

With few exceptions, e.g., vitamins D and B_{12}, vitamins are plant products. The discovery that plant-derived vitamins are essential components of human diets is a major achievement of Western pharmacology and medicine. It does, however, also represent a conceptual breakthrough. From the historical perspective, it can be looked upon as the confirmation of a principle that has been accepted by non-Western societies for millennia. That principle has two parts: (1) plants contain compounds capable of inducing specific effects in humans, and (2) careful selection of the plants used to provide extracts can yield products that are beneficial to humans. We now consider some examples of these plant products and their effects.

Effects of Plant Products on Humans: Ancient Lore

Benefits from plant products were often obtained unwittingly in societies less technically sophisticated than our own. Vitamins are good examples of plant products that were consumed without any knowledge of them or their effects. Many ancient cultures knew, however, the specific effect that could be induced in humans by specially prepared extracts from particular plants or by some type of plant preparation. Their knowledge did not extend to the nature of the actual factors responsible: such knowledge came later with the application of analytical chemistry techniques. The key fact to grasp at this point is that ancient societies could correlate a specific response in humans with ingestion, or application, of an extract from a particular type of plant. And they knew that the response was reproducible in trial after trial. In some ways, the ancient pharmacologists were remarkably successful and skillful.

Perhaps the oldest documented case of the deliberate preparation of an active plant extract occurs in Sumerian clay tablets. The compound was alcohol and the mode of preparation involved brewing or fermenting barley. Other societies recognized the hallucinogenic properties of certain cacti such as *peyote* (*Lophophora williamsii*) in Mexico; *Ariocarpus* spp., *Coryphantha* spp., and *Mammillaria trichocereus* in South America (Schultes and Hofmann 1980); and fly agaric (*Amanita muscaria*) in Europe, or they were aware of the ability of extracts of seeds of wild or bitter melon (*Trichosanthes kirilowii*) to induce abortions. The Sumerians also appear to have known about the sedation induced by opium by about 3500 B.C. Its properties were described as early as 1500 B.C. in the *Ebers Papyrus* (Bianchini and Corbetta 1975).

The significance of these examples, for the present discussion, is this. First, they demonstrate that ancient societies had a body of knowledge—from empirical observations—that products from specific plants are capable of inducing particular responses in humans. Second, they show that the range of types of response induced is quite wide. These examples are also useful in that they illustrate various aspects of (1) the attitudes of ancient societies to plant products capable of eliciting known, i.e., identifiable and reproducible responses, in humans; (2) how that knowledge was obtained; and (3) how that knowledge was transmitted.

The first point that emerges is that the exploration of plant products in ancient societies was not confined solely to a search for cures for specific diseases. Their interests must have extended to such materials, given the normal levels of infections in all societies, but they obviously recognized, and were willing to use, any useful response. (N.B.: the origin of the concept of disease resistance or cure is philosophically and linguistically of great interest but is outside the scope of this discussion.)

Among many examples of the successes of older societies in identifying plant extracts with specific therapeutic, i.e., curative, effects we may cite the antimalarial drug quinine, antibiotics against fungal infections used by ancient Chinese and Mayan societies, and reserpine from various species of *Rauvolfia* (Bianchini and Corbetta 1975). Older societies probably searched diligently for beneficial plant products. The successes they achieved are remarkable, especially when we consider the heavily weighted odds against them. The source of their difficulties is this: any traditional society, especially in tropical or subtropical regions, is surrounded by thousands of plant species. These include fungi, algae, mosses, ferns, and herbs, and shrubs and trees of higher plants. How did individuals of ancient societies arrive at the idea that plants could provide them with extracts that were, in some way, beneficial or therapeutic? And how did they select specific plants as possible sources for extracts that could yield certain responses? We can do no more than speculate about the processes involved and the number of tests that must have been carried out. One thing is certain, however: the test experiments—for they were in a primitive way experiments—must have been largely hit-and-miss, lacking any rational basis.

Untold numbers of tests must have been performed before any useful or valid results were obtained. And for many of the subjects involved in such tests the results must have been disastrous or even fatal. But time, and patience, yielded results. The method of trial and error, though time consuming and prone to mistake, yielded tangible results, however slowly.

With time, a variety of active plant products that had specific effects on humans became known. To the already-cited examples were gradually added the extracts from hallucinogenic fungi, lethal poisons from fungi and higher plants, and codeine and morphine from opium poppies. As Farnsworth (1990) has noted, 74% of 119 prescription drugs currently in use in Western medicine were identified by screening extracts from plants identified by native societies as having therapeutic effects. With all these examples, the effects on human subjects are clear-cut. In some cases, they are dramatic and immediately visible. And they involve the use of refined pharmaceuticals: what were originally crude extracts have been fractionated and refined. The result is that we are now in a position to equate a specific response with a treatment using a particular, and purified, compound.

Traditional societies, we conclude, were able to establish the important principle that there is a causal relationship between the application of extracts from specific plants and the precise nature of the response shown by human subjects under treatment. Not all claims made by these societies concerning the efficacy of plant extracts are as readily confirmed as those we have cited here. But in light of the successes they achieved, it is evident that not all their claims should be dismissed as mere superstition. The important step bridging the older and the newer worlds of pharmacological medicine is to make a useful "extract" yield its active constituent(s). The lore of the ancients indicates where our modern technology would be usefully applied (Lee 1987; Eisner 1991; Schultes and Raffauf 1990).

How Was Ancient Lore Transmitted?

In native societies, knowledge of the special properties of particular plants was often the speciality of certain individuals—such as shamans or, in Western terminology, traditional healers. Their knowledge was transmitted by actual demonstration and orally: i.e., identification of particular plants and the methods of preparing extracts. For generations, therefore, as knowledge was accumulated, it was stored only in the memory of unique and specialized individuals, and it was transmitted orally. This process is, at best, risky and prone to error. With the development of written alphabets, however, it became possible to record what was known of plant products and their effects. This knowledge could then diffuse within a tribe or even between tribes. As the level of literacy increased, herbals were produced: each is a compendium of descriptions of plants, or parts of plants—how to identify them and what effects their products induce. Written herbals were produced in China, India, and Europe. One compendium of medicinal plants, entitled *Yellow Prince's Classic of Internal Medicine (Huangdi Neijing),* was produced in China about 4,000 years ago. As additional studies added new knowledge, the original herbals were modified and extended, and the variety of plants with pharmacological properties was increased. This has widened the range of plants from which Western medicine is now poised to draw new pharmaceuticals.

Much of the information recorded in written herbals is, admittedly, general. It would be both easy and tempting to dismiss it as mere folklore or superstition. Nevertheless, herbals based on knowledge developed and orally transmitted over thousands of years contain clear evidence that primitive societies were in possession of specific knowledge of the products of some plants. The herbals, unlike some modern scientific publications, do not record the trials, with some plants, that failed: only the successes were recorded and transmitted as part of the lore of a society.

Parallel trials established that other plant products gave pleasant taste sensations; these include spice and flavor extracts such as pepper, nutmeg, basil, and garlic.

These additional examples confirm that plants contain a range of different compounds of use, or of benefit, to humans. The number of plant products used by humans is, however, a mere fraction of the actual number of compounds present in plants. And of the thousands of plant compounds already identified, only a small number have been tested for their possible use in therapeutic or medical treatments. This suggests an alternative approach: to evaluate as many different plants as possible. Thus we, as others, propose the following: plants are a rich, and largely untapped, source of compounds with many potentially new applications of benefit to humans.

THE ROLE OF BIODIVERSITY

In addition to the evaluation of ethnobotanicals, there are four other valid strategies: the taxonomic, phytochemical, chemosystematic, and random approaches to collection of plants. All these strategies embrace the vital importance of the concept of the utilization (and the preservation) of biodiversity. The last builds on the philosophy that the more plants studied and/or the more new plants evaluated through pharmacological screens, the greater the opportunity for discovery of novel lead compounds. Indeed, many of our most important pharmaceuticals have been discovered by random screening of microorganisms. Important, more recently discovered active factors present in microbes include potent antibiotics, e.g., the penicillins and streptomycins, and immunosuppressive agents from fungi, e.g., cyclosporin.

This random approach has been embraced by a number of academic and industrial research organizations and has resulted in the formation of commercial offshore laboratories for the collection, identification, and extraction of plant specimens for evaluation in pharmacological screens. These laboratories involve scientists in the fields of taxonomy, ecology, and natural products chemistry. The latest technologies are being used for this work, including satellite technology for precise location. Modern screening tests, which may involve specific receptors or enzymes isolated from cells, provide a rapid and effective means of identifying compounds with potential pharmacological applications. Through these techniques, coupled with advances in purification and spectroscopic technologies (to rapidly determine the nature of the active material), thousands of extracts can be rapidly screened, making the random plant collection approach to drug discovery feasible; tests on living organisms, which are expensive and time consuming, are no longer necessary in the initial screening process. They are needed only when a compound has passed all the early screening tests.

In addition, it is now generally accepted that the diversity of plant life is decreasing at an alarmingly high rate; unless active programs are undertaken now to study the available biodiversity, this resource will be lost forever. In addition to this consideration, we propose that it is equally important to recognize the importance of studies of integrated biodiversity. Most organisms live in intimate association with others—if higher plant species are lost through extinction, then many associated organisms are also lost. It goes without saying that time is therefore of the essence.

In some cases, a plant may turn out to contain only a low concentration of a specific active compound. Then currently available techniques of plant micropropagation, breeding from elite genotypes, and in vitro selection can be used to increase yields. In some cases, it may be more cost-effective to use the synthetic machinery of plant cells to make a compound, especially if its synthesis is a complex, multistep process, than to produce the compound chemically. Plant cell propagation, with fermenter scale-up, will then be useful. In most cases, however, chemical synthesis may be more cost-effective.

WHY USE PLANTS?

Now is an appropriate time to intensify efforts in the identification of new drugs from plants. Two main approaches seem valid: to build upon the leads provided by folk medicine and herbals and to undertake a larger, more widespread screening.

The knowledge consolidated in folk medicine has accumulated over thousands of years and represents a gigantic series of screening tests with humans used as a bioassay. Its results could serve modern societies well, if used judiciously; at minimum, the data of folk medicine could point to those plants deserving of further study and analysis. This approach has not, however, yielded many novel therapeutics. The real need in the pharmaceutical industry is for truly novel chemistries that can be exploited by medicinal chemistry to produce compounds with the appropriate therapeutic, toxicological, and pharmacokinetic profiles to become commercial drugs.

For these reasons, we advocate the broader approach of wide screening. Very large biological evaluation programs are feasible now because of technological advances.

Contemporary modifications of extraction, fractionation, and purification technologies, coupled with rapid, miniaturized pharmacological screening techniques, will all speed up the process of selection. The extensive use of data bases and advanced spectroscopic analysis (now possible on very small samples) complement these technologies and allow rapid distinguishing between useless and useful plant extracts. All these make a large-scale, random plant collection program completely feasible.

This, added to the issues of the alarming denuding of the earth's biological diversity, points to the value of large-scale screening methods in the rapid identification of new and valuable therapeutically active agents for human welfare.

2: The Opportunity for Commercial Development

MAGNITUDE OF THE OPPORTUNITY

New compounds with high levels of pharmacological activity are urgently required for a wide range of human disorders and diseases. Equally urgent is the need for a broad-based intensive plant-screening effort using all the strategies discussed earlier.

Interesting leads have been provided, by folk medicine, to plants with active extracts. Large-scale screening has also resulted in the discovery of important compounds (e.g., taxol). The number of plants, and the number of compounds that have been tested is, however, small; it is only a fraction of the species and the compounds available for study. The integration of traditional and Western medicine, botany, taxonomy, ecology, natural products chemistry, and screening technology presents an opportunity for the development of new pharmacological agents. How can this opportunity be grasped?

An important source of information on potential sources of new drugs is contained in written herbals. The second comes from ongoing exploration of formerly isolated regions of the world, e.g., remote areas in subtropical and tropical areas. This exploration is providing access to a rich history of traditional medicine and diversity of plant material. By integrating these resources with recent advances in natural products chemistry, pharmacology, and screening technology, we anticipate that ever-increasing numbers of active ingredients in plants will be isolated, identified, and tested. Studies of this type have been under way for some years. Well-equipped research centers engaged in the identification of plant pharmaceuticals are established in a number of leading institutions (some of which are listed in table 3.1); these are institutions in which modern technology is being integrated

TABLE 3.1   *Institutions with Active Programs of Research Into Plant-Based Pharmaceuticals*

The New York Botanical Garden
Royal Botanic Gardens, Kew
Missouri Botanical Garden
The Chinese Academy of Sciences and the Institutes of Biological Sciences
The Chinese Academy of Medical Sciences
National Cancer Institute
University of Illinois at Chicago

with knowledge from folk medicine, ecology, and plant systematics in the search for new therapeutically active compounds.

In more remote areas, located primarily in subtropical and tropical regions, transmission of folk medicine knowledge is still largely oral. But as these areas are opened up, ethnobotanists and anthropologists are working there to produce written records of the plants. They are building up inventories of the plants used in folk medicine and, in many cases, producing the first descriptions and taxonomy of the species. As this new phase of exploration proceeds, the written records that are produced will extend our knowledge of herbal plants from societies of the Pacific Rim, China, India, the former Soviet Union, and Central and South America. The evaluation of extracts from the plants singled out by folk doctors, by use of modern, rapid-input pharmacological screens, will be the means of discovering novel lead compounds and new pharmaceuticals.

Many well-known diseases or disorders in humans lack satisfactory cures or relief. And as new diseases appear, e.g., AIDS, new challenges are presented to medical science. The road to curing these various diseases and disorders lies in the discovery of new compounds and new modes of treatment. In part, new therapeutic agents will probably be isolated from the compound-rich pharmacies of herbal medicine. But even with new drugs, it is likely that new approaches to treatment will be adopted; these include the multiple-drug therapy regimens, or the "cocktail approach." This approach has been proposed as an alternative method to conquer many prevalent contemporary diseases; this represents a merger of the philosophies of traditional and Western medicine.

The methodologies and infrastructure for drug discovery from medicinally used plants are already in place. Applying these methods to the large-scale screening of the plant kingdom offers the next opportunity for drug discovery. Given this background, it is obvious that an opportunity exists for the emergence of a new generation of medical biotechnology companies built on a foundation of herbal pharmacies and random plant collections with large-scale plant screens. These resources, coupled with modern chemistry, pharmacology, and biotechnology, will allow this new generation of medical biotechnology companies to fill their pipelines with new classes of pharmaceutical compounds. As we have already discussed, modern chemistry provides us with the technology for extrac-

tion, separation, and evaluation of natural compounds. The high-technology pharmacological screens provided through biotechnology allow for the rapid robotic
screening of thousands of materials for multiple indications within short time
frames.

The plant side of the equation we are considering has two components. The
first is to identify plants containing useful compounds, while the second is to select
and improve the cultivated lines to maximize compound production. We have
already described the complementary approaches of plant selection in addressing
the first component. With regard to the second aspect, advanced techniques of
breeding selection and improvement allow elite genotypes in new strains of plants
to be established rapidly. Once high-yielding lines have been developed they will
be grown and harvested; the method of growing will have to be adapted to the
type of plant and the type of compound. For example:

1. In some cases conventional methods of agricultural production or growth by
   hydroponics in greenhouses will give satisfactory yields of the compound.
2. An alternative approach would be to use tissue or cell cultures grown in large-
   scale fermenter vessels. Slow-growing and long-lived species may make compound extraction from intact plants economically, or environmentally, infea-
   sible. The solution would be to use cultures of cells with the desired synthetic
   capabilities and so produce the compound of choice on an economically practical scale.
3. Another approach would be to sidestep breeding and selection techniques
   and proceed along the path of genetic engineering. In this approach, which
   involves gene transfer, the genetic information that directs synthesis of the
   compound of choice is moved into a new cell type or a new organism. This
   approach has already been applied successfully with tobacco plants (*Nicotiana*) and yeast cells (*Saccharomyces*). The additional advantage of this approach
   is that it can be adapted to obtain the directed synthesis, within cells, of compounds that are difficult to manufacture, or whose manufacture would not
   be economically feasible. The necessary tools of plant biotechnology and cell
   culture are available. The need is to achieve an interfacing between two types
   of companies or institutions, i.e., those with the appropriate background in
   plant biotechnology and those with expertise in developing, testing, and marketing new drug treatments.

THE COMMERCIAL OPPORTUNITY

We are confident that an opportunity exists to link the knowledge base accumulated from traditional medicine and the systematic random collection of plant
material to modern drug discovery programs. Recently a number of collaborative
research relationships have been put in place between the major pharmaceutical
companies and academic centers in regard to the screening of natural products.
Parallel with this, a number of small biotechnology companies have been involved
in the identification of active compounds from plants (table 3.2). Examples of

TABLE 3.2   *Leading Companies with Active Programs of Research Into Plant-Based*
Pharmaceuticals

1. Biosource Genetics Corporation	Tobacco mosaic virus (TMV)/alien gene/host plant channeling infection/host cell synthetic machinery channeled/new pharmaceutical product production
2. Calgene, Inc.	Antisense technology
3. DNA Plant Technology Corporation	
4. Genelabs, Inc.	Development of Compound Q, a plant-based compound from Chinese cucumber; now successfully synthesized
5. Glaxo Holdings, Ltd.	Screening of plant compound and extract libraries for the discovery of novel lead compounds for drug development
6. HKIB/Syntex Ltd.	
7. Merck, Sharp & Dohme	
8. SmithKline Beecham	
9. Hauser Chemical Research, Inc.	Extraction of phytochemicals
10. Indena SpA	
11. Penick Corporation	
12. PGS/Corvas Merger	Plant genetic engineering approach to drug compound discovery and production
13. PHYTOpharmaceuticals, Inc., subsidiary of ESCAgenetics Corporation	Screening of plant libraries for the discovery of novel lead compounds for drug development and taxol production via plant cell/bioreactor propagation
14. Shaman Pharmaceuticals, Inc.	Ethnobotany/herbal pharmacopoeia approach to pharmaceutical compound development
15. VimRx Pharmaceuticals, Inc.	Development of Hypericin, a compound discovered from St. Johns Wort, and its successful synthesis
16. Xenova Ltd.	Screening of fungal libraries for the discovery of novel lead compounds for drug development

compounds they have studied include hypericin, Compound Q, and taxol. Few of these fledgling companies have combined the key resources for the emergence of a fully integrated pharmaceutical company with a focus on drug development based on novel lead compounds discovered from plants. Such a company combines modern chemistry, pharmacology, biotechnology, natural product chemistry, and plant libraries of the world. Our discussion will now focus on a plan for development of such a company.

The scientific business environment is ripe for development of such a company because, for the most part, the pharmaceutical companies are staffed primarily with organic chemists, pharmacologists, and biotechnology-oriented scientists in the microbe- and animal-related areas. There is, however, a shortfall in the numbers of scientists with expertise in natural products chemistry and the plant-related sciences. The situation is not dissimilar to the scientific staffing situation more than a decade ago when most of the scientists in eukaryotic cell biology, cell culture, monoclonal antibody technology, and genetic engineering were housed within the walls of the ivory tower, not within industry. The marriage of the key scientists and advanced technologies in the biological sciences from the universities and research institutes and venture capital in the early eighties allowed for the infant technologies of biotechnology to be embraced and become the cornerstones of the new fledgling biotechnology companies and for the further development of the technologies and the resulting product pipelines.

With time, these companies, after proving the value of the new technologies in the production of novel medical products, were embraced by the large pharmaceutical companies. This resulted in collaborative research relationships, joint ventures, marketing relationships, and acquisition of the companies that became operating divisions within the multinational pharmaceutical companies. The lesson to be learned here is that the major research-oriented companies undergo scientific growth through the development of collaborative relationships or through acquisition of small companies that have the new emerging technologies in place as well as the scientific teams that are up and running; the opposite approach is to build groups from within. This acquisition mode of operation also improves the odds of success for the large company, both from the standpoint of building successful research teams and also from the standpoint of staying ahead of the competition. It is our feeling that the same scenario will be played out in regard to the emergence of a cluster of biotechnology companies built on the foundation of natural products chemistry and plant libraries. One of the essential steps in new company development, however, will be an objective assessment of their competitors.

THE COMPETITION

Before the organization of a new biotechnology company, it is essential that the potential investors assess the competition. In this case, the assessment needs to be made in regard to those companies with activities related to plant-based pharmaceuticals. Table 3.2 is a list of some companies currently active in this field. These companies can be segregated into the following categories based on their activities in plant-based pharmaceuticals: (1) screening of natural product compound and extract libraries by use of the company's proprietary screens, (2) ethnobotanical research approach to the discovery of novel lead compounds, (3) establishment of proprietary collections of organisms for the production of extracts for screening in the company's proprietary screens, (4) use of plant tissue culture for the large-scale manufacturing of plant-based pharmaceutical compounds, (5) use of plant molecular genetics for the creation of novel lead compounds and/or the manufacturing of plant-based pharmaceutical compounds, (6) plant pharmaceutical compound extraction, and (7) development of a novel compound.

A number of the multinational pharmaceutical companies have recently begun to evaluate natural-product-based extracts and compounds in their proprietary screens for discovery of novel lead compounds. A compound will progress in the research program of these companies only if sufficient natural product is available for elucidation of compound structures; moreover, the novel compound or the analogue therefrom must lend itself to a simple synthesis.

Alternative approaches to increasing inventories of natural products needed for the elucidation of structures or alternatives to conventional synthesis are usually not considered. This is for good reason because the major pharmaceutical companies have few scientists with expertise in the plant sciences and natural product chemistry and consequently do not have access to the high-technology approaches available in the plant sciences, e.g., tissue culture, clonal propagation, advanced breeding, and molecular genetics. The plant science approaches appear to be quite applicable to the pharmaceutical industry because of the renewed interest in the screening of natural products including plants. We expect that plant science technology will be the next technology to be integrated into the technology pool used by the pharmaceutical industry for the discovery and synthesis of novel compounds.

ORGANIZING THE COMPANY

It seems apparent that over the next few years a number of additional plant-based pharmaceutical companies will form. Some new companies will probably grow out of collaborative relationships between existing companies with different, but complementary, technologies and proprietary collections of plant taxa, extracts, and compounds. Productive synergistic interactions would develop out of the appropriate matching of proprietary compounds against proprietary screens and a parallel matching of breeding and selection techniques, molecular biology, tissue culture, and natural product and synthetic chemistry. Other companies will develop out of interactions among leading research institutions, plant collection programs, and companies with strong commitments to drug discovery programs. A key factor for success may, however, require more than the melding together of different technologies; it may depend on the integration of traditional Western medical approaches, e.g., less dependence on single drug treatments and more extended periods of therapy with lower doses of drugs.

The de novo approach.   Opportunities exist for the organization of biotechnology companies with a focus on the evaluation of herbal pharmacies, the teachings of traditional medicine and/or random plant collections, natural products chemistry, and biotechnology coupled with the approaches of Western medicine for discovery of novel lead compounds for new drug development. A first step would be the identification of an established scientist with a research background that emphasizes an integrated approach to new drug development involving both traditional and Western medicine.

The second step would be to develop a relationship between the principal scientist and a lead venture capitalist (LVC) who would assume the responsibility for bringing together the necessary financial resources and management talents for the formation of the company. The LVC would put together the appropriate licensing transactions to bring the proprietary technology and drug compounds into the company. In addition, the LVC would enter into the appropriate collaborative relationships with key academic institutions and scientific advisors. The objective would be to develop a team of outstanding scientific experts at appropriate research institutions to work with the principal scientist and LVC in development of the research and profit plans for the company.

Usually the LVC is willing to invest "seed money" into the company to hire the principal scientist and an office staff and to lease headquarters for the company. Some of the principal scientists hired from an academic institution would go on a part-time appointment at the academic institution or take a one-year leave of absence in order to have appropriate time to work with the LVC in the organization of the company. This kind of relationship provides the principal scientist with a security backup blanket in the event that the company is not successful with its financing. In this situation, the principal scientist would have the option of returning to the academic institution.

A general law firm and a patent law firm need to be engaged to handle the various legal issues pertaining to the formation of the company and various contractual relationships with employees, consultants, and institutions. Legal matters include the drafting and execution of licensing agreements, collaborative agreements, consultant agreements, scientific advisory agreements, and licensing of key technologies and compounds.

An ideal environment for a start-up biotechnology company is the leasing of space in a university incubator or science park. This arrangement usually serves to minimize leasing costs and provides access to secretarial pools, equipment facilities, libraries, computers, and the resources of the academic institution.

The next step is the development of a business plan that will involve the efforts of the LVC, the principal scientist, consultants, and the scientific advisory board. The business plan usually consists of the following: (1) executive summary; (2) table of contents; (3) the company: introduction, industry overview, and, in this case, an overview both of traditional and Western medicine; (4) objective and strategy: a statement of the company's mission in new drug development that outlines an approach to drug use that involves the integration of traditional and Western medical methods of treatment and evaluates herbal pharmacies, the knowledge base of traditional medicine, key collaborative relationships, proprietary technologies, natural product chemistry, and the biotechnology, coupled to Western medicine, for establishing a pipeline of novel drug compounds for the company; (5) products and markets; (6) proprietary analysis; (7) operating plan; (8) financing; (9) the people: management, board of directors, scientific advisory board, and key scientific staff.

Usually, upon completion of the business plan, formation of the company, and execution of the appropriate agreements, e.g., human resources and technology-related collaborative agreements, the LVC introduces the company to its allied venture capital companies and provides them with an opportunity to participate in a private placement involving the LVC and usually two to five allied venture capital companies. A typical private placement of this kind might provide a company with $3–5 million of capital.

Upon completion of a successful private placement the company is in a position to recruit key personnel, including a chief executive officer (CEO). The CEO recruited for a biotechnology company is usually a retired senior executive from a Fortune 500 company, with the experience to manage the development of a high-technology company. In the early years of the company's growth this involves consummating research and marketing agreements with the appropriate major pharmaceutical companies. Such research and marketing agreements provide the fledging biotechnology company with substantial research monies and/or an infusion of capital in the event that the collaborating pharmaceutical company elects to take an equity position in the company. These relationships are critical to the eventual success of such companies by providing an appropriate partner for the company to take certain categories of pharmaceuticals to the market. Moreover, the collaborating pharmaceutical company has the resources needed to take compounds through the regulatory process and then into the marketplace. These corporate relationships also provide a company with credibility in the pharmaceutical industry. This is critical to the company in regard to the success of future private offerings or an initial public offering (IPO) for raising additional capital for the company.

The spin-off approach.   PHYTOpharmaceuticals, Inc., (PPI) is an example of the spin-off approach to the start-up of a plant-based pharmaceutical company. ESCAgenetics Corporation is an agricultural biotechnology company organized in 1986 as a successor to IPRI, The International Plant Research Institute, which was founded in 1976. IPRI was the first agricultural biotechnology company to form in the United States. The ESCAgenetics Corporation technology portfolio has a seventeen-year history of plant science research including a global germ plasm collection, plant breeding, chemistry, plant cell tissue culture, and fermentation process sciences.

ESCAgenetics held discussions with the National Cancer Institute (NCI) during 1990 in regard to the possibility of producing taxol by using the company's fermentation process technology, which the company had successfully applied to the scale-up of several high-value plant-based chemicals for the food industry. The company was awarded a grant from the NCI to investigate the feasibility of the plant cell tissue culture scale-up and economic production of taxol, beginning in September 1991. The success of the project forced the company to make a business decision in regard to either licensing the taxol fermentation technology to a pharmaceutical company or leveraging the taxol technology as a building block for the launch of a new plant-based pharmaceutical company. The company elected to pursue the commercial scale-up of taxol and to license the relevant technologies for the creation of a plant-based pharmaceutical company subsidiary.

The company had the good fortune to have former Fortune 100 pharmaceutical executives on the board of directors to provide counsel in the development of the plant-based pharmaceutical company. The initial step was to hire a human resource manager with experience in plant-based pharmaceuticals. This individual was assigned to put together a first draft of a business plan including a resource development plan for the new plant-based pharmaceutical company, which was to be named PHYTOpharmaceuticals, Inc.

The PPI mission was to become a plant-based drug discovery company. PPI was to combine biodiversity and biotechnology for the discovery, development, and commercialization of novel human therapeutics. It was decided that the five key technical pillars required for building PPI consisted of the following: (1) plant biology including cell biology, plant cell tissue culture, and systematics; (2) plant sourcing with offshore laboratories for collecting and preparing extracts; (3) chemistry; (4) natural products chemistry; and (5) pharmacology, including an in-house screening capability. The offshore laboratories would allow for the preparation of certified plant extracts from well-documented plant collections. The extracts were to be screened in the company's proprietary screens or those of pharmaceutical company partners. The plant cell tissue culture is important to PPI in the provision of adequate plant material for those plants in short supply, the generation of chemical diversity, and the commercial scale-up of pharmaceutical compounds when appropriate. This, coupled with natural chemistry, provides the company with a unique position for drug discovery.

The spin-off approach to the start-up of PPI had certain advantages, including: (1) available financial resources, (2) a professional management, (3) business infrastructure, (4) laboratory space availability, (5) human resource management, (6) information resource services, and (7) opportunities to acquire certain technical assets in cell biology and chemistry.

The next steps were to form PPI, and this occurred in late 1992 concurrently with the appointment of a board of directors with experienced management from the pharmaceutical industry as well as a chairman and chief executive officer. Shortly thereafter, PPI appointed a chief scientist and research director and later a president and chief operating officer. The research department was reorganized into four departments: cell biology, chemistry, natural products chemistry, and pharmacology. PPI is at present financed by the parent company but in the future will consider other modes of financing such as a private placement or an IPO.

THE BIOTECHNOLOGY TRIANGLE

The lessons of the eighties have demonstrated that the most efficient way to move a scientific advance in regard to new technologies and/or products in the biological and medical sciences is through the forging of relationships between academic institutions and venture capital companies. Such relationships smooth the path for the movement of a key technology and/or product(s) from the academic institution to the private sector. The key to allowing the technology transfer to occur is the establishment of an appropriate business relationship with the academic institution and the principal academic scientist(s) in order to move the technology, product(s), and scientists from the institution to a biotechnology company. The financing for the biotechnology company is usually accomplished through a private placement of $3–5 million involving the lead venture capital company and two to five allied venture capital companies. These relationships are usually beneficial to the academic institution(s) at all levels, i.e., faculty, students, and administration. We refer to the biotechnology company, the academic institution, and the venture capital company(s) as the biotechnology triangle.

ACADEMIC INSTITUTIONS

Biological and medical research activities at academic institutions have traditionally been funded through grants from government, private research foundations, gifts, and, recently, grants from the biotechnology industry. This research advances in regard to new technology and resulting products: germ plasm, lead compounds, and early stage products, which, until very recently, were the subject of research papers. Often, however, these scientific advances failed to be commercialized because the intellectual property was improperly protected. This situation changed during the eighties, when the venture capital companies began courting the academic institutions and their scientific staff in the spawning of biotechnology companies. This resulted in accountability in regard to intellectual property resulting from research activities at the academic institutions and the establishment of patent and licensing offices. The academic institutions have become quite sophisticated in dealing with the private sector during recent years.

Two textbook examples in regard to the spawning of biotechnology companies from academic institutions and private research institutions that are often cited in the literature are the Genentech Corporation, formed by Dr. H. Boyer, a molecular biologist from the University of California, San Francisco, and Robert Swanson, the venture capitalist; and Genetic Systems, formed by Dr. Robert Nowinski, the monoclonal antibody scientist from the Fred Hutchinson Institute of the University of Washington, and David and Isaac Blech, the venture capitalists responsible for the establishment of a myriad of biotechnology companies.

VENTURE CAPITAL INDUSTRY

The resurgence of the venture capital industry as king in the eighties was the result of a lowering in the capital gains tax rate, which resulted in appealing acquisition prices for small companies, especially ones in technology, as well as the revitalization of the public equity market for emerging growth businesses (Schilit 1991). The venture capital industry was successful in raising more than $26 billion between 1982 and 1988, of which substantial monies resulted in the start-up of about 110 biotechnology companies. Twenty-five percent of the companies have now achieved profitability with sales of about $1 billion. It is expected that the sales figure will triple over the next five years.

The recent tax reform act has put a damper on the raising of venture capital funds and has slowed the start-up of new venture capital companies. This requires emerging companies to be of high quality with promise of having a product pipeline within a reasonable time frame.

MULTINATIONAL COMPANY/BIOTECHNOLOGY COMPANY RELATIONSHIPS

One asks why the multinational corporations have embraced the fledgling biotechnology companies and have entered into a myriad of collaborative research relationships, licensing agreements, joint ventures, marketing relationships, and acquisitions. Why did these multinationals not opt to deal directly with the academic institutions and their scientific staffs? The answer to the question resides in the difference in the missions of the academic institution and the biotechnology company. The academic institutions have a primary mission of teaching and training undergraduates, graduates, and postdoctoral fellows. They have secondary missions of conducting research and, in more recent years, protecting intellectual property resulting from the research and entering into appropriate commercial relationships. The biotechnology company has a commitment to further develop new technologies and promising products for commercialization. These companies tend to be astute in their approach to selecting the promising technologies and products and protecting their intellectual property. The companies tend to be made up of young, energetic, driven individuals with lives built around the research laboratory.

The multinationals embraced the youthful biotechnology companies because of their energy and creative approach to scientific discovery and development. The establishment of collaborative relationships with the biotechnology companies provides a number of advantages to the multinationals such as: (1) research conducted in private security-conscious laboratories, (2) research teams with a focus on development, (3) opportunity to finance off balance sheet research through equity participation in the biotechnology company, and (4) opportunity to evaluate emerging scientific advances for determination of the commercial opportunity without interfering with the company's corporate research organization or the risk of staffing up unproven research areas.

THE BIOTECHNOLOGY COMPANY/UNIVERSITY RELATIONSHIP

The biotechnology company/academic relationships have flourished over the past decade, and the majority of the myriad relationships have been of mutual benefit. The key to success has been the bringing of appropriate officials from the academic institution and/or government officials into early-stage discussions. In situations where the relationships failed to bear fruit, the management of the biotechnology company has sometimes failed to understand the chain of command and organizational structure of academic institutions.

Not only have the fledging biotechnology companies relied on academic institutions for the licensing of technology and early-stage products and recruitment of scientific teams, but also, to a large extent, they have located the company's headquarters and laboratory facilities in close proximity to major academic institutions. This has often resulted in a so-called incubator situation (Schilit 1991).

Incubators.   The incubator is a structure that enables entrepreneurs to develop their business skills in an environment conducive to fostering technical creativity (Schilit 1991). Incubators, which are often university related, generally provide low-cost laboratory and office space, state-of-the-art techniques and equipment, administrative support, and computer and library facilities for a nominal fee. In addition, these incubators enhance public-private-industry-university relations and often result in economic benefits to all parties involved. According to Schilit (1991), incubators have been a growth industry. In 1984, there were 40 incubators nationwide. Today, there are more than 300, with the greatest number found in Pennsylvania, New York, and Illinois.

The prototype university-related incubator and research center is the University City Science Center (UCSC) in Philadelphia. UCSC, which is affiliated with twenty-eight universities, colleges, and medical schools in the Philadelphia area (including the University of Pennsylvania, the Philadelphia General Hospital, the Philadelphia College of Pharmacy and Science, the Presbyterian University of Philadelphia Medical Center, Drexel University, and Villanova University), is the only entirely urban research park in the country. UCSC has the capacity to house nearly 100 companies in its 1 million-square-foot facility. Most of the current tenants are in high-tech industries.

Other similar, but much smaller, university-related programs include Western Pennsylvania Advanced Center in Pittsburgh and Carnegie-Mellon University; Georgia Advanced Technology Program in Atlanta; Rensselaer Polytechnic Institute (RPI), in Troy, New York; Utah Innovation Center (UIC), in Salt Lake City, which has had a relationship with the University of Utah; and the Institute for Ventures in Technology (INVENT), which is sponsored by Texas A & M University.

The incubators allow for an orderly movement of new technology or a developing product from a university research laboratory into a new and developing company. The incubator provides obvious benefits to both the university and the early-stage company. First, it provides an opportunity for the inventor to keep a watchful eye on ongoing research and to work with the company in regard to the proper protection of the intellectual property. At the same time it allows the academic institution to retain the faculty member and the scientific team.

The incubator relationship allows the company to develop in an environment of intellectually rich scientific resources while, at the same time, it is working with limited financial resources. Thus, this setup provides: (1) the opportunity to develop business skills in an academic environment; (2) low-cost laboratory and office space and access to equipment, administrative support, computer facilities, and libraries; (3) human resources, including faculty, postdoctoral fellows, graduate students, undergraduate assistants, and support staff, together with business and law school resources.

The benefits of the biotechnology company/academic institution relationships have occurred at the departmental, college, and institutional levels. These benefits have consisted of (1) supplemental research monies, (2) supplements to faculty salaries, (3) fellowships, and (4) licensing fees, benchmark payments, and royalties from patents and intellectual property.

Other arrangements beneficial to the faculty and their laboratories and departments have been: (1) appointment of faculty members to the scientific advisory boards of the company, (2) establishment of consultant positions, (3) part-time appointments as members of the company's scientific team and participation in collaborative research projects with funding to the faculty members' laboratory, (4) eligibility for government grants-in-aid for research conducted jointly between the fledging biotechnology companies and the academic institution research centers, and (5) fellowships and research support at postdoctoral, graduate student, and undergraduate levels. Thus, management and scientific staffs have been in a position to make significant contributions to the academic institutions.

These contributions have been important because of recent trends: (1) the greater number of graduates seeking positions in the private sector, (2) the declining number of positions available at academic institutions, and (3) the change in emphasis at academic institutions from pure research to research with an eye on the commercial benefits of a given project.

The managements and senior scientists of the biotechnology companies have been appointed to (1) policy-making boards, (2) research and academic program-steering committees, (3) adjunct professorships, (4) graduate committee membership, and (5) search committee membership for recruitment of faculty members when appropriate. These collaborative relationships between companies and leading research scientists and institutions will play an increasingly important role in establishing and strengthening fledging companies.

Private-sector incubators.   Schilit (1991) also discusses examples of private-sector incubators. These, like university-related incubators, provide laboratory and office space, administrative support, and an entrepreneurial atmosphere to entrepreneurs. They differ, however, from university-related centers in that (1) the funding is strictly from private, rather than public, sources; and (2) the primary goals are profit—job creation and community economic development. Some examples cited as typical private incubators are the Technology Center (Montgomeryville, Pennsylvania) and The Rubicon Group (Austin, Texas).

The Future

The basis, as we have tried to show here, now exists for an active and rapid expansion in the supply of new pharmaceutical compounds from plant sources. We are, perhaps, optimistic in our view that this area will expand rapidly, but there are no grounds, we suggest, to question the potential that exists for the development of a supply of new, plant-based therapies. The one point on which we feel some degree of pessimism concerns the shortage of research scientists in key areas of pharmacology and medicine. One result, which may be fruitful, is that this shortage will lead to increased cooperation between biotechnology companies and academic institutions in the future.

Another result, already becoming apparent, is that there will be an increase in the concentration of specific types of scientists in certain companies. In a survey of 231 biotechnology companies it was found that 47–48% of the companies have a market concentration in either medical therapeutics or medical diagnostics (Holden 1991). The statistics show that in the 1980s, the populations of scientists and engineers in the United States nearly doubled, increasing to well over four million (Holden 1991). The demographic forecasts for the late 1990s suggest, however, that the demand for scientists will rise sharply in the late 1990s and early 2000s. Part of the demand will be to replace academics hired in the period 1950–1965 who are now close to retirement. But there will also be a demand for scientists to staff expanding research and development programs outside universities. The output of Ph.D.s has remained flat for the past two decades, and no signs of an increase are apparent. These data have led the National Science Foundation to project a shortage of half a million scientists and engineers by the year 2000.

Another trend that supports a need for enhancing the bonding between the biotechnology companies beyond the apparent manpower shortage that will soon be approaching is that government funding for research is declining. The *Science* survey (Holden 1991) discusses the situation at NIH as an example; although the national research budget in the United States has increased by more than 50% since 1980, the number of grants awarded annually has fallen by almost one third. At the National Science Foundation (NSF), only 30% of those who apply for grants will be funded. Over the past ten years there has been a decline in the percentage of Ph.D.s employed by educational institutions and government agencies while there have been substantial increases in the number employed by business and industry or in those who are self-employed.

In order to realize, as fully as possible, the potential that exists for the development of new plant-based pharmaceuticals, government, academic, and research institutions and the business community must be willing to commit resources of manpower and financial support. Analysis and review of ongoing programs will need to be acute and searching. We maintain that the potential exists and that, with care, the benefits and rewards will fully justify the investments that have been made.

REFERENCES

Bianchini, F. and F. Corbetta. 1975. *Health Plants of the World: Atlas of Medicinal Plants.* New York: Newsweek Books.

Eisner, R. 1991. ''Botanists Ply Trade in Tropics: Seeking Plant-Based Medicinals.'' *The Scientist* 5 (12):1–25.

Farnsworth, N. R. 1990. ''The Role of Ethnopharmacology in Drug Development.'' In D. J. Chadwick and J. Marsh, eds., *Bioactive Compounds from Plants,* pp. 2–21. Chichester: Wiley.

Holden, C. 1991. ''Career Trends for the 90's.'' *Science* 252:1110–47.

Lee, S. L. 1987. *Medicinals and Other Chemicals from Plants: Status and Prospects.* Battelle Technical Inputs to Planning/Report no. 52, 30 pp.

Schilit, W. K. 1991. ''Dream Makers & Deal Breakers: Inside the Venture Capital Industry.'' Englewood Cliffs, N.J.: Prentice-Hall.

Schultes, R. E. and A. Hofmann. 1980. *The Botany and Chemistry of Hallucinogens,* 2d ed. Springfield, Ill.: Charles C Thomas.

Schultes, R. E. and R. F. Raffauf. 1990. *The Healing Forest: Medicinal and Toxic Plants of the Northwest Amazonia.* Portland, Ore.: Dioscorides Press.

4

Chemical Approaches to the Study of Ethnomedicines

Domingos Sávio Nunes

THE vast amount of information on the use of medicinal plants worldwide necessitates the development of a method to facilitate the huge task of evaluating their therapeutic value scientifically. These uses are associated with beliefs and traditions that are part of local cultures, many of which are in danger of rapid disappearance. This lends an urgency to accomplishing research efforts that guarantee the transfer of this knowledge to relevant scientific areas.

The proper botanical identification of the species is condition sine qua non for the beginning of any study on medicinal plants, regardless of the further approaches to be used, and constitutes the first link between traditional knowledge and contemporary science. Because of the relationship between taxonomy and chemical profile, the correct identification is also important as a base to build up the working hypothesis. At the same time, a need exists for complete information on the mode of preparation, posology of administration, and symptoms treated with the traditional remedy being considered for laboratory analysis; otherwise, it is impossible to define the chemical and pharmacological profile of a traditional drug. In this context it is ideal to collect the botanical material along with the traditional healers one is working with, in order to avoid errors in interpreting the original information. The particularities of each traditional preparation are better understood when analyzed comprehensively in their ethnological, pharmacological, and chemical aspects, all covered by the ethnopharmacological approach. In collecting information among users, it is possible to obtain precious data on the habitat of the species, optimum season for harvesting, management and conservation of the collected material, specific parts to be used, and other aspects relevant to the effectiveness of a vegetable drug.

Undoubtedly, the interdisciplinary character inherent to the ethnopharmacological approach is what brings together the fundamental needs for a scientific evaluation of the therapeutic value of the traditionally used phytotherapies and provides the initial basis for the standardization of galenic formulations (Elisabetsky 1986). The purpose of this paper is to discuss the chemical aspects to be considered in the study of the various types of traditional drugs, as part of the ethnopharmacological approach.

The Role of Phytochemistry in the Ethnopharmacological Method

Medicinal plants might have in their composition a mixture of major active principals, secondary active compounds, and other chemical substances—all of which can eventually alter the beneficial biological activity and/or induce unwanted side effects. Among the various factors that can, isolated or together, cause variability in the chemical composition of secondary metabolites in any given species are the following: intraspecies variability or genetic degradation, seasonal variation, soil composition and humidity (as well as other climatic conditions), postharvest storage, and conservation techniques (Mika 1962). The variability in the chemical composition of plant species necessarily renders phytotherapy, using official or non-official drugs, less secure than therapies that make use of isolated compounds, natural or synthetic (Bock 1983). The quality control methods for phytotherapeutic drugs are much more complex than those used for well-characterized substances, since each botanical sample could have been altered by the above-mentioned factors, and this can affect the expected chemical composition and therapeutic result.

The botanical identification opens the first door to cope with this challenge by permitting access to the published phytochemical and chemotaxonomic data. These have to be combined with the ethnopharmacological information regarding the mode of preparation of the traditional remedy in order to generate a realistic hypothesis regarding the active compounds. Given that usually there is limited or no medical follow-up on the actual effects of traditional drugs, the ethnopharmacological field information becomes the basic premise for the study. This fact necessitates that extracts be pharmacologically evaluated in a form resembling their original state as used in traditional medicine. Chemical spot tests to detect the occurrence of different classes of compounds in the specific part of the species actually used in the traditional formulation itself can lead to new insights and allow for a critical appraisal of the type of chemical compounds that could be responsible for the therapeutic claims or biological activity. Generation of hypotheses based solely on chemotaxonomic relationships of the species is less accurate, since not all substances present in the species must be present in the traditional drug and therefore absorbed by the patients. The information about traditional mode of preparation, when analyzed from a chemical point of view, can strongly contribute to establishment of the original hypothesis regarding the identity of the main active principal or introduce corrections in the hypothesis.

Criteria for handling the botanical material and optimization of the chemical methods of obtaining extracts are chosen according to the analytical results of the traditional preparation. The various extracts obtained can be compared by spectrometric, chromatographic, and chemical analysis with the traditional preparation in order to detect major differences in composition. Preliminary chemical tests, especially color reactions on thin-layer chromatography (TLC) and spot tests, can be highly valuable in planning the separation into fractions. A close interaction between pharmacologists and chemists is nevertheless needed, since each purification step depends on pharmacological results as much as chemical analysis. The increase or decrease in the biological activity of each fraction exerts major influence on the phytochemical methods to be adopted as the next step in the process of isolation of active compounds.

Besides playing a major role in the ethnopharmacological method, especially in the isolation and identification of active compounds, phytochemistry is also important in developing methods for the production of the target substances in sufficient amounts to guarantee future clinical evaluation.

Phytochemical Strategies

Each traditional formulation is a unique example of chemical composition. The traditional mode of preparation usually reflects the long experience of users. It is reasonable, therefore, to expect that the mode of preparation include basic rules of manipulation of the ingredients that lead to the liberation or concentration of active compounds. In the following sections, the most frequently used modes of preparation found among Amazonian communities are discussed in regard to their chemical significance.

Aromatic teas. Aromatic plants in enormous variety are traditionally used as medicines, usually prepared as teas. The botanical material is added to hot water, the tea is covered (*abafado*) for some minutes, and ingested shortly thereafter.

In these cases the likely presence of essential oil in the preparation should be considered; it is also reasonable to suppose that other organic compounds of various polarities were extracted, including glycosidic bound volatile compounds (Svendsen and Merkx 1989). Besides, inorganic and organic salts might be present owing to their greater solubility in water, although this factor per se does not always determine the presence or absence of chemical substances in teas. For instance, components of essential oils are normally fairly insoluble in water, even if hot, but their occurrence in teas is announced by the aroma, and their chemical composition is perfectly quantifiable by capillary gas chromatography (Harnisch-feger 1985).

In teas made of aromatic plants, the volatile components of essential oils stand as likely candidates responsible for biological activity, since there are many ex-amples of bioactive essential oils (Wagner 1985). The oil obtained by steam distil-lation should be chosen as a priority for pharmacological evaluation. The method of choice for qualitative and quantitative analysis of essential oils is gas chroma-tography coupled to mass spectrometry (GC-MS), owing to its practicality, sen-sitivity, and accuracy. For analysis of complex essential oils by GC-MS, a previous separation into fractions by dry-column chromatography could be recommended (Hostettmann, Hostettmann, and Marston 1986).

Nonaromatic teas.   The botanical material is added to water at room temper-ature or boiling water for variable amounts of time, indicating that volatile sub-stances are not important. Once discounting the presence of essential oil in the traditional preparation, this group of substances is ruled out as an active principal.

The ideal sample for chemical reactions for classes of compounds and prelim-inary pharmacological evaluation is a freeze-dried aqueous extract obtained by following rigorously the traditional mode of preparation. This strategy aims to preserve the qualities of the original formulation and allows quantifying the dose used traditionally. If pharmacological activity is confirmed at this point, the phy-tochemical routines to be chosen are the ones that favor the obtaining of purified extracts that concentrate substances of the same class or similar polarity.

If there is indication of presence of alkaloids in the aqueous extract (or tradi-tional preparation), these become the first priority for pharmacological evaluation. In general, alkaloids deserve such attention owing to the many known cases of medicinal or toxic plants in which they are responsible for strong biological activ-ities (Schultes and Raffauf 1990).

Alkaloids might be present in teas as free bases; as glycosides; as salts of pri-mary, secondary, or tertiary amines; or as quaternary ammonium salts. An alka-loid extract obtained from a freeze-dried tea by means of an organic solvent at pH 7 or greater could contain the free bases, as well as other bases released in basic pH. For a future standardization of the drug under study, it is important to quantify the total alkaloid content of the traditional preparation. The possibility of differences in biological activity observed for an alkaloid as free base or as salt cannot be ruled out without further testing. These differences may be more dra-matic when the pharmacological activity of aglycones and glycosides is compared, pointing to the importance of isolating the active substances as they are found in the traditional preparation. Moreover, even substances of very similar chemical structures can present very different pharmacological effects (Gilman et al. 1990). Qualitative and/or quantitative chromatographic analysis (TLC, GC, GC-MS, or HPLC) of alkaloid extracts obtained from freeze-dried teas and directly from bo-tanical material, combined with pharmacological results, is useful for verifying any important differences in the chemical composition of the various extracts and identifying the most appropriate phytochemical strategy for fractioning.

When the freeze-dried teas are devoid of alkaloids, these (or the plant materials) might be further extracted by using a sequence of organic solvents of increasing polarity, culminating with water. In most cases this strategy results in a reasonable separation of chemical components by polarity ranges and allows for constructing a picture of the bioactivity potential of various extracts.

In the chemical analysis of the extracts obtained by sequencing of organic solvents of increasing polarity, the occurrence of highly water-soluble substances is sometimes observed in the least polar extract. This is the case, for instance, with high proportions of common sugars such as fructose and saccharose found in the room temperature hexane extract of the bark of *Dalbergia monetaria* L. (Nunes 1988). In other instances, the same substance might appear in all extracts of the series, such as the relatively low polar furanocoumarines from rhizomes of *Dorstenia asaroides* Gard. (Elisabetsky and Nunes 1990). Substances of plant origin, insoluble in a given solvent, may be extracted by this very solvent if saponins are present in the plant material (Woo 1959).

The cases discussed above show that besides its solubility in the solvent utilized, the presence of a substance in an extract might depend on factors related to the morphology of the species, the state in which the secondary metabolites are accumulated in the plant, the degree of humidity of the material, the size of the grain obtained in the grinding process, and other factors. It is not a rare event that chemical transformation occurs in any phase of the extraction procedure, generating artifacts that might be absent in the traditional preparation.

Garrafadas.   These are single or mixed species prepared in alcohol and sold in bottles. The plant material is loosely ground and added to alcoholic beverages such as white or red wine or *cachaça* (an alcoholic beverage distilled from sugar cane) and the resulting infusion is left to mature for some days.

For a preliminary evaluation of pharmacological activity of this type of remedy, it is suggested that the plant be extracted by use of water:ethanol (9:1) for *garrafadas* prepared with wine and water. Water:ethanol (up to 1:1) is suggested for those prepared with *cachaça*. The pharmacological evaluation is carried out after distillation under vacuum of the ethanol portion and freeze-drying of the aqueous solution. Very often several plants are used in a single *garrafada*. It is reasonable to expect that the bioactivity could be caused by the interaction of more than one active compound. Chemical and pharmacological analyses of each species of the mixture are therefore needed.

Baths.   External baths, on specific parts of the body or the whole body, are a frequent way to utilize traditional remedies in the Amazon. Aromatic and non-aromatic baths are used with the preparation at room temperature or even hotter. The obvious hypothetical absorption routes of active compounds are the respiratory tract (volatile substances carried by water vapor) and the skin. Many aromatic baths are known in the Pará State as *banhos de cheiro* (fragrant baths), to which magical properties are attributed (Amorozo and Gély 1988). It could be argued that users might not realize that they are actually ingesting a drug and, therefore, credit its effects to magical or occult forces. The majority of remedies of the Tiriyó, an Amerindian group living in the upper Paru de Oeste River, close to the Brazilian border with Suriname, are used as baths (Cavalcante and Frikel 1973). Besides analysis of volatile components, the standardization of medicinal baths requires general chemical studies.

Saps.   There are many plant species in which the fresh botanical material is pressed and the sap is used medicinally. In these cases any class of chemical compounds usually found in plants might be present. There is no selection of active principles, and the stability of the preparation is not affected by exposure to heat. The traditional use of the sap without further processing possibly indicates the presence of very unstable active substances.

In our study of *Aeollanthus suaveolens* Spreng., from which a sap obtained from fresh plants is used traditionally in various places in the Brazilian Amazon as an antiepileptic agent, a major part of the anticonvulsant activity found in the essential oil was due to the presence of the lactone of 5-hydroxy-2-decenoic-acid (Elisabetsky et al., in press). The α,β-unsaturated-δ-lactones are not present in fresh plants but are released readily as the unstable glycosides split due to increase in temperature (Tschesche et al. 1971). Examples such as this suggest that pharmacological activity in such cases should be sought in the sap itself after filtration and freeze-drying.

Syrups.   Syrups are prepared by cooking medicinal plants with sugar and a small amount of water. They are generally used for respiratory diseases. A syrup might contain components of essential oils as well as others of higher molecular weight, of low or high polarity.

Aromatic medicinal plants used in syrups require analysis by GC-MS of the oils obtained by steam distillation. The results can then be compared with GC analysis of the syrup essence itself. The preliminary evaluation of pharmacological activity of nonaromatic syrups can be done by use of the aqueous freeze-dried extract. The next logical step is the chemical and pharmacological study of extracts obtained with a sequence of solvents of increasing polarity or extracts for specific chemical substances.

Exudates.   The latexes of various species of trees are obtained directly from the plants and ingested as such. Important examples of this type of remedy are two Apocynaceae species: *Parahancornia amapa* (Huber) Ducke (known as *amapá*) and *Himatanthus sucuuba* (Spruce) Woodson (known as *sucuuba*). These two latexes are used in the Amazon as tonics, pulmonary fortifiers, and antiinflammatories. No collection of these latexes is made between May and August, when they are considered to be toxic and, therefore, improper for use (Amorozo and Gély 1988). The chemical approach to these materials cannot be specific and the standardization must necessarily satisfy the safety requirements regarding seasonal toxicity.

In the study of traditional phytotherapies facilitated by ethnopharmacology, researchers must pay special attention to information on traditional modes of preparation, through which active substances are selected and dosages defined. Such information plays an important role since it is the basis for comparing the chemical composition of the traditional remedy with extracts obtained in laboratories. Moreover, the traditional mode of preparation provides clues regarding the active substances, enabling a short cut to the establishment of the research strategy, including the choice of analytical techniques and the sequences of steps that successfully lead to the isolation of active substances.

REFERENCES

Amorozo, C. and A. Gély. 1988. "Uso de plantas medicinais por caboclos do Baixo Amazonas, Barcarena, PA, Brasil." *Boletim do Museu Goeldi, Série Botânica* 1 (4):47–131.
Bock, H. E. 1983. "Die Phytotherapie und ihre medizinische Relevanz." In H. G. Menβen, ed., *Phytotherapeutische Welt*, pp. 5–14. Frankfurt pmi-pharm & medical inform: Verlags-GmbH.
Cavalcante, P. B. and P. Frikel. 1973. *A farmacopeia Tiriyó: Estudo etnobotânico.* Belém: *Publicações Avulsas do Museu Paraense Emilio Goeldi,* no. 24, 157 pp.
Elisabetsky, E. 1986. "New Directions in Ethnopharmacology." *Journal of Ethnobiology* 21 (6):121–28.
Elisabetsky, E. and D. S. Nunes. 1990. "Ethnopharmacology and Its Role in Third World Countries." *Ambio* 19 (8):419–21.
Gilman, A. G., T. W. Rall, S. A. Nies, and P. Taylor, eds. 1990. *Goodman and Gilman's— The Pharmacological Basis of Therapeutics,* 8th ed. New York: Pergamon.
Harnischfeger, G., ed. 1985. *Qualitatskontrolle von Phytopharmaka.* Stuttgart: George Thieme Verlag.
Hostettmann, K., M. Hostettmann, and A. Marston. 1986. *Preparative Chromatography Techniques: Applications in Natural Product Isolation.* Berlin: Springer-Verlag.
Mika, E. S. 1962. "Selected Aspects on the Effect of Environment and Heredity on the Chemical Composition of Seed Plants." *Lloydia* 25 (4):291–95.
Nunes, D. S. 1988. "Phytochemische Untersuchungen an *Dalbergia monetaria* Inhaltsstoffen." Ph.D. diss., the Universität Erlangen-Nurnberg, Germany.
Schultes, R. E. and R. F. Raffauf. 1990. *The Healing Forest: Medicinal and Toxic Plants of the Northwest Amazonia.* Portland, Ore.: Dioscorides Press.
Svendsen, A. B. and I. J. M. Merkx. 1989. "A Simple Method for Screening of Fresh Plant Material for Glycosidic Bound Volatile Compounds." *Planta Medica* 55:38–40.
Tschesche, R., H. J. Hoppe, G. Snatzke, G. Wulff, and H. W. Fehlhaber. 1971. "Glycosides with Lactone-Forming Aglycones. Parasorboside, the Glycoside Precursor of Parasorbic Acid from Mountain Ash Berries." *Chem. Ber.* 104:1420.
Wagner, H. 1985. *Pharmazeutische Biologie: 2. Drogen und ihre Inhaltsstoffe,* 3d ed. Stuttgart: Gustav Fischer Verlag.
Woo, L. K. 1959. "Influence of Saponin on the Extraction of Insoluble Compounds." *Seoul University Journal* 8:322–24.

5

The Contribution of the Physician to Medicinal Plant Research

Douglas C. Daly and Charles F. Limbach

MEDICINAL plant research has attracted increasing attention in recent years, owing partly to its scientific interest but owing also to its relevance to much more than just the health aspects of current debates surrounding economic development and conservation in the developing world. Ethnobotany, once a mostly academic pursuit, has become an increasingly complex endeavor encompassing new environmental, cultural, legal, political, ethical, and even commercial concerns. Planning medicinal plant research has therefore become more problematic.

More physicians are beginning to participate in ethnopharmacological projects and in issues related to medicinal plant use. This participation might be viewed with skepticism, given the difficulty of reconciling traditional medical systems with Western medicine's often dogmatic concepts of illness and health. If certain fundamental limitations are recognized, however, the Western-trained physician may add valuable contributions and insights in several key areas of medicinal plant research.

The Research Team

Creating the ideal study in medical botany challenges the investigators' ability to define and compose an adequate research team. The components of a medicinal plant research team can be extremely difficult to assemble. Rarely if ever has it been possible to join a botanist, anthropologist, physician, pharmacist, pharmacologist, and natural products chemist on a long-term project, owing to the difficulty of locating representatives of all these disciplines who are interested in medicinal plant research and in the particular project, capable of performing their functions in the project, and available to devote sufficient time to it. It is fortunate that more physicians and natural products chemists are becoming interested enough to participate in ethnopharmacological projects and other research related to medicinal plant use, but they are still rather scarce.

Omission of key disciplines from the research team can compromise the completeness or even the validity of the results. As Alexiades and Wood Sheldon (in press) aptly and diplomatically put it,

> While the interdisciplinary nature of ethnobotany allows for many approaches and applications, it also poses a challenge to workers approaching the field from any one particular discipline. . . . Training in botany or medicine will introduce different "filters" which will predispose the botanist or doctor to notice and interpret things differently.

There is no doubt that most projects and publications about medicinal plant use and ethnobotany in general suffer from lack of rigor in one or more of the component disciplines. Botanists decry the sketchy field data and scraps of vegetable matter brought to them by anthropologists or physicians seeking identification of medicinal plants. Anthropologists rightfully criticize the "car-window ethnobotany" published by botanists that consists of anecdotal information compiled unsystematically and in a cultural vacuum. Physicians are not interested in examining case studies and other health-related elements of a medicinal plant study if they are not based on laboratory reports or at least reliable field diagnoses.

The botanist may be a more dispensable member of a medicinal plant research team than the anthropologist or physician. Medical botany without a valid medical component is only botany, as is ethnobotany that skirts the cultural setting. Anthropology is the principal limiting factor in any study of plant uses by people. Collaborations between anthropologists and botanists have produced some of the more successful ethnobotanical studies in general (e.g., Berlin, Breedlove, and Raven 1974; Franquemont et al. 1990; Vickers and Plowman 1984) as well as studies of medicinal plant use (e.g., Davis and Yost 1983, who made use of recent medical reports on the tribe they studied).

The botanical component of a medicinal plant use study consists primarily of recognizing the plant parts used and making accurate taxonomic identifications of the species. Botanical training is useful for morphological descriptions or for making observations on the ecology of the species, especially considering the phenotypic (including chemical) variation in plant populations that occurs in response to environmental variation (e.g., Wayne and Bazzaz 1991). For the most part, however, only the actual identification requires specialized skills. It is not difficult to teach an anthropologist or physician to make good herbarium specimens accompanied by the necessary field observations, and the final identifications can be carried out by botanists in the herbarium subsequent to the fieldwork. The converse is not true, that is, there is no substitute in the field for more than rudimentary training in medicine and anthropology. A poor herbarium specimen can still be identified in most cases, but a botched interview or diagnosis can compromise the validity of the entire project.

Collaborations between specialists with interdisciplinary training can compensate at least partially for less than complete research teams. One now encounters botanists with strong backgrounds in anthropology (e.g., Alexiades and Wood Sheldon, in press), anthropologists with a decent understanding of systematics (e.g., Balée 1986), and physicians interested in ethnomedicine (e.g., Limbach and Daly, in preparation).

The physician can play a key role in studies of medicinal plant use, but is continually presented with challenges to his or her conceptual framework and therefore, in a sense, faces the greatest task. The physician must be able to understand traditional/indigenous medical paradigms sufficiently to examine them for similarities to Western medicine without sacrificing basic tenets of either.

Limiting Factors

The complexity of medicinal plant use in traditional health care systems should not be underestimated, nor should a research project in this area be undertaken without extensive preparation for understanding the cultural context. There is a good deal of truth to Elisabetsky and Setzer's (1985:245) assertion that "detailed ethnographic research is crucial for the understanding of drug use and medical practices, since these cannot be isolated from more general levels of integration, such as religion, rituals, social relations and so forth." Ultimately, no substitute is available for developing a strong ethnological background, assembling an interdisciplinary research team, and making a commitment to a long-term study involving a significant amount of participant observation.

The relevance of and need for emphasizing the cultural context in studies of medicinal plant use, even for those coming from the natural sciences, are understandable when one considers that medical treatment in all societies is based on their understanding and concepts of disease. Therapeutic regimens reflect etiology, such that an illness perceived as being caused by intrusion of a disease object or disease-causing spirit is treated by extraction or exorcism (Hughes 1978). In the majority of traditional medical systems, the most important factor in a disease is not the subjacent pathological process but rather its etiology (Foster 1976).

Hughes (1978) cites five of the most common folk etiologies explaining incidence of disease: sorcery, breach of taboo, intrusion of a disease object, intrusion of a disease-causing spirit, and loss of soul. In a specific example, a mixed-heritage riverine (*caboclo*) community in Amazonian Brazil sees the causes of disease as *ramo de ar* (literally, branch of air), *flecha de bicho* (arrow wound by an animal), *quebranto* (essentially the evil eye), witchcraft, and *caruani* (syncretic religious entities), as well as temperature shocks, ingestion of "greasy foods" (*comidas remosas*), or blood texture, which can result in a tendency to certain diseases (Elisabetsky and Setzer 1985). Not much room exists here for Western parallels.

Most folk etiologies view disease as a manifestation of disharmony in humankind's overall relation to the universe: "Theories of disease generally have major relevance to the moral order, that is, to the control of man's behavior in society. Disease is frequently seen as a warning sign, a visitation from punishing agents for a broken taboo, a hostile impulse, or an aberrant urge to depart from the approved way" (Hughes 1978). Interestingly enough, this principle prevailed among the ancient Greeks, the spiritual ancestors of Western medicine. Parallels may be drawn here with those in the West who blame the AIDS epidemic on aberrant sexual behavior or who blame the high incidence of many cancers on the offenses committed by Western society against the environment. The principles of disharmony and transgression of taboos figure prominently in traditional Chinese medicine, perhaps the most elaborate and certainly the best studied of the world's non-Western medical systems. There, the causes of disease have been placed into three categories: exogenous (the six excesses, or climatic factors), endogenous (the seven emotions), and "neither exogenous nor endogenous." In addition to several factors more familiar to Westerners, these include irregular diet, excess of sexual activity or physical exertion, and conditions of excess phlegm and stagnant blood (now classified as endogenous). Under pestilence, Chinese traditional medicine has always recognized "epidemic noxious factors" as a cause of disease (Liu 1988). Possible Western parallels with this latter factor should be examined carefully.

The great differences between traditional and Western etiologies are reflected in their thinking about treatment. Logan and Hunt's (1978:149) observation that "the use of botanicals is not, however, a purely empirical matter" is an understatement. The Kayapó of northern Brazil, for example, do not regard medicinal plants simply as curative agents; rather, they believe that plants have the capacity to alter the state of the body, modifying its resistance to attacks by spirits and illnesses, and that plants can also repel undesirable spiritual elements (Elisabetsky 1985).

The conceptual frontier between Western and traditional medical systems is rugged enough given their widely diverging sets of etiologies; it is made even less passable by the ways in which the conceptual frameworks are preserved and passed on. Traditional societies often have "complex ways of encoding and transmitting knowledge . . . legends, myths, and tales may be the symbolic expression of observed biological phenomena" (Elisabetsky and Setzer 1985:248).

Behind the Stereotypes

The role and potential contribution of the physician in studies of medicinal plant use can be distorted by two stereotypes. One is the physician, rigidly faithful to the infallibility of Western medicine, disdainful of the validity of traditional health care systems, skeptical of their practical effectiveness, and incapable of developing and unwilling to attempt to develop avenues of communication with the traditional healer. The rigid physician is pitted against the stereotypical shaman: secretive, inaccessible, superstitious, inscrutable, intuitive more than empirical, rarely effective—and, when effective, only because of luck, self-healing of the patient, or a long history of trial-and-error rather than to any understanding of "real" disease or of a treatment's mode of action.

These stereotypes do a disservice to both the physician and the traditional healer and exaggerate the difficulties of communication between them. One should not underestimate the diversity of types of traditional healers, the accessibility of many of them, the internal consistency of their conceptual frameworks, the "sophistication" (from a Western viewpoint) of their understanding of diseases and treatments, and the effectiveness of traditional health care systems. For example, much has been made of the Eskimos' knowledge of anatomy and of the use of surgery by the Masai (Hughes 1978).

Similarly, one should not underestimate the degree to which the experiences and even part of the training of many Western physicians increase their adaptability to other conceptual frameworks for health, disease, and treatment, as well as their ability to understand and apply (or at least participate effectively in) rigorous ethnological methods of inquiry. Given a reasonable background on the culture being studied, a physician can carry out valid if limited research on medicinal plant use by carefully selecting the types of healers to work with, the types of diseases to study, and the investigative methods to apply.

Many Western-trained physicians are far more prepared for medicinal plant research than one might suppose. It is discouraging that neither this subject nor even pharmacognosy figures in medical school curricula in the United States; on the other hand, some aspects of Western medical training and experience can be applied directly in research on medicinal plants.

In multicultural societies such as the United States, residents and staff physicians in many hospitals, clinics, and local practices frequently face many of the challenges of ethnomedical fieldwork, including language barriers, suspicions and/or fears of Western physicians, foreign concepts of health and disease, and taboos. Dietary restrictions, so often associated with treatment in traditional societies, are familiar to any Western-trained physician: management of many common illnesses, including diabetes, heart disease, hepatitis, and hypertension, is based on dietary modifications.

The Western physician is not quick to doubt diseases with unclear or unknown origins. Various common conditions, including schizophrenia, asthma, diabetes, and cancer *sensu lato,* have poorly understood etiologies. Some of the more curious of today's medical researchers are beginning to venture into areas uncharted by Western science but well known to traditional societies. The relatively new field of psychoneuroimmunology is a good example.

Finally, Western-trained physicians appreciate the importance of interviews, because a thorough, consistently applied interview is just as much of a mainstay in Western medicine as it is in ethnomedicine and ethnobotany, even if the nature of the interviews is rather different. Contrary to the "high-tech" image of modern medicine in the West, perhaps 75% of a physician's diagnostic information comes from interviewing and examining the patient. Similarly, carefully prepared and conducted interviews are crucial in any ethnobotanical fieldwork; they constitute "a necessary step in moving away from the superficial compilation of ethnobotanical 'anecdotes' that characterizes many ethnobotanical studies" (Alexiades and Wood Sheldon, in press).

Botanists' affinity with traditional healers, and often their access to each other, stems from their appreciation and understanding of plants. Traditional healers and physicians—Western healers—also share interests and purposes, and in many circumstances they may be making the same observations and asking the same questions. For example, once one of us (CFL) gave a typical case presentation for an oral cancer to a Shuar traditional healer in Amazonian Ecuador, who recognized the symptoms as belonging to a disease familiar to him and gave a description of the disease's progression that could grace a textbook. If a person has diarrhea, both physicians and many traditional healers will want to know the frequency of the bowel movements, whether they are painful, whether the stools are watery or bloody, and so on.

The skepticism that a physician might bring to a study of medicinal plants can be turned into an advantage when it is applied to improving the rigor of the project. For example, when the results of the interviews in the same study of Shuar healers in Amazonian Ecuador were written up, the data recorded for each medicinal plant voucher included the Shuar name for the ailment(s) involved and possible Western counterparts, always with the phrase "used to treat symptoms resembling" (Limbach and Daly, in preparation). This approach avoided making false synonymies or implied assertions of efficacy. For a contrasting example, we have seen the herbarium labels for a collection of medicinal plants used by a Spanish-speaking Amerindian group in Bolivia, on which a forester recorded the informant's assertions about the plant in question—including such bold phrases as "cures cancer"—and using other Western terminology that may not be translatable, either conceptually or linguistically, from the traditional disease concepts into Spanish or from the local use of Spanish into English.

Solutions

A conceptual chasm appears to exist between Western and traditional medical systems that researchers can begin to bridge only after years of laying an ethnological foundation. While such an approach should be taken whenever possible, we argue that in many circumstances the access of physicians and other Westerners to traditional medical systems is better than might be assumed given the vast differences in etiologies and in transmitting medical knowledge. As mentioned above, some of the approaches to health care taken by Western and traditional healers often show fundamental similarities. It can be relatively easy to reach and to communicate with certain types of healers. In many cultures, there are categories of illnesses for which the etiologies are not so foreign to the Western perspective. Finally, in a given floristic region many of the same plant species may be widely known and figure prominently in the pharmacopeias of distinct communities and cultures, thus facilitating the work of researchers seeking to study interesting bioactive plants.

Similarities

Traditional medical systems have concepts of the causes of disease, explanations of treatments, and means of passing on medical knowledge that are so different as to hinder communication with physicians or other researchers coming from a Western background, but there are characteristics shared by all medical systems that can permit a degree of communication among them. In all systems, diseases are diagnosed and named; Hughes (1978:155) pointed out that "an effective cultural response to disease requires patterned discrimination and categorization of disease symptoms." All have a pharmacopeia. There must be some internal consistency, and there must be some degree of success or efficacy. Hughes (1978:155) also pointed out that "the inductive epistemological framework of folk medicine is essentially similar in structure to that of modern scientific medicine" and that traditional medicine employs "therapeutic and preventive practices, many of which are empirically efficacious by standards of modern medicine."

One must assume that the physiology of the human organism, including its essential metabolic and catabolic processes as well as its general response to illness, is fundamentally consistent regardless of cultural milieu. The physician's task in this situation is to separate what could be a straightforward disease entity, known by a different name in the traditional setting but otherwise characteristic of a Western medical diagnosis, from what one must inevitably describe as "culture-bound syndromes" for which no Western equivalent exists.

A visiting physician may observe activities related to disease treatment and prevention that make perfect sense from a Western perspective, even if the motivation or explanation in the folk medicine context is completely different:

A great part of the task of folk medicine . . . is borne by cultural practices which, although oriented to different social purposes, have important functional implications for health. Thus, notable hygienic purposes are served by many religious and magical practices, such as avoidance of the house in which a death has occurred, theories of contagious "bad body humors" which necessitate daily bathing, distinctions of "hot" and "cold" food and water which require boiling or cooking, hiding of fecal and other bodily waste through fear of their use by sorcerers or witches, and numerous others. (Hughes 1978:154)

Layers of Knowledge

It is something of a fallacy to assume that all useful information in traditional medicine rests with the mysterious shaman. In any society, everyone has at least rudimentary medical knowledge, so perhaps it would be beneficial in some instances to focus not on specialists but rather on other categories of healers or even "lay" persons. The more specialized the specialists, the more difficult access to and communication with them may be.

Traditional medical systems often have several types or levels of healers, just as in the West. Among the Kayapó of Brazil, 5% of the population are considered shamans (*wayanga*), but another 26% are held to be specialists in one or more medicinal plants and the correlated illnesses (Elisabetsky 1985). In eastern Amazonian *caboclo* communities, for example, there are *pajés* (essentially shamans), *benzedoras* (literally, blessers), *puxadores* (massagers), *parteiras* (midwives), and *raizeiros*, who specialize in planting, collecting, prescribing, preparing, and trading medicinal plants (Elisabetsky and Setzer 1985).

The physician might have more ready access to a *raizeiro* than to a *pajé*. Moreover, important portions of the traditional medical knowledge may reside in the general population, as noted by Elisabetsky and Setzer (1985:253) among the *caboclos*:

> It is noteworthy that the knowledge and use of medicinal plants utilized for *common* ailments are shared and are in the public domain; they are not dependent upon special training with experts. This fact is important for ethnopharmacological data collection, since these people are generally more readily available and cooperative than *pajés* or other specialists.

Disease Classification

Some classes of ailments in a given cultural context may be relatively accessible to the physician or other Western thinker, not only because of easier access to the types of traditional healers who treat them, but also because their classification and etiologies may be more similar to Western counterparts. There is evidence that, at least in some traditional medical systems, categories of disease exist that are attributed to "natural causes" at least partly intelligible to Westerners; physicians interested in studying traditional plant medicines should—and can more legitimately—focus on these categories.

Foster (1976) perceived two basic types of medical systems, personalistic and naturalistic. In the former, illness is seen as being caused by intervention of an external agent (human, nonhuman, or supernatural); in the second type, illness is caused by natural forces or conditions such as cold, heat, wind, or food. In these latter systems, the shaman is more of an herbalist.

In traditional Chinese medicine, the category of diseases referred to as "neither exogenous nor endogenous" contains some ailments relatively easily grasped by Westerners. These include traumatic injuries, insect or animal bites, and parasitic infection (now classed as exogenous). Traumatic injuries refer to any "external mechanical violence," including harm caused by cuts, falls, contusions, strains, and burns (Liu 1988).

Among several Amazonian indigenous groups studied by Elisabetsky (1985), certain illnesses are related to natural causes: cold, heat, stings, bad food, etc. The Kayapó distinguish between common illnesses (*kanê*) and those related to spirits (*mekaron kanê*). Moreover, they distinguish remedies from *feitiços* (spells). Also among the Kayapó, illnesses caused by spirits are considered graver and more difficult to treat. A correlation may exist in many cultures between more recalcitrant, more serious disease on the one hand and more complex etiologies on the other. Health problems that are straightforward or easy to diagnose are also likely to present fewer conceptual barriers; not much translation is needed to explain such problems as insect stings, cuts, some skin disorders, and burns. On the other hand, understanding the nomenclature, etiology, and treatment for many internal disorders is likely to be much more challenging.

Some Approaches

The investigator well versed in Western medicine may use treatments for relatively simple disorders as clues for discovering plant remedies with significant biological activities. Elisabetsky and Gély (1987) took this approach in their study of medicinal plant use by the Kayapó. In order to seek plants with principles useful for treating allergic processes, they focused on plants indicated for asthma, insect bites/stings, and itching; for antiinflammatories, they focused on plants indicated for boils, sores, inflammation (erisipela), fever, rheumatism, earache, and painful urination. Their search for plants with potential in treating thrombosis presented a much greater ethnological challenge; for these, they focused on plants indicated for purification of blood, and for curing the *doença que entorta* and *ramo do ar* (branch of air).

Projective aids (e.g., Berlin, Breedlove, and Raven 1974; Ellen 1984) can also be used to circumvent some of the same barriers to communication. One of us (CFL) recently had an opportunity to work with several traditional healers in a partially Spanish-speaking Shuar community in Amazonian Ecuador (Limbach and Daly, in preparation). In the context of long discussions and unstructured interviews, they were shown clinical photographs of ailments with prominent external manifestations. In some instances, a traditional healer would recognize an ailment and provide a description of it that would leave no doubt about its Western equivalent. In other cases the presentation was not recognized, actually a positive sign indicating forthrightness of the informants. In still other cases, there was some measure of uncertainty, calling for careful interpretation by the physician. This type of approach, while no substitute for more complete ethnomedical studies, addresses some of the problems associated with etiologies, disease nomenclature, diagnosis, vernacular names of plants, and accurate botanical identification.

The physician may be fortunate enough to observe diagnosis, treatment, and results in the field. Opportunities for such ideal research conditions are rare, because traditional healers usually work in areas of very low population density, where patients may appear at very irregular intervals. Clearly, sufficient participant observation can be achieved only in long-term projects. Traditional healers who operate in towns and cities may be busier, but there traditional practices are more likely to have been altered by influences foreign to the original cultural context.

Congruence

Evidence exists that some of the best known and most widely used medicinal plants in a given region are those more likely to contain interesting active principles. Foxglove (*Digitalis purpurea* L.) in northern Europe, may apple (*Podophyllum peltatum* L.) among Amerindians in northeastern North America (e.g., O'Dwyer et al. 1984, 1985), and *sangre de drago* (*Croton lechleri* Muell. Arg.) in western Amazonia (e.g., Vaisberg et al. 1989) are examples of species that are or were widely used as medicinals in their native range and that have yielded significant compounds for Western medicine. Moreover, each species is or was used rather consistently for the same purpose(s) over a large geographic area and even across some cultural and linguistic barriers.

A number of investigators in industry as well as in public health have stressed congruence of use in their research design (e.g., Steven R. King, personal communication 1993; Xavier Lozoya, personal communication 1992). Through a review of the literature or other forms of data on medicinal plant uses from a given region, a pattern of bioactivity may begin to emerge. When such information is compiled before the physician enters the field, it can help guide the interviews as well as reveal some of the major diagnostic flaws that abound in the ethnobotanical literature and that lead other researchers astray.

Other Contributions of the Physician

The contribution of the physician to fieldwork in medicinal plant studies need not and should not be solely intellectual. Since it has become clear as ethnobotany has developed that "field work is a cooperative venture between the researcher and local consultants" (Alexiades and Wood Sheldon, in press), it is essential to consider carefully what will be the return to the community where the fieldwork is taking place, in fair exchange or compensation for their time and cooperation and for any disruption caused by the research.

Where needed, the physician can make contributions to the community by carrying out primary health care, assessing and compiling regional epidemiological data, and providing educational services in public health. This is, in fact, the job description of primary health care practitioners in our society.

Such work may be very rewarding, but it is also difficult and may present some risks. The physician must remain keenly aware of the limitations imposed by working alone and without the amenities of medical practice in the developed world. Great caution should be exercised in considering "heroic" efforts, because interfering with life and death in many traditional societies is tantamount to accepting culpability in case of a therapeutic failure. Still, many nonlife-threatening problems can be effectively treated, or appropriate care for them can be arranged in a regional medical center. Such collaborative involvement in a community often helps promote a spirit of cooperation and trust, and brings some tangible and immediate benefit to the host community.

Not only can contributing primary health care fulfill an obligation on the part of the physician and build trust in the host community; it can also provide insights into the prevalent local health problems and even serve as a vehicle for the medicinal plant research. One of us (DCD) once designed a collaboration in Amazonian Peru between a Peruvian forester from Iquitos and a physician, then working for a Spanish international aid mission, who was going to run a rural clinic along a new road. As the physician diagnosed and treated illnesses, she would conduct structured interviews related principally to the nomenclature and etiologies that local persons associated with those illnesses and to the plant preparations used to treat them. The forester would visit the communities with the most intensive and interesting uses of medicinal plants, go into the forest with the ex-patients or the traditional healers who had treated them, and collect botanical vouchers of the medicinal plants revealed by the interviews.

Physicians can and should help ensure that any medicinal plant study in which they participate is structured in such a way that the health and other aspects of the host community's well-being benefit from any discoveries or developments achieved by the study itself or by any research program linked to it. As Elisabetsky and Setzer (1985:263), among others, have pointed out, "It should be possible to return ethnopharmacological knowledge, improved through scientific analysis, to the people that most contributed to and most desperately need it." Such contributions help make the research arrangement more than just a one-sided, one-way relationship that is more contractual than collaborative.

Criticisms and Responses

The contribution of primary health care in the course of fieldwork on medicinal plants has been criticized in several ways, and these criticisms must be addressed. First is the idea that such activities are merely Band-Aid measures that do nothing to solve the underlying conditions that ultimately compromise the health of the community. This is true only if the physician neglects the responsibility to assess major public health issues such as sanitation, exposure to introduced diseases, and access to in-country health facilities. Investigation of and reporting on these conditions should be standard procedure for medical botany fieldwork. Just as it is customary to deposit duplicates of vouchers in local herbaria, the physician should prepare reports for appropriate government authorities, nongovernmental organizations, and/or regional associations, apprising them of the status of public health in the study areas.

Another criticism is that the information and treatment supplied by the physician are not commensurate with the potentially invaluable information being supplied by traditional communities. The physician must, of course, exercise caution and integrity in the selection and execution of research projects, but the physician alone cannot be made responsible for all reciprocal activities. Any academic and/or commercial interest that undertakes the research and ultimately benefits from it must be responsible for arranging avenues of long-term reciprocity with regional governments and local communities. The physician's activities must be viewed as only a small part of an overall arrangement, an effort of good will in an overarching agreement between the research group and the traditional community.

There is a real danger that the presence and activities of a physician could contribute to the erosion of the community's faith in and use of traditional health care. This can be damaging, because erosion of traditional beliefs of illness and health weakens the cultural integrity of a community at a fundamental level. Physicians visiting very remote areas must be aware of this danger; one must not merely "splash down," unpack one's medical kit bag, and begin consultation. Besides blatantly invalidating local healing practices, such actions may incite suspicion or even anger in local healers who may view the visitor as a rival.

To a large extent, the relationship between the physician and the traditional healer will be determined by the physician's attitude. Skepticism and condescension will justifiably be met by hostility. The traditional healer may still feel threatened by a well-meaning physician. As a rule of thumb, the physician should be wary of practicing Western medicine in communities with little exposure to it. Even where Western medicine is not a novelty, the physician should avoid any activity or statements that could impugn the validity of the traditional medical system.

It is imperative that local healers and leaders be advised of the physician's visit and the purpose of the physician's activities, preferably well in advance. When the physician's professional intervention would be unwelcome, it must not be attempted even in life-and-death situations. Such a constraint may be agonizing; however, the physician must honor the autonomy of traditional societies to take care of their own and manage the transitions of life and death.

Those who would criticize the physician's exercise of primary health care under any circumstances in a traditional community should consider that, in many cases, outside diseases have already crept in. Western diseases may require Western medical procedures, because in such situations traditional therapies may be lacking. Cholera, tuberculosis, and resistant strains of malaria are but a few examples. The physician may be of service in such areas by educating people about new diseases, providing treatment, and instituting preventive measures such as immunizations. Ideally, this can be done in such a way that traditional healers and practices are not threatened. If some aspects of Western medicine have already been adopted locally, the physician should work toward integrating Western and traditional medical systems, such that the community reaps the benefits of both while preserving the knowledge inherent in the traditional medical system.

Researchers undertaking a study of medicinal plant use in a traditional health care system should make every effort to make their study as uncompromising as they can: they should assemble as nearly complete an ethnobotanical or ethnopharmacological team as possible, and they should design and undertake a long-term study that considers every cultural and scientific aspect of medicinal plant use. Often this is not possible, but interdisciplinary training—and interdisciplinary thinking—can compensate for at least some of the limitations imposed by practical realities. Physicians participating in any such study must develop an adequate background on the cultural context. They need to collaborate with healers who will be accessible to them in all senses. They should focus on disease systems that the team can manage conceptually. Finally, they must use investigative methods appropriate to the anthropological skills of the research team.

Many reasons can be given why physicians should be invited to collaborate in medicinal plant research. Clinical skills are undoubtedly needed in efforts to translate a disease from one cultural context to another. The physician can help define and compare the experience of illness in different cultures; with a fundamental understanding of human physiology, the similarities and unique qualities of various diseases can be clarified.

The physician may also be in the best position to suggest the probable pharmacological activity as well as the efficacy of traditional treatments observed in the field. When research efforts are focused on discovery of potentially useful compounds, such insights may be invaluable.

Where appropriate, the physician can make other contributions, in the form of primary health care, collection and reporting of epidemiological and public health data, teaching in various health-related subjects, and helping to achieve a harmonious integration of traditional and Western medical practices. The cultural context must always be considered and the services structured accordingly.

Under these circumstances, the physician can make important contributions not only to medicinal plant research but also to the health of the communities being studied and to the preservation of traditional knowledge about medicinal plants. It is hoped that increasing numbers of interested and culturally perspicacious physicians will engage in medicinal plant research.

ACKNOWLEDGMENTS

We thank Miguel Alexiades for his insights and suggestions. The National Cancer Institute provided support for fieldwork carried out by both authors.

REFERENCES

Alexiades, M. and J. Wood Sheldon, eds. (in press). "Selected Guidelines for Ethnobotanical Research: A Field Manual." *Advances in Economic Botany,* The New York Botanical Garden.

Balée, W. 1986. "Análise preliminar de inventário florestal e a etnobotânica Ka'apor (Maranhão)." *Bol. Mus. Paraense, Bot.* 2 (2):141–67.

Berlin, B., D. E. Breedlove, and P. H. Raven. 1974. *Principles of Tzeltal Plant Classification; an Introduction to the Botanical Ethnography of a Mayan-Speaking People of Highland Chiapas.* New York: Academic Press.

Davis, E. W. and J. A. Yost. 1983. "The Ethnomedicine of the Waorani of Amazonian Ecuador." *Journal of Ethnopharmacology* 9:273–97.

Elisabetsky, E. 1985. "Etnofarmacologia." In D. Ribeiro, ed. *Suma etnológica brasileira 1. Etnobiologia* [B. G. Ribeiro, "coordinator"], pp. 135–40. Petrópolis, Brazil: Vozes/Financiadora de Estudos e Projetos (FINEP).

Elisabetsky, E. and A. Gély. 1987. "Plantes médicinales utilisées en Amazonia comme fond potentiel de nouveaux agents thérapeutiques dans les cas d'allergie, thrombose et inflammation." *Journal d'Agronomie Tropical et de Botanique Apliquée* 34:143–51.

Elisabetsky, E. and R. Setzer. 1985. "Caboclo Concepts of Disease, Diagnosis, and Therapy: Implications for Ethnopharmacology and Health Systems in Amazonia." In E. P. Parker, ed. *The Amazon Caboclo: Historical and Contemporary Perspectives,* pp. 243–78. Studies in Third World Societies Series, no. 32. Williamsburg, Va.: College of William and Mary department of anthropology.

Ellen, R. S., ed. 1984. *Ethnographic Research—a Guide to General Conduct.* New York: Academic Press.

Foster, G. M. 1976. "Disease Etiologies in Non-Western Medical Systems." *American Anthropologist* 78:773–82.

Franquemont, C., T. Plowman, E. Franquemont, S. R. King, C. Niezgoda, E. W. Davis, and C. R. Sperling. 1990. "The Ethnobotany of Chinchero, an Andean Community in Southern Peru." *Fieldiana, Botany* (n.s.) 24:1–126.

Hughes, C. C. 1978. "Medical Care: Ethnomedicine." In M. H. Logan and E. E. Hunt, eds. *Health and the Human Condition: Perspectives on Medical Anthropology,* pp. 150–58. Belmont, Calif.: Wadsworth (reprinted from a 1968 article).

Limbach, C. F. and D. C. Daly (in preparation). "Medicinal Plant Study of a Shuar Community in the Oriente of Ecuador."

Liu, Yanchi. 1988. *The Essential Book of Traditional Chinese Medicine. Theory,* vol. 1. New York: Columbia University Press.

Logan, M. H. and E. E. Hunt, Jr., eds. 1978. *Health and the Human Condition: Perspectives on Medical Anthropology.* Belmont, Calif.: Wadsworth.

O'Dwyer, P. J., M. T. Alonso, B. Leyland-Jones, and S. Marsoni. 1984. "Teniposide: A Review of 12 Years of Experience." *Cancer Treatment Reports* 68:1455–66.

O'Dwyer, P. J., B. Leyland-Jones, M. T. Alonso, S. Marsoni, and R. E. Wittes. 1985. "Etoposide (VP–16–213)—Current Status of an Active Anticancer Drug." *New England Journal of Medicine* 312:692–700.

Vaisberg, A. J., M. Milla, M. C. Planas, J. L. Cordova, E. R. Augsti, R. Ferreyra, M. C. Mustiga, L. Carlin, and G. B. Hammond. 1989. "Taspine Is the Cicatrizant Principle in Sangre de Grado Extracted from *Croton lechleri.*" *Planta Medica* 55:140–43.

Vickers, W. T. and T. F. Plowman. 1984. "Useful Plants of the Siona and Secoya Indians of Eastern Ecuador." *Fieldiana, Botany* (n.s.) 15:1–37.

Wayne, P. M. and F. A. Bazzaz. 1991. "Assessing Diversity in Plant Communities: The Importance of Within-Species Variation." *Trends in Ecology and Evolution* 6:400–4.

6

Conservation and Tropical Medicinal Plant Research

Steven R. King

PEOPLE in the tropical forests of the world have utilized plants as part of their primary health care systems for millennia. In the New World tropics archaeological remains of plants used as medicine have been dated to 8000 B.C. This human-plant medical interdependence continues today for at least 80% of the world's population.

Both medicinal plant knowledge systems and tropical forest ecosystems are being erased at an unprecedented and unacceptable rate. The loss of this biocultural diversity is producing the greatest immediate impact on the people of the tropical forest. In the future the loss of biocultural diversity will have a negative effect on the entire global population as we search for treatments for new diseases such as AIDS (Schultes 1991).

Plants used as medicine are often the most accessible and appropriate therapy for a wide diversity of health problems. Indigenous and local people often cultivate and transplant wild medicinal plants in and around their homes and villages. Plant-derived medicines are commonly employed to treat fevers, fungal infections, burns, gastrointestinal problems, pain, respiratory problems, and wounds and are used as antidotes to toxins from organisms such as poisonous snakes and as remedies for many other health problems.

A significant proportion of the urban populations in tropical regions of Asia, Africa, and Latin America also depend on plants as therapeutic agents on a daily basis. Increasing numbers of people in both rural and urban tropical areas are also educating visiting researchers about the spiritual value of tropical forest biosystems and plants to both individuals and communities (Balick 1990).

One of the primary causes of tropical forest loss is poverty. People seeking to feed, clothe, and care for their families often have few viable alternatives except clearing new areas of forests every two to three years or clearing land for large landowners. Without reasonable economic alternatives both protected areas such as national parks and unprotected tropical forests will continue to be destroyed.

This paper is intended to describe the importance of tropical biological diversity to the health care and medical systems of local and indigenous people throughout the tropics of the world.

The Historical Context

More than five millennia ago, people throughout the world were utilizing plants as the basis of their primary medicine. This includes the widely documented Chinese medical system and Indian Ayurvedic medical systems. Five centuries ago the Old and the New World had not yet come into contact. Shortly after the initial journeys of Europeans to the New World, two medical systems in which plants played an important role came into direct collision. In 1492, at the time of the first voyage to the New World, the *materia medica* of Europe used plants extensively. The royal pharmacy of Spain maintained a considerable botanical apothecary that provided the foundation for medical treatment to the royal family and the clergy. Botanists and pharmacists were often the same individual as they created plant medicines utilizing the state-of-the-art knowledge at that time. This knowledge had been, of course, handed down over many centuries through various cultures and medical systems to that time. These plants were as yet unknown to people in the New World.

At the time of contact there existed complex medical systems in the New World as well. Indigenous people from the Arctic to Tierra del Fuego were using an extraordinary diversity of medical practices including a tremendous profusion of plants used as medicines. The Aztec and Maya peoples of middle and central America had extensive pharmacopeias as did the Inca, the people whom the Inca conquered in South America, and the tropical forest cultures. A number of these plants were documented by the early naturalists who arrived after the first Europeans in the New World (Spruce 1908). One image by muralist Diego Rivera depicts an Aztec Indian woman preparing medicinal plants in collaboration with another Aztec healer along with a profusion of plants with Nahuatl names on a mural. On the other side of the mural is an image of scientists working with an electron microscope to analyze the chemical constituents of these compounds (Viola and Margolis 1991).

The first explorers to come to South America encountered indigenous peoples utilizing a vast array of techniques to solve health problems. These included vapor baths with medicinal plants and other systems that are similar to the currently evolving dermal delivery systems for drug absorption.

One of the first cases of plant medicines to move from the New World to the Old World is that of *Cinchona officinalis* L. The first collection of *Cinchona* bark came from the high rain forest region of several Andean countries. It was shipped back to Spain, where it gained great notoriety in a short period of time as a cure-all for fevers. It was first known as "Quina-Quina"—bark of barks—in the regional indigenous language. It was subsequently referred to as Indian fever bark and eventually was renamed Jesuit fever bark. *Cinchona* bark became so valuable as a medicinal plant in Europe that it obtained the equivalent value by weight of silver. The demand became so great that thousands of pounds of *Cinchona* bark were shipped in sewn leather bundles from ports in Ecuador, Peru, and Colombia to Spain and other European ports.

The tremendous demand for this bark caused what is undoubtedly the first conservation crisis for a medicinal plant harvested from the tropics of the New World. Numerous scientific expeditions were commissioned by the royal family in Spain to examine, analyze, and describe the variation present in the species of *Cinchona* trees that were supplying bark. There was little control of the species variation and even less control on the long-term impact of massive harvesting of this material. Indigenous people recognized the variation present in the *Cinchona* trees and helped some of the early scientists such as Ruiz and Pavón, a botanist/ pharmacist team, to distinguish the sources of bark. A number of the varieties of bark had a low content of the active alkaloids with little or no therapeutic value and these trees were harvested inappropriately to fulfill the demand in Europe.

Ironically, it was the transferral of germplasm of the species from the New to the Old World that may have saved *Cinchona* species from extinction or extreme genetic impoverishment. The planting of seedlings in India, Sri Lanka, and Southeast Asia by the Dutch and British eventually supplanted the need for harvesting raw material from the wild. This saved the species from serious long-term ecological and genetic consequences. This example is given to remind interested scientists and development workers that the push to develop natural products from the tropical forests can have devastating consequences if not managed by utilizing ecologically, economically, and socially sound methods.

The exploitation of these kinds of natural products, as mentioned previously, is not without grave potential consequences both for the environment and local people. The early history of exploitation of natural rubber, *Hevea brasiliensis,* was horrendous. There was a period of time in which the voracious worldwide demand for natural latex from rubber trees stimulated slave-like concentration camp atmospheres in the northwestern Amazon of South America. It took an extensive investigation by the British counsel, Sir Roger Casement, to document the atrocities committed by rubber collection camps and rubber barons in the Putumayo region of the northwestern Amazon and expose to the world one of the worst examples of human behavior. This behavior included punishments that were imposed on native people such as the removal of limbs, fingers, and other parts of the body for not meeting the collection quotas (Hardenburg 1912).

The Present

Today only a small percent of the drugs approved are new compounds. In 1988 less than 25% of new molecular entities were approved as drugs by the Food and

Drug Administration in the United States. There is little doubt, however, that the great diversity of chemical compounds found in nature and particularly in tropical forest species could increase the number of new molecular entities approved as therapeutic agents. That would be of great value to the entire global population provided that the development and benefits gained from new molecular entities derived from tropical forests are equally distributed both to people who need the medication and to the countries and regions from which they have been discovered.

One of the methods utilized by Shaman Pharmaceuticals, Inc., a company that develops new drugs from ethnobotanical leads, to ensure that the appropriate distribution of benefits takes place has been the formation of a nonprofit conservation organization called the Healing Forest Conservancy (Moran 1993). Its charter is to (1) maintain medicinal plant biological diversity and (2) provide a structure whereby a portion of the profits generated by the commercialization of plant-derived compounds can and will be distributed to countries who participate in the process of plant collection and other collaborative activities. It is not difficult to establish what are the needs and priorities of native and local people within the tropical countries with whom we are working. One only needs to ask.

One of the Waorani Indian collaborators with whom we worked in January 1991, Alfredo Gaya Nenguimo, was very articulate about the needs of his family and community in the Ecuadorian Amazon. He expressed a need and a desire to have better access to health care, particularly clinics and hospitals, in cases of illness that the community or individuals were not able to cure. That also includes education and information about how to deal with afflictions such as cholera, which has taken thousands of lives in the countries of Peru and Ecuador already. They also expressed interest in having more routine access to health care providers such as physicians in more remote regions who would be sensitive to their cultural medicine and local needs.

One of the approaches used in a recent Shaman Pharmaceuticals collection expedition was to bring a physician to provide health care to community members. This physician, Dr. Charles Limbach, also collaborated in the process of understanding the context and application of traditional medicine in this region (fig. 6.1). There is also a strong interest in many indigenous communities for methods to provide for the continuation of medicinal plant knowledge. As part of the 1991 Ecuador expedition sponsored by Shaman Pharmaceuticals, data were left on all the plants collected for the local school and schoolteacher to duplicate and utilize in teaching on a routine basis. This was something requested by the local community; they have explicit interest in preserving their traditional medical knowledge.

During one of our collecting journeys in the forest we were taught about the use of a potent antifungal plant by an elder Waorani Indian. This gentleman, Huepe Coba, taught us and his son about this plant. His son, who was twenty-one years old, was not familiar with the name or use of this particular plant. Subsequent laboratory analysis has shown this collection to be a potent antifungal agent (fig. 6.2).

FIGURE 6.1 As part of the January 1991 research expedition, Dr. Charles F. Limbach provided health care in two Waorani villages as part of an exchange of Waorani and Western medicine.

These are some of the issues that have been identified by indigenous peoples as important to them and their cultures. They also expressed a strong desire to maintain both a legal claim to their land and the ecological integrity of their environment. They are extremely aware of the importance of an intact, relatively undisturbed, environment to provide them with food and game as well as access to regional plant medicines.

During this field visit Dr. Limbach and I used a number of methods, including images from textbooks of dermatologic diseases, while discussing the use of plants for skin and other fungal afflictions. This was an extremely effective way to stimulate a dialogue and discussion between a Western-trained healer and local healers about the use of plants for fungal afflictions.

We have found that 69% of the plants that were used as antifungal medicine by indigenous people in the tropics of the world have shown activity in our antifungal assays. These include both skin fungal assays and systemic fungal assays. That does not come as a great surprise to ethnobiologists who have worked closely with indigenous and local people throughout the tropics. Their knowledge of the qualities of plants, particularly for fungal afflictions, is profound. An overall idea of the product pipeline is presented in figure 6.3.

We also have used a similar approach in the antiviral area. When working in the field with people we have asked them about the variety of potential symptoms that may well be treated with plants with antiviral activity. These symptoms include fevers, respiratory problems, jaundice, wounds, mouth sores, blindness, malaria, measles, herpes, and warts. Whereas these symptoms may appear to be too diverse and perhaps produced by many, many different diseases, there are precedents in current therapeutics for a wide-spectrum treatment of health problems by single compounds. Corticosteroids are one of the best examples of this. Corticosteroids are used to treat at least a dozen different disorders including endocrine, rheumatic, collagen, dermatologic, allergic, ophthalmic, respiratory, hematologic, neoplastic, and nervous system disorders. All these states are treated with the exact same molecular entity and indicate that our acceptance of indigenous and local knowledge regarding the healing properties of plants requires an open mind.

One example of an ethnomedical profile of an antiviral plant includes a plant utilized for diarrhea, pulmonary problems, cuts, skin irritations, rheumatism, tonsillitis, enhanced fertility, tuberculosis, coughs and influenza, hemorrhoids, contraception, and sore muscles. This plant, which is used for so many diverse symptoms, is now in human clinical trials as part of our antiviral development program.

FIGURE 6.2 During a January 1991 research and collecting expedition to Amazonian Ecuador a young Waorani, Nama Coba, learned, from his father, Huepe Coba, about the antiinfective medicinal applications of a plant that was previously unknown to him. The results of this research and collecting expedition are being integrated into the school curriculum of this village.

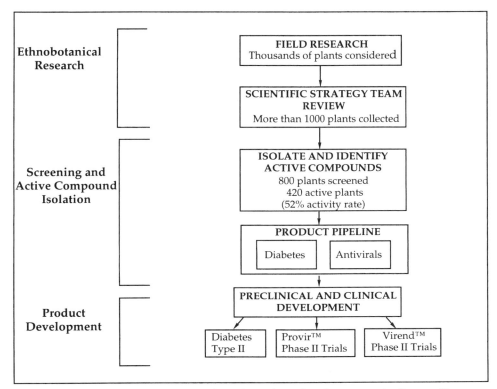

FIGURE 6.3 Ethnobotanical research and product development pipeline at Shaman Pharmaceuticals.

This plant has yielded a molecule, SP–303, which shows strong in vitro and in vivo activity against respiratory syncytial virus as well as influenza A and B. This particular molecule is nonsynthesizable owing to its complex structure (Ubillas et al. 1994). In order to bring this plant to market we will be relying upon natural sources from a number of Latin American countries (King 1994).

That approach, one that respects the knowledge of local and indigenous people and the forest, has helped bring Shaman Pharmaceuticals to the phase I human clinical trials of an antiviral agent in a short time span of sixteen months. Indigenous knowledge about the chemical potential of tropical forest species has been brought back to our laboratory, where sophisticated scientific techniques are used to analyze and screen these compounds (King and Tempesta 1994).

Sustainability

This compound, SP–303, occurs naturally in ten tropical countries and after harvesting regenerates rapidly with minimal management. The plant is a pioneer species and establishes itself quickly where land has been cleared, especially old garden sites and road sites. SP–303 is an ideal addition to buffer zones around protected areas and is one component of agroforestry systems.

Shaman Pharmaceuticals requires that all plant collections be conducted in a sustainable manner, which includes management and replanting when intensive wild harvesting is conducted. Research attempts to develop new natural products from tropical forests need to pay particular attention to species that already have these kinds of growth characteristics: rapid maturation and consistently high levels of active compound. It is advisable to examine and work with species that are already integrated into the mosaic of gardens, secondary forests, and forests managed by humans. Profiles of secondary forests that are undergoing succession often indicate a high density of species that are well adapted to proliferate in secondary vegetation.

The Future

Working with indigenous peoples in tropical forests in the search for new potential therapeutic agents will indeed yield new medicines. It is very important, however, that in the process of doing so local and native people are the beneficiaries and the guardians of the forest (Boom 1990). One of the ways that this can be accomplished is through applying economics to the conservation of biological diversity. This includes strategies to save and develop tropical forests by integrating nontimber forest products into extractive reserves in agroforestry systems (Peters, Gentry, and Mendelsohn 1989; Balick and Mendelsohn 1992). Nontimber or nonwood forest products have become extremely vital areas of research and development for organizations such as the Food and Agriculture Organization (FAO) of the United Nations and numerous independent researchers working in the tropics of Asia, Africa, and Latin America (FAO 1991; Dixon, Roditi, and Silverman 1991). At the same time literally billions of people in dozens of countries in the tropics depend upon plant medicines for primary and routine health care. The plant medicines known as Jamu in Indonesia are consumed by nearly 200 million people. These are medicines derived from plantations and wild collections throughout the Indonesian archipelago. In South America, traditional medicines include plants sold widely in markets in capital cities and remote areas of countries such as Colombia, Ecuador, Peru, Bolivia, Paraguay, Venezuela, Brazil, and many others.

The interest in and enthusiasm for the use of these plants have in the past few decades spread dramatically to the countries in North America, Europe, and Asia. One of the many tropical forest plant medicines reaching the American markets today is Pau D'Arco, which comes from several *Tabebuia* species. This herbal remedy is marketed by a number of health food distributors. This particular plant is the extract of a tree bark, and several companies marketing this product describe it as being harvested in a sustainable nondestructive fashion. This system is described as using only the small amount of cambium layer of the bark of the tree. It is not entirely clear how this is accomplished without destroying the tree, and information clarifying this type of harvesting system must be better explained wherever and whenever it can be done in an effective fashion. The controlled stripping of bark in West Africa has been done without destroying trees of the genus *Prunus,* but activities conducted over the past few years have seriously threatened the diversity and abundance of this species (Cunningham and Mbenkum 1993).

The product, Pau D'Arco, is only one of numerous natural products that have entered the health food market of Europe, North America, and parts of Asia. Increasing numbers of plants and herbal medicines are being brought to the world from people of tropical forest regions. A number of these plants are utilized in very small quantities and could be very important income-generating sources for people in tropical forests. Among the products that use plants in small quantities are those from aromatic plants. Some aromatic plants are utilized in inhalers for a new kind of health food market consumer. Other products such as *Cephaelis ipecacuanha* and *Cinchona* are used in extraordinarily small quantities as part of homeopathic medical preparations.

A voracious hunger exists for products made with plants that are both natural in base and derived from sustainably harvested systems. These include natural body care products, which are estimated to be a 1-billion-dollar market by the year 1996 (*Green Market Alert* 1992). Many other food products, such as Rainforest Crunch, marketed by Cultural Survival, Inc., of Cambridge, Massachusetts, are providing income to local people and educating consumers about rain forest issues.

One of the most sustainably produced products from the tropical forest are paintings by students of the USKO Amazonian School of Painting in Pucalpa, Peru (Luna and Amaringo 1991). In this school, several hundred students observe plants and learn about medicinal properties of plants and then paint them as part of landscapes. These images are sold as postcards and paintings throughout Europe and North America and constitute the most sustainable use of tropical forests—the painting of its beauty and marketing of it without destroying it.

All these products from natural forests can and are being integrated into sustainable systems. The primary goal and most important aspect of this entire type of development are people. Human beings must be the beneficiaries of these systems, for they are both the guardians and the ones who depend upon the often fragile biological diversity for their survival. These are the people who have been living in these environments for literally millennia and who have profound knowledge about their properties while being dependent upon them.

A meeting in 1989 of natural scientists and conservationists in Manaus, Brazil, sponsored by Conservation International, established a complex map of the Amazon Basin indicating areas of greatest and lowest priority for biodiversity conservation activities. These priority areas were based upon the regions of greatest diversity and density of biological diversity. Clearly, any such attempt to create priorities for conservation would have to integrate data on human population, density, social issues associated with the movement of those human populations, and the ways that the people living in these regions could be a part of systems to manage biological diversity. This includes access to and acknowledgment of the importance of tropical forests as sources of plants for health care. The ever-increasing concern and interest of people in the regions of North America, Europe, and parts of Asia about the disappearing tropical forests is very well founded. Ecotourism in tropical forests enables people from other regions to experience the tropical forests for themselves, where they often express an expanded concern for the welfare of this environment.

One of the problems associated with the current public attention toward tropical forests is that it does not include adequate concern for the local people who live in and around tropical forest ecosystems. In order for conservation activities to be successful, they will need to take into account and work with the needs of local people in both rural and urban areas of tropical regions. This mandate includes policymakers in Washington, D.C., and development institutions worldwide, which are increasingly realizing the value and importance of biological diversity in tropical forest regions (King, Carlson, and Moran 1995).

Simultaneously, imagery that has flooded the media over the past several decades about the relationship of scientists to native peoples and of native peoples to their local and national environments needs to be revised. At this time indigenous leaders are addressing world financial institutions such as the International Monetary Fund (IMF), the World Bank, and the U.S. Agency for International Development (USAID) and public press organizations such as the National Press Club to describe their needs and concerns about the environmental protection movement. They are especially concerned about their lack of inclusion in the design of conservation programs in tropical forests (King 1990). Many indigenous federations and organizations have indicated their strong interest in becoming involved with the management and protection of tropical forests. Land title control is one of the most important issues for indigenous peoples of the tropical regions of the world at this time (SAIIC 1990). The development of traditional medicines from these regions can contribute to both an income and a protection strategy for these lands.

In conclusion, it is important to remember that when the first Europeans came five centuries ago to the New World they brought with them diseases that decimated indigenous populations. Bernardino de Sahagun has written (Verano and Ubelaker 1992):

> . . . and a great plague came. Many died everywhere. It was the smallpox. Never had it been suffered in Mexico. It showed on the faces of everyone. No longer were the dead buried, they could only cast them into the water.

Today, nearly five hundred years later, similar events are still taking place in parts of northern Amazonian South America, where Yanomami Indians are dying of exposure to introduced diseases including chloroquine-resistant strains of malaria. They are also experiencing a degraded environment owing to massive influx of gold miners. The time is critical both for these people and their environment and for many similar cultures. The impact of malaria is still very powerful in other regions of Amazonian South America, and it was unknown to the New World prior to the contact. There exists a strong ethical and moral obligation for all parties involved in conservation activities in tropical forests to work with and address the needs and concerns of local indigenous people who inhabit those tropical forests.

Numerous medicines have been derived from the knowledge of tropical forest people and clearly there will be more in the future. This alone is reason enough for any and all programs to be concerned with the conservation, development, and protection of tropical forest regions. Human needs and problems are a primary component of any conservation program. This focus on human needs requires assessing the importance of regional forests in traditional systems of medicine, and it also requires provisions that allow for any activities to have minimal negative impact on the accessibility to these medical resources. Conversely, any and all activities that seek to develop natural products from these regions need to incorporate explicit reciprocal benefit programs in early phases of their planning for the people and places from which the products come. It is clear that our global interdependence is increasing every day, and one of our primary commitments to maintaining biological diversity in the tropics requires acknowledging the value of indigenous knowledge and the importance of traditional medicine to people throughout the tropics.

ACKNOWLEDGMENTS

The author and Shaman Pharmaceuticals, Inc., would like to gratefully acknowledge the intellectual collaboration, guidance, and counsel of the following people: Huepe Coba, Tiro Coba, Namé Coba, Coweña, Illias Gualinga, Cesar Gualinga, and the Gualinga families. We would also like to acknowledge the meetings and guidance provided by COICA, AIDESEP, and multiple indigenous and local people in the tropical forest in Latin America, Nigeria, Tanzania, Indonesia, Papua New Guinea, and many other countries.

REFERENCES

Balick, M. J. 1990. "Ethnobotany and the Identification of New Drugs." In D. Chadwick and J. Marsh, eds., *Bioactive Compounds from Plants*, pp. 23–39. Ciba Foundation Symposium 154. Chichester: Wiley.

Balick, Michael J. and Robert Mendelsohn. 1992. "Assessing the Economic Value of Traditional Medicines from Tropical Rain Forests." *Conservation Biology* 6 (1):128–30.

Boom, B. 1990. "Ethics in Ethnopharmacology." In E. Elisabetsky, ed., *Proceedings of the*

First Congress of Ethnobiology, vol. 2, part F. Belém, Pará: Museu Paraense Emilio Goeldi.

Cunningham, A. B., and F. T. Mbenkum. 1993. "Sustainability of Harvesting *Prunas africana* Bark in Cameroon." People and Plants Working Paper 2, UNESCO Presse, France.

Dixon, Anthony, Hannah Roditi, and Lee Silverman. 1991. *From Forest to Market: A Feasibility Study of the Development of Selected Non-Timber Forest Products from Borneo for the U.S. Market,* vol. I and II. Cambridge, Mass.: Project Borneo.

Food and Agricultural Organization (FAO) of the United Nations. 1991. *Non-Wood Forest Products: The Way Ahead.* Rome: FAO paper no. 97.

Green Market Alert. Jan. 1992, vol. 3, no. 1, Carl Frankel, ed.

Hardenburg, W. E. 1912. In R. Enock, ed. *The Putumayo: The Devil's Paradise.* London.

King, S. R. 1990. "Why Conservation Makes Sense." *Garden Magazine* (Nov.–Dec.). New York Botanical Garden.

King, Steven R. 1994."Establishing Reciprocity: Biodiversity, Conservation, and New Models for Cooperation Between Forest-Dwelling Peoples and the Pharmaceutical Industry." In *Intellectual Property Rights for Indigenous Peoples, A Source Book.* The Society for Applied Anthropology, pp. 69–82.

King, S., T. Carlson, and K. Moran. 1995. "Biological Diversity, Indigenous Knowledge, Drug Discovery, and Intellectual Property Rights" In *Indigenous Knowledge and Intellectual Property Rights,* S. Brush and D. Stabinsky, eds. Island Press.

King, S. and M. Tempesta. 1994. "From Shaman to Human Clinical Trials: The Role of Industry in Ethnobotany, Conservation, and Community Reciprocity." *Ciba Foundation Symposium No. 185.* John Wiley Publishers, pp. 197–213.

Luna, L. and P. Amaringo. 1991. *Ayahuasca Visions. The Religious Iconogrophy of a Peruvian Shaman.* Berkeley: North Atlantic Books.

Moran, K. 1993. "Managing Biological and Cultural Diversity Through the Healing Forest Conservancy." *Intellectual Property Rights for Indigenous Peoples, A Source Book.* The Society for Applied Anthropology, pp. 99–109.

Peters, C. M., A. H. Gentry, and R. Mendelsohn. 1989. "Valuation of an Amazonian Rainforest." *Nature* 339:655–56.

Schultes, R. E. 1991. "Dwindling Forests: Medicinal Plants of the Amazon." *Harvard Medical Alumni Bulletin,* vol. 65, no. 1.

South and Meso-American Indian Information Center (SAIIC) Newsletter (Fall 1989 and Winter 1990), vol. 5, nos. 2 and 3.

Spruce, R. 1908. *Notes of a Botanist on the Amazon and Andes.* London: MacMillan.

Ubillas, R. et al. 1994. "SP–303, an Antiviral Oligomeric Proanthocyanidin from the Latex of *Croton lechleri* (Sangre de Drago)." *Phytomedicine* 1, (2) (September 1994): Gustaf Fischer Verlag, Stuttgart-Jena-New York, pp. 77–106.

Verano, John W. and Douglas H. Ubelaker, eds. 1992. *Disease and Demography in the Americas: Changing Patterns Before and After 1492.* Washington, D.C.: Smithsonian Institution Press.

Viola, H. and C. Margolis. 1991. *Seeds of Change.* Washington, D.C.: Smithsonian Institution Press.

7

Higher Plants Versus Microorganisms: Their Future in Pharmaceutical Research

Georg Albers-Schönberg

THE discovery of new medicines in a tropical rain forest, a wetland, or any wilderness area would remind the world of how valuable these resources are. These areas are also the source of the traditional medicines on which primary health care in the developing world so much depends. We must spare no effort to protect these resources. An active interest on the part of the pharmaceutical industry could make an important contribution toward this goal.

At Merck we have screened plants in the past with little success, but we know that they should be looked at again with the eyes of molecular cell biology and modern screening technologies. Therefore, when The New York Botanical Garden's Institute of Economic Botany—at that time under Dr. Ghillian Prance, now under Dr. Michael Balick—approached us with the proposal to screen tropical plants within their program of "conservation through sustainable use," the opportunity to make our contribution to conservation had come. Recently, we have decided to expand on this concept by entering into a collaboration with Costa Rica's National Institute of Biodiversity (INBio). This is the topic of another paper in this volume.

The search for medically useful natural products is expensive and fraught with the risk of failure. Even large organizations can search for many years and still fail. Since the discovery of penicillin and streptomycin some fifty years ago, the pharmaceutical industry has mostly concentrated on microorganisms. They seemed not only a new and promising source of potentially interesting compounds but also a much more convenient source than labor-intensive plants. However, even though probably hundreds of millions of species of microorganisms have been screened for many different applications, only a handful have yielded important compounds, too few to allow a valid comparison with other sources.

The known drugs from plants are not representative either, though for a very different reason. Most of them have been discovered before the middle of our century and have then been our best medicines. But few of them satisfy modern requirements of safety and efficacy. We still use them because we have decades of experience with them and nothing yet to replace them with. Even the newest anticancer drugs from plants, such as Taxol, while extremely valuable, are not the magic bullets that hit only malignant cells. Whether screening plants is more or less promising than screening microorganisms is therefore hard to say. One thing, however, seems clear to me: besides modern screening technologies and cell biology, we also need new screening strategies.

Many microbiologists argue that microbial natural products are metabolic aberrations and have no useful functions for the organisms that produce them. Microbial screening is therefore often justified simply by the multitude and variety of structures that nature has to offer. To look at plants as merely a reservoir of structures seems equally tenuous. We know today the structure of over one hundred thousand natural products. Why have so few among them become useful drugs? I propose that it is precisely because we have spent our efforts on random approaches and have completely neglected ecological points of view.

We should not be interested in natural products as a random collection of diverse structures. Just like pharmaceutical chemists, nature optimizes structures for specific biochemical functions. We should therefore search for compounds for which the applications that we intend correlate with their biochemical functions as intended by nature. To speculate about this, let me give you a few examples from our own laboratory. These are well-known microbial products that have become "blockbuster" drugs, but the thesis undoubtedly holds also for useful products from plants or other sources.

The microorganism *Streptomyces cattleya* goes to great length to synthesize three different β-lactam antibiotics—by one process a penicillin and a cephalosporin, by a separate process the carbapenem thienamycin, the source of Primaxin®. The organism must have very good reasons for investing so much in two independent biosynthetic pathways and the associated regulatory mechanisms. Perhaps *S. cattleya* has to defend itself in its natural habitat against infections by other microorganisms that are particularly susceptible to this type of antibiotics.

We know of an incredible number of toxic terpenoid natural products. Could it be that the ability to prevent the formation of such compounds in their immediate environment confers a distinct advantage on organisms that can block the synthesis of these toxins? The fungi *Aspergillus terreus* and *Monascus ruber* produce the very potent and effective cholesterol-lowering drug Mevacor®, which specifically inhibits the synthesis of mevalonic acid, a key intermediate in the synthesis of cholesterol as well as of those toxic terpenes.

Avermectin has been discovered as an incredibly potent, broad-spectrum, and safe agent against intestinal helmintic worms and other parasites. Its dihydro-derivative Ivermectin® is used worldwide for veterinary applications and, under the name Ivomec®, for the treatment of onchocerciasis (River Blindness) in people. Can one speculate that the soil organism which produces Avermectin, *Streptomyces avermitilis,* must defend itself against common soil helmints or itself feeds on them?

There are no data that support, or contradict, these postulated ecological functions, and no such speculation played any role in the discoveries of the compounds. But in hindsight, the high potencies of these compounds, their target specificities and, at least in the case of Mevacor® and thienamycin, their structures insinuate that they are not random products. The search for functional relationships may well be the key to new discoveries of such extraordinary natural products as the ones I have just cited, and may become far more successful than massive random screening. Coincidence of ecological and intended pharmaceutical function does not, of course, guarantee pharmaceutical usefulness, but would make it much more likely. Initially this is a "long-shot" approach requiring much basic research. We should get to work as long as some unspoiled resources still exist.

You will now say that the topic of my remarks should have been "Higher plants *and* microorganisms" rather than "Higher plants *versus* microorganisms." You are right. And yet, *versus* alludes to a widespread and counterproductive misunderstanding regarding pharmaceutical research. Many people believe that traditional "natural" plant medicines are better for us than what the industry discovers in its laboratories. But the microbial products penicillin, Primaxin, Mevacor, and Ivomec are also natural and examples of some of the most effective and safest medicines that we have. Furthermore, the ideas for many, if not most, of our modern synthetic drugs can be traced to natural products—the active ingredient of a traditional medicine, or a compound found by screening, or one of our own hormones or neurotransmitters. They are but versions of these that have been structurally and functionally optimized for efficacy and safety. One of the very best examples of synthetic drugs that resulted from the careful study of the biochemistry of a natural product are today's antihypertensive angiotensin converting enzyme (ACE) inhibitors. They trace back to the venom of a Brazilian viper.

We are closing the circle. The topic of this brief paper is the future of compounds from higher plants *and* microorganisms *and* other sources—in short: natural products—in pharmaceutical research. I believe their future is very bright, but they are very difficult to find. We must develop better discovery strategies than we are now using. The understanding of interspecies relationships appears to me to be of foremost importance. Our concern about deforestation anywhere in the world is not only about magnificent trees but about all the species that interact with each other in very specific ways and that live on and in and under the scaffolding of trees. We lose these fragile and yet so valuable ecologies forever when we cut the trees that support and protect them.

8

Topotecan Development: An Example of the Evolution of Natural Product Drug Discovery Research

Brad K. Carté and Randall K. Johnson

DURING the last decade natural product drug discovery research has evolved from an empirical search for antimicrobial and cytotoxic compounds to a more mechanism-based approach. The various stages of development of topotecan, a semisynthetic derivative of the plant alkaloid camptothecin, currently in phase II clinical trials in collaboration with the National Cancer Institute (NCI) as a potential anticancer agent, provides a good example of this evolution to a more mechanism-based search for inhibitors of specific enzymes and antagonists of specific receptors. The importance of the natural resources contained in areas of high species biodiversity to the success of natural products drug research as it stands today will also be discussed.

Discovery of the Antitumor Alkaloid Camptothecin

Natural product research has played an important role in the discovery of drugs for the chemotherapy of cancer. The NCI began an organized program to screen for new anticancer agents in 1955 with the founding of the Cancer Chemotherapy National Service Center (CCNSC). Over the next twenty-five years more than 100,000 plant extracts were screened in a variety of primary assays, predominantly against the L1210 and P388 in vivo leukemia models and the KB cell line in vitro assay (Suffness and Douros 1979). The in vivo leukemia models had the advantages of being more predictive of compounds with potential clinical utility but the disadvantages of being very cumbersome and expensive for natural product screening. These assays required large amounts of material for testing and had a very slow turnaround time for obtaining activity results. The end result was that it often required several years and several hundred kilograms of plant material to isolate and identify a bioactive plant metabolite by using these screens. The in vitro KB cell line cytotoxicity assay was more amenable to high-throughput screening of natural product extracts but had the disadvantage of not being predictive of in vivo antitumor activity. Many common classes of plant natural products such as lignans, saponins, flavonoids, and sesquiterpene lactones were found to be active in the KB cytotoxicity assay, but most had no selectivity of toxicity toward tumor cells as opposed to normal cells and were therefore of no clinical utility. Despite some of the problems with the bioassays used in the NCI program during this time, the program has been quite successful. Today, two of the most exciting new developments in cancer chemotherapy, taxol and second-generation camptothecin derivatives, are a direct result of this NCI program begun in the mid-1950s.

In the late 1950s crude extracts of *Camptotheca acuminata,* a fast-growing deciduous tree indigenous to southern China, was shown to have activity in several of the NCI's animal tumor models. By 1965 the active component of this extract had been isolated and identified as a novel pyrroloquinoline alkaloid that was given the name camptothecin (Wall et al. 1966). Four years later anticancer clinical trials were initiated with the water-soluble sodium salt of the lactone-hydrolyzed form of camptothecin. Although solid tumor responses were reported in phase I clinical trials, in more extensive phase II trials no substantial clinical effect was observed and the trials were terminated in 1972 owing to hemorrhagic cystitis and unpredictable and severe myelosuppression and gastrointestinal toxicity (Moertel et al. 1972; Gottlieb and Luce 1972).

This is where the development of camptothecin ended for the next ten years until the mechanism of action of the antitumor activity of camptothecin was understood. During this same ten-year period natural product research in general also evolved from an empirical search for cytotoxic and antimicrobial compounds to a more mechanism-based approach.

Mechanism-Based Natural Product Screening in General

The evolution of natural products drug discovery research has resulted in a resurgence of industrial interest in natural products as a source of new drug candidates. This has been made possible by several advances in basic science. The first has been advances in molecular and biochemical pharmacology that allow one to understand the molecular and biochemical basis for disease pathogenesis. Through this knowledge it is possible to choose molecular targets, the interference of which may inhibit disease progression. The second major advance contributing to the development of mechanism-based natural product drug discovery research has been the progress in recombinant DNA technology that allows the production of the necessary reagents, enzymes, their natural substrates and receptors, and their natural ligands to develop selective high-throughput mechanism-based assays for the screening of natural products. Finally, since one is looking for compounds that interact at the active site of a specific enzyme or the binding site of a specific receptor, the "hit rate" in these specific assays should be very low, and it is therefore necessary to screen many samples to obtain a lead. This has been made possible through advances in microtiter technology, microcomputers, and robotics, which allow automation of several of the time-consuming steps of mechanism-based screening of natural products.

The example of the modern-day search for drugs to treat hypertension provides a good example of what is meant by mechanism-based natural products drug discovery research. Several decades ago, to search for potential blood-pressure-lowering agents from natural sources, one would screen natural products for the ability to relax vascular smooth muscle in in vivo animal models or in organ culture. While many active substances would likely be found, one would have no idea of the mechanism by which a drop in blood pressure was observed and most likely there would be many observed, often serious, side effects. Today, the knowledge of the involvement of the renin-angiotensin system in hypertension (figure 8.1) allows the development of specific mechanism-based screens to discover potential antihypertensive agents (Timmermans et al. 1991a, b). Angiotensin II (AII) is an octapeptide that, upon binding to specific AII receptors in arteries, causes vasoconstriction with a concomitant increase in blood pressure. A mechanistic approach to the discovery of potential antihypertensive agents would be to block this action by either antagonizing the action of AII at its receptor or by blocking the biosynthesis of AII. AII is biosynthesized from the circulating glycoprotein angiotensinogen by the action of the aspartyl protease enzyme renin to give the biologically inactive decapeptide angiotensin I. AI is further hydrolyzed to AII by the action of the dipeptidyl carboxypeptidase, angiotensin-converting enzyme (ACE). Potential molecular targets would therefore be enzyme inhibitors of either renin or ACE or an antagonist of the AII receptor. Research into renin inhibitors has resulted in several potent inhibitors of the enzyme, although all are peptidic and suffer from poor bioavailability and short duration of action and therefore have not found clinical utility. Research on inhibitors of ACE has been more successful, and one of the most clinically important classes of antihypertensive agents are the ACE inhibitors such as captopril and enalapril. Some of the side effects seen with ACE inhibitors, such as dry cough, are believed to be due to the multisubstrate action of ACE, which is a nonselective peptidyl-dipeptide hydrolase that also inactivates other physiologically active peptides such as the enkephalins and bradykinin. AII receptor antagonists may therefore represent a more selective class of antihypertensive agents, and several nonpeptide AII receptor antagonists

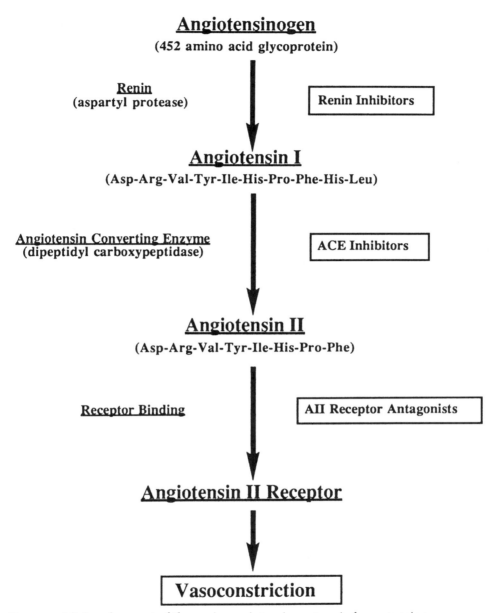

FIGURE 8.1 Involvement of the renin-angiotensin system in hypertension.

are in early stages of clinical trials. This discussion provides a good example of what is meant by mechanism-based drug discovery. A high-throughput screen to discover a potential antagonist of the AII receptor is one of a variety of mechanism-based screens used by SmithKline Beecham Pharmaceuticals for natural product screening.

Mechanism-Based Natural Product Drug Discovery Research at SmithKline Beecham Pharmaceuticals

SmithKline Beecham Pharmaceuticals (SB) has had a very active program in mechanism-based natural products drug discovery research since 1988. We believe that by incorporating a variety of natural product sources in our screening program (table 8.1) we will be screening the widest spectrum of natural product structural types and will therefore increase our chances for success in these efforts.

Extracts of plant material are currently received from five collaborations. One of the major suppliers of extracts of plants from tropical forests areas to SB is Biotics, an independent biotechnology consultancy founded in 1983. Biotics acts as a liaison between the pharmaceutical and agrochemical industries and developing Third World countries where much of the world's biodiversity exists. Biotics currently provides SB with plant extracts from Ghana, Malaysia, and Costa Rica. Collaborators at the Community College of Micronesia provide SB with Micronesian medicinal plants and randomly collected plants endemic to the islands of Micronesia in the Western Pacific. The Morris Arboretum in Philadelphia, Pennsylvania, provides plant material from species found in the northeastern United States and other geographical areas with similar climates. The Royal Botanic Gardens, Kew, in London provides plant extracts of many tropical rain forest species from a variety of worldwide locations. Finally, through a collaboration with Professor Sidney Hecht at the University of Virginia, we have available a very large randomly collected sample of plants from the National Cancer Institute's original plant collections, again from a variety of worldwide geographic locations.

The plant extracts from these sources, along with extracts of marine and microbial natural products from a variety of sources, are screened in a series of enzyme inhibition and receptor-binding assays. The enzyme inhibition assays can be grouped into three major classes based on the nature of the enzyme substrate, whether it be nucleic acid such as for topoisomerases and HIV reverse transcriptase, a protein substrate such as HIV protease, or a small molecule substrate as is the case with phospholipase A_2. Likewise, the receptor antagonist assays can be grouped into three major categories depending on the nature of the natural receptor ligand whether it be a protein such as for the TGFα receptor, an oligopeptide such as for the angiotensin II receptor described in the previous section, or a nonpeptide small-molecule ligand as is the case with leukotriene receptors. The results as of the end of 1991 for screening plant extracts in these assays are shown in table 8.2 (enzyme inhibition assays) and table 8.3 (receptor antagonists assays). A lead compound or group of compounds is not defined as an active hit in the primary assay but must possess all the characteristics necessary for one to consider putting a significant amount of effort in developing the lead as a potential drug candidate. For example, in the angiotensin II receptor antagonist assay, a lead

TABLE 8.1   *Natural Product Sources for Mechanism-Based Screening at SmithKline Beecham*

I.   Plant extracts
  • Biotics (Ghana and Malaysia)
  • CCM (Federated States of Micronesia)
  • Morris Arboretum (NE United States)
  • Royal Botanic Gardens, Kew
  • University of Virginia (old NCI collections)

II. Marine organisms

III. Fermentation sources

TABLE 8.2   *Mechanism-Based Screening of Plant Extracts: Enzyme Inhibitors*

Target	No. Screened	Leads
Nucleic acid substrates		
HIV reverse transcriptase	1,680	0*
HIV ribonuclease H	1,260	0
"DNA damage induction"	7,100	4*
Recombination repair	3,100	2*
Topoisomerase I and II	7,100	2*
Protein substrates		
HIV protease	2,620	0*
Fucosyltransferase	1,200	0
Protein kinase C	2,320	0*
Small-molecule substrates		
ATP citrate lyase	3,950	1*
Phospholipase A$_2$	540	0

*Leads also identified from other natural product sources (i.e., marine or microbial fermentation).

compound must potently inhibit the binding of AII to its receptor in a dose-related manner. In addition, it must be selective in its action and not inhibit the binding of other biologically active small peptides such as substance P, endothelin, or vasopressin to their specific receptors. Finally, the lead compound must show antagonist activity in a biological or functional assay. For AII, the lead must antagonize the AII-induced contraction in isolated aortic strips but not the contraction induced by other agents such as potassium or norepinephrine. Only after a compound has passed all the criteria of selective and potent inhibition and appropriate activity in a panel of secondary assays is it considered to be a true lead worthy of further development. As indicated in tables 8.2 and 8.3, SB has been successful in identifying leads from plant natural products in a variety of mechanism-based screening assays.

Table 8.3 *Mechanism-Based Screening of Plant Extracts: Receptor Antagonists*

Target	No. Screened	Leads
Protein ligands		
Interleukin-1α	2,800	0
Transforming growth factor α	4,400	0
Fibrinogen	760	0
HIV gp120	1,620	0*
Peptide ligands		
Substance P	2,550	0*
Angiotensin II	1,820	4*
Endothelin	1,940	2*
Vasopressin	680	0*
Nonpeptide ligands		
Leukotriene B4	2,600	1*
Leukotriene D4	3,900	2*
Immunophillins	7,100	0*

*Leads also identified from other natural product sources (i.e., marine or microbial fermentation).

Mechanism-Based Drug Discovery Research and the Conservation of Biodiversity

From previous discussions it is evident that, in mechanism-based natural products drug discovery research, one is searching for compounds that selectively interact at the active site of specific enzymes or the binding site of specific receptors, and one should therefore see a very low hit rate. This is the case as seen from the results of plant extract screening at SB in tables 8.2 and 8.3 in the previous section. From more than 61,000 primary screening assays in 21 different mechanism-based assays a hit rate of less than 0.03% for true leads was observed. For success in such a mechanism-based screening program it is advantageous to screen a source of structurally diverse chemicals with a potential to interact in a selective manner with specific enzymes or receptors. Natural products are an excellent source of such a class of chemicals.

The chemistry of living organisms can be divided into two main groups, the primary metabolites and the secondary metabolites, often referred to as natural products (Geissman and Crout 1969). Primary metabolites are the products of primary metabolic processes and are therefore required for the survival of the organisms. These compounds are participants in the cellular activities of nearly all living organisms and include low-molecular-weight carboxylic acids, common amino acids, fats, lipids, sugars, and sugar derivatives. Secondary metabolites or natural products are more restricted in their distribution, being characteristic of a particular taxonomic group whether it be a particular family, genus, or species. Natural products are of relatively complex structure and include classes of compounds such as the alkaloids, terpenoids, phenolics, and rare amino acids and sugars. While natural products largely have no recognized function in the metabolic activity of the producing organism and do not appear to be necessary for the survival of the organism, it is felt they give the organism an adaptive advantage. In other words, they serve an ecological function.

Table 8.4 lists some of the roles natural products can play in the chemical ecology of an organism (Harborne 1986, 1989). While space considerations do not allow discussions of all the potential roles of natural products, several points important to the role of the potential of natural products in providing new drug leads in mechanism-based screening programs can be made. The prime basis for the biological success of any organism is its ability to compete for the necessities of life. In areas of high biodiversity, such as tropical forests and coral reef communities, there is an intense competition between organisms and it becomes advantageous for any organism to expend the metabolic energy required to develop chemical methods to increase its ability to compete and its chances for continued survival. Therefore, areas of high biodiversity are good sources of a diverse collection of natural products.

When one looks at specific examples of the interactions listed in table 8.4 one finds that many of these natural products exert their ecological effect by interaction on a molecular level with specific enzymes or receptors. Take, for example, plant-animal hormonal interactions. Juvenile hormones are insect hormones that control the normal metamorphosis and development of various larval and adult stages of insects. Many plants produce natural products that are specific receptor antagonists of the juvenile hormones and that interfere with the normal metamorphosis and development of the insects that feed on these plants (Williams 1970). These natural products then act as a specific natural insecticide that, through lack of

TABLE 8.4   *Potential Interactions in Chemical Ecology*

Plant-microbe interactions
  • Mycotoxins
  • Signal molecules
  • Phytotoxins
  • Antimicrobials

Plant-plant interactions
  • Allelopathic agents
  • Host-parasite interactions

Plant-animal interactions
  • Antifeedants (animal and insect)
  • Insecticides
  • Hormonal interactions
  • Attractants (pollination interactions)

Animal-animal interactions
  • Chemical defense
  • Trail-following pheremones
  • Alarm pheremones
  • Sexual attractants

predation by herbivorous insects, provides the producing plant with an adaptive advantage over competing plants that lack this defense.

Another important point concerning the potential for drug development from areas of high species biodiversity concerns the nonplant sources of potentially useful natural products. Most discussions concerning the medical resources contained in tropical forests tend to focus only on plant resources, which are only a part of the available resources to be found in these areas. Tropical forests also have a very high degree of microorganism (bacteria and fungi) and insect biodiversity, all of which have evolved biologically active natural products of potential use in drug discovery efforts. An example would be some of the low-molecular-weight insect toxins produced by spiders. Spiders make their living by capturing insects and some have evolved toxins that are receptor antagonists of excitatory amino acids (EAAs), the predominant transmitter at insect neuromuscular junctions. These EAA receptor antagonists cause instant paralysis when injected in insects. EAAs have also been implicated in the pathogenesis of a number of human neurological disorders such as epilepsy and Huntington's disease. These spider toxins may therefore be useful in the development of agents to control these disorders (Jackson and Usherwood 1988).

In conclusion, areas of high biodiversity by definition contain a large number of different species that, owing to differences in biochemical pathways, produce compounds of diverse structural types, many of which have evolved to exert specific interactions at the molecular level of specific enzymes and receptors (Williams et al. 1989). These are just the types of compounds one wishes to screen in a mechanism-based natural product drug discovery program. The natural resources contained in areas of high biodiversity and their protection are absolutely vital to the future success of this research.

Preclinical Development of Topotecan from the Lead Compound Camptothecin

The idea of mechanism-based screening is that through a careful selection of a molecular target one will improve the selectivity of a resulting drug and therefore improve its therapeutic index. For antineoplastic drugs the criterion of selectivity is to selectively kill malignant cells over normal cells. One mechanism-based target for antineoplastic drug discovery is inhibition of topoisomerase enzymes. Topoisomerases are enzymes that bind double-helix DNA and interconvert various topological forms of DNA. There are two classes of topoisomerases (I & II), which differ in the mechanism by which they accomplish this interconversion. Since these enzymes are necessary for DNA replication and transcription during cell division, and since malignant cells are rapidly proliferating cells, the hypothesis is that malignant and nonmalignant cells differ in quantity, isozyme expression, or the regulation of topoisomerases. Therefore, selective intervention may be possible with topoisomerase active drugs (Liu 1989).

To test this hypothesis, various antitumor drugs with unknown mechanism of action were tested for their ability to interact with topoisomerase enzymes. In support of the finding was the discovery that the mechanism of antitumor activity of several clinically useful drugs was inhibition of topoisomerase II (figure 8.2). Doxorubicin and actinomycin D are two microbial natural products isolated from

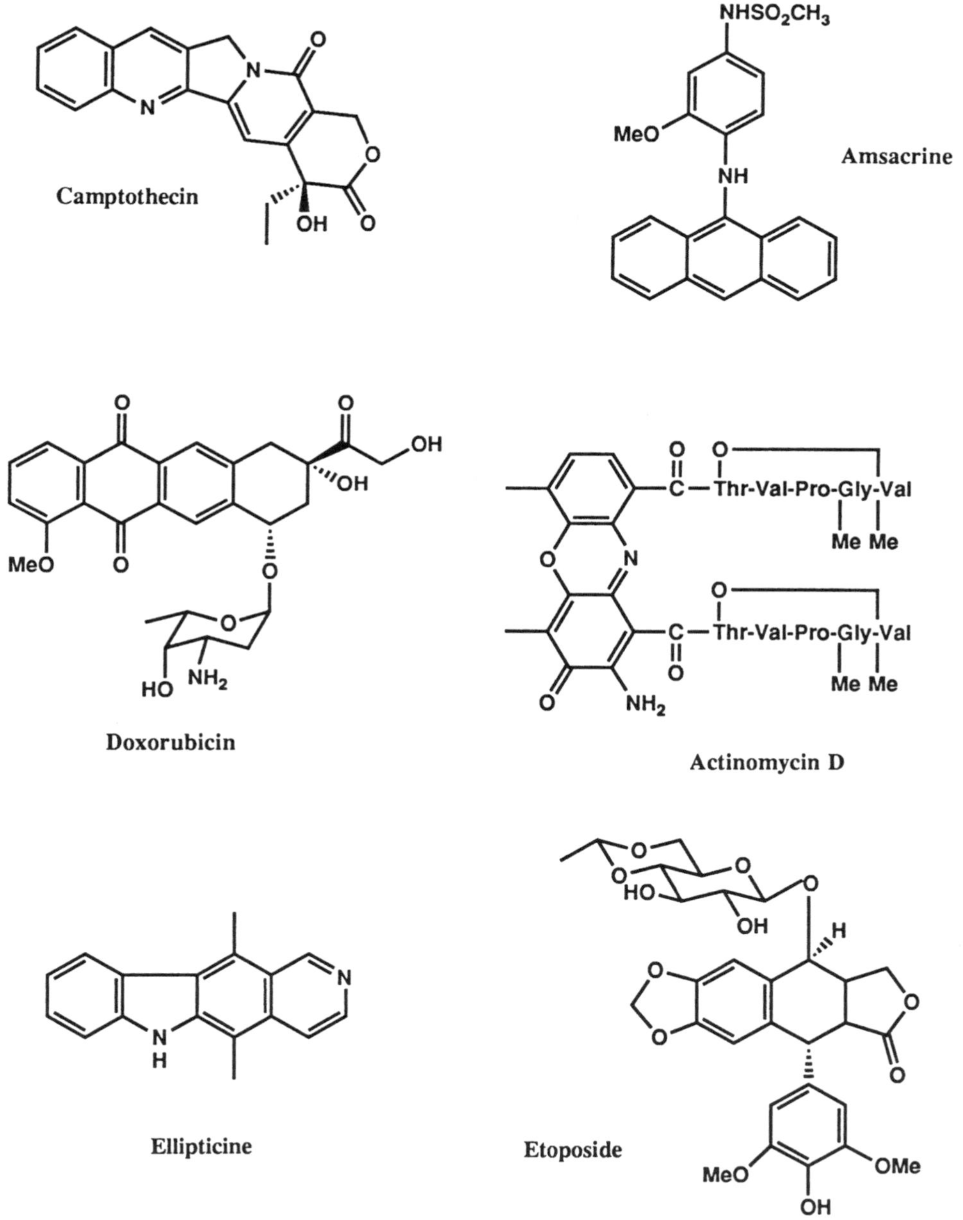

FIGURE 8.2 Structures of some chemotherapeutic drugs that inhibit the action of DNA topoisomerase I or topoisomerase II.

Streptomyces spp., amsacrine is a synthetic compound, and ellipticine and etoposide are naturally occurring or semisynthetic plant natural products. All these compounds are potent and selective inhibitors of topoisomerase II and all except ellipticine have found clinical utility in the treatment of cancers. In addition, it was found that the mechanism of action of the plant alkaloid camptothecin was inhibition of topoisomerase I (Hsiang et al. 1985).

With an understanding of the mechanism of action of the antitumor activity of camptothecin it was possible to design derivatives that might have lower toxicity and better selectivity than camptothecin itself. It was proposed that the severe toxicity associated with camptothecin, which resulted in its being dropped from clinical trials in 1972, was due, at least in part, to its poor water solubility. At SB our strategy was to design water-soluble derivatives of camptothecin that would retain its potent and selective activity against topoisomerase I and its broad spectrum in vivo antitumor activity (Kingsbury et al. 1991). Figure 8.3 illustrates the results of an extensive medicinal chemistry effort to determine where substituents were permitted on the camptothecin nucleus without adversely affecting its topoisomerase I inhibition activity.

From this structure-activity relationship (SAR) study the 10-hydroxy-9-dimethylaminomethyl derivative of camptothecin, topotecan, was chosen for further clinical development. The hydrochloride salt of the dimethylamino side chain of topotecan is water soluble, retains activity as a potent and selective inhibitor of

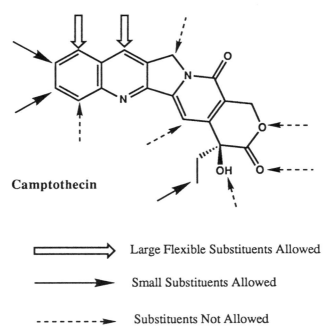

Large Flexible Substituents Allowed

Small Substituents Allowed

Substituents Not Allowed

FIGURE 8.3 Structure-activity relationships of camptothecin analogs for inhibition of mammalian topoisomerase I.

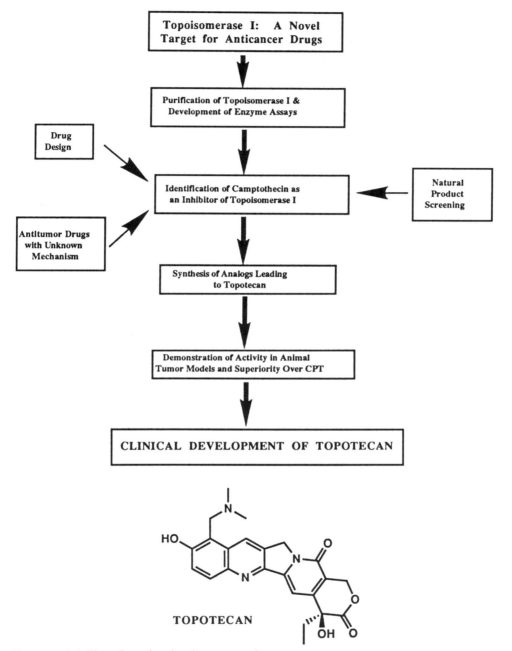

FIGURE 8.4 Flowchart for the discovery of topotecan.

mammalian topoisomerase I, and exhibits broad-spectrum antitumor activity in animal models superior to that found for the parent compound camptothecin. Figure 8.4 illustrates schematically the steps involved in the discovery of topotecan.

Clinical Development of Topotecan

In preclinical studies topotecan exhibited excellent activity in a broad spectrum of preclinical tumor models (Johnson et al. 1992). It was broadly effective in both transplantable solid tumors and leukemias and was curative in several models. Of most importance was the fact that, since topotecan has a unique mechanism of action, it is effective in tumor models that have developed resistance to established drugs. Topotecan was therefore chosen as a candidate for anticancer clinical trials.

Unlike the situation with taxol, the supply of topotecan should not be an issue for clinical trials or commercial production if it should be established as effective in the clinic. Several total syntheses exist for camptothecin (Cai and Hutchinson 1983), and yields for synthetic material are constantly improving. However, synthetic routes to topotecan are still not competitive with semisynthetic production from the natural product camptothecin. Camptothecin is found in significant yields in both *Camptotheca acuminata* and *Nothapodytes foetida,* rapidly growing deciduous trees indigenous to southern China and India, respectively. SmithKline Beecham currently obtains natural camptothecin from both Chinese and Indian pharmaceutical concerns and produces topotecan semisynthetically in an efficient three-step synthesis with an overall yield of more than 50%. In addition to these foreign supplies of camptothecin, the U.S. Department of Agriculture (USDA) has demonstrated the feasibility of the economic production of camptothecin by domestic cultivation of *C. acuminata.* Supply of topotecan will not, therefore, be an issue, for it is economically available from renewable sources.

The first step in the clinical development of topotecan was phase I studies, which are small-scale studies with a limited number of patients designed to determine the maximum tolerated dose (MTD) on a variety of dosing schedules, to identify and quantitate the dose-limiting toxicity on each schedule, and to look for initial evidence of clinical responses. The results of several phase I studies are presented in table 8.5. Regardless of the dosing schedule, the dose-limiting toxicity has been predictable and manageable neutropenia or a drop in white blood cell count. Evidence of activity was seen in a phase I trial conducted at The Johns Hopkins University on a schedule in which topotecan was administered once per day for five days every three weeks (qd $\times$ 5 q3–4 wk). The maximally tolerated dose was 2.0 mg/m^2/day. Responses were seen in patients with advanced ovarian cancer and nonsmall-cell lung cancer. Because of the evidence of activity and the predictable myelosuppression observed on this schedule, phase II studies have focused on the daily treatment regimen.

TABLE 8.5 *Phase I Clinical Studies with Topotecan*

Schedule	Study (Sites)	MTD (Dose-Limiting-Toxicity)
Q3 wk	Univ. Texas at San Antonio (UTSA)	22.5 mg/m^2 (neutropenia)
Qd $\times$ 5 q3–4 wk	The Johns Hopkins University, Memorial Sloan Kettering Cancer Center (MSKCC), Finsen Inst., Rotterdam	2.0 mg/m^2-day (neutropenia)
24 Hr CI q3 wk	M. D. Anderson Hospital, Free University of Amsterdam, Mayo Clinic	5–8 mg/m^2 (neutropenia)
24 Hr CI q1 wk	Fox Chase Cancer Center	Ongoing (neutropenia)
72 Hr CI q3 wk	UTSA, Case Western University	Ongoing (neutropenia)
120 Hr CI q3 wk	(UTSA)	0.68 mg/m^2/day (neutropenia)
Qd $\times$ 5 + gCSF	The Johns Hopkins University	Ongoing
Qd $\times$ 7>10>14 ETC	New York University	Ongoing
Qd $\times$ 5 + taxol	Gynecologic Oncology Group (GOG)	Planned
Qd $\times$ 5 + cisplatin	Cancer and Acute Leukemia Group B (CALGB)	Planned
Qd $\times$ 5 + etoposide	UTSA	Planned

Note: gCSF = granulocyte colony-stimulating factor.

Phase II clinical trials are expanded studies using a larger patient group and are designed to look for clinical efficacy. A number of phase II studies at a variety of cancer treatment centers have been planned using the qd $\times$ 5 q5d dosing schedule. The studies against the most clinically important cancers are shown in table 8.6. These studies are planned to begin during 1992. Additional studies against less common cancers, not shown in table 8.6, are also planned.

Natural products drug discovery research has evolved over the last few decades from an empirical search for antimicrobial and cytotoxic compounds to a more mechanism-based search for inhibitors of specific enzymes or antagonists of specific receptors. The natural product resources contained in areas of high species diversity, such as tropical forests, are vital to the success of this research. SmithKline Beecham Pharmaceuticals has been successful in discovering a number of new drug leads from plant extracts in a variety of mechanism-based enzyme inhibition and receptor antagonists screens. The discovery of the mechanism of action of the well-known antitumor compound camptothecin allowed the development of a second-generation semisynthetic camptothecin analog, topotecan, with improved antitumor activity and decreased toxicity as compared with camptothecin itself. Topotecan is currently in phase II clinical trials as an anticancer agent. The results of these clinical trials will determine whether we are warranted in presenting topotecan in a section on success stories in plant-derived medicine.

TABLE 8.6   *Phase II Clinical Studies Planned with Topotecan 30 Min. Infusion Daily x q3 wk*

Target Cancer	Study Site(s)
Colon	European Org. Research and Treatment of Cancer (EORTC), Case Western University, M. D. Anderson Hospital
Nonsmall-cell lung	M. D. Anderson Hospital, Dana Farber, UTSA (in combination with cisplatin), EORTC (with gCSF)
Small-cell lung	M. D. Anderson Hospital, EORTC, Eastern Cooperative Oncology Group
Ovarian	The Johns Hopkins University, M. D. Anderson Hospital
Cervix	GOG
Breast	French Multicenter, University of Rochester
Prostate	Fox Chase Cancer Center
Melanoma	Ohio State University, NCI (with gCSF)
Renal	MSKCC, NCI

Note: UTSA = University of Texas at San Antonio, GOC = Gynecologic Oncology Group, NCI = National Cancer Institute, MSKCC = Memorial Sloan Kettering Cancer Center, gCSF = granulocyte colony-stimulating factor.

Finally, the future success of natural products drug discovery research depends heavily on our ability to preserve and protect the natural resources contained in the vast biodiversity found throughout the world.

REFERENCES

Cai, J. C. and C. R. Hutchinson. 1983. "Camptothecin." A. Brossi, ed, *The Alkaloids*, 21:101–37. New York: Academic Press.
Geissman, T. A. and D. H. G. Crout. 1969. *Organic Chemistry of Secondary Plant Metabolism*, pp. 5–8. San Francisco: Freeman, Cooper.
Gottlieb, J. A. and J. K. Luce. 1972. "Treatment of Malignant Melanoma with Camptothecin." *Cancer Chemotherapy Reports* 56 (1):103–5.
Harborne, J. B. 1986. "Recent Advances in Chemical Ecology." *Natural Product Reports* 3:323–44.
Harborne, J. B. 1989. "Recent Advances in Chemical Ecology." *Natural Product Reports* 6:85–109.
Hsiang, Y. H., R. Hertzberg, S. M. Hecht, and L. F. Liu. 1985. "Camptothecin Induces Protein-Linked DNA Breaks Via Mammalian DNA Topoisomerase I." *Journal of Biological Chemistry* 260:14873–78.
Jackson, H., and P. N. R. Usherwood. 1988. "Spider Toxins as Tools for Dissecting Elements of Excitatory Amino Acid Transmission." *Trends in Neurosciences* 11 (6):278–83.
Johnson, R. K., F. L. McCabe, G. Gallagher, J. Wood, and R. P. Hertzberg. 1992. "Comparative Efficacy of Topotecan, Irinotecan, Camptothecin, and 9-Aminocamptothecin in Preclinical Tumor Models," p. 85. 7th NCI-EORTC Symposium on New Drugs in Cancer Therapy.
Kingsbury, W. D., J. C. Boehm, D. R. Jakas, K. G. Holden, S. M. Hecht, G. Gallagher, M. J. Caranfa, F. L. McCabe, L. F. Faucette, R. K. Johnson, and R. P. Hertzberg. 1991. "Synthesis of Water-Soluble (Aminoalkyl)camptothecin Analogues: Inhibition of Topoisomerase I and Antitumor Activity." *Journal of Medicinal Chemistry* 34 (1):98–107.
Liu, L. F. 1989. "DNA Topoisomerase Poisons as Antitumor Drugs." *Annual Reviews Biochemistry* 58:351–75.

Moertel, C. G., A. J. Schutt, R. J. Reitmeier, and R. G. Hahn. 1972. "Phase II Study of Camptothecin in the Treatment of Advanced Gastrointestinal Cancer." *Cancer Chemotherapy Reports* 56 (1):95–101.

Suffness, M. and J. Douros. 1979. "Drugs of Plant Origin." In V. T. DeVita Jr., and H. Busch, eds., *Methods in Cancer Research* 16:73–126. New York: Academic Press.

Timmermans, P. B. M. W. M., D. J. Carini, A. T. Chiu, J. V. Duncia, W. A. Jr. Price, G. J. Wells, P. C. Wong, R. R. Wexler, and A. L. Johnson. 1991a. "Angiotensin II Receptor Antagonists: From Discovery to Antihypertensive Drugs." *Hypertension* (Supplement III) 18 (5):136–42.

Timmermans, P. B. M. W. M., P. C. Wong, A. T. Chiu, and W. F. Herblin. 1991b. "Nonpeptide Angiotensin II Receptor Antagonists." *Trends in Pharmacological Sciences* 12:55–62.

Wall, M. E., M. C. Wani, C. E. Cook, K. H. Palmer, A. T. McPhail, and G. A. Sim. 1966. "Plant Antitumor Agents I. The Isolation and Structure of Camptothecin, a Novel Alkaloidal Leukemia and Tumor Inhibitor from *Camptotheca acuminata*." *Journal of the American Chemical Society* 88:3888–90.

Williams, C. R. 1970. "Hormonal Interactions Between Plants and Insects." E. Sondheimer and J. B. Simeone, eds., *Chemical Ecology*, ch. 6, pp. 103–32. New York: Academic Press.

Williams, D. H., M. J. Stone, P. R. Hauck, and S. K. Rahman. 1989. "Why Are Secondary Metabolites (Natural Products) Biosynthesized?" *Journal of Natural Products* 52 (6):1189–1208.

9

Shaman Pharmaceuticals' Approach to Drug Development

Lisa A. Conte

SINCE the first Earth Day, nations worldwide have rallied to address environmental issues. Ever escalating, the forces behind the "green" movement have penetrated almost all walks of life—from the corporate bastion to the single-family home. Today even branded consumer packaged goods use "green" labels and eco-driven marketing campaigns to vie for shoppers' increasingly scarce dollars.

Given this context, it is almost incomprehensible that in 1989, the vision of a business combining capitalism, a commitment to world health, and a dedication to sustaining global biocultural diversity was met with broad-based skepticism. When Shaman Pharmaceuticals first committed to a fund-raising path targeting traditional venture capitalists, there were simply more nonbelievers than potential investors. Today Shaman Pharmaceuticals has the distinction of having raised more than $86 million in less than four years—more than $27 million in venture capital and the remainder in 1993 through two public equity offerings. Although the company is still developing products, Shaman commands a market valuation of more than $50 million, with its common stock publicly traded on the NASDAQ exchange. As of March 31, 1995, Shaman had eighty-three employees, seventy-five of whom are in research and development, including twenty-six Ph.D.s and two M.D.s. Its unique concept and its successful implementation bear strong testimony to the persistence and sheer determination of a community of dedicated individuals who believed they could combine state-of-the-art science with traditional medicinal plant knowledge to play a part in staving off destruction of the world's tropical rain forests and in developing novel pharmaceuticals for unmet medical needs as well.

Shaman's novel discovery strategy has achieved significant time and cost savings while advancing two drugs into the clinic in less than three years. However, to provide tangible evidence that its strategy will also lead to time and cost savings in overall pharmaceutical product development, Shaman's most immediate challenge is advancing these products through the rigorous Food and Drug Administration (FDA) approval process.

Throughout Shaman there is a commitment to accomplishing that goal and to ultimately commercializing novel pharmaceutical products that will fulfill unmet medical needs in cost-sensitive environments. Concomitant to this commitment is a dedication to returning benefits to rain-forest-dwelling peoples, to establishing new models of reciprocity, and to creating models for the sustainable harvesting of nontimber forest products. Success at Shaman will not be defined solely by the traditional financial measures of the pharmaceutical industry. Even in today's more environmentally sensitive world, Shaman will also measure its success in creating industries that are individually owned by forest-dwelling peoples and creating positive environmental impacts in the rain forests of the world.

The Company

Shaman Pharmaceuticals discovers and develops novel human pharmaceutical products. The cornerstone for Shaman's work is a unique drug discovery platform focused on isolating active compounds from tropical plants with a history of medicinal use. At Shaman, "ethnobotany-based" discovery methodologies are combined with natural product chemistry, sophisticated screening capabilities, and modern medicine to create efficiencies in drug discovery and development.

By screening plants used by native healers as remedies for select disease categories, Shaman is producing plant-based drug candidates with diversity of both chemical class and mechanism of action. In this way, the company expects to identify potential human therapeutics with oral activity and safety faster and more efficiently than random mass-screening technologies. In the first two years of its operation, Shaman advanced two infectious disease products from discovery concept to human clinical development. Both are currently being studied in Phase II trials. In late 1994 the company focused its in-house research efforts on diabetes.

The Discovery Process

Shaman's unique drug discovery approach is based on two key interrelated steps. First, it identifies candidate plant materials through fieldwork done by a network of ethnobotanists and physicians who seek out plant remedies used by generations of native peoples. Second, the company investigates candidate plant materials through close cooperation between these ethnobotanists and Shaman's natural product chemists, who have extensive experience in isolating and identifying active compounds from plant materials. This close cooperation allows the company to identify plants likely to have activity in our current therapeutic target areas—antivirals and antidiabetics—and to give priority to the resulting pharmaceutical development opportunities. This prioritization takes into account raw material supply and involves a multidisciplinary exchange among ethnobotanists, plant natural product chemists, pharmacologists, physicians, and pharmacists.

There are three major phases in Shaman's product discovery and development process: (1) ethnobotanical research, (2) screening and active compound isolation, and (3) product development.

ETHNOBOTANICAL RESEARCH

The company's drug discovery process begins with ethnobotanists and physicians collecting comparative data on traditional medicinal uses of plants from geographically diverse tropical areas. Shaman's ethnobotanists and physicians have conducted field expeditions in areas of Africa, Southeast Asia, and Latin and South America where traditional medicines are relatively undocumented and under-analyzed. The tropical rain forests of these areas have vast plant diversity, with more than half of the world's estimated 500,000 plant species. Yet, less than 1 percent of these plants have been researched for medicinal activity. Physicians typically accompany the ethnobotanists on their expeditions to assist in the di-agnosis and documentation of the illnesses and infections that the native people are treating. The ethnobotanist records the specific plants and plant parts used medicinally, form of use (dried, brewed, fresh), duration and method of treatment, and location and abundance of the plant.

In giving priority to certain plants, Shaman notes whether medicinal plants of interest are used to treat similar ailments in geographically diverse cultures. The field-derived information is also cross-checked through literature searches in re-gard to chemical constituents, previously discovered biological activity, and other reported medicinal uses. In the next stage of the prioritization process, these plants are evaluated by Shaman's scientific strategy team (SST). Members of the SST apply their individual area of expertise to the plant selection criteria established and identify the high-priority plants that are targeted for collection and specific activity testing. In Shaman's multidisciplinary environment, the ethnobotanists continue to work with other scientists after the expedition phase in the later stages of drug discovery to assist in directing activity screens.

SCREENING AND ACTIVE COMPOUND ISOLATION

The company's core competencies in ethnomedical investigation, natural product chemistry, and sophisticated animal screening provide the foundation for a unique up-front screening process—a process targeted at generating drug leads with a regularity and diversity that cannot be duplicated by traditional pharma-ceutical industry paradigms. Moreover, using ethnobotany-based drug discovery to identify a small but highly prioritized group of starting materials, Shaman utilizes its sophisticated drug-screening capabilities to reduce the risks normally associated with new drug research and to discover compounds that demonstrate diversity in both chemical class and in mechanism of action, that are active by the oral route of administration, and that show early indications of safety.

Shaman collects high-priority plants from various countries through its net-work of ethnobotanists, botanical gardens, local communities, and cooperatives around the world. It then isolates and identifies the active compounds from plant extracts by testing for activity at each fractionation step of its analytical process. An in-house group is responsible for preparing the plant extracts and the subse-quent isolation and identification of active compounds. Its natural product chem-ists use modern chromatography and spectroscopy and apply proven technology to define new methodologies for identifying and isolating compounds and structures.

By combining its drug discovery and drug-screening capabilities, Shaman has developed a distinct competency which may be applied to potential therapeutic areas. Its focus on diseases with multiple abnormalities for which there are whole animal models that are predictive of the human condition enables the company to identify lead compounds more efficiently than companies that rely on high-throughput screening methods targeted to an individual molecular site. These lead compounds typically exhibit both chemical diversity and diversity in underlying mechanisms of action.

Product Development

Once a pure compound has demonstrated a promising pharmacological profile, it is subject to the same product regulatory requirements as potential drugs from other sources. These requirements include preclinical good laboratory practices (GLP) testing, clinical trials, and FDA filings. Shaman's current products in development have been tested in animal models that have historically been predictive of the indications in humans. Appropriate clinical studies are designed by the company's product development team in consultation with regulatory, toxicology, and pharmacokinetic experts as necessary.

Shaman currently has two products in clinical trials: Provir™, an oral product for the treatment of respiratory viral infections; and Virend™, a topical antiviral product for the treatment of herpes.

Respiratory antiviral product.   Provir, an orally administered product, has demonstrated efficacy in preclinical animal trials against a broad range of respiratory viruses. Shaman is currently studying Provir in hospitalized children with respiratory syncytial virus (RSV). SP–303, the active compound in Provir, is derived from a plant that grows naturally in several countries in South and Latin America, where it has been used medicinally for centuries. The medicinal plant remains a popular local remedy for cold and flu symptoms even in many areas where modern medicines are readily accessible.

Phase I clinical trials of Provir were conducted in more than 120 adults, in both single and multiple doses. The results indicate no significant adverse effects of the drug. In the spring of 1993, Shaman conducted a challenge study to affirm the safety of Provir in experimentally infected adults prior to initiating a clinical program in RSV-infected children. The results of the challenge study, reported in September 1993, confirmed the safety of Provir established in the Phase I trials. In January 1994, the company continued its Phase II development program to further evaluate the safety of Provir in hospitalized, RSV-infected children three to twenty-four months of age. The initial part of this Phase II program is designed to establish the safety and pharmacokinetics of Provir, while the second part is designed to assess preliminary indications of efficacy and dosing requirements of Provir. Shaman ultimately plans to develop the Provir for outpatient use in children with RSV.

Herpes antiviral product.   Virend is a topical formulation of SP–303 for the treatment of herpes simplex virus. This compound has shown activity in animal models and in vitro against various strains of herpes, including those resistant to aciclovir, the only presently approved treatment for herpes. The plant from which this compound is derived also has a long history of folk use in South and Latin America for the topical treatment of wounds and lesions associated with herpes, and is covered by the United States composition-of-matter patent for SP–303 issued to Shaman.

Shaman completed a phase I/II pilot study in immunocompromised patients with aciclovir-resistant herpes in 1993. This study involved a very sick and small patient population in which improvement was reported in more than half of the lesions evaluated after fourteen days of treatment. The results of this Phase I/II study supported the company's decision to begin a double-blind, placebo-controlled Phase II study involving approximately forty patients in December 1993. This study expanded the Virend program to include patients who are immunocompromised and have recurrent herpes virus infections, not just those with aciclovir-resistance. Unlike the pilot trial, this study will evaluate Virend as a first-line therapy rather than as a treatment of last resort for patients who have failed all conventional therapy. Once safety and preliminary indications of efficacy have been determined in a controlled setting, Shaman intends to begin a pivotal trial of Virend in immunocompromised patients in the United States. Shaman intends to develop the current formulation of Virend for the treatment of herpes infections in immunocompromised patients and to out-license Virend for herpes infections in the general population.

Drug discovery research. In late 1994, basic research in diabetes became the centerpiece of the company's research efforts. The process of selecting diabetes as the centerpiece of the company's research program was the direct result of a strategic review that incorporated the knowledge Shaman had gained since its founding, as well as the opportunities and research results made possible by a distinctive drug discovery platform. Diabetes is a disease that is not well managed by available therapies, and the market for an effective oral therapeutic agent is large; its underlying pathophysiology is complicated, with multiple abnormalities that can lead to the disease; whole animal models are predictive of the diabetic disease state in humans; and the disease has symptoms that are easily observed in the field and currently treated by traditional healers with plant-based remedies. This therapeutic target embraces all the concepts that clearly differentiate Shaman's expertise and capabilities and set the company apart from those focused on random high-throughput technologies based on in vitro discovery.

Diabetes mellitus is a chronic disease in which the body does not produce or respond to insulin, a hormone produced by the pancreas to metabolize glucose. When insulin is absent or ineffective, high levels of glucose appear in the blood. The two major types of diabetes mellitus are insulin-dependent diabetes mellitus (IDDM or Type I, also called juvenile onset diabetes) and non-insulin dependent diabetes mellitus (NIDDM or Type II). Type II diabetes, the focus of Shaman's research, accounts for up to 95% of all cases.

Shaman's current diabetes program involves in vivo screening of plants by oral administration in parallel with, or followed by, in vitro assays; the fractionation of active extracts; the isolation and identification of active compounds; and the capability to profile and prioritize promising candidates for clinical development. The company filed its first United States patent application in this program in September 1994, and through the end of March 1995 had identified two more lead compounds that lower blood glucose in mouse models with the expectation of filing United States patent applications on these compounds as well.

Corporate Partners

In September 1991, Shaman formed a three-part corporate alliance with Inverni della Beffa (Inverni), one of the world's leading manufacturers of plant-derived pharmaceuticals. Shaman granted Inverni a nonexclusive license to sell SP–303 in Italy. Inverni will pay Shaman a royalty on products derived from SP–303 and distributed by Inverni in Italy. In addition, there is a long-term manufacturing agreement, under which Inverni is obligated to scale-up Shaman's manufacturing of SP–303 bulk drug at Inverni's expense.

Shaman believes that potential pharmaceutical partners will look to our discovery technology (a) to reduce much of the time normally required to take potential compounds to the point of demonstrating relevant in vivo activity and (b) to reduce the risk of a joint research and development program that is limited by chemical class or mechanism of action. Indeed, it is this very process, or methodology, that Shaman expects to serve as a model for its ongoing research efforts. Over time, Shaman expects that its proprietary methodologies will distinguish it as a pharmaceutical company with a drug discovery platform that is robust, risk-diversified, and sustainable.

The Healing Forest Conservancy

Shaman formed the Healing Forest Conservancy (HFC), a California nonprofit corporation dedicated to maintaining global plant biodiversity, as part of its founding activities. The HFC focuses on conserving plants that have been used traditionally for medicinal purposes. Early on, Shaman committed to donating funds from product profits to provide benefits to indigenous peoples in the countries where Shaman's source plants are obtained. Currently, the nonprofit is soliciting private donations to fund its operations and conservation efforts.

Both Shaman and HFC are philosophically committed to the principle that compensation for indigenous peoples should not be delayed for five to ten years, pending commercialization of a potential product. Both organizations feel that a "waiting period" does not serve the immediate short- and medium-term needs of the forest-dwelling peoples, especially in light of the fact that commercialization of pharmaceutical products can be relatively protracted. Throughout both the company's and the nonprofit's activities over the past three years, there have been tangible and explicit short-, medium-, and long-term reciprocal benefits returned to the people and places where work has been done. This protects the communities where research is conducted but does not lead to a product.

The Shaman and HFC reciprocity solutions are three-pronged. Shaman intends to provide a portion of the profits of any and all products to all the communities and countries in which it has worked. This spreads out the risk and ensures a more rapid return of resources for all collaborators. Even a product licensed from another company, at such time as it is revenue generating, will contribute to the pool of distributable resources.

The second part of the solution is the mechanism. The HFC was designed to help determine, with an independent board of advisers, the appropriate distribution of resources to the communities and government organizations. Representatives from the various countries will participate in this process of discussion and decision making, all independent of Shaman.

The third part of returning benefits involves the creation of new sustainable natural product supply industries in the countries in which Shaman works. The development of new sustainable supply industry in tropical countries is considered to be a vital part of economic development by the governments and local people and many countries throughout the tropics. Such an industry is in progress in four Latin American countries at this time, providing premium prices and managed by local forest-dwelling people in those countries.

Additionally, because of the typically long development period for pharmaceutical products, Shaman is returning benefits immediately to any and all groups with which it works. This is accomplished simply by asking the people with whom the company works what their immediate needs are, and this is done in advance of any given research project. This reflects a core philosophy; Shaman strongly believes in according adequate compensation for the intellectual property of forest-dwelling peoples and it reinforces its commitment by contributing reciprocal benefits based on the requests of local people in the early, middle, and later stages of a collaboration. In sum, we are working to reverse and reorient some of the culturally and environmentally destructive patterns of well-intended developmental programs that work with local and indigenous people throughout the world.

The work at Shaman today is laying the foundation for the company's future. Yet, even with clear vision of the objectives that we hope to achieve, there is much to learn and much uncertainty that will undoubtedly shape our history. As the two products now in the clinic advance in development and as new products enter the clinical arena, external market conditions, new therapeutic developments, regulatory concerns, and even political issues may come to bear on the future of Shaman.

We cannot, admittedly, claim to envision all the scenarios that we may face in the future. But our commitment to bringing greater efficiency to drug discovery and development, to developing novel drugs for cost-sensitive environments, and to creating industries in forest-dwelling communities will continue to shape the paths we choose to take.

We intend to lead, to remain faithful to our cause, and to responsibly create models for businesses of the future. We intend to continue to be activists, to take our messages to all audiences whether similarly inclined or not. It is our hope that Shaman has begun to pave a road down which many environmentally sensitive businesses will follow to rescue the valuable natural resources of the rain forests and to bring new, sorely needed products to the global marketplace.

10

Drug Discovery and Development at the National Cancer Institute: The Role of Natural Products of Plant Origin

Gordon M. Cragg and Michael R. Boyd

THE United States National Cancer Institute (NCI) was established in 1937, its mission being "to provide for, foster and aid in coordinating research related to cancer." In 1955 NCI set up the Cancer Chemotherapy National Service Center (CCNSC) to coordinate a national voluntary cooperative cancer chemotherapy program, involving the procurement of drugs, screening, preclinical studies, and clinical evaluation of new agents. By 1958 the initial service nature of the organization had evolved into a drug research and development program with input from academic sources and massive participation of the pharmaceutical industry. The responsibility for drug discovery and preclinical development at NCI now rests with the Developmental Therapeutics Program (DTP), a major component of the Division of Cancer Treatment (DCT). Thus, NCI has, for the past forty years, provided a resource for the preclinical screening of compounds and materials submitted by grantees, contractors, pharmaceutical and chemical companies, and other scientists and institutions, public and private, worldwide, and has played a major role in the discovery and development of many of the available commercial and investigational anticancer agents (Driscoll 1984). During this period, more than 400,000 chemicals, both synthetic and natural, have been screened for antitumor activity.

With the emergence of acquired immunodeficiency syndrome (AIDS) as a global epidemic in the 1980s, DTP initiated a major new program within NCI for the discovery and preclinical development of anti-HIV agents (Boyd 1988). DTP developed a high-flux screen capable of accommodating more than 40,000 samples per year and, since 1988, has provided a national resource that permits scientists from academic and industrial organizations worldwide to submit compounds for anti-HIV testing (Boyd 1988; Weislow et al. 1989).

During the early years of the CCNSC, the screening of natural products was concerned mainly with the testing of fermentation products, and, prior to 1960, only about 1,500 plant extracts were screened for antitumor activity. The establishment of an interagency agreement with the United States Department of Agriculture (USDA) in 1960 for the collection of plants for screening in the CCNSC program marked the start of the systematic effort toward the development of anticancer agents from plant sources. Initially collections were made in the United States and Mexico, but these were later expanded to about sixty countries through both field collections by USDA personnel and procurements from contract suppliers. Between 1960 and the termination of the collection program in 1982, some 114,000 extracts of an estimated 35,000 plants were screened against a range of tumor systems used as a primary screen, principally the L1210 and P388 mouse leukemias. A discussion of the scope and achievements of this program is not the subject of this paper, but it has been reviewed in depth in earlier reports (Perdue 1976; Suffness and Douros 1979, 1982).

Screening Methods Used at NCI

PRECLINICAL ANTICANCER SCREENING

In vivo animal tumor models, 1955–1985. Since the inception of the NCI new drug program in 1955 a number of in vivo tumor models have been examined as potential screens (Driscoll 1984; Venditti, Wesley, and Plowman 1984), but before 1985, major reliance was placed on the murine leukemias, L1210 and P388. From 1956 to 1975, the L1210 model served as the primary screen; from 1975 to 1985 it was replaced by the more sensitive P388 model. After 1975, agents exhibiting significant activity against the P388 were tested further against a secondary tumor panel comprising four to eight other models, including animal tumors and a few human tumor xenografts. Those agents showing potent, broad-spectrum activity in the secondary panel were generally given highest priority for preclinical development and eventual advancement to disease-oriented clinical trials (figure 10.1).

In assessing the performance of these screens it is clear that they have done well in detecting a diverse range of compounds having a variety of mechanisms of actions. These compounds include: alkylating agents; purine and pyrimidine antimetabolites; antifolates; mitotic inhibitors; DNA-interactive compounds, including intercalators, alkylators, minor groove binders, single- and double-strand breakers, DNA polymerase inhibitors, and topoisomerase inhibitors; and inhibitors of protein synthesis (Chabner and Collin 1990). A substantial number of active drugs have been identified (Driscoll 1984), but useful clinical activity has been restricted to leukemias and lymphomas in the majority of cases. A serious defi-

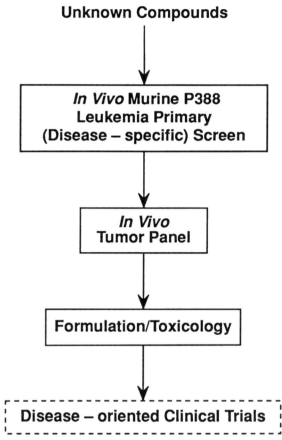

FIGURE 10.1 Schematic representation of drug discovery and development strategy using the P388 primary screen.

ciency exists, however, in the chemotherapy of slow-growing adult solid tumors, such as lung, colon, advanced breast, prostatic, pancreatic, and brain tumors. In retrospect, these results might be attributed to the use of a single disease-specific model as the primary screen that filtered out those agents with potential specificity against tumors other than mouse leukemia or closely related human diseases.

In an attempt to overcome this deficiency, NCI has, over the past five years, developed an alternative disease-oriented preclinical anticancer drug discovery strategy aimed at the discovery of new agents for disease-specific clinical trials in relevant cancer patient populations (Boyd 1986, 1989, 1993).

Disease-oriented in vitro human tumor cell line primary screen. Cancer comprises an extremely complex and diverse group of diseases that share some common biological characteristics, collectively defined as malignancy. Specific forms of cancer, however, often exhibit distinctive characteristics reflected by differences in heterogeneity, accessibility, size and diffuseness, histologic appear-ance, growth rates, and other features. From the point of view of chemotherapy, the most critical difference among animal (including human) tumors is that of drug sensitivity. No single drug can be considered truly broad spectrum, and often apparently similar tumors exhibit markedly different drug response patterns. The nature of cancer thus presents serious problems in the development of suitable screening models.

A disease-oriented screening strategy should employ multiple disease-specific (e.g., tumor-type specific) models and should permit the detection of either broad-spectrum or disease-specific activity. The use of multiple in vivo animal models for such a screen is not practical, given the scope of requirements for adequate screening capacity and specific tumor-type representation. The availability of a wide variety of human tumor cell lines representing many different forms of hu-man cancer offered, however, a suitable basis for development of a disease-oriented in vitro primary screen. Moreover, since many established human tumor cell lines can be propagated in vivo in athymic, nude mice, there existed the basis for secondary in vivo testing of any agents exhibiting line- or panel-selective cy-totoxicity in the primary screen. Such agents would be evaluated in vivo in se-lected cell lines from the primary screen and, if shown to be sufficiently effective in vivo, could be advanced through preclinical development (formulation, phar-macology, toxicology) to disease-specific clinical trials (fig. 10.2) (Boyd 1989).

Pilot screening operations were started in 1989 using a panel comprising a total of sixty human tumor cell lines derived from seven cancer types (Monks et al. 1991). The panel cell lines are organized into subpanels representing lung, colon, melanoma, renal, ovarian, brain, and leukemia (Stinson et al. 1992). Each cell line meets minimal quality assurance criteria (testing for mycoplasma, membrane-associated proteins [MAP], human isoenzyme, karyology, in vivo tumorigenicity) and is adaptable to a single growth medium. Mass stocks of each line were pre-pared and cryopreserved, and these provide reservoirs for replacement of the corresponding lines used for screening after no more than twenty passages in the screening laboratory. After extensive investigation of alternative assays (Alley et al. 1988; Scudiero et al. 1988; Monks et al. 1991; Rubinstein et al. 1990), a protein-staining procedure using sulforhodamine B (SRB) (Skehan et al. 1990) was selected as a suitable method for determination of cellular growth and viability in the screen (Monks et al. 1991). Repetitive screening of a set of 175 known compounds, comprising commercially marketed (NDA-approved) anticancer agents, investi-gational (INDA-approved) anticancer agents, and other candidate antitumor agents in preclinical development, has established the reproducibility of the screening data and permitted development of procedures for quality control moni-toring.

In the routine primary screening, each agent is tested over a broad concentra-tion range against every cell line in the current panel. All lines are inoculated onto a series of standard ninety-six-well microtiter plates on day zero, in the majority

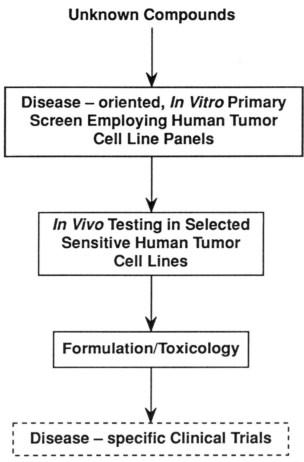

FIGURE 10.2 Schematic representation of drug discovery and development strategy using the new in vitro disease-oriented primary screen.

of cases at 20,000 cells/well, then preincubated in absence of drug for twenty-four hours. Test drugs are then added in five tenfold dilutions, starting from the highest desired concentration, and incubated for a further forty-eight hours. Following this, the cells are fixed in situ, washed, and dried. SRB is added, followed by further washing and drying of the stained adherent cell mass. The bound stain is solubilized and measured spectrophotometrically on automatic plate readers interfaced with microcomputers, which in turn are interfaced to a mainframe computer. While the overall concept of the screen and the technical aspects of the assay methodology appear simple and straightforward, the technical, logistical, and managerial challenges to operation of the screen at the desired capacity have been great. Data management and analysis have also presented unprecedented challenges (Boyd, Paull, and Rubenstein 1991). Further details of how all these challenges have been addressed are beyond the scope of this review but are described in the various references cited above. Currently, the primary screening laboratory is capable of testing compounds at a rate of 400 per week against a 60-line panel.

The optimal strategies for analysis and display of the screening data, and the determination of optimal criteria for selection and ranking of novel active compounds, are subjects of continuing investigation. However, one simple way to obtain a measure of the relative cell line sensitivities to a particular agent is to compare the relative drug concentrations required to produce the same level of response (e.g., GI_{50}, TGI, LC_{50}; the concentrations producing 50% growth inhibition, total growth inhibition, or 50% cell killing, respectively) in each cell line (Boyd, Paull, and Rubenstein 1991; Monks et al. 1991; Paull et al. 1989).

One approach to visual presentation of such a comparison is the so-called mean graph display (Paull et al. 1989). As an example, a mean graph from the screening of one of our interesting crude plant extracts is shown in figure 10.3. In this instance the mean graph was constructed by projecting bars, one for each cell line (listed by an identifier on the left of the graph), to the right or left of a central line depicting the arithmetic mean of the logarithm of the GI_{50} values for all the cell line responses measured for the compound; those bars projecting to the right of the mean represent cell lines more sensitive to the compound, while those to the left represent lines less sensitive to the compound. The length of a bar is proportional to the difference between the logarithm of the individual cell line GI_{50} and the mean. For example, a bar projecting two log units to the right of the mean reflects a cellular sensitivity 100 times that of the average of all the cellular responses to the compound. Interesting features of the screening fingerprint of this extract are the relatively lower sensitivities of the leukemia lines compared with many of the solid tumor lines and the apparent clustering of in vitro activity among the melanoma cancer lines. This extract is presently being subjected to bioassay-guided fractionation to isolate and identify the pure active constituent(s).

A potentially valuable application of the mean graph representation is the ability to match the mean graph fingerprints of natural product extracts with those of known agents recorded in the NCI standard agent data base. A family of computer programs called COMPARE have been developed for this purpose (e.g., see Paull et al. 1989). COMPARE has already proved useful in the dereplication of a number of plant extracts being investigated in the current NCI natural products program. Dereplication is the identification of compounds or chemical classes (replicates) previously isolated and reported in the literature (Suffness, Newman, and Snader 1989). The need for dereplication at an early stage is particularly important in natural products research in order to avoid waste of effort in the isolation and structural elucidation of known structure types of no special current interest. The application of the COMPARE program is illustrated by the example of a recent investigation of extracts of the plant *Anthriscus sylvestris* (L.) Hoffm. A COMPARE analysis of the mean graph fingerprint of the organic extract (provided to us by Professor Won S. Woo of Seoul National University as part of a collaboration in the study of Korean medicinal plants) against the current screening data

Panel/Cell Line	Log_{10} GI50	GI50
Leukemia		
CCRF-CEM	-4.58	
HL-60(TB)	-4.88	
K-562	-4.64	
MOLT-4	-4.73	
RPMI-8226	-4.77	
SR	-4.67	
Non-Small Cell Lung Cancer		
A549/ATCC	-5.71	
EKVX	-4.68	
HOP-18	-5.65	
HOP-62	-4.97	
HOP-92	-4.68	
NCI-H226	-5.26	
NCI-H23	-6.30	
NCI-H322M	-5.36	
NCI-H460	-5.61	
NCI-H522	-4.82	
LXFL 529	-4.79	
Small Cell Lung Cancer		
DMS 114	-5.42	
DMS 273	-5.26	
Colon Cancer		
COLO 205	-5.66	
DLD-1	-4.80	
HCC-2998	-4.88	
HCT-116	-4.75	
HCT-15		
HT29	-5.50	
KM12	-5.00	
KM20L2	-5.33	
SW-620	-5.08	
CNS Cancer		
SF-268	-4.59	
SF-295	-5.38	
SF-539	-5.11	
SNB-19	-4.92	
SNB-75	-5.42	
SNB-78	-4.53	
U251	-4.87	
XF 498	-4.70	
Melanoma		
LOX IMVI	-5.88	
MALME-3M	-5.94	
M14	-5.94	
M19-MEL	-6.70	
SK-MEL-28	-5.50	
UACC-257	-5.64	
UACC-62	-5.97	
Ovarian Cancer		
IGROV1	-4.62	
OVCAR-3	-4.80	
OVCAR-4	-4.85	
OVCAR-5	-4.57	
OVCAR-8	-4.60	
SK-OV-3	-4.79	
Renal Cancer		
786-0	-4.55	
A498	-4.90	
ACHN	-4.82	
CAKI-1	-4.44	
RXF-393	-4.67	
RXF-631	-4.93	
SN12C	-5.15	
TK-10	-4.12	
UO-31	-4.73	
MG_MID	-5.08	
Delta	1.62	
Range	2.58	

+3 +2 +1 0 -1 -2 -3

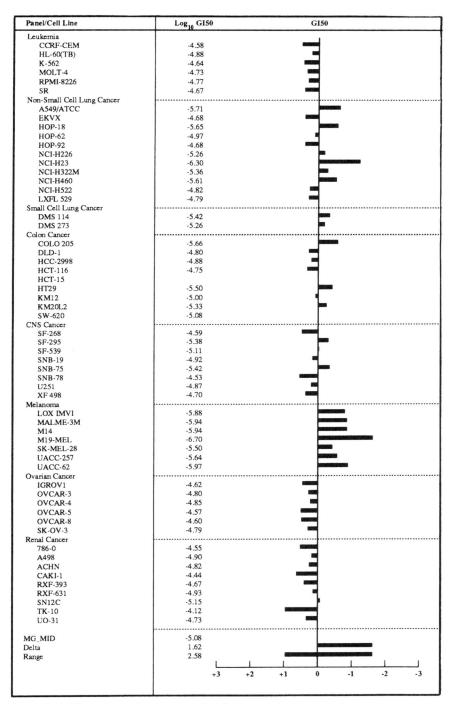

FIGURE 10.3 GI_{50}-centered mean graph of plant extract.

Note: MG-MID is the calculated mean graph-mean inhibitory dose expressed in micrograms. The bar charts are graphic descriptions of the difference in sensitivity of each cell line from the average response of all. When dose responses are plotted for each cell line, the intercept where the dose reduces the cell response to 50% of the original is measured (the GI_{50}). The GI_{50}s from all the cell lines are then averaged to calculate the mean (the MG-MID). The delta value is the difference between the GI_{50} and the mean, and the range is the total difference (summed positive and negative) between the maximum GI_{50} and the minimum GI_{50}.

base of pure compounds showed close correlations with the mean graphs of the plant-derived tubulin binder podophyllotoxin (fig. 10.4) and other related compounds. Reference to the literature revealed that the closely related compound deoxypodophyllotoxin had previously been reported from extracts of *A. sylvestris* (L.) Hoffm. (Inamori et al. 1985), and NCI chemists rapidly isolated this compound and confirmed it as the agent responsible for the observed activity (M. Tischler, J. Cardellina et al., unpublished).

A major goal of the new primary screen is to search for agents giving new biological activity profiles of interest. The discovery of new agents having clinical utility against any or all of the various forms of cancer represented in the screen will be the ultimate measure of success of this new strategy. The scope of the current interim sixty-cell-line panel is limited by the size of the disease-related subpanels and, for technical reasons, the absence of subpanels representing certain major cancer types, such as breast and prostate cancer. Special emphasis is being placed on the acquisition of cell lines representing these cancer types; in addition, efforts are being made to expand and improve the current disease-related subpanels by acquisition of more adequately documented and more representative cell lines. During the next few years we anticipate that the panel may be fully expanded to include as many as ten to twelve different major cancer types with as many as ten lines or more in each subpanel.

PRECLINICAL ANTI-HIV SCREENING

As part of the response of the National Institutes of Health (NIH) to the AIDS epidemic, the DTP of the NCI developed a screening program for the large-scale testing of synthetic and natural products for anti-HIV activity (Boyd 1988). The anti-HIV screening assay (Boyd 1988; Weislow et al. 1989) uses somewhat similar technology for determination of cellular growth or viability as the in vitro human tumor cell line primary screen described above. Human lymphoblastoid cells (CEM-SS cells) are grown in microtiter plate wells in the presence or absence of the human immunodeficiency virus (HIV-1) and in the presence or absence of test material. Anti-HIV activity is indicated by an enhanced growth or survival of the virus-infected cells in the presence of the test material. As an important control, the relative growth or survival of uninfected cells in the presence of the test material gives a measure of the direct cytotoxicity of the test material to the host cells. The degree of cell survival is measured quantitatively by a colorimetric procedure (Scudiero et al. 1988; Weislow et al. 1989) using a soluble tetrazolium reagent (XTT) (Paull et al. 1988), which is metabolically reduced by viable cells to yield a soluble, colored formazan product. Uninfected, viable cells, or cells that are protected from the cytopathic effects of the virus by the test material and have continued to proliferate, produce the soluble orange formazan, and these cultures give high optical densities (OD). Cells not protected by the test material are killed by the virus and do not proliferate, resulting in less formazan production and

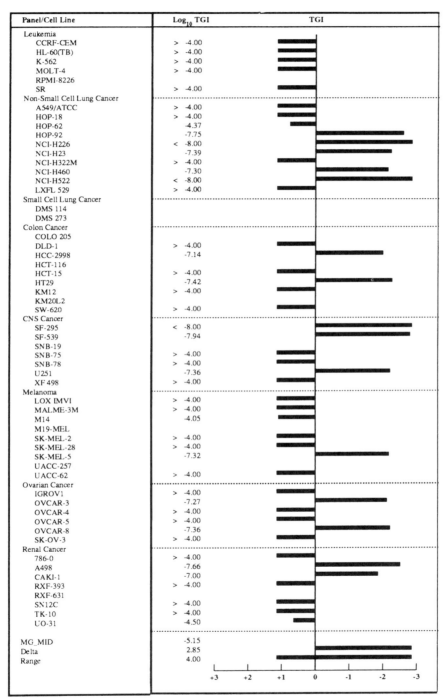

Panel/Cell Line	Log$_{10}$ TGI		TGI
Leukemia			
CCRF-CEM	>	-4.00	
HL-60(TB)	>	-4.00	
K-562	>	-4.00	
MOLT-4	>	-4.00	
RPMI-8226			
SR	>	-4.00	
Non-Small Cell Lung Cancer			
A549/ATCC	>	-4.00	
HOP-18	>	-4.00	
HOP-62		-4.37	
HOP-92		-7.75	
NCI-H226	<	-8.00	
NCI-H23		-7.39	
NCI-H322M	>	-4.00	
NCI-H460		-7.30	
NCI-H522	<	-8.00	
LXFL 529	>	-4.00	
Small Cell Lung Cancer			
DMS 114			
DMS 273			
Colon Cancer			
COLO 205			
DLD-1	>	-4.00	
HCC-2998		-7.14	
HCT-116			
HCT-15	>	-4.00	
HT29		-7.42	
KM12	>	-4.00	
KM20L2			
SW-620	>	-4.00	
CNS Cancer			
SF-295	<	-8.00	
SF-539		-7.94	
SNB-19			
SNB-75	>	-4.00	
SNB-78	>	-4.00	
U251		-7.36	
XF 498	>	-4.00	
Melanoma			
LOX IMVI	>	-4.00	
MALME-3M	>	-4.00	
M14		-4.05	
M19-MEL			
SK-MEL-2	>	-4.00	
SK-MEL-28	>	-4.00	
SK-MEL-5		-7.32	
UACC-257			
UACC-62	>	-4.00	
Ovarian Cancer			
IGROV1	>	-4.00	
OVCAR-3		-7.27	
OVCAR-4	>	-4.00	
OVCAR-5	>	-4.00	
OVCAR-8		-7.36	
SK-OV-3	>	-4.00	
Renal Cancer			
786-0	>	-4.00	
A498		-7.66	
CAKI-1		-7.00	
RXF-393	>	-4.00	
RXF-631			
SN12C	>	-4.00	
TK-10	>	-4.00	
UO-31		-4.50	
MG_MID		-5.15	
Delta		2.85	
Range		4.00	

+3   +2   +1   0   -1   -2   -3

FIGURE 10.4 GI$_{50}$-centered mean graph of podophyllotoxin.

Note: See note to figure 10.3.

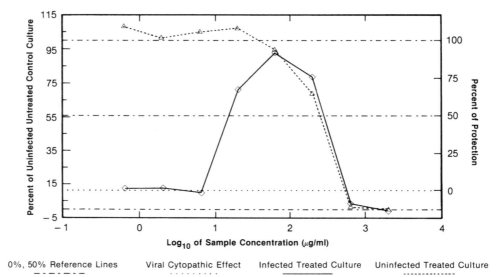

FIGURE 10.5 Anti-HIV activity graph of plant extract.

lower OD. Data are expressed as percent of formazan produced by untreated control cells, as determined by the equation:

$$\text{Percentage untreated control formazan} = \frac{Test\ OD}{Control\ OD} \times 100.$$

Results may be expressed graphically as exemplified in figure 10.5 for a typical in vitro active crude extract. A plot of the percentage untreated control formazan for treated uninfected cells against the log concentration (upper curve) gives a measure of cytotoxicity; the concentration that inhibits formazan production to 50% of that in untreated, uninfected control cells is called the IC_{50} value (IC = inhibitory concentration). A plot of the percentage untreated control formazan for treated infected cells against the log concentration (lower curve) gives a measure of protective ability; the concentration that increases formazan production to 50% of that in untreated, uninfected control cells is called the EC_{50} value (EC = effective concentration). At present, the capacity of the microculture anti-HIV screen is close to 40,000 samples per annum, and, as of December 1994, more than 30,000 plant extracts had been tested.

Plant Acquisition Program

From 1960 to 1980 approximately 35,000 samples of terrestrial plants were collected and screened for anticancer activity through an interagency agreement between the NCI and the USDA (Suffness and Douros 1979). The USDA collection strategy has been reviewed by Perdue (1976). In the early 1980s this program was discontinued, since it was perceived that few novel active leads were being isolated from natural sources. Although a number of active plant-derived antitumor compounds were discovered (e.g., see Suffness and Douros 1979; Suffness 1987 for reviews), the continued testing of plant extracts in the primary P388 mouse leukemia screen appeared to be detecting only known active compounds or chemical structure types having little or no activity against human solid tumors. The same conclusions were drawn for other natural product extracts, such as those derived from marine and microbial sources, and resulted in a general de-emphasis of natural products as potential sources of novel antitumor agents.

The apparent failure of natural products to yield novel agents possessing activity against the more resistant solid tumors could, however, be attributed more to the nature of the primary screen being used at the time, rather than to a deficiency on the part of Nature. Suspicion of this potential weakness led to revision of the antitumor-screening strategy and to approval by the NCI Division of Cancer Treatment Board of Scientific Counselors in 1985 of development of the new in vitro human cancer cell line screen (Boyd 1986; Boyd et al. 1988, 1989). At the same time, the Board approved a number of new natural product concepts involving initiation of new procurement, extraction, and isolation programs. DTP's subsequent initiation of a major new program for anti-HIV drug discovery and development (Boyd 1988) provided yet further impetus and resources for the revitalization of NCI's focus on natural products.

CONTRACT COLLECTIONS

In September 1986, three five-year contracts were awarded for collections of plants in tropical and subtropical regions worldwide. The three contractors and their respective collection regions were: Missouri Botanical Garden in tropical and subtropical regions of Africa, Madagascar, and neighboring islands; New York Botanical Garden in Central and South America, with emphasis on rain forest regions; and the University of Illinois at Chicago (assisted by the Arnold Arboretum at Harvard University and the Bishop Museum in Honolulu) in Southeast Asia. These contracts were subjected to recompetition in 1990, and five-year contracts were awarded to the same organizations in September 1991.

Each contract called for the collection of 1,500 samples of 0.3–1.0 kg (dry weight) per year. Different plant parts could constitute separate, discrete samples; thus, a tree could yield three or more samples, while a small shrub or herb might only yield one (whole plant; PL) sample. In general, emphasis has been placed on the collection of leaves (LF), bark (BK), roots (RT), and wood (WD), but significant numbers of samples of flowers (FL), fruits (FR), and twigs (TW) or branches (BR) have also been collected. Detailed documentation of each sample is obtained, including taxonomy (family, genus, species), plant part, date and location of collection (including geographic coordinates), habitat, hazards (e.g., thorny, irritant), and, when available, any information concerning medicinal uses and methods of preparation of plant material for administration to patients (e.g., water infusion or decoction, tea, etc.). Each sample is assigned a unique NCI collection number, expressed in the form of a bar code label, which is attached to the sample bag in the field. In addition, at least five voucher specimens of each plant species are collected and carefully prepared according to standard herbarium practices. One voucher specimen is donated to the national herbarium in the country of collection, while another is sent to the Botany Department of the Smithsonian Institution Museum of Natural History in Washington, D.C.; this latter collection serves as the official national and NCI collection that can be referenced if needed for recollections of active species. As of December 1994, more than 40,000 samples had been collected. The logistics and problems associated with undertaking these collections are discussed elsewhere in this volume in the paper by Soejarto et al.

SELECTION OF PLANTS

In awarding the collection contracts, NCI specified that, when reliable information is available, emphasis should be placed on the collection of plants reputed to have medicinal use, but that the collections should also encompass a broad taxonomic diversity. The latter specification stemmed from the recognition that cancer generally has been poorly defined in terms of folklore and traditional medicine, and hence, effective plant-derived treatments probably remain to be discovered. The same reasoning applies to the more recent NCI mission of discovery of novel anti-HIV agents. The potential of traditional medicine systems is, however, appreciated, and contract botanists are encouraged to collect plants reputed to be used in the treatment of various ailments, such as fungal and parasitic diseases. The importance of considering an apparently unrelated medicinal use is highlighted by the isolation of the two efficacious anticancer drugs vinblastine and vincristine from *Catharanthus roseus* (L.) G. Don f. (rosy periwinkle), which was initially studied as a possible source of antidiabetic agents (Neuss and Neuss 1990). The use of plant folklore as a possible means of predicting sources of antitumor agents has been reviewed by Spjut and Perdue (1976), and the potential problems of this approach have been discussed by Suffness and Douros (1979). The important role to be played by ethnobotanical and ethnopharmacological research in drug discovery is receiving increasing attention (Schultes and Raffauf 1990; Balick 1990; Cox 1990; Farnsworth 1990) and future analysis of NCI data should provide valuable insight into possible applications to anticancer and anti-HIV drug discovery. Note, however, that none of the anticancer agents presently in clinical use or being developed toward clinical trials has been isolated from a plant having a history of use in the treatment of cancer.

COLLABORATIONS AND COMPENSATION

The recognition of the value of the natural resources (plant, marine, and microbial) being investigated by NCI, and the significant contribution made by traditional healers in the selection of bioactive plants, led NCI to formulate measures aimed at collaboration with, and compensation of, countries participating in the NCI drug discovery program. The need to draft such measures was emphasized by the reluctance, or even refusal, of some countries to grant collection and export permits without establishing an agreement safeguarding their rights to some form of compensation in the event of discovery of an efficacious drug from a locally collected organism. In many instances, there appeared to be suspicion of the motives of drug discovery and development organizations in developed nations, particularly pharmaceutical companies, based on previous exploitation of developing-nation natural resources (NAPRECA Newsletter 1990).

The letter of collection formulated by NCI contains both short-term and long-term measures aimed at assuring countries participating in NCI-funded collections of its good intentions (National Cancer Institute, unpublished). In the short term, NCI periodically invites appropriate officials or scientists from local scientific organizations to visit the drug discovery facilities in Frederick, Maryland, to discuss the goals of the drug discovery and development program. When laboratory space and resources permit, suitably qualified scientists are invited to spend periods of up to a year working with scientists in NCI facilities on the bioassay-guided isolation and structure determination of active agents, preferably from organisms collected in their countries. To date, scientists from twelve countries have visited NCI and U.S. Collection contractor facilities for periods of one to two weeks, and scientists from eleven countries have carried out collaborative research projects with scientists in NCI facilities.

As screening test data become available, these are provided to collection contractors for dissemination to interested scientists in countries participating in their collection programs. Each country receives only data obtained from organisms collected within its own borders, and scientists are requested to keep data on active organisms confidential until NCI has had sufficient time to assess the potential for development of new agents from such organisms. The request for confidentiality is related to the possibility of obtaining patents on these new agents; in the event of a patent being licensed to a pharmaceutical company for development and eventual marketing of a drug, NCI requires the successful licensee to negotiate an agreement(s) with an appropriate organization and/or government agency in the source country of the organism yielding the drug. Such an agreement(s) will ensure that the source country receives acceptable royalties and other forms of compensation, as appropriate. This form of compensation is regarded as a potential long-term benefit, since development of a drug to the stage of marketing can take from ten to twenty years from its time of discovery. Another potential benefit to the country of origin is the development of a large-scale cultivation program to supply sufficient raw material for bulk production of the drug. In licensing a patent on a new drug to a pharmaceutical company, NCI will require the company to seek, as its first source of supply, the natural product produced in the country of origin.

The letter of collection already has formed the basis for agreements between NCI and organizations in nine countries for the collection of plants for evaluation as potential sources of novel anticancer and anti-HIV agents. It has also been used in establishing formal collaborations with research organizations in countries not formally participating in current NCI contract collections.

STORAGE AND EXTRACTION OF PLANT MATERIALS

After collection and drying, each plant sample is stored in a suitable cloth bag and labeled with the NCI code number, available taxonomy data, and hazard information. Sample bags are packed in large containers (burlap bags or cardboard boxes) and shipped by air freight to the NCI Natural Products Repository (NPR) in Frederick, Maryland. An import permit has been provided to the contractor maintaining the repository (Program Resources, Inc.; PRI) by the Animal and Plant Health Inspection Service (APHIS) of the USDA, which has provided excellent support to NCI in facilitating the import of thousands of plant samples. On arrival at the NPR, the samples are stored in large −20°C walk-in freezers for at least forty-eight hours; this freezing of samples is required by APHIS in order to minimize the survival of plant pests and pathogens.

After freezing, the samples are transferred to the Extraction and Grinding Laboratory (EGL; also operated by PRI), where they are ground; the ground material is stored in plastic containers labeled with the appropriate NCI collection number. The containers are either retained at −20°C in the EGL for immediate extraction or returned to the NPR for storage at −20°C and later extraction. After evaluation of a number of different extraction procedures (McCloud et al. 1988), the following sequential procedure was adopted for preparation of organic and aqueous extracts. The ground plant material is steeped in a percolator at room temperature for about twelve hours in a 1:1 mixture of methanol and methylene chloride. After draining of the extract, the residual plant material (marc) is washed with methanol, and a gentle vacuum is applied to the percolator to remove as much of the organic solvent as possible. The methanol wash is combined with the original extract and concentrated under vacuum at less than 40°C on a rotary evaporator; the viscous residue is transferred to a tared bottle, which is placed under high vacuum to remove the last traces of solvent, to give the organic extract. The marc remaining in the percolator is then steeped in water at room temperature for about twelve hours. The water is drained and lyophilized and the residue transferred to a tared bottle to give the water extract.

Five 100-mg samples of each extract are weighed out into small vials to give aliquots suitable for screening, while the remaining materials are kept as bulk samples suitable for subsequent fractionation and isolation studies, if necessary. All extract samples are assigned discrete NCI sample numbers and are returned to the NPR for storage at −20°C until requested for screening and further investigation.

Drug Discovery and Development

FRACTIONATION AND ISOLATION STUDIES

Extracts found to exhibit anti-HIV activity or a cytotoxicity profile of interest in the human tumor cell line screen are subjected to bioassay-guided fractionation by a team of NCI chemists and biologists to isolate the pure compounds responsible for the observed activity. In bioassay-guided fractionation, all fractions produced at each stage of the separation are tested for activity in the relevant bioassay, and the subsequent fractionations are performed only on the active fraction(s). This process of fractionation and testing is continued until the pure active component(s) is isolated. The process is illustrated schematically in figure 10.6. Bioassay-guided fractionation is essential since, in most instances, the active compounds are present in only minute amounts in the crude extracts and are generally isolated in yields of 0.01% or less, based on mass of dried plant material.

Use of solvent partitions in the early stages of fractionation eliminates much of the mass of inactive material to give active fractions that, nevertheless, are still extremely complex chemical mixtures (e.g., see Suffness and Douros 1979). Further fractionation and purification of the active component(s) generally involves extensive use of various forms of chromatography (adsorption, reversed-phase, ion-exchange, gel permeation), using techniques, such as thin-layer, high-pressure liquid, and counter-current chromatography (Hostettmann, Hostettmann, and Marston 1986).

Application of modern spectroscopic techniques usually permits the structural elucidation of the biologically active compound, even if only milligram quantities are available; determination of the final absolute stereochemistry might, however, require an x-ray crystallographic study of the compound itself or a suitable derivative thereof.

LARGE-SCALE PRODUCTION OF NATURAL PRODUCTS

The initial plant collection sample (0.3–1.0 kg) will generally yield enough extract (10–40 g) to permit isolation of the pure, active constituent in sufficient milligram quantity for complete structural elucidation. Subsequent secondary testing and preclinical studies (pharmacology, formulation, toxicology) might, however, require gram or even kilogram quantities, depending on the degree of activity and toxicity of the active agent (Driscoll 1984).

In order to obtain sufficient quantities of an active agent for early preclinical development, recollections of 5–50 kg of the dried plant material are carried out, preferably from the original site of collection. If the preclinical studies justify development of the agent toward clinical trials, considerably larger amounts of plant material would be required, and data on the distribution and abundance, as well as the drug content of the various plant parts, would need to be collected. In

DISCOVERY OF NEW NATURAL PRODUCTS

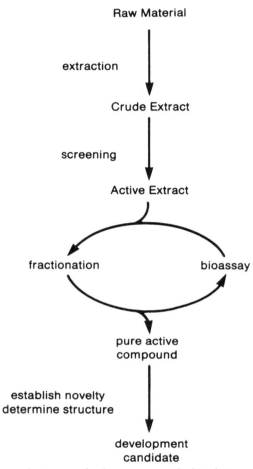

FIGURE 10.6 General strategy for bioassay-guided isolation of natural products.

addition, the potential for mass cultivation of the plant would need to be assessed. If problems are encountered owing to lack of abundance or inability to adapt the plant to cultivation, a search for alternative sources would be necessary. Other species of the same genus or of closely related genera can be analyzed for drug content, and techniques, such as plant tissue culture, can be investigated. Although total synthesis must always be considered as a potential route for bulk production of the active agent, the structures of most bioactive natural products are extremely complex, and bench-scale syntheses are generally not readily adapted to large-scale economic production.

In carrying out large-scale recollections and studying the feasibility of mass cultivation, NCI and its collection contractors will endeavor to work in close collaboration with the country of origin of the active source plant. In addition, NCI will make its best effort to promote the use of the plant grown in the country of origin as the first source of supply by any company licensed to produce an NCI-patented drug.

A typical procurement problem is that associated with the large-scale production of the promising new anticancer drug taxol (Rowinsky, Cazenave, and Donehower 1990). Taxol is isolated from the bark of *Taxus brevifolia* Nutt. (Pacific or Western Yew), which occurs in the northwestern Pacific regions of the United States and Canada. *T. brevifolia* Nutt. is a very slow-growing understory tree that tends to grow in a scattered manner. The average yield of taxol is of the order of 0.01% based on dried bark. Early preclinical and clinical development required modest quantities of up to 5 kg, but discovery of its efficacy in the treatment of refractory ovarian cancer has increased the demand to more than 25 kg per year. Ongoing clinical studies indicate potential activity against several other serious cancers, and this could further escalate the demand to hundreds of kilograms per year. Based on current yields, at least 320,000 kg of dried bark are required to produce sufficient drug to treat patients with ovarian cancer; this represents more than 35,000 trees. Given the relative lack of abundance of the tree, other sources are being investigated. Fortunately, the needles of *Taxus brevifolia* Nutt. and other *Taxus* species also contain taxol, albeit in lower yields than the bark; however, the needles also contain a key precursor, baccatin III, which can be converted readily to taxol (Denis et al. 1988). Various *Taxus* species, such as *baccata* L., and *cuspidata* Sieb. & Zucc., grow in temperate regions in a number of countries, and the needles of these species are being developed as a renewable source of the drug. In addition, a variety of *Taxus* cultivars are grown on a large scale as ornamental plants in nurseries in the United States and elsewhere, and the regular pruning of these plants could provide yet another renewable resource. Other projects aimed at the mass cultivation of high-yielding genotypes of *T. brevifolia* Nutt. and other *Taxus* species have been initiated, and some early results from *Taxus* tissue culture experiments indicate potential for this method of large-scale production.

Procurement of sufficient plant material constitutes only one part of the overall problem of large-scale production of the active agent. The other aspect requiring considerable research and development is the adaptation of the initial bench-scale isolation process to pilot-scale production. Problems can be encountered in the scale-up of processes involving extensive chromatography, but, once the structure of the active agent is known, more efficient processes can be developed based on a knowledge of functional groups present in the molecule. Discussion of these problems and challenges is beyond the scope of the present review, but the case of the large-scale production of maytansine discussed by Suffness and Douros (1979) serves as a suitable illustration. The processes used for the bulk production of clinical drugs have to follow good manufacturing practices (GMP) and must be carried out in facilities approved by the United States Food and Drug Administration (FDA). Any modification to a process requires new FDA approval.

PRECLINICAL DRUG DEVELOPMENT

The isolation and structural elucidation of a potential new agent are but the first phase in a lengthy process of development toward clinical trials and possible general clinical use. Depending on the physical and biological properties of the agent, this process can span anything from ten to twenty years and can cost in excess of $200 million. The challenges associated with large-scale procurement of raw material and the isolation of bulk quantities of the agent have been discussed in the previous section.

Drug formulation studies involve the development of suitable preparations for administration of the drugs to patients. The route of administration is frequently intravenous, and the drugs need to be sufficiently soluble and stable in acceptable delivery vehicles. Acceptable vehicles are usually predominantly aqueous, and many natural product agents typically pose considerable formulation problems owing to their very low degree of water solubility. Such problems can generally be overcome by the use of salts, cosolvents, or emulsifying agents (surfactants) or, in certain instances, by the synthesis of soluble prodrugs that are converted to the drugs in the body (Davignon and Cradock 1987). Problems can occur also with instability of the drugs in the administration vehicles. The short-term and long-term stabilities (shelf lives) of the formulated drugs need to be monitored.

Another phase of preclinical development involves detailed pharmacological evaluation in suitable preclinical animal models. Data are developed to determine the route and schedule of administration that give optimal activity. Sensitive, selective analytical techniques are developed to enable the quantitative determination of the drug and its metabolites in biological fluids such as blood, plasma, and urine; analytical methods used during the chemical isolation and purification procedures might not be suitable, since the compounds of interest often occur only in trace quantities in the biological fluids. Pharmacokinetic studies determine the half-lives, bioavailability, and effective concentrations of the drugs in blood and plasma as well as their rates of clearance, excretion routes, and metabolism. The identity and rates of formation of metabolites can provide insight into the possible mechanisms of action whereby the drugs exert their therapeutic and toxicological effects (Cragg and Suffness 1988). Pharmacokinetic and metabolism data can be used to design analogs and congeners of lead compounds with the aim of enhancing activity and/or decreasing toxicity.

The final phase is a toxicological evaluation to determine the type and degree of major toxicities in rodent and dog models and to develop data for the determination of safe starting doses in humans. Studies are designed to determine the relationship of toxicity to dose and schedule of administration and to establish the reversibility of observed toxic effects.

CLINICAL DRUG DEVELOPMENT

On completion of a successful toxicological study and a favorable review by program staff, all the preclinical data are presented to the NCI Cancer Therapy Evaluation Program (CTEP), which is responsible for the clinical development of new anticancer drugs. In the case of potential anti-HIV drugs, the National Institute for Allergy and Infectious Diseases (NIAID) may assume the primary responsibility for clinical development. For potential anticancer drugs, CTEP collates all the necessary data and files an INDA with the FDA. Once the FDA has approved an INDA, the various phases of clinical development may begin.

Phase I clinical trials are conducted to determine the maximum tolerated dose (MTD) of a drug in humans and observe the sites and reversibilities of toxic effects. The starting doses administered are generally well below the lethal dose$_{10}$ (LD$_{10}$) determined for mice, and doses are gradually escalated until toxic effects are observed. Phase I trial patients are most often terminally ill and, as with all trials, they are entered on a voluntary basis. Owing to the advanced state of disease, meaningful responses of the patients to drug treatment in phase I trials may not occur, though instances of partial and occasionally complete remissions of various cancers have been noted with certain drugs, such as taxol (Rowinsky et al. 1990).

Once the MTD has been determined, and CTEP staff are satisfied that no serious problems exist with toxicities, the drug advances to phase II clinical trials. The trials are generally conducted to test the efficacy of the drug against a range of different cancer disease types. As many as thirty disease types may be selected, though once new agents discovered by way of the new disease-oriented in vitro primary screen advance to the clinical development stage, disease-specific clinical trials, based on observations in the primary screen, will be given priority (fig. 10.2). In phase II trials, doses at, or close to, the MTD level are administered, and patients are evaluated for meaningful response to the drug treatment. Additional confirmatory phase II trials may be conducted against those disease types showing meaningful responses. Phase III clinical trials are conducted against those disease types responding to the new drug treatment, and the efficacy of the drug is compared with that of the best chemotherapeutic agents currently available for those disease types. In addition, the new drug may be tried in combination with other effective agents to determine whether the efficacy of the combined regimen exceeds that of the individual drugs used alone.

Once sufficient evidence has been accumulated indicating that the new drug is effective for a particular disease type, all the necessary information may be assembled and filed as an NDA with the FDA. The NDA will generally apply only to the particular responsive disease type, and approval by the FDA usually permits marketing of the drug only for use in the treatment of that disease type.

Current Status of Plant-Derived Agents

ANTICANCER AGENTS

The chemical classes of plant products that have shown significant activity in earlier NCI screening programs have been reviewed by Suffness and Douros (1979). The new in vitro human cancer cell line primary screen has only recently begun operating in a routine testing mode; it is, therefore, too early to assess which chemical classes will exhibit significant selective cytotoxicity patterns in this screen, though it seems probable that a diverse range of new active structure types may be discovered.

A number of plant-derived agents are either in regular clinical use or are presently under clinical or preclinical evaluation or development. The so-called Vinca alkaloids, vinblastine and vincristine (fig. 10.7), isolated from the Madagascar periwinkle, *Catharanthus roseus* (L.) G. Don f., still remain the best known of the plant-derived anticancer agents. The chemistry, pharmacology, and therapeutic use of these and related bisindole alkaloids from *C. roseus* (L.) G. Don f. have been comprehensively reviewed in the recent volume, *The Alkaloids: Antitumor Bisindole Alkaloids from Catharanthus roseus* (L.) G. Don f. (Neuss et al. 1990). These alkaloids first became available in the 1960s and are now used extensively, most often in combination with other agents, in the treatment of a wide variety of different cancer disease types (Neuss et al. 1990). Long-term, disease-free survivals have been observed in the treatment of various lymphomas and leukemias, bladder cancer, and testicular cancer, while significant palliative benefits have been seen in patients with breast cancer, melanoma, and small-cell lung cancer. A typical combination chemotherapeutic regimen is MOPP (nitrogen mustard, vincristine, procarbazine, and prednisone), which has achieved complete responses in more than 70% of patients with Hodgkin's disease. There is still great interest in the synthesis of analogs of these agents, and several promising new agents have been developed (Neuss and Neuss 1990).

Two other agents in clinical use are the lignan derivatives etoposide (VP–16) and teniposide (VM–26) (fig. 10.8). These are semisynthetic derivatives of epipodophyllotoxin, an epimer of podophyllotoxin isolated from *Podophyllum peltatum* L. or *Podophyllum hexandrum* Royle. Etoposide shows clinical activity against small-cell lung and testicular cancers, as well as lymphomas and leukemias (O'Dwyer et al. 1985). Teniposide is active against acute lymphocytic leukemia and neuroblastoma in children and non-Hodgkin's lymphoma and brain tumors in adults (O'Dwyer et al. 1984).

Camptothecin (fig. 10.9) is an alkaloid isolated from *Camptotheca acuminata* Decne, an ornamental tree grown in many regions in China. The compound has been shown to be a potent inhibitor of DNA synthesis by a unique mechanism of action, and clinical studies in China, using a fine suspension of microparticles, have shown responses among patients with liver, gastric, head and neck, and

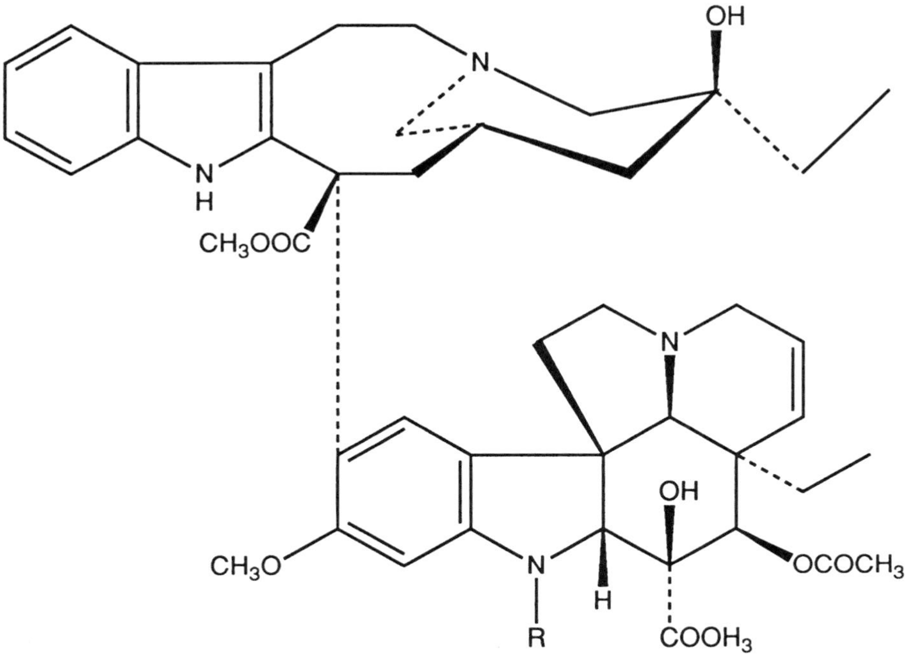

Vincristine : R = CHO

Vinblastine : R = CH₃

FIGURE 10.7 Structures of vincristine and vinblastine.

bladder cancers. Clinical trials in the United States in the early 1970s using the more soluble sodium salt were, however, terminated owing to severe toxicity, despite observation of some responses in patients with gastrointestinal tumors (Suffness and Cordell 1985). The synthesis of more soluble derivatives of camptothecin having superior antitumor activity and reduced toxicity in preclinical animal systems has revived interest in this group of compounds, and a number of derivatives are now undergoing clinical trials. One such derivative, CPT–11 (fig. 10.9), has been shown to be effective against refractory leukemia and lymphoma in a phase II trial in Japan (Ohno et al. 1990), and another derivative, topotecan (fig. 10.9), is showing activity against ovarian and various lung cancers (Kingsbury et al. 1991).

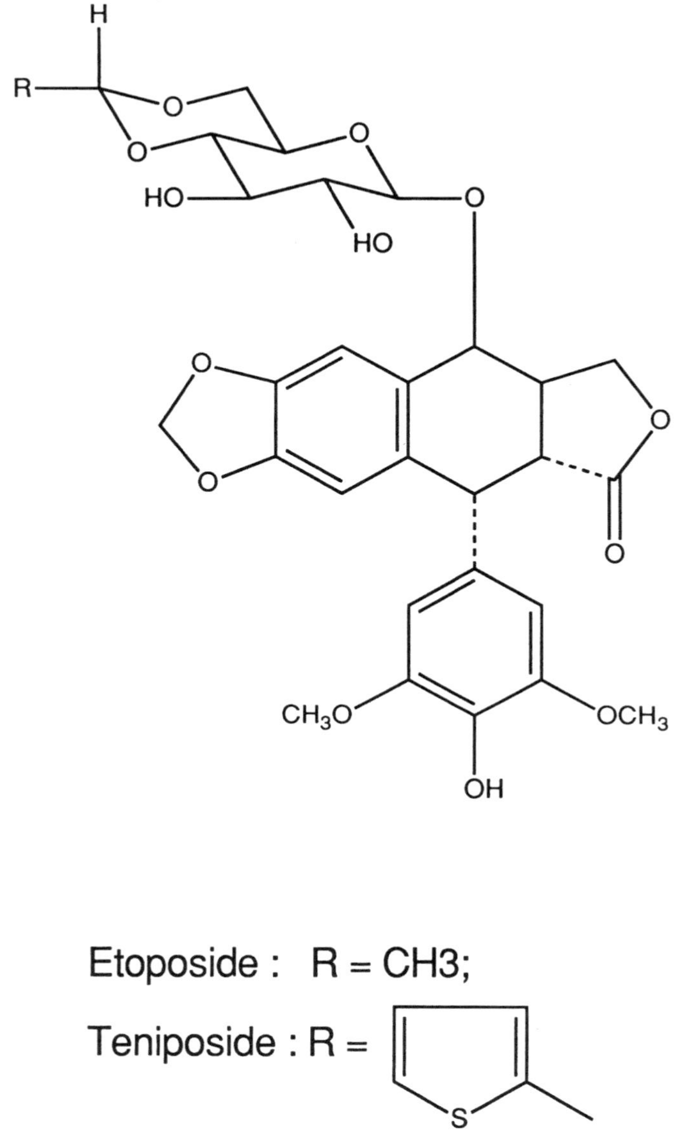

FIGURE **10.8** Structures of etoposide and teniposide.

Combretastatin A-4 (fig. 10.10) is a stilbene derivative, isolated from *Combretum caffrum* Kuntze (= Salicifolium E. Mey ex hook) (Pettit et al. 1989). Combretastatin A-4 is a potent inhibitor of microtubular action and has shown activity against various human colon cancer cell lines. It has been selected for advanced preclinical development in the United Kingdom and is undergoing formulation studies before entering preclinical toxicology.

9-Hydroxy-2-methylellipticinium acetate (elliptinium; fig. 10.11) is undergoing phase II clinical trials in Europe, and responses have been reported in the treatment of thyroid and renal cancer and soft-tissue sarcomas (Rousse et al. 1981). Activity has also been observed in the treatment of bone metastases resulting from advanced breast cancer (Juret et al. 1982; Clarysse et al. 1984), though a later trial demonstrated that the agent has only minimal activity against advanced breast cancer (Treat et al. 1989). This agent is a semisynthetic derivative of the alkaloid ellipticine, which is isolated from species of the Apocynaceae family, including *Ochrosia* species, *Bleekeria vitiensis* (Markgraf) A. C. Smith, and *Aspidosperma subicanum* Mart. (Suffness and Cordell 1985).

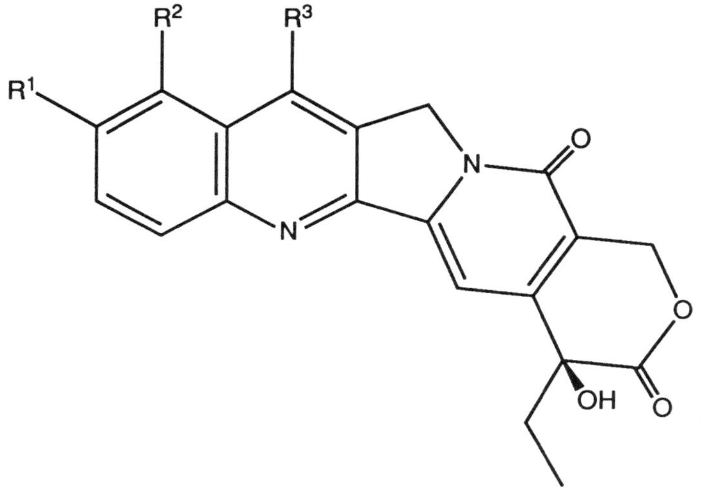

Camptothecin : $R^1 = R^2 = R^3 = H$

CPT–11: $R^1 =$

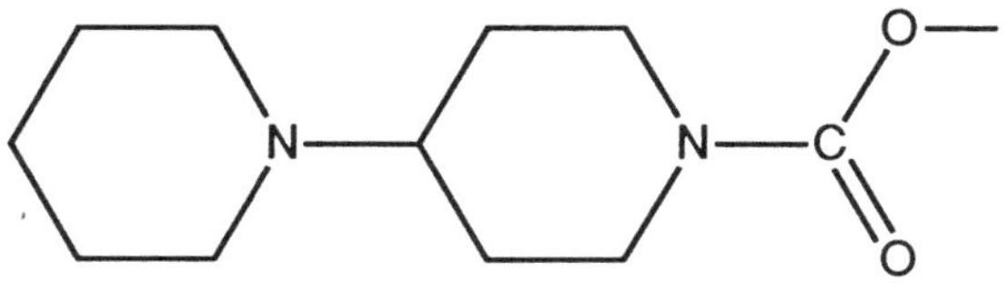

$R^2 = H$; $R^3 = CH_3CH_2$

Topotecan: $R^1 = OH$; $R^2 = CH_2N(CH_3)_2$; $R^3 = H$

FIGURE 10.9 Structures of camptothecin and derivatives CPT–11 and topotecan.

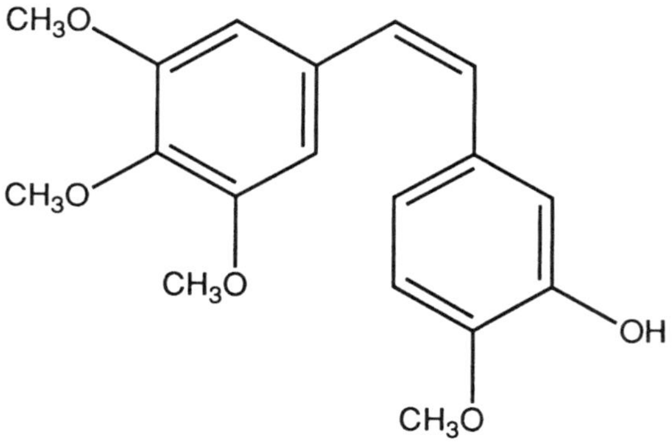

Combretastatin A–4

FIGURE 10.10 Structure of combretastatin A–4.

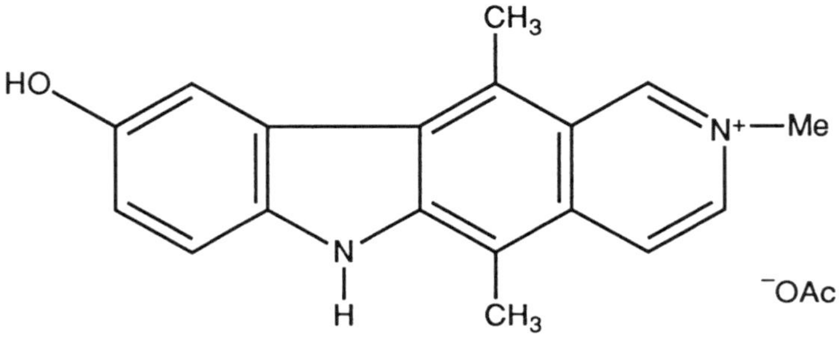

9–Hydroxy–2–Methylellipticinium Acetate

FIGURE 10.11 Structure of 9-hydroxy-2-methylellipticinium acetate.

Harringtonine and homoharringtonine (fig. 10.12) are alkaloids isolated from *Cephalotaxus harringtonia* (D. Don) C. Koch, a small evergreen tree native to Japan and China, as well as from other *Cephalotaxus* species (Suffness and Cordell 1985). Observations of clinical activity against leukemias in Chinese studies have been confirmed in phase II clinical trials in the United States (O'Dwyer et al. 1986).

4-Ipomeanol (fig. 10.13) is one of four pneumotoxic furan derivatives produced by sweet potatoes (*Ipomoea batatas* [L.] Lam.) infected by the fungus, *Fusarium solani* (Martius) Saccardo (Boyd et al. 1974). These toxins were isolated during an investigation of several incidents of fatal lung injury observed in cattle that had ingested moldy sweet potatoes. There is convincing evidence that the toxic furans, or precursors thereof, are actually biosynthesized as stress metabolites by the sweet

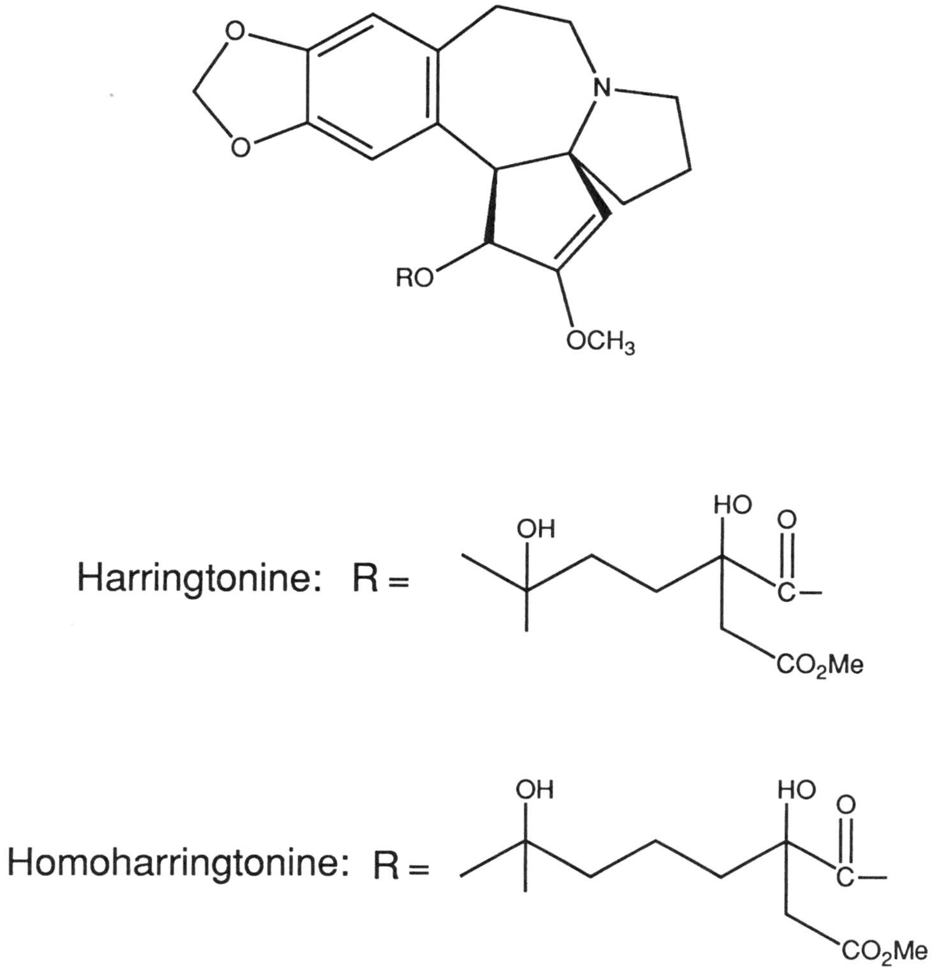

FIGURE 10.12 Structures of harringtonine and homoharringtonine.

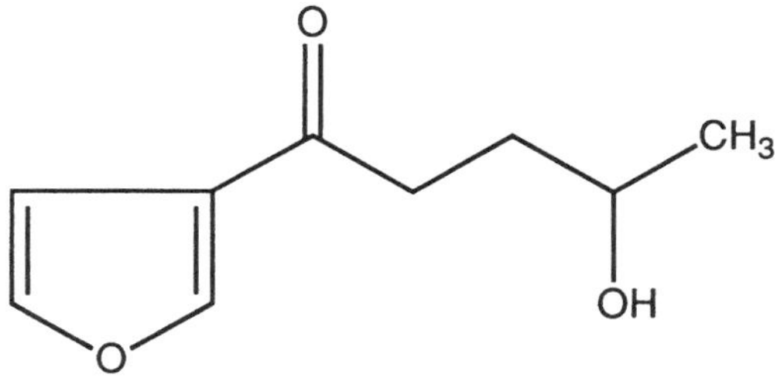

Ipomeanol

FIGURE 10.13 Structure of ipomeanol.

potato and are not primary fungal metabolites, though the fungus does play a key role in the biosynthetic process (Burka et al. 1978). The lung toxicity of 4-ipomeanol to cattle and other warm-blooded species is due to metabolic activation of the compound in the lung, especially in cells of Clara origin (Boyd 1977, 1980). The compound has been shown to be activated by metabolism and to exert cytotoxicity to human lung cancer cell lines (Falzon et al. 1986; McLemore et al. 1990). The rationale for testing 4-ipomeanol against lung cancer was first conceived and proposed more than a decade ago (Boyd 1977). The preclinical development of the agent has subsequently been completed and phase I trials initiated (for review, see Christian et al. 1989).

Pancratistatin (fig. 10.14) is an alkaloid isolated from the bulbs of *Pancratium littorale* Jacq. (Pettit et al. 1986). Significant in vitro activity was observed against breast, lung, melanoma, and stomach cell lines, as well as the M5076 ovarian sarcoma in mice. The agent is particularly insoluble and is currently undergoing formulation studies in the United Kingdom. Preclinical toxicology and advancement to clinical trials are dependent on development of an acceptable formulation.

Phyllanthoside (fig. 10.15) is a terpene glycoside isolated from the Central American tree *Phyllanthus acuminatus* Vahl (Pettit et al. 1984). The agent exhibits cytotoxicity against tumor cell lines at low nanomolar concentrations and is a potent inhibitor of protein synthesis (DTP, unpublished). It has advanced through preclinical toxicology studies in the United States and currently is in phase I clinical trials in the United Kingdom.

The isolation and characterization of the diterpenoid taxol (fig. 10.16), from the bark of the Pacific yew *Taxus brevifolia* Nutt., was reported in 1971 by Wani, Taylor,

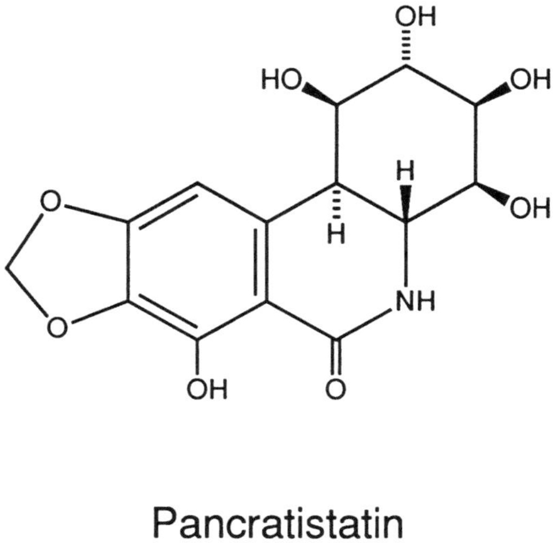

Pancratistatin

FIGURE 10.14 Structure of pancratistatin.

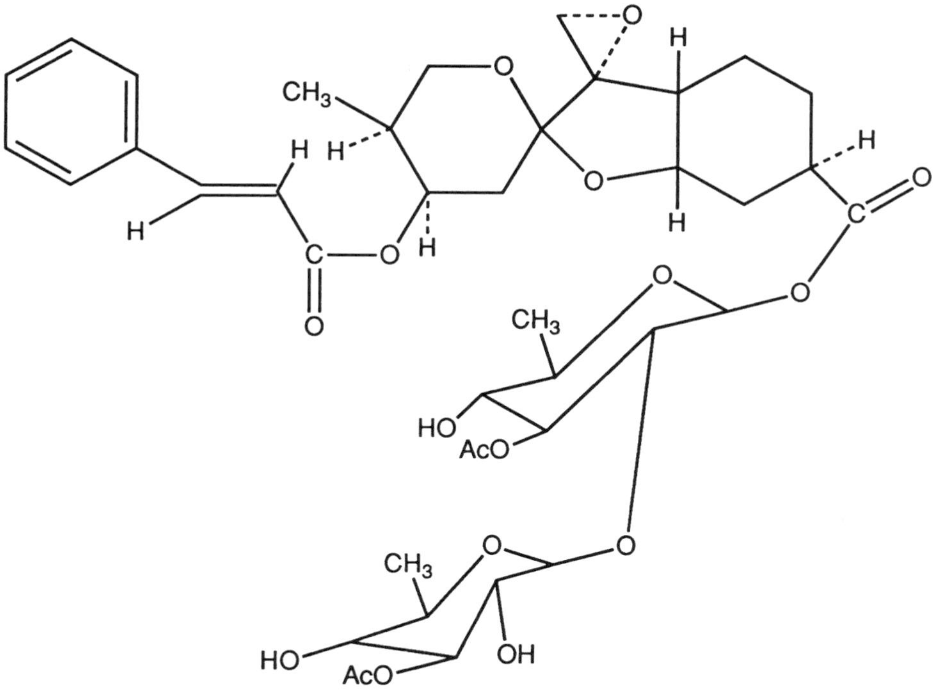

Phyllanthoside (Ac = CH$_3$CO)

FIGURE 10.15 Structure of phyllanthoside.

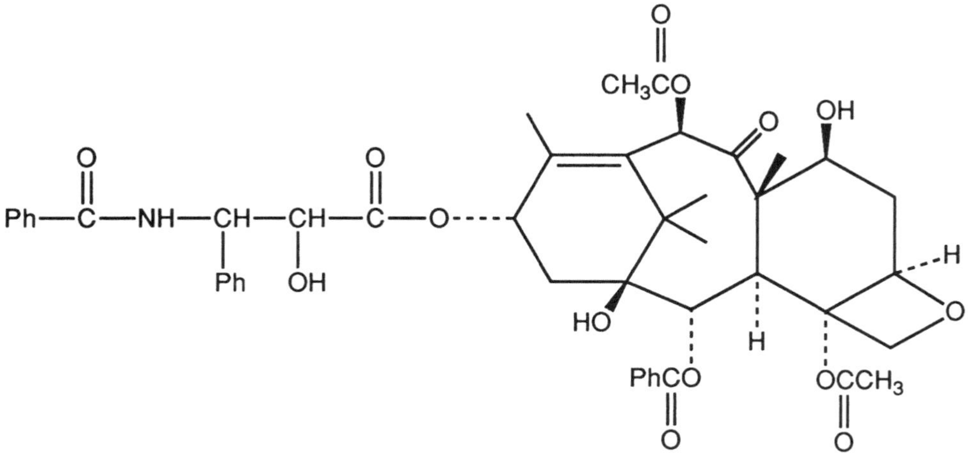

Taxol (Ph = Phenyl)

FIGURE 10.16 Structure of taxol.

and Wall. It has a unique mode of action, promoting polymerization of tubulin to form microtubules that are stabilized against standard depolymerization processes (Manfredi and Horwitz 1984). It was selected for advanced preclinical and clinical development in 1977, and most of the phase I clinical trials were completed in 1985. Significant responses have been observed in phase II trials in patients with refractory ovarian cancer (Rowinsky, Cazenave, and Donehower 1990), and promising activity has recently been observed against other cancer disease types. The problems encountered in the procurement of sufficient raw material for production of adequate quantities of taxol for expanded phase II trials have been discussed earlier in this chapter, but it appears that such problems will be solved in the long term by mass cultivation of a suitable *Taxus* species. It seems likely that this drug will find use, either alone or in combination with other agents, in the primary treatment of ovarian cancer.

ANTI-HIV AGENTS

Since the introduction of the large-scale NCI anti-HIV screen in late 1987 (Boyd 1988), more than 20,000 plant extracts and more than 1,600 characterized natural products have been tested for anti-HIV activity. The potential of plants and other organisms as sources of anti-HIV drugs has recently been reviewed (Lednicer and Snader 1991), and readers are referred to this article for details of those natural products exhibiting preliminary activity.

In general, approximately 5% of the organic plant extracts have exhibited in vitro activity in the NCI screen, but the positive response for aqueous extracts has been substantially higher. This high level of activity can, in most cases, be associated with the presence of various biopolymers, such as polysaccharides and tannins.

Sulfated polysaccharides, such as dextran sulfate, exhibit significant in vitro anti-HIV activity, and various carrageenins, present in many marine algae, are very potent in the in vitro assay. These biopolymers are not generally bioavailable when administered orally owing to internal degradation, and toxic anticoagulant effects preclude intravenous administration. The selective fragmentation of these polymeric anions might, however, yield active entities that merit further study. The potential of tannins as cancer chemotherapeutic agents was discounted in early studies in the NCI anticancer drug discovery program, but the possibility of developing this class of chemicals as potential anti-HIV agents continues to be investigated elsewhere (Nishizawa et al. 1989).

A purified preparation of the protein trichosanthin, isolated from the Chinese cucumber *Trichosanthes kiriliwii* Maxim., has received publicity as a potential anti-HIV agent. This and other proteins, such as conconavalin A isolated from the jack bean (*Canavalia ensiformis* [L.] DC.), are still being investigated, and it remains to be seen whether the adverse effects caused to the immune system by such agents can be outweighed by beneficial anti-HIV effects.

Of the pure plant-derived agents reported thus far, hypericin, pseudohypericin, and castanospermine have probably received most attention. Hypericin and pseudohypericin (fig. 10.17), isolated from *Hypericum* species, are reported to exhibit activity against various retroviruses (Meruelo, Lavie, and Lavie 1988), though significant activity has not been observed in the NCI screen. A clinical trial of hypericin has been initiated. The alkaloid castanospermine (fig. 10.18), isolated from the seed of *Castanospermum australe* A. Cunn. & C. Fraser., shows strong inhibition of the mammalian alpha glucosidase enzyme, and it has been proposed that it interferes with the normal processing of viral glycoproteins; however, only weak activity has been observed in the NCI in vitro screen. This class of com-

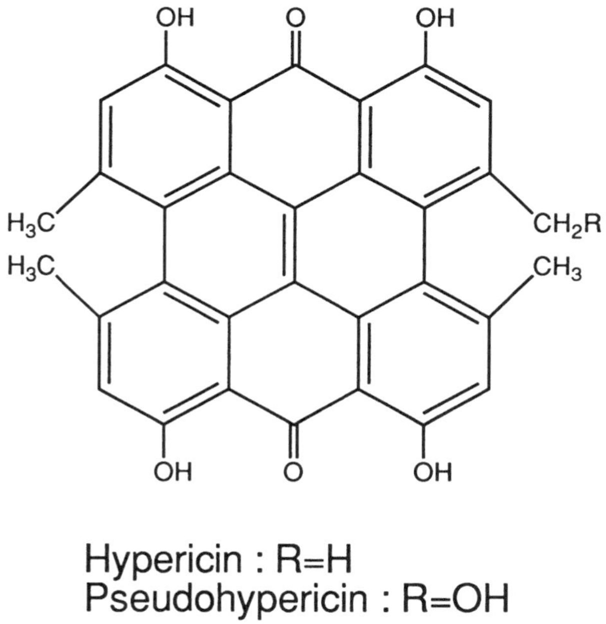

Hypericin : R=H
Pseudohypericin : R=OH

FIGURE 10.17 Structures of hypericin and pseudodohypericin.

Castanospermine

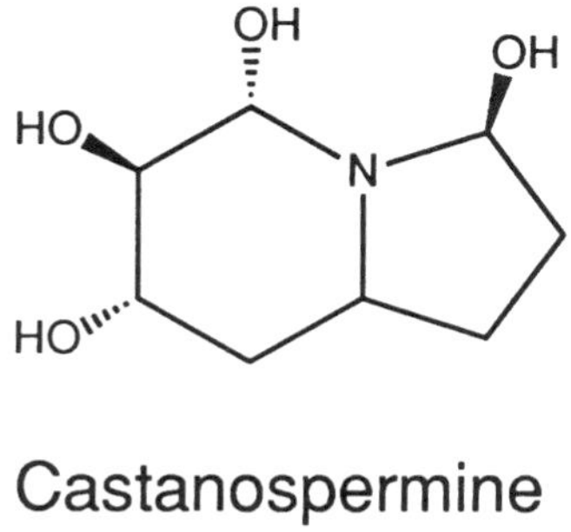

FIGURE 10.18 Structure of castanospermine.

pounds is, nevertheless, of considerable interest, and structure-activity relationships are being extensively investigated.

Sulfolipid compounds (fig. 10.19) isolated from extracts of cyanobacteria (blue-green algae) have been reported to have anti-HIV activity (Gustafson et al. 1989). Sulfolipids are ubiquitous constituents of plant chloroplasts; however, there presently are no reports of plants having anti-HIV activity that could be accountable specifically to the presence of sulfolipids.

The phorbol compound prostratin (fig. 10.20), isolated from the Samoan medicinal plant *Homalanthus nutans* Guillo, has been reported to have potent anti-HIV activity (Gustafson et al. 1992). Phorbols frequently exhibit significant tumor-promoting properties, which usually preclude their development as chemotherapeutic agents. Prostratin does not, however, appear to be associated with such properties, and extensive studies are under way to substantiate this observation.

The dimeric alkaloid michellamine B (fig. 10.21), isolated from a Cameroonian *Ancistrocladus* sp. plant, exhibits significant in vitro activity against both HIV-1 and HIV-2 (Manfredi et al. 1991). The absolute stereochemistry of this novel alkaloid has recently been determined (Bringmann et al. 1993). Apart from the nucleosides, such as AZT, no other class of compounds has been reported to date that exhibits equivalent activity against both viruses. Interestingly, the corresponding monomeric alkaloids isolated from this and other *Ancistrocladus* species do not show anti-HIV activity (Manfredi et al. 1991).

Calanolide A (fig. 10.22) is a novel coumarin isolated from the twigs and leaves of the tree *Calophyllum lanigerum* Miq. var. *austrocariaceum* (T. C. Whitmore) P. F. Stevens, collected in Sarawak, Malaysia (Kashman et al. 1992). Calanolide A and several related coumarins exhibit significant in vitro activity against HIV-1 and several resistant forms of this virus.

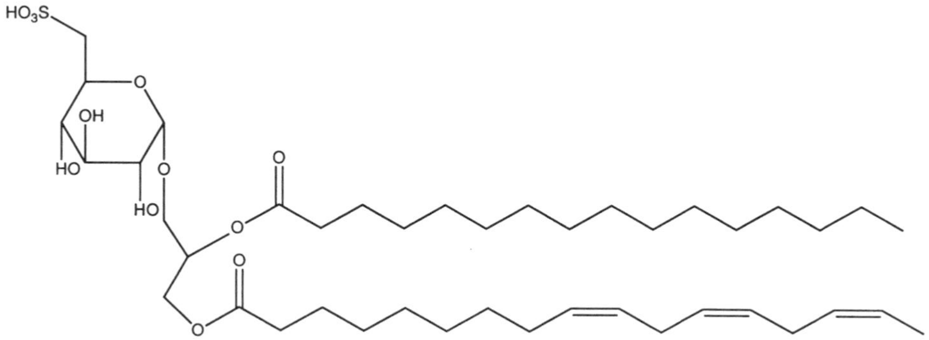

Sulfolipid

FIGURE 10.19 Structure of sulfolipid.

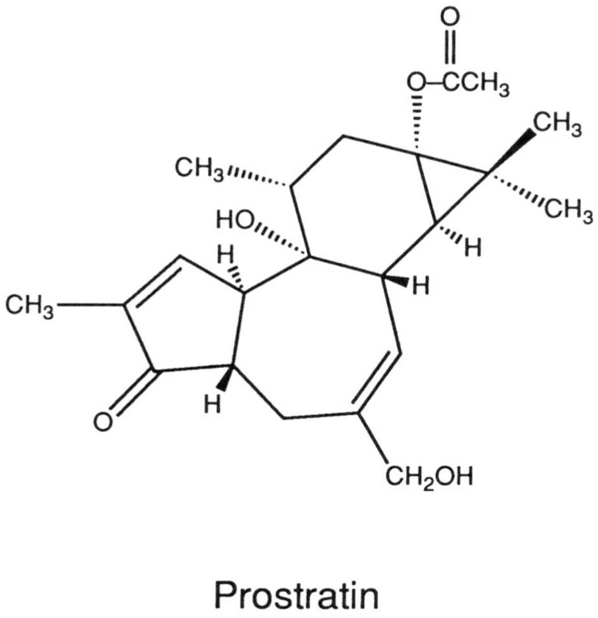

Prostratin

FIGURE 10.20 Structure of prostratin.

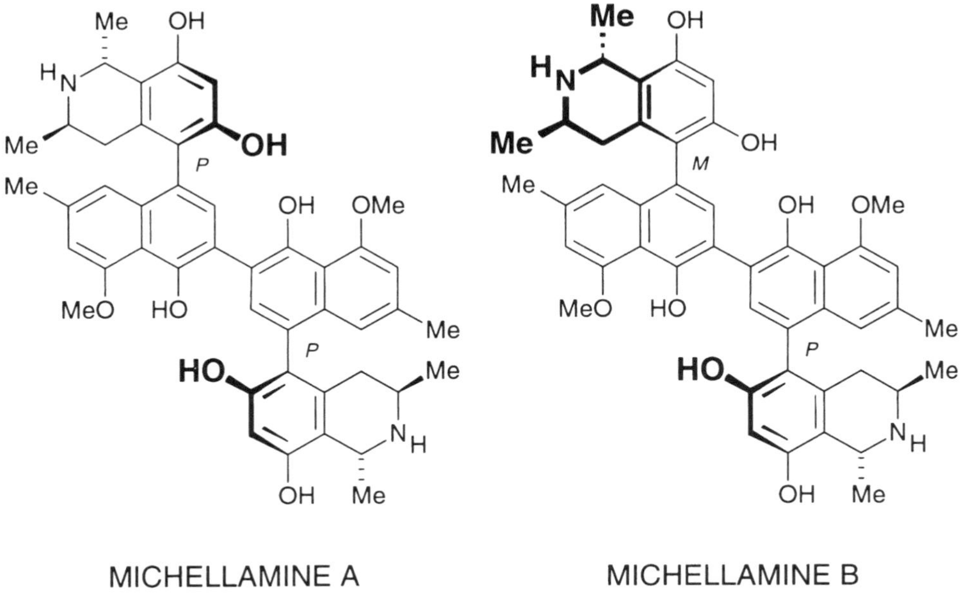

MICHELLAMINE A   MICHELLAMINE B

FIGURE 10.21 Structure of michellamine A and B.

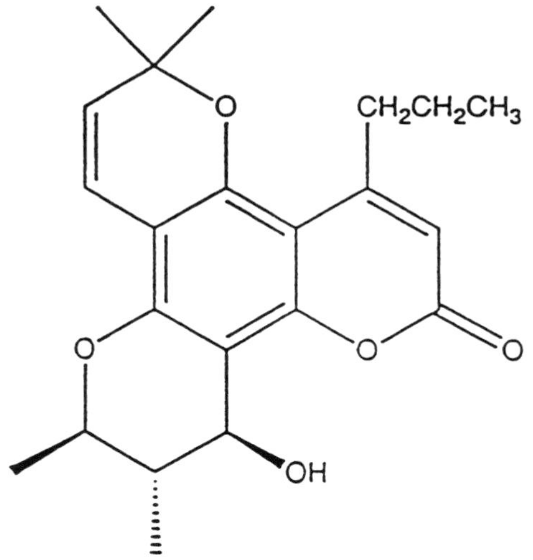

Calanolide A

FIGURE **10.22** Structure of calanolide A.

REFERENCES

Alley, M. C., D. A. Scudiero, A. Monks, M. L. Hursey, M. J. Czerwinski, D. L. Fine, B. J. Abbott, J. G. Mayo, R. H. Shoemaker, and M. R. Boyd. 1988. "Feasibility of Drug Screening with Panels of Human Tumor Cell Lines Using a Microculture Tetrazolium Assay." *Cancer Research* 48:589–601.

Balick, M. J. 1990. "Ethnobotany and the Identification of Therapeutic Agents from the Rainforest." In D. J. Chadwick and J. Marsh, eds., *Bioactive Compounds from Plants,* pp. 22–39. Ciba Foundation Symposium 154. Chichester: Wiley.

Boyd, M. R. 1977. "Evidence for the Clara Cell as a Site of Cytochrome P450-Dependent Mixed-Function Oxidase Activity in Lung." *Nature* 269:713–15.

Boyd, M. R. 1980. "Biochemical Mechanisms of Chemical-Induced Lung Injury: Roles of Metabolic Activation." *CRC Critical Review of Toxicology* 7:103–76.

Boyd, M. R. 1986. "National Cancer Institute Drug Discovery and Development." In E. J. Frei and E. J. Freireich, eds., *Accomplishments in Oncology. Cancer Therapy: Where Do We Go from Here?* 1 (1):68–76. Philadelphia: Lippincott.

Boyd, M. R. 1988. "Strategies for the Identification of New Agents for the Treatment of AIDS: A National Program to Facilitate the Discovery and Preclinical Development of New Drug Candidates for Clinical Evaluation." In V. T. Devita, S. Hellman, and S. A. Rosenberg, eds., *AIDS: Etiology, Diagnosis, Treatment, and Prevention,* pp. 305–19. Philadelphia: Lippincott.

Boyd, M. R. 1989. "Status of the NCI Preclinical Antitumor Drug Discovery Screen." In V. T. Devita, S. Hellman, and S. A. Rosenberg, eds., *Principles and Practice of Oncology Updates,* 3 (10):1–12. Philadelphia: Lippincott.

Boyd, M. R. 1993. "The Future of New Drug Development." In J. E. Niederhuber, ed., *Current Therapy in Oncology,* pp. 11–22. Philadelphia: Decker.

Boyd, M. R., L. T. Burka, T. M. Harris, and B. J. Wilson. 1974. "Lung-Toxic Furanoterpenoids Produced by Sweet Potatoes (*Ipomoea batatas*) Following Microbial Infection." *Biochim. Biophys. Acta.* 337:184–95.

Boyd, M. R., K. D. Paull, and L. R. Rubinstein. 1991. "Data Display and Analysis Strategies for the NCI Disease-Oriented *in Vitro* Antitumor Drug Screen." In F. A. Valeriote, T. Corbett, and L. Baker, eds., *Cytotoxic Antitumor Drugs: Models and Concepts for Discovery and Development*, pp. 11–34. Amsterdam: Kluwer Academic Publishers.

Boyd, M. R., R. H. Shoemaker, G. M. Cragg, and M. Suffness. 1988. "New Avenues of Investigation of Marine Biologicals in the Anticancer Drug Discovery Program of the National Cancer Institute." In C. W. Jefford, K. L. Rinehart, and L. S. Shield, eds., *Pharmaceuticals and the Sea*, pp. 27–44. Lancaster, Penn.: Technomic Publishing AG.

Boyd, M. R., R. H. Shoemaker, T. L. McLemore, M. R. Johnston, M. C. Alley, D. A. Scudiero, A. Monks, D. L. Fine, J. G. Mayo, and B. A. Chabner. 1989. "New Drug Development." In J. A. Roth, J. C. Ruckdeschel, and T. H. Weisenburger, eds., *Thoracic Oncology*, ch. 49, pp. 711–21. Philadelphia: Saunders.

Bringmann, G., Zagst, R., Schäffer, M., Hallock, Y. F., Cardellina, J. H. II, and Boyd, M. R. 1993. "The Absolute Configuration of Michellamine B, a Dimeric Anti-HIV Active Napthylisoquinoline Alkaloid." *Angewandt Chemie*, International Edition [English] 32:1190–91.

Burka, L. T., L. Kuhnert, B. J. Wilson, and T. M. Harris. 1978. "Biogenesis of Lung-Toxic Furans Produced During Microbial Infection of Sweet Potatoes (*Ipomoea batatas*)." *Journal of the American Chemical Society* 99:2302–5.

Chabner, B. A. and J. M. Collin. 1990. *Cancer Chemotherapy: Principles and Practice*. Philadelphia: Lippincott.

Christian, M. C., R. E. Wittes, B. Leyland-Jones, T. L. McLemore, A. C. Smith, C. K. Grieshaber, B. A. Chabner, and M. R. Boyd. 1989. "4-Ipomeanol: A Novel Investigational New Drug for Lung Cancer." *Journal of the National Cancer Institute* 81:1133–43.

Clarysse, A., A. Brugarolas, P. Siegenthaler, R. Abele, F. Cavalli, R. De Jager, G. Renard, M. Rozencweig, and H. H. Hansen. 1984. "Phase II Study of 9-Hydroxy-2N-Methylellipticinium Acetate." *European Journal of Clinical Oncology* 20:243–47.

Cox, P. A. 1990. "Ethnopharmacology and the Search for New Drugs." In D. J. Chadwick and J. Marsh, eds., *Bioactive Compounds from Plants*, pp. 40–55. Ciba Foundation Symposium 154. Chichester: Wiley.

Cragg, G. and M. Suffness. 1988. "Metabolism of Plant-Derived Anticancer Agents." In G. Powis, ed., *Pharmac. Ther.* 37:425–61. Oxford: Pergamon.

Davignon, J. P. and J. C. Cradock. 1987. "The Formulation of Anticancer Drugs." In S. K. Carter and K. Hellman, eds., *Principles of Chemotherapy*, pp. 212–27. New York: McGraw-Hill.

Denis J. N., A. E. Green, D. Guenard, F. Gueritte-Voegelein, L. Mangatol, and P. Potier. 1988. "A Highly Efficient, Practical Approach to Natural Taxol." *Journal of the American Chemical Society* 110:5917–19.

Driscoll, J. S. 1984. "The Preclinical New Drug Research Program of the National Cancer Institute." *Cancer Treatment Reports* 68:63–76.

Falzon, M., J. B. McMahon, H. M. Schuller, and M. R. Boyd. 1986. "Metabolic Activation and Cytotoxicity of 4-Ipomeanol in Human Non-Small Cell Lung Cancer Lines." *Cancer Research* 46:3484–89.

Farnsworth, N. R. 1990. "The Role of Ethnopharmacology in Drug Development." In D. J. Chadwick and J. Marsh, eds., *Bioactive Compounds from Plants*, pp. 2–21. Ciba Foundation Symposium 154. Chichester: Wiley.

Gustafson, K. R., J. H. Cardellina II, R. W. Fuller, O. S. Weislow, R. F. Kiser, K. M. Snader, G. L. Patterson, and M. R. Boyd. 1989. "AIDS-Antiviral Sulfolipids from Cyanobacteria (Blue-Green Algae)." *Journal of the National Cancer Institute* 81:1254–58.

Gustafson, K. R., J. H. Cardellina II, J. B. McMahon, R. J. Gulakowski, J. Ishitoya, Z. Szallasi, N. E. Lewin, P. M. Blumberg, O. S. Weislow, J. A. Beutler, R. W. Buckheit Jr., G. M. Cragg, P. A. Cox, J. P. Bader, and M. R. Boyd. 1992. "A Nonpromoting Phorbol from the Samoan Medicinal Plant *Homalanthus nutans* Inhibits Cell Killing by HIV-1." *Journal of Medicinal Chemistry* 35:1978–86.

Hostettmann, K., M. Hostettmann, and A. Marston. 1986. *Preparative Chromatography Techniques: Applications in Natural Products Isolation.* Berlin: Springer-Verlag.

Inamori, Y., Y. Kato, M. Kubo, K. Baba, T. Ishida, K. Nomoto, and M. Kozawa. 1985. *Chemical Pharmacology Bulletin* 33:704–9.

Juret, P., J. F. Heron, J. E. Couette, T. Delozier, and J. Y. LeTalaer. 1982. "Hydroxy-9-Methyl-2-Ellipticinium for Osseous Metastases from Breast Cancer: A 5-Year Experience." *Cancer Treatment Reports* 66:1909–16.

Kashman, Y., K. R. Gustafson, R. W. Fuller, J. H. Cardellina II, J. B. McMahon, M. J. Currens, R. W. Buckheit Jr., S. H. Hughes, G. M. Cragg, and M. R. Boyd. 1992. "The Calanolides. A Novel HIV-Inhibitory Class of Coumarin Derivatives from the Tropical Rainforest Tree, *Calophyllum lanigerum*." *Journal of Medicinal Chemistry* 35:2735–43.

Kingsbury, W. D., J. C. Boehm, D. R. Jakas, K. H. Holden, S. M. Hecht, G. Gallagher, M. J. Caranfa, F. L. McCabe, L. F. Faucette, R. K. Johnson, and R. P. Hertzberg. 1991. "Synthesis of Water-Soluble (Aminoalkyl) Camptothecin Analogues: Inhibition of Topoisomerase I and Antitumor Activity." *Journal Medicinal Chemistry* 34:98–107.

Lednicer, D. and K. M. Snader. 1991. "Plants and Other Organisms as a Source of Anti-HIV Drugs." In H. Wagner and N. R. Farnsworth, ed., *Economic and Medicinal Plant Research,* 5:1–20. London: Academic Press.

Manfredi, J. J. and S. B. Horwitz. 1984. "Taxol: An Antimitotic Agent with a New Mechanism of Action." *Pharmac. Ther.* 25:83–125.

Manfredi, K. P., J. W. Blunt, J. H. Cardellina II, J. B. McMahon, L. K. Pannell, G. M. Cragg, and M. R. Boyd. 1991. "Novel Alkaloids from the Tropical Plant *Ancistrocladus abbreviatus* Inhibit Cell-Killing by HIV-1 and HIV-2." *Journal of Medicinal Chemistry* 34:3402–5.

McCloud, T, J. Nemec, G. Muschik, H. G. Sheffield, P. Quesenberry, M. Suffness, G. M. Cragg, and J. Thompson. 1988. "Extraction of Bioactive Molecules from Higher Plants." Abstract. *International Congress on Natural Products Research.* Park City, Utah.

McLemore, T. L., C. L. Litterst, B. P. Coudert, M. C. Liu, W. C. Hubbard, S. Adelberg, M. Czerwinski, N. A. McMahon, J. C. Eggleston, and M. R. Boyd. 1990. "Metabolic Activation of 4-Ipomeanol in Human Lung, Primary Pulmonary Carcinomas and Established Human Pulmonary Carcinoma Cell Lines." *Journal of the National Cancer Institute* 82:1420–26.

Meruelo, D., G. Lavie, and D. Lavie. 1988. "Therapeutic Agents with Dramatic Antiretroviral Activity and Little Toxicity at Effective Doses: Aromatic Polycyclic Diones Hypericin and Pseudohypericin." *Proceedings of the National Academy of Science USA* 85:5230–34.

Monks, A., D. Scudiero, P. Skehan, R. Shoemaker, K. Paull, D. Vistica, C. Hose, J. Langley, P. Cronise, A. Vaigro-Wolff, M. Gray-Goodrich, H. Campbell, and M. Boyd. 1991. "Feasibility of a High-Flux Anticancer Drug Screen Utilizing a Diverse Panel of Human Tumor Cell Lines in Culture." *Journal of the National Cancer Institute* 83:757–66.

NAPRECA Newsletter 7:2. 1990. "Researchers Want Clear Policies on Traditional Herbs." International Conference of Experts of Developing Countries on Traditional Medicinal Plants, Arusha, Tanzania.

Neuss, N. and M. N. Neuss. 1990. "Therapeutic Use of Bisindole Alkaloids from *Catharanthus*." In A. Brossi and M. Suffness, eds., *The Alkaloids* 37:229–39. New York: Academic Press.

Nishizawa, M., T. Yamagishi, G. E. Dutschman, W. B. Parker, A. J. Bodner, R. E. Kilku-skie, Y-C. Cheng, and K-H. Lee. 1989. "Anti-AIDS Agents 1. Isolation and Characteri-zation of Four New Tetragalloylquinic Acids as a New Class of HIV Reverse Transcrip-tase Inhibitors from Tannic Acid." *Journal of Natural Products* 52:762–68.

O'Dwyer, P., M. T. Alonso, B. Leyland-Jones, and S. Marsoni. 1984. "Teniposide. A Re-view of 12 Years of Experience." *Cancer Treatment Reports* 68:1455–66.

O'Dwyer, P., S. A. King, D. F. Hoth, M. Suffness, and B. Leyland-Jones. 1986. "Homohar-ringtonine—Perspectives on an Active New Natural Product." *Journal of Clinical Oncol-ogy* 4:1563–68.

O'Dwyer, P., B. Leyland-Jones, M. T. Alonso, S. Marsoni, and R. E. Wittes. 1985. "Etopo-side (VP–16–213). Current Status of an Active Anticancer Drug." *New England Journal of Medicine* 312:692–700.

Ohno, R., K. Okada, T. Masaoka, A. Kuramoto, T. Arima, Y. Yoshida, H. Ariyashi, M. Ichimaru, Y. Sakai, M. Oguro, Y. Ito, Y. Morishima, S. Yokomaku, and K. Ota. 1990. "An Early Phase II Study of CPT-11: A New Derivative of Camptothecin, for the Treat-ment of Leukemia and Lymphoma." *Journal of Clinical Oncology* 8:1907–12.

Paull, K. D., R. H. Shoemaker, M. R. Boyd, J. L. Parsons, P. A. Risbood, W. A. Barbera, M. N. Sharman, D. C. Baker, E. Hand, D. A. Scudiero, A. Monks, M. C. Alley, and M. Grote. 1988. "The Synthesis of XTT—A New Tetrazolium Reagent That Is Bioreducible to a Water-Soluble Formazan." *Journal of Heterocyclic Chemistry* 25:911–14.

Paull, K. D., R. H. Shoemaker, L. Hodes, A. Monks, D. A. Scudiero, L. Rubinstein, J. Plowman, and M. R. Boyd. 1989. "Display and Analysis of Patterns of Differential Ac-tivity of Drugs Against Human Tumor Cell Lines: Development of Mean Graph and COMPARE Algorithm." *Journal of the National Cancer Institute* 81:1088–92.

Perdue, R. E. Jr. 1976. "Procurement of Plant Materials for Antitumor Screening." *Cancer Treatment Reports* 60:987–98.

Pettit, G. R., G. M. Cragg, M. Suffness, D. Gust, F. E. Boettner, M. Williams, J. A. Saenz-Renauld, P. Brown, J. M. Schmidt, and P. D. Ellis. 1984. "Antineoplastic Agents. 104. Isolation and Structure of the *Phyllanthus acuminatus* Vahl (Euphorbiaceae) Glycosides." *Journal of Organic Chemistry* 49:4258–66.

Pettit, G. R., V. Gaddamidi, D. L. Herald, S. B. Singh, G. M. Cragg, and J. M. Schmidt. 1986. "Antineoplastic Agents 120. *Pancratium littorale.*" *Journal of Natural Products* 49:995–1002.

Pettit, G. R., S. B. Singh, E. Hamel, C. M. Lin, D. S. Alberts, and D. Garcia-Kendall. 1989. "Isolation and Structure of the Strong Cell Growth and Tubulin Inhibitor, Combretasta-tin A–4." *Experientia* 45:209–11.

Rousse, J., T. Tursz, T. Le Chevalier, D. Huertas, J. L. Amiel, G. Brule, B. Callet, J. P. Droz, P. M. Voisin, H. Sancho-Garnier, J. B. Le Pecq, and C. Paoletti. 1981. "Interet de la 2N-methyl-9-hydroxyellipticine (NSC 264137) dans le traitement des cancers metas-tases." *Nouv. Presse Med.* 10:1997–99.

Rowinsky, E. K., L. A. Cazenave, and R. C. Donehower. 1990. "Taxol: A Novel Investiga-tional Antimicrotubule Agent." *Journal of the National Cancer Institute* 82:1247–59.

Rubinstein, L. V., R. H. Shoemaker, K. D. Paull, R. M. Simon, S. Tosini, P. Skehan, D. Scudiero, A. Monks, and M. R. Boyd. 1990. "Comparison of *in Vitro* Anticancer-Drug-Screening Data Generated with a Tetrazolium Assay Versus a Protein Assay Against a Diverse Panel of Human Tumor Cell Lines." *Journal of the National Cancer Institute* 82:1113–18.

Schultes, R. E. and R. F. Raffauf. 1990. *The Healing Forest. Medicinal and Toxic Plants of the Northwest Amazonia.* Portland, Ore.: Dioscorides Press.

Scudiero, D. A., R. H. Shoemaker, K. D. Paull, A. Monks, S. Tierney, T. H. Nobziger, M.

J. Currens, D. Seniff, and M. R. Boyd. 1988. "Evaluation of a Soluble Tetrazolium/For-mazan Assay for Cell Growth and Drug Sensitivity in Culture Using Human and Other Tumor Cell Lines." *Cancer Research* 48:4827–33.

Skehan, P., R. Storeng, D. Scudiero, A. Monks, J. McMahon, D. Vistica, J. T. Warren, H. Bokesch, S. Kenney, and M. R. Boyd. 1990. "New Colorimetric Cytotoxicity Assay for Anticancer-Drug Screening." *Journal of the National Cancer Institute* 82:1107–12.

Spjut, R. W. and R. E. Perdue. 1976. "Plant Folklore: A Tool for Predicting Sources of Antitumor Activity?" *Cancer Treatment Reports* 60:979–85.

Stinson, S. F., M. C. Alley, H. Fiebig, L. M. Mullendore, S. Kenney, J. Keller, and M. R. Boyd. 1992. "Morphologic and Immunocytochemical Characteristics of Human Tumor Cell Lines for Use in an Anticancer Drug Screen." *Anticancer Research* 12:1035–54.

Suffness, M. 1987. "New Approaches to the Discovery of Antitumor Agents." In K. Hos-tettmann and P. J. Lea, eds., *Biologically Active Natural Products. Annual Proceedings of the Phytochemical Society of Europe,* pp. 85–104. Oxford: Clarendon Press.

Suffness, M. and G. A. Cordell. 1985. "Antitumor Alkaloids." In A. Brossi, ed. *The Alka-loids* 25:1–325. New York: Academic Press.

Suffness, M. and J. Douros. 1979. "Drugs of Plant Origin," ch. 3. In V. T. DeVita and H. Busch, eds., *Methods in Cancer Research,* 16:73–125. New York: Academic Press.

——. 1982. "Current Status of the NCI Plant and Animal Product Program." *Journal of Natural Products* 45:1–14.

Suffness, M., D. J. Newman, and K. Snader. 1989. "Discovery and Development of Anti-neoplastic Agents from Natural Sources." In P. J. Scheuer, ed., *Bioorganic Marine Chem-istry,* 3:132–68, Berlin: Springer-Verlag.

Treat, J., A. Greenspan, A. Rahman, M. S. McCabe, and P. J. Byrne. 1989. "Elliptinium: Phase II Study in Advanced Measurable Breast Cancer." *Investigational New Drugs* 7:231–34.

Venditti, J. M., R. A. Wesley, and J. Plowman. 1984. "Current NCI Preclinical Antitumor Screening *in Vivo.* Results of Tumor Panel Screening 1976–1982, and Future Direc-tions." *Advances in Pharmacology and Chemotherapeutics* 20:1–20.

Wani, M. C., H. L. Taylor, and M. E. Wall. 1971. "Plant Antitumor Agents. VI. The Isola-tion and Structure of Taxol, a Novel Antileukemic and Antitumor Agent from *Taxus brevifolia.*" *Journal of the American Chemical Society* 93:2325–27.

Weislow, O. S., R. Kiser, D. L. Fine, J. Bader, R. H. Shoemaker, and M. R. Boyd. 1989. "New Soluble-Formazan Assay for HIV-1 Cytopathic Effects: Application to High-Flux Screening of Synthetic and Natural Products for AIDS-Antiviral Activity." *Journal of the National Cancer Institute* 81:577–86.

11

The Merck/INBio Agreement: A Pharmaceutical Company Perspective

Lynn Helena Caporale

To begin, I would like to establish a context for the Merck/INBio agreement by describing how a pharmaceutical company discovers a drug, and thus I hope to provide a perspective on what we do.

Even though Merck is now the world's largest pharmaceutical company, about 95% of the pharmaceuticals sold in the world are sold by others. Because one company does not dominate, opportunity exists for different approaches.

Our large size does allow us to run clinical trials simultaneously around the world for several different diseases. I would like to describe some of our recent work. In the last decade we introduced treatments for cardiovascular disease, a major international killer. Among these is Vasotec®, a treatment for hypertension. Because high blood pressure is readily treatable, without side effects that stop people from taking their medicine, the rate of stroke and other debilitating cardiovascular diseases has decreased. A recent large clinical trial demonstrated that the risk of heart failure, in people whose hearts may be at special risk for failure, is decreased by taking Vasotec. My colleague Dr. Georg Albers-Schönberg has written in this volume about Mevacor®, a natural product that was discovered in a soil sample and that lowers blood cholesterol, thus decreasing atherosclerosis; recently (in a major and fairly expensive clinical trial) it was demonstrated that Mevacor can reverse preexisting atherosclerosis.

Broad-spectrum antibiotics play an important role in control of bacterial diseases. We donated Mectizan® (an antiparasitic compound originally discovered in a soil sample by our animal health research program) to the World Health Organization to prevent river blindness.

Another major area of our work involves vaccines, which include those for mumps, measles, rubella, and hepatitis B. The recent increased incidence of measles in inadequately vaccinated populations in the United States, where eighty-nine people died from measles in 1990, brings home to us what an important role vaccination plays in saving lives.

Although these are success stories, many serious diseases remain for which there is currently no adequate treatment. We lack adequate therapy for AIDS; cancer is still a scourge around the world; the immediate aftereffects of heart attack and the protection of tissue at risk of damage by the presence of a blood clot, in spite of great recent progress with plasminogen activators, are problems still not solved; Alzheimer's disease is a devastating disease that increases in incidence as people live longer (it is estimated that a majority of people more than eighty years of age will have some cognitive deficit related to the kinds of plaque seen in Alzheimer's disease). Diabetics remain at risk for the devastating effects of neuropathy, blindness, and kidney failure.

These are examples of major unsolved medical problems. Merck is working on all of them, as are others around the world; I believe we can agree that all those working to find treatments should do the best they can in the best way they can.

How do we at Merck work to find treatments for these diseases? I will give HIV as an example because this program has had some very clear milestones. Why is HIV so difficult? Because a virus uses many of the cell's own molecules to survive, it is very hard to kill a virus without killing the cell it has infected. (Remember that in Western medicine there is no cure for the common cold.) However, viruses do have a few of their own proteins that we can target. Once HIV had been isolated and its DNA sequenced, some people recognized within the sequence the code for a string of amino acids that looked familiar to them, that looked like part of a type of enzyme called a protease. Based on analogy with other viral diseases the prediction was made that if we were able to knock out the HIV protease the virus would not be able to function. To test this hypothesis we (and others) undertook genetic engineering experiments, in which a single amino acid within the hundreds of amino acids in the AIDS virus was changed to inactivate the protease. These experiments demonstrated that when the protease is inactivated the virus cannot spread.

Once we tested this biochemical hypothesis for treating AIDS, that if you knock out the protease you kill the virus, we mounted a major effort to discover inhibitors of that protease. We looked in as many different kinds of places as possible. At first, we recognized the similarity of the HIV protease to the protease renin, involved in blood pressure regulation. Since many pharmaceutical companies had been working to inhibit renin to treat hypertension, we all began to look for molecules related to the inhibitors of renin that we had on our shelves, to see whether they might be the starting point to design a molecule that will inhibit the HIV protease specifically. While the chemists could begin with ideas such as these to synthesize new molecules to test as inhibitors, they are also eager to learn about new types of molecules to help them design better inhibitors.

In all our programs we are open to suggestions from people outside Merck. When someone comes to us with an idea, whether a new small biotech company, or a professor at a university, or someone who is familiar with an ethnomedicine tradition, we take them all seriously and evaluate them the same way. To leap ahead for a moment to compensation issues, the biotech company might want us to purchase stock, the professor is likely to request his or her support for laboratory research, and the ethnobotanist may need money to protect indigenous people and/or the land (or there may be other needs; we work out an equitable arrangement in the course of negotiations); we would like the information to help us to discover drugs, and we understand that our new collaborators have their own needs.

In addition to searching for new ideas inside and outside Merck, we remain humble in the face of these very clever viruses; there are limits to our knowledge, and limits to other peoples' knowledge, so we also screen. Some find it hard at first to accept this random screening approach, but since we have demonstrated that if we can inhibit the HIV protease in a sustained way we can stop the spread of the virus, we consider it important enough to search by this approach as well. We put samples of the protease (and other viral enzymes) in thousands and tens of thousands of test tubes and reach for as wide a variety of substances as we can to place in those test tubes, until we find new molecules that inhibit the protease. When we find a molecule with useful properties, such as one that knocks out that protease while sparing other important proteases people need to survive, we begin to develop it as a drug. It is very likely that the molecule we find in the screen may not be able to get into the bloodstream, or it might not last long enough in the blood to kill the virus (further, with HIV there is also the problem of rapid development of resistance to certain molecules). But we do not discard these imperfect inhibitors; chemists design better molecules based on what they learn from these leads.

It is widely quoted that chemists synthesize 10,000 compounds for one that is good enough to take into the clinic, but the other 9,999 compounds are not all wasted time, wasted money. Each new compound teaches us how to make a better compound. We learn that if we modify this end of the molecule we lose all activity against the enzyme, but certain changes on another side of the molecule may significantly improve activity against the enzyme. Chemists and others study this molecule, learning how to make a better inhibitor of the enzyme, learning how to make it orally active or to have a long lifetime in the blood so that it does not disappear as soon as a patient swallows it.

While we are screening an extract against the AIDS protease, we screen the same extract against thirty or so other targets directed at diseases such as cancer and diabetes. Diversity is important for screening, for the more different kinds of molecules we test, the more likely we are to find a lead, an idea, to treat one of the diseases on which we are working.

Why did we decide to enter into a collaboration with INBio as a source of diverse molecules? Our reasons include the great diversity of Costa Rican organisms, the strong commitment of Costa Rica to conservation and education, and the strong scientific foundation of INBio. There is tremendous diversity in Costa Rica, which has more than 5% of the world's species, owing in part to its location as a land bridge between the North and South American continents and between the Atlantic and Pacific Oceans, and yet it is very accessible. Diversity is a reflection not only of the flow of species but also of the variety of Costa Rica's environments, including rain forests, dry forests, cloud forests, active volcanoes, and tropical beaches. We believe biodiversity is a reflection of underlying molecular diversity.

In addition to their tremendous diversity, Costa Rica's commitment to conservation can be seen by the fact that a quarter of the land has been put aside in these conservation areas. Their commitment to education has provided a strong base of very well trained local people; through the parataxonomist program local people are trained to become authorities on organisms in the conserved lands around where they live. Thus there is a strong scientific foundation to this collaboration, with INBio's survey of Costa Rican biodiversity. We have very well informed collectors in a variety of sites in Costa Rica. We know what we have been sent.

This strong scientific tradition and the inventory help our collaboration in another way. If, for example, we were to find a molecule in a particular beetle that was good but not optimal, we might want to look at one of the related beetles to see whether there was a similar molecule with better properties. All this makes INBio a very attractive partner.

Further, one reason we are working with INBio is that they approached us. I believe the way in which they approached us grows in part out of Costa Rica's tradition of conflict resolution, the belief that there does not always have to be a winner and a loser in every conflict but rather that we can find common goals in any potential conflict and work together toward a solution. One apparent conflict in the world today is that between conservation and the economic needs of local people, but does there need to be such a conflict? INBio approached us knowing that Merck is experienced in designing drug discovery programs and that it would be of value to both Merck and INBio to work together to find new organisms for our screens.

In this specific agreement, there will be a royalty on any products that we discover and that we will sell around the world. Even if a screen is successful, it will take a long time for profits to appear, for many years are invested in development, and yet money is needed in the interim in Costa Rica to support conservation and to support training; these were INBio's needs and thus Merck agreed to pay a significant amount of money in the first two years. Some of this money supports collection and training for work related to science and to sustainable development. In addition, 10% of the money goes directly to conservation in Costa

Rica. For example, funds from this agreement provide an endowment for Cocos Island National Park, a unique ecosystem off the coast of Costa Rica.

While a strong scientific base exists in Costa Rica, we are specialists in pharmaceutical discovery and development. Therefore, part of the agreement involves technology transfer from Merck to INBio. Among the first steps in this agreement was our establishment of an extraction laboratory in Costa Rica by the donation of $150,000 in equipment. Two of Merck's key natural products chemists in Costa Rica worked together with Costa Rican natural products chemists to set up this extraction laboratory. The laboratory now runs independently in Costa Rica. Further, Costa Rican scientists come to Merck to see from inside the pharmaceutical industry in the United States how we discover and develop a new medicine.

This is not something we have to do for the developing world. Trained scientists are there who need resources so they can do this for themselves. We see potential partnerships as true collaborations. And we do not see Costa Rica becoming dependent on this collaboration in order to move its science and conservation plans forward.

This agreement has received a great deal of attention. On our side it was undertaken as a way to obtain diverse samples for screening to help us in our work of discovering new treatments for serious diseases. Costa Rica has created in INBio a mechanism by which our need for diverse identified samples can be used to support local needs for conservation and sustainable development.

12

Biodiversity Prospecting

Walter V. Reid, Sarah A. Laird, Carrie A. Meyer,
Rodrigo Gámez, Ana Sittenfeld, Daniel Janzen,
Michael A. Gollin, and Calestous Juma

In September 1991, Costa Rica's National Biodiversity Institute (INBio)—a private, nonprofit organization—and the U.S.-based pharmaceutical firm Merck & Co., Ltd., announced an agreement under which INBio would provide Merck with chemical extracts from wild plants, insects, and microorganisms from Costa Rica's conserved wildlands for Merck's drug-screening program in return for a two-year research and sampling budget of $1,135,000 and royalties on any resulting commercial products. INBio agreed to contribute 10% of the budget and 50% of any royalties to the government's National Park Fund for the conservation of national parks in Costa Rica, and Merck agreed to provide technical assistance and training to help establish drug research capacity in Costa Rica (Aldhous 1991).

This agreement represents a watershed in the history of ''biodiversity prospecting''—the exploration of biodiversity for commercially valuable genetic and biochemical resources. (See Eisner 1989, 1992.) For decades, ecologists and environmentalists have been arguing that pharmaceutical and other commercial applications of biodiversity should help justify its conservation. However, industry investment in natural products research since the mid-1960s has been small, and it actually declined in the pharmaceutical industry during the 1960s and 1970s. Clearly, the INBio-Merck agreement demonstrates a shift in industry focus and the true economic potential of these resources.

This ground-breaking agreement also shows how companies can return a por-

This paper is excerpted from W. V. Reid et al. ''A New Lease on Life.'' In W. V. Reid, et al., eds., *Biodiversity Prospecting: Using Genetic Resources for Sustainable Development*, pp. 1–52. Washington, D.C.: World Resources Institute, 1993.

tion of the benefits of pharmaceutical development to the developing country where the chemical compounds originated. Further, it ensures that some of these proceeds will directly finance conservation while the remainder will indirectly finance conservation through biodiversity research, development, and industry in association with the national parks. Coming as it did during the final negotiations of the International Convention on Biological Diversity, the Merck-INBio agreement validated what was becoming—after heated debate—an underlying tenet of the convention: the fair and equitable distribution of the benefits of the use of genetic resources among *all* those who invest in their continued existence.

Although its close link to conservation efforts has earned it exceptional attention, the Merck-INBio agreement is just one of a rapidly growing number of biodiversity-prospecting ventures. Japan has launched a major biodiversity research program in Micronesia, the U.S. National Institutes of Health is screening wild species for compounds active against HIV and cancer, and both Indonesia and Kenya are establishing inventory programs similar to INBio's and are exploring possible biodiversity-prospecting activities.

This flurry of interest and enthusiasm in biodiversity prospecting is taking place in a policy vacuum. Virtually no precedent exists for national policies and legislation to govern and regulate wildland biodiversity prospecting. Yet, the more than 150 countries that signed the International Convention on Biological Diversity in 1992 now must pass implementing legislation that establishes just such a policy framework.

The stakes are high as countries begin to fill this policy vacuum. Done well, biodiversity prospecting can contribute greatly to environmentally sound development and return benefits to the custodians of genetic resources—the national public at large, the staff of conservation units, the farmers, the forest dwellers, and the indigenous people who maintain or tolerate the resources involved. But carried out in the mold of previous resource-exploitation ventures, biodiversity prospecting can have a negligible or potentially harmful effect on biodiversity conservation and environmentally sound development.

This chapter offers suggestions to governments, nongovernmental organizations, scientists, and industry on designing effective and equitable biodiversity-prospecting programs, with a particular focus on the use of biodiversity in the pharmaceutical industry. The chapter's premise is that appropriate policies and institutions are needed to ensure that the commercial value obtained from genetic and biochemical resources is a positive force for development and conservation. In particular, three problems must be overcome if biodiversity prospecting is to contribute to national sustainable development and the long-term survival of wildland biodiversity.

First, growing commercial interest in biodiversity will not necessarily fuel increased investment in resource conservation. Genetic and biochemical resources are often described by economists as "nonrival public goods." In other words, their use by one individual does not reduce their value to others who use them.

Because any user benefits from investments in their conservation, market forces will lead to less conservation of the resource than its value to society warrants.[1] In fact, unregulated biodiversity prospecting and drug development could speed the destruction of the resource.

Second, there is no guarantee that the institutions created to capture the benefits of biodiversity will contribute to economic growth in developing countries. Quite the opposite has been the case historically. The chief commercial beneficiaries of genetic and biochemical resources found in developing countries have been the developed countries able to explore for valuable resources, develop new technologies based on the resources, and commercialize the products. The Convention on Biological Diversity provides a framework that may boost developing countries' negotiating strength and foster needed investments in conservation, but it will be up to individual nations to pass the laws and establish the regulations needed to achieve these benefits. From a conservation standpoint, unless developing countries do realize benefits from these resources, summoning the political will to conserve them will be difficult.

Finally, biodiversity prospecting is just one of many forms of biodiversity development that could take place in the countryside to help raise living standards there. In most countries, the people living side by side with wildland biodiversity—farmers and villagers, indigenous peoples, forest dwellers, medicinal healers, and fisherfolk—hold the key to its survival. If the local and national citizens do not get something out of maintaining wildland habitats, the habitats will be converted to timber plantations, farms, or other productive uses harmful to biodiversity. Yet, in many cases sustainably managed wildlands do not yield enough direct economic benefits to support large local populations, so governments will have to ensure that a share of the national benefits from activities such as biodiversity prospecting are used to meet rural development needs. How well biodiversity-prospecting institutions contribute to sustainable development thus ultimately depends on effective local and national government policies for conservation and development—a big question in many countries.

Growing Demand for Genetic and Biochemical Resources

The driving forces behind the evolution of new biodiversity-prospecting institutions have been the growing demand for new genes and chemicals and a growing awareness that an abundant and virtually untapped supply of these resources exists in wildland biodiversity. Whereas genetic and biochemical resources have long been important raw materials in agriculture and medicine, biotechnology is opening a new frontier. Furthermore, democratization and economic development in many developing countries have fanned interest in the local development of in-country resources.

In the pharmaceutical industry, after a hiatus in natural products research in the 1970s, interest has intensified over the past decade. As a source of novel chemical compounds, natural products research is an important complement to "rational drug design"—the chemical synthesis of new drugs. Natural products research has been revived by the development of efficient automated receptor-based screening techniques that have increased a hundredfold the speed with which chemicals can be tested. Although only one in about 10,000 chemicals yields a potentially valuable "lead" (McChesney, this volume; Principe, this volume), these new techniques have made large natural products screening programs affordable. Researchers are thus returning to such natural sources of biologically active chemicals as plants, insects, marine invertebrates, fungi, and bacteria.

Another and quite different stimulus to natural products research has come from decades-old ethnopharmacology—the study of medicines used by traditional communities. Leads based on the use of plants or animals in traditional medicine can greatly increase the probability of finding a commercially valuable drug. For small pharmaceutical companies, drug exploration based on this indigenous knowledge may be more cost-effective than attempting to compete in expensive random screening ventures. For example, Shaman Pharmaceuticals—a small company in California—bases all its drug exploration on plants used in traditional medicine (King, this volume). One of its most promising products is an antifungal agent derived from a species commonly used as a folk remedy for wound healing in Peru and parts of Mexico. Other examples of natural products research programs now under way include the U.S. National Cancer Institute's five-year $8-million program to screen 10,000 substances against 100 cancer cell lines and HIV, and new screening programs at SmithKline Beecham, Merck & Co., Inc., Monsanto, and Glaxo (see table 12.1).

In the United States, some 25% of prescriptions are filled with drugs whose active ingredients are extracted or derived from plants. Sales of these plant-based drugs amounted to some $4.5 billion in 1980 and an estimated $15.5 billion in 1990 (Principe, this volume). In Europe, Japan, Australia, Canada, and the United States, the market value for both prescription and over-the-counter drugs based on plants in 1985 was estimated to be $43 billion (Principe 1989).

Biotechnology has also opened the door to greater use of biodiversity in agriculture. Genetic diversity has always been a key raw material in agricultural research, accounting for roughly one half of the gains in U.S. agricultural yields from 1930 to 1980 (OTA 1987). But whereas previously only close relatives of crops could be used in breeding programs, now the genes from the entire world's biota are within reach.

The products of agricultural biotechnology are just now entering the marketplace, but by the year 2000, farm-level sales are expected to reach at least $10 billion and possibly as much as $100 billion annually, nearly equal to the total world market for agrochemicals and seeds in 1987 (World Bank 1991). Research

TABLE 12.1 *A Sample of Companies Active in Plant and Other Natural Product Collection and Screening*

Abbott Laboratories
  Active since: 1950
  Collectors: University of Illinois, independent collectors
  Capacity: 20–50 primary screens
  Natural product focus: microbes, plants
  Therapeutic groups: antiinfective, cardiovascular, neuroscience, and immunoscience

Boehringer Ingelheim
  Active since: 1986–89
  Collectors: University of Illinois, New York Botanical Garden (pilot program in 1986), and
    independent collectors
  Capacity: 8–12 screens; 5,000 compounds per year
  Natural product focus: plants, microbes
  Therapeutic groups: cardiovascular, respiratory, and gastroenterology

Bristol-Myers Squibb
  Active since: company established
  Collectors: Scripps Institute of Oceanography, Oncogen (pokeweed protein), and independent
    collectors
  Capacity: not available
  Natural product focus: fungi, microbes, marine, and plants
  Therapeutic groups: antiinfective, cancer, and antiviral

Ciba-Geigy
  Active since: 1989 (marine); 1992 (tropical plants)
  Collectors: Chinese Academy of Sciences, Harbor Branch Oceanographic Institute, and independent
    collectors
  Capacity: 4,000 samples tested (1991)
  Natural product focus: microbes, marine, and plants
  Therapeutic groups: cancer, cardiovascular, antiinflammatory, CNS, respiratory, and antiallergy

Eli Lilly
  Active since: active in 1950s and 1960s
  Collectors: now collaborates with NCI, Shaman Pharmaceuticals, and independent researchers
  Capacity: not available
  Natural product focus: plants, algae
  Therapeutic groups: antiinfective, diabetes, cardiovascular, cancer, CNS, pulmonary, antiviral, and
    skeletal diseases

Glaxo Group Research
  Active since: 1988
  Collectors: Royal Botanic Gardens, Kew; Chelsea Physic Garden; Institute of Medicinal Plant
    Development (Beijing); Biotics, Ltd.; and University of Illinois/NCI
  Capacity: not available to the public
  Natural product focus: fungi, microbes, marine, and plants
  Therapeutic groups: gastrointestinal, respiratory, antiinfective, cardiovascular, dermatology,
    metabolic diseases, cancer, antiinflammatory, and infectious diseases

Inverni della Beffa
  Active since: late 1950s
  Collectors: in-house and independent collectors in Asia, Africa, and South America
  Capacity: in-house screening of hundreds of samples per year
  Natural product focus: plants
  Therapeutic groups: cardiovascular, gastroenterologic, and antiinflammatory

Merck & Co., Inc.
  Active since: 1991
  Collectors: INBio, New York Botanical Garden, and MYCOsearch
  Capacity: not available to the public
  Natural product focus: fungi, microbes, marine, and plants
  Therapeutic groups: respiratory, antiallergy, antiinflammatory, cancer, cardiovascular, antiinfective,
    antiviral, gastrointestinal, prostate, and bone disease

TABLE 12.1 *Continued.*

Miles, Inc.
  Active since: 1991
  Collectors: contract companies, independent collectors
  Capacity: not available to the public
  Natural product focus: microbes, plants, marine, and fungi
  Therapeutic groups: CNS, antiinfectives, cardiovascular, antidiabetes, and rheumatic diseases

Monsanto
  Active since: 1989
  Collectors: Missouri Botanical Garden
  Capacity: 9,000 samples per year, mainly from North America and Puerto Rico; number of screens
    is not available to the public
  Natural product focus: plants, microbes
  Therapeutic groups: antiinfectants, cardiovascular, and antiinflammatory

National Cancer Institute
  Active since: 1960–1980, 1986–present
  Collectors: U.S. Department of Agriculture (1960–80); Missouri Botanical Garden; New York
    Botanical Garden; University of Illinois; Kunming Institute of Botany, China; Central Drug
    Research Institute, India; Brigham Young University; Harbor Branch Oceanographic Institute;
    Australian Institute of Marine Sciences; Coral Reef Research Foundation; Smithsonian
    Oceanographic; University of Connecticut; University of Hawaii at Manoa; University of Miami;
    Michigan Biotechnology Institute; and Tel Aviv University
  Capacity: 1960–1980: received almost 35,000 species of plants, 16,000 marine extracts, and 180,000
    microbe extracts; under current program, receives almost 10,000 plant, marine, invertebrate, fungi,
    and algae samples per year
  Natural product focus: plants, microbes, insects, marine, and fungi
  Therapeutic groups: cancer, AIDS, antivirals

Pfizer
  Active since: not available
  Collectors: Natural Product Sciences (now lapsed); New York Botanical Garden
  Capacity: not available to the public
  Natural product focus: plants, spider venom
  Therapeutic groups: cardiovascular, antiinflammatory, antiinfective, psychotherapeutic,
    antidiabetes, atherosclerosis, cancer, gastrointestinal, and immunoscience

Pharmagenesis
  Active since: 1990
  Collectors: in-house experts in herbal medicine and more than fifteen collaborating entities
    throughout China and Asia
  Capacity: 2,000–3,000 samples per year; 50 screens per year
  Natural product focus: natural products used in traditional Asian medicine
  Therapeutic groups: immune, endocrine, CNS, and cardiovascular

Phytopharmaceuticals
  Active since: 1992
  Collectors: University of São Paulo, Brazil; Chinese Academy of Sciences; independent collectors
  Capacity: not available
  Natural product focus: plants
  Therapeutic groups: cancer

Rhone-Poulene Rorer
  Active since: 1991
  Collectors: University of Hawaii; Beijing Medical University; Shanghai Medical University; Tianjin
    Plant Institute, China; and independent collectors
  Capacity: hundreds of samples per year; 9–20 screens
  Natural product focus: plants, marine, and microbes
  Therapeutic groups: cardiovascular, antiinfective, AIDS, CNS, respiratory, bone disease, and cancer

(continued)

Table 12.1 *Continued.*

Shaman Pharmaceuticals, Inc.
  Active since: 1989
  Collectors: in-house botanists and a network of collaborators in Africa, Asia, and South America
  Capacity: 200 samples per year
  Natural product focus: plants
  Therapeutic groups: antiviral, antifungal, analgesics, and diabetes

SmithKline Beecham
  Active since: 1987
  Collectors: Biotics, Ltd.; Royal Botanic Gardens, Kew; University of Virginia; Scripps Institution of
    Oceanography; Morris Arboretum, University of Pennsylvania; MYCOsearch; and in-house
    collectors
  Capacity: 2–3,000 samples per year; in-house library of 17,800 natural product extracts; and 10–15
    screens
  Natural product focus: microbes, plants, and marine
  Therapeutic groups: antiinfective, cardiopulmonary, CNS, gastrointestinal, and antiinflammatory

Sphinx Pharmaceuticals
  Active since: 1990
  Collectors: Biotics, Ltd.; independent collectors
  Capacity: 15,000 samples per year; 3 screens
  Natural product focus: plants, marine, fungi, and algae
  Therapeutic groups: psoriasis, antifungal, and cancer

Sterling Winthrop
  Active since: 1988
  Collectors: Mississippi State University, Brigham Young University, New York Botanical Garden
    (one shipment), independent collectors
  Capacity: few hundred samples per year
  Natural product focus: microbes, plants, and marine
  Therapeutic groups: cancer, antiinflammatory

Syntex Laboratories
  Active since: 1986
  Collectors: Chinese Academy of Sciences
  Capacity: receive 10,000 plant extracts per year; 10 screens
  Natural product focus: plants, microbes
  Therapeutic groups: antiinflammatory, bone diseases, immunology, cancer, gastroenterology,
    cardiovascular, antiviral, dermatology, and oral contraceptives

Upjohn Company
  Active since: 1986–87
  Collectors: Shanghai Institute of Materia Medica
  Natural product focus: microbes, plants
  Therapeutic groups: CNS, cardiovascular, antiinfectives, and AIDS

Source: Reid et al. 1993.

expenditures are equally striking. In 1987, total R & D expenditure on agricultural biotechnology was estimated at $900 million (Giddings and Persley 1990).

Growth in this "biotechnology industry" foretells increasing demands for novel genetic and biochemical resources. Between 1985 and 1990, the number of biotechnology patent applications filed in the United States grew by 15% annually—by 9,385 in 1990 alone (Raines 1991). Total product sales for the U.S. biotechnology industry in 1991 totaled approximately $4 billion—a 38% increase over 1990—and by the year 2000, sales are expected to have grown more than tenfold to some $50 billion (IBA 1992).

What Is at Stake?

All else being equal, the growing demand for genetic and biochemical resources should increase the potential market value of the raw material. But, given the high revenues generated from the final products developed in the agricultural and pharmaceutical industries, it is easy to misjudge how much money might actually be involved.

Many of the industries using genetic and biochemical resources produce high-value commodities and thus enjoy substantial gross earnings from the commercial product. Two drugs derived from the rosy periwinkle—vincristine and vinblastine—alone earned $100 million annually for Eli Lilly (Farnsworth 1988)—a figure that is sometimes erroneously cited as the "value" of the rosy periwinkle. But sales of a product provide little indication of the potential market value of the unimproved genetic material in the source country. Most of the industries using these resources are capital-intensive ventures that invest substantial time and money in the production of a commercial product, and most are far removed from the original source of the genetic or biochemical material.

In the U.S. pharmaceutical industry, a commercially marketable drug requires an estimated $231 million and twelve years on average to develop (DiMasi et al. 1991). These costs cover the processes of screening candidate compounds, isolating active compounds, testing for possible toxicity, and undertaking clinical trials, as well as failed attempts to discover and produce a new drug. Developing agricultural products through genetic engineering also entails substantial costs. For example, the successful introduction of Bt genes into plants took several years and cost some $1.5 million to $3 million (Collinson and Wright 1991).

In any given trial, the likelihood of discovering a valuable compound for the pharmaceutical industry is quite low. By most estimates, only about 1 in 10,000 chemicals yields a promising lead, and less than one fourth of the chemicals reaching clinical trials will ever be approved as a new drug (McChesney, this volume; DiMasi et al. 1991; Principe, this volume). For example, of 50,000 extracts put through an HIV screen in the natural products research program of the National Cancer Institute, only 3 are likely to wind up in clinical trials, and of 33,000 extracts screened for cancer, only 5 are receiving further study (Sears 1992).[2]

Given the high value added in both the pharmaceutical industry and agriculture, the abundance of unimproved genetic and biochemical resources, and the low probability that any specific sample will have commercial value, the holders of unimproved material are likely to receive a relatively low payment for access to the resource, current heightened demand notwithstanding. In agriculture, Barton (1991) estimates that the total revenue that might be gained if developing countries sought royalties for unimproved genetic material could amount to less than $100 million annually.[3]

Even in the pharmaceutical industry, possible earnings from the sale of raw materials are smaller than might be thought given the industry's worldwide sales of roughly $200 billion—more than thirty times that of the seed industry (Lisansky and Coombs 1989). In this industry, typical royalties paid for samples of unknown clinical activity (e.g., new synthetic chemicals) amount to only 1–5% of net sales— a range of royalties likely to apply to natural products as well. Consider an institution that supplies 1,000 chemicals to a pharmaceutical company in return for a 3% royalty on the net sales of any commercial product. Given the need to screen roughly 10,000 chemicals to find a single lead, a one in four chance of a lead being developed into a commercial product, a 5% discount rate, a ten-year wait before a product is ready to be marketed, and fifteen years of patent protection while it is being marketed, and on the assumption that a drug, if discovered, generates $10 million net annual revenues, the present value of the agreement to the supplier is only $52,500.[4] More sobering, there is a 97.5% chance that the 1,000 chemicals will not turn up any commercial product at all, and if they do, royalty payments will not begin until more than a decade after chemical screening commences.

However, the prospects for success are raised with natural products, since any extract from a species will contain hundreds or thousands of different chemicals that might result in a pharmaceutical "lead." Moreover, the probability of success can be increased through the use of multiple—and higher quality—screens. Thus, for natural products research using current technologies, the probability of success could easily be ten times that of the example above and thus produce promising leads at a rate of about 1 per 1,000 samples.[5] The probability of developing at least one commercial product in the example above would then grow from 2.5% to 22%, and the present value of the agreement would grow accordingly, to $461,000. And if a "blockbuster" drug—earning $1 billion in sales annually—happens to be discovered under this scenario, that value would swell to $46 million.

Biodiversity prospecting does involve financial risks. With the odds against striking it rich, it often makes economic sense for biodiversity prospectors to hedge their bets by seeking advance payments and relatively small royalties rather than forgo collecting fees and hold out for higher royalties that may never materialize. Moreover, a risk exists that the market for natural products could quickly become saturated. While a number of pharmaceutical firms have natural products research efforts under way (see table 12.1), most are small in scale, and the demand for chemical extracts from plants, animals, and microbes might be saturated by a handful of large-scale suppliers. As, say, Costa Rica, Indonesia, India, Brazil, and Mexico establish biodiversity-prospecting institutes, the growing supply may well lead to steadily declining prices for raw materials.

Finally, there is no sure way of projecting future demand for biological samples on the part of the pharmaceutical industry. Within a decade or two, advances in synthetic chemistry, biotechnology, and medical sciences may curtail interest in natural products. On the other hand, wild species will continue to be a source of novel genes and proteins, as well as a source of insights into chemical and physiological processes. Nobody knows whether natural products will fall from favor in several decades or become even more valuable in medicine and in industrial applications.

In sum, while biodiversity prospecting can return profits to source countries, institutions, and communities, the amounts involved are likely to be small relative to the market value of the final products, a decade or more may pass before significant revenues materialize, a good chance exists that no commercial drugs will be produced, and latecomers may find a market already saturated with suppliers. On the other hand, given the scale of revenues generated in the pharmaceutical industry, even a relatively small share of net profits may amount to extremely large revenues for a developing country. And if nations add value to genetic resources domestically and build technical capacity for improving the resource themselves, biodiversity prospecting could become an important component of a nation's economic development strategy.

The Evolution of Biodiversity-Prospecting Institutions

The increasing value of wildland genetic resources to private industry—combined with many countries' growing sense of national identity and desire for greater control over their destiny—has created incentives for new kinds of institutional arrangements for capturing the return on investment in the use of biodiversity. In particular, genetic resource property rights, international agreements, and the use of intermediary organizations are three critical institutional arrangements whose evolution must be guided to ensure the sustainable and equitable use of biodiversity. (For wildland biodiversity, a "sustainable use" is one that does not diminish the diversity of wild species through time.)

PROPERTY RIGHTS

For decades, the major trend in the evolution of intellectual property rights for improved genetic and biochemical resources has been a gradual expansion in the scope and strength of ownership. As a result, two different systems now govern ownership and access to genetic and biochemical resources. On the one hand, "unimproved genetic material"—wild species and traditional varieties of crops and livestock grown by farmers—is treated as an ownerless, open-access resource.[6] On the other hand, Intellectual Property Rights (IPR) regimes—including patents, Plant Breeders' Rights (PBR), and trade secrets—establish ownership for new varieties of plants and animals developed by commercial breeders and chemicals isolated and developed by pharmaceutical firms.

The biodiversity-prospecting "industry" falls squarely between these two systems inasmuch as it seeks to locate wild resources with commercial potential. Not surprisingly, considerable controversy surrounds the applicability of property rights to wild biodiversity and to information about its potential use.

Historically, unimproved genetic and biochemical resources were regarded as the common heritage of humankind, freely accessible to anyone. Scattered efforts to control ownership amounted to what would today be considered "trade secret" protection. Brazil, for example, tried unsuccessfully to prevent the export of rubber tree seeds, and for good reason. Just twenty years after the first rubber trees were established in Malaysia, the Brazilian rubber industry that had once commanded 98% of the world supply was exporting virtually nothing, while Singapore became the rubber capital of the world (Brockway 1988). Similarly, Andean nations' attempts to prevent the export of *Cinchona*—the source of an antimalarial compound—were eventually overcome, again by British plant explorers (Juma 1989).

As early as 1873, however, a new type of ownership was extended to certain genetic resources: the patent. In that year, Louis Pasteur was awarded a patent in the United States for a yeast culture, giving him a limited monopoly over the culture, enforced by the state, in recognition of his intellectual contribution to the creation of the product (Juma 1989).

Beginning in 1930, IPR for genetic and biochemical resources began to expand rapidly in breadth and scope. In 1930, the United States passed the Plant Patent Act, which allowed patenting of asexually reproduced plants such as roses, other ornamentals, and fruit trees. In the 1940s, European countries established Plant Breeders' Rights protecting sexually reproduced plants, and the United States followed suit in 1970 with its Plant Variety Protection Act.[7] To address issues arising from international trade in species protected by PBR, the International Convention for the Protection of New Varieties of Plants—commonly referred to as the UPOV Convention—was adopted in 1961.[8]

The most significant step in the expansion of IPR coverage for genetic resources took place in 1980, when the U.S. Supreme Court ruled in the case of *Diamond* v. *Chakrabarty* that a genetically altered bacterium could be granted a utility patent under standard patent law (U.S. Supreme Court 1980, 447 U.S. 303). Then, in 1985, the U.S. Patent and Trademark office ruled that a corn plant containing an increased level of a particular amino acid could also receive a utility patent. In 1988, the first animal was patented—a mouse carrying a human cancer gene used in medical research. The extension of patents to human life took place over the same period. Human cells—cancerous cells taken from a leukemia patient—were first patented in 1984. In 1991, the U.S. National Institutes of Health filed patent applications for the structure of 337 human gene fragments identified with an automated sequencing machine and in 1992 applied for patents on a further 2,375 gene fragments (Roberts 1992). (The first of these applications was rejected by the U.S. Patent and Trademark Office in 1992.)

Countries differ widely in the patent protection they offer for living material. At one end of the spectrum, the United States grants patents on novel DNA sequences, genes, plant parts, plant or animal varieties, and biotechnological processes. In contrast, while they do grant patents for plant and animal genes, European countries have only recently extended patent protection to plant varieties. Recently, a patent was also granted for the Harvard mouse in the United Kingdom, though the court decision allowing the patent indicated that a criterion of clear human benefit must be used in determining the patentability of an animal. Many developing countries exempt biological processes and products entirely from their patent regimes.

Chemical compounds and processes have long been subject to patent protection in most industrialized countries, though drugs and other types of chemical products are sometimes excluded from patentability. For example, patent protection for pharmaceutical products was extended only in 1958 in France, 1968 in the Federal Republic of Germany, 1976 in Japan (when it ranked second in world drug production), and 1978 in Italy (Chudnovsky 1983). As recently as 1990, Finland, Norway, and Spain did not patent pharmaceutical processes and products (Lesser 1990).

The gradual expansion of IPR protection raises an important and fundamental question: How can anyone "own" genes or biochemicals that occur in nature? In most fields, patents are granted only for innovations, not for discoveries. Is it right for someone to possess an exclusive right to a naturally occurring gene or chemical?

No uniform standards exist for the treatment of discoveries by intellectual property regimes in different countries, particularly for discoveries relating to natural products like genes and chemicals. In many industrialized countries, patents are allowed if the discovery requires notable input of human effort and ingenuity (Lesser 1990). For instance, in the case of agriculture, a gene will usually be patentable only if it is used in a species in which it did not evolve or which it could not have been transferred to through conventional breeding (Barton 1991). Similarly, a long-standing U.S. legal doctrine holds that the purified form of a chemical can be patented if the chemical is found in nature only in an unpurified form (Barton 1991). Thus, in the United States, Europe, and Japan, pharmaceutical companies can patent chemicals derived from natural sources and genes that have been transferred to unrelated organisms.[9] In contrast, a number of developing countries exclude drugs and/or biological materials from patent protection.

INTERNATIONAL AGREEMENTS

Even as the scope of property rights for improved genetic resources expanded over the past century, unimproved genetic resources retained their "common heritage" status until well into the 1980s. Beginning in the mid-1970s, however, questions surfaced in international forums over the nature of the institutions governing access to these resources.

In agriculture, a significant fraction of so-called unimproved genetic resources was actually the product of the hard work and ingenuity of farmers as they selected and bred crop varieties fit to local conditions and tastes (Mooney 1983; Fowler and Mooney 1990). Similarly, many pharmaceutical products developed from natural products were first "discovered" by traditional healers. Why, more people began to wonder, did not these intellectual contributions receive the same

IPR protection as the contributions of plant breeders and pharmaceutical companies? Or, alternatively, if these contributions were freely available to all, should not the same apply to the products developed by pharmaceutical firms and seed companies?

A second concern revolves around ownership of the genes, seeds, and chemicals themselves. Developing countries began to question why individuals and companies based in the gene-poor developed countries were obtaining resources free of charge from the gene-rich developing countries, then patenting the genes and chemicals and selling the patented products back to the country where they originated. Since these were the raw materials used in agricultural breeding and pharmaceutical development, why should not companies pay for them just as they would pay for, say, coal or oil?

In the agricultural arena, these debates quickly escalated in the early 1980s into a bitter "seed war" between the North and the South. Since then, the resolution of this dispute through international mechanisms has moved at a glacial pace. In 1983, a Commission on Plant Genetic Resources was established through the Food and Agriculture Organization (FAO) of the United Nations and the "International Undertaking on Plant Genetic Resources" was signed by most developing countries and some industrialized countries. This undertaking initially held that all genetic resources (including the elite lines of private plant breeders) should be considered common heritage and thus freely accessible. Needless to say, few developed countries with established seed industries supported the undertaking.

In 1987 the Commission on Plant Genetic Resources accepted the legitimacy of IPR protection for breeders in exchange for recognition of the concept of "farmers' rights." These were defined to be communal rights, vested in the international community through the International Undertaking on Plant Genetic Resources, recognizing the contributions of local communities and farmers in creating and maintaining genetic resources. In this same year, the commission established a "Fund for Plant Genetic Resources" to fulfill the obligations inherent in the concept of farmers' rights by compensating developing countries for the use of their genetic resources, though donor countries have never provided more than token sums for this fund.

The debate over ownership and access to genetic resources shifted venue in the late 1980s to the negotiations for a Convention on Biological Diversity. Here, countries quickly agreed to recognize that biodiversity was a sovereign national resource and a "common concern" of humankind—not a common heritage. But up until the very end of the negotiations, developed and developing countries could not agree on mechanisms for protecting intellectual property and for allocating the benefits of the use of biodiversity. The final convention, signed by more than 150 nations at the Earth Summit in June 1992, recognizes nations' obligations to ensure that both the countries supplying biodiversity and those using it receive economic benefits and even notes that countries should encourage the "equitable sharing of the benefits arising from the utilization of [the knowledge, innovations, and practices of indigenous and local communities]."

Biodiversity-Prospecting Intermediaries

The final element of the evolution of biodiversity-prospecting institutions has been the recent emergence of new intermediary arrangements to facilitate access to genetic and biochemical resources and their transfer to the pharmaceutical, agriculture, or biotechnology industry. A wide range of such institutions already exists, and many more are being planned.

One outstanding example is Costa Rica's INBio. This private, nonprofit organization was established to facilitate the conservation and sustainable use of biodiversity. It uses its income and donations to support a wide array of conservation actions—from carrying out the national biodiversity inventory in collaboration with the Ministry of Natural Resources, Energy, and Mines (MIRENEM) to conducting and facilitating biodiversity-prospecting activities to support its conservation mission. Many other private, nonprofit intermediaries are based in developed countries. For example, The New York Botanical Garden, the Missouri Botanical Garden, and the University of Chicago have all contracted with private pharmaceutical companies and with public research organizations to provide samples of biodiversity for pharmaceutical development. Increasingly, these intermediaries also enter into contractual relationships with the countries—or appropriate institutions within the country—where they pursue their collecting activities.

Private for-profit intermediaries also exist in both developed and developing countries. Biotics, Ltd., a private firm based in the United Kingdom, works as a broker, providing pharmaceutical companies with plant genetic resources. Biotics buys samples and, through a contract, agrees to share any royalties with the source country institution. Similar contracts are drawn up between Biotics and the pharmaceutical firms, which would ultimately hold the patent on any discovery. Numerous collectors in developing countries also make a business of supplying plant and animal samples to industry. While most large pharmaceutical companies rely on other organizations to collect natural products, smaller firms—such as Shaman Pharmaceuticals—may both collect biodiversity samples and develop drugs.

Public organizations have also begun to serve as intermediaries. Mexico's National Biodiversity Commission—established in February 1992—may seek to play much the same role for Mexico that INBio does for Costa Rica. Similarly, Indonesia—and the Asian Development Bank—have considered establishing a Biodiversity Marketing and Commercialization Board. Elsewhere, the U.S.–Japan Environmental Partnership will be providing $20 million annually from 1994 to 1997 to establish several Natural Resource Conservation and Management Centers in Asia, some of which may undertake biodiversity prospecting. And three U.S. government agencies established a program in 1992 to fund "International Cooperative Biodiversity Groups" designed to "promote conservation of biological diversity through the discovery of bioactive agents from natural products, and to ensure that equitable economic benefits from these discoveries accrue to the country of origin" (NIH et al. 1992:3).

Finally, some collaborative efforts between the public and private sector have been established. For example, twenty-four Japanese corporations—including Suntory, Nippon Steel, and the Kyowa Hakko Pharmaceutical Company—and the Ministry of International Trade and Industry have established the Marine Biotechnology Institute in Japan. Researchers at this institute, with some eighty employees, two research laboratories, and a research vessel, are looking for new antibiofouling agents, oil-eating bacteria, phytoplankton that fix atmospheric carbon dioxide, and new pharmaceutical compounds in marine and coastal waters near Japan and Micronesia. No arrangements have been made to share royalties with Micronesia or to pay an exploration fee (Sochaczewski 1992).

Biodiversity-prospecting intermediaries have been established for various purposes. Some are strictly money-making ventures. Others carry out basic research or spur conservation or economic development. But nearly all the commercial collection programs of these institutions are young and thus by nature experimental.

Biodiversity-Prospecting Guidelines

Although the mission of some organizations engaged in biodiversity prospecting is primarily one of conservation, most have evolved primarily in response to growing commercial demand for the resource, rent seeking by commercial ventures, and public policies designed to foster innovation through the extension of IPR. None of these factors provides a sufficient incentive for resource conservation, the survey and description of biodiversity, local economic development, or the distribution of the benefits from biodiversity to those who pay the direct or opportunity costs for developing and maintaining it.

Biodiversity prospecting has attracted the interest of environmentalists and developing countries because it may provide significant incentives and funds for conservation and could contribute to economic development in regions rich in genetic and biochemical resources. But this dual potential will not be realized unless new policies are established to steer the evolution of the institutions toward these ends.

The remainder of this paper summarizes general principles that can guide the development of such policies. These guidelines, derived from more detailed chapters in Reid et al. (1993) and based largely on the experiences of INBio in Costa Rica, should help governments, nongovernmental organizations (NGOs), and industry develop appropriate property rights regimes, intermediary institutions, collecting agreements, contracts, collecting regulations, and technology policies. In the absence of detailed empirical and theoretical studies, these conclusions are tentative and must be modified to fit specific circumstances. But taken as a whole, they approximate the "state-of-the-art" of biodiversity-prospecting policies today.

ROLE OF INTERMEDIARIES

Whether through one or more organizations, countries should establish the capability to identify and locate biodiversity, to save representative samples of wild biodiversity in protected wildlands, and to use it nondestructively for the public good.

Few generalizations about the diverse intermediary organizations involved in biodiversity prospecting hold. Intermediaries can support—or undermine—the conservation and sustainable use of biodiversity, whether they are public or private and whether they are located in the source country or in a foreign land.

Nevertheless, more than any other component of biodiversity-prospecting programs, well-designed intermediaries have the potential to promote conservation, development, and equity. As a pioneering institution, INBio's activity as a biodiversity-prospecting intermediary has received particular attention as a "model." The founders of INBio reject the assertion that INBio is a model but accept that it is an instructive "pilot project" (Gámez et al. 1993).

Perhaps the most important insight from INBio's experience is that biodiversity-prospecting activities are only a means to an end. INBio was established to help identify and inventory Costa Rica's biodiversity and to integrate its nondestructive use into the intellectual and economic fabric of the society. Biodiversity prospecting helps fund conservation, but, more important, it demonstrates the economic value of biodiversity and thus helps convince policymakers that biodiversity conservation should figure centrally into all development planning.

Whatever intermediary organizations are established, the array of institutions involved in biodiversity activities should fill three basic needs: saving representative samples of wild biodiversity in protected wildlands, knowing what this biodiversity is and where it is to be found in those wildlands, and using biodiversity nondestructively for societal aims. If biodiversity is to survive, the society in whose custody it resides must perceive it as an asset. That will happen only through understanding what biodiversity is and seeking ways to use it to satisfy local and national social and economic needs.

Any effort to save, know, and use biodiversity requires the joint efforts of widely different sectors of society—including universities, museums, conservation ministries, commercial firms, and rural communities. But INBio's experience demonstrates that one organization can catalyze the integration of these sectors. INBio's inventory of Costa Rica's species provides employment for rural people as technicians—"parataxonomists"—in this venture. The institute is generating abundant information that is needed to wisely manage the country's biodiversity for a wide variety of users, developing the capacity to undertake chemical screening and pharmaceutical development, and working with Merck & Co., Inc., and other corporations to develop—and share the benefits from—new products based on that biodiversity. In essence, INBio closes the loop between studying, saving, and using biodiversity.

In other countries, biodiversity management institutions may or may not be involved in biodiversity prospecting. They may build on existing public-sector institutions like universities, environment ministries, and national museums, or they may take the form of new public or private institutions. Multinational management and prospecting organizations may make sense in some regions, while provincial or state-level organizations may be needed in others.

Clearly, institutions designed to gather information on biodiversity management and to develop new products of value to the biotechnology or pharmaceutical industry address only one portion of biodiversity conservation needs. For example, such institutions can create some employment in rural communities and may develop new products that local entrepreneurs can market, but it is unlikely that they could make rural development their mission. Yet, actions to reduce poverty in rural areas and to provide alternatives to habitat conversion that meet the needs of rural communities rank at the top of biodiversity conservation priorities (WRI et al. 1992). By contributing to economic and technological development and by contributing user fees or taxes directly to the public sector, biodiversity-prospecting initiatives can provide a share of the resources needed to meet this broader array of conservation and development needs, but the responsibility rests with national and local governments to ensure that these resources are used appropriately. When governments are unable to meet these responsibilities, the potential for success of biodiversity prospecting will be diminished.

One serious concern is that the revenues governments earn from biodiversity prospecting and the economic gains stimulated by commercialization of new products based on biodiversity may sometimes enrich the few rather than contribute to rural development. Certainly, biodiversity-prospecting institutions often return some benefits directly to the individuals, landowners, and communities involved in biodiversity-collecting activities. But, more typically, as when biodiversity is collected from public lands or without the benefit of local information, there is no alternative to effective public-sector mechanisms for returning benefits to local communities. For those countries that have shown a commitment to biodiversity conservation and the development needs of rural communities, biodiversity-prospecting intermediaries can be a valuable element of biodiversity conservation policies. Without such a national commitment, biodiversity prospecting may be nothing more than the newest unsustainable resource commercialization venture.

COMPANY-COLLECTOR CONTRACTS

Contracts between companies and collectors can help ensure that the exchange of biological materials generates both immediate and long-term benefits for the source countries and communities.

Contracts are an important means of distributing the costs, benefits, and risks between the collecting organization and the companies interested in developing products from genetic and biochemical resources. Through them, the portion of benefits that will return to the country that possesses the biodiversity can be determined. Contracts can be established even if countries lack intellectual property regimes or legislation governing the activities of collectors. They are an extremely flexible form of agreement that could, in theory, be used to ensure that the source country receives financial returns from biodiversity prospecting and that these funds are used to promote resource conservation.

However, contracts alone will not make a country's conservation and development objectives materialize (Laird 1993). Such agreements can be expensive and difficult to draft, negotiate, and enforce, and any company negotiating such a contract is motivated by the desire to acquire useful samples for screening,[10] not to conserve resources. As a result, any provisions for conservation, the return of benefits to local communities, technology transfer, and so forth are likely to be limited (even if they are the collecting organization's primary goals).

Company-collector contracts typically involve a fee for samples and, occasionally, advance payments to the collector. In such cases, the collector must determine how to disperse these in the country of collection. As countries begin regulating access to genetic resources, the collectors' obligations to in-country collaborators and to collecting regions are likely to become more stringently defined. Laird (1993) notes that while most collectors take responsibility for determining equitable relationships with their in-country collaborators, collecting regulations must be developed that will hold up regardless of whether personal relationships do.

One of the most striking aspects of the Merck-INBio contract was the size of the advance payment to INBio for services. Customarily, pharmaceutical plant collectors receive payments of $50 to $200 per sample. In sharp contrast, the $1.1 million paid by Merck in exchange for samples is nearly ten times the traditional service payment. Merck and Co. were asked to pay virtually all the real costs of a sample, rather than be subsidized by the social and institutional backup that a pharmaceutical collector normally receives but does not charge to the company. From Merck and Co.'s standpoint, this sum is warranted by the greatly increased quality of the samples that it receives from INBio during the initial two-year agreement and in future years if the agreement is renewed. How often payments of this magnitude will be made depends on how often sourcing institutions can offer samples of such quality, whether all collectors choose to charge all the real costs to the purchaser, and whether competition among collectors drives prices to below-cost levels. As in many other markets, product quality is likely to be strongly proportional to the price paid for the sample and its associated services.

Many provisions could be included in company-collector contracts to further conservation, development, and equity. For example, contracts could specify that future supplies of raw material would be obtained from the country of origin, that royalties would be distributed to individuals (such as traditional healers) that provided information on the resource, or that a specified fraction of royalties would be dedicated to conservation. While such stipulations may currently be uncommon, the rules of biodiversity prospecting are changing rapidly. For example, all INBio commercial contracts state explicitly what portion of the research and royalty budget goes directly to the National Park Fund at the Ministry of Natural Resources, Energy, and Mines and what portion is used for other kinds of wildland conservation activities. Similarly, all INBio samples must come from inside the conserved wildlands so that there is no contest over where the funds should be spent.

Property Rights

There is no more fundamental and divisive issue related to biodiversity prospecting than the question of who owns biodiversity. Developing countries have long been frustrated with a system that labels their resources as "open access" but then establishes private property rights for improved products based on those resources. Is it possible to modify IPR regimes to internalize the cost of biodiversity loss and management and ensure that the source countries and the custodians of biodiversity within them receive more of the economic returns from its development?

> *It is uncertain whether Intellectual Property Rights can be extended to wild genetic and biochemical resources and whether such rights would hurt or help the objectives of conservation and development.*

On the surface, the idea of extending IPR protection to wild species would seem to resolve the apparent imbalance between the rights of ownership for improved and unimproved genetic resources, thereby providing an incentive for resource conservation. Just as the individual who purifies a naturally occurring chemical is able to patent it, the individual (or nation) first spending the time and money needed to identify a new species and bearing the cost of maintaining that species could be granted exclusive rights to its use or sale (Sedjo 1988; Sedjo 1992). By assigning such rights, some would argue, the opportunity cost of the loss of the resource could be internalized and market forces and legislation might then lead to an "optimal" investment in conservation, at least with respect to biodiversity's genetic and biochemical value.

However, the extension of IPR to wild species is unworkable at present (Gollin 1993). From a pragmatic standpoint, patent offices would be deluged with speculative claims on species whose utility was unknown. But, more important, such a step would place more of the "public domain" in private hands than would be justified to maximize social benefits, Gollin concludes.

More generally, the various types of IPR that exist today are of limited use in promoting the conservation of wild species (but also do not necessarily hasten the loss of biodiversity). On the other hand, IPR can help stimulate domestic innovation and technology acquisition, thus providing an incentive for the sustainable development of the resource within the source country and generating economic benefits that may then be used to support conservation or to compensate the custodians of biodiversity.

The most promising immediate opportunities for capturing greater benefits from biodiversity involve access regulations, contracts, and value-added industries.

If extending IPR to unimproved genetic resources fails to capture benefits from the use of the resources, what other mechanisms are possible? Three mechanisms are described in this chapter: contracts, access regulations (see below), and the promotion of value-added industries. Efforts to add value to biochemical and genetic resources may be particularly rewarding since they contribute directly to the development of the source country's technological capacity. Strengthened capacity, in turn, allows source-country institutions to enter into more profitable partnerships with technology-intensive industries.

The economic returns generated from biodiversity can be enhanced either by providing a service related to the unimproved resource or by improving the resource itself. For example, in its agreement with Merck, INBio is basically selling biodiversity-prospecting services, not any IPR that it holds. Among the services it offers are sample identification, ready access to further samples from the same species and of the same quality, and known and user-sensitive sample-processing methods. The Merck-INBio agreement is not exclusive. Merck is free to buy samples from others in Costa Rica, INBio can provide samples to other organizations, and other organizations can collect the same samples and sell them to Merck or any other user. Although INBio's agreements include stipulations that for six months to two years it will not send the same sample to a competing company, in no sense does INBio control access to—or "own"—the resource.

Institutions can also increase economic returns by developing information about the resource. A biodiversity-prospecting institution could undertake preliminary chemical screening of samples to identify those with promising biological activity, thereby raising their potential market value. Such work could be undertaken with no intent to seek a patent; indeed it could be undertaken in a country with no patent protection for biological materials. The increased commercial value would stem from the new information on the materials' potential use. In the pharmaceutical industry, for example, it is common to receive royalties of 1–6% of net sales for unscreened chemical samples, 5–10% for material backed by preclinical information on its medical activity, and 10–15% for fractionated and identified material with efficacy data.

Indigenous people, farmers, and traditional healers can and sometimes should seek IPR protection. As a supplement to these property rights, formal and informal contracts will often be a more promising avenue for ensuring just compensation for their knowledge. National collecting regulations can help ensure that equitable contracts are negotiated.

Today, traditional knowledge is rarely involved in the development of new pharmaceutical products from biodiversity. Natural products chemistry today is based primarily on research by scientists, physicians, and pharmacologists. The screening programs used by large pharmaceutical companies are more likely to make use of phylogenetic information—screening organisms related to those that have proven their pharmaceutical worth—than indigenous knowledge, and new genes for agricultural breeding are increasingly found among wild species where farmers have played little role. But in some cases, the discovery of new medicines or promising genes is due in part to the knowledge of traditional healers or the work of generations of farmers. In such cases, how can these people be equitably compensated?

Knowledge of the therapeutic properties of wild species is often held in confidence by traditional societies, both because considerable training is needed before the materials can be used safely and effectively and because widespread knowledge of the cures would undermine the healers' vocation. Historically, ethnopharmacologists have not seen the need to protect these secrets (though often researchers have attempted to negotiate compensation for the information provided). For example, the author of *Medicinal Plants of East Africa* (which gives complete descriptions of the taxonomy, distribution, and uses of the medicinal plants) writes in the foreword:

> Many of the herbal medicine men will not like this book since it may deprive them of their profession once their secrets are revealed. The majority of them were reluctant to show me the drug plants as a whole for this reason. In most cases, I was given the leaves or root of the plant already crushed or picked. But after some persuasion, I was shown the plant on the condition that I would not reveal it to anyone else. (Kokwaro 1976)

Though such practices were once commonplace, today this would be considered a misappropriation of trade secrets that could and should be prevented by legal means, including lawsuits.[11]

Issues of equity in the distribution of benefits from the use of traditional medicines and traditional crop varieties have underlain international debates over biodiversity for more than a decade (Mooney 1983; Elisabetsky 1991). And today, the issue of what represents "just compensation" for the holders of traditional knowledge is far from resolved. Some of the questions that arise include: How can the efforts of generations of farmers be equitably compensated through their descendants for developments in agriculture? Should a traditional healer be compensated for indigenous knowledge, or should the debt be paid to the community or to the state? Is a one-time payment to the deserving party or group enough, or do the bearers of traditional knowledge have a basic right to the fruits of their inspiration that goes beyond the labor effort involved?

The subjectivity of any definition of equitable compensation ensures that no mechanism for allocating benefits will appear "just" to all. And North-South questions of equity will be particularly troublesome. In a cohesive and well-integrated society where it can be shown that privatizing specific types of knowledge leads to greater public good, this "implicit" compensation ensures reasonable equity in the distribution of benefits (Brush 1991). For example, when the United States grants a patent to a U.S. drug company that develops an anticancer compound made from a local plant, "implicit" social benefits accrue nationally in the form of a lessened incidence of cancer. But it is hardly surprising that equity issues come up when the actors are traditional healers living outside market economies in Brazil on the one hand and genetic engineers in the United States on the other. What benefits return to a remote region of the Amazon from a new drug designed to fight diseases common only in the developed world and too expensive for purchase by local people in any event?

One mechanism for meeting global obligations to the generations of farmers and healers who have developed and protected the genetic and biochemical resources now used in industry is through an international financial mechanism such as the Fund for Plant Genetic Resources or the Convention on Biological Diversity (Fowler and Mooney 1990). But can other mechanisms complement such international agreements? Specifically, can IPR be used to protect the knowledge of indigenous people, traditional healers, and farmers?

The answer is "sometimes." Most current IPR regimes would, in principle, allow the extension of IPR to cover the innovations and knowledge of traditional healers and farmers. Traditional healers could be granted patents for novel uses of a compound under most systems of patent protection. As a corollary, if a traditional medicinal use of a compound is public knowledge, then patent laws should be applied to prevent others from patenting that compound for the same purpose. Similarly, there is no compelling reason why a farmer who breeds a new variety of plant could not receive protection under most systems of IPR.

Any number of practical problems crop up, however, when IPR are extended to these "informal" innovations and promoting their use in this context is somewhat disingenuous. The scope of protection of IPR is generally as much a function of the political and economic power of those seeking protection as it is of wise or just economic policy. Moreover, the utility of IPR regimes is always a function of the enforceability of the rights. Society can establish the legal framework governing such disputes, but, ultimately, the rights holder must be able to identify infringements and challenge the infringing party. Clearly, a traditional healer in Brazil or a farmer in Ethiopia can rarely do either. Farmers and traditional healers cannot effectively claim ownership to a resource if they cannot control access to it, and they are in no financial position to challenge IPR claims made by others.

Finally, the costs of enforcing the right may often outweigh any benefits. A farmer might well be able to file for Plant Variety Protection on a new plant variety, but why bother if the new variety is locally adapted to just one small region of the country? The market for the variety simply will not be big enough to repay the effort.

Thus, while farmers and traditional healers are in a position to seek formal intellectual property protection (in countries that provide it), seeking compensation for their knowledge and inventions more directly through contracts and informal agreements usually makes more sense. For example, by refusing access to knowledge or traditional seed varieties, individuals can at least establish a framework for negotiating an equitable settlement (WRI et al. 1992). These two avenues for compensation are not mutually exclusive, and indeed, recognition of the legal right may encourage formal negotiations for compensation.

National legislation regulating biodiversity-collecting activities provides another, more formal, mechanism for ensuring that the rights of local communities and source countries are respected. Collecting permits could, for example, require collectors to get prior informed consent from local communities before collecting begins and, in some cases, to negotiate the terms by which they would be given access to land or to local knowledge.

Legal Guarantees

Each of the policy tools discussed above—organizational design, company-collector contracts, and IPR—can help achieve the objectives of conservation, development, and equity. However, without effective national regulation, the attainment of these objectives may be the exception rather than the rule. Private intermediaries are more likely to be established with profit, rather than conservation, in mind. The parties to contracts will rarely agree on both the need for conservation and technology transfer. And it will be easy for commercial collectors and companies to slight the contributions of farmers and traditional healers to new medicines and crop varieties.

The best means available to ensure that biodiversity prospecting does meet these broader social objectives is national policy, specifically biodiversity-collecting regulations (Janzen et al. 1993). Such regulations should be part of legislation established by countries to implement the Convention on Biological Diversity. Costa Rica, for example, adopted a Wild Life Protection law on October 12, 1992, which declares all wild plants and animals to be "national patrimony" and requires collectors to submit an application for a license that details their collection plans, deposit voucher samples with the national collection, and send copies of publications resulting from the work to the national library. Collection for non-scientific purposes requires a special license and must involve the use of public bids, concessions, or contracts.

The agreement reached between a biodiversity collector and society is, in essence, a research contract. Where past collecting activity has been regulated informally, if at all, the state should now ensure that in return for access to genetic and biochemical resources the collector assumes certain obligations with regard to conduct, liability, and payments. The most critical elements of such regulation are: (1) user fees for access to genetic or biochemical resources on public or private land and (2) requirements that collectors negotiate equitable arrangements with the local communities, the wildland administrators, the private landowners, the farmers, and healers who were the custodians of the biodiversity collected or who contributed to the discovery or development of valuable genetic or biochemical resources.

To increase the benefits they receive from biodiversity, countries and local communities should regulate access to the resource and charge "user fees" where appropriate.

Critics have charged that private biodiversity-prospecting intermediaries inappropriately exploit the public domain for private benefit (Kloppenburg and Rodriguez 1992). This criticism is often valid: private commercial collectors do often obtain genetic resources freely from the public domain and sell them for private gain. Public policies should thus seek to ensure that private collectors pay local or national governments for access to biodiversity.

Nobody would expect a nation to allow a private timber company to use public timber resources free of charge or to mine on public land without reimbursing the state. A similar system of user fees—or biodiversity-prospecting concessions— should be established for access to public lands for biodiversity-prospecting ventures (Sedjo 1990; Simpson 1992). Ideally, such fees would be used to maintain the biodiversity, thereby internalizing part of the costs of conservation. INBio, by investing 10% of Merck's initial payment of $1 million in traditional conservation activities and agreeing to spend half of all royalties on conservation through MIRENEM, the remainder on conservation through its own activities, and by conducting all its activities as development of the conservation areas, basically paid such a user fee, even though no national legislation required it at the time.

The time has come for *all* research on biodiversity—whether commercial or scientific—to be strictly regulated by public institutions (or their designated representatives) (Janzen et al. 1993). This does not mean that all researchers must pay user fees. For example, scientists carrying out basic research on biodiversity— such as inventory and taxonomic work—return "in-kind" benefits to a nation instead of direct payments. Similarly, governments might set lower fees for local (as opposed to foreign) collectors, thus giving them an incentive to develop local industries based on these resources.[12]

The nature of compensation for access to biodiversity must be based on what the researcher has to provide, which is not necessarily money. Nonetheless, some user fees may be appropriate even for those engaged in "basic" rather than commercial research. Scientists readily accept the notion that they must contribute to the overhead of their home institutions; they should not object to the idea that they should also contribute to the "overhead" of their research sites. (Nor should their granting agencies discourage such expenses.)

An alternative to systems of user fees would be for the state to control all aspects of the commercialization of the resource. Genetic and biochemical resources do have unique attributes that set them apart from other elements of a nation's patrimony—among them, its timber, minerals, and fisheries. For example, the sale of rights to a gene or chemical to a foreign company exhausts the local rights and control over the resource. Whereas local communities or future generations may have an opportunity to challenge forest or mineral leases, for genetic resources the deal is final. And the real value of the resource lies in the information contained in the genes or chemicals, not in its physical properties. Though an intermediary may be selling only a service related to the resource, its actions may make it easier for individuals with technological expertise not available in the source country to establish private property rights for that information.

But whether stronger control by national governments would better serve national interests is far from clear. Such a system could run into tremendous practical problems. For example, INBio is paid for the service and information it provides, not for licenses to intellectual property rights. A system that retains national control over all such information and services—as well as the right to the resource itself—would be unwieldy at best and fraught with inefficiency and corruption at worst. In many countries, the balance between local and national control over resources has shifted too far toward the latter, undermining prospects for sustainable use and equitable distribution of the benefits from resource use. With too much national control, for example, indigenous groups would lose their right to contract with a pharmaceutical company for the use of their knowledge. In an ideal world, the national government might assume that right and make sure that the local community is compensated equitably, but in most countries the retention of local control is more likely to achieve the social objectives.

In any event, where private biodiversity prospecting is allowed, governments should protect the public interest by regulating access to the resource, charging appropriate fees for that access, and using the revenue so generated to support conservation and rural communities near protected wildlands.

Biodiversity prospecting on private lands should be subject to regulation and "user fees."

The need for user fees is relatively clear on public lands but somewhat problematic when applied to biodiversity collected on private lands. Almost all countries, for example, consider plants growing on private land to belong to the landowner, though animals are the property of the state. Individuals can cut a tree on land they own without the state's permission but—because wild animals move across property lines—must follow state regulations governing the harvest of wildlife.

The issue of ownership and access to genetic and biochemical resources is closer to that of the right to harvest wild animals on private lands than to that of plant ownership. When an individual cuts and sells a tree, nothing prevents another individual from cutting another tree of the same species on adjacent land and selling it. But only the first individual who sells a chemical extract that is later developed into a drug will receive the economic benefit associated with the discovery and associated property right.

Thus, following the same policy that governs the harvest of wild animals, nations should not allow all rights to these resources to be "bundled" with private property rights in land. While local landowners may regulate access to the resource and charge collecting fees, local and national governments should also regulate the exploitation of these resources and charge user fees where appropriate.

TECHNOLOGY POLICY

Developing Countries should establish technology policies that better enable them to benefit directly from their genetic and biochemical resources.

Their long-term contribution to economic development, conservation, and the equitable sharing of benefits from genetic resources may be greatest if biodiversity-prospecting policies foster the development of national capacity in biotechnology. Efforts that do not will fall victim to the historical mistakes of other export industries based on raw materials in developing countries.

A narrow focus on the sharing of returns on the sale of products derived from biological material is misguided (Juma 1993). This approach can give developing countries financial incentives to conserve biological diversity, but even longer-term benefits will stem from technological cooperation and capacity building in science and technology. For this reason, biodiversity prospecting should be considered part of the larger issue of national biotechnology policy and should be treated as a capacity-building activity.

IPR do not pose as great an obstacle to access to new technologies as is often feared (Juma 1993). Most of the technologies needed by developing countries to build capacity in these fields are already in the public domain. The obstacle is not proprietary rights, despite the attention they receive in international debates.

IPR should be viewed as a tool for enlarging technological capacity in developing countries. IPR regimes established without due consideration to the need for effective legal, political, and economic systems conducive to private business activity and the protection of private property rarely serve their stated ends (Evenson 1990). IPR protection—tailored to a nation's development needs—can foster advances in technological innovation, but that protection must be coupled with other institutional changes to increase knowledge of public domain technologies, upgrade technical training, and provide access to the credit needed to develop new technologies and markets.

Even small countries with limited industrial capacity can move to the frontiers of biotechnology in specific fields by enhancing their human resource capacity. By investing in training, establishing systems that provide ready access to information about both biodiversity and new technologies, and seeking ways to add value to genetic resources through screening and characterization, developing countries can turn short-term economic benefits into a long-term development strategy.

International Agreements

The Convention on Biological Diversity and other multilateral agreements are important foundations for sustainable and equitable biodiversity prospecting programs.

A central theme of this paper is that a variety of national and subnational actions and policies can help biodiversity prospecting contribute to sustainable development. Rather than rely strictly on multilateral agreements, therefore, countries, institutions, and individuals can use contracts, institutional design, national legislation, and common sense to steer the evolution of biodiversity-prospecting institutions. Some have even argued that national policies and bilateral agreements like that between Merck and INBio are sufficient and that no multilateral action is necessary. In 1992, the United States used this argument as one justification for its refusal to sign the Convention on Biological Diversity.

In fact, multilateral agreements are necessary for several reasons. First, by themselves, bilateral biodiversity-prospecting agreements are likely to result in conservation and development benefits for only a limited number of countries. Countries that are quick to enter the market as suppliers of biodiversity and that have the necessary technical capacity to compete may reap substantial gains. But for most developing countries—and the bulk of the world's biodiversity—multilateral mechanisms are needed to provide financial and technical support for biodiversity conservation and technological development.

Second, the value of many of the economic benefits provided by biodiversity— clean water, healthy ecosystems, aesthetic pleasure—is not fully reflected in the market, so market-based strategies like biodiversity prospecting can only complement public-sector financial support for conservation. While some of these benefits are strictly local or national, others—like the maintenance of healthy forest and marine ecosystems—are global and justify multilateral action.

Third, multilateral agreements will help increase the benefits that source countries can derive from their genetic resources. As suppliers of biodiversity saturate the market, the price for genetic and biochemical resources will fall. The interests of source countries could be better served if uniform conditions were developed through multilateral agreements to govern access to biodiversity.

On the other hand, the ability of source countries to form effective genetic and biochemical resource cartels is probably limited. The demand for biochemical resources for the pharmaceutical industry, for example, is likely to be very elastic in response to price changes. Today's resurgence in natural products research is due in part to the decline in costs resulting from new screening technologies. If the price for access to natural products rises, pharmaceutical firms could respond with increased investment in synthetic chemistry and reduced investment in natural products research. In principle, the establishment of cartels is more likely in the case of genetic resources used in agriculture, but the relatively low value of the seed industry (compared with the pharmaceutical industry) could mean that the costs of creating a cartel, restricting the flow of crop genetic resources, and pursuing royalties and payments for these resources might easily exceed the economic benefits. Short of a cartel, though, countries could agree to establish minimum obligations for companies engaging in biodiversity prospecting.

Fourth, multilateral agreements can help level the playing field so that bilateral agreements can be negotiated fairly. Clearly, institutions in developing countries may have less negotiating experience than multinational corporations. Under a multilateral agreement, mechanisms could be established to provide information, legal advice, or the services of an ombudsman to help ensure equitable negotiations.

Many developing countries also lack the ability to effectively regulate access to genetic resources within the country. Without such capacity, laws requiring collecting permits or user fees could easily be circumvented by international collectors. By requiring prior informed consent of the source country for access to biodiversity, the Convention on Biological Diversity will help shift some responsibility for enforcement to the developed countries. Parties to the Convention, for example, could pass laws requiring that gene or biochemical patent applications within their country include evidence that the material in question was collected with the prior informed consent of the source country.

Finally, an international agreement such as the Convention on Biological Diversity sets the stage for a "Grand Bargain" whereby developing countries would seek strengthened IPR so as to profit from their biological resources while the developed world would concede the possibility that each nation may tailor its intellectual property laws to meet its own conservation, development, and equity needs. Rather than weaken intellectual property laws—a fear that the United States cited when it refused to sign the convention—this new bargain is likely to strengthen them.

NOTES

1. That is, the private returns of conserving the resource are less than the social returns.

2. These five include taxol, the most promising drug of the decade for treating breast, ovarian, and lung cancer. Since the success rate for cancer screening is based on technologies used in the 1960s, current technologies are likely to yield higher rates of "hits."

3. This estimate is based on his 1979 calculation (Barton and Christensen 1988) of the U.S. markup of seed sales derived from proprietary protection, extrapolated to the 1990s and to the global market (totaling $1.5 to 2 billion). With a 5% royalty returning to the suppliers of the genetic material, this would amount to $75 million to $100 million.

4. If p is the probability of a single chemical yielding a useful lead, q is the probability that a lead will result in a commercial product, and n is the number of chemicals screened, then the probability of producing one commercial product (C) is $C = 1 - (1 - (p \times q))^n$. In this example, $p = .0001$, $q = .25$, $n = 1000$, and $C = .0247$. If $R =$ the present value of the royalties from a single commercial product, then the present value of the agreement is calculated as $C \times R$.

5. Even this figure may be conservative. At a January 1986 workshop involving representatives of American and Swiss pharmaceutical companies involved in plant-based drug development, a consensus was reached that the probability of any plant yielding a *marketable* pharmaceutical (not simply a "lead") ranged from 1 in 1,000 to 1 in 10,000 (Principe, personal communication 1993).

6. Clearly, a local crop variety bred by farmers is an "improved" variety even though it has not been commercialized. Similarly, the investment that a nation makes in conserving wild species or in inventorying and identifying its species arguably results in an "improvement" in that species analogous to that made by commercial breeders.

7. Plant Breeders' Rights grant an individual exclusive right to sell a specific variety but traditionally do not prevent farmers from saving and replanting the seed of the variety (farmer plantback) or breeders from using that variety in a breeding program (breeders' exemption). Many in the plant-breeding industry have argued that this level of protection provides an insufficient incentive for research investment and have advocated closing "loopholes" related to both farmer plantback and the breeder exemption. (In response, the March 1991 revision of UPOV allowed countries to restrict farmer plantback and alters the breeders' exemption so that "essentially derived" varieties—that is, new varieties based largely on the genetic makeup of a protected variety—must obtain a license from the owner of the protected variety.)

8. All UPOV members were West European until 1978. Since that time, other countries, including Australia, Czechoslovakia, Canada, Hungary, Israel, Poland, South Africa, and the United States, have joined, and some developing countries are considering joining.

9. Typically, drugs developed from natural products are altered from their natural forms during the drug development process and these derivatives are also patentable. The trail of patents filed during drug development can help in determining whether wholly or partially synthesized drugs originated from natural precursors.

10. A number of companies now recognize the need for conservation in their policies, but generally support for conservation is contributed through philanthropic foundations associated with the company. However, these foundations cannot legally donate money to institutions involved in a commercial arrangement with the parent company.

11. Several professional societies are developing ethical guidelines seeking to ensure that the rights of holders of traditional knowledge are respected and that just compensation is provided to local communities for access to such information.

12. This difference in treatment might raise red flags under international trade agreements. On the other hand, many countries already have two-tiered user fees for access to national parks, with foreign nationals paying higher fees than local residents.

REFERENCES

Aldhous, Peter. 1991. "'Hunting License' for Drugs." *Nature* 353:290.
Barton, John H. 1991. "Relating Scientific and the Commercial Worlds in Genetic Resource Negotiation." Paper presented at the Symposium on Property Rights, Biotechnology, and Genetic Resource, African Centre for Technology Studies and World Resources Institute, Nairobi, Kenya. June 10–14.

Barton, John H. and Eric Christensen. 1988. "Diversity Compensation Systems: Ways to Compensate Developing Nations for Providing Genetic Materials." In J. R. Kloppenburg, *Seeds and Sovereignty*, pp. 339–55. Durham: Duke University Press.

Brockway, Lucile H. 1988. "Plant Science and Colonial Expansion: The Botanical Chess Game." In J. R. Kloppenburg, ed., *Seeds and Sovereignty*, pp. 49–66. Durham: Duke University Press.

Brush, Stephen B. 1991. "Intellectual Property and Traditional Agriculture in the Third World." Paper presented at the Roundtable on Intellectual Property Rights and Indigenous Peoples. Society for Applied Anthropology. Charleston, South Carolina.

Chudnovsky, Daniel. 1983. "Patents and Trademarks in Pharmaceuticals." *World Development* 2 (3):187–93.

Collinson, M. P. and K. L. Wright. 1991. *Biotechnology and the International Agriculture Research Centers of the CGIAR.* 21st Conference of the International Association of Agricultural Economists. Tokyo, Japan, August 22–29, 1991.

DiMasi, Joseph A., Ronald W. Hansen, Henry G. Grabowski, and Louis Lasagna. 1991. "Cost of Innovation in the Pharmaceutical Industry." *Journal of Health Economics* 10:107–42.

Eisner, Thomas. 1989. "Prospecting for Nature's Chemical Riches." *Issues in Science and Technology* 6 (2):31–34.

Eisner, Thomas. 1992. "Chemical Prospecting: A Proposal for Action." In F. H. Bormann and S. R. Kellert, eds., *Ecology, Economics, and Ethics: The Broken Circle*, pp. 196–202. New Haven: Yale University Press.

Elisabetsky, E. 1991. "Sociopolitical, Economic, and Ethical Issues in Medicinal Plant Research." *Journal of Ethnopharmacology* 32:235–39.

Evenson, R. E. 1990. "Survey of Empirical Results." In W. E. Siebeck, ed., *Strengthening Protection of Intellectual Property in Developing Countries*, pp. 33–46. World Bank Discussion Paper 112. Washington, D.C.: World Bank.

Farnsworth, Norman R. 1988. "Screening Plants for New Medicines." In E. O. Wilson and Francis M. Peters, eds., *Biodiversity*, pp. 83–97. Washington, D.C.: National Academy Press.

Fowler, C. and P. Mooney. 1990. *Shattering: Food, Politics, and the Loss of Genetic Diversity.* Tucson: University of Arizona Press.

Gámez, Rodrigo, Alfio Piva, Ana Sittenfeld, Eugenia Leon, Jorge Jimenez, and Gerando Mirabelli. 1993. "Costa Rica's Conservation Program and National Biodiversity Institute (INBio)." In W. Reid et al., eds., *Biodiversity Prospecting: Using Genetic Resources for Sustainable Development.* Washington, D.C.: World Resources Institute.

Giddings, Luthar Val and Gabrielle Persley. 1990. "Biotechnology and Biodiversity." Unpublished manuscript prepared for the UNEP Negotiations on the Convention on Biological Diversity. U.S. Department of Agriculture, Hyattsville, Md., and International Service for National Agricultural Research, The Hague, Netherlands.

Gollin, Michael A. 1993. "An Intellectual Property Rights Framework for Biodiversity Prospecting." In W. Reid et al., eds., *Biodiversity Prospecting: Using Genetic Resources for Sustainable Development.* Washington, D.C.: World Resources Institute.

IBA [Industrial Biotechnology Association]. 1992. "U.S. Biotechnology Industry Fact Sheet." Washington, D.C.: IBA.

Janzen, Daniel H., Winnie Hallwachs, Rodrigo Gámez, Ana Sittenfeld, Jorge Jimenez. 1993. "Research Management Policies: Permits for Collecting and Research in the Tropics." In W. Reid et al., eds., *Biodiversity Prospecting: Using Genetic Resources for Sustainable Development.* Washington, D.C.: World Resources Institute.

Juma, Calestous. 1989. *The Gene Hunters: Biotechnology and the Scramble for Seeds.* Princeton: Princeton University Press.

Juma, Calestous. 1993. "Policy Options for Scientific and Technological Capacity-Building." In W. Reid et al., eds., *Biodiversity Prospecting: Using Genetic Resources for Sustainable Development.* Washington, D.C.: World Resources Institute.

King, Steven R. 1992. "Conservation and Tropical Medicinal Plant Research." Mimeo, Shaman Pharmaceuticals, Inc.

Kloppenburg, Jack and Silvia Rodriguez. 1992. "Conservationists or Corsairs?" *Seedling* 9 (2–3):12–17.

Kokwaro, J. O. 1976. *Medicinal Plants of East Africa.* Kampala, Nairobi, Dar es Salaam: East African Literature Bureau.

Laird, Sarah A. 1993. "Contracts for Biodiversity Prospecting." In W. Reid et al., eds., *Biodiversity Prospecting: Using Genetic Resources for Sustainable Development.* Washington, D.C.: World Resources Institute.

Lesser, William. 1990. "An Overview of Intellectual Property Systems." In W. E. Siebeck, ed., *Strengthening Protection of Intellectual Property in Developing Countries,* pp. 5–15. World Bank Discussion Paper 112. Washington, D.C.: World Bank.

Lisansky, S. G. and J. Coombs. 1989. *Funding Mechanisms for the Fund for Biological Diversity.* Newbury, U.K.: CPL Scientific Limited.

McChesney, James. 1992. "Biological Diversity, Chemical Diversity, and the Search for New Pharmaceuticals." Paper presented at the Symposium on Tropical Forest Medical Resources and the Conservation of Biodiversity, Rainforest Alliance, New York, January 1992.

Mooney, Pat Roy. 1983. "The Law of the Seed." *Development Dialogue* 1983 (1–2):1–172.

NIH [National Institutes of Health], National Institute of Mental Health, National Science Foundation, and U.S. Agency for International Development. 1992. International Cooperative Biodiversity Groups: Request for Applications. June 12, Washington, D.C.

Office of Technology Assessment (OTA). 1987. *Technologies to Maintain Biological Diversity.* Washington, D.C.: U.S. Congress, U.S. Government Printing Office.

Principe, Peter P. 1989. "The Economic Significance of Plants and Their Constituents as Drugs." In H. Wagner, H. Hikino, and N. R. Farnsworth, eds., *Economic and Medicinal Plant Research,* vol. 3, pp. 1–17. London: Academic Press.

Principe, Peter P. Unpublished manuscript. "Monetizing the Pharmacological Benefits of Plants."

Raines, Lisa J. 1991. "Protecting Biotechnology's Pioneers." *Issues in Science and Technology.* Winter 1991–92, pp. 33–39.

Reid, Walter V., Sarah A. Laird, Carrie A. Meyer, Rodrigo Gámez, Ana Sittenfeld, Daniel Janzen, Michael A. Gollin, and Calestous Juma, eds. 1993. *Biodiversity Prospecting: Using Genetic Resources for Sustainable Development.* Washington, D.C.: World Resources Institute.

Roberts, Leslie. 1992. "NIH Gene Patents, Round Two." *Science* 255:912–13.

Sears, Cathy. 1992. "Jungle Potions." *American Health* (October).

Sedjo, Roger A. 1988. "Property Rights and the Protection of Plant Genetic Resources." In J. R. Kloppenburg, ed., *Seeds and Sovereignty,* pp. 293–314. Durham: Duke University Press.

Sedjo, Roger A. 1990. "Property Rights, Genetic Resources, and the Protection of Biotechnological Development." Unpublished manuscript, Resources for the Future, Washington, D.C., January 3.

Sedjo, Roger A. 1992. "Property Rights, Genetic Resources, and Biotechnological Change." *Journal of Law and Economics* 35:199–213.

Simpson, R. David. 1992. ''Transactional Arrangements and the Commercialization of Tropical Biodiversity.'' Resources for the Future Discussion Paper, Washington, D.C.

Sochaczewski, Paul Spencer. 1992. ''Marine Biodiversity: Who Benefits, Who Pays?'' Unpublished manuscript. Gland, Switzerland: World Wide Fund for Nature.

U.S. Supreme Court. 1980. United States Supreme Court Cases 447 U.S. 303. Washington, D.C.: U.S. Government Printing Office.

World Bank. 1991. *Agricultural Biotechnology: The Next Green Revolution?* World Bank Technical Paper no. 133. Washington, D.C.

World Resources Institute (WRI) et al. 1992. *Global Biodiversity Strategy.* Washington, D.C.: WRI, IUCN, UNEP.

13

Property Rights and Genetic Resources: A Framework for Analysis

Jack R. Kloppenburg Jr. and Michael J. Balick

THAT the world is losing biological diversity at an unprecedented rate is no longer any more surprising than the persistence of warfare in the post–Cold War era. Having failed to learn charity toward each other, can anyone find it remarkable that we are unable to treat our fellow species with care or respect? This is not to say, however, that humankind is indifferent to the loss of genetic diversity. What it does mean is that the global rationale for the preservation of threatened toucans and bromeliads and sponges is moving toward utilitarian as well as ethical issues. Relating to each other principally through the instrumentality of the market, we now apply the principles of the General Agreement on Tariffs and Trade (GATT) and the North American Free Trade Agreement (NAFTA) to other species. Much of the overriding theme of the discourse regarding the loss of organisms now has to do with the loss of potential utility associated with disappearing organisms, not with integrity of the creatures themselves.

Increasing scarcity alone might have been expected to enhance the perceived value of biochemical and genetic materials. And this valorization through restriction of the supply of biochemical and genetic resources is occurring precisely at the moment when the vast bulk of those resources is becoming accessible to us. Before 1975, the genetic information embodied in the toucan was pretty much locked up in the toucan. As such, it was almost exclusively useful in its capacity to reproduce toucans. With biotechnology and genetic engineering, it becomes possible to move that information around and combine it with the DNA from other organisms. Suddenly, organisms such as the toucan are of interest for their potential as sources of industrial, agricultural, and medical substances. Hence the emergence of broad corporate and governmental concern with biodiversity and the simultaneous development of the "chemical prospecting" (Clifford 1993; Eisner 1989) in which the academic-industrial complex is now so busily engaged (see, e.g., National Institutes of Health 1993; Plotkin and Famolare 1992; Reid et al. 1993).

The World Resources Institute (WRI) may be right; biochemical and genetic resources may well be the "oil of the information age." And if those toucans and bromeliads are indeed the essential raw materials of the genetic engineers, then the distribution of rights in and access to those materials is a matter of great importance. As the value of genetic materials of all kinds—crop germplasm, wild medicinal plants, diseased human tissue—increases, there is struggle over the social arrangements in place to regulate access to and ownership of those materials (Kloppenburg 1988; Fowler and Mooney 1990).

Genetic and biochemical resources have long been collected from peasant farmers and indigenous peoples as the "common heritage of mankind," a public good for which no payment was appropriate or necessary (Wilkes 1983). Though the industrialized North has enjoyed uncountable benefits from access to such materials, there have not historically been mechanisms for systematically ensuring a reciprocal flow of benefit to those who have supplied genetic or cultural information in the first place. If we in the North are in a position to make ourselves better off by using resources supplied by others, is it not ethically appropriate to make sure that they are better off as well? And if ethics is not persuasive to the corporate and foundation practitioners of conservation realpolitik, may they not find good pragmatic reasons to ensure such a reciprocal flow of benefit? If preservation of biodiversity is an objective, what better way to accomplish this than to reward people for its production, reproduction, and maintenance? Moreover, whatever ethical or instrumental stance is favored by representatives of the North, farmers and indigenous communities are increasingly demanding that those who come to take are also obligated to give (Shiva 1990; Suhai 1992).

The resulting transition to a new problematic in the "seed wars" is best exemplified by the now well-known arrangement between Costa Rica's National Biodiversity Institute (INBio) and the pharmaceutical multinational Merck and Co., Inc. (Blum 1993; Kloppenburg and Rodriguez 1993). In this arrangement a nongovernmental organization (NGO) and a company are voluntarily adhering to the principle that access to genetic materials merits compensation. Further, that compensation is not merely rhetorical but also material. The INBio-Merck arrangement is the first instance of systematic, contractual conjoining of both the willingness to sell genetic materials and the willingness to pay for them.

Over the last few years, a wide variety of other arrangements for acquisition of biochemical and genetic materials from farmers and indigenous peoples have been developed. These range from detailed and highly legalistic models typical of Western patent law to frameworks that are more like a treaty than a contract. The parties to the agreements may be—on the suppliers' side—individual shamans, communities, peoples, or nations. The parties on the receiving end may be government agencies, companies, or individual scientists. Mediating the exchange are often NGOs and activist/advocacy groups. The situation is extremely complex. Whatever their form, all such agreements purport to manage the exchange of genetic resources on a legitimate, equitable, and compensatory basis.

The central issue is no longer whether or not compensation is appropriate but under what conditions compensation will be paid and—most importantly—which social groups or institutions will have the right to determine those conditions. We can expect continuing proliferation of models. If indeed the world is going to move to a truly new and more just regime for the exchange of biochemical and genetic materials, we will need to think critically about the models that arise. Our purpose in this article is to provide a conceptual framework to facilitate clear analysis of the diverse arrangements now being promulgated.

The Convergence of the Twain

We first met in debate over these issues at an annual meeting of the Society for Economic Botany. At the time, both of us had recognized the legitimacy of "compensation," but our attentions were focused on the problem at different levels. Kloppenburg had taken a global perspective, viewing the question principally in the context of North/South structural relations (e.g., Kloppenburg and Kleinman 1987). Balick, on the other hand, had been involved quite personally in the collection of genetic and cultural information and had focused on needs at the community and individual levels. Both of us initially had a difficult time accepting the relevance of the other's point of view. Nevertheless, in discussion, we both came to see that our positions were incomplete.

In particular, we have come to believe that the stickiest issues, and the most complicated analysis, will come not at the level of global regimes or individual rights, but at a wide variety of levels in between. We have chosen to refer to this terrain between the individual and the global as the "middle ground." Only rarely will questions of rights to access to genetic materials involve individuals as independent actors. The shaman is a member of a community; the collector is an employee of a company or a government agency. The interests of those collective groups or institutions are what will generally be at issue. At the other extreme, while much concern has been focused on intergovernmental and geopolitical maneuvering, the exchange of genetic materials will most typically occur at a lower level of organization.

Allocation of property rights in genetic resources will involve not only a variety of social levels (international, national, ethnic, community, individual) but also a wide variety of different social actors (academics, NGO representatives, officials, farmers, indigenous peoples) and different institutional actors (international organizations, NGOs, government offices, companies, popular organizations, indigenous organizations). While global and individual dimensions will remain important, we believe that most of the critical action will take place at levels that are less abstract than the global and more complex than the individual.

The fundamental question is "Whom does one compensate and how?" We cannot answer that question phrased at that level of generality, for an adequate answer will be a function of the diverse circumstances in which exchanges may occur. We do hope that our analysis will be of value in helping people to locate the social actors in an exchange. We also hope that this concrete evidence of interdisciplinary collaboration might be an encouragement to those who may be contemplating the possibility of such work. A sociologist and an ethnobotanist, respectively, we are from two quite different disciplines with very different training, and, indeed, we work from very different political positions. Yet we have learned from each other and have established a productive working relationship. We would like to think that our joint work represents a methodological example for the generation of solutions: interdisciplinary work and discussion between those with quite different views.

It ought to be clear that the foundation for our cooperation is our agreement on one essential point: compensation for the appropriation and use of "raw" genetic materials is appropriate in principle. Accepting the principle of compensation provides the necessary "equitability" or "symmetry" needed to develop a politically practicable new regime of germplasm exchange.

A Framework for Analysis

But given agreement that compensation is appropriate, who is to be compensated? And how? We are really talking about how to foster conditions for a just exchange: those who supply genetic or cultural information should receive some reciprocal flow of benefit from the recipients of genetic and cultural information. A useful first step toward grappling effectively with the problem is to identify the participants—the "social actors"—in the exchange. In figures 13.1, 13.2, and 13.3, we present graphic representations of a framework we have found heuristically useful in engaging the issues that arise in our own work.

In figure 13.1 we identify six classes of social actors who frequently participate in such exchanges. These actors are placed in a grid that should facilitate conceptualization or visualization of their participation in the process of exchange of biochemical and genetic information. Each social actor may be either a supplier (donor) or a recipient (demander) of germplasm. Our model encompasses all types of germplasm from wild species to landraces and commercial seed, to bulk samples of medicinal plants. We have established our classes of social actors based on the different objectives and interests that the social actors have. That is, companies (e.g., Monsanto, Merck, Shaman Pharmaceuticals, Pioneer Hi-Bred) have different interests than NGOs (e.g., New York Botanical Garden, Nature Conservancy, Conservation International), which in turn have different interests than government agencies (e.g., United States Department of Agriculture [USDA], National Cancer Institute [NCI], Brazil's National Center for Genetic Resources and Biotechnology—CENARGEN), which in turn have different interests than international

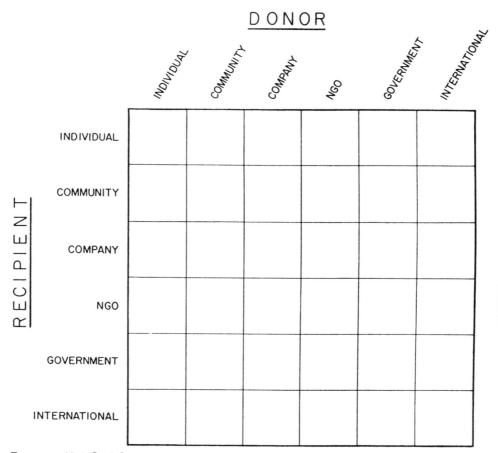

FIGURE 13.1 Social actors in genetic resource exchange regimes.

agencies (e.g., United Nations Environmental Program, Food and Agricultural Organization [FAO] of the United Nations [UN], international germplasm centers).

In figure 13.2, we use our framework to illustrate the types of germplasm exchange regimes that have operated until recently. For centuries, germplasm has been supplied by individuals and communities. Over the last hundred years there have emerged in the advanced industrial nations a range of companies, NGOs, and national and international government organizations with an interest in collecting such materials. Concentration of seeds and cuttings and whole plants in the gene and plant banks of the North has proceeded apace since the "Golden Age of Plant Hunting" in the late nineteenth century (Klose 1950; Brockway 1979). The bulk of such collection has been accomplished not by private companies, but by individual scientists working for such government agencies as the USDA's Plant Introduction Office and the Consultative Group on International Agricultural Research (CGIAR's) network of Green Revolution research centers. More recently, such agriculturally oriented work has been supplemented by herbaria, botanical gardens, and medical research agencies more interested in medicinal and industrial than in agricultural uses of plants.

We term this collection of materials by (mostly) ethnobotanists and agronomists *free appropriation* because the plants and seeds were obtained free of charge or at limited cost, principally from peasant farmers and traditional and tribal peoples in the Third World. The unrecompensed appropriation of these materials has been predicated on a widely accepted ideology that has defined germplasm as the "common heritage of mankind" (Wilkes 1983). As "common heritage," biochemical and genetic information has been looked upon as a public good for which no payment is necessary or appropriate.

But though nothing (or relatively little) was paid for them, those seeds and plant cuttings were extremely valuable. And the individuals doing the collecting were rewarded for their skill at extracting and appropriating those seeds and

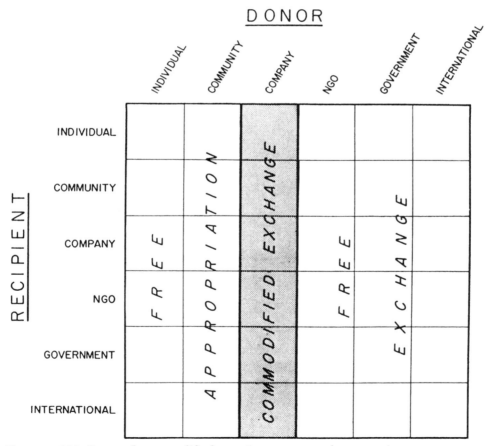

FIGURE 13.2 Free and commodified genetic resource exchange regimes.

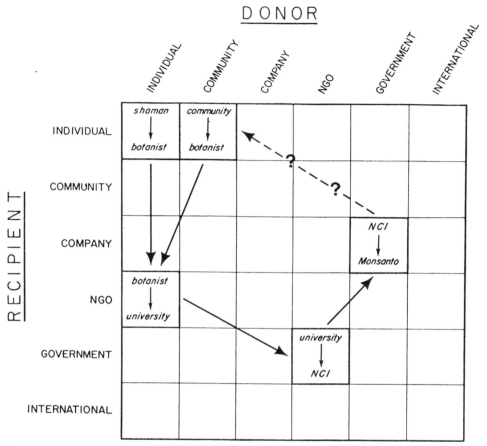

FIGURE 13.3 Information and benefit flows associated with biodiversity prospecting.

plants. The ethnobotanists and agronomists of the USDA, the Missouri Botanical Garden, the University of Wisconsin department of horticulture, or the International Rice Research Institute receive salaries for their work. They obtain grants, produce publications, and achieve professional advancement and prestige for their recovery and analysis of materials they collect from the lands and peoples of the Third World.

Note that they are paid directly, not for the plants but for the labor they are engaged in: collection and analysis. While the scientists and professionals of the collecting organizations benefit from their biological prospecting, they are rewarded indirectly rather than directly for their work. Nor do they necessarily retain the plant materials or the rights to these materials. In fact, after being collected, seeds stored in "gene banks" are made available to any qualified (i.e., another scientist or professional) person who wishes to use or further work on the material. Thus, the NGOs, government offices, universities, and international agencies that do the bulk of collecting supply the materials they collect to other NGOs, government offices, universities, international agencies, and—a new actor—companies, on demand. This is done freely, with no more than a shipping charge assessed of the recipient. We term this type of interchange "free exchange" in figure 13.2. Note that while this arrangement appears equitable—Third World farmers could theoretically ask for a sample of seed collected in another part of the world, Third World plant breeders can have access to the USDA's gene banks—in practice free exchange benefits the North disproportionately. This is because the capacity to benefit from access to a resource is a function of the capacity to use that resource. Since that technical capacity exists overwhelmingly in the North, "free exchange" is not the even-handed opportunity its proponents have made it out to be, and the benefits of collecting biochemical and genetic information have accrued to the North in extremely disproportionate fashion.

The appearance of companies—profit-making commercial businesses—in the equation marks the demarcation of yet a third form of exchange. While they are recipients of materials under free exchange, seed and pharmaceutical companies are less interested in academic publications than they are in the development of new products from the information they receive. Companies exist to sell products in a market. They are suppliers of germplasm under free exchange only in very limited circumstances associated with public relations and the maintenance of preferential relations with scientists and institutions whose cooperation they value highly. The business of business is business. Companies process biochemical and genetic information received under the regime of free exchange and sell those products as commodities. This simple social fact is illustrated in the "commodified exchange" section of figure 13.2. Companies are suppliers of germplasm at a price in the form of commercial seed or drugs or they do not make materials available at all for proprietary reasons. Effectively, companies have had free access to the genetic resources of the globe, but their germplasm is available only for a price.

A New International Genetic Order?

These regimes of exchange are now in flux as a variety of events and forces reshape the social and biological terrain in which genetic resources are embedded. A number of factors have combined to galvanize the emergence of global political conflict around the increasingly apparent asymmetries and inequities associated with the distinctions between the forms of exchange we represented graphically in figure 13.2.

Over the last fifteen years there has been a growing awareness that global processes of industrial and agricultural development have often resulted in substantial environmental externalities. One of the most serious of these has been the accelerating destruction of biological diversity. General concern over the broad problem of biological destruction helped focus attention on the question of plant genetic resources in particular. On the one hand it has been recognized that one of the consequences of the Green Revolution has been the gradual displacement of the traditional landraces upon which the development of high-yielding varieties of Northern industrial agriculture have been based (Frankel 1970). On the other hand there is the more recent revival of interest in the potential therapeutic applications of the many organisms that are now threatened with extinction. The principal rationale for developed-nation support for biological conservation in the Third World is now the potential utility and economic value of the genetic resources located there, a point that has not been lost on developing nations.

Additionally, in order to facilitate creation of a world market for commodities— including seeds and pharmaceuticals—the companies and nations of the North have sought global extension of a legal framework that would give them proprietary rights to the new seed varieties and drugs they are developing for sale. One of the most contentious components of the GATT is the issue of Trade-Related Intellectual Property Rights (GRAIN 1993). Controversy over the possible impact of the extension of patent rights necessarily has entailed consideration of the commercial value of the various forms of biochemical and genetic information.

Attention to questions of value and property rights in germplasm has been further emphasized by the emergence of the cluster of new genetic technologies commonly referred to as "biotechnology." Germplasm is the fundamental raw material of the genetic engineer, and as Winston Brill (then an executive of the American biotechnology firm Agracetus) observed, with the development of such techniques as rDNA transfer and protoplast fusion, "genetic wealth, . . . until now a relatively inaccessible trust fund, is becoming a currency with high immediate value" (quoted in Myers 1983:218).

As a result of this constellation of factors, there has been a growing unease with the established structure of the global genetic order among Third World politicians, diplomats, scientists, and farmers. Indigenous peoples have also become aware of these issues as the process of "chemical prospecting" finds the knowledge of traditional peoples and their healers to be one of the most efficient and effective routes to the identification of which species are endowed with possible therapeutic or industrial characteristics of relevance to humans.

Third World nations and peoples are now asserting what they see as their right to insist upon an end to the unrecompensed appropriation of cultural, biochemical, and genetic information and to require that chemical, cultural, and biological prospecting be undertaken in accord with well-defined rules that assure the suppliers of a reciprocal flow of benefit (e.g., Shiva 1990). In response to the ethical and practical principles now being affirmed in the Third World, Northern governments, companies, universities, and other organizations with an interest in maintaining access to Southern biodiversity are finding innovative ways to provide this reciprocal flow of benefits. What those rules should be is a matter of struggle. It is no surprise that questions regarding biotechnology and access to genetic resources were the two foci of disagreement in Rio de Janeiro and continue to be the pivots around which global cooperation in the Biodiversity Treaty will depend (Athanasiou 1992).

In brief, what is happening now is that with recognition of the possible value of germplasm and genetic resources, characteristics of commodified exchange are beginning to penetrate the areas of figure 13.2 previously restricted to free appropriation or free exchange. Some form of a "New International Genetic Order" is clearly in the offing. The degree to which this altered order is truly "new," or whether it is simply a kinder and gentler version of the old exploitative relationships, remains to be seen.

Questions of Compensation

If a new set of rules—a new regime—for the exchange of biochemical and genetic information is to be developed, what should those rules be? We are particularly concerned with individuals and communities in their roles as suppliers. We privilege these social actors, as it were. Individuals and communities are prime sources for the collection of "new" or unidentified genetic material. Farmers are the producers and reproducers of crop genetic variability. Indigenous peoples' communities are frequently the social integument through which useful materials are identified, domesticated, and distributed. Traditional healers are the source through which useful species of medicinal plants are identified and dispensed. Yet farmers, indigenous communities, and traditional healers usually receive limited medium- and long-term benefits for the services they provide to others. But consideration of how the rights of such peoples and communities may be protected means analysis at a number of levels.

For example, let us assume that a botanist obtains a plant from a shaman that ultimately becomes the drug of choice for AIDS therapy. Figure 13.3 illustrates a hypothetical flow of information through a series of exchanges that run from the shaman to the botanist, who in turn transmits the plant to a university, whose researchers' preliminary analysis suggests the plant might be useful in cancer therapies and who provide the material to the NCI, where NCI scientists isolate a substance from the plant that is appropriate for AIDS treatment, and finally the NCI licenses the active principle in the plant to Monsanto for development of a commercially available drug. All the participants in the various transformations of the shaman's information are rewarded for their activities in some fashion, except that the shaman provided the plant free or for a relatively small amount of money, to reflect his/her labor involved in the collection. Our concern is to see that some of the benefits are enjoyed at all nodes in the flow of information.

The Individual and Community Level: The Point of Appropriation

Collection of genetic materials frequently implies contact between individuals—a supplier and a collector. Certainly those choosing to donate genetic and cultural information deserve respect and some immediate concrete reward: the results of research, an acknowledgment of their contribution in cash or kind, or recognition in nonmaterial fashion such as a day of celebration for a shaman. The decision about what form such compensation should take must be determined by the people from whom genetic and cultural information is being collected. This implies a condition of informed consent. People should know what might be done with information they provide and must be given the opportunity to place their own restrictions on how that information is used. Researchers and collectors are becoming more sensitized to these imperatives. For example, the Society for Economic Botany has developed a code of ethics for collection and the FAO of the UN has already developed such a model protocol (FAO 1993b).

Evidence exists that indigenous peoples can act effectively in defense of their resources, though the effectiveness of such regulation is crucially dependent on the strength and character of indigenous rights over the land on which the resources are located and on the exigencies of national laws. For example, the Kuna people of Panama require payments from scientists wanting to engage in collection or research activities on Kuna land. Moreover, recognizing that real control of genetic information lies ultimately in knowing more about what it is and especially about how it might be used (and what it might be worth) in an industrial society, the Kuna require that an indigenous assistant accompany the scientists and that reports resulting from the research or collection be made available to them.

Such bilateral arrangements between a community or a people and an outside entity will surely be useful if intelligently crafted. But these community-based agreements also could well be subject to abuses, especially when the indigenous group has little experience with legalisms and when substantial commercial as well as academic applications of knowledge are a real possibility. Moreover, indigenous and other communities are not necessarily the homogeneous, solidarist, stable entities that some analysts romantically imagine. Not only are they subject to strains resulting from external pressures, they may also be characterized—as are most societies—by various gender and status divisions. Indigenous, rural, peripheral, farm, and peasant communities have had all manner of rural developers try to "do the right thing" as they saw it, or thought they saw it—almost always with little success (Chambers 1983). Effective consultation with a "community" is no more a simple matter when access to genetic resources is at stake than when any other issue arises.

In this regard, we note the possibly problematic approach to compensation recently introduced by the environmental NGO Conservation International in its plans for a project in Surinam. That project envisions the possibility that patent rights could be allocated to specific shamans (Stone 1993). We regard all knowledge production as social, and this is nowhere clearer than in indigenous communities. Unreflective imposition of Western individual property rights on non-Western communities in the name of Western concepts of "equity" has possibly been more destructive than the unthinking introduction of technologies. Is introduction of individual patent rights appropriate? Or will such "inappropriate social rules" join "inappropriate technology" as a force eroding the very culture they purport to protect? Conservation International's approach might be considered in light of a vote taken recently by the Belize Association of Traditional Healers (BATH). BATH decided that any arrangements with the pharmaceutical industry for access to their plants should be returned, not to an individual shaman, but to the community of traditional healers via BATH (BATH n.d.).

THE MIDDLE GROUND

As complex as the issues are at the individual and community level, they become considerably more complicated at what we are calling the "middle ground." In fact, agreements simply involving two parties—an individual or community supplier and a single nonlocal recipient—will probably be the exception rather than the rule. Often, we may expect that no single person or ethnic group or community will be associated with a particular plant of interest because of the plant's ubiquity. The plant may be used regionally, by more than one community or social group, and have different uses in different communities. And what of plants that the chemical prospectors may find to be valuable but are not actually used by the people on whose land it is found? In yet other cases, communities may not have the legal, technical, social, or political expertise or power to effectively structure an exchange in their own interests and may require the assistance of other organizations such as activist NGOs (Kloppenburg and Gonzales 1994). These sorts of situations involve supraindividual and supracommunity rights and interests, and there appears to be no clear-cut approach to the problem of equitably managing exchange.

A considerable amount of activity is now evident on this middle ground. As Northern corporations and research agencies become more interested in chemical prospecting, and as Southern nations and indigenous and peasant communities become aware of the need to defend their rights, a host of NGOs has stepped in to facilitate or manage the creation of new exchange mechanisms with an enhanced legitimacy that is derived from the inclusion of various forms of compensation for suppliers of biochemical and genetic information.

The Rainforest Alliance and WRI have developed a model contract that represents a valuable attempt to encompass the many legal issues that arise (Downes et al. 1993). But the complexity of the model may limit its usefulness to most indigenous or peasant communities. The NCI has, to its credit, felt an obligation to engage these issues and has developed a policy that includes provisions for the transfer of "knowledge, expertise and technology" developed during the discovery process to the country where the organism was collected. Another clause in this document "requires the successful licensee to negotiate and enter into agreement(s) with the appropriate source country government agencies. These agreement(s) will address the concern on the part of the source country government that pertinent agencies, institutions, and/or persons receive royalties and other forms of compensation, as appropriate" (NCI, n.d.). Additional "up front" and long-term benefits are offered to the source country through this agreement. The NCI requires that if a promising compound is licensed to a company, the company is required to "negotiate and enter into agreement(s) with the appropriate source country Government agency(ies)." A similar version of this agreement has been recently signed between the NCI and Awa people of Ecuador (H. T. Beck, personal communication).

Another type of agreement, by Shaman Pharmaceuticals, Inc., seeks to compensate *all* parties in all countries who have entered into collaboration with the company since its inception, through the formation of a nonprofit foundation, the Healing Forest Conservancy (discussed elsewhere in this volume). Yet another approach has been developed by Darrell Posey (1994), who has drafted "A covenant on intellectual, cultural, and scientific property: A basic code of ethics and conduct for equitable partnerships between responsible corporations, scientists, or institutions, and indigenous groups." More like a treaty than a contract, an altered version of this model has apparently been implemented in an agreement between the Kayapó people of Brazil and the well-known company The Body Shop International (Foundation for Ethnobiology 1993).

The United States Agency for International Development (USAID), the National Institutes of Health (NIH), and the National Science Foundation (NSF) are embarking on a program of biodiversity prospecting. These three agencies have just funded five consortia—or, as they phrase it, International Cooperative Biodiversity Groups (ICBGs)—in a $12-million, five-year program of chemical prospecting. These ICBGs comprise alliances of corporate, NGO, and academic organizations focusing on "the selection and acquisition of natural products derived from biological diversity as potential therapeutic agents" (NIH 1993). This work will be carried on by such well-known companies as Monsanto, American Cyanamid, Bristol-Myers Squibb, and Shaman Pharmaceuticals. Assisting these companies will be organizations like the Missouri Botanical Garden, Washington University, INBio, Cornell University, Conservation International, and the Walter Reed Army Institute. Projects will be carried out in Asia, Africa, and Latin America. According to the NIH, "Intellectual property agreements have been negotiated among participating institutions so that economic benefits from these discoveries are equitably shared and accrue to local communities and indigenous peoples involved in the discovery of the natural product" (NIH 1993:2). At this point, we cannot assess these arrangements since they are considered to be proprietary information. Certainly, these projects will bear watching in the future.

THE INTERNATIONAL LEVEL

While the immediate appeal of such contracts for (some) farmers and indigenous people is considerable, they will work only in rather restricted circumstances: where a particular people/community/region can be unambiguously associated (i.e., have clear tenure) with a particular genetic component or organism with substantial value. We fear that this condition may hold rather less often than many people now anticipate. We have two concerns.

First, nearly all genetic contributions are very small. Yet in aggregate they are very large. Take the example of wheat in the U.S. It has benefited tremendously from genes from all over the world. But each piece of the genetic "stew" that is a modern wheat variety contributes rather little and has value only in interaction with millions of other genes. While there is no convenient way to follow each and every contribution, it is clear that in aggregate the South is a large net contributor of genetic materials. On the other hand, the North (with its superior capacity to use those materials) benefits enormously. Moreover, because the North benefits disproportionately from access to global genetic resources, it has a greater interest in ensuring—and a greater ethical responsibility to ensure—the preservation of those materials. For these reasons, it is appropriate that there be a concrete recognition of the North's greater debt. But this can be accomplished only through some global mechanism that does not depend on a detailed accounting of genetic contributions of peoples, communities, or nations.

Second, only a global framework can provide for compensation for materials for which there is no unique ethnic or geographic provenance. The neem tree (*Azadirachta indica*) is an example here. Native to Asia, its useful properties have long been understood by peasant farmers. These properties have also been recognized by companies. Extract of neem has been synthesized. Moreover, the synthesized extract has been patented and is now being produced commercially as a biopesticide by the agropharmaceutical transnational W. R. Grace (Burrows 1993). But there has been no reciprocal flow of benefit to Indian farmers. And even if there were, it is not clear who should be compensated: some Indian farmers, all Indian farmers, NGOs claiming to represent Indian farmers, or the Indian government? Additionally, the neem now grows in Africa and elsewhere. Should African farmers receive benefits as well? We may find that there are relatively few biological materials that can be clearly assigned to a community or even a region. It may be that most value will ultimately be transferred to the North in materials like neem and that the situation in which a particular ethnic group or community or even country can be compensated will be quite rare. In addition, companies will be looking for alternate suppliers for any material that has significant commercial value. Without a compensation mechanism at the global level, relatively little compensation may ever flow to the South.

The Convention on Biological Diversity concluded in Rio de Janeiro recently is the obvious candidate for the global mechanism that we believe is required. However, as it stands, the convention is clearly inadequate (Athanasiou 1992; Shiva 1992). Rio was more a biological GATT than anything else, a debate over how the earth's resources would be exploited rather than protected. The convention established the global hegemony of the existing legal framework for the appropriation and patenting of biochemical and genetic material. On the other hand, it failed to deal with materials already appropriated and stored in gene banks and, even more critically, neglected to concretely engage the question of "farmers rights" to the genetic resources they produce and reproduce every day (GRAIN 1994). The FAO, which pioneered the concept of farmers rights in its International Undertaking on Plant Genetic Resources, is now in the process of revising its undertaking to make it compatible with the Biodiversity Convention (FAO 1993a). This initiative might provide an avenue for the institutionalization of a compensation mechanism appropriate to the global level as a means of facilitating a flow of benefit to communities of farmers and indigenous peoples who supply genetic materials. If the FAO initiative should show promise, a similar arrangement might be developed with regard to medicinal plants. The Convention on Biological Diversity may not be much, but it is now the only game in town.

Intellectual property rights agreements in the medicinal plant arena are evolving and proliferating at considerable speed, with new approaches being suggested or implemented every few months. It is appropriate that those developing the agreements have a clear understanding of the issues involved, as well as the complex interactions between the various "social actors"—individuals, communities, companies, and institutions, both local and international. If we are to achieve maximum benefits from the employment of "utilitarian" agreements for biodiversity conservation, then mechanisms must be worked out that recognize and include all the parties involved in the process of biodiversity prospecting in its broadest sense.

This will not be easy. Different arrangements are required for different levels, and at any one level no single approach will necessarily be appropriate. The diversity of initiatives and arrangements now emerging at least has the virtue of reflecting the principle of "tactical pluralism" that Michael Soulé (1991:748) believes to be the most appropriate path for concrete efforts at conservation. The variability of the social as well as the biological world appears to require diverse strategies. We need to develop innovative models, monitor those models, and have the courage and the political will to modify them as necessary to realize a just as well as a utilitarian regime of exchange of biochemical and genetic materials.

REFERENCES

Athanasiou, Tom. 1992. "After the Summit." *Socialist Review* 22 (4) (October–December):57–92.
Belize Association of Traditional Healers (BATH), n.d. "Intellectual Property Rights in Belize." 4 pp.
Blum, Elissa. 1993. "Making Biodiversity Conservation Profitable: A Case Study of the Merck/INBio Agreement." *Environment* 35 (4) (May):16–20, 38–45.
Brockway, Lucile. 1979. *Science and Colonial Expansion: The Role of the British Royal Botanic Garden.* New York: Academic Press.
Burrows, Beth. 1993. "Patenting Neem: Intellectual Property Rights or Modern Piracy." *Journal of Pesticide Reform* 13 (3) (fall):21.
Chambers, Robert. 1983. *Rural Development: Putting the Last First.* New York: Wiley.
Clifford, Harlan. 1993. "Chemical Prospecting." *Profiles* (July):53–60.
Downes, D., S. A. Laird, C. Klein, and B. Kramer Carney. 1993. "Contract for Biodiversity Prospecting." In Walter V. Reid et al., eds., *Biodiversity Prospecting*, pp. 255–88. Washington, D.C.: World Resources Institute.
Eisner, Thomas. 1989. "Prospecting for Nature's Chemical Riches." *Issues in Science and Technology* 6 (2):31–34.
Food and Agriculture Organization of the United Nations (FAO). 1993a. *Implications of UNCED for the Global System on PGR.* CPGR, January 7, 1993. Rome: FAO.
Food and Agriculture Organization of the United Nations (FAO). 1993b. *Draft International Code of Conduct For Plant Germplasm Collecting and Transfer.* CPGR, January 8, 1993. Rome: FAO.
Foundation for Ethnobiology. 1993. "Covenant Between a Responsible Corporation, Scientist, or Scientific Institution and an Indigenous Group." London: Foundation for Ethnobiology.
Fowler, Cary and Pat Mooney. 1990. *Shattering: Food, Politics, and the Loss of Genetic Diversity.* Tucson: University of Arizona Press.
Frankel, O. H. 1970. "Genetic Dangers in the Green Revolution." *World Agriculture* 19 (3):9–13.
Genetic Resources Action International (GRAIN). 1993. "GATT, NAFTA, and Intellectual Property Rights." *Seedling* 10 (4) (December):2–6.
Genetic Resources Action International (GRAIN). 1994. "Packaging an Ag Biodiversity Plan." *Seedling* 12 (1) (March):19–22.
Kloppenburg, Jack, Jr. 1988. *First the Seed: The Political Economy of Plant Biotechnology, 1492–2000.* New York: Cambridge University Press.
Kloppenburg, Jack, Jr. and Tirso Gonzales. 1994. "Between State and Capital: NGOs as Allies of Indigenous Peoples." In Thomas Greaves, ed., *Intellectual Property Rights for Indigenous Peoples: A Sourcebook.* Oklahoma City: American Anthropological Association.
Kloppenburg, Jack, Jr. and Daniel Lee Kleinman. 1987. "Seed Wars: Common Heritage, Private Property, and Political Strategy." *Socialist Review* 95 (September/October):7–41.
Kloppenburg, Jack, Jr. and Silvia Rodriguez. 1993. "Conservationists or Corsairs?" *Seedling* vol. 9 (June/July):12–17.
Klose, Norman. 1950. *America's Crop Heritage: The History of Foreign Plant Introduction by the Federal Government.* Ames: Iowa State College Press.
Myers, Norman. 1983. *A Wealth of Wild Species.* Boulder: Westview Press.
National Cancer Institute (NCI), n.d. "Agreement Between Source Country and Developmental Therapeutics Programs." Washington, D.C.: Division of Cancer Treatment, National Cancer Institute, 5 pp.

National Institutes of Health (NIH). 1993. "First Five Year Awards are Announced Under Interagency Biodiversity Program." *NIH News* (December 7).

Plotkin, Mark and Lisa Famolare, eds. 1992. *Sustainable Harvest and Marketing of Rain Forest Products*. Washington, D.C.: Island Press.

Posey, Darrell. 1994. "A Covenant on Intellectual, Cultural, and Scientific Property: A Basic Code of Ethics and Conduct for Equitable Partnerships Between Responsible Corporations, Scientists, or Institutions, and Indigenous Groups." In Tom Greaves, ed., *Intellectual Property Rights for Indigenous Peoples*, appendix 1. Oklahoma City: Society for Applied Anthropology.

Reid, Walter V., Sarah A. Laird, Carrie A. Meyer, Rodrigo Gámez, Ana Sittenfeld, Daniel Janzen, Michael A. Gollin, and Calestous Juma, eds. 1993. *Biodiversity Prospecting: Using Genetic Resources for Sustainable Development*. Washington, D.C.: World Resources Institute.

Shiva, Vandana. 1990. "Biodiversity, Biotechnology, and Profit: The Need for a Peoples' Plan to Protect Biological Diversity." *The Ecologist* 20 (2) (March/April):44–47.

Shiva, Vandana. 1992. "Why Biodiversity Convention May Harm the South." *Third World Resurgence* 24/25 (August/September):16–18.

Soulé, Michael, 1991. "Conservation: Tactics for a Constant Crisis." *Science* 253 (August 16):744–48.

Stone, Richard. 1993. "NIH Biodiversity Grants Could Benefit Shamans." *Science* 262 (December 10):1635.

Suhai, Suman. 1992. "Patenting of Life Forms: What It Implies." *Economic and Political Weekly* (April 25):878–79.

Wilkes, Garrison. 1983. "The Current Status of Crop Germplasm." *Critical Reviews in the Plant Sciences* 1:133–81.

14

Monetizing the Pharmacological Benefits of Plants

Peter P. Principe

THE primary purpose of this paper is to describe methods for estimating and monetizing the benefits provided by existing medicinal plants and the potential pharmacological benefits that might be realized from as-yet-undiscovered phytochemicals.[1] These monetized benefits are essential for public policymaking based on benefit-cost analyses and constitute the first step in developing more nearly comprehensive benefits estimates for ecosystems. Similarly, the estimates derived herein should be viewed as the first step in developing more sophisticated data and methods for valuing the pharmacological benefits of plants. Toward that end, the methods are described as transparently as possible so that as better data or assumptions become available, they can be readily substituted to generate better estimates.

The Importance of Valuing the Benefits of Medicinal Plants

Plants have always had a major role in medicine and public health, and the significance of that role has hardly diminished over time, even in the developed countries. In developing countries, fully 80% of the population depends on traditional (plant-based) medicine (Farnsworth et al. 1985), and in the United States, 25% of the prescriptions are filled with drugs based on phytochemicals (Farnsworth and Soejarto 1985). While the emphasis in pharmaceutical research has been on drug synthesis (rational drug design) and biotechnology, plant-based drugs are regularly being discovered and brought to market (Principe 1991). Recently, the pharmaceutical industry has had a resurgence of interest in natural products as a result of some disappointment with the lack of major successes from rational drug design research.

Naturally, the value of these plant-based drugs to the national economy and to the maintenance and improvement of public health is considerable. The market value of plant-based prescriptions filled in the United States in 1980 has been estimated to exceed $8 billion (Farnsworth and Soejarto 1985), and the market value for both prescription and over-the-counter drugs based on plants in 1985 for the OECD countries[2] has been estimated to be about $43 billion (Principe 1989). When an attempt is made to estimate the economic value (the difference between market value and economic value is discussed below) of plant-based drugs, the values increase significantly. Considering only the benefits derived from saving lives of people afflicted with cancer, the economic value of plant-based drugs in the United States has been estimated to be about $250 billion annually (Principe 1989). The derivation of these economic values is discussed below, and they are updated to reflect the most recently available data.

As interesting as these numbers may be, they can be helpful in the public debate only if they are placed within a context that makes their relevance clear to public policymakers. One of the goals of this analysis is to provide the basis for deciding whether the preservation of biodiversity is in the economic self-interest of all governments, whether in developed or developing countries. Regardless of the intrinsic merit of preserving biodiversity, governmental actions necessary to preserve biodiversity will not be forthcoming unless this economic self-interest is clearly demonstrated. Further, even if the magnitude of the self-interest is clear, action may be slow or stillborn because of countervailing interests. However, worrying about the latter issue is pointless unless the former can be accomplished.

Much uncertainty is associated with these analyses—about the data, about the economic theory and its application, and about the quantification of qualitative judgments and measures. But this uncertainty is inherent in any effort to estimate benefits. While it must be acknowledged and, to the extent possible, quantified, it should not be accepted as a rationale for delaying the analysis or for not acknowledging the results. Understanding its nature and source provides important insight into how to best use the estimates and where to direct future research.

Since uncertainty is always a factor in governmental decisions, its presence should not surprise or deter decision makers. At least with respect to biodiversity, one aspect is certain: extinction is irreversible. This lends considerable weight to the case for preserving biodiversity. Even absent a comprehensive quantification of benefits, the fact that a potential action will cause this irreversible result, thereby precluding any future exploitation of the species' potential benefits, should create a substantial presumption against taking the action. Nonetheless, sufficient weight is seldom given to the benefits forgone when biodiversity is lost, so the estimation of its benefits assumes a critical role in terms of helping to establish that the intuitive value of biodiversity can be substantiated.

It is essential that the estimation of benefits include the forgone benefits that could be realized from currently unused plants, since it is unlikely that a plant or animal that is currently providing a benefit would be permitted to become extinct. Thus, while current market value estimates serve a valuable purpose in describing the existing value of biodiversity, they incompletely describe the total magnitude of benefits because the forgone benefits are likely to be far greater in magnitude. Furthermore, the loss of diversity is unlikely to diminish the current market values (except insofar as plant-based drugs are replaced with drugs derived from other sources).

If one accepts the notion that quantifying and monetizing the current or potential pharmaceutical value of plants is useful for policymaking related to biodiversity, it is hardly a leap of faith to posit the utility of this value as an indicator of ecosystem value. When one argues to preserve biodiversity, one is simultaneously arguing to preserve ecosystems. There are at least four reasons this is so:

1. Biodiversity can be preserved and sustained successfully only in situ.
2. The many species that comprise an ecosystem are jointly responsible for the sustenance of that ecosystem's biodiversity—so trying to preserve individual species ex situ is at best a desperate attempt to save a species, but it is not a means of saving biodiversity or those unique characteristics that sustain biodiversity and the natural change attendant upon biodiversity.
3. In most ecosystems, there are a large number of species that we have not identified or of which we are only vaguely knowledgeable, and attempting to preserve all these species ex situ would be impossible.
4. Biodiversity and the tremendous variety of phytochemicals we find in nature result from the complex interactions within ecosystems, so to preserve the biodiversity without preserving the ecosystem is an oxymoron.

While it is obvious that the pharmaceutical value of an ecosystem's plants represents only one component of the ecosystem's total value, the other aspects of that value are likely to be far more difficult to quantify. So this value, while not completely characterizing the entire aggregate of values associated with an ecosystem, may be useful as an indicator of the value of a given ecosystem relative to other ecosystems or as an indicator of the lower bound estimate of an ecosystem's value. Clearly, this indicator would be most useful at a highly aggregated level when the survival of a particular ecosystem is in question. It is much less clear that this indicator would be useful at lower levels of aggregation, such as trying to assess the marginal value of changes in the ecosystem. Further work would be necessary to acquire data and develop methodologies to refine the indicator for uses in such situations.

The Special Role of Medicinal Plants

Plants, and in particular their pharmacological properties, provide an especially important indicator of value for biodiversity and ecosystems. With respect to the need to preserve biodiversity, our inability to predict which plants will provide useful drugs demonstrates the obvious need to preserve the maximum biodiversity possible. Furthermore, new uses are always being found for plants and their chemicals, even those that have been available for many years: "It must be taken into account that one can never completely discount any plant, no matter how exhaustively it has been tested for biological effects, as being completely devoid of one or more useful drugs" (Farnsworth and Soejarto 1985). One well-publicized example is the recently discovered effectiveness of aspirin in reducing risks of second (and in some cases, first) heart attacks. It has often been argued that all the potential pharmaceutical products have already been squeezed out of temperate-climate plants. Yet drugs derived from temperate-climate plants are still being discovered (e.g., taxol [Rowinsky et al. 1989; McGuire et al. 1989] and artemisinin [Klayman 1985, 1989]). As a result, there is a clear need to preserve as many species of plants as possible since whenever a plant becomes extinct, the potential loss could be of enormous magnitude.

Another reason that plants have a special role in estimating ecosystem benefits is that many of the market and societal values they provide (such as agricultural and pharmaceutical benefits) are (relatively) more easily quantified than many other benefits provided by ecosystems. For example, it is easier to place a value on a particular drug than on the benefit provided by benthic organisms as part of the food chain or by the Amazonian rain forest in removing atmospheric pollutants.

What Counts in Valuing Ecosystems?

In assessing the value of tropical forests, many commentators focus exclusively on the value of raw materials extracted from the forests or exclusively on those materials or products currently being used. This narrow focus leads to an underestimation of benefits for at least three reasons:

1. The value of tropical forests is grossly underestimated because their value is far greater than just that represented by the raw products we currently extract from them (e.g., the value of the raw products hardly reflects the economic value [using "economic value" to mean the total of all societal benefits] associated with the finished products [especially medicinal products], the various environmental benefits provided by forests such as pollutant scrubbing, and the existence value of the forests).
2. The potential value of as-yet-undiscovered products (notably in the medicinal area) is far greater than these current values (see below).
3. The focus on current products could easily lead to the implementation of conservation strategies that lead to the preservation of currently utilized plants to the detriment of programs that preserve larger numbers of species or that encourage research to develop new products.

With respect to the first issue, it is not simply what the crude vegetal products are worth that defines the value of the plants or forests to either the countries in which the forests exist or the countries that use the forests' products. Even if we limit our discussion to the medicinal value of tropical forests, the value of the crude products represents only a small portion of the total value of these forests (Principe 1989).

With respect to the second issue, it is misleading to base a valuation of the pharmaceutical potential of tropical forests on the current use of tropical plants. Most of the plant-based drugs we currently use are based on temperate plants since the presynthetic pharmacopoeia was based on plants that were familiar to our ancestors, who mostly lived in temperate climates. However, the number of new drugs that might come from tropical moist forests is potentially very large. Not only are more species found in these forests but also these species live under greater stress from competition and predation, which leads to a higher probability of there being pharmacologically active phytochemicals because the biological response to that stress results in more complex chemical defenses.

Given our extremely limited knowledge of tropical forest phytochemistry ("it has been estimated that nothing is known about the chemistry of more than 99 per cent of the plant species comprised by the flora of Brazil" [Balandrin et al. 1985]), it would seem overly conservative to suggest that the current percentage of tropical-forest-derived drugs should be viewed as the maximum likely. This would be true only if no screening and follow-up at all took place in the future. It is important to recognize the immense potential that the tropical forests represent. They should be viewed as a resource much like mineral or oil reserves—except that the forests and the species that comprise them are a renewable, yet delicate, resource. (Whether genetic resources should be viewed as renewable or nonrenewable resources is a consideration that would exceed the limits of the present discussion.)

Adopting a narrow focus is an easy trap within which to become ensnared, especially if one permits the problem to be defined a priori rather than insist on a careful examination of the underlying assumptions. It is essential that the definition of value be expanded to include the total economic value of the tropical forests (or the plants therein). Further, the huge potential value must be asserted, for in this untapped reserve the vast bulk of potential benefits to society resides.

The use of benefit-cost analysis for public policymaking raises some similar issues. Benefit-cost analyses often have two major flaws: first, benefit quantification is exceedingly difficult, which results in total benefits usually being unestimated or underestimated (and those estimates that are made are usually limited to market values rather than economic values); and, second, costs are usually overestimated since opportunities for cost reduction or cost offsetting are unrecognized or ignored at the time of the decision. Consequently, the resulting benefit-cost analyses are usually heavily weighted against any action that has a large nonmarket-value component. Controversy also surrounds the appropriateness of discounting the value of future benefits against current costs (e.g., preventing a death seventy years from now by imposing a cost today can rarely be justified if the benefit [assuming it can be estimated] is discounted).

Another example of a too-narrow focus is the view that a drug must have a vegetal component to be considered plant derived. A more satisfactory definition would include the following three categories described more than twenty years ago (Hänsel 1972):

1. Constituents isolated from plants that are used directly as therapeutic agents. Examples of such natural substances are digitoxin, strophanthin, morphine, and atropine. . . .
2. Plant constituents that are used as starting materials for the synthesis of useful drugs. For example, adrenal cortex and other steroid hormones are normally synthesized from plant steroidal sapogenins, and the "synthetic" penicillins from natural penicillin.
3. Natural products that serve as models for pharmacologically active compounds in the field of drug synthesis. There are numerous reasons why plant constituents that are potentially useful drugs cannot be employed directly. The plant material may be either unavailable or available only in limited quantity; furthermore, the plant may not lend itself to cultivation. Frequently, the side effects of a natural product often prevent its use in medicine and can be resolved only by preparation of a synthetic derivative—for example, cocaine, which led to the development of modern local anesthetics; the coumarins as precursors of modern antithrombins; and the modification of colchicine and of podophyllotoxin to obtain antitumor preparations.

A plant-based drug originates from a phytochemical—there is not merely some post facto similarity to a phytochemical.

Economic Value/Benefits Estimation

While several different methods exist for valuing the contribution of plants to medicine and the pharmaceutical industry, no one method is either completely inclusive or without weakness. Further, as might be expected, many unfortunate gaps exist in the publicly available data, and a variety of assumptions must be made to bridge them. While the robustness of these assumptions varies, the most important consideration is that they be stated plainly so that it is clear where the data leave off and the conjecture begins and so that as better information or data become available they can be substituted to improve the analysis.

One important distinction that must be understood is that between market value and economic value. Market value is most easily viewed as the sales of the commodity and its derivatives in the marketplace. In contrast, economic value consists of all societal benefits of a commodity, including its market value. In the case of a drug, economic value would include the value of its sales (its market value) plus the value of decreases in morbidity or mortality realized through its use and the value of its contribution to public health and productivity. Consequently, the economic value of a drug is substantially larger than its market value, but the economic value is far more difficult to estimate in a manner that does not create considerable dispute. For this reason, market values are much more commonly found in benefit-cost analyses, but it is imperative that the consequence of this choice (i.e., underestimation of benefits) is made clear. The following section deals with the development of a variety of estimates of market value, and some of the elements of the calculus of economic value are considered in the section following that.

Estimates of Market Value

There are three ways of viewing the market value of plant-based pharmaceuticals. The first is to estimate the market value of plant-based prescriptions. This method relies on estimates of the retail pharmaceutical sales and of the percentage of plant-based prescriptions. The second is to estimate the potential forgone market value of drugs that will not be discovered and brought to market because species have become extinct before their utility could be discovered and exploited. The third is to estimate the present value of the forgone market value of the plant-based drugs that will not be brought to market because of extinction. These three views represent quite different measures: the first shows past and present market value of existing plant-based pharmaceuticals; the second shows the speculative future value of as-yet-undiscovered plant-based pharmaceuticals; and the third shows what might be a reasonable minimum expenditure today to preserve the plants that would provide the undiscovered drugs of the future. The development of estimates for these three valuations is described below.

PHARMACEUTICAL SALES DATA

There are three major sources of pharmaceutical sales data for the United States: (1) the Pharmaceutical Manufacturers Association (PMA); (2) the U.S. Bureau of Census; and (3) IMS America, Ltd., a private data-collection company. Since only the first two sources are in the public domain (only private subscribers can obtain the IMS data), this discussion will be limited to those two. The PMA data for U.S. sales include "finished prescription and 'OTC ethical' dosage forms," "OTC ethical" drugs being defined as "a drug product sold over the counter but primarily promoted to the profession. This does not include proprietary drugs (i.e., OTC products on display for purchase by consumers)" (PMA 1990). The PMA data cover the entire U.S. industry, not just PMA members, but the contributions of nonmembers are only estimates. The PMA data are in manufacturers' prices and are available going back to 1954.

The census data are substantially more complex to use and interpret. These data comprise the four major product areas shown in table 14.1. The medicinals and botanicals class is composed of two major segments: the manufacture of bulk organic and inorganic medicinal chemicals and their derivatives and the processing of bulk botanical drugs and herbs (including isolating plant alkaloids). The

TABLE 14.1 *Bureau of Census Drug Industry Product Classifications*

SIC[a] Code	Product Class
2833	Medicinals and botanicals
2834	Pharmaceutical preparations
2835	Diagnostic substances
2836	Biological products, except diagnostic

[a]SIC: Standard Industrial Classification.

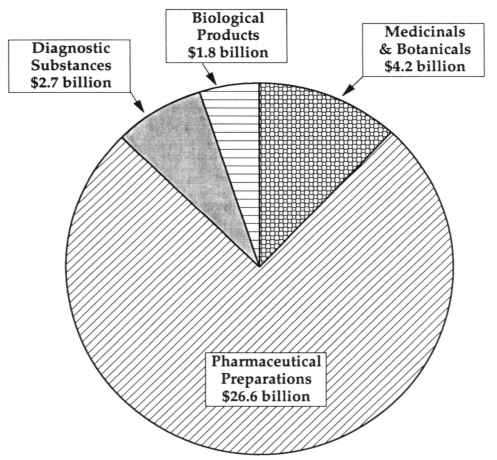

FIGURE 14.1 Sales in drug product classes in manufacturers' prices for 1987.
Source: Bureau of Census (1990c).

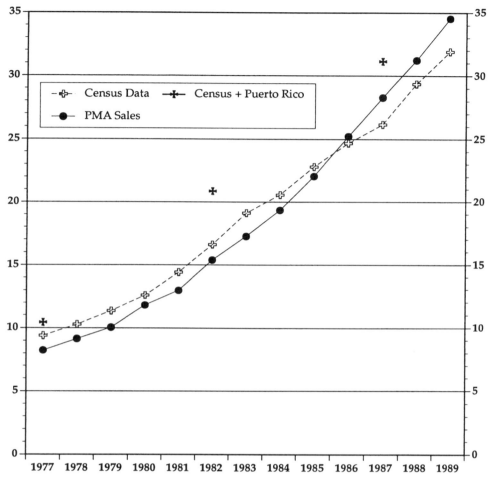

FIGURE 14.2 U.S. pharmaceutical sales data (in $ billion current at manufacturers' prices).

Source: PMA (1990); Bureau of Census (1977, 1982, 1985, 1987a, 1987b, 1990a, 1990b).

pharmaceutical preparations class is what would normally be thought of as the drug industry: the manufacture, fabrication, and processing of pharmaceuticals for human or veterinary use. The diagnostic substances class is engaged in the manufacture of in vitro and in vivo diagnostic substances. Finally, the biological products class produces vaccines and blood products (U.S. Bureau of Census 1990c). The relative size of these product classes in 1987 is shown in figure 14.1.

The PMA data are probably most comparable to the census data for the pharmaceutical preparations class. These data are compared in figure 14.2. As can be seen, the data are quite comparable, but the crossover of the trend lines in 1986 is somewhat puzzling. It appears that this might be explained by the fact that considerable pharmaceutical manufacturing was moved from the continental United

States to Puerto Rico in the middle to late 1980s. The census data do not include manufacturing data from Puerto Rico, so the noticeable change in growth rate for the census data from about 1984 to 1987 could be attributable to the movement of manufacturing capability to Puerto Rico. Unfortunately, data for pharmaceutical manufacturing in Puerto Rico are available only at five-year intervals (U.S. Bureau of Census 1977, 1982, 1987b), and these data have been added to the Census data for those three years and are also shown in figure 14.2. But even with the Puerto Rican sales added to the U.S. census data, the PMA data still seem to be growing at a more rapid rate. This can be seen in the graph: the PMA line steadily moves closer to the census plus Puerto Rico data over time. Given the uncertainty at this point about the stability of the census data, the PMA data would appear to provide a somewhat better basis for subsequent projections.

CONVERTING MANUFACTURERS' PRICES TO RETAIL PRICES

One of the difficulties in quantifying the value of medicinal plants has been moving along the chain from raw materials prices to retail prices. Among the more difficult steps has been converting data on pharmaceutical market sales from manufacturers' prices to retail prices. This conversion is important since most analyses (especially those directed toward public policymaking) use retail prices because of their familiarity and because they afford a well-understood benchmark. However, much of the available information is expressed in terms of manufacturers' prices. The difficulty in effecting the conversion arises from the fact that the industry considers much of the necessary data to be proprietary, for reasons of both market strategy and public image.

One study done for the Pharmaceutical Manufacturers Association (Trapnell, Genuardi, and O'Brian 1983) provides some insight into the relationship between manufacturers' prices and retail prices. This study provides data showing the relationship between prices at the three levels of the distribution chain (i.e., manufacturers, wholesalers, and retailers) for the ten-year period 1971–1980. These data are shown in figure 14.3. As can be seen, the retailers' share of the final drug price steadily decreased during the decade from 44.4% to 33.0%, while the manufacturers' share rose from 51.3% to 62.1%. The wholesalers' share of the final price increased only slightly over the decade, moving from 4.3% to 4.9%.

The study attributes the distribution system's diminishing share to three factors: (1) the increasing size of the average prescription, (2) automation-related economies from smaller inventories, and (3) a shift in retail sales from community pharmacies to lower-priced outlets. The effect of this trend on the estimation of retail prices is straightforward: as manufacturers' prices increased their share of the final retail prices of pharmaceuticals, total sales figures based on manufacturers' prices become better indicators of retail sales, and the extrapolation error should have a smaller effect on the outcome.

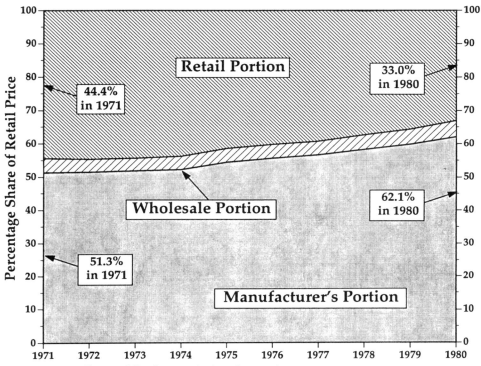

FIGURE 14.3 Share of final prescription drug prices.
Source: Trapnell, Genuardi, and O'Brian (1983).

Since the Trapnell, Genuardi, and O'Brian data do not go beyond 1980, deciding how to convert the sales data of the 1980s presents a problem. As can be seen from figure 14.4, the trends of the share-of-final-price indicate that significant changes were underway in the late 1970s: while both manufacturers' and wholesalers' shares were increasing, the retailers' share was diminishing. However, given the fairly large magnitude of the rates of change for all three shares, extrapolation would quickly lead to unrealistic outcomes. Unfortunately, these data do not clearly indicate the likely levels at which the shares would plateau in the 1980s.

Nevertheless, for estimating retail sales in the 1980s, a range of possibilities can be evaluated to determine how sensitive the outcome is to the initial assumption. Two of the market-share scenarios fall readily to hand: (1) the ten-year average of the market shares and (2) the market shares of the last year of the series (1980). A third possibility is that the end-of-period trends would continue for a period of time before reaching a plateau. With use of round numbers, a market-share ratio of 70:5:25 (manufacture-wholesale-retail) was assumed rather than 65:5:30 to emphasize the degree of sensitivity of the data to the assumption. The three scenarios are shown in table 14.2.

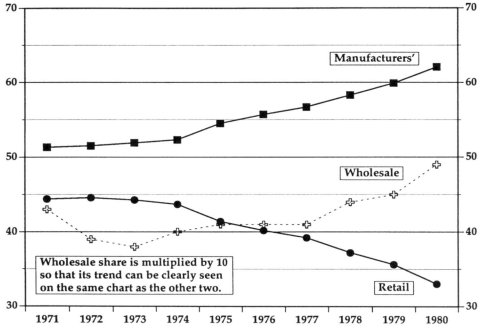

FIGURE 14.4 Trends in percentage shares of retail drug price for manufacturers, wholesalers, and retailers.   *Source: Trapnell, Genuardi, and O'Brian (1983).*

TABLE 14.2   *Three Scenarios for Estimating Retail Value of U.S. Drug Sales from Sales Data in Manufacturers' Prices*

	Share of Retail Price		
	Manufacturer	Wholesale	Retail
Ten-year (1971–1980) average shares	55.4%	4.2%	40.4%
Last-year (1980) shares	62.1%	4.9%	33.0%
High-rate scenario	70.0%	5.0%	25.0%

The results of applying these three scenarios to pharmaceutical sales data are shown in figure 14.5. The projected retail sales values for 1990 increase in $7 billion increments. The value based on the ten-year average probably has the least credibility given the trends shown by the data during the 1970s and given that the underlying causes of those trends were not reversed during the 1980s. The other two scenarios probably define a reasonable range ($55 billion–$62 billion) for the expected value. The last-year trend line would carry somewhat more weight since it is based on actual data rather than simply an estimate developed for testing the sensitivity of the extrapolation.

Another set of data lead to a quite different conclusion regarding the extrapolation to retail prices. Based on data from the National Prescription Audit (from

IMS America), the number of prescriptions filled in community pharmacies in 1973 was determined to be 1.532 billion, with an average cost in retail prices of $4.13 per prescription (Farnsworth and Soejarto 1985). Simple multiplication leads to a retail value of $6.33 billion for prescriptions filled and refilled from community pharmacies. However, community pharmacies represent only a part of the whole market, and the same data led Farnsworth and Soejarto to conclude that community pharmacies represented 50% of the market. Therefore, the entire retail market would be about $12.66 billion in 1973. This estimate is one-third higher than the one developed by Trapnell, Genuardi, and O'Brian of $9.5 billion.

The same methodology was used by Farnsworth and Soejarto to derive an estimate of 2.0 billion prescriptions filled or refilled in community pharmacies in 1980 with an average cost of about $8.00 per prescription. By use of the same correction factor to extrapolate from prescriptions filled by community pharmacies to all prescriptions, the retail value of the prescription drug market in 1980

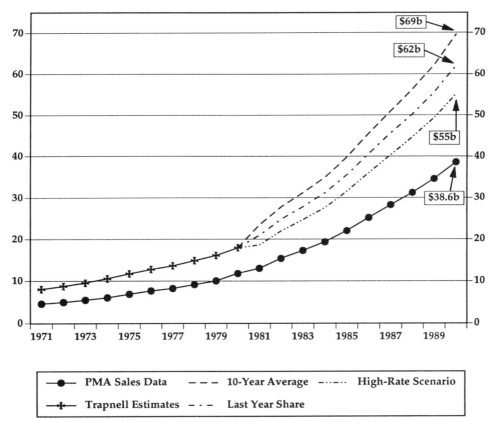

FIGURE 14.5 Projected retail pharmaceutical sales in the United States under three different scenarios in $ billion current.

Source: PMA (1990); Trapnell, Genuardi, and O'Brian (1983).

was estimated to be $32 billion. This estimate is 79% higher than that of Trapnell et al. for the same year. However, by taking advantage of market-share information provided by Trapnell et al. for 1980 and by reading from a graph in Farnsworth and Soejarto, a lower estimate that might be more accurate can be developed. Figure 1 in Farnsworth and Soejarto shows that the actual number of prescriptions filled at community pharmacies (without their correction for market-share changes) was between 1.35 and 1.40 billion, and the estimated average cost per prescription was $8. The market share of community pharmacies in 1980 given by Trapnell et al. is 60.9%. Simple arithmetic yields an estimate of total retail value of prescription drugs in 1980 of about $18 billion, which is, for all intents and purposes, identical to the Trapnell et al. estimate of $17.9 billion.

VALUE OF PRESCRIPTIONS DERIVED FROM PLANTS

Considerable research directed by Farnsworth during the 1970s and 1980s has resulted in authoritative estimates of the percentage of prescriptions that were filled with plant-based pharmaceuticals. On the basis of survey data for the years 1959–1973, plant-based drugs comprised just more than 25% of all prescriptions dispensed from community pharmacies (Farnsworth and Soejarto 1985). The range of annual values during this period was 23.12% to 28.22%. Farnsworth and Soejarto determined the number of prescriptions filled, the percentage filled with plant-based drugs, and the average cost per prescription. For 1973, they estimated that the value of plant-based prescriptions was $3.2 billion, and this value increased to about $8.112 billion in 1980. However, as discussed above, more recent data indicate that the market share of community pharmacies is larger than that estimated by Farnsworth and Soejarto. In assuming that the two sets of data can be used together, the effect is to lower the estimated value of plant-based prescriptions in 1980 to about $4.5 million. Taking the estimate of retail sales in 1990 of $62 billion and applying the 25% factor for plant-based prescriptions yields an estimate of $15.5 billion as the retail value of plant-based prescription pharmaceuticals in 1990.

POTENTIAL FORGONE MARKET VALUE

The forgone market value that is being estimated herein is the market value that would have been realized if some plants had not become extinct. In other words, if the plants were still around to have their pharmacologically active chemicals discovered and brought to market, there would be an increase in the sales of pharmaceuticals in the future. However, if the plants become extinct, that increase will not be realized, and that constitutes a forgone benefit.

The U.S. National Institutes of Health (NIH) conducted a plant-screening program for anticancer drugs from 1960 to 1981, and it was found that between 9 and 13% of the plants had some biological activity, and somewhat more than 1 in 1,000 plants contained chemicals that had commercial promise (Suffness and Douros

1979, 1982). This range is difficult to use because the screens used were intended only to detect anticancer activity, so other pharmacological effects would not have been detected, and the screens' ability to detect anticancer activity is now considered suspect (e.g., vincristine and vinblastine went undetected). Another difficulty is that "commercial promise" does not equal "marketable." Therefore, the range could be thought to be too low or too high. A consensus view of a roundtable of drug development professionals was that a reasonable estimate of the probability that any given plant would yield a marketable prescription drug would be in the range of 1 in 1,000 to 1 in 10,000 (Principe 1991). For the purposes of developing an estimate of forgone benefits in this analysis, that range's midpoint, 5:10,000, will be used.

The Worldwide Fund for Nature (WWF [formerly the World Wildlife Fund]) and the International Union for Conservation of Nature and Natural Resources (IUCN) estimate that there are approximately 250,000 plant species[3] and that about 25% of these will be extinct by the year 2050 [Heywood and Synge, personal communication]. On the assumption, for the sake of simplicity, that all those 62,500 species will become extinct between 1991 and 2050 and that they will conveniently expire at a constant rate, 1,059 species will become extinct annually during this period. Given the probable yield of marketable drugs of 5:10,000, the upshot of this species loss estimate is that about 30 plants that could yield marketable pharmaceuticals will be lost or, put another way, 1 marketable drug will be lost in every two-year period (5:10,000 reduces to 1:2,000 and about 2,118 plants will be lost in any given two-year period).

The next step is to estimate the forgone benefits of this loss of a marketable drug every other year. Farnsworth and Soejarto (1985) have stated that all the plant-based prescriptions in the United States in 1980 were derived from only forty plants. If it is assumed that the prescription sales in 1990 were based on the same number of plants, then the average contribution per plant was just less than $390 million ($15.5 billion divided by 40). Therefore, the forgone benefit in the first year can be estimated to be close to $200 million, increasing every year during the period by that same amount, so that the forgone benefit in the year 2050 will be between $11 billion and 12 billion in the United States (in 1990 dollars). The limits of this estimate are described above and more extensively elsewhere (Farnsworth and Soejarto 1985; Principe 1989, 1991).

THE PRESENT VALUE OF FORGONE MARKET VALUE

The present value describes the value today of benefits received in the future. The present value is estimated by choosing a discount rate that reflects the rate of return that would be expected if the cost incurred to achieve the benefits had been invested elsewhere (e.g., in a savings account or in real estate). Using and choosing discount rates in environmental analyses has engendered considerable controversy, but the economic basis for their use is clear (Pearce and Turner 1990).

In the instant analysis, the present value of the forgone market value calculated in the previous section will be determined. This present value could be used to determine what level of spending today would be appropriate to preserve the market value that would otherwise be forgone as a result of extinction of plant species. On the assumption of a 5% discount rate (which is the lower end of the range suggested by Pearce and Turner), the present value (in 1991) of the $11 billion–12 billion forgone benefit in 2050 is more than $3.5 billion. While this estimate may seem low to some, this is the present value of only the forgone retail sales of the pharmaceutical products—it does not include any economic values (e.g., the value of lives saved or extended, productivity, ecosystem benefits, or a variety of economic values such as existence value). Incorporation of these economic values would tend to increase this estimate (see below).

Given the variety of assumptions that underlie this value, a series of curves is shown in figure 14.6. These curves show the effect of making different assumptions regarding the discount rate and the number of plant species extant. In ad-

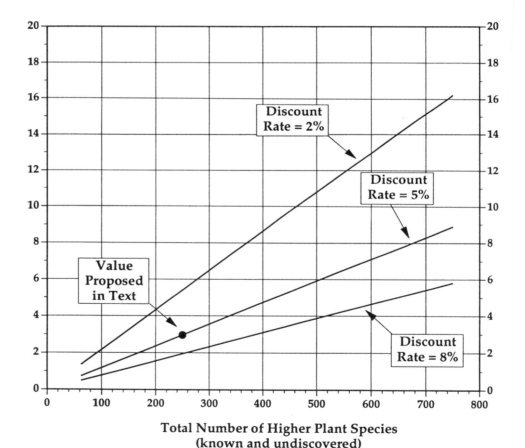

**Total Number of Higher Plant Species
(known and undiscovered)**

FIGURE 14.6 Present value in 1991 of benefits forgone in 2050 not realized from pharmaceutical sales as a result of plant extinctions (in billions of 1990 dollars).

dition, the number of species can be used as a surrogate for other variables, such as the percent of species to become extinct or the value of a species that is a source of a marketable pharmaceutical.

Issues Related to the Estimation of Economic Value

Estimating economic values is not a straightforward task, especially for something as complex as an ecosystem. Plants provide a whole variety of benefits, including chemicals that can be used as pharmaceuticals. Even limiting the consideration to just this one economic benefit barely simplifies the analysis. Estimating economic value requires three steps: (1) identifying the benefits, (2) quantifying the benefits, and (3) monetizing the benefits. While the first two steps are exceedingly difficult, the third is the most troublesome on which to achieve a consensus. The one question that most typifies the problem is: How much is a human life worth? There are others just as difficult, such as: How much is a few extra months of life worth? How much is "good health" worth? (And what is good health?) Because of the complexity of these issues, they will not be explored in any depth here, but an attempt will be made to describe some of the issues and how they could be addressed in specific instances.

AN EARLIER ESTIMATE OF ECONOMIC VALUE

Several years ago, the economic value of plant-based anticancer drugs was estimated to be about $250 billion annually in the United States (Principe 1989). Examining how this estimate was developed and some of the underlying assumptions can usefully illustrate the difficulties inherent in developing such estimates.

The development began with number of deaths caused by cancer each year in the United States (500,000). Then, with a value per life of $8 million (in 1983 dollars), the value of those lives was estimated to be about $4 trillion. Using estimates of the percentage of lives saved by anticancer drugs (15%) and of the percentage of anticancer drugs that were plant based (40%), approximately 30,000 lives per year were estimated to be saved by plant-based anticancer drugs. Simple multiplication of value per life and lives saved yielded an estimated economic value of $250 billion (simple multiplication actually yields $240 billion, but it was rounded to $250 billion to remove any misplaced sense of accuracy that might be imparted by using a number less obviously a rounded estimate—it might be better not to use Arabic numbers at all and simply refer to the estimate as "about a quarter of a trillion dollars," but the eye and mind would be inappropriately drawn to "trillion").

Quite clearly, this estimate is a simple one using very aggregated data—a back-of-the-envelope calculation that combines reasonably accurate estimates with some heroic assumptions. However, a fairly extensive undertaking to acquire and analyze the available data in a variety of areas and to develop methodologies to transform those data into meaningful statistics would be required to make major enhancements of the estimate's accuracy. In addition, the accuracy of any estimate will always be a subject of debate since certain linchpins like the dollar value of life can never be as precise as sales data. An analogy might be using a value of π accurate to ten decimal places to estimate the area of a circle whose radius has been estimated by eye from ten feet away. Nevertheless, society is rarely amenable to making major, discomfiting policy choices (such as those required to preserve biodiversity) without the greatest accuracy possible, even if the estimate errors are only marginally smaller.

MORTALITY, MORBIDITY, AND DEBILITY

Three types of indirect benefits are associated with any health-related program or product: (1) reduction of premature death (mortality), (2) avoidance of lost working time (morbidity), and (3) avoidance of reduced working capacity (debility)[4] (Eastaugh 1981). The balance of the value of indirect benefits between avoiding mortality and avoiding morbidity depends upon the nature of the disease: in skin diseases, avoidance of morbidity represents 90% of the indirect benefits while in cancer, avoidance of mortality represents 90% of indirect benefits (Eastaugh 1981).

With respect to cancer mortality, the estimate of 500,000 in the original analysis is supported by 1985 data on cancer deaths in the United States. In that year, 461,563 people died of cancer, and by 1988, an estimated 494,000 died (American Cancer Society 1988). The American Cancer Society also estimates that 40% of people who were diagnosed with cancer in 1988 would be alive five years later. They also provide what is a more useful statistic for the purposes of this analysis: that upon taking into account normal life expectancy, 49% of those diagnosed with cancer in 1988 will be alive five years later. Thus, of the estimated 985,000 people to be diagnosed with cancer in 1988, about 483,000 would survive the cancer for five years (and this number might be expected to increase as changes in treatment methods improve survival rates).

These 483,000 survivors could be considered "lives saved," but only an extensive analysis of cancer incidence data for different organ systems and survival rates by cancer type and treatment regimen would permit estimating the percentage of those lives saved by plant-based anticancer drugs. In all likelihood, there would not be a clear answer since many current treatment regimens have more than one component. For example, treatment with radiation will be followed by chemotherapy, or chemotherapy will be followed by surgery (neoadjuvant chemotherapy). In addition, many chemotherapy regimens consist of combinations of up to five different drugs, each having a particular effect. Consequently, there will be no straightforward answer in estimating the lives saved by plant-based anticancer drugs, and analyses will have to rely on estimates by experts, such as the one used in the original analysis.

Another aspect of the economic value of plant-based anticancer drugs not considered in the original analysis is that there is a benefit even in those instances where life is extended but not to the extent that it would be considered a life saved. There are many instances where life expectancy is increased from months to a year or more. Developing a methodology to estimate these benefits will be fairly complicated, especially given the many different types of cancer and the complex treatment regimens referred to above. Note that this is the sort of difficulty that has caused these values to remain unestimated.

VALUE OF LIFE

Once the estimation of lives saved has been successfully completed, the next step is to apply a value per life to establish the monetized benefit. The question of how large a dollar value should be placed on a human life is a hotly debated question with an extensive literature. Most estimates were developed within the occupational framework of workman's compensation and risk preferences as demonstrated in job choice. These hedonic wage-risk studies are usually based on preferences and choices made by blue-collar workers and tend to suggest a fairly low value of life. More recently, research has attempted to quantify people's willingness to pay (WTP) and their willingness to accept (WTA) through contingent valuation studies. WTP is a measure of how much a person is willing to pay or give up to achieve a certain end, whether that be to reduce the risk of disease or to keep a national park open. In contrast, WTA is a measure of how much a person would have to be compensated for agreeing to accept a higher risk of an adverse outcome, such as the risk of getting a disease or the closing of a national park.

One of the difficulties in extending some of the findings of the value-of-life studies outside the occupational arena is that they reflect the valuation of voluntary risks rather than involuntary risks. That is, the acceptance of a job and the risk it entails is quite a different matter than not having a drug available to treat a disease. The available information indicates that the values estimated in these studies should be viewed as a lower bound for valuing life in the involuntary risk situations found in analyzing the environmental consequences of market decisions (Violette and Chestnut 1989). For these reasons, it would seem that the contingent valuation studies should be used as the base from which to develop value-of-life estimates for involuntary risks. Note, however, that other, more conservative, views exist regarding the likely differences between life values in voluntary and involuntary risk situations (Pearce and Markandya 1987).

Violette and Chestnut (1989) state that the well-established range of value-of-life for occupational risks is $1.5–8 million (in 1983 dollars), and this is the range they believe should be considered the lower bound for environmental policymaking. The range for the wage-risk studies was $0.8–6.5 million (the range for "judgmental best estimate" was $1.6–6.4 million) and for the contingent valuation studies was $2.1–7.8 million ($2.7–3.0 million for judgmental best estimate).

In a specific comparison, WTP values and WTA values were quite consistent between different groups of workers. As shown in table 14.3, the WTP values range between $2 million and 3 million and the WTA values range between

TABLE **14.3** *Value-of-Life (VOL) Estimates from Contingent Valuation Studies (in 1983 Dollars)*

	Mean Risk Level[t]	Mean VOL—WTP	Mean VOL—WTA
Union white-collar	1.8	$2,030,000	$7,156,000
Nonunion white-colar	1.6	$2,531,000	$7,436,000
Union blue-collar	4.0	$2,952,000	$7,480,000
Nonunion blue-collar	3.7	$2,544,000	$7,342,000
All union	3.3	$2,789,000	$7,384,000
All workers	2.6	$2,558,000	$7,404,000

[t]Number of deaths per 4,000 workers. WTA = willingness to accept; WTP = willingness to pay.
Source: Gegax, Gerking, and Schulze (1985). Table adapted from Violette and Chestnut (1989).

$7 million and 8 million. Violette and Chestnut (1989) state that the WTA values have been shown to be biased upward. Remember, however, that these values are for voluntary, occupational risks. Another factor may be that most people have a very different view of alternatives when they themselves are directly affected. In comparing responses of cancer patients with other patients and medical and nursing professionals, it has been found that most cancer patients are willing to accept intensive chemotherapy for a very small chance of benefit as compared with the other sample populations, which were less inclined to accept radical treatment for minimal benefit (Slevin et al. 1990). This reaction would seem to indicate that most individuals would be disinclined to forgo future drugs that might extend or ameliorate their lives.

Taking all of this information into account, the original analysis chose a value-of-life of $8 million. While this represents the high end of the range for voluntary, occupational risks, it should be viewed as a conservative, lower bound for involuntary risks such as those presented by the loss of species, the loss of pharmaceutical products, and the subsequent forgoing of the benefits these things provide.

For the purposes of the analysis herein, this $8 million in 1983 dollars should be converted to 1990 dollars. Using the OECD price indices,[5] the value-of-life estimate becomes $12.4 million in 1990 dollars. Note that other countries are likely to have quite different values of life. One survey has suggested a minimum value of life in the United Kingdom of £2 million (Marin 1986).

One issue that must be dealt with is how to prorate the value of life in estimating the economic benefit or whether this is appropriate. Normally, the value of a child's life would be assigned a higher value than that of an elderly person. Certainly, if the basis of estimating the value of life is the hedonic wage-risk studies, the logic is straightforward—the older a person is, the less in wages that person has left to earn before retirement or death. It would seem, however, that that logic becomes weak when one considers those past retirement because the inexorable conclusion is that a life without wages is a life without value (albeit stated a bit harshly). Leaving aside the all-or-nothing approach, it would seem illogical to assign the same value to all people regardless of age, but developing a methodology to achieve an allocation that is fair in both perception and economics is likely to be difficult.

Even if one believes that all lives should be assigned the same value regardless of age, there remains the question of how to value extensions of life. For example, for many cancers, it is rare or impossible to achieve a complete remission or cure, so chemotherapy can extend life only by a matter of months or a year or two. A simplistic approach would simply divide the value-of-life estimate by the standard life expectancy (in months) then multiply by the mean or median (another choice!) life extension. It may not be possible to do much better than that. The quality of the life extension should also be considered—the debility of treatment versus the benefit of extra life. Since most people choose treatment, it must be assumed that the benefits outweigh the debility. While there is qualitative evidence that the extra time of life extensions is valuable (Lubeck and Yelin 1988; Slevin et al. 1990), quantitative data are lacking to move beyond the simple estimation method just described. However, it seems clear that the marginal utility of life extensions generally rises as one gets closer to death.

THE PRESENT VALUE OF ECONOMIC VALUE

By use of the same methodology described for estimating the present value of forgone market value, the present value of the economic value of the anticancer benefits of plant-based drugs can be estimated. Given the complications discussed above, it would be prudent to view these estimates as fairly gross estimates (toward that end, the values given in table 14.4 are shown as integers). With use of the previously developed economic value of $250 billion (1983 dollars), which is an annual value, the present value of the total benefit accumulated through 2050 is about $5 trillion on the assumption of a 5% discount rate. If the economic value is expressed in 1990 dollars ($370 billion), the present value through 2050 with the same discount rate rises to $7 trillion. These values as well as those assuming discount rates of 2% and 8% are shown in table 14.4. These represent substantial increases over the present value estimated for forgone market value, as might be expected given the substantially higher starting value.

The major assumptions inherent in this estimate should not be overlooked. In addition to the difficulties in estimating a value of life and the appropriate share attributable to plant-based drugs and only partial remissions, to develop this estimate it must be assumed that the economic value remains stable throughout the period. In addition, further work is required to assess the extent to which projected

TABLE 14.4   *Present Value in 1991 of Forgone Economic Value of Plant-Based Anticancer Drugs Through 2050*

	Discount Rate		
	2%	5%	8%
1983 Dollars	$ 9 Trillion	$5 Trillion	$3 Trillion
1990 Dollars	$13 Trillion	$7 Trillion	$5 Trillion

benefits are diminished by nonplant replacements or are increased by a growing population. Finally, remember that this estimate of economic value is based solely on value-of-life estimates and does not include other economic values of the market value of the drugs themselves.

Application of the Methods and Estimates

LIMITATIONS OF THE METHODS AND UNDERLYING DATA

The description, quantification, and monetization of benefits always comes to a less satisfactory conclusion than the parallel exercise for costs. Not only is the enumeration of benefits far more difficult but also their quantification and monetization is far less certain than on the cost side. Because benefits estimation is a far less developed area than cost estimation, it is essential that the method described above be viewed as a starting point for the development of far more refined estimates. The use of any such method involves choices, both implicit and explicit, and some of those choices are described below along with the weaknesses in the underlying data.

One of the more obvious choices is that ranges have been only rarely used in the analysis above. The primary reason for not including ranges is that since virtually all the data can be described only in terms of a range, the arithmetic manipulation of ranges leads only to broader and broader ranges until the resulting range is so broad that it has little or no utility. Consequently, in most instances, a single value that was considered most appropriate was chosen from the range. In many instances, other equally defensible choices could have been made. One of the goals of future research should be to reduce the breadth of these ranges or to add more certainty to the choice of a particular value within the range.

The estimation method deals with six distinct elements of the valuation: (1) the market value and (2) the economic value of existing plant-based pharmaceuticals; (3) the projected future market value and (4) the projected future economic value of existing plant-based pharmaceuticals; and (5) the projected future market value and (6) the projected future economic value of potential plant-based pharmaceuticals. While each of these elements has distinct difficulties associated with its estimation, the economic values and the value associated with potential plant-based pharmaceuticals are clearly more speculative.

With respect to the market value of existing plant-based pharmaceuticals (element 1), the problems associated with the underlying sales data have already been described above. Converting these data to retail prices requires that share-of-final-price data ten to twenty years old be used. It would be very useful to examine more recent data so that the manufacturers'-to-retail conversion done at the aggregate level could be done with more recent data. It would also be helpful if data were available to indicate whether plant-based pharmaceuticals followed the industry average in this conversion. Finally, for the estimate of the plant-based pharmaceutical value, it would be helpful if Farnsworth's earlier research were repeated for the 1980s. At the moment, there is no other estimate of the percentage of plant-based pharmaceuticals, but the data are now twenty to thirty years old, and repeating the study could lay to rest questions about the effect of the evolving pharmaceutical market.

The future market value of existing plant-based pharmaceuticals (element 3) has not been addressed in this analysis, but rather than simply project current market values, it would be useful to determine whether any expected changes in current usage levels can be foreseen. In addition, changes in patent status might have a significant effect on the retail price of some pharmaceuticals.

Projecting the potential market value of as-yet-undiscovered pharmaceuticals (element 5) requires the development of a framework of assumptions, most of which have more than one reasonable value. The probability that any given plant is likely to yield a marketable pharmaceutical is not likely to be refined since there are so many factors that affect this probability and those factors are constantly changing. Even so, the range and the selection of its midpoint for analytical purposes warrant further research. In a slightly different vein, the number of plant species and the percentage of those species expected to become extinct are the subject of considerably more debate, the resolution of which is unlikely in the near future. While this analysis need not depend upon the outcome of the current debate among taxonomists between the ''lumpers'' and the ''splitters'' (see note[3]), that debate could lead to a better estimation of the number of species/subspecies/ varieties that is appropriate to use in this analysis. Finally, if the data were available, it would be useful to determine the distribution of individual market values for each of the forty plants identified by Farnsworth and Soejarto (1985) rather than use the average value calculated by dividing the estimated plant-based market total by forty. It might be more appropriate to use the median rather than the mean for the purposes of this analysis. It would also be useful to develop a complete history of individual medicinal plants to determine their net value, by taking into account the development, manufacturing, and marketing costs balanced against the sales revenue and economic benefits.

With respect to the economic value of existing and potential plant-based pharmaceuticals (elements 2, 4, and 6), many issues are not likely to be easily resolved. At the aggregate level, it is fairly difficult to estimate the number of lives that have been ''saved'' by anticancer drugs. Rather than try to develop better aggregate measures, it may be best to concentrate on developing estimates for individual drugs and then aggregating these values. A major issue that goes beyond this analysis is the valuation of life extension (i.e., adding several months or years of life when remission is not achieved). Intertwined with life extension is the issue of valuing quality of life, especially for diseases such as cancer. The quality-of-life issue also extends to the development of values for those drugs that are used to treat nonterminal diseases or symptoms.

Naturally, the issue that dwarfs all these other issues is the valuation of life. The questions surrounding this issue have been touched upon above, but given its importance, both notionally and arithmetically, in the analysis, further research and debate are necessary to provide a better basis for valuation for policymaking purposes. It would also be helpful to address the role that the value of life has in different sectors of public policy (e.g., the differences between the environmental sector and the public health sector). For consistency in public policymaking, a similar valuation of life for instances of involuntary risk across all sectors would seem to be a necessary goal (a separate, but consistent, value for voluntary risk would also be useful).

Finally, the issue of discounting future benefits needs to be addressed in a more formalized manner within the context of public policymaking. As described above, the theoretical basis for discounting has been adequately described, but the choice of an appropriate discount rate is a policy choice that needs to be made. In the absence of governmental guidance, the range of possible present values of future benefits is too great to be very useful, and choosing a single value opens the analysis to criticism from those who would choose a different discount rate.

LIMITS AND IMPLICATIONS OF THE ESTIMATES

The estimates that have been developed must be used with care—it is very important that appropriate caveats be used with the estimates, the limitations described immediately above being kept in mind. Further, remember that the estimates are not precise; rather, they are more order-of-magnitude estimates that are best used to provide a sense of the magnitude of the benefits involved. Note that the number of significant digits has intentionally been reduced to the minimum possible to avoid conveying an unwarranted sense of accuracy. There would appear, however, little need to apologize for the estimates since the methodology, while simple, is transparent and uses the best available data.

That said, it must be clear that the magnitude of the pharmaceutical benefits from plants is very large. Even if these benefits are diminished by several orders of magnitude, they are still exceedingly large. Further, note that many other benefits are provided by plants that, when quantified and monetized, would cause the values to increase even further.

The large value of the benefits would seem to indicate that any action that would diminish the diversity of plant species would have to have a commensurately large benefit associated with it. Since such a situation is unlikely, logic suggests that virtually no such action could be justified. Taken from a different perspective, it could further be argued that given the very large present value of future benefits, almost any current action to preserve plant biodiversity could be justified economically.

This state of affairs presents a paradox—the benefit values are so large that they are likely to be ignored in policymaking since they render impotent the standard tool used by policymakers: the benefit-cost analysis. Note, however, that few if any benefit-cost analyses include all the economic value associated with taking a particular action (e.g., the benefit attributable to the mental well-being of having a job as contrasted with being unemployed). Perhaps if all economic values were considered, large-magnitude values would be more commonplace. But the estimation of these other economic values would constitute a considerable additional burden and would be subject to many of the same sorts of uncertainty that have been described above. The solution is not readily apparent.

From this confusion of data and assumptions, simplicity and complexity, several transcendent notions are paramount. First and foremost is that the extinction of species is likely to result in very large forgone benefits, and public policymaking processes rely on analytical methods that do not adequately consider this factor. Second, to the extent that the consequences of extinction can be characterized and quantified, underestimation of the total benefits of ecosystem preservation will be minimized and public policy decision making will be improved. Third, there is not a straightforward methodology that permits complete quantification of the benefits because of the large number of data gaps and the nascent development of quantification techniques. Fourth, given the first factor, the absence of a complete quantification of benefits should not inhibit the development of partial estimates to provide some measure of balance in decision making. Finally, methods and data are needed to permit a much better estimation of species and ecosystem benefits.

Based on the analyses described above, the estimated market value of total U.S. sales of plant-based pharmaceuticals at retail prices in 1990 is about $15 billion. If currently expected rates of plant extinction should occur, the market value of sales of new pharmaceuticals forgone because species became extinct can be expected to approach $12 billion annually by the middle of the next century. The present value of those forgone sales can be estimated to be about $3.5 billion annually on the assumption of a 5% discount rate. This means that an annual expenditure of $3.5 billion could be justified to preserve these benefits alone, without consideration of other benefits provided by plant species and their ecosystems.

The market values described in the previous paragraph are relatively easy to derive as compared with economic values, which are far more complete measures of benefits. An earlier estimate of the economic value of plant-based anticancer drugs ($250 billion annually, in 1983 dollars) cannot be improved upon for the moment. But more extensive analyses may permit a refinement of this estimate. Projecting out to the middle of the next century, the present value of this benefit is estimated to be about $5 trillion (in 1983 dollars with a 5% discount rate). By converting value to 1990 dollars, this increases to about $7 trillion. The sheer magnitude of this number should raise doubts about the underlying methodology, which is certainly not without weaknesses. However, significant discounting would still yield a very large number. As described in the previous section, more work is needed to refine these estimates.

In the end, these estimates of benefits would not be very useful in making specific public policy decisions except in terms of the broadest characterization of the benefits of ecosystems. Their current utility lies more in characterizing the potential magnitude of these benefits and in defining areas where additional research is necessary so that decisions based on benefit-cost analyses reflect not only cost considerations but also as complete a characterization as possible of the quantified benefits of ecosystems.

NOTES

1. The information in this document has been funded in part by the United States Environmental Protection Agency. It has been subjected to agency review and approved for publication. Mention of trade names or commercial products does not constitute endorsement or recommendation for use.

2. At the time this estimate was developed the Organization for Economic Cooperation and Development (OECD) had twenty-four member countries: Australia, Austria, Belgium, Canada, Denmark, Finland, France, Germany, Greece, Iceland, Ireland, Italy, Japan, Luxembourg, the Netherlands, New Zealand, Norway, Portugal, Spain, Sweden, Switzerland, Turkey, the United Kingdom, and the United States. Yugoslavia was an associate member.

3. The question of how many species of higher plants exist is not especially clear-cut. The WWF and IUCN are fairly firm in their belief in the soundness of their estimate. The traditionally cited estimate has been 250,000 known species with up to another 250,000 undiscovered species (Schultes 1972). More recently, it has been suggested that the upper end of the range of total species could be as high as 750,000 (Svoboda 1983; Balandrin et al. 1985). However, the number of species is really only a surrogate for different phytochemical systems. For the purposes of drug discovery, it hardly matters whether a plant harboring a particular chemical (or a sufficiently high concentration of that chemical to permit identification and extraction) is a distinct species or a subspecies or a variety.

Naturally, the estimate of forgone benefits will be dramatically different depending upon which estimate is chosen. Since the analysis uses the WWF estimates of plant extinction, their estimate of the number of plant species has been used for the sake of consistency. Note, however, that this choice could result in a substantial underestimate of the forgone benefits. Caveat lector.

4. Eastaugh's constraining of his definition of morbidity and debility to work-related benefits, while traditional, is not very accurate. While it is true that work-related benefits are relatively more easy to measure than nonwork benefits and that traditional benefit quantification methodologies rely on this ease of measurement, the nonwork benefits of reduced or eliminated morbidity and debility are significant. For example, an individual who is not morbid or debilitated presents several benefits, such as: (1) the individual can contribute to the maintenance of the household; (2) the morbidity and debility is not a physical or mental burden to the spouse or children of the individual; and (3) the inner well-being of the individual is enhanced (once again, the value of "good health" or the cost of "bad health"). This view is substantiated by the findings of a recent study that found that maintaining social contacts and personal relationships, shopping, running errands, and

doing chores for their family and themselves were much more important than work-related activities.

5. By use of consumer price indices from the OECD (OECD 1990a, 1990b), 1980 prices can be converted to 1990 prices by first converting the 1980 prices to 1985 prices by using a factor of 77.6 and then converting 1985 prices to 1990 prices by using a factor of 120.1 (based on the first ten months of 1990). Since these indices are based on all prices, they are likely to underestimate the increase in prices of prescriptions at the retail level since health care costs routinely increase faster than other consumer prices.

REFERENCES

American Cancer Society. 1988. *Cancer Facts & Figures—1988.* New York.
Balandrin, Manuel F., James A. Klocke, Eve Syrkin Wurtele, and William Hugh Bollinger. 1985. "Natural Plant Chemicals: Sources of Industrial and Medicinal Materials," *Science* 228 (June 7):1154–60.
Eastaugh, Steven R. 1981. *Medical Economics and Health Finance.* Boston: Auburn House.
Farnsworth, Norman R. and Djala Doel Soejarto. 1985. "Potential Consequence of Plant Extinction in the United States on the Current and Future Availability of Prescription Drugs." *Economic Botany* 39 (3):231–40.
Farnsworth, Norman R., Olayiwola Akerele, Audrey S. Bingel, Djala D. Soejarto, and Zhengang Guo. 1985. "Medicinal Plants in Therapy." *Bulletin of the World Health Organization* 63 (6):965–81.
Gegax, D., S. Gerking, and W. Schulze. 1985. "Perceived Risk and the Marginal Value of Safety." Working paper prepared for the U.S. Environmental Protection Agency, July 1985, as cited in Violette and Chestnut (1989).
Hänsel, Rudolf. 1972. "Medicinal Plants and Empirical Drug Research." In Tony Swain, ed., *Plants in the Development of Modern Medicine.* Cambridge: Harvard University Press.
Heywood, Vernon H. and Hugh Synge. Personal communication. IUCN Plant Conservation Office, Kew, United Kingdom.
Klayman, Daniel L. 1985. "*Qinghaosu* (Artemisinin): An Antimalarial Drug from China." *Science* 228 (May 31):1049–55.
Klayman, Daniel L. 1989. "Weeding Out Malaria." *Natural History* 98 (10):18–26.
Lubeck, D. P. and E. H. Yelin. 1988. "A Question of Value: Measuring the Impact of Chronic Disease." *Milbank Quarterly* 66 (3):444–64.
Marin, A. 1986. "Commodity, the Bias of the World." *Science of the Total Environment* 56 (November 15):77–87.
McGuire, W. P., E. K. Rowinsky, N. B. Rosenshein, F. C. Grumbine, D. S. Ettinger, D. K. Armstrong, and R. C. Donehower. 1989. "*Taxol:* A Unique Antineoplastic Agent with Significant Activity in Advanced Ovarian Epithelial Neoplasms." *Annals of Internal Medicine* 111 (4) (August 15):273–9.
Organization for Economic Cooperation and Development (OECD). 1990a. *Main Economic Indicators, Historical Statistics, 1969–1990.* Paris.
Organization for Economic Cooperation and Development. 1990b. *Main Economic Indicators, December 1990.* Paris.
Pearce, David W. and R. Kerry Turner. 1990. *Economics of Natural Resources and the Environment.* Baltimore: The Johns Hopkins University Press.
Pearce, David W. and Anil Markandya. 1987. *The Benefits of Environmental Policy: An Appraisal of the Economic Value of Environmental Improvement and the Economic Cost of Environmental Damage.* Paris: Organization for Economic Cooperation and Development.

Pharmaceutical Manufacturers Association (PMA) (October). 1990. *Annual Survey Report, 1988–1990.* Washington, D.C.

Principe, Peter P. 1989. "The Economic Significance of Plants and Their Constituents as Drugs." In H. Wagner, H. Hikino, and N. R. Farnsworth, eds., *Economic and Medicinal Plant Research,* vol. 3. London: Academic Press.

Principe, Peter P. 1991. "Valuing Diversity of Medicinal Plants." In O. Akerele, V. Heywood, and H. Synge, eds., *Conservation of Medicinal Plants.* Cambridge: Cambridge University Press.

Rowinsky, E. K., P. J. Burke, J. E. Karp, R. W. Tucker, D. S, Ettinger, and R. C. Donehower. 1989. "Phase I and Pharmacodynamic Study of *Taxol* in Refractory Acute Leukemias." *Cancer Research* 49 (16) (August 15):4640–47.

Schultes, R. E. 1972. "The Future of Plants as Sources of New Biodynamic Compounds." In Tony Swain, ed., *Plants in the Development of Modern Medicine.* Cambridge: Harvard University Press.

Slevin, M. L., L. Stubbs, H. J. Plant, P. Wilson, W. M. Gregory, P. J. Armes, and S. M. Downer. 1990. "Attitudes to Chemotherapy: Comparing Views of Patients with Cancer with Those of Doctors, Nurses, and General Public." *British Medical Journal* 300 (6737) (June 2):1458–60.

Suffness, Matthew and John Douros. 1979. "Drugs of Plant Origin," ch. 3. In *Methods of Cancer Research,* vol. 16. New York: Academic Press.

Suffness, Matthew and John Douros. 1982. "Current Status of the NCI Plant and Animal Product Program." *J. Natural Products* 45 (1):1–14.

Svoboda, Gordon, H. (September) 1983. "The Role of the Alkaloids of *Catharanthus roseus* (L.) G. Don (*Vinca rosea*) and Their Derivatives in Cancer Chemotherapy." In *Plants: The Potentials for Extracting Protein, Medicines, and Other Useful Chemicals, Workshop Proceedings.* Washington, D.C.: U.S. Congress, Office of Technology Assessment, OTA–BP–F–23.

Trapnell, Gordon R., James S. Genuardi, and Joan O'Brian. (September 9) 1983. "Consumer Expenditures for Ethical Drugs." Washington, D.C.: Pharmaceutical Manufacturers Association.

United States Bureau of Census. 1985, 1987a, 1990a, 1990b. "Current Industrial Reports. Pharmaceutical Preparations, Except Biologicals." MA28G(84)–1, MA28G(86)–1, MA28G(88)–1, MA28G(89)–1. Washington, D.C.: U.S. Department of Commerce.

United States Bureau of Census. 1977, 1982, 1987b. "Economic Censuses of Outlying Areas—Puerto Rico." OA77–E–4, OA82–E–4, OA87–E–4 (issued July 1990). Washington, D.C.: U.S. Department of Commerce.

United States Bureau of Census. 1990c. "1987 Census of Manufactures, Industry Series, Drugs." MC87–I–28C (issued April 1990). Washington, D.C.: U.S. Department of Commerce.

Violette, Daniel M. and Lauraine G. Chestnut. 1989. *Valuing Risks: New Information on the Willingness to Pay for Changes in Fatal Risk.* Report to the U.S. Environmental Protection Agency, EPA–230–06–86–016. Washington,

15

Capturing the Pharmaceutical Value of Species Information: Opportunities for Developing Countries

Bruce A. Aylward

THERE is currently a resurgence of interest in the use of biodiversity as a source of novel chemical compounds for the development of new pharmaceuticals. A growing number of pharmaceutical companies are initiating or upgrading research programs that screen microbial sources, higher plants, and other taxonomic groups for useful activity against disease targets. On the supply side, developing country governments, development agencies, and nongovernmental organizations are increasingly interested in assisting developing country institutions to capture the pharmaceutical value of biodiversity.

Some potential misunderstandings exist, however, in the view that pharmaceutical prospecting can serve as a mechanism by developing countries to extract compensation for conservation of their biodiversity. In an effort to clarify the pharmaceutical value of biodiversity and species information, this article investigates the economic relationships involved in pharmaceutical prospecting, which is the process of deriving marketable pharmaceuticals from natural products. I argue that an overemphasis on the question of how to capture the value of biodiversity misses the key development question—that of how to invest in the generation of information about biodiversity.

The divergence of views on this subject comes from the failure to draw a clear distinction between biodiversity as the raw material in the production process and information about biodiversity—the intellectual property that drives innovation. As a raw material, biodiversity is typically treated as a free good. As a consequence, pharmaceutical prospecting provides little in the way of financial incentives for a developing country to invest in biodiversity protection. On the other hand, the ability to patent novel chemical compounds does provide an incentive to generate information about species that is useful in producing new and marketable drugs. The economic link between biodiversity and pharmaceuticals is the development of information about species and their chemical constituents.

To capture the pharmaceutical value of biodiversity, developing countries need to come up with a practical mechanism for controlling access to the country's biodiversity. Through the effective implementation of their sovereignty over national biological resources, developing countries could establish their ability to derive just compensation (or payment) from the market for biodiversity samples. An alternative means of establishing a fair share of the returns from the raw material is to move into information-generating activities that involve exclusive rights over biotic samples provided by collectors. Generating species information in-country may be a more practical means of capturing the pharmaceutical value of biodiversity. In addition, such investment enables the country to appropriate a larger share of value added in the drug development process.

Pharmaceutical Prospecting as an Economic Activity

Novel chemical compounds with marketable potential as prescription drugs are currently derived either from natural sources or by chemical synthesis in the laboratory. Historically, however, all medicinal preparations were derived directly from nature. Since the 1800s interest in the research and development (R & D) of natural-product-based pharmaceuticals has been cyclical as synthetic chemistry and, more recently, efforts at rational drug design based on knowledge of biomolecular processes have led researchers to abandon the use of natural products. In the past few years, new technological developments—including advances in receptor- and mechanism-based screening technology—have rekindled the interest of pharmaceutical companies in the exploration of plants, marine organisms, microbial sources, and insects for novel chemical compounds.

Farnsworth and Morris (1976) point out that although guesstimates can be made about the untapped potential of biodiversity, it is practically impossible to actually determine when a particular species has been fully investigated for its pharmaceutical properties. For example, Douros and Suffness (1980) report that in the first natural-products-screening program by the National Cancer Institute (NCI), 35,000 species of plants were screened for anticancer activity. In other words, in the most extensive pharmacological investigation of plants ever recorded, only a fraction of the total number of plant species were evaluated for a single type of activity (Farnsworth and Morris 1976). In addition, these plants were tested only against a particular set of cancer screens. In its new program initiated in 1986, NCI is testing natural products against a revised set of disease-oriented screens (Suffness, Newman, and Snader 1989). Hence, it is possible to conclude that owing to improvements in NCI's screening technology the original 35,000 species of plants are once again uninvestigated sources of anticancer compounds.

Improvements in screening technology and the development of new screens clearly extend the potential applications of the chemical diversity resident in natural products. New screens are a response not only to scientific and technological advances in isolating disease targets but also to the continued evolution of diseases. Increasing levels of disease resistance to commonly used drugs is of particular concern in the case of tuberculosis, pneumonia, meningitis, and other infectious diseases. The scourge of new and evolving diseases affects both the developed and the developing world. AIDS is a global epidemic, while resistance to traditional malarial drugs plagues the tropics. In the United States, population shifts to outer-edge suburbs and rural areas combined with increasing deer and tick populations have led to increasing dangers from Lyme disease (*U.S. News and World Report* 1992).

Thus the sheer scale of the resource—on the order of 10 to 100 million species—and the continuing evolution of screens, screening technologies, and disease targets implies that biodiversity will never be fully explored or exploited for its pharmaceutical potential. This suggests that the chemical properties of biodiversity represent a potentially limitless (relative to demand) renewable resource pool for use in the development of new pharmaceuticals. The real threat to this resource is on the supply side—the competing uses of land and natural habitat and the failure to protect areas rich in biodiversity, particularly in the developing world.

Pharmaceutical prospecting—the process of generating new pharmaceuticals from natural products—begins with biodiversity and ends with the production of a marketable drug. A number of activities are involved in this process, including:

- protection of biodiversity
- collection and identification of biotic samples
- extraction and screening of biotic samples
- isolation and structural determination of lead compounds
- additional preclinical research including laboratory and animal testing
- clinical research
- development of mass-production techniques for marketable compounds

Pharmaceutical prospecting does not necessarily proceed in a linear, stepwise fashion as outlined above. However, the process generally involves adding information to the raw material of biodiversity and its subsequent forms.

In economic terms pharmaceutical prospecting activities can be segregated according to three major types of investment:

1. investment in protection of biodiversity
2. investment in collection and identification of biotic samples and
3. investment in pharmaceutical R & D

The economic outputs of these investments are

- the raw material for pharmaceutical prospecting—biodiversity
- species information and the processed product—biotic samples

- information about a species's pharmaceutical properties and the final product—a marketable compound.

In the remainder of the paper I focus on the principal economic ingredients of pharmaceutical prospecting—biodiversity and species information.

Capturing the Value of Pharmaceutical Prospecting

An initial analysis of the economic characteristics of biodiversity and species information reveals obstacles that impede society's ability to obtain an optimal level of investment in the production of these goods. I then discuss evolving and potential market and policy solutions to these incentive problems, which may assist developing countries in capturing the value of pharmaceutical prospecting.

THE PROTECTION OF BIODIVERSITY

The protection, or maintenance, of biodiversity must be included in an economic analysis of pharmaceutical prospecting because the supply of this raw material input involves a significant social cost. The social costs of protecting biodiversity are the direct costs of protection and the opportunity cost of allocating land to the production of biodiversity. Because economically profitable alternative land uses may exist for lands currently functioning as reservoirs of tropical biodiversity, it is important that the production of biodiversity be capable of generating real economic benefits. Otherwise, little economic incentive exists for society to protect biodiversity.

The use of the raw material input in pharmaceutical prospecting may involve three different interventions at the level of the biological resource itself:

- initial collection for identification to the species level
- further collection for further research and development
- "mass" collection or cultivation if a marketable drug results

Depending on the case, only the first or second collections may be required. But all three interventions may be necessary if, as Balandrin et al. (1985) suggest, most natural product leads are secondary metabolites. From a technical perspective secondary metabolites will be difficult—and therefore costly—to synthesize. Collection of microbial species in the form of a single environmental sample typically yields enough starter material for researchers to develop methods for culturing species that show promise in early screens. Prospecting with plants, on the other hand, will usually involve all three interventions.

For the initial collection of biotic samples the raw material input of biodiversity is generally a nonrival resource. Collection by one individual rarely impedes the ability of another potential consumer to collect the same species. However, in the case of endangered species, species of limited size, or species making it through to further stages of testing and development, biodiversity may prove to be rival owing to the effects of congestion on the resource. The intensity of collection activities relative to the prevalence of the species may cause the quantity or quality of the remaining stock to be degraded to the point where it impairs the ability of another collector to gather the same species. Rivalness in the later stages of pharmaceutical prospecting may imply absolute limits on the successful development of promising new compounds and raises concerns regarding the extinction of such species. I limit the discussion to the initial provision of the nonrival raw material input.

Nonintensive collection of biotic samples from public wildlands in developing countries is not subject to much in the way of government restriction or control. Collecting permits are required in some countries; fees payable to public authorities expressly for the privilege of collection are virtually unheard of. The difficulty and cost of asserting exclusivity to biological resources have left public authorities with little effective control over access to biodiversity. In this context, biodiversity is a nonexclusive, as well as nonrival resource, and fits the definition of a public good. As a result, biodiversity is often left in a state of open access and is freely collected by all comers—biodiversity is treated as a free good by collectors. It is, therefore, extremely difficult for the state or an individual, firm, or other societal group to capture the value of pharmaceutical prospecting that is attributable to biodiversity itself. The outcome of this market failure is that the actual returns to maintaining biodiversity are less than the social returns. Given these conditions, pharmaceutical prospecting provides no incentive for continued investment in the protection of biodiversity, alternative land uses appear more favorable, and land will be taken out of the production of biodiversity.

SPECIES INFORMATION: COLLECTION AND IDENTIFICATION OF BIOTIC SAMPLES

In producing biotic samples for use in pharmaceutical R & D, a number of different types of information about species may be generated. This information often guides the selection of species for screening and includes:

- collection information—date, location, site conditions, etc.
- taxonomic classification of the organism
- ecological data indicating biochemical activity
- ethnobotanical information about traditional medicinal uses of plants
- reports of biochemical activity for a given species, genus, or family

The rest of the paper focuses on the task of generating species information in collection and taxonomic identification activities, which are essential inputs in pharmaceutical prospecting.

Information, or knowledge, of all kinds is nonrival—consumption of knowledge (learning) does not reduce the opportunity of the next consumer to learn the same information. Species information—whether taxonomic, ecological, ethno-botanical, or otherwise—is no exception. However, the ability of a potential consumer to learn or acquire a particular set of information does depend on the exclusivity accorded to

- the knowledge already gained by another consumer
- the raw material or raw data behind the knowledge
- the finished product generated by the application of the knowledge

In the latter two cases, a lack of exclusivity may, respectively, enable a potential consumer to reinvent the wheel or reverse engineer nonrival information.

Access to species information—the taxonomic classification and details regarding the collecting—and to the physical specimen itself is typically kept confidential by the collector and the buyer of biotic samples. Collectors of biotic materials are competing for market share and are unlikely to share species information with other collectors. In addition, pharmaceutical companies may request or require that collectors keep descriptions of collected species confidential. Collectors of biotic samples are, therefore, certain to exert exclusivity over the species information and physical specimens they collect. In addition, pharmaceutical companies are likely to restrict access to biotic samples and their associated information while they are under investigation. It thus becomes practically impossible for competing collectors to reverse engineer taxonomic information or biotic samples.

In sum, market failure is not an inescapable result of the nonrivalness of collection and taxonomic information. Because of the exclusivity exerted over both the information and the associated biotic samples, competitors do not necessarily generate a cost advantage by reinventing the wheel, and reverse engineering of biotic samples becomes impossible. Commercial collectors operate in a competitive end-use market and are able to appropriate the profit, or producer surplus, generated by their investment in species information.

The implicit assumption of the preceding discussion is that collectors are generating species information on their own. However, collectors often rely on existing natural history museums or botanic gardens for a number of services—which are often received free of charge. These taxonomic inputs are often an important element in the production of biotic samples. Market failure in this input, or factor, market may lead to a reduced incentive to invest in the broader base of taxonomic knowledge itself.

In the case of known species, commercial collectors may use existing reference collections to gather data on collection sites or to confirm the identification of a specimen already collected. In the case of species that are not held in local collections or that are outside the area of expertise of a collector, the collector may actually submit a sample to one of the large public institutions in the North (or South) that has the taxonomic expertise necessary to make an identification.

It is the investment of such institutions in developing the expertise of their staff, the physical collections, and the information contained in collections and data bases that goes unrewarded by pharmaceutical prospecting. These inputs make an important contribution to the commercial endeavor of producing biotic samples for sale to the pharmaceutical industry. Whether this unpaid social cost is interpreted as an external factor of production that does not enter the market calculus or as an implicit government subsidy (since most collection facilities are funded by public bodies) is not important. The point is that carrying out such activities for free is a drain on already scarce taxonomic resources.

In sum, collectors may be able to capture the full value of their investment in information generation by competing in the market for biotic samples, but there is a hidden social cost that goes unpaid. The market in biotic samples, thus, fails to provide the requisite incentive to invest in the generation of the larger body of taxonomic knowledge that is essential to pharmaceutical prospecting. In addition, the exchange of biotic samples between collectors and pharmaceutical companies rarely includes specific requirements for sharing benefits with biodiversity protection per se. Such arrangements, therefore, do not actually enable organizations directly involved in biodiversity protection to "capture" a fair share of biodiversity's pharmaceutical value.

Species Information: Pharmaceutical R & D

The objective of pharmaceutical R & D into natural products is to generate the requisite amount of knowledge about a species and its chemical constituents to ascertain whether any of these compounds has potential as a marketable drug. As with species information generated during the collection stage, this information is nonrival. In general, those engaging in pharmaceutical R & D guard the information they generate very closely. Despite the assertion of exclusivity over this information, other potential consumers of this knowledge are—in theory—still able to reinvent the wheel or reverse engineer the information through access to the original raw material or the final product.

As a result, a second pharmaceutical company could reproduce a drug developed by another company and corner the market by selling the drug at a lower price than its competitor. The second company could sell at a lower price because, presumably, it would have lower R & D costs to recoup from its product sales by virtue of having clues as to what information to generate. In this fashion, the nonrival nature of the information derived in pharmaceutical R & D conspires to reduce the returns to investments in drug innovation, leading to a less than optimal rate of drug innovation and provision of pharmaceutical products.

In the case of drugs derived from natural products the practical difficulty of generating identical information leading to the development of the same drug should not be understated. Reinventing the wheel involves retracing a number of complex steps including collection of the same species and development of comparable screens that search for the same disease target. It is unclear how such a process would generate a significant cost advantage for a potential competitor. Reverse engineering involves working backward from the marketed drug to the structural determination of the chemical compound. As noted earlier, however, naturally produced compounds are often difficult to commercially synthesize. If this is the case, then reverse engineering would require a company to work backward from a chemical compound to the original and unknown species. The ability to exclude others from the taxonomic and collection information generated earlier in the prospecting process would make this a difficult feat—akin to looking for a needle in a haystack.

POLICY ISSUES

Policy solutions to these incentives problems should enable individuals, firms, communal groups, institutions, or governments in developing countries to capture an appropriate portion of the value of pharmaceutical prospecting. In the case of biodiversity this value should be determined by the demand for the raw material and the supply costs of biodiversity protection. In the case of species information the value should reflect the demand for the innovative end product, the marginal production costs of this end product, and the costs of the investment made in information generation.

In order to resolve the incentives problem posed by the nonrivalness of information produced in pharmaceutical R & D, most developed countries have legislated intellectual property rights that provide patent protection for novel compounds. In obtaining a patent, a company gives up its exclusivity over the information it has generated in return for a legal guarantee of exclusive rights (over a set time period) to sell the product itself. Thus a company will reap monopoly profits from its investment in R & D if any of its lead compounds should prove to be of commercial value.

As described above, difficulties in reinventing the wheel and reverse engineering information reduce the extent of the incentives problem encountered in pharmaceutical prospecting relative to that found in the case of R & D based on compounds fabricated in the laboratory. Patenting might, therefore, be less important in the case of pharmaceutical prospecting. It is unlikely, however, that this situation would justify a separate policy approach for natural-product-derived pharmaceuticals—particularly as advances in basic science and technology may render natural product compounds more amenable to commercial synthesis.

Solutions to the incentives problem posed by the nonrival and nonexclusive characteristics of biodiversity and species information—generated during collection and identification of biotic samples—involve either government intervention to provide these public goods or the development of means to enable the private appropriation of their value. Although public funding of biodiversity protection and the generation of species information has a long tradition, both budgetary limitations and the increasing commercialization of biodiversity suggest that methods for privatizing these activities are worth exploring. Put another way, since pharmaceutical companies are receiving monopoly profits from materials originating in biodiversity-rich developing countries, these countries must have some claim on a share of these profits.

In order to capture the value of biodiversity—the raw material in pharmaceutical prospecting—developing countries are beginning to develop their capacity to exclude potential collectors from public wildlands. Such exclusion might involve some combination of the institution and enforcement of legal property rights over species found in public wildlands or effective managerial control over these wildlands. If it is possible to exclude potential consumers from access to biodiversity—or some subset of species—effective control over the benefits of the resource may be assured through the institution of a system for charging potential collectors for access to the resource.

Unlike the case with information, nonrivalness of species means little if access is not possible. Information may be recreated by reinventing the wheel or reverse engineering, but species cannot be regenerated if access is not permitted. The potential stumbling block to this approach is the existence of pantropical species. Since many species are not endemic to a single country, it may prove difficult for a country to effectively exclude a collector from access to a particular species (known or unknown) that is found within its borders.

A second method of capturing the value of biodiversity protection and species information is the establishment of contracts with biodiversity brokers or pharmaceutical companies that guarantee such buyers exclusivity over the biotic samples for a limited period of time. Granting exclusivity over the sample gives users only a degree of exclusivity over the resource itself. Nonetheless, existing contractual arrangements indicate that this is sufficient to allow suppliers to receive royalties that appear to be a reasonable compensation for the "raw material" and "information" components of biotic samples (Aylward 1993). While this approach may allow local collectors in developing countries to capture biodiversity's pharmaceutical value it does not mean that protection activities will themselves be rewarded. Until developing countries are capable of asserting property rights over biodiversity (as discussed above) there is likely to be little incentive for private collectors to share royalty rights with those involved in biodiversity protection.

Regarding the market failure that arises in the provision of taxonomic information—which is essentially a free good—one solution would be for taxonomists to begin charging fees for their services (Townes 1992). These fees should reflect not only the costs of generating biotic samples but also the costs of identification (Townes 1992). As mentioned above, classification work that is farmed out to other specialists is carried out for free, and the cost of these activities is rarely represented in taxonomists' budgets and is not charged to third parties who purchase biotic samples, such as pharmaceutical companies. Charging fees would still permit the circulation of information; however, the generation of such information would be priced in an open and competitive market. Clearly, such an innovation might take time to implement given current attitudes and methods of doing business in the systematics profession.

Collectors of biotic samples may also enter directly into contracts that access future monopoly profits of successful products or provide nonmonetary benefits. Laird (1992) provides a detailed description of a number of emerging contractual arrangements between pharmaceutical companies and the suppliers of biotic samples. As these contracts are negotiated directly with pharmaceutical companies the ability of a developing country to invest in the development of the human resources necessary for collection and identification of species will allow a country to gain a large share of the returns from pharmaceutical prospecting.

In a similar vein, contractual arrangements or vertically integrated operations in which the initial stages of pharmaceutical R & D are performed in-country provide additional opportunities to capture more of the value of pharmaceutical prospecting. Developing countries wishing to capture a larger share of the value generated by pharmaceutical prospecting should, therefore, consider investing in developing internal capabilities in pharmaceutical R & D or attracting external investment by existing pharmaceutical companies.

Finally, there may be synergies between efforts made at different stages in the pharmaceutical-prospecting process. The ability on the part of a developing country to control access to its biodiversity might also limit any problem posed by the nonrivalness of species information generated during collection and identification. Collectors that are guaranteed exclusive access to particular species are in a much better contractual negotiating position. It may also be the case that by investing in the generation of species information and striking contracts with pharmaceutical companies, a developing country may be able to capture the value attributable to its biodiversity without the need to engage in developing potentially costly mechanisms of exclusion.

In sum, there may be a number of ways that a developing country can try to capture the value of pharmaceutical prospecting. Drawing the distinction between the three stages in pharmaceutical prospecting suggests that the value of conservation does not lie simply in protecting, or saving, biodiversity. Throughout the entire process of pharmaceutical prospecting, information—and consequently value—is being added to the species under investigation. If a developing country wants to appropriate a large share of the value added from pharmaceutical prospecting it must invest—or encourage outsiders to invest—in the generation of species information within the country.

Recognition of the distinction between biodiversity and species information suggests that the processes of getting to know and sustainably use biodiversity are rewarding endeavors of economic merit in their own right. Indeed, as described elsewhere, investments in biodiversity protection and species information are likely to be complementary activities (Aylward and Barbier 1992). Thus, if conservation of biodiversity is to be a meaningful concept, and sustainable over the longer term, it must be understood as a process involving the complementary steps of "saving, knowing, and sustainably using" biodiversity (Janzen 1990; WRI 1992).

ACKNOWLEDGMENTS

This article draws upon research undertaken by the International Institute for Environment and Development in collaboration with Costa Rica's National Biodiversity Institute and the Tropical Science Center. Support for the study, "The Economic Value of Species Information and Its Role in Biodiversity Conservation: Case Studies of Costa Rica's National Biodiversity Institute and Pharmaceutical Prospecting," came from the Swedish International Development Authority. I am grateful to comments by Edward B. Barbier, Joshua Bishop, Jo Burgess, and David Simpson on earlier versions of this paper.

REFERENCES

Aylward, B. 1993. *The Economic Value of Pharmaceutical Prospecting and Its Role in Biodiversity Conservation.* LEEC Discussion Paper Series 93–05. London: International Institute for Environment and Development.

Aylward, B. and E. B. Barbier. 1992. *What Is Biodiversity Worth to a Developing Country? Capturing the Pharmaceutical Value of Species Information.* LEEC Discussion Paper Series 92–05. London: International Institute for Environment and Development.

Balandrin, M., J. Klocke, E. Wurtele, and W. Bollinger. 1985. "Natural Plant Chemicals: Sources of Industrial and Medicinal Materials." *Science* 288:1154.

Douros, J. and M. Suffness. 1980. "The National Cancer Institute's Natural Products Antineoplastic Development Program." In S. K. Carter and Y. Sakurai, eds., *Recent Results in Cancer Research* 70:21–44. Berlin: Springer-Verlag.

Farnsworth, N. and R. Morris. 1976. "Higher Plants—the Sleeping Giant of Drug Development." *American Journal of Pharmacy* 148 (2):46–52.

Janzen, D. 1990. "A South-North Perspective on Science in the Management, Use, and Economic Development of Biodiversity." Paper prepared for the International Conference on Conservation of Genetic Resources for Sustainable Development, Roros, Norway, September 10–14.

Laird, S. 1992. "The Commercialization of Biological Samples: Contracts for the Prospecting of Biodiversity." Draft paper prepared by the Periwinkle Project of the Rainforest Alliance, New York.

Suffness, M., D. J. Newman, and K. Snader. 1989. "Discovery and Development of Antineoplastic Agents from Natural Sources." In *Bioorganic Marine Chemistry* 3:131–68. Berlin: Springer-Verlag.

Townes, H. K. 1992. "Charging Fees for Taxonomic Services." *Association of Systematics Collections Newsletter* 20 (4):129–31.

U.S. News and World Report. 1992. "The Troubling Ghosts of Scourges Past" (October 26), pp. 70–71.

World Resource Institute (WRI). 1992. *Global Biodiversity Strategy.* Washington, D.C.: WRI.

PART TWO

Country and Regional Programs in Medicinal Plant Research and Health Care

16

Resource Utilization and Conservation of Biodiversity in Africa

Maurice M. Iwu

THE sound management of biological resources is an essential requirement for economic development. When used in a sustainable manner natural resources can be a feasible tool for social and economic development. Although a nexus between sustainable use of natural resources, conservation of biodiversity, and economic development is generally recognized, no proper articulation or agreement on a suitable framework for addressing this connectivity has been made. Another type of relationship also exists between advances in biotechnology and the valuation, depreciation, and conservation of the natural resource base of developing countries. The linkage between developments in biotechnology and biodiversity conservation may in fact prove to be the most important determinant factor in understanding the dynamics of biodiversity loss and the future of the tropical ecosystem.

To provide an operational mechanism for an integrated approach to conservation of biological diversity and economic development, some African scientists, nongovernmental organizations, and the private sector established a consortium, the Biotech Development Agency (BDA). We have explored these linkages, analyzed their implications for Africa's future development, and assessed their effects on the conservation of biodiversity. This contribution will focus primarily on two case studies based on a program in Nigeria. To adequately discuss the activities of our program, I shall outline some of the fundamental frameworks that formed the basis of most of our decisions. I shall briefly summarize the state of the environmental problems in Africa and shall also use some examples to illustrate our view that the present environmental problems were caused essentially by inappropriate development strategies of the past. The paper also addresses the conflicts in perceptions and global economic relationship that, from our viewpoint, are fundamental issues to be dealt with in any program to preserve biodiversity.

In sub-Sahara Africa, environmental crisis presents a complex economic and social problem of dimensions unlike those seen anywhere else in the world. The problem has many aspects, some interrelated, others caused or worsened by ill-conceived solutions, with a net result that there is now an accelerated depletion of Africa's natural resources with a concomitant deterioration of living standards.

The need to conserve biological diversity is perhaps of utmost importance in Africa where the lives of humans are intricately linked to the environment in a symbiotic relationship in which each species cannot survive without the essential contributions from the whole. As has been pointed out by Vandana Shiva, bio-diversity erosion starts a chain reaction. The disappearance of a species is related to the extinction of innumerable other species and in most cases threatens the life-support systems and livelihoods of millions of people in Third World countries (Shiva 1992).

African tradition had a balanced relationship among nature, culture, and religion that favored the judicious use of natural resources. Humans were part of the environment and were content with adaptive existence rather than conquest of their habitat. The totems, taboos, and other prohibitions were essential for the protection of various exotic species of plants and animals. Certain springs and waterways were considered sacred and were protected from human activities. Protection was also accorded to some forests, caves, and burial grounds.

A common assumption is that most of the taboos and restrictions were based on the belief in magic and the primitive respect for the unknown. Nothing can be further from the truth. While it is correct that some of the taboos had religious significance, most of the proscriptions were based on the collective decision of the elders, who were respected for their accumulated wisdom and knowledge. If a river is the only source of drinking water for the village, for example, it was not only valued for its water but also treated with respect for its spirit, its life. A strong sense of communal responsibility demanded the subjugation of individual needs to those of the larger group. Every life was treated with respect. To an African, every object has an in-dwelling spirit that forms part of a cosmic relationship with the entire community, and this linkage was considered too fragile to be perturbed by overconsumption.

From an African viewpoint, the greatest threat to the protection of biodiversity is the biphasic issue of poverty and affluence. Separately and through their inter-action both conditions will continue to cause rapid depletion of biological diversity. Poverty and the destruction of the environment are readily traceable to poor management of global resources and poor adaptation to a changed environment.

While some general agreement exists in regard to what causes loss of biological diversity, serious differences appear in the conception of the motivating factors behind depletion of biological diversity. Disagreement also arises about the most appropriate methods for solving global environmental problems. Conservation programs are directed to isolated forest wilderness rather than to habitats that are able to sustain diverse species, including human, over a long time without serious environmental damage.

For people living in the so-called Third World countries, it is imperative that any genuine conservation strategy be linked to the related issues of economic development.

The tropical environment is not exactly the perfect human habitat being made out by social activists. Preservation of biodiversity also includes the conservation of malaria, leishmaniasis, onchocerciasis, trypanosomiasis, and a wide range of disease-causing zoonotic parasites. We must enhance the competitive advantage of rural Africans in their natural habitat.

From our perspective the primary causes of destruction of biological diversity in Africa include the following:

1. Habitat destruction due to pressure on land to accommodate increased in-dustrial demand for cheap tropical plants and the cultivation of cash crops in place of subsistence farming.
2. Declining market value for major crops—hence, increased pressure on land to produce greater quantity to achieve previous level of income.
3. Social impact of previous policies on technological capability of indigenous staff.
4. Structural imbalance in the present system of international trade and patent laws.
5. Introduction of homogenous system of agriculture and the replacement of diverse plant species and land races with monocultures. In some cases these monocultures are grown only for biomass or industrial raw materials and their products are incapable of replicating themselves owing to genetic ma-nipulation.
6. The change in traditional reverence and respect for women owing to the in-fluence of imported religions and culture, which have in turn deprived tra-ditional societies of the leadership, vision, and valor associated with that gender.

Dimension of the African Environmental Situation

Africa is confronted with several environmental problems, most of which are traceable to the dynamics of tropical ecology and to the increased demand for agricultural products as industrial feedstock for developed nations at prices de-termined by so-called market forces. In attempts apparently aimed at improving agricultural production in Africa, several well-meaning organizations have com-pounded the situation by importing into Africa inappropriate models of agricul-ture used in ecologically different areas of the world. The result of these experi-ments has been an unmitigated disaster of such magnitude that the human suffering caused by these agencies has no parallel in human history. In a recent paper presented in Ota, Nigeria, the former World Bank president, Robert McNamara (1991), summed up the situation thus:

A child born today in Sub-Saharan Africa faces a bleak set of statistics. The odds are one in 10 that he or she will not live more than one year; the odds are one in 20 that the child's mother will die giving birth. The child born today in Sub-Saharan Africa can expect to live for only 51 years—26 years less than children in the high-income countries and 12 years less than in India and China. The newborn African child enters a world in which one person in five does not receive [enough] food to lead a productive, healthy life. There is only one doctor for every 24,000 people, compared with one for every 470 people in the high-income countries.

The puzzle is that no one seems to understand the problem, and the following sobering reflections of a former World Bank president holds true even today.

> We [the World Bank], along with other donors have failed in Africa. We have not understood the problems, we have not identified the priorities, we have not always designed our projects to fit the agroclimatic conditions of Africa and the social, cultural and political frameworks of Africa. . . . We and everybody else are still unclear about what can be done in agriculture in Africa. (Stern 1984)

The saddest aspect of the situation is that the frustration caused by the inability to understand the African situation has increasingly driven many critics to the desperate situation of blaming the victims of failed attempts to eradicate poverty in Africa.

Many eloquent solutions have been formulated; Africa has been a fertile testing ground for many untested hypotheses. Often brilliant, but faulty, rationalizations and sweeping generalizations have been made in order to provide excuses for the unexpected failures, and attempts have been made to justify the collective global mistake. The population pressure, for example, has often been given as an alibi for almost every conceivable problem in Africa. The population bogey has been blamed for the present poverty in the continent, for the erosion of the top soil, and for the expansion of the Sahara desert.

The common refrain reads thus: "This pressure of people, combined with traditional practices, is causing environmental degradation at an alarming pace—desertification, soil erosion, destruction of vegetable cover, and biodiversity loss."

With no reliable census figures, one is at a loss as to the origin of the base data for the alarming population projections. Population estimates made by armchair pundits outside the continent are being recycled so often that they have become accepted as actual figures. The population of Nigeria, for example, has variously been stated to be between 100 to 120 million by international organizations. These figures were supposedly based on the 1965 census, without taking into consideration the effect of the 1968–70 civil war and the actual decline in population growth in the middle-income, educated urban dwellers. A 1992 census, monitored by independent demographers, returned a population of less than 90 million. Africa remains the only continent in the world whose population pressure has not been moderated by mass emigration to lesser populated continents. The population density of Europe lessened during the last 100 years, not by adherence to birth control measures, but largely by the availability of lands in the Americas and Australia for resettlement of Europeans and by changes in European attitudes toward childbearing as a consequence of the economic boom that followed industrialization.

The point being made here is that while birth control and family planning are very important factors in solving the problem of global poverty, the issue is far more complex than the experts are prepared to acknowledge. Projections made solely on static models have failed woefully to address the African environment problem, since the variables used in such studies are considered as changes across space rather than as time-determinant factors. This approach has resulted in a situation where indigenous populations are increasingly viewed as part of the problem rather than as the key to the solution. Poverty and the destruction of the environment are two sad symptoms of the same disease; they are products of the structural imbalance in our present system of international trade, in which farmers and rural dwellers are poor because they receive unfair prices for their commodity and labor. They in turn are forced to increase their agricultural production in order to maintain their share of the commodity market and earn needed foreign exchange. The resultant effect is habitat loss (of more than 70% in Africa, see table 16.1) and a high rate of deforestation.

It should be a matter of great concern to all of us that since 1900, the number of people inhabiting the earth has multiplied more than three times. But the world economy expanded twenty times within the same period. The industrial produc-

TABLE **16.1**   *Wildlife Habitat Loss in West and Central Africa*

Country	Original Wildlife Habitat (1,000 ha.)	Amount Remaining (1,000 ha.)	Habitat Loss (%)
Benin	11,580	4,632	60
Burkina Faso	27,380	5,476	80
Burundi	2,570	359	86
Cameroon	46,940	19,245	59
Central African Republic	62,300	27,412	56
Chad	72,080	17,299	76
Congo	34,200	17,422	49
Cote d'Ivoire	31,800	6,678	79
Equatorial Guinea	2,500	920	63
Gabon	26,700	17,355	35
Gambia	1,130	124	89
Ghana	23,000	4,600	80
Guinea	24,590	7,377	70
Guinea Bissau	3,610	794	78
Liberia	11,140	1,448	87
Niger	56,600	12,780	77
Nigeria	91,980	22,995	75
Rwanda	2,510	326	87
Senegal	19,620	3,532	82
Sierra Leone	7,170	1,076	85

Source: IUCN/UNEP. 1986. Adapted from McNeely et al. 1990. *Conserving the World's Biological Diversity,* p. 46. IUCN, WRI, CI, WWF, and World Bank publication.

tion increased fifty times, with four-fifths of that increase occurring since 1950. The consumption of fossil fuels has grown by a factor of thirty (MacNeil 1990). The poverty, the inequities, and social instability that have become characteristic of the existing world order are therefore direct products of the system of distribution of global wealth, not the scarcity of resources.

Africa's share of the world market has fallen to about 50% of what it was in 1970. While the rest of the world seems to benefit from "liberalization" of international trade and improvements in the means of production, Africa has been harmed by these developments. The general feeling within the continent is that any meaningful solution to Africa's environment has to be developed from within the continent. As had been noted by Awori (1992): "Africa has had enough of unworkable development formulae and technical fixes hatched from outside. Enough of sustainable development sweet-talk from the North. . . . What the region requires is true and tangible resource support by way of substantial investment and development capital."

Some people even suggest that most biodiversity conservation programs are part of a plot hatched by scientists in developed countries so that the continent will remain forever underdeveloped. The contention is that history is being distorted and facts mangled to portray Africa as a miserable place where hope is elusive and that its problems are beyond solution. African policymakers are sensitive, therefore, to projects conceived outside the continent that, when they fail, may provide further ammunition for those who mock the continent for its environmental problems. For example, the U.S.-based weekly magazine *Time*, which in no small measure helped fan the embers of the ideological wars that contributed immensely to the refugee problems of the continent, wasted little time at the end of the Cold War to paint a miserable picture of the continent. Every imaginable ill, including "overpopulation, tribal conflict, drought, starvation, bureaucratic mismanagement and political corruption," was blamed for the crisis, but the magazine failed to mention even once that the continent was the arena for seventeen major wars during the so-called Cold War. According to *Time*'s Lance Morrow (1992): "Africa has a genius for extremes, for the beginning and the end. . . . Nowhere is there a continent more miserable. Africa . . . has begun to look like an immense illustration of chaos theory, . . . has turned into a battleground of contending dooms, . . . a vast continent in free fall." While Africa has its problems, articles such as the one by *Time* can only hurt by causing erosion of investors' confidence and capital flight—more so in this technology era when perceptions created by misinformation are often mistaken for reality. As the executive secretary of the Organization of African Unity, Salim A. Salim, stated at the International Public Relations Conference in Nairobi, this type of distortion and willingness to subordinate the truth and objectivity is often driven by the selfish motive to create sensational headlines, which in turn will help sell the papers and promote the career of the writer (Salim 1992). The twin problem of environmental degradation and poverty caused by unequal access to global resources poses the single greatest threat to world peace and stability.

Biotechnology and Product Substitution

The progress made by biotechnology and improved agriculture, rather than help alleviate the negative pressure on African biological resources, has worsened the situation by further depriving the continent of any competitive advantage it had in the world market of certain crops. I have chosen two major crops from Nigeria, oil palm and cocoa, to illustrate this. In 1970, Africa supplied about 78% of the world palm oil needs; by 1980 the share of the market had dropped to 40%, and by 1990, Africa has only a little less than 20% of the world market. The major cause of this shift is that researchers at Nigerian's Institute for Oil Palm Research had developed an improved variety of oil palm seeds, which was introduced into Malaysia. And the rest is history. Cocoa is another crop in which the African share in the world market has steadily declined since 1970. It is even more depressing to observe that improved seeds based on genetic materials derived from inputs from the whole global environment are not only patented by a few companies but also are sold at prices far beyond the financial means of most developing countries.

Another disturbing issue in the management of tropical resources is that studies in plant molecular biology in industrialized countries are targeted mainly on tropical crops. The results of these efforts have led to substitution of plant-based products with genetically engineered equivalents. These new products will ultimately rob millions of farmers in tropical countries of their livelihood. Laboratories in industrialized countries are presently engaged in the development of alternatives to natural flavorings, cooking oils, industrial oils, and nutrients. Both the EEC and OECD have expressed similar concerns on the possible negative impact of biotechnology on the economy of Third World countries, as shown in the following statements.

> Thanks to biotechnology it will gradually become possible to replace tropical agriculture commodities such as palm oil or manioc with products grown in the community and other industrialized countries. This could considerably upset agricultural commodity markets and spell disaster for third world countries dependent on them if nothing is done. (European commission, document Com (86) 550 final/2, 1986)

> Given the technological and industrial preponderance of OECD countries . . . there is strong evidence that developing countries, notably those heavily engaged in agriculture, will bear the brunt of trade impacts for a long time to come. (OECD, "Biotechnology: Economic and Wider Impacts," Paris: OECD, 1989, p. 81)

The substitution of vanilla with the tissue culture fermentation product, for example, will deprive the poor island country of Madagascar of a major export. A similar fate faces Nigeria, Ghana, and a host of other palm-producing countries if palm oil and its kernel oil are replaced with genetically altered rapeseed. The coastal towns in East and West Africa along with the Pacific islands of Vanuatu will confront an even harder problem when coconut oil is replaced with biotechnology products. In the case of Vanuatu the replacement of coconut oil will result in a loss of 80% of that poor country's export earnings. East African pyrethrum farmers and processors will also give up their source of livelihood as soon as the genetically engineered microbes can produce enough of this natural insecticide. These are urgent issues.

Biotechnology could be beneficial to the farmers in tropical countries since it generates an improved variety of seeds. But through the existing mechanism of international trade, such as the IMF, African labor and resources are undervalued so much that the farmers in rural villages are unlikely to be able to afford the cost of improved seed variety. From our perspective, the loss of biological diversity will continue, even at increased rate, unless the problem of resource management in the tropics is considered seriously.

In the context of the reality of these predicaments we have initiated some programs to address African environmental problems within the framework of economic development. This paper briefly discusses two case studies of conservation projects linked to economic development. I have outlined some of our observations in the design and implementation of the program that may have implications for similar projects elsewhere. The focus is Africa, a continent that has remained a mystery to many people. Our operational base is presently limited to Nigeria.

Salvage Ethnography Project

In 1982, the Institute of African Studies, the Faculty of Arts, and the Department of Pharmacognosy, all of the University of Nigeria, Nsukka, initiated a salvage ethnography project (SEP) aimed at providing documentation on the Nka-na-Nzere of the Igbo people of southeastern Nigeria. Nka-na-Nzere does not have an equivalent phrase in English but a rough translation is "a documentation of the art and norms of the Igbo people." Art in this context included the representative and creative arts, as well as the symbolic components, or what in Western thought is grouped as arts, science, and technology. The project was executed with the help of undergraduate students who were trained in field data collection and sent to their villages to gather base data on the human interaction with the environment, among other areas of inquiry. One of the results of the project is that in nearly all the cases of taboos and other forms of restrictions, species conservation was a major factor in the impositions.

The project also allowed us the opportunity to develop a framework for the interdisciplinary collaboration that was essential for the objectives we had set for ourselves. Under the general direction of the late Dr. Donatus Nwoga, a professor of English and folk Igbo literature, the project collected data on proverbs, music, oral history, ethnobotany, indigenous biotechnology, ethnomedicine, literature, foods, customs, visual arts, and other aspects of life in Igbo land.

Among the important lessons learned from that project is that meaningful community participation was essential for the success of any project. Organizational innovations were formulated to integrate efforts of the various disciplines involved in the program and also to circumvent the traditional bureaucracy and crippling compartmentalization of the administrative structures in academic institutions.

One major handicap was that we had no access to computers at that time, and this resulted in poor data handling and loss of some of the materials we had collected. We also underestimated the magnitude and cost of the project and were therefore unable to process most of the materials we had collected. We had many cassette tapes that were not transcribed, films that were not developed, and artifacts we could not preserve.

Even with the meager budget, the project was very successful. It has initiated a process that may produce some tangible results in the future. The following are some of the observable gains from the study.

1. Two data bases were established, one by Prof. Nwoga on Igbo proverbs and another on Igbo medicinal and culinary plants started by me. The medicinal and culinary plants data base included entries on the botanical identification, medicinal uses, local names, nutritional use, methods of processing for food and medicine, chemical constituents, and reported pharmacological activities and toxicity profile.
2. A written form of communication, not similar to Nsibidi, was discovered during the project period. A follow-up project was initiated by Prof. Nwoga in association with a medium, Mazi Aneke, to study this script by using modern linguistics methods.
3. The project rekindled interest in traditional knowledge in the university, which led to the introduction of courses in indigenous arts and science. In the Faculty of Pharmacy, a mandatory course in African traditional medicine was offered as a part of the pharmacy undergraduate training. This requirement has since become integrated into the training programs of all the schools of pharmacy in the country.
4. The SEP has generated several follow-up interdisciplinary research projects in many faculties at the University of Nigeria, Nsukka, in which social scientists and biologist collaborate in a complementary manner.
5. It has also led to a critical reevaluation of the ethnobiological information as a method for the selection of medicinal plants as sources of biologically active compounds. In diseases that are well known to the medicine men, the correlation between traditional use and experimental biological activity is as high as 80%.

Biotechnology Development Agency (BDA)

The second project was based on the realization that the economic development of the country is directly linked to the state of its environment. A consortium was established by a group of scientists, nongovernmental agencies, and the private sector to articulate a program of resource management based on application of modern biological techniques.

Economic underdevelopment of Africa and the protection of the environment are recognized as two sides of the same coin. It was clear to us that a fundamental factor in the threat to the African biodiversity is the declining economic value of the environment-based resources. In a broad outline, the BDA program aims at the use of available human and material resources in Nigeria for the conservation of the biodiversity through establishment of extractive forestry research parks, initiation of village-based social forestry projects, and investigation into the uses of biological resources in the development of novel pharmaceuticals, cosmetics, and food additives. Private sector participation is encouraged in all aspects of BDA activity. Although BDA was conceptualized as a not-for-profit, nongovernmental institution, the program was designed to generate its own funds and sustain its activities through grants and, eventually, through royalties accruing from its patents and publications. Some of the projects are, however, designed as commercial ventures and are expected to be commercially feasible.

The major objectives of the cooperative program include:

- To collect, collate, and codify available information on the uses of African plants, with special reference to indigenous food crops, medicinal and aromatic plants, and industrial crops.
- To encourage basic research on the chemistry, biology, and industrial application of indigenous natural resources.
- To stimulate public awareness and concern about the vanishing resource base of tropical agriculture and to support the activities of public-interest groups that are working on these issues and foster cooperation and communication between them.
- To stimulate the activities and policies that lead to a better assessment of the new emerging technologies and highlight their implications for African natural resources.
- To initiate and encourage efforts for the conservation of biodiversity as a feasible tool and exploitable resource for sustainable economic development.
- To encourage the establishment of small-scale agroindustrial and marketing enterprises and of technologies in related industries. It is expected that such projects should not only tap the existing local markets but should also specifically establish overseas marketing outlets.

In order to realize these goals, some pilot projects have been initiated and several others are being formulated with scientists from Africa and non-Africans interested in the continent. A major aspect of this program is the KIBORD (Kates Institute of Bio-Organic Research and Development) project.

KIBORD Project

KIBORD is a private-sector initiative, which in collaboration with the Department of Pharmacognosy, University of Nigeria, Nsukka, has been investigating tropical African plants as possible raw materials for the cosmetics, pharmaceutical, and food flavor industries. The overall development objective is to increase the exploitation of indigenous raw materials and establish more efficient processing facilities to bring about the sustained development of the living standard of the people. The project will help to raise the hygienic standard of local populations, to increase and diversify the industrial production, and to develop new household and cosmetic products. Field studies have been carried out and research projects have already been undertaken by various Nigerian universities to evaluate the medicinal plants growing in Nigeria and their potential for industrial use.

The project has yielded some interesting results including plant isolates for the treatment of viral infections, two new antiparasitic agents, a greaseless body oil, an antiplaque and antihalitosis agent, two antifungal agents, and a substitute for hops used in beer brewing that possesses the advantage of protecting the liver against alcohol-induced cirrhosis.

The Phytotherapy Research Laboratory, at the University of Nigeria, Nsukka, has provided phytochemical support for this project and arranged for the screening of selected plant extracts and isolates through research collaborations with government and private laboratories in the United States, Italy, and England. It is a major policy of the program that plants have to be carefully selected and cultivation has to be initiated before any pilot plant is started, and accordingly a base farm has already been started for three of the selected plants. A second base farm is planned in the next planting season in collaboration with an Italian firm for the cultivation of a plant that yields an experimental drug used for the treatment of Alzheimer's disease. A central processing facility and laboratory is proposed as a core element of this project. A project formulation framework has already been prepared and approved by the relevant national authorities. Sources of funding are presently being explored to enable work to start on this facility, which will be capable of providing assistance and technical training for medium-level staff not only in Nigeria but also throughout the Economic Community of West African States (ECOWAS) subregion.

Certain determinant factors were identified in the KIBORD project and include:

- Availability of a critical mass of scientists trained in various aspects of plant science, processing engineering, and formulation science
- Presence of local demand for the anticipated products
- Conservation of efforts by use of existing institutions and facilities
- Participation of the private sector and nongovernmental organizations, which guarantees minimal governmental interference

Other Projects Planned Under the BDA Program

INFORMATION MANAGEMENT

Access to relevant information on previous projects on tropical plant utilization and conservation was considered as one of the most important aspects of the program. An off-line data base is being maintained on the species of interest. Our list presently has more than 1,000 entries of major medicinal and aromatic plants used in the entire continent (Iwu 1993). We also have access through our collaborators to commercial natural products data bases in the United States. The documentation of medicinal uses of African plants is becoming increasingly urgent because of the rapid loss of the natural habitat for some of these plants due to anthropogenic activities. The continent is estimated to have about 216,634,000 ha. of closed forest areas and with a calculated annual loss of about 1% due to deforestation, many of the medicinal plants and other genetic materials become extinct before they are even documented. Africa has one of the highest rates of deforestation in the world; for example, Cote d'Ivoire and Nigeria have 6.5% and 5.0% deforestation per year (table 16.2), respectively, as against a global rate of 0.6%. Habitat conversion threatens not only the loss of plant resources but also traditional community life, cultural diversity, and the accompanying knowledge of the medicinal value of several endemic species. A majority of the plants found in Africa are endemic to that continent, the Republic of Malagasy having the highest rate of endemism (82%).

TABLE 16.2 *Estimates of Forest Areas and Deforestation Rates in Selected African Countries*

Country	Closed Forest Area (1,000 ha.)	Percent Deforested per Year
Benin	47	2.6
Burundi	26	2.7
Cameroon	17,920	0.4
Central African Republic	3,590	0.2
Congo	21,340	0.1
Cote d'Ivoire	4,458	6.5
Equatorial Guinea	1,295	0.2
Gabon	20,500	0.1
Ghana	1,718	1.3
Guinea	2,050	1.8
Guinea Bissau	660	2.6
Liberia	2,000	2.3
Kenya	1,105	1.7
Nigeria	5,950	5.0
Zaire	105,750	0.2

Source: FAO. 1981. Adapted from McNeely et al. 1990. *Conserving the World's Biological Diversity,* p. 44. IUCN, WRI, CI, WWF, and World Bank publication.

SOCIAL FORESTRY PROJECTS

As part of our second objective, it is planned that communities will be assisted in cultivating tree crops for food, fuel wood, and as barriers in farms to check erosion and land degradation. Although no such project has been initiated to date on a commercial scale, a pilot project has been formulated with active participation of rural dwellers, and we hope to recommend it as a model for other interested parties.

We have selected the following plants as possible species for cultivation by villagers in the main vegetation zones of the country (see map, fig. 16.1).

MANGROVE SWAMPS
Anthocleista vogelii Planch
Carapa procera DC.
Crudia klainei Pierre ex De Wild.
Uapaca guinensis Muell. Arg.

RAIN FOREST
Albizia lebbeck Benth.
Anogeissus leiocarpus (DC.) Guill. & Perr.
Borassus aethiopum Mart.
Butyrospermum parkii (G. Don) Kotschy
Casuarina equisetifolia Forst.
Dalbergia heudelotti Stapf.
Dracaena mannii Baker
Erythrina milbraedii Harms.
Garcinia kola Heckel
Irvingia gabonensis Baill
Physostigma venenosum Balfour
Picralima nitida (Stapf.) Th. & H. Dur
Tamarindus indica Linn.
Zanthoxylum zanthoxyloides Waterman

RELIC RAIN FOREST
Adansonia digitata Linn.
Azadirachta indica A. Juss.
Bauhinia purpurea Linn.
Cassia alata Linn.
Eucalyptus citrioda Hook
Ficus capensis Thunb.
Salvadora persica Linn.

GUINEA SAVANNA
Acacia spp. L.
Anacardium occidentale Linn.
Annona senegalensis Pers.

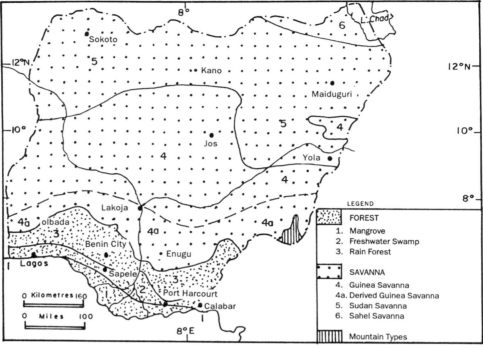

FIGURE 16.1 Nigeria: ecological zones.

Euphorbia balsamifera Ait.
Parkia biglobosa Benth.
Scerocarya birrea (A. Rich) Hochst

SAHEL SAVANNA
Acacia albida Del.
Acacia senegal (L.) Willd.
Balanites aegyptiaca (L.) Del.
Boscia senegalensis Lam.-Holl.
Commiphora molmol Engl.
Parkinsonia aculeata Linn.
Prosopis africana Taub.
Terminalia catapa Linn.
Zizyphus mucronata Willd.

Although the plants were selected for their positive impact on conservation of soil and yield of undercrop, the material benefit to the farmers is direct by giving them a regular supply of wood and fruits, and some of the plants are known sources of local medicines.

FOREST BASE FARMS

Farms are proposed for selected plants found useful as possible raw materials for industrial production. Our present effort is concentrated in a 50-ha. farm in which we have seeded the medicinally important plant Calabar bean (*Physostigma venonosum*) in its natural environment with minimal disturbance on the ecosystem of the area. In another location in the southeastern region of Nigeria we have introduced the planting of selected medicinal plants as fallow crops. Annuals and vines are most suitable for such farms since the farmers are bound to return to the land for the cultivation of regular food crops after a few years.

BIORESOURCES DEVELOPMENT AND CONSERVATION PROGRAM (BDCP)

The BDCP is the conservation wing of the BDA. Its present project focuses on the southeastern rain forest region of Nigeria, in the Cross-River/Niger/Imo river basin. The area represents the western boundary of a contiguous rain forest range that stretches up to central Africa, including the rain forests of Cameroon, Gabon, Equatorial Guinea, and Congo. The eastern region of Nigeria presents varied ecological zones (see map, fig. 16.2), and by maintaining biodiversity plots in several areas of the region we hope to have access to diverse plant species for future drug development work. The program was designed from the beginning to address the real concerns of the rural dwellers whose plight was often linked to previous top-down experiments designed and implemented with minimal input from those whose lives were directly affected. It adopts a bottom-up approach in its efforts to empower the poor and powerless rural dwellers to enable them to derive maximum benefits from their environment-based resources and their labor.

Two major conservation activities have been formulated under this project. The first is the compilation of the inventory of species at the Oban-Boshi-Okwangwo forest complex, and the second project is the economic value assessment of the species in the forest complex.

CONSERVED AREAS

The BDCP also plans to establish parks, nature reserves, and biological gardens. Our objective is to acquire species-rich habitats and manage them jointly with the communities that live near the area. Present efforts are limited to acquisition of land titles on sacred groves and shrines in order to maintain their existing seclusion from human activities.

Relevance of BDA to Similar Projects

It is perhaps too early to assess the long-term impact of BDCP programs, but within its short period of operation we have observed some tangible results. We

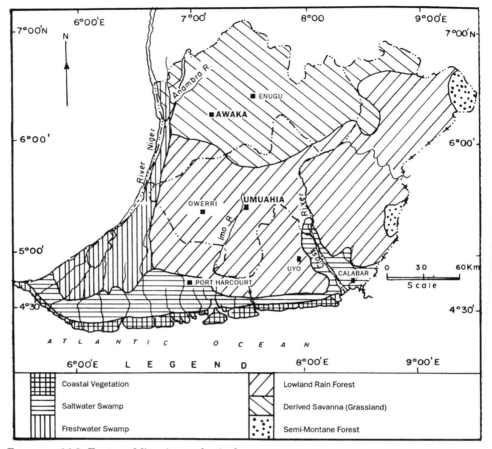

FIGURE 16.2 Eastern Nigeria: ecological zones.

do not yet have a finished product, but we have begun a process with a clear vision of its probable outcome. A major difference from similar efforts in other parts of the continent is that the program was home grown, initiated and managed in its entirety by indigenous staff. It was therefore possible to internalize the decision-making process. Science and technology are viewed as useful tools to be adapted to the cultural framework of productive activities, not as a modern alternative to the contributions of members of the community.

In our analysis of earlier projects we identified some features that may have contributed to their success (see table 16.3). A similar analysis of projects that failed also revealed some weaknesses that may have contributed to their failure (table 16.4). We considered it very useful to learn from the experiences gained by others in previous projects. In all the projects adopted by the BDCP careful consideration was given to possible social impact of the projects. For the strictly economic development projects, the environmental orientation was established as outlined in table 16.5.

One approach to which we did not accord any serious consideration is the rigid maintenance of the environmental status quo and the absolute ban on the use of tropical products. This strategy is based on the hope that the resultant lack of patrons will have a shadow effect of stopping the deforestation. Accordingly, major campaigns have begun in many parts of the world for a boycott of tropical products (especially those derived from the rain forests) as a means of protecting the forests. This approach ignores the legitimate needs of rural people whose lives are linked inextricably with the forests. People who for thousands of years coexisted with nature and exploited the bounty of the forests in a sustainable and environmentally responsible manner will be forced to economic stagnation by this strategy. Local community leaders are becoming increasingly skeptical about conservation strategies in which their interests are not adequately addressed and have expressed concern about what they refer to as "the burden of conservation." The first priority of any conservation program should be to feed the world's population. It would be unrealistic to expect rural people to protect natural resources and the environment and concern themselves with the well-being of future generations when their immediate survival is at stake.

TABLE 16.3 *Indicators of a Successful Project*

1. Broad, long-term, and comprehensive view of development process
2. Appropriate, affordable, understandable, serviceable, and adaptable technology
3. Feasible "internalization" strategy, confidence and support of the local stake holders
4. Relatively disinterested examination of the inputs, methods, and technology adopted in the project by controlling agencies
5. A critical mass of local scientists and technicians in the relevant disciplines

TABLE 16.4 *Characteristics of Failed Projects*

1. Short-term and narrow view of development taken, funding for project only for a few years
2. Top-down approach taken in both the design and execution of projects
3. High-technology options chosen that cannot be sustained after the withdrawal of external funding or foreign participation
4. Single-minded pursuit of a particular goal that blocks all other objectives
5. Vested interest of funding agency in the method of development and the choice of materials that conflicts with project mission

TABLE 16.5 *Project Environmental Orientation*

1. What is short-term impact of the project in 0–5 years?
2. What will be the environmental outcome in fifty years if the project is continued?
3. What would be the position if the project were to be widely replicated?
4. Does the project support policies or programs that have particular environmental orientations?
5. Does the project planning utilize local knowledge regarding likely environmental issues, or is it dependent totally on transferring experience?

REFERENCES

Awori, Achoka. 1992. "Africa: Surfacing from the Debris of Global Development." *Resources, Journal of Sustainable Development in Africa* 2:1.

Iwu, M. M. 1993. *Handbook of African Medicinal Plants*, p. 435. Boca Raton: CRC Press.

MacNeil, J. 1990. "Strategies for Sustainable Economic Development." In *Managing Planet Earth: Readings from Scientific American Magazine*, p. 109. New York: W. H. Freeman.

McNamara, Robert S. 1991. *Africa's Development Crisis: Agricultural Stagnation, Population Explosion, and Environmental Degradation.* Paper presented at the African Leadership Forum, Ota (Nigeria), June 21, 1990.

Morrow, Lance. 1992. "Africa: The Scramble for Existence." *Time* 140 (10) (September 7):40.

Salim, Ahmed Salim. 1992. Lecture delivered to the International Public Relations Conference. Reproduced in *Resources, Journal of Sustainable Development in Africa,* 2 (3):9–17.

Shiva, Vandana. 1992. *Biodiversity, A Third World Perspective.* Penang, Malaysia: Third World Network.

Stern, Ernest. 1984. "The Evolving Role of the Bank in the 1980s." Washington, D.C., January 12, 1984. Cited in A. O. Anya (1991). *Discourses of the Nigerian Academy of Science* 9:67.

17

The Economic Value and Potential for Plant-Derived Pharmaceuticals from Ghana

G. T. Odamtten, E. Laing, and D. K. Abbiw

THE last two decades have seen increased research in many countries in search of active ingredients in plants for use in pharmaceutical products. Plant medicine is a broad category of medicaments that include drugs used in traditional systems of medicine, folklore and ethnomedical products, and drugs discovered from plants having no documented therapeutic use (Wijesekera 1991). In Africa, herbal therapy has for many years formed the basis of treatment of many diseases. The flora of Ghana is replete with plant species that can be used or are being used in treatment of a wide spectrum of diseases (Ayitey-Smith 1989; Abbiw 1990). Plants provide about a quarter of our medicines in Ghana, and they could provide much more if a careful search were made (Findeisen and Laird 1991).

Once a plant has been identified as effective against specific disease(s), there is the need to carry out biological screening (1) to find new drugs, (2) to discover lead molecules (essentially novel chemical moieties) that can be modified through chemical means into new drugs, and (3) to provide a rationale for clinical use of traditional drugs even if activity is not of a high enough order to warrant development of the active moiety as a new drug. In many laboratories, pharmacological studies are heavily biased toward plants used in traditional systems of medicines or having some ethnomedical data available.

Undoubtedly, medicinal plants and the drugs derived from them constitute great economic and strategic value for the African continent (Mahran 1967; Anon. 1985). Currently, there is a quest by African research scientists to collaborate with others in the development of new drugs from medicinal plants. Priority has now been given by the Organization of African Unity to operational work oriented toward the validation or invalidation of popular knowledge with the aid of scientific research.

Systematic exploration of rain forests with funding from pharmaceutical companies or other interested nongovernmental agencies (NGOs) for commercial screening programs have many advantages. First, the funding agencies are able to tap into the knowledge of the indigenous populations through their local counterparts to identify, survey, gather, and prepare plant samples for shipment. They are also familiar with local export regulations. Many of the local counterparts spend time with native herbalists and get vital information on ethnomedical use for cancer, parasitic diseases, efficacy in wound healing, and other infectious diseases—to mention but a few. Such information may lead to identification of plants that have not been chemically investigated; these plants will probably be unusual and will therefore produce unusual compounds (Findeisen and Laird 1991).

This paper reports findings from a survey commissioned by the International Trade Center, Geneva, Switzerland. We surveyed the availability of twenty-seven selected medicinal plants in Ghana. The economic export potential and possible uses in plant-derived pharmaceuticals were also studied. The crucial question of sustainable exploitation and conservation strategies to benefit both the indigenous people and the importers is highlighted here.

The Nationwide Survey

The survey was carried out from 1986 to 1989. The availability of twenty-seven medicinal plants was aimed at giving us an overview of occurrence and product profile for each—including item of commerce, active constituents, therapeutic applications, and export potential. The starting list of plants for the survey is presented in table 17.1. Of these, medicinal plants available in commercial quantities that simply require export promotion are *Griffonia simplicifolia*, *Voacanga africana*, *Catharanthus roseus*, *Rauvolfia vomitoria*, *Penianthus zenkeri*, *Sphenocentrum jollyanum*, and *Clausena anisata*. Plants that require intensive agronomic studies and cultivation for sustainable exploitation are *Calotropis procera*, *Carica papaya*, *Datura metel*, *Datura stramonium*, *Xylopia spp.*, *Physostigma venenosum*, and *Zanthoxylum xanthoxyloides*.

Table 17.2 summarizes the items of commerce, active constituents, therapeutic applications, and export potential. This tabulation shows the potential use of many Ghanaian medicinal plants in plant-derived pharmaceuticals for the treatment of Hodgkin's disease, acute chronic leukemia, breast cancer, syphilis, leprosy, rheumatism, psychotic disorders, heart diseases, diabetes, asthmatic cases, bronchitis, gastrointestinal disorders, hypertension, and many others.

Some medicinal plants, e.g., *Rauvolfia vomitoria*, *Griffonia simplicifolia*, and *Voacanga africana*, can be exploited continuously because of their ability to regenerate themselves. Others, like *Catharanthus roseus* and *Physostigma venenosum*, have to be cultivated in large quantities, especially when the roots form the bulk of item of commerce.

TABLE 17.1   *List of Medicinal Plants Selected for the Supply Survey*

Name of Plant	Common Name	Family
1. *Dennetia tripetala* Bak.f.		Annonaceae
2. *Xylopia aethiopica* Dunal A.Rich	Ethiopian pepper	Annonaceae
3. *X. quintasii* Engl & Diels		Annonaceae
4. *X acutiflora* Engl. & Diels		Annonaceae
5. *X. parviflora* (A.Rich.) Benth.		Annonaceae
6. *X. staudtii* Engl. & Diels		Annonaceae
7. *Catharanthus roseus* (Linn.) G.Don	Periwinkle	Apocynaceae
8. *Rauvolfia vomitoria* Afzel.		Apocynaceae
9. *Voacanga africana* Stapf.		Apocynaceae
10. *Calotropis procera* (Ait.)Ait.f.	Sodom apple	Asclepiadaceae
11. *Ehretia cymosa* Thonning		Boraginaceae
12. *Ehretia trachyphylla* C. H. Wright		Boraginaceae
13. *Heliotropium indicum* Linn.	Indian heliotrope	Boraginaceae
14. *Griffonia simplicifolia* (Vahl ex DC.) Baill.		Caesalpiniaceae
15. *Carica papaya* Linn.		Caricaceae
16. *Thaumatococcus daniellii* (Benn.) Benth.	Katamfe	Marantaceae
17. *Dioscoreophyllum cumminsii* Diels	Serendipity berries	Menispermaceae
18. *Penianthus zenkeri* (Engl.) Diels		Menispermaceae
19. *Sphenocentrum jollyanum* Pierre		Menispermaceae
20. *Physostigma venenosum* Balfour	Calabar bean	Papilionaceae
21. *Mitragyna inermis* (Willd.) Ktze.		Rubiaceae
22. *Clausena anisata* (Willd.) Hook.f.ex Benth.	Mosquito plant	Rutaceae
23. *Zanthoxylum gilletii* (*Z. macrophylla*) (DeWild.) Waterman		Rutaceae
24. *Z. xanthoxyloides* (Lam.) Waterman		Rutaceae
25. *Synsepalum dulcificum*	Miraculous fruit, berry	Sapotaceae
26. *Datura stramonium* Linn.	Trumpet stramonium	Solanaceae
27. *D. metel* Linn.	Jimson weed or metel	Solanaceae

Source: Odamtten, Laing, and Abbiw 1989.

Total earnings from medicinal plants exported overseas from Ghana rose steadily from almost nothing in 1986, reaching a peak value of U.S. $450,000 in 1989. But this was followed by a sharp decline in 1990 and 1991. The marketing of potentially exportable botanicals from Ghana is carried out in trickles by many small-scale companies and business houses, depending on demand from the importers. From 1986 to 1989, the bulk of the export earnings (mainly from *V. africana, R. vomitoria,* and *G. simplicifolia*) was to European Community countries and other developed countries, e.g., Switzerland, United States, etc. Export to the remaining trading areas is more erratic. Furthermore, marketing research is required to enable us to find means of regularizing export to prospective buyers. Regulation of supply is also particularly important, for a large oversupply of plants will often destabilize the market and cause prices to decline to such an extent that it will no longer be profitable to produce or trade in those medicinal plants. The foreign exchange money accruing to Ghana could be increased substantially when appropriate market survey information is available.

In addition to medicinal plants, the tree sweeteners *S. dulcificum, D. cumminsii,* and *T. daniellii* are exported in commercial quantities from Ghana. Leaves of *T. daniellii* are also used as wrapping for many local food products. The problem of

TABLE 17.2 *Item of Commerce, Active Constituents, Therapeutic Applications, and Economic Potential of Listed Medicinal Plants from Ghana*

Name of Plant	Family	Item of Commerce	Active Constituents	Therapeutic Applications	Export Potential
1. *Catharanthus roseus* (Linn.) G.Don	Apocynaceae	Roots, leaves, stems	About seventy alkaloids known, e.g., vinblastine, vincristine (Velban) (Oncovin) ajmalicine, serpetine (Raubistine), vindesine (from seed and leaves)	Treatment of Hodgkin's disease, lymphosarcoma, choriocarcinoma, carcinoma of breast, acute chronic leukemias, neuropathic effects, etc.	Occurs in commercial quantities
2. *Calotropis procera* (Ait.) Ait.f.	Asclepiadaceae	Leaves, bark root, latex	Mudarin (bark), glycoside calotropin, calotropain, nontoxic proteolytic enzyme	Emetocathartic effect; fresh leaves used as arrow poison: rheumatism, toothache, chest complaint; root used for syphilis and leprosy	Available but needs to be cultivated from seed or otherwise
3. *Clausena anisata* (Willd.) Hook.f. ex Benth.	Rutaceae	Leaves, stems, roots	Volatile oils (74.3–89.6% anethole), charvicol methyl ether; roots contain coumarines (helletin and imperatorin and scoparone producing quiescence and diminution of locomotor activity)	Leaf as a parasiticide and purgative; burnt to keep mosquitoes away; root used as anthelminthic	Occurs in commercial quantities

Plant	Family	Parts used	Chemical constituents	Uses	Remarks
4. *Datura metel* 5. *Datura stramonium*	Solanaceae Solanaceae	Leaves, fruits, seeds, flowers	Alkaloids, e.g., hyoscyamine, atropine, hyoscine (scopolamine)	Antiemetic and sedative action; hyoscine (5 × as active as atropine) produces mydriasis; mainly used as antimotion sickness drug, in gastric disorders (duodenal ulcers); antispasmodic action in asthma treatment; sedative in acute mania and delirium, parasympatholytic, anticholinergic	Has economic potential but needs to be cultivated
6. *Griffonia simplicifolia* (Vahl. ex DC.) Baill.	Caesalpinaceae	All parts, especially seeds	5-hydroxyl-L-tryptophan (5-HTP) in mature seed; 5-hydroxytryptamine (5-HT) or serotonin; indole-3-acetyl-aspartic acid 1AAA; 5-hydroxyindole-3-acetic acid (or 5-HIAA)	Reputed medicinal value contains chemicals similar in action to that of LSD; aphrodisiac action; leaf juice used as enema and for kidney disease remedies; treats vomiting, diarrhea and constipation; various parts for treatment of constipation; used in medical diagnostic kit	Has economic potential but needs to be cultivated
7. *Penianthus zenkeri* (Engl.) Diels	Menispermaceae	Roots	Not known	Roots chewed as aphrodisiac; cure for constipation and loss of appetite	Promising but needs to be organized
8. *Sphenocentrum jollyanum* Pierre	Menispermaceae	Roots	Not known	Roots chewed as aphrodisiac; cure for constipation and loss of appetite	Promising but needs to be organized
9. *Physostigma venenosum* Balfour	Papilionaceae	Beans and aerial parts	Eserine; stigmasterin; physostigmine	Used medicinally for ophthalmia; a wide class of pesticides; the carbamates have been developed from physostigmine	Needs intensive cultivation to boost export

(continued)

TABLE 17.2 *Continued.*

Name of Plant	Family	Item of Commerce	Active Constituents	Therapeutic Applications	Export Potential
10. *Rauvolfia vomitoria* Afzel.	Apocynaceae	All parts (root, bark, stem, leaves, fruit, latex)	More than fifty alkaloids, including reserpine, ajmaline, ajmalicine, serpertine, vellosimine, ajmalinol, etc.	Reserpine is a tranquilizer used in psychiatric disorders; roots used in treatment of jaundice; ajmalicine used in treatment of cardiac arrhythmia	Of commercial importance and exported in large quantities
11. *Voacanga africana* Stapf.	Apocynaceae	Leaves, bark, seeds	All parts rich in alkaloids, e.g., voacamine (major); voacangine, voacangrine, voacarine, and vobtusine	Alkaloids are hypotensive with ventricular cardiostimulant action and a slight action on sympathetic and parasympathetic nervous system; plant used for treating sores, furuncles, abscesses, fungal infections, filaria, and eczema	One of the most exploited commercially
12. *Xylopia aethiopica* (Dunal) A.Rich	Annonaceae	Fruits (mostly), leaves, roots, bark	Anonaceine (alkaloid resembling morphine), volatile oil, rutin	Bronchitis, dysenteric conditions, biliousness; bark used for asthma, rheumatism, stomach ache; fruits used in cough medicine	Available but requires cultivation

	Family	Part traded	Chemical constituents	Uses	Remarks
13. *Zanthoxylum xanthoxyloides* (Lam.) Waterman)	Rutaceae	All parts are traded	Mostly alkaloids: furoquinolines, 1-benzyltetrahydroisoquinolines, orthocoupled aporphines, paracoupled benzophenanthrides, protoberberines, amides, bicyclic coumarines, furancoumarines, pyrancoumarins; cinamic acid derivatives	Used in treatment of paralysis; roots chewed for toothache	Promising but needs to be cultivated
14. *Carica papaya* Linn.	Caricaceae	Roots, leaves, and fruits	Papain, chymopapain; roots contain enzyme myrosin and potassium myronate; latex contains alkaloid carpine and pseudocarpine used as heart depressant in treatment of heart disease	Abortifacient, hernia, affection of urogenital system; blennorrnea, orchitis, chancre, febrifuge, diabetes, purgative, yaws, venereal diseases, piles, anthelmintic on *Ascaris, Trichinia, Enterobius*	Hardly any commercial cultivation but has tremendous potential
Sweeteners					
15. *Synsepalum dulcificum* (Schum & Thom) Danieli	Sapotaceae	Fruit	Miraculin	In dietetic foods	High export potential
16. *Dioscoreophyllum cumminsii* Diels	Menispermaceae	Fruit	Proteinaceous monellin	In dietetic foods	High export potential
17. *Thaumatococcus daniellii* (Benn) Benth.	Menispermaceae	Fruit	Thaumatin	In dietetic foods	High export potential

ensuring freshness of fruits at port of delivery has been a hard nut to crack, and many exporters lose heavily because goods shipped in good condition arrive in bad condition. The best packaging and shelf-life extension method should be found to enable us to curtail this problem.

Cultivation and Conservation of Medicinal Plants

Deforestation and the global demand for medicinal plants will continue to put intense pressure on many wild plant populations. The problem in Ghana is accentuated by the spate of bush fires that take a heavy annual tool of endangered species in the forest—further eroding the stock of medicinal plants. Cultivating or sustainably harvesting these plants could be a way to provide environmentally sound income for people in the tropics. It could also ensure a steady supply of valuable medicine to both the developed and the developing nations. If collectors take more than can be naturally replaced, however, it might have a disastrous effect on the health delivery systems of the developing world because the World Health Organization has estimated that up to 80% of those living in the developing world rely on plant-derived medicines for their primary health care (Malakoff 1991).

A few examples of overexploitation of plants in Ghana may suffice. The bark of the mahogany tree (*Khaya senegalensis*) is useful in herbal preparation as blood tonic. It also yields valuable gums. The debarking of the plant has become the order of the day, and some plants die as a result of excessive exploitation of bark. Some species of yams (*Dioscorea spp.*) are hard to come by because of overexploitation and erosion by bush fires. It is essential to heed the lesson of Mt. Oku in Cameroon. There, bark of *Pygeum africanus* is used to make a drug that helps control urinary problems associated with enlarged prostate glands. The threat of overexploitation required management practices that limited removal of only half the bark of a tree every five years (Malakoff 1991).

Tropical plant species in Ghana have yielded and will continue to yield important medical compounds, including vincristine, vinblastine, reserpine, ajmalicine, colchicine, papyotin, leurocristine, atanisatine, physostigmine, eserine, eseranine, calabarine, stimmianin, mudarin, asclepin, etc. And yet, less than 1% of tropical Ghanian species have been examined for their medical potential. The list provided in table 17.3 can form the basis of a future survey of distribution and economic potential of plant-derived compounds for use in drug therapy. The combination of floral and microbial diversity and lack of previous exploration indicates that our forest holds enormous potential for industrial screening programs, including the search for a cure for AIDS in plant-derived pharmaceuticals. As companies aim at profitable discovery and marketing of new drugs, they should not lose

TABLE 17.3   *List of Plants Used in the Traditional Systems of Healing Diseases in Ghana but Not Included in the Survey List*

Plant Used	Family	Disease(s) Cured
Treculia africana	Moraceae	Abdominal pains after childbirth
Lannea welwitschii	Anacardiaceae	
Piliostigma thonningii	Caesalpiniaceae	
Corynanthe pachyceras	Rubiaceae	Abscess or boil
Combretodendron africanum	Lecythidaceae	
Palisota hirsuta	Commelinaceae	
Baphia nitida	Papilionaceae	
Cassia occidentalis	Caesalpiniaceae	
Dissotis rotundifolia	Melastomataceae	Asthma
Oxyanthus speciosus	Rubiaceae	
Momordica charantia	Cucurbitaceae	
Desmodium adscendens	Papilionaceae	
Spondias monbin	Anacardiaceae	Epidermophyton of skin
Microdesmis puberula	Euphorbiaceae	
Euphorbia hirta	Euphorbiaceae	Diarrhea in children
Desmodium adscendens	Papilionaceae	
Paulinia pinnata	Sapindaceae	
Sterculia tragacantha	Sterculiaceae	
Ficus capensis	Moraceae	Dysentery
Alchornea cordifolia	Euphorbiaceae	
Pupalia lappacea	Amaranthaceae	
Psidium guajava	Myrtaceae	
Hoslundia oppositum	Labiatae	Herpes zoster
Picralima nitida	Apocynaceae	
Lannea welwitschii	Anacardiaceae	
Pterocarpus erinaceus	Papilionaceae	
Alternanthera repens	Amaranthaceae	
Vernonia biafrae	Compositae	Piles
Combretodendron macrocarpum	Lecythidiaceae	
Ficus capensis	Moraceae	
Mitragyna stimpulosa	Rubiaceae	Ulcer
Lippia multiflora	Verbenaceae	Jaundice
Strophanthus hispidus	Apocynaceae	Heart stimulant
Picralima nitida	Apocynaceae	
Capparis erythrocarpus	Capparidaceae	
Indigofera arrecta	Papilionaceae	
Gloriosa superba	Liliaceae	Gout, leprosy, colchicine, skin diseases

sight of the conservation and sustainability of the flora. It is important to discover through appropriate agronomic studies how these selected plants grow, where to cultivate them for maximum yield, how to have a sustainable harvest, and (last but not least) how to ensure payment of royalties for rain forest plants. Such agreements for royalties should be beneficial to the country involved. Royalties are typically negotiated based on value of the product to the marketing company, the investment made by the originator, and the risk borne by each (Findeisen and Laird 1991). For a sustainable and profitable arrangement, all parties would need to work toward a compromise that would ensure the ultimate availability of good health and essential drugs for all by the year 2000.

ACKNOWLEDGMENTS

We are deeply indebted to the Ghana Export Promotion Council, the Rainforest Alliance Periwinkle Project, and Bioresources, Inc., for financial support. The typing assistance of Mr. B. A. Impraim, Botany Department, University of Ghana, is also gratefully acknowledged.

REFERENCES

Abbiw, D. K. 1990. *Useful Plants of Ghana.* Kew, U.K.: Intermediate Technology Publications and Royal Botanic Gardens.
Anonymous. 1985. *African Pharmacopoeia* 1985, vol. 1. OAU/STRC.
Ayitey-Smith, E. 1989. *Prospects and Scope of Plant Medicine in Health Care.* Ghana Universities Press.
Findeisen, C. and S. A. Laird. 1991. ''Natural Products Research and the Potential Role of the Pharmaceutical Industry in Tropical Forest Conservation.'' Unpublished report. New York: The Periwinkle Project of the Rainforest Alliance.
Mahran, G. H. 1967. *Medicinal Plants.* Cairo: Anglo-Egyptian Bookshop.
Malakoff, D. 1991. ''Cultivating the Rainforest.'' In *The Canopy* (Summer), pp. 4–5.
Wijesekera, R. O. B. 1991. *The Medicinal Plant Industry.* Boca Raton: CRC Press.

18

The Rwanda Experience in Enhancing and Commercializing the Use of Traditional Medicinal Plants

Luc Van Puyvelde

RWANDA, one of the smallest and poorest Central African countries, has a rich and still very popular traditional medicine. Even nowadays, the major part of the population initially consults the traditional healer before calling on the primary health care or hospital facilities.

In order to evaluate the native medicine and flora of Rwanda, researchers of the faculty of medicine (National University of Rwanda) started, at the end of 1971, with the study of Rwandese traditional medicine. In 1977, an interfaculty and interdisciplinary research group was founded, which led to the creation of a research center in 1980: CURPHAMETRA (Centre de recherche sur la pharmacopée et la médecine traditionelle). CURPHAMETRA is part of the Institut de recherche scientifique et technologique (IRST). The institute was created by the Rwandese government in 1989 in order to stimulate and to improve useful research programs for the country.

The primary objective of CURPHAMETRA is the development and production of drugs starting from traditional medicine and medicinal plants. In developing countries—where the need for drugs becomes urgent in light of the difficult economic situation—the research, development, and production of drugs starting from local material offers an attractive alternative to expensive medicines on the world market. There are other significant advantages as well:

- validation of ancestral knowledge
- limitation of import, thus resulting in a reduction of the national debt
- creation of employment at various levels
- accessibility to valuable low-cost drugs for the population

- export possibilities
- protection and conservation of the natural environment

CURPHAMETRA has a dispensary of traditional medicine, an interdisciplinary research program, and a small plant for the production of drugs derived from medicinal plants. A six-step work scheme has been elaborated: (1) integration of traditional medicine, (2) use of official medicinal plants, (3) acclimatization of foreign medicinal plants, (4) production of solvents and excipients, (5) exploitation of economically interesting plants, and (6) research on new drugs. Each of these steps is described in the remainder of this article.

Integration of Traditional Medicine

Between 60% and 80% of the Rwandese initially consult a traditional healer before calling on the primary health care or hospital facilities. Thus, an effort to integrate healers into the primary health care system (by improving their knowledge of scientific and technologic options) would be advantageous.

We started ethnopharmacognostic studies throughout the country and created a dispensary of traditional medicine within CURPHAMETRA. In this dispensary, organized as a cooperative, five traditional healers carry out their profession while a medical team (medical doctor and medical assistant) provides follow-up of the patients before and after treatment. To verify the efficacy and toxicity of the traditional remedies, a biological screening program was set up.

On the basis of results obtained in the ethnopharmacognostic studies (frequency of use of a remedy in the country), clinical observation in our dispensary, and biological and toxicological studies, we can propose a number of remedies that may be pursued by recognized traditional healers who should be integrated into the primary health care system.

These remedies can, for example, be promoted as medical teas. In the near future, CURPHAMETRA will commercialize several teas, such as a hepatoprotective tea, an antiulcer tea, and an antidiarrhea tea.

Use of Official Medicinal Plants

We first started production of plant-derived drugs based on well-known medicinal plants—those used or not used in the native medicine—which were already growing in the country. These plants have been categorized as "official medicinal plants," for they are found in different pharmacopoeias (European, Belgian, French, American). Methods of extraction, analysis, dosage, etc., are already described. Thus, we avoid expensive and long research. The following extracts of official medicinal plants are in production:

- tincture of the leaves of *Datura stramonium* L. (antispasmodic)
- tincture and essential oil of the leaves of *Eucalyptus globulus* Labill. (pulmonary disinfectant)
- liquid extract of the fruits of *Capsicum frutescens* L. (revulsive)
- liquid extract of the leaves of *Plantago lanceolata* L. (anticough)

For the production of extracts and drugs, CURPHAMETRA has a small plant with dryers, mills, percolators, extractors, concentrators, and distillators, as well as equipment for the formulation of syrups, ointments, tablets, etc. There are also a laboratory for analysis and control and 100 hectares of ground for cultivation.

Acclimatization of Foreign Medicinal Plants

In order to increase the number of official medicinal plants for our production, we introduced several well-known plants. Three plants are now being grown and processed:

- tincture and liquid extract of the flower of *Calendula officinalis* L. (antiinflammatory and for wound healing)
- tincture and liquid extract of the herb of *Thymus vulgaris* L. (anticough)
- essential oil of the leaves of *Mentha saccharinensis* (carminative)

For the moment, CURPHAMETRA produces several drugs with the official medicinal plants described above:

- a disinfectant for the mouth
- two anticough syrups and a solution
- an antispasmodic syrup
- an antiinflammatory and wound-healing ointment
- four medicinal teas

All these drugs are produced in bulk for hospitals, health centers, and dispensaries. Smaller quantities are prepared for pharmacies.

A second series of drugs based on additional well-known plants will be developed and produced in the near future.

Production of Solvents and Excipients

The development and production of plant-derived drugs depend on the use of solvents and excipients, which account for a great part of the total production costs. Some examples of solvents are:

- Ethyl alcohol. We produce this alcohol from the molasses of the sugar cane factory. The alcohol is used in processing our medicinal plants and is further commercialized as a disinfectant alcohol. We now produce 12,000 L/year; with the extension of our plant we will produce 45,000 L/year.

- Petroleum ether. For the needs of our laboratory we distill petroleum ether from gasoline.

Necessary excipients include:

- Starch. We produce starch from manioc in a pilot-scale facility. A larger facility will be built later for full-scale production.
- Beeswax. Beeswax is produced in several parts of the country and will be used in the preparation of ointments.

Exploitation of Economically Interesting Plants

One of the research programs of CURPHAMETRA aims at exploitation of essential oils for local production and for export. Currently, we produce for medical purposes the essential oils of *Eucalyptus globulus* Lab., *E. smithii* R. T. Baker, and *Mentha saccharinensis*. For mosquito repellent, we process into cream and candle form the essential oils of *Pelargonium graveolens* L'Hérit, *Eucalyptus citriodora* Hook, and *Cymbopogon citratus* (Nees) Stapf.

With the arrival of two big extractors, we will produce essential oils for the Rwandese cosmetic industry. Our research team will also try to install extractors in other parts of the country in order to stimulate dispersed cultivation and exploitation of essential-oil-bearing plants.

Several plants were analyzed for their tannin content in order to replace the vegetal tannins imported by the local tanneries.

Methods to extract colchicine from *Gloriosa simplex* Linn. and berberine from *Thalictrum rhynchocarpum* Q. Dillon & A. Rich were finalized.

Research on New Drugs

Our research on the Rwandese traditional medicine resulted in the development of several new drugs.

The first original Rwandese pharmaceutical preparation is an antiscabies solution and ointment prepared with an alcoholic extract from the tuber of *Neorautanenia mitis* (A. Rich.) Verdc. This tuber has traditionally been used by Rwandese farmers to treat scabies of calves. A biological screening showed substantial acaricidal and antiscabies activity. A bioguided phytochemical study led to the isolation of seven isoflavone-type compounds with 7α hydroxyrotenone as active principle. A solution and ointment were prepared and tested on more than 500 patients affected with scabies. This antiscabies drug is now commercialized in Rwanda. An acaricidal preparation is now under investigation.

Tetradenia riparia (Hochst.) L. E. Codd. is one of the most popular Rwandese medicinal plants. The people cultivate the plant around their houses and use it as a remedy against a wide range of diseases including malaria, angina, cough, diarrhea, several kinds of fevers, and aches. The leaves are also employed for the conservation of beans in the silos. Upon biological screening, substantial antimicrobial, antispasmodic, antitrichomonas, and insecticidal activities were found in the leaves. This led to the isolation of four new α pyrones and a new diterpenediol with several biological activities. An extract of the plant will also be used as a pesticide against *Pseudomonas solanacearum,* which causes a bacterial disease that afflicts potato crops.

An antifungal ointment from an extract of the roots of *Pentas longiflora* Oliver has been developed and will be commercialized soon. This plant is used by one of the traditional healers of our dispensary at CURPHAMETRA to treat pityriasis versicolor.

Other new preparations, such as an ointment for hemorrhoids and several medicinal teas, are in development. We are also working on plants with antiprotozoan activity and on antimicrobial plants active against AIDS-opportunistic infections (fungal meningitis, tuberculosis).

19

The Role of Medicinal Plants in Health Care in India

James A. Duke

JUST returned from the Pongal celebration (an equivalent of our Thanksgiving), I have elected to stress neem (*Azadirachta indica* A. Juss.) as one of the thousands of medicinal plants of great economic and health importance to the millions of tribal people in India.

Although some authors put India's medicinal exports at only about $10 million, Sundaresh (1982) puts the value at closer to $50 million for 1978 (table 19.1). Whether you accept the $50 million value for India's medicinal exports or $10 million (Subramanian, Venkatasubramanian, and Sasidharan 1991), the internal value of the neem plant, not listed among the exports, is at least an order of magnitude greater. Assigning a dental value of $2 per person/year to neem sticks indicates a value of $1 billion for the half-billion people reported to use neem as a toothbrush.

My Indian counterpart stressed computerization of traditional and tribal medicinal knowledge before it is lost. This is, of course, a field that holds great interest for me, but at the moment, it would be low in agricultural research service priorities, except as it led to preservation of endangered economic plants and their wild relatives. We are already involved in this type of work in Ecuador and Peru. There are so many parallels between Asian Indian and American tribal medicines, and the loss of knowledge as the shamans lose their sons and daughters to urbanization, that I see a new and bigger meaning for the term *all-India project*. I have already computerized all the medicinal plants in the eleven-volume *The Wealth of India* and could readily expand it, in the same format, to include Asian Indian tribals. I have started computerizing Kirtikar, Basu, and An (1975) and entered *Medicinal Plants of India* (Satyavati, Raina, and Sharma 1976) into my Father Nature's Farmacy (FNF) data base.

We are currently computerizing Amerindian medicinal plants as part of our

TABLE 19.1   *Medicinal Exports of India, 1978 (After Sundaresh 1982)*

Product	Tons	Value ($ U.S.)*
Opium	2,132	35,000,000
Psyllium	29,910	12,000,000
Menthol	200	1,600,000
Cinchona alkaloids	50	760,000
Senna	3,800	600,000
Diosgenin	20	400,000
Strychnos alkaloids	16	100,000
Rauvolfia alkaloids	3	60,000
Ergot	16	40,000
Xanthotoxin	0.1	40,000
Berberine	3	25,000
Ipecac	20	20,000
Belladonna	28	8,000
Pyrethrum flowers	16	6,000
Total		50,000,000

*Assumes 1 lakh rupee = $4,000; well rounded.

tropical biodiversity program in Amazonian America, and we could expand on this, stressing comparisons and differences in the ethnomedicine of the two Indian components of our all-India project.

Agroforestry (and Nonwood Forest Products)

India and other tropical Asian countries have also long been masters of intercropping, including agroforestry. I remember well a Laotian field I visited with more than twenty-five species of economic plants, some trees, some vines, some perennial herbs, and some annual herbs (including the annual poppy).

Global Warming

I enjoyed visits to the following stations:

Coimbatore	Tropical very dry forest life zone, 600 mm rain, 26°C mean temperature
Delhi	Tropical very dry forest life zone, 700 mm rain, 25°C mean temperature
Dehra Dun	Subtropical wet forest life zone, 2300 mm rain, 22°C mean temperature

These three stations circumscribe the ecological amplitude of neem, which can be grown in drier areas, e.g., Jeddah, with irrigation. Dehra Dun would be close to the colder limits for neem. It was clear to me that hundreds of economic plant species are growing under the specific climatic (and soil) conditions of each of the study areas. Many of these economic plants are not cultivated in the United States today but could be, wherever similar soil and climatic conditions prevail, on the assumption that latitudal problems did not arise. For example, neem could squeak through in the United States today in nearly frost-free areas of Arizona, California, Florida, Georgia, Hawaii, and Texas, not to mention Puerto Rico.

More important, in the various global warming scenarios, these tropical life zones are projected to move to other areas in the United States. For that reason, table 19.2 shows the ecological and geographical characteristics of areas where neem is grown today (Beckstrom-Sternberg and Duke 1992).

Cataloging the economic plants and their wild relatives (including nonwood forest species, as well as timber species), along with associated climatic data (as we have done for neem), would enable us to predict where in the United States these economic plants could be grown under the various global warming scenarios. Hence, I could see merit in collaborating with the government of India (GOI) in cataloging the ecological distribution of their economic species. Such a catalog could prove useful in all the mentioned avenues of collaboration. I published an initial effort in this direction in Atal and Kapur (1982) with my chapter "Ecosystematic Data on Medicinal Plants." This could readily be expanded to include new data, such as a listing of the numerous species at Coimbatore and Dehra Dunn, with the attendant climatic data. This computerized data base could be tied to another computerized data base on tribal uses of the economic plants, a theme apparently of great interest to some Indians.

TABLE 19.2 *Average Annual Rainfall and Temperature of Neem-Growing Locations*

Country	Station	Precipitation (mm)	Temperature (° C)
Saudi Arabia	Jeddah	60	28.0
Sudan	Khartoum	164	29.6
Pakistan	Lahore	490	24.0
India	Coimbatore	612	26.4
India	New Delhi	714	25.2
Nigeria	Sokoto	734	28.1
India	Bangalore	889	24.0
Nigeria	Samaru	1095	25.0
Kenya	Mombasa	1191	26.7
India	Madras	1215	28.6
Nigeria	Ibadan	1227	26.4
India	Nagpur	1242	26.9
Nigeria	Agege	1359	26.1
United States	Miami	1401	23.9
India	Dehra Dun	2269	21.8

The United States imports more than a million dollars a month each in senna and psyllium from India, both of which could be grown in the United States. In June 1992, we imported more than 1,500 MT psyllium worth more then $3,000,000 (Anon. 1992). We could grow all the species mentioned in these pages, albeit in limited quantities in the United States, but it is often cheaper to import from India. The importance of herbal medicine in India probably parallels that in China. An estimated 30–50% of Chinese medicines are herbal, a figure that may be 70–90% in the mountainous regions. My counterpart's estimates in India ranged from 50% (70% of people are tribal and 70% of their medicine is herbal) (Tandon, personal communication) to 99 + % (Subramanian, personal communication). Even in the United States, an increasing percentage of the population cannot afford health insurance, hospitalization, and prescription drugs. I like the figure 50% for temperate, 75% for tropical people, largely using traditional medicines.

Medicinal and Aromatic Plants

My Indian counterparts mentioned a Tibetan friend in Himachal Pradesh (HP) who knew all the Tibetan medicinal plants, perhaps the traditional medicinal flora in greatest peril of extinction. Cataloging these data should be of great interest to conservational organizations like Conservation International, The Rainforest Alliance, World Wildlife Fund, and perhaps even the World Bank, which has recently expressed possible interest in a center for study of endangered medicinal species in the Indian subcontinent. Japanese markets almost extinguished the Indian rhinoceros; Chinese, the snow leopard. Chinese consumption led to endangerment of American ginseng; Euroamerican consumption (Sandoz and Bristol-Myers) may have led to endangerment of Asian may apple. Aliens and Indians led to endangerment of Indian snakeroot (*Rauvolfia*), Americans are leading to endangerment of the Western Yew (*Taxus brevifolia* Nutt.), and deforestation endangers the Himalayan yew. One pharmaceutical firm started a plantation of wild yams (*Dioscorea* spp.). They could then truthfully say they were using cultivated *Dioscorea* as a source of steroids. Still, I am told, they also purchased wild root so that it was all but extirpated in the wild. Steroids still constitute about 15% of the world's prescription drugs, suggesting a value of $15 to $22.5 billion for the world's steroid drugs. The temperate *Glycine* has largely replaced tropical *Dioscorea* as a source of steroid starter material.

My counterparts tell me that a similar thing happened with the composite kuth root, *Saussurea lappa* C. B. Clarke, source of an essential oil heavily exported (ca. $70,000) in 1988/89. With legitimate cultivated crops established, the tribals still found it attractive to harvest the wild material too, while they waited for their slow-growing cultivated material to grow.

This rather parallels what is happening with threatened American ginseng, exports (mostly to China) of which totaled close to $75 million in 1990. In many states, it is illegal to harvest ginseng on private or public property without specific permit. Hypothetically, a West Virginia grower could establish a cultivated plot of ginseng and then commingle illegally harvested wild ginseng (which commands three times the price, perhaps more than $200/lb) with the legal cultivated ginseng. A few astute oriental buyers can tell the difference between legal cultivated ginseng and illegal wild harvested ginseng. Hence, the establishment of more ginseng farms will not necessarily save it in the wild. Dr. Bennett, at Dehra Dun, showed me specimens of *Panax* from India, rare and variable.

In their quest for the elusive elixir of aphrodisia, Chinese may be contributing to the endangerment of American ginseng (*Panax quinquefolius* L.) just as Japanese are contributing to the endangerment of the Indian rhinoceros. As early as 1982, exports of *Coptis teeta, Dioscorea deltoidea* Wall., *D. frazeri, Podophyllum hexandrum* Royle, *Rauvolfia serpentina* Benth., *Rheum emodi* Wall., and *Saussurea lappa* C. B. Clarke were "virtually banned" from India.

There are 1,000 to 2,000 tribal ethnic groups here, each with its own dialect and suite of economic plants and phytomedicinals. (Could we not say that about the Americas, too?) These peoples are themselves often as endangered as their forest medicinal plants. The people and their traditional medicines are being lost before ethnobotanists and medical botanists record which of these endangered species are used for what.

We know that American/European consumerism has driven one species, *Podophyllum hexandrum* (alias *P. emodi* Wallich ex Hook F. & T. Thomas) to the brink of extinction, such that it was listed by the CITES only in 1990, about six years after etoposide (alias VePesid®) was approved by the FDA for cancer of the testicles and four to five years after it was approved for lung cancer, which takes more than 100,000 American lives a year. The same year that the species was listed by CITES in South Asia, sales of VePesid were more than $100 million/year for the first time. VePesid is the semisynthetic derivative of a lignan that occurs in the rhizomes and roots of the endangered unAmerican species, *Podophyllum hexandrum,* and the unendangered American may apple, *P. peltatum.* But VePesid apparently still depends on plants for starter material. Sandoz and its American producer of VePesid, Bristol-Myers, probably found it cheaper to obtain their starter material from Asian rather than American may apple. The CITES listing may not change this. While it is illegal, under the convention, to trade in the plant, extracts and/or podophyllotoxin, like reserpine, are still legal exports (at least according to some interpretations I have heard). If this latter sentence is true, and trade in podophyllotoxin and reserpine is still permitted, then the convention will do little to save *Rauvolfia* and *Podophyllum* in the wild in India. It could be predicted that pharmaceutical firms will establish farms for these species so they can say they are helping, as they continue to purchase wild-crafted herb to commingle with the more expensive cultivated herb.

Both internal and external consumption of reserpine from the Indian snakeroot (*Rauvolfia serpentina*) contributed to its dimunition. Y. K. Sarin (1982) ranked the snakeroot among the most important medicinal plants native to India. In 1955, the GOI put a ban on the export of the raw drug. Around 1980, India was harvesting 25 to 27 tons of root from the wild, but "annual supplies can be increased to about 70 tonnes of materials per annum, if the demand picks up." Cultivated snakeroot in India added up to little more than 5 tons per year. But India's requirements for hypotensive alkaloid (ca 200 kg/yr) will require a minimum of 50 tons. For the external market, Sarin (1982) suggests 100–150 tons/year. Since the snakeroot is native to sal forests (*Shorea floribunda* Kurz.), it might be intercropped with commercial sal, itself a good earner of foreign exchange.

Neither Madagascar nor India receives much today from the Madagascar periwinkle (*Catharanthus roseus* [L.] G. Don.), much of which is now grown for Eli Lilly in Texas. But Singh, Rao, and Atal (1982) report that 1,000 tons of *Catharanthus* leaves were exported annually to the United States and Hungary, and 600 tons of roots were exported to other European states. About 1,500 ha. were being cultivated at that time. Singh, Raos, and Atal estimated 3,500 kg ajmalicine as natural production, estimating a price of 25,000 rupees per kg. At today's conversion rates (25 rupees per dollar), that figures $3,500,000 for the world value of ajmalicine. Vincristine/vinblastine sales probably top $100 million.

In their search for cancer cures, American pharmaceutical firms, specifically Bristol-Myers, may be endangering somewhat America's western yew, *Taxus brevifolia* Nutt., bark of which is the source of taxol, the most exciting new potential drug in the war against cancer, especially cancer of the ovaries, which takes 10,000–12,500 American lives. Bark of the western yew, which averages 100 ppm taxol, is being nonrenewably harvested for the production of taxol, 25 kg of which are needed a year, just for the ovarian cancer studies. Taxol is so important that the National Cancer Institute (NCI) now has $2.5 million in taxol research and development grants. Ironically the western yew was used by American tribals for lung ailments, and now taxol is also showing promise in lung cancer, which takes 143,000 American lives a year. Taxol holds promise in the cancers mentioned in table 19.3.

Small wonder that some women with terminal ovarian cancer, yet unable to

TABLE 19.3 *Cancers Against Which Taxol Holds Promise*

Promise	Lung cancer	143,000 deaths a year
	Colorectal	60,500 deaths a year
	Breast cancer	44,500 deaths a year
	Ovarian cancer	12,500 deaths a year
Potential	Prostate cancer	32,000 deaths a year
	Melanoma	6,000 deaths a year
Total		ca. 300,000 deaths a year

get taxol, suggest that their lives are more important than the lives of a few western yews. Taxol is worth about a half million dollars per kilogram today. Many kilograms are available, renewably, in the Himalayas, I predict. Once needle-derived taxol is approved, as bark-derived taxol is now approved on the New Drug Application (NDA), the Himalayan yew, yet another forest tree, *Taxus wallichiana* Zucc., may be of interest. Perhaps nothing more than a narrow-leaved variant of the common yew, *Taxus wallichiana* could conceivably contain as much taxol in its renewable needles as the nonrenewable bark of *Taxus brevifolia.*

Conversations with Dr. Subramanian revealed that he would be happy to collaborate on medicinal plant programs, e.g., a survey of taxol in Himalayan yews, and a survey of camptothecin in Ghat *Alangiums* and *Mappia.* These are priority compounds of the American NCI.

Conservation of Chemotypes

Clearly we need to conserve all species of *Taxus,* seeking out the ones that can produce the most taxol/hectare renewably. We know, for example, that the bark of *T. brevifolia* may contain, rounded, 1 to 700 ppm taxol. Now if it takes four large "average" yew trees to yield enough taxol to treat one woman for ovarian cancer, and if the average tree bark contains 100 ppm taxol, then it would take 400 of the low-taxol trees, or less than one high-taxol tree to nonrenewably yield the bark-derived taxol per patient. Prudence would dictate conservation of the 700-ppm tree, if you can find it, and if the loggers have not hauled it away yet.

I expect there is equally dramatic variation in the taxol content of the renewable needles. Suspicious of the taxonomy, I report variation of 30–154 ppm in needles reported (or suspected by me) to be *Taxus baccata* L., 0.3–51 ppm in *T. brevifolia,* 90 ppm in *T. canadensis* Marsh., 80 ppm in *T. cuspidata* Siebold & Zucc., and 20–134 ppm in *T. media* Rehd. I predict that when needles of these species have been studied as intensively as the bark of *T. brevifolia* has been studied, we shall find comparable chemotypic variability, i.e., a range from 1 to 700 ppm in renewable needles. Thus the Himalayan yew, *T. wallichiana,* from its endangered Himalayan forest habitat (and it is said to be dependent on shade for reproduction), *may* be higher in taxol, quicker growing, and easily coppiceable, so that it *may* be a more promising source of taxol than our cultivated species.

I am told that the NCI now arranges for a portion of the proceeds of any new natural product drug to return to the county of origin. India is justifiably sensitive about their germ plasm and raw materials. Dr. Mohammed Khalil reminds us that overzealous collection of Kenya's *Maytenus buchananii* (Loes.) R. Wilczek has all but removed that shrub from the local pharmacopoeia. As Perdue (1976) notes, 20,000 pounds of the stems of this "uncommon, if not rare" species were needed as a source of maytensine. "In early 1974, 2 years after the massive collection, there was little evidence of regeneration" (Perdue 1976).

As noted by Sundaresh (1982), though India is "the foremost supplier of medicinal plants in the world, its exports of the derivatives/active principles pale into insignificance." Sundaresh notes that the big six (United States, Japan, Germany, United Kingdom, France, and Switzerland) exported only $22.3 million in crude medicinals (remember that United States exported $75 million in ginseng in 1990), but their value-added medicinal exports were ten times more ($260 million). It was vice versa in India, in 1974, exporting 31 crore rupees (ca. $12 million) in crude botanicals compared with only 4.5 crore rupees (ca. $2 million) in value-added derivatives and active compounds.

"First World" scientists in this volume may not hold much respect for the crude botanicals or extracts, preferring, as United States pharmaceutical firms do, the "silver bullet." But Dhawan, in this volume, shows how extracts of *Bacopa, Commiphora, Curcuma, Picrorrhiza, Sapindus,* and *Streblus* are proportionately more effective than their isolated ingredients, suggesting synergies in the crude extractives, widely available on the Indian subcontinent. Clearly taxol is the most exciting drug to the NCI in the last two decades, but camptothecin is of almost equal promise. Camptothecin is derived from the Chinese Happy Tree, *Camptotheca acuminata* Decne., plantations of which were established by the U.S. Department of Agriculture (USDA), years ago, in Chico, California. Those plantations were abandoned, but the tree still persists in various botanical gardens in California. It is not listed in the published holdings of the Dehra Dun Arboretum, but the tree should be imported there. *Nothopodytes,* alias *Mappia foetida* Miers, an Indian member of the Icacinaceae, is little known even among the Indians, but it also contains camptothecin.

India also grows some *Fritillaria imperalis* L. (*Petilium* is an alternative name for *Fritillaria,* the imperial lily), a prime source of imperialine. Bulbs of imperial fritillary, *Fritillaria imperialis* L., are reported to contain 800–1,200 ppm imperialine. The bulbs are rather large, attaining 100 grams or so. That means that with near perfect extraction, one might get 1 gram of imperialine from ten bulbs weighing a kilogram. The bulbs run about $5.00 each. A pharmacist at Georgetown is eager to get imperialine for diagnostic properties, based on its antimuscarinic potential. There is a remote possibility this could lead to bigger markets for imperialine, noted for bronchiorelaxant, myorelaxant, spasmolytic, and uterorelaxant properties (Duke 1992a).

The related alkaloids may have hypotensive activities. The minor alkaloidal fraction is said to be cardiotonic and antifibrillatory, like guanidine, and spasmolytic, like papaverine. This book also says, "Imperatine [sic], the major alkaloid isolated from the plant exerted relaxant and spasmolytic actions against various spasmogens on uterine, intestinal, bronchial, tracheal, and vascular muscles." The minor alkaloidal fraction also lowered the blood pressure of anesthesized dogs owing to cardiac depression and peripheral vasodilation. Compounds reported from *Fritillaria* include cevacine, cevanine, imperialine, imperoline, imperonine, isobaimonidine, peiminine, and starch (Duke 1992b).

Perhaps the NCI should cosponsor a chemotaxonomic survey of the genus *Mappia* (*Nothopodytes*) in South India to parallel the chemotaxonomic survey of Himalayan *Taxus* in Northern India, if vouchered germ plasm (for research only) is provided the USDA for trials in Puerto Rico and/or Peru, where we would also like to consider neem (*Azadirachta indica* A. Juss.) as an alternative crop to *Erythroxylum*. Neem seeds are reported to vary as widely as 50–90,000 ppm in azadirachtin content. The high-azadirachtin plants need to be identified and conserved.

Tyler (in this volume) mentioned the mythical discovery of quinine's febrifugal activity in America, long before the Columbian exchange had stimulated the introduction of malaria from Africa. Now the malaria organism is resistant to quinine and quickly becoming resistant to chloroquine. The Food and Agriculture Organization (FAO) is supporting studies of compounds derived from *Artemisia annua* L., also grown as a cultivar and weed in India, for chloroquine-resistant malaria. Early in 1992 (Duke 1992c) I predicted that the malaria organism would prove resistant to the *Artemisia* compounds within ten to twenty years after they were introduced on a wide scale.[1] Then we would go back to Mother Nature, knocking on her door, and pleading again, this time for a cure for artemisinin-resistant malaria. The more we deplete the species of the world's flora, the less the likelihood that Mother Nature can help again.

Lisa Conte (in this volume) mentioned the hope that Shaman's SP–303 might hold the answer to acyclovir-resistant herpes. If so, might we predict an SP–303-resistant herpes, ten to twenty years down the road?

As conservationists, we must remember that disease organisms, with very short generation times, evolve much faster than the higher plants from which we hope to elicit pharmaceuticals. AIDS, herpes, malaria, measles, and tuberculosis are just a few of the evolving diseases. It is said that almost every AIDS virus is different from its "parent." Will we become more alarmed if a sneeze-transmitted AIDS evolves? Will we then have 250,000 or 125,000 or 25,000 higher plants to screen for the anti-AIDS compounds? Will the cure come from some now unknown species or from some *Aloe, Castanospermum, Glycyrrhiza, Hypericum, Hyptis, Phytolacca, Podophyllum, Prunella, Ricinus, or Viola* now cultivated in India? Or will the last of the endangered species containing the magical medicine have fallen to the axe?

Neem

There is some controversy about the neem, not at all endangered, but very important, culturally, medicinally, and pesticidally in the Indian subcontinent. What value do we assign to a tree that provides toothbrush; soap; sacrament; protection to stored grains, pulses, and rice; and even spiritual food to many of India's 800 to 900 million people? Conservationists ask what right an American firm has to patent a neem product, not sharing any of the profits with India. The

United States does have, of course, many patent and copyright disputes with India and China.

C. M. Ketkar (1982) adds amebicide, antiallergic, antidermatitic, antieczemic, antifeedant, antifungal, antifuruncular, antigingivitic, antihistaminic, antiinflammatory, antiperiodontitic, antipyorrheic, antiscabic, antiseborrhoic, antitubercular, antiviral, bactericidal, cardiac, diuretic, insecticidal, larvicidal, nematicidal, piscicidal, and spermicidal to the biological activities attributed to neem or its derivatives. India has many patents of its own on neem and has the potential to produce renewably 80,000 tons of neem oil and 330,000 tons neem cake from 420,000 tons seed from 13.8 million neem trees. About 18,000 tons neem oil was used in soap manufacture in 1975 (Ketkar 1982). Ironically, experiments planned at Coimbatore forced our Indian counterparts to import neem extracts from Germany and the United States (for forest spraying in the optimistic belief that "natural" pesticides would not upset the ecological balance in the forest).

Mike Benge (personal communication 1992) suggests a wholesale price of $80–$160/kg azadirachtin and shows data suggesting that seeds may vary from 50 to 90,000 ppm azadirachtin. Assume that a tree yields 50 kg fruit, which contains 25 kg seed, with 4% azadirachtin (40,000 ppm) means 1 kilogram of azadirachtin worth $80–$160, per tree, following Benge's assumptions. A tree can bear 50 kg fruit, which will bring 4 cents per kg at the neem plant, making the unprocessed fruit of one tree worth $2.00. Depulped and undried seed brings 8 cents per kg, depulped dried seed, 10 cents per kg. The dried kernels smell just like some pickled onions I had for lunch at Coimbatore.

Larson (1989) notes that half a billion people use neem as a toothbrush. The average toothbrush and a tube of toothpaste at my local drug store each costs more than a dollar. Does this make the toothbrush application a billion-dollar business? If so, the neem's value as a chewstick toothbrush is worth magnitudes more than the medicinal exports of India.

Azadirachtin, like margosan, is for the monied First World, leaving the traditional neem branch in the bean and rice containers for the Third World, a cheaper and probably healthier approach. Nearly half of Asia's rice crop is lost to pests, many of which can be deterred, if not completely repelled, by neem. What value do we assign a natural antifeedant that saves 1%, 10%, or maybe even half the stored grains of India? Two to 5 kg dried neem leaves are added to 100 kg grain, or they soak their feed bags in water containing 2–10 kg neem leaves/100 liters water, drying these sacks for storing their grain. Other farmers mix neem-leaf paste with mud to make earthen repellant pots. Leaves placed in books, mattresses, and woolens are said to repel vermin. Asian neem extract is synergistic with American custard apple (*Annona squamosa*), the combination 0.5–1 times as effective as DDT against pulse beetles, grain borers, and houseflies (Ketkar 1982). Yamasaki and Klocke (1989) compared the natural antifeedant salannin with fourteen derivatives, some of which were more than forty times more potent than salannin. Azadirachtin was more than four times more potent than salannin. The compound gedunin from neem bark and seeds has proven antimalarial activity, roughly equivalent to that of quinine.

One interesting Saudi project was to plant 50,000 trees in the Plains of Arafat to provide shade to nearly 2 million Muslim pilgrims during their annual Haj rites (Ahmed, Bamofleh, and Munshi 1989). Under Saudi Arabia's arid conditions, neem is usually watered for the first ten to twelve years, after which it taps ground water. Traditional Hindus eat neem leaves on their New Year. Neem is important in the Tamil "Thanksgiving," called Pongal. Neem and mango leaves are hung ceremonially to dispel evil spirits.

There are certain caveats to use of neem oil. Unrefined neem oil may contain between 50 and 1,000 ppb aflatoxin compared with 25 ppb for refined oil. Malaysian infants given oral doses up to 5 mL neem oil experienced vomiting, drowsiness, metabolic acidosis, and encephalopathy. A four-month-old Indian given 12 mL oil died after twelve days (Jacobson 1989).

Extracts have the high acute oral toxicity of 13,000 mg/kg, indicating a low oral toxicity (caffeine has an oral LD_{50} of 192 mg/kg, suggesting that caffeine is nearly 100 times more toxic than neem extracts).

While hard currency exports are important to India, medicinal plants have much greater value internally in India than in the export markets. Internal and external markets lead to exploitation of these crops. Poor people make poor conservationists. We still import many botanicals from India, including neem, psyllium, senna, possibly extracts of Indian mayapple, and snakeroot.

Like China, India is one of those countries where more citizens rely on traditional medicinal plants than on modern synthetics. Farming for the export market does not necessarily relieve intense harvesting pressures on such plants. A Third World mother with a starving child is more likely to sell the last yew to a pharmaceutical firm than a well-fed First-World matron is, unless that matron is dying of cancer.

NOTE

1. Dr. L. Alstatt, retired, M.D., Walter Reed Army Research Institute, tells me (personal communication, 1992) that artemisinin-resistant malaria has already evolved in Thailand.

REFERENCES

Ahmed, S., S. Bamofleh, and M. Munshi. 1989. "Cultivation of Neem (*Azadirachta indica*, Meliaceae) in Saudi Arabia." *Economic Botany* 43 (1):35–38.
Anon. 1992. "Botanical Drug Imports: June." *Chemical Marketing Reporter* (September 21): 14.
Atal, C. K. and B. M. Kapur, eds. 1982. *Cultivation and Utilization of Medicinal Plants.* Jammu Tawi, India: Regional Research Laboratory. 877 pp.
Beckstrom-Sternberg, S. M. and J. A. Duke, 1992. "Sister-Site Selection for the Neem Tree

Using the ORACLE® Climate-Crop Data Base." In *ARS–102, USDA,* p. 59 (March). Proceedings of BARC Poster Day.

Duke, J. A. 1992a. *Handbook of Biologically Active Phytochemicals and Their Activities.* Boca Raton: CRC Press, 183 pp. Also available in a data base format.

Duke, J. A. 1992b. *Handbook of Phytochemical Constituents of GRAS Herbs and Other Economic Plants.* Boca Raton: CRC Press, 654 pp. Also available in a data base format.

Duke J. A. 1992c. *CRC Handbook of Edible Weeds.* Boca Raton: CRC Press, 246 pp.

Jacobson, M. 1989. "Pharmacology and Toxicology of Neem." In M. Jacobson, ed., *Focus on Phytochemical Pesticides,* vol. 1: *The Neem Tree,* ch. 8. Boca Raton, Fla.: CRC Press, 178 pp.

Ketkar, C. M. 1982. "Properties and Uses of Neem (*Azadirachta indica* Juss.)—Its Products and Byproducts." In C. K. Atal and B. M. Kapur, eds., *Cultivation and Utilization of Medicinal Plants,* pp. 483–94. Jammu Tawi, India: Regional Research Laboratory, 877 pp.

Kirtikar, K. R., B. D. Basu, and I. C. S. An. 1975 (reprint). *Indian Medicinal Plants,* 4 vols. text, 4 vols. plates. Delhi: Jayyed Press.

Larson, R. O. 1989. "The Commercialization of Neem." In M. Jacobson, ed., *Focus on Phytochemical Pesticides,* pp. 155–67. Boca Raton: CRC Press, 178 pp.

Perdue, R. E. 1976. "Procurement of Plant Materials for Antitumor Screening." *Cancer Treatment Reports* 60 (8):987–98.

Sarin, Y. K. 1982. "Cultivation and Utilization of *Rauvolfia serpentina* in India." In C. K. Atal and B. M. Kapur, eds., *Cultivation and Utilization of Medicinal Plants,* pp. 288–94. Jammu Tawi, India: Regional Research Laboratory, 877 pp.

Satyavati, G. V., M. K. Raina, and M. Sharma, eds. 1976. *Medicinal Plants of India,* vol. 1. New Delhi: Indian Council of Medicinal Research, 487 pp.

Singh, J., P. R. Rao, and C. K. Atal. 1982. "Ajmalicine (Raubasine) a Medicinally Important Alkaloid from *Catharanthus roseus (Vinca rosea)*." In C. K. Atal and B. M. Kapur, eds., *Cultivation and Utilization of Medicinal Plants,* pp. 284–87. Jammu Tawi, India: Regional Research Laboratory, 877 pp.

Subramanian, K. N., N. Venkatasubramanian, and K. R. Sasidharan. 1991. "Conservation of Wild Germplasm of Medicinal Plants and Its Relevance to Tribal Welfare and Development." *Indian Journal of Minor Forest Produce* 1 (1–2):52–57.

Sundaresh, I. 1982. "Export Potential of Medicinal Plants and Their Derivatives from India." In C. K. Atal and B. M. Kapur, eds., *Cultivation and Utilization of Medicinal Plants,* pp. 800–23. Jammu Tawi, India: Regional Research Laboratory, 877 pp.

Yamasaki, R. B. and J. A. Klocke. 1989. "Structure-Bioactivity Relationships of Salannin as an Antifeedant Against the Colorado Potato Beetle (*Leptinotarsa decemlineata*)." *Journal of Agricultural Food Chemistry* 37:1118–24.

20

A Standardized Commiphora wightii *Preparation for Management of Hyperlipidemic Disorders*

B. N. Dhawan

THE introduction of numerous new synthetic drugs has not solved many contemporary problems of human health, and at the same time, the progress of civilization has increased the risk of falling ill, including iatrogenic diseases caused by modern drugs. The use of herbs linked with traditional systems of medicine fills a gap that appears in modern medicine in treatment of diseases like atherosclerosis. It is being realized that drugs of natural origin may be acting less efficiently and rather slowly but are better related to human physiology since over the centuries *Homo sapiens* has worked out adaptation to them, leading to better tolerance. At the same time, humans are not sufficiently adapted to "aggressive interference of (new) chemical drugs" (Kuznicka 1989).

Gugulipid is a standardized extract of the gum oleoresin obtained from *Commiphora wightii* (Arnott) Bhandari (previously called *C. mukul*), a tree growing in various parts of the Indian subcontinent and containing steroidal constituents. The major steroids have been isolated and characterized by Sukh Dev and his colleagues and include the Z- and the E-guggulsterone (figure 20.1). The chemical studies have been reviewed by Sukh Dev (1988). The total content of these two major guggulsterones in gugulipid is 4%.

The gum resin (called guggul or guggulu) has been used in India for treatment of gout and other forms of arthritis and for reducing body weight in cases of obesity and lipid disorders, and has been mentioned in ancient texts. Thirty-three compound preparations containing the gum as a resin are described in an ancient Ayurvedic treatise *Bhavprakash Nighantu*. The hypolipidemic activity was first experimentally observed by Satyavati, Dwarkanath, and Tripathi (1969). The earlier

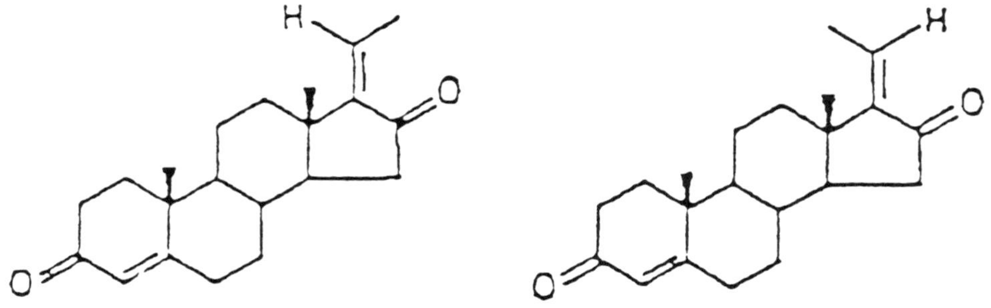

Z–GUGGULSTERONE   E–GUGGULSTERONE

FIGURE 20.1 Chemical structure of Z-guggulsterone and E-guggulsterone.

work has been comprehensively reviewed by Satyavati (1989, 1991) and Dhawan (1989).

The work at the Central Drug Research Institute was started in 1969, the chemical work being undertaken by Dr. Sukh Dev at the National Chemical Laboratory, Poona. It soon became evident that the gum could be fractionated in an ethyl-acetate-soluble fraction having antiinflammatory and hypocholesterolemic activity and in an inactive insoluble fraction, which was also toxic. A neutral fraction was obtained from the ethyl acetate extract that lowered serum cholesterol, and this activity could further be narrowed to a ketonic fraction having about twenty constituents (Nityanand and Kapoor 1973). It was observed that activity did not significantly improve with the pure sterones, and the decision was made, therefore, to develop this standardized fraction as a drug and to name it gugulipid. Assay methods have been developed based on ultraviolet absorption, high-pressure liquid chromatography (HPLC), and thin-layer chromatography (TLC) and confirmed by bioassays.

Pharmacological Studies

1. *Hypolipidemic activity:* The hypolipidemic activity of gugulipid has been demonstrated in normal and hyperlipidemic rats, rabbits, and monkeys. A dose-related lowering of serum cholesterol and triglycerides was observed in normal rats by oral feeding of 25–100 mg gugulipid for thirty days. The effect was more marked in animals made hypolipidemic with Triton (200 mg/kg) and evident even with a single dose of gugulipid (Nityanand and Kapoor 1973, 1975). It is also antagonized diet-induced hyperlipidemia in rats and rabbits as well as ethanol-induced hyperlipidemia in rats (unpublished observation). There was a regression of atheromatous lesions and lowering of tissue lipids in hyperlipidemic monkeys.

Gugulipid produced a significant inhibition in hepatic cholesterol synthesis and decreased free fatty acid release following epinephrine-induced lipolysis in fat cells and heart slices of male rats (Kapoor and Nityanand 1978). Chronic administration produced twofold increased fecal excretion of total bile acids, cholic acid, and deoxycholic acid in rats, rabbits, and monkeys.

2. *Inhibition of platelet aggregation:* Gugulipid (10^{-4} M) was equiactive with pure E- and Z-guggulsterones and clofibrate in inhibiting adenosine diphosphate (ADP)-induced platelet aggregation. The guggulsterones also antagonized aggregation induced by adrenaline and serotonin (Mester, Mester, and Nityanand 1979).

3. *Effect on isoprenaline-induced myocardial necrosis:* Pretreatment of rats with gugulipid (100 mg/kg) improved survival and reduced the intensity of isoprenaline-induced myocardial necrosis. The studies have been repeated with guggulsterones also (Kapoor and Nityanand 1980). Clofibrate was inactive.

4. *Effect on catecholamine biosynthesis:* Chronic oral administration of gugulipid increased dopamine and norepinephrine concentration of heart and brain in the rhesus monkey associated with increased dopamine-β-hydroxylase activity (Srivastava, Nityanand, and Kapoor 1984). Similar results have been obtained with pure guggulsterones in the rats except that dopamine-β-hydroxylase activity in the brain was decreased. This was associated with decreased dopamine and norepinephrine concentration. Reverse changes were observed in serotonin and histamine concentrations in the two tissues (Srivastava and Kapoor 1986).

5. *Hormonal activity:* Gugulipid as well as the pure guggulsterones (E and Z) were devoid of estrogenic, antiestrogenic, progestational, or antiprogestational activity (Dossier 1986).

6. *Other pharmacological actions:* Gugulipid had mild antiinflammatory activity. It had no effect on food/water intake, gross behavior, and other organ systems.

Toxicology

1. *Acute toxicity:* Gugulipid is very safe and has a high lethal dose$_{50}$ (LD$_{50}$) in mice and rat by both oral and intraperitoneal routes (>1.6 g/kg).

2. *Subacute and chronic toxicity:* The studies were conducted in rats, beagle dogs, and rhesus monkey at 2.5–10 times the effective doses. No toxic effects were observed in gross behavior or in hematological, biochemical, macroscopic, or histological observations on various organ functions.

3. *Teratological studies:* The experimental animals were rats and rabbits, the drug being administered during the period of organogenesis. No embryotoxic, fetotoxic, or teratogenic effects were observed in either species.

4. *Mutagenic activity:* Gugulipid was devoid of mutagenic activity in *Salmonella typhimurium* by the Ames (1971) test.

Clinical Studies

The clinical studies were carried out as envisaged by the Central Drug Standard Organization of the Government of India after informed consent of participating volunteers and patients was obtained.

1. *Clinical pharmacology:* Clinical pharmacology (phase I clinical study) was studied in healthy adult volunteers. In the single-dose study, volunteers received 200–2400 mg gugulipid in a double-blind manner. The multiple-dose study employed a daily dose of 1,200 or 1,500 mg for four weeks. Gugulipid was safe and well tolerated. The chronic administration of the higher dose produced a 29% reduction in serum cholesterol and a 15–20% reduction in low-density lipoproteins (Nityanand et al. 1980, 1981; Agarwal et al. 1986).

2. *Phase II clinical trial:* The phase II clinical trial was an open trial in 50 cases wherein a dose of 500 mg was given thrice daily for a period of twelve weeks to patients with hyperlipidemia (Agarwal et al. 1986; Nityanand, Srivastava, and Asthana 1989). The patients had persistent minimum fasting serum cholesterol levels of 220 mg/dl and/or triglycerides 150 mg/dl with no secondary causes of hyperlipidemia. There was no effect on biochemical indicators of liver and kidney function by gugulipid therapy. A significant lowering in serum cholesterol (27%) and triglycerides (22%) was observed. The degree of hypocholestremic effect appeared to depend on the initial serum cholesterol level (Dhawan 1989).

The results showed that patients suffering from Type II B or Type IV hyperlipidemia responded to gugulipid more effectively.

3. *Multicentric (phase III) clinical trials:* These trials were conducted in two parts. In part A, phase II trials were extended to three other centers and results were obtained from 250 patients. Basically, the results were similar. About 88% of patients responded in six to eighteen weeks. The fall in cholesterol and triglycerides ranged between 14% and 30% and 13.5% and 40%, respectively, associated with a 14–27% increase in high-density lipoprotein (HDL) cholesterol. The part B was a double-blind crossover comparison between the effects of gugulipid and clofibrate. Enough washout period was allowed between the two drugs. The sequence of two drugs was decided on a double-blind, randomized basis. Detailed results have been described by Dhawan (1989) and are summarized in table 20.1.

In most patients gugulipid was more effective except in hypertriglyceridemia, where clofibrate appeared somewhat better. Moreover, no side effects were obtained with gugulipid, whereas 2 patients receiving clofibrate had to be withdrawn from the trial because of the occurrence of a flu-like syndrome. Mean changes in important parameters in patients during treatment with gugulipid and clofibrate are summarized in table 20.2.

TABLE 20.1   *Distribution of Total Cases and Responders in Double-Blind, Multicentric, Crossover Comparison of Gugulipid and Clofibrate*

Parameter	Gugulipid	Clofibrate
Total cases	125	108
Percent responders:		
Mixed hyperlipidemia	94.5	89.3
Hypertriglyceridemia	66.5	86.6
Hypercholesterolemia	80.0	36.6
Total	88.0	83.3

TABLE 20.2   *Comparative Percent Changes in Serum Lipids with Gugulipid and Clofibrate*

Parameter	Gugulipid	Clofibrate
Total cholesterol	−12.6	−14.7
Triglycerides	−16.4	−23.2
HDL cholesterol	+16.1	+ 7.8
LDL cholesterol	−16.7	−13.2
LDL/HDL ratio	−27.6	− 5.1
Total cholesterol/HDL	−22.9	− 9.2

Gugulipid produced a significantly greater increase in HDL cholesterol and a marginally greater fall in LDL cholesterol. As a result there is significantly greater improvement in LDL/HDL and total cholesterol/HDL ratios with gugulipid, thus clearly establishing its superiority over clofibrate along with absence of side effects.

4. *Other clinical studies:* Recently gugulipid (500 mg thrice daily) has been given for six to twelve months in 12 controlled cases of diabetes mellitus with hyperlipidemia. There was a mean weight reduction of 4.7 kg associated with 34.5% and 54.1% reduction in cholesterol and triglyceride, respectively (Dhawan 1989).

The studies have confirmed Ayurvedic claims of effectiveness of *Commiphora wightii* in management of atherosclerosis and hyperlipidemia and established gugulipid as a safe and effective hypolipidemic agent. This is a useful addition to physicians' armamentarium for treatment of this difficult, serious, and common disease utilizing a renewable natural resource. The Drug Controller, Government of India, has permitted its marketing as a new drug, and it has been commercially available as a prescription drug in tablets containing 500 mg gugulipid for nearly six years. The World Wildlife Fund (Switzerland) Biological Diversity Campaign in 1989 included gugulipid among nine new natural products for the cure of our ills.

REFERENCES

Agarwal, R. C., S. P. Singh, R. K. Saran, S. K. Das, N. Sinha, O. P. Asthana, P. P. Gupta, S. Nityanand, B. N. Dhawan, and S. S. Agarwal. 1986. "Clinical Trial of Gugulipid—a New Hypolipidemic Agent of Plant Origin." *Indian Journal of Medical Research* 84:626–34.

Ames, B. N. 1971. "The Detection of Chemical Mutagens with Enteric Bacteria." In A. Hollander, ed., *Chemical Mutagens: Principles and Methods for Their Detection,* pp. 267–82. New York: Plenum.

Bhavaprakash Nighantu. 1924. *"English Commentary,"* 3d ed., p. 107. V. N. Dwivedi, ed. Banaras: Motilal Banarasi Das.

Dev, Sukh. 1988. "Ayurveda and Modern Drug Development." *Proceedings of the Indian National Science Academy* 54A:12–42.

Dhawan, B. N. 1989. *Le Gugulipide,* pp. 27–35. Nice: Compete Rendu du Congress Internationale de Phytotherapie.

"Dossier on Gugulipid, Phase III Clinical Data and Summary of Preclinical and Phase I and II Data," p. 71. Central Drug Research Institute. 1986. Submitted to the Drug Controller, Government of India, New Delhi.

Kapoor, N. K. and S. Nityanand. 1978. "Effect of Guggul Steroids in Cholesterol Biosynthesis in Rats." *Indian Journal of Biochemistry and Biophysics* 15 (Suppl.):75.

Kapoor, N. K. and S. Nityanand. 1980. "Guggulsterones in Isoproterenol Induced Myocardial Necrosis." *Indian Journal of Heart Research* 1 (Suppl. 1):22.

Kuznicka, B. 1989. "The Role of Ethnopharmacy and Ethnopharmacology in Light of the Historical Studies." In B. Kuznicka, ed., *The History of Natural Drugs,* p. 20. Warsaw: Polish Academy of Science.

Mester, L., M. Mester, and S. Nityanand. 1979. "Inhibition of Platelet Aggregation by Guggul Steroids." *Planta Medica* 37:367–77.

Nityanand, S. and N. K. Kapoor. 1973. "Cholesterol Lowering Activity of the Various Fractions of the Guggal." *Indian Journal of Experimental Biology* 11:395–96.

Nityanand, S. and N. K. Kapoor. 1975. "Hypolipidemic Effect of Ethyl Acetate Fraction of *Commiphora mukul* (Guggal) in Rats." *Indian Journal of Pharmacology* 7:106.

Nityanand, S., O. P. Asthana, S. S. Agarwal, P. P. Gupta, A. N. Tangri, S. Dev, V. Puri, and B. N. Dhawan. 1980. "Tolerance and Hypolipidemic Activity of Gugulipid—the Steroidal Fraction of *Commiphora mukul.*" *Abstracts of the World Conference on Clinical Pharmacology and Therapeutics,* London, no. 0667.

Nityanand, S., O. P. Asthana, P. P. Gupta, N. K. Kapoor, and B. N. Dhawan. 1981. "Clinical Studies with Gugulipid, a New Hypolipidemic Agent." *Indian Journal of Pharmacology* 13:59–60.

Nityanand, S., J. S. Srivastava, and O. P. Asthana. 1989. "Clinical Trials with Gugulipid—a New Hypolipidemic Agent." *Journal of the Association of Physicians of India* 37:323–28.

Satyavati, G. V. 1989. "Gum Guggul (*Commiphora mukul*)—the Success Story of an Ancient Insight Leading to a Modern Discovery." *Indian Journal of Medical Research* 87:327–35.

Satyavati, G. V. 1991. "Gugulipid: A Promising Hypolipidaemic Agent from Gum Guggul (*Commiphora wightii*)." *Economical and Medicinal Plants Research* 5:47–82.

Satyavati, G. V., C. Dwarkanath, and S. N. Tripathi. 1969. "Experimental Studies on the Hypocholesterolemic Effect of *Commiphora mukul* Engl. (Guggul)." *Indian Journal of Medical Research* 57:1950–62.

Srivastava, M. and N. K. Kapoor. 1986. "Guggulsterone Induced Changes in the Levels of Biogenic Monoamines and Dopamine Beta-Hydroxylase Activity of Rat Tissues." *Journal of Bioscience* 10:15–19.

Srivastava, M., S. Nityanand, and N. K. Kapoor. 1984. "Effect of Gugulipid on Norepinephrine Biosynthesis of Monkey Tissues." *Current Science* 53:131–33.

21

Plant Explorations in Asia Under the Sponsorship of the National Cancer Institute, 1986–1991: An Overview

Djaja Doel Soejarto, Charlotte Gyllenhaal, Peter S. Ashton, and S. H. Sohmer

THE Program for Collaborative Research in the Pharmaceutical Sciences (PCRPS) at the University of Illinois at Chicago (UIC) has been involved since 1977 in three major areas of plant-derived drug discovery, namely, the search for anticancer agents, the search for agents to regulate fertility, and the search for vegetal sweeteners as possible sugar substitutes. To fill the needs of these projects, plant collections in different parts of the world (Africa, America, and Asia) were carried out. Research funding has come primarily from the National Cancer Institute (NCI) of the National Institutes of Health (NIH), from the World Health Organization (WHO), and from the National Institute of Dental Research (NIDR) of NIH. Funds have also been obtained from the industrial and private sectors.

The PCRPS represents a unique multidisciplinary research team, consisting of chemists, pharmacognosists, pharmacologists, biochemists, and botanists. Aside from chemical, pharmacological, and cell culture facilities at the University of Illinois at Chicago under the direct control of PCRPS, the institution has a close tie with the Botany Department of the Field Museum of Natural History, whose facilities (among which is a 2.5-million-specimen herbarium collection) are at the disposal of PCRPS for use in plant collection, identification, curation, and safekeeping.

On December 2, 1985, in response to a request for proposal (REP) from the NCI, PCRPS, in collaboration with the Arnold Arboretum of Harvard University (Cambridge, Massachusetts) and the Bishop Museum (Honolulu, Hawaii), submitted a proposal to carry out a plant collection program in Southeast Asia for anticancer evaluation at the Frederick Cancer Research and Development Center, Frederick, Maryland. The Arnold Arboretum, a botanical institution specializing in the flora of Asia, is also endowed with a large herbarium collection holding (1,430,000 specimens, integrated curatorially with other Harvard herbaria, comprising a total collection holding of some 5 million specimens), of which 50% (ca. 700,000 specimens) consists of plants of East and Southeast Asia. The UIC-Harvard University team was further strengthened by the affiliation of the botany department of the Bishop Museum, Honolulu, Hawaii, which has active plant collection programs in the Pacific and Papua New Guinea and a herbarium collection holding of more than 450,000 specimens.

On September 29, 1986, the NCI awarded the PCRPS a research contract (Contract No. NO1–CM–67925) to carry out plant explorations in Southeast Asia for the period of September 1, 1986, through August 31, 1991. Unless otherwise stated, the term *NCI contract* used throughout this chapter refers to this particular contract number. A plant-collecting expedition was initiated in March 1987 to the Philippines by the PCRPS/UIC-Arnold Arboretum/Harvard University staff and was later followed by many others.

This chapter discusses the strategy, methodology, accomplishments, and status of this NCI-sponsored plant exploration program up to the close of its five-year cycle, August 31, 1991 as well as other plant collection efforts and considerations of personal health, safety, and politics.

Methodology

GENERAL STRATEGY

The geographic area covered in the present plant exploration program extends, in the main part, from Thailand east to New Guinea, comprising the Malesian biogeographic region. Explorations and plant collections were targeted to the tropical rain forest areas, with Malaysia, Indonesia, the Philippines, and Papua New Guinea as the major focus. Collection work started in western Malesia during the earlier stages and extended to eastern Malesia in the later stages.

Long before the initiation of a plant-collecting expedition, all the necessary arrangements were made to secure visas and other permits that would allow entry into a particular country to carry out field research (including collection of plant material in, and its export from, the country). The modus operandi that has been adopted for the project was to carry out joint botanical fieldwork with a host botanical institution, as well as to support local plant exploration projects.

In every plant-collecting expedition, the primary objective was to collect plant samples in amounts of 300–1,000 g dry weight each, to be subsequently used for bioassays, initially intended to detect any cancer-arresting properties of the plant extracts, but later also to be tested for their anti-AIDS activity. Emphasis of the collection was given to the flowering plant taxa. As used here, the term *sample* is defined as a plant part or combination of parts, in the amount indicated; thus, we have leaf sample, leaf plus twig sample, stembark sample, root sample, and whole-plant sample (the latter in case of herbaceous plants), etc. Normally, three samples (leaves + twigs, stembark, root) were collected from a single tree. The collection of more than one type of sample per plant, especially in the case of trees, is advisable, since the occurrence of chemical compounds may vary in different plant parts. Thus, by separating the different parts, the exact location of any biologically active principle(s) would be known with certainty. All samples were documented by a series of voucher herbarium specimens for identification or confirmation of identification of the species, as well as for future reference.

Only fertile materials were collected when the on-the-spot taxonomic identity of the plant species was not known. For plants whose specific identity in the field was known with certainty, sterile materials were permitted for collection. If several collecting expeditions were made to one site, such as an island or province, attempts were made to carry out collection work at different seasons of the year, in order to capture the full flowering and fruiting spectrum of the plant species, and hence, a maximum percentage of the species in the flora.

Selection Criteria

Plants were collected based on two major criteria. The first was to provide a high taxonomic diversity and novelty to the collection. The rationale behind this selection criterion is that a high taxonomic diversity will provide a high diversity of types or classes of chemical structures, which would increase the chances of hitting active species in the screening process. The second was to collect plants based on information on medicinal uses as recorded in the field. Information on medicinal use suggests the presence of biologically active principles in the plant, thus serving as a guide that may help in discovering anticancer and anti-AIDS compounds.

In order to achieve a high taxonomic diversity, a list of plants from each area to be explored was prepared based on existing floras and/or checklists. At the onset of the program, such a floristic list was compared with a list of species that the NCI considered as plants of low priority for collection called GESOC (genera extensively screened or completed), in order to produce a "high-priority" list of plants to collect for a particular geographic area. This (high-priority) list was provided to and used by collectors as a field guide. When the NCI decided to evaluate all plants collected in the program against HIV (human immunodeficiency virus, the causative agent of AIDS) two years later, in addition to cancer cell lines, the practice of generating "high-priority" lists of plants was abandoned. Since we did not have any model of plants to treat AIDS or any previous record of plants screened against HIV, we would miss plants that would give active anti-HIV tests if we selected only plants that appear in such a "high-priority" list. However, we continued to generate floristic lists.

In addition to the "random" collection of preselected species, inquiries were routinely performed during plant-collecting fieldwork on plants that are used for medicinal purposes in the area of collection. Based on these field ethnomedical data, plants were collected without regard to priority. Thus, except for three occasions when focused ethnobotanical inquiries were conducted, namely, during fieldwork in Nepal, Balochistan, and Irian Jaya, sporadic field inquiries on the local uses of plants for medicine were routinely performed as an integral part of all the plant-collecting expeditions for the project.

As the collection work progressed, an increasingly large list of previously collected plants was developed. This list, called the TOVLIFOC list (taxa of very little interest for collection), comprises all plants that have been collected for the project up to a particular date. All plants appearing in the TOVLIFOC list were to be avoided, as much as possible. Thus, in the later stages of the plant-collecting operation, floristic lists and the TOVLIFOC lists were used as a guide for collection.

PRECOLLECTION DOCUMENTATION

In order to assure the collection of a preselected species, a number of measures must be taken before, during, and after the collection process. Thus, following the preparation of the various lists mentioned above, "botanical profiles" of these species were prepared. Such profiles included, among others, distribution maps, taxonomic descriptions and/or keys, photographs, line drawings or good photocopies of herbarium specimens, and common name(s) of the plants in the local language of the area to be explored.

Because of the large number of plants to be collected during a particular expedition, the extent and amount of precollection documentation were left to the discretion of individual collectors. The cooperation and help of resident botanists in the country of collection who are knowledgeable on the local flora reduced the load of precollection documentation and facilitated the collection work.

FIELD METHODS

In our plant collection program, the host collaborating institution has always been the primary headquarters for the field operation. In these institutions all preparations for the field operation were finalized. There, also, herbarium specimens collected were later dried, packed, and shipped to the United States. Similarly, following the conclusion of a particular plant-collecting expedition, preliminary taxonomic determination was performed in the host institutions.

Since most collaborating host institutions were located in the capital city or near the capital city of the country of collection, it was necessary to transfer expedition technical personnel from this location to a town located near the collection site(s). This was done either by the use of commercial airlines, roadways (depending on the location and distance), or passenger ships. Once the expedition area was reached, the next step was to find and set up a semipermanent field base (fig. 21.1a). From such a base, collecting forays were made into forest areas; one or more temporary (two to three days) collecting bases (tents) were also set up, as needed, in a forest edge or clearing, where a stream was found nearby (fig. 21.1b). Because of the nature of sample collecting for bioassays and chemical analyses (namely, bulky material and voluminous loads), the availability of such a semipermanent base with access to transportation, either by road or waterway, was a primary consideration. Thus, a dependable mode of transportation that would provide mobility to the collecting party was a necessity. Transportation was usually in the form of a motorized vehicle (fig. 21.1c) or boat, but one that was big enough to transport expedition crew, expedition supplies, and the voluminous plant materials collected.

Certain expedition supplies (twine, metal bar to dig roots, used newsprint to press voucher herbarium specimens, denatured alcohol to fix specimens, cutting tools, etc.) and provisions were normally acquired in a town near the expedition site, while basic field equipment and supplies, such as a camera, altimeter, field binoculars, branch clippers, plastic bags, notebook, specimen tags, etc., were normally brought from the headquarters.

In our field operation, a crew of five to twelve or so, depending on local conditions, was usually assembled (fig. 21.1d). The crew was headed by the expedition leader, who was responsible for overall coordination and for spotting and determining which plants to collect (fig. 21.1e). Other crew members were the coleader (typically the collaborating botanist from the host institution), herbarium technicians from the host institution, tree climbers, general-purpose workers, and other helpers (local authority, guide, driver, cook). In addition, five to ten temporary porters (fig. 21.1f) to carry expedition supplies and plant materials collected were employed, if vehicles could not penetrate deep into or near collecting sites. A large crew became necessary when time was a constraint, such as in collecting 200–400 samples within a period of one month.

One problem to be faced in collecting plant samples for biological and chemical studies is to determine the type of drying method to be used in the field and to find a space to dry the plant materials collected. Drying either a large number of small-size plant samples simultaneously (batches of thirty to sixty samples of approximately 1 kg dry weight each) or a large amount of only one type of plant sample (for example, 100 kg dry weight of leaves) is a real logistical challenge. Several drying methods exist (see, e.g., Perdue, Jr. 1976); however, the most efficient method appears to be one we used widely in our operation. To begin with, during the collecting process, samples were chopped into small pieces by means of a branch clipper, a large cutting tool, or a specially constructed chopper (fig. 21.2a). Chopping samples reduces bulk and facilitates packing; it also speeds drying. Chopped samples were packed into specially made zippered nylon net or mesh bags. These bags were then placed under the sun on a concrete floor or on

FIGURE 21.1 (a) A base station in Puerto Princesa (Palawan, Philippines) during 1988 and 1989 collecting expeditions. (b) A camp site in central Palawan. (c) A motorized vehicle provides mobility to the expedition crew. (d) Expedition crew on its way to a collecting site. (e) An expedition leader (D. D. Soejarto, Palawan) with a pair of field binoculars to spot plants to collect; his camera is slung around his waist. (f) Additional porters were often employed to carry field supplies and plant materials collected, when a motorized vehicle could not penetrate to camp sites.

Photos by D. D. Soejarto.

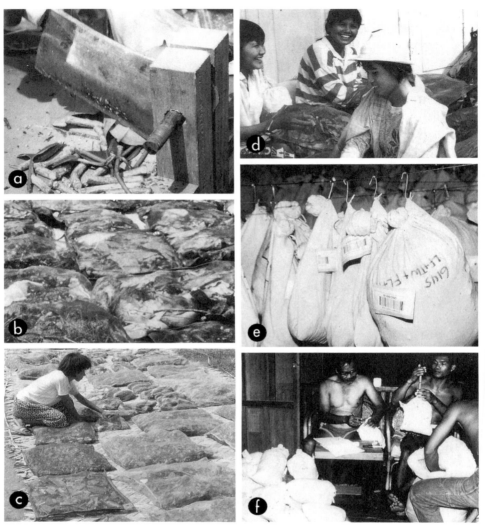

FIGURE 21.2 (a) A plant "chopper" widely utilized in the NCI-sponsored Southeast Asia plant-collecting operation; a 2 m × 2 m tarpaulin is used as a base mat to keep chopped samples uncontaminated. (b) and (c) Different samples in oversized nylon mesh bags are being dried on a concrete floor (b) and on a bamboo mat (c). (d) Bone-dry samples are transferred into white cloth (packing) bags. (e) Bar-coded, dried, packed samples are hung along wires in a well-ventilated place to prevent molding and sample deterioration. (f) Weighing, inventorying, and packing samples for shipment from the field base to the host institution.

Photos by D. D. Soejarto.

bamboo mats (figs. 21.2b, 21.2c). In our experience, plastic zippers lasted longer than metal ones. The size of the mesh bags was large enough (e.g., 60–80 cm by 80–100 cm) to accommodate 1–3 kg fresh weight of plant materials in a loose-fitting manner, which facilitated the shaking and movement of the sample. Shaking and turning the bags over occasionally are necessary in order to speed the drying process and to obtain an evenly dried sample. Smaller mesh bags may be used for less bulky plant materials, such as stembark, root, fruit, etc. Processed this way, a sample may dry within two to seven days in a strong sun, depending on sample texture and fleshiness. During the rainy season, however, a different drying method was used. This included constructing temporary drying chambers, using either electricity or charcoal as a source of heat, and providing ventilation. The combined ingenuity of the collector(s) and members of the field crew usually helped provide solutions and overcome the drying problems in adverse situations.

Completely dried samples were transferred and packed into white cloth bags (fig. 21.2d). The mesh bags could then be reused. To each white cloth bag containing a particular sample, an NCI code number (a bar-code label) was attached by way of a Tyvek tag sewn to the bag or by way of a shipping tag fastened to the bag by a thin wire or nylon string. Dried samples packed this way were temporarily hung along wires in a well-ventilated location (fig. 21.2e), before final packing and shipment. If electricity was available, an electric fan was placed in this location to help maintain a better air circulation. Because of the high air humidity in the tropical rain forest areas where the collection work was performed, this measure was intended to prevent sample molding and deterioration. Near the end of the fieldwork, dried bagged samples were weighed, inventoried (fig. 21.2f), and packed in burlap sacks or carton boxes for shipment or transport to a major city (normally, the city of the host institution), where an international air shipper or shipping consolidator was located. In the end, all samples (in white cloth bags) were packed in carton boxes (fig. 21.3a) for shipment by air cargo through a shipping consolidator to the Frederick Cancer Research and Development Center at Frederick, Maryland. Samples were imported under a special departmental permit held by the NCI. Upon receipt at Frederick, samples were kept in walk-in freezers at a temperature of $-20°C$ (fig. 21.3b), until they could be extracted for testing.

THE CONSERVATION CHALLENGE

A challenge to be faced in collecting plants for anticancer and anti-HIV evaluation is the performance of the collection work without endangering the environment and/or the species collected. Our plant-collecting practices have been developed with this conservation challenge in mind; minimal disturbance to the forest habitat was given a high priority in the collection process. This was achieved primarily by using tree climbers (fig. 21.3c) to collect the aerial parts of a tree, by making a narrow longitudinal strip (fig. 21.3d) cut on one side of a tree in collecting the

FIGURE 21.3 (a) Samples being packed in carton boxes for shipment by air cargo from the country of collection to the United States (NCI). (b) Upon arrival at the NCI's Frederick Repository, samples are kept in walk-in freezers at a temperature of −20° C. (c) and (d) Nondestructive collecting methods: a tree climber on his way up a 40-m-tall tree to get leaf, twig, and fruit samples (c), and workers in the process of collecting a small strip of the bark and a small piece of the root of a large tree (d). (e) In the collecting site, voucher herbarium specimens are prepared and pressed in the same way as in any botanical collecting expedition. (f) At the Field Museum of Natural History in Chicago, voucher herbarium specimens are sorted, labeled, and distributed to designated herbarium institutions.   *Photos by D.D. Soejarto.*

stembark, by tracing the root to a distance (2–3 m) from the tree base in collecting the root, by leaving a collecting site in the same condition as it was found, and by extinguishing all campfires completely. In cases of rare species and small herbaceous plants, measures were taken not to harvest all plants of a species from a single population.

POSTCOLLECTION DOCUMENTATION

Voucher herbarium specimens were prepared and processed in a routine manner as done by all botanists in plant collection work (fig. 21.3e). Because of the large number of specimens involved, field drying of these specimens was not considered. Rather, the wet method, whereby specimens are routinely fixed in denatured alcohol, was used. In this method, bundles of freshly collected specimens in newsprints were placed in a strong (heavy duty) plastic bag in a vertical position and an adequate quantity of diluted ethanol (approximately 50:50 v/v) was poured into and through the specimens, until the material was well soaked. Such treated herbarium specimens were later opened upon receipt at the host institution to be dried in its drying facility. Dried unmounted specimens were shipped from a host institution to the University of Illinois at Chicago to be forwarded to the John G. Searle Herbarium, Field Museum of Natural History, Chicago.

At the field museum, these specimens were processed (sorted, labeled, and distributed to designated herbarium institutions; fig. 21.3f). In all cases, one set of voucher herbarium specimens was deposited in the herbarium institution in the host country where the collection work was carried out. Other duplicate sets were distributed to, among others, the following herbaria: A (Arnold Arboretum of Harvard University, Cambridge, Massachusetts), F (Field Museum of Natural History, Chicago), L (Rijksherbarium at Leiden, the Netherlands), and US (National Herbarium of the Smithsonian Institution, Washington, D.C.).

Botanical and ethnomedical field data of the plants collected were recorded in a field notebook at the time of collection. Preprinted blank field labels (each with a carbon copy) (fig. 21.4) were later completed by longhand. Batches of such handwritten field labels were dispatched separately and, if possible, before the voucher herbarium specimens, from field bases to the project's headquarters in Chicago. Upon receipt, the field data were entered into a computerized plant data base, and printed field labels were generated. Following data entry, a diskette containing a set of botanical field data was sent to NCI. New diskettes were periodically sent to NCI as the data base was updated with new determinations or redeterminations.

TAXONOMIC DETERMINATION

Taxonomic determination and/or confirmation of taxonomic identity of the plants collected were started in a herbarium institution located in the host country. For

PLANTS OF _____

This is a voucher specimen for
anticancer testing: YES ____ NO ____

Fam.:

Det. by: Date:

Field characters:

Loc.:

Lat.:   Long.:   Alt.:

Habitat:

Loc. name(s):

Med. use(s):

Part(s) used:

General notes:

Hazard notes:

Collector(s):

            No.:   Date:

Sample plant part(s):

NCI code number(s):

Collected under the auspices of:
  U.S. National Cancer Institute, Bethesda, MD.
  University of Illinois at Chicago, Chicago, IL.
  Arnold Arboretum, Harvard University, Cambridge, MA.
  Field Museum of Natural History, Chicago, IL.

  Host Institution:

FIGURE 21.4 A blank field label used in the Southeast Asia plant collection operation. This label must be completed by longhand in the field; a batch of completed labels is to be sent to the program's headquarters in Chicago by separate air mail by the collector from the country of collection.

certain collections, further attempts at determination were made at the herbarium of the Field Museum of Natural History, Chicago. In both cases, continuing determination took place at the herbarium of the Arnold Arboretum, Harvard University. Final attempts at determination were made at the Rijksherbarium at Leiden, and if a specimen remained undetermined, the assistance of a taxonomic specialist was sought.

AVOIDANCE OF DUPLICATION

In order to avoid or minimize the duplication of plants collected, each member of the network of collectors in the project was provided with a computer-generated list (TOVLIFOC list, see above) of plants that had been collected up to a particular date. This list was updated periodically.

Accomplishments

Up to August 31, 1991, at the close of the first five-year collection cycle, thirty-five botanical expeditions in various regions of Asia, but primarily Southeast Asia, were completed under the sponsorship of the NCI (Contract NO1–CM–67925). More than 10,000 screening-sized samples were collected during this five-year project period, distributed in 3,535 collection numbers belonging to more than 2,000 species, in more than 200 families of flowering plants (based on concept of families as used in Willis and Airy Shaw 1980). These numbers may, however, change when the taxonomic determination of all plants collected is completed.

Fifty-one percent of the samples collected consisted of leaves and twig parts, 21% of stem parts, 17% of reproductive parts (flowers, fruits, seeds), and 9% of underground parts (roots, rhizomes, etc.), and the remainder consisted of entire plants. The low number of underground plant parts and entire plants (herbaceous species) sampled reflects the difficulty of obtaining these parts in an adequate quantity for biological evaluation.

Figure 21.5 gives an idea of the sample collection volume (number of samples collected) and sample collection intensity achieved during the period 1986–1991. In this figure, the cumulative number of samples (sample volume) collected per country or island and the total voucher herbarium collection numbers (not necessarily the number of species) per country or island are shown. It is immediately obvious from this figure that a high volume of sample collection has been made in the Philippines, Indonesia, Malaysia, and Papua New Guinea. The relationship between sample collection intensity for a particular area vs. sample collection volume gives an index that indicates the degree of taxonomic diversity of the samples collected. Such an index is referred to as TDI (taxonomic diversity index). For example, for Taiwan, with a collection number of 43, comprising 68 samples,

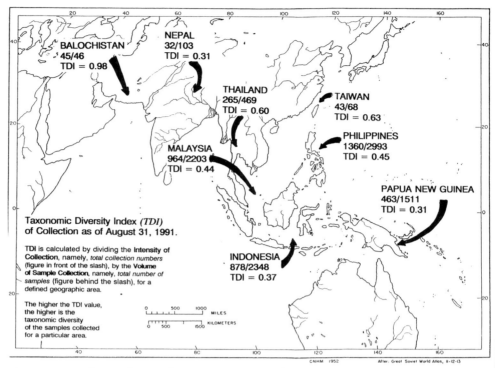

FIGURE 21.5 Map of Asia showing countries where the NCI-sponsored plant-collecting operation has been completed.

the TDI is $43/68 = 0.63$; for Thailand, the TDI is $265/469 = 0.56$; for Sumatra $116/402 = 0.29$; etc. The higher the TDI, the higher the taxonomic diversity of the samples collected; the lower the TDI, the lower the diversity. An optimum TDI for tree species is 0.3, namely, when an average of three samples per plant (normally, leaf + twig, stembark, and root samples) have been collected; the highest possible TDI is 1.0, when only one sample type per plant was collected. The overall TDI of the collection is 0.35.

The TDI is not, of course, a full measure of the taxonomic variation of the samples collected, since it is based on collection numbers, rather than on actual numbers of species collected. Measurements based on species numbers will not be available until all specimens have been fully identified. However, we estimate that for a single expedition, 90–100% of the samples collected represent different species, so that the TDI and the actual taxonomic diversity of the collection will be highly correlated. The TDI provides a preliminary approximation that enables us to monitor progress toward our simultaneous goals of achieving high taxonomic diversity in our collections and including a range of different plant parts for analysis.

Overview of Status

Although the objective of this plant exploration program was to collect plants to be submitted for anticancer and anti-HIV evaluation, the scientific significance of the program goes beyond drug discovery.

One direct contribution it makes is to demonstrate to the host country the potential value that its forests may have in medicine. Although detailed results of this endeavor will not be available until a few years to come, some encouraging indications may be noted. Of the more than 10,000 samples collected, only about 3,000 (belonging to more than 700 species) had been tested against HIV by August 31, 1991. More than 100 of these species showed active test results. Further analysis of these data is under way to evaluate the validity of the approach used in the exploration effort and to demonstrate any correlation that may exist between ethnomedical information and test results. Meanwhile, further evaluation of the remainder of samples and in-depth studies of those that have shown high-priority activity continue at NCI's laboratories. Because of the complex screening procedure for anticancer activity, results of anticancer evaluation of only a small fraction of all samples collected are available. Analysis of these results will be performed when more data accumulate.

Another obvious scientific spinoff of this project is the contribution it makes to the floristic and biogeographic knowledge data base of Southeast Asia, through the rich and new herbarium collections that have been made. An overview on the status of the exploration program at the end of this five-year cycle is provided below. In the discussion, reference is continuously made to figure 21.5.

INDONESIA

An archipelagic nation of more than 13,000 islands, Indonesia still has one of the richest floras in the world and has the largest and richest share of tropical rain forests in Asia. In 1982, the Food and Agriculture Organization (FAO) estimated that there are 10,000 tree species in Indonesia (Anon. 1982). In terms of vascular plant species, a reliable estimate of the number for the country is not available. When we consider, however, that 25,000 flowering plant species are believed to occur in Malesia (van Steenis 1971), not less than 15,000 must occur in Indonesia. Because of the richness of the species, our knowledge of its flora is still far from complete.

Although the study of the flora of Indonesia is the responsibility of Indonesian botanical institutions, there is insufficient scientific staff in Indonesia to complete floristic treatments and taxonomic revisions in the foreseeable future (Ashton 1989). For example, the national botanical institution of Indonesia, the Herbarium Bogoriense, at Bogor, West Java, with a collection holding of more than 1,600,000 specimens, has only two Ph.D. taxonomists (flowering plants) and no research budget. As a result, the Flora Malesiana Foundation headquartered in Leiden, the Netherlands, has led the study of the flora of Indonesia, as a major portion of the study of the entire Malesian region. Yet, despite fifty years of hard work, only about 60% of the monographic treatments of the flowering plant families of this region have been completed.

An ample herbarium specimen base is fundamental to the completion of definitive taxonomic treatments, but no significant plant-collecting programs were undertaken by the Herbarium Bogoriense for many years. Under these circumstances, the NCI-sponsored plant exploration work in Indonesia has helped boost floristic inventory in this country. For the period 1986–1991, seven major botanical expeditions were carried out by the UIC-Harvard team, in cooperation with the Bogor Herbarium: two expeditions to Kalimantan, two to Sumatra, one to Sulawesi, one to Seram, and one to Irian Jaya. In addition, the following special collection efforts were made: "Jamu" traditional medicine collection in Java in 1988, an ethnobotanically focused expedition in the Arfak Mts. of Irian Jaya, a small plant collection effort in Krakatau in August 1989, and one Sulawesi expedition participation in 1991. A total of 878 collection numbers, comprising 2,348 samples, were obtained, for a 0.37 TDI (fig. 21.5).

Aside from these botanical collecting expeditions, a small ethnopharmacology project under the title of "Field Studies of Indonesian Medicinal Plants," funded by the World Wildlife Fund (WWF) U.S. (Grant 6262) was carried out jointly with three of the NCI-sponsored expeditions, namely, in 1988 (Central Kalimantan and Sumatra) and in 1989 (West Kalimantan). The primary goal of the WWF U.S.-funded work was to identify ethnomedical leads for follow-up collection by the NCI-funded team during each of the three expeditions (Warsita Mahyar et al. 1991).

The host institution for all our exploration work in Indonesia was Herbarium Bogoriense in Bogor. This institution is a subdivision of the Research and Development Center for Biology (PPPB), which, in turn, is a Division of the Council for Sciences of Indonesia (LIPI). The director and staff at these three levels of administration actively cooperated and provided generous support to the UIC-Harvard University personnel (primarily J. S. Burley) throughout all the expeditions.

PHILIPPINES

Another island nation, the Philippines, consists of more than 7,000 islands, most of which have been partly deforested. Nevertheless, its rich flora is estimated to consist of about 8,000 flowering plant species, with a high degree of endemism (Merrill 1926; Madulid 1982).

Although the study of the flora of the Philippines should be the primary responsibility of Philippine botanical institutions, there are not enough scientific staff in the country to carry out the floristic treatments and taxonomic revisions needed. For example, the Philippine National Herbarium (PNH) in Manila, with collection holdings of 180,000 specimens (formerly more than 500,000 specimens, the greater part of which were destroyed during World War II; Madulid, personal communication) is currently staffed by only two Ph.D. botanists. At the same time, funds had not been adequate to permit extensive and continuing plant collection programs. As a result, studies on the flora of the Philippines have also been led by Leiden, as part of the Flora Malesiana project. In mid-1990, work on a Flora of the Philippines project, organized through the joint efforts of the Bishop Museum and the Philippine National Herbarium, was implemented, with funding from the United States National Science Foundation (NSF). At present, the inventory stage of this project is ongoing.

Under these circumstances, the NCI-sponsored plant collection work in the Philippines, initiated in 1987, has significantly contributed to plant exploration efforts in that country. Ten plant-collecting expeditions, large and small, were carried out during the period 1986–1991 under this sponsorship. Collection work has been done on the islands of Luzon, Visayas, Mindoro, Panay, and Palawan, from which a total of 1,360 collection numbers, comprising 2,993 samples (TDI = 0.45), have been collected for anticancer and anti-AIDS evaluation. The largest number of samples came from Palawan, followed by Luzon, then Panay, Visayas, and Mindoro. Unquestionably, specimens collected under the NCI sponsorship represent a significant addition to the existing collection holdings of the PNH and provide a substantial contribution toward the writing of the recently implemented Flora of the Philippines project. All NCI-sponsored plant collection work in the Philippines has been performed jointly with the PNH.

Explorations of Palawan for the NCI screening program started in 1988 (Soejarto 1989). A total of 788 collection numbers from this island, comprising 1,493 samples (TDI = 0.53), has been accumulated up to August 31, 1991. Although these figures represent a large number for the island, work to collect plants from Palawan should continue. The reasons for this continued interest are that (1) Palawan is the only major island in the Philippines with more than 60% of its land surface still covered by good forests (only 10–30% good forest cover still remains in other larger islands). (2) The flora of this island is rich (current estimate: 1,700 species of flowering plants in an area of 1.2 million hectares), with a high degree of endemism: the present collection represents perhaps less than 20% of the flora. (3) The local logistics are ideal. (4) The cooperation received from both the local authorities in Palawan (Bureau of Forest Development or BFD and Palawan Integrated Area Development Project or PIADPO), as well as from the Philippine National Museum, Manila, has been excellent.

Among the activities of current interest being undertaken in Palawan is the implementation of a plot study for the NCI anticancer and anti-HIV evaluation program. This study represents a follow-up of the recommendations proposed by the 1984 Palawan Botanical Expedition team (Podzorski 1985), concerning the conservation of the forests in central Palawan, which cover the Mt. Beaufort/Mt. Thumb system. This expedition team proposed that, in order to protect the forests of central Palawan, a conservation scheme consisting of a central genetic reserve should be surrounded by a forested area to be called a buffer zone, which in turn is to be encircled by a forest utilization area to be called an agroforestry zone.

A 1-hectare plot was established in a semievergreen tropical rain forest (in the so-called buffer zone conservation area) at 350 m altitude in the Mt. Beaufort/Mt. Thumb mountain system of central Palawan, in May 1989. To facilitate the study, trees with a diameter at breast height of 10 cm or more were marked with an easily visible number, registered, and mapped. Two additional plots of 0.1 hectare size each were later added in different forest subtypes located in the so-called gene conservation zone, one at 200 m altitude, the other at 650 m, for purposes of comparison. Sample collections were made from all numbered trees to be submitted for the cancer and HIV screens. The benefit of plot collecting to the NCI program is obvious: numbered trees facilitate the relocation of biologically active species (hence, of pharmaceutical interest) in case of recollection, even when the plant identity has not been determined definitively.

The purpose of the plot study was to obtain a semiquantitative estimate of the potential medicinal value of the Beaufort/Thumb forest cover, whose area has been estimated at 6,000 hectares, as well as of Palawan as a whole. Furthermore, plants collected from the plot are being examined for various chemical compounds at the University of the Philippines, Manila (School of Pharmacy, Department of Pharmacognosy), and in collaboration with the Kobe Women's College of Pharmacy, Kobe, Japan. This plot-collecting work may turn out to have even more significance in the near future, because of the great interest being shown by the Philippine government in its policy of conservation for sustainable development.

As a result of the NCI-sponsored efforts, our knowledge of the flora of this island has been enriched. Further, through a cooperation between the PNH and PCRPS, a Palawan floristic data base is being built based on the PNH's and the field museum's herbarium collection holdings.

Aside from the collecting expeditions, in 1989 the NCI directly provided support to a small project in the Philippines, namely, upgrading the curatorial facilities and operation of the PNH in Manila.

MALAYSIA

Malaysia consists of two physically separated divisions: the Malay Peninsula (western Malaysia) and Sarawak and Sabah, in the west and in the northeast of Borneo, respectively (eastern Malaysia). As a country, no estimate is available on the species richness of its total land surface; estimates are available, however, for the Malay Peninsula and for Borneo, respectively. For the former, the estimate is 7,500 flowering plant species, of which about 3,000 comprise tree species (Whitmore 1973; Keng 1978), while for the latter (Borneo as a whole) the estimate is 10,000–15,000 species (Ashton 1989).

The study of the flora of the Malay Peninsula has been and is partly under the charge of the Forest Research Institute of Malaysia (FRIM) at Kepong, where a well-staffed forest herbarium with 300,000 specimens is located. There is a smaller herbarium at the Department of Botany, University of Malaya, Petaling Jaya. Exploration of the flora of Sarawak is actively being undertaken by the Forest Department in Kuching, whose herbarium collection holding is 80,000 specimens. Similarly, plant exploration of the flora of Sabah is being undertaken by the Forest Department at Sandakan, where the Sandakan herbarium contains more than 80,000 specimens (Ashton 1989). Although there is no national program at present for a comprehensive study of the flora of Malaysia as a whole, this task is being undertaken as a part of the Flora Malesiana project in Leiden.

A plant-collecting collaboration between the NCI-sponsored personnel and the Malaysian botanical institutions was implemented starting in 1987. Three collecting expeditions in Sarawak jointly with the Sarawak Forest Department in Kuching, three collecting expeditions in Sabah with the Sandakan Forest Department staff, and one short collecting trip in the Malay Peninsula with the Kepong FRIM's staff were completed. Also, a collection program by the Institute of Advanced Studies of the University of Malaya at Petaling Jaya was funded through this contract. Altogether, a total of 964 collection numbers, comprising 2,203 screening-sized samples (TDI = 0.44) were collected (fig. 21.5).

Although the collaborating Malaysian botanical institutions have been active themselves in the exploration of their floras, plant-collecting activities undertaken under the project's sponsorship have contributed further to the enrichment of the herbarium collection holdings at these institutions and in augmenting our knowledge of the floras.

PAPUA NEW GUINEA

Papua New Guinea (PNG) is the eastern half of the large island of New Guinea, located at the eastern extremity of the Malesian biogeographic region. The western portion of this island is known as Irian Jaya and is a province of Indonesia. No estimates are available for the species richness of the flora of PNG. However, the island as a whole is believed to contain at least 9,000 flowering plant species, of which about 90% may be endemic (Good 1960). The entire island is luxuriantly covered with tropical rain forests of various types; in Papua New Guinea the forest cover is estimated to be about 85% (Davis et al. 1986).

Plant-collecting programs and floristic studies of the flora of PNG have been actively pursued by botanists from institutions located inside, as well as outside the country, since before 1920 (Stevens 1989); exploration work accelerated since the initiation of the Flora Malesiana project in late 1940s. One of the botanical institutions inside PNG that has been active in exploration work is the Lae National Herbarium of the Department of Forests, Lae (now, Herbarium of the Forest Research Institute, Lae), with a collection of more than 200,000 specimens. One of the botanical institutions outside PNG that has had an active plant-collecting program in this country is the Botany Department of the Bishop Museum, Honolulu. In the 1960s, this latter institution established the Bishop Museum Field Station in Wau (now, the Wau Ecology Institute), with a goal of strengthening the institution's research efforts in the documentation of the flora and fauna of PNG. Through the activities of Wau Ecology Institute and also through its relationship with the Division of Botany (FRI), Bishop Museum has been able to create one of the best records of the PNG fauna and flora.

Two long-term residency expeditions were made in 1988 and 1989 under the sponsorship of the NCI. A third expedition was initiated in June 1990, and the fourth, and last, was in May 1991. For the first expedition, residence was established at Wau (Wau Ecology Institute); for the second, at the Lae National Herbarium. Both the Wau Ecology Institute and the FRI Herbarium have provided excellent and generous cooperation. To date, a total of 463 collection numbers, comprising 1,511 screening-sized samples (TDI = 0.31) have been collected from PNG (fig. 21.5). Collections have been concentrated in the eastern and northeastern Morobe and Madang Provinces, respectively, in diverse types of vegetation. These include *Castanopsis-*, as well as *Nothofagus*-dominated forests, mossy montane forest in the Kuper Range, cloud forest at Ekuti Divide near the Pass, seasonally dry grassland, lowland primary forest, and secondary forests.

NCI's sponsorship has helped boost the plant exploration programs of the Bishop Museum in PNG, particularly in furthering the museum's efforts to document and interpret the plant life of PNG, considered to be one of the most important remaining natural history resources in the Pacific. In addition to furthering this research effort, this sponsorship has permitted the implementation of an even closer collaborative research program between the museum and the Division of Forests, which resulted in an institutional strengthening of the latter. The accomplishment of this collaborative program, thus far, goes beyond the actual collections that have been made: it has enabled these institutions to help interpret the biological diversity through the materials collected.

The NCI-sponsored plant explorations in PNG have also helped another project, under way at the Wau Ecology Institute, to achieve its objectives. Data from the plant exploration work contributed to the completion of a project on tree canopy fogging, an effort to examine the richness of insect life in the forest canopies of PNG.

THAILAND

Close to 12,000 flowering plant species may be found in Thailand (Larsen 1979), whose diverse vegetation cover includes evergreen tropical rain forests (in the peninsular and southeast section of the country), dry evergreen forest with dipterocarps, hill evergreen forest, dry deciduous dipterocarp forest with bamboos, deciduous teak forests, freshwater swamp forest, and mangrove formation, among others.

Exploration of the flora started in 1778, and many botanists, both Thai and foreigners, have since collected at least 116,000 plant specimens from the country (Smitinand 1989). Very active plant collecting was undertaken especially since 1957, when a Thai-Danish Botanical Cooperation was established. This cooperation lasted until 1968. At present, the study of the flora of Thailand is under the charge of the Forest Herbarium of the Royal Forest Department, Bangkok, staffed by seven active taxonomists. Its collection includes more than 60,000 specimens. The primary botanical activity of this institution is the preparation of the *Flora of Thailand,* which was initiated in 1970.

Since the flora of Thailand is distinct from that of Malesia (van Steenis 1950), an NCI-sponsored plant collection in Thailand was considered important in order to increase the taxonomic diversity of samples to be submitted for anticancer evaluation. A collecting trip was implemented in 1987 with the cooperation of the Forest Herbarium. A total of 265 collection numbers, comprising 469 screening-sized samples, were collected during this fieldwork. The following vegetation types were explored: evergreen tropical rain forest, dry evergreen and deciduous dipterocarp forests; deciduous teak forest, mixed deciduous forests; and mangrove forests. Localities between Nakhon Ratchasima and the international boundary with Malaysia, as well as the Kanchanaburi area (southeastern Thailand) were visited.

Although only one collecting trip was made in Thailand, the array of taxa collected did indeed considerably enrich the taxonomic diversity of the plants collected for the NCI plant-screening program. In terms of taxonomic diversity, the TDI of the Thai collection is quite high (TDI = 0.60) (fig. 21.5). The plant material collected during this fieldwork has also contributed to enriching the herbarium data base at the Forest Herbarium and to the elucidation of some taxonomic problems of the flora (Smitinand 1987).

Fieldwork in Thailand was performed jointly with the staff of the Forest Herbarium, who provided excellent cooperation, scientifically, as well as logistically.

TAIWAN (REPUBLIC OF CHINA)

Taiwan is located at the northern edge of the tropical rain forest belt, right on the Tropic of Cancer. As a consequence of its geographic location, the island has different types of vegetation ranging from low-statured evergreen tropical rain forests (Lanyu Island, southern tip of Taiwan) to seasonal deciduous and evergreen forests in the lowlands, broadleaved evergreen forests at medium altitudes, mixed and coniferous forests above 1,800 m, and grasslands above 2,500 m. Despite the small size of the island, Taiwan has a rich flora.

The flora of Taiwan has been well studied, and a floristic treatment (Li et al. 1975–1979) is available. The number of flowering plant species in this country is estimated to be 2,992 (Huang 1979), with a high degree of endemism. A strong floristic relationship exists between the flora of Taiwan and that of southern China, on the one hand, and with those of the Philippines and western Malesia, on the other.

Large collection holdings of the flora of Taiwan are found both inside and outside the country. The National Herbarium at the Taiwan National University has a collection holding of more than 160,000 specimens (Wang, Chen, and Wang 1989). A much smaller holding is found at the herbarium of the Tropical Botanical Garden located at Kenting, in the Heng-chun Peninsula at the southern tip of the island.

Currently, work is ongoing, by the Missouri Botanical Garden in cooperation with Chinese and Taiwanese botanical institutions, to write an eighteen-volume abridged treatment in English of the *Flora of China,* which will include Taiwan. This will be based on the 118-volume national flora in Chinese, which is scheduled for completion in three years. As a result of the project, collecting activities will again be intensified in Taiwan to enrich the existing collection holdings for the writing of the new *Flora.*

A short plant-collecting field trip was undertaken in Taiwan in late 1989 under the sponsorship of the NCI contract. Excellent cooperation during fieldwork was provided by the Heng-chun Peninsula Tropical Botanical Garden, by the Herbarium of the Taiwan National University, and by the Department of Pharmacognosy of the China Medical College, Taichung. Collections were made in the Wuhse montane forest of central Taiwan and in the tropical forests in the Heng-chun Peninsula. Sample collections (43 collection numbers, 68 samples) of high taxonomic diversity (TDI = 0.63) were obtained during this short period of collecting.

The primary objective of this collecting trip was to survey the potential importance that the flora of Taiwan could contribute in increasing the taxonomic diversity of the NCI samples collected from Southeast Asia as a whole, as well as to establish contacts with the Taiwanese botanical institutions. The small number of plants collected did indeed show the novelty of the taxa, primarily those representing endemics and elements from southern (tropical) China.

Other Plant-Collection Efforts

NEPAL

Nepal is located outside the geographical tropics, approximately 27° N latitude, but its climate is partly tropical on account of the high-pressure zone north of the Himalayas, which draws hot, humid southerly winds off the Indian Ocean. The vegetation of Nepal ranges from tropical evergreen forest in the valleys below 1,000 m in the east to alpine meadows at elevations above 4,000 m. The flora of this country is quite rich: it is estimated to contain 6,500 species of flowering plants, with about 5% endemism (Stearn 1978).

Field studies of medicinal plants in Nepal have been pursued by a number of scientific institutions, in Nepal as well as in India. The center of study in Nepal is the Department of Medicinal Plants, Thapathali, Kathmandu.

In 1987 NCI funds were made available to provide partial support for the implementation of a plant-collecting expedition in Nepal by a graduate student of the School of Forestry and Environmental Sciences, Yale University, New Haven. Collecting was done by using folk medicinal uses as a guide in the selection of plants to collect. Collection work was undertaken in the tropical moist deciduous forest of eastern Nepal, in the Terai, and in the lower Arun River Valley. Excellent cooperation of the Department of Medicinal Plants in Kathmandu was received during the collecting operation. A total of 33 collection numbers, comprising 103 screening-sized samples were collected (fig. 21.5), all with some type of information on their folk medicinal uses.

Aside from ethnomedically oriented sample collections, the purpose of the Nepal collection was to increase the taxonomic diversity of samples to be submitted for biological evaluation by the NCI. A set of anti-HIV test results of plants collected in Nepal has been provided to the Department of Medicinal Plants in Kathmandu.

BALOCHISTAN

Balochistan is an autonomous province of Pakistan located in the southwestern corner of the country along the border with Iran. The area falls north of 25° N latitude. The vegetation cover of southern Balochistan is semidesert and desert, with tropical thorn scrubs such as *Acacia, Capparis,* and *Prosopis.*

An ethnobotanical study of the Makrani Baloch was made by a staff member of the Field Museum of Natural History in the spring of 1990. Based on a prior agreement, a small amount of funds from the NCI contract was made available to provide partial support for this ethnobotanical fieldwork, in order to permit the collection of plant samples for anticancer and anti-HIV evaluation. Only plants with field ethnomedical uses were to be collected for the NCI screening program.

This ethnobotanical field study was completed with approximately 1,000 collection numbers, of which about 200 have detailed ethnobotanical data. Forty species of these 200 were collected for the NCI screening program, comprising 46 samples.

Fieldwork in Balochistan was done with the cooperation of the Department of Botany of the University of Karachi.

KUNMING (PEOPLE'S REPUBLIC OF CHINA)

As part of an NCI program to study traditional Chinese medicine and Chinese medicinal plants, a collaboration has been established between the Kunming Institute of Botany and the NCI in the evaluation of medicinal plants from Yunnan and other southern Chinese provinces for anticancer and anti-HIV activities.

Plants are selected and collected by Kunming botanists, based on their documented medicinal use or on evidence provided by local peoples. Organic and aqueous extracts are subjected to bioassay-guided fractionation in NCI laboratories, and where possible, Kunming and NCI chemists collaborate in the isolation and structure elucidation of the active agents (Cragg 1990).

Personal Health and Safety

Sickness, accidents, robbery, political upheaval with hostile consequences, exposure to toxic plants, encounters with poisonous animals, and other misfortunes may befall anyone carrying out botanical fieldwork. Although one or more of these did happen to members of the Southeast Asia field teams in the conduct of their duties, no life-threatening situations arose.

The most common complaints received were bouts of diarrhea, animal and insect bites, and exposure to poisonous plants (mostly contact dermatitis). To minimize infections and the possibility of contracting sickness in the field, members who do botanical fieldwork routinely receive vaccinations and other prophylactic measures, before departure and during the expedition (typhoid, malaria, etc.).

In spite of the precautions taken, health and security problems were experienced by fieldwork crews. For example, one member of the 1989 Palawan expedition (Philippines) contracted malaria, others suffered animal bites, and still others suffered bacterial and fungal infections, as well as exposures to poisonous plants (contact dermatitis). All of them received medical attention in local hospitals and later in clinics in Manila.

Political Considerations

The major political consideration in a plant collection program for drug discovery involves issues on the question of property rights and compensation to the people in the country of collection. In recent years, there has been an increasing awareness in many countries on issues of benefit return, namely, that some type of compensation should be provided in exchange for the collection of biological materials from a particular country. Such an awareness has been awakened, in part, by concerned scientists, who, through ethical considerations, feel justly that plant and animal resources of a country belong to the people of that country and that indigenous knowledge of the medicinal uses of plants belongs to the people who originally discovered it, through eons of trial and error, and who are now providing such potentially valuable information, which may lead to the discovery and development of new drugs. Thus, a share of the monetary gain should be returned to the country of collection or to the people who gave the information responsible for the discovery. Proof of this concern is expressed by, among others, the Declaration of Belem, the Kunming Action Plan, and the Hipolito Unanue Agreement (Anon. 1992), the Göteborg Resolution (Eisner and Meinwald 1991), the Chiang Mai Declaration (Akerele, Heywood, and Synge 1991), the United States Agency of International Development–National Institute of Health–National Science Foundation joint Commentary (statement) (Schweitzer et al. 1991), and articles such as "Folklore, Tradition, or Know-How" (Elisabetsky 1991) and "No Hunting" (Kloppenburg, Jr. 1991).

Among the measures that have been implemented in the Southeast Asia plant-collecting program to respond to such issues are the training of technicians and junior scientists in field and herbarium techniques; the deposit of a set of duplicates of voucher herbarium specimens in the host (normally, national) herbarium institution; the provision of relevant test results for plants collected in a particular country to appropriate governmental agencies (primarily the host institution) in that country; the provision of curatorial support to host botanical institutions; and the sponsorship of travel for scientists from the country of collection to visit the NCI laboratories and other facilities of U.S. institutions that have connections with the NCI-sponsored program.

Other measures include assurance to the country of collection of a share of future financial benefit, if a drug derived from a plant collected in that particular country should be developed and marketed, within the policy guidelines as provided by the NCI. A provision is also in force for a selected junior scientist (primarily natural products scientist) in the country of collection to undertake special training in the NCI's laboratories at Frederick or in other laboratories in the United States under the NCI's sponsorship.

Starting with the second cycle of the new plant collection program (1991–1996), the NCI, additionally, provides a letter of intent (agreement), which represents a legal document to strengthen any pledge to return share of possible future monetary benefits to the country of collection.

Plant explorations in Asia, in particular Southeast Asia, to collect samples for anticancer and anti-HIV evaluation under the sponsorship of the NCI for the period of 1986–1991 have been successfully completed. A great taxonomic diversity of samples collected has been achieved, and many taxa belonging to genera that have never been evaluated in the NCI's previous program were included. Although field ethnobotanical inquiries on the medicinal uses of plants collected, as a selection criterion, have not been made extensively, many plants collected do have data on their folk medicinal uses. When one considers that there are probably 25,000–30,000 species of flowering plants in tropical Asia (van Steenis 1971; Prance 1977), the accomplishments of this first five-year plant collection cycle represent but a fraction (7–8%) of the flora.

When one also considers the rate of tropical rain forest decimation that is taking place throughout the tropical belt, and particularly in the Asian tropics (Myers 1984), one cannot help but feel that plant explorations for mass biological evaluation programs in the search for new drugs to treat diseases, for which we have no satisfactory cures at present, are definitely needed. Without such bold action, as has been stated elsewhere (Soejarto and Farnsworth 1989), it will soon be too late to attempt to discover what new clinically useful pharmaceuticals the rich tropical rain forests, still little explored for this purpose, can offer to humanity. In Southeast Asia, where the tropical rain forest conversion rate is one of the fastest, it has been predicted (Myers 1984) that if the rate continues unabated, much of the lowland forests of Indonesia, Malaysia, and the Philippines will be gone between the years 1990 and 2000. It is indeed timely, therefore, that the United States National Cancer Institute implemented a program to return to the plant world in the search for the cure of the dreaded diseases of cancer and AIDS.

Aside from its goal and eventual benefit of finding clinically useful drugs to treat cancer and AIDS, the NCI-sponsored plant explorations in Asia have contributed to the advancement of our botanical and biogeographic knowledge of the flora of the region through the large number of new collections, estimated to comprise at least 60,000 new herbarium specimens.

Directly or indirectly, the NCI-sponsored plant exploration program has also helped stimulate and strengthen further research activities, both in the plant sciences and in the elucidation of tropical rain forest biological diversity, as well as in other scientific efforts that may lead to the discovery of new drugs.

ACKNOWLEDGMENTS

This plant exploration program, with emphasis in the Malesian region, has been funded by the United States National Cancer Institute through Contract NO1–CM–67925 to the University of Illinois at Chicago.

To the following scientists, who have successfully performed botanical expeditions for the project during the period, we want to express our thanks and appreciation: Dr. John S. Burley (formerly research associate, PCRPS, University of Illinois at Chicago; presently research director, Arnold Arboretum, Harvard University), Dr. David G. Frodin (formerly of the Academy of Natural Sciences, Philadelphia), Dr. Domingo A. Madulid (curator, Philippine National Herbarium, Manila), Dr. Willem Meijer (Department of Biological Sciences, University of Kentucky, Lexington), Dr. E. Soepadmo (Department of Botany, University of Malaya, Kuala Lumpur), Dr. Benjamin C. Stone (formerly of the Academy of Natural Sciences, Philadelphia, presently at the Bishop Museum, Honolulu), Dr. Wayne Takeuchi (Department of Botany, Bishop Museum, Honolulu), Dr. Gunapathy S. Varadarajan (formerly a research associate, PCRPS, University of Illinois at Chicago, Chicago), Dr. W. J. J. O. de Wilde (Rijksherbarium, Leiden, The Netherlands), Dr. Elizabeth A. Widjaja (Herbarium Bogoriense, Bogor, Indonesia), Dr. Mark Bush (Ohio State University, Columbus), Ms. Alison Church (Arnold Arboretum, Harvard University), Mr. William Condon (formerly a graduate student at Yale School of Forestry and Environmental Sciences, presently at Winrock International, Asia Division, Morrilton, Arkansas), and Mr. Steven M. Goodman (field biologist, Field Museum of Natural History, Chicago).

The generous cooperation of the following scientists in Southeast Asia during the various stages of fieldwork gratefully acknowledged: Dr. Domingo A. Madulid (Philippine National Herbarium, Manila, Philippines), Dr. Soedarsono Riswan (Herbarium Bogoriense, Bogor, Indonesia), Dr. Justo Rojo (Forest Products Research and Development Institute, Los Banos, Philippines), Dr. E. Soepadmo (Department of Botany of the University of Malaya, Kuala Lumpur), Dr. Yuan-Shiun Chang and Mr. Liao (Department of Pharmacognosy of China Medical College, Taichung, Taiwan), Mr. Feng-Chi Ho (Hengchun Tropical Botanical Garden, Kenting, Taiwan), Drs. Tem Smitinand, Thawatchai Santisuk, and Chamlong Phengklai (Royal Forest Herbarium, Bangkok, Thailand), Dr. Francis Ng (Forest Research Institute of Malaysia, Kuala Lumpur), Mr. Lee Hua Seng (Sarawak Forest Department, Kuching, Sarawak), Datuk Miller Munang (Director General, Sabah Forest Department, Sandakan, Sabah), Dr. Simon Saulei (Forest Research Institute, Lae, Papua New Guinea), Drs. S. B. Malla, K. R. Rajbhandari, and N. P. Manandhar (formerly Department of Medicinal Plants, presently Department of Forestry and Plant Research, Kathmandu, Nepal), and Drs. S. I. Ali and Abdul Gafoor (Department of Botany, University of Karachi, Pakistan).

To individuals who have collaborated in one way or another in the implementation of this plant exploration program, and in particular to Dr. M. M. J. van Balgooy, who assisted in the taxonomic determination of the collection, we also express our thanks and appreciation.

REFERENCES

Akerele, O., V. Heywood, and H. Synge, eds. 1991. *The Conservation of Medicinal Plants.* Cambridge, U.K.: Cambridge University Press.
Anon. 1982. *National Conservation Plan for Indonesia: Field Report of UNDP/FAO National Parks Development Project Ins/78/061,* 8 vols. Bogor, Indonesia: UNDP/FAO.
Anon. 1992. "Declaration of Belem. Kunming Action Plan. Hipolito Unanue Agreement." *International Traditional Medicine Newsletter* 4 (2):1–2, 4.
Ashton, P. S. 1989. "Sundaland." In D. G. Campbell and H. D. Hammond, eds., *Floristic Inventory of Tropical Countries,* pp. 91–99. New York: The New York Botanical Garden.
Cragg, G. M. 1990. Personal communication. Dr. G. M. Cragg, Chief, Natural Products Branch, DTP, DCT, National Cancer Institute, Frederick Cancer Research and Development Center, Frederick, MD 21702–1201.
Davis, S. D., S. J. M. Droop, P. Gregerson, L. Henson, C. J. Leon, J. L. Villa-Lobos, H. Synge, and J. Zantovska. 1986. *Plants in Danger,* p. 277. Gland, Switzerland, and Cambridge, U.K.: International Union for Conservation of Nature and Natural Resources.
Eisner, T. and J. Meinwald. 1991. "The Göteborg Resolution." *Chemoecology* 1:38.
Elisabetsky, E. 1991. "Folklore, Tradition, or Know-How." *Cultural Survival Quarterly* (Summer):9–13.
Good, R. G. 1960. "On the Geographical Relationships of the Angiosperm Flora of New Guinea." *Bulletin of the British Museum (Natural History), Botany* 2 (8):205–26.
Huang, T.-C. 1979. "Statistics of Taxa." In H.-L. Li, T. S. Liu, T.-C. Huang, T. Koyama, and C. E. DeVol, eds., *Flora of Taiwan,* 6:1–2. Taipei: Epoch Publishing Co.
Keng, H. 1978. *Orders and Families of Malayan Seed Plants,* p. xxvii. Singapore: Singapore University Press.
Kloppenburg, J. Jr. 1991. "No Hunting." *Cultural Survival Quarterly* (Summer), pp. 14–18.
Larsen, K. 1979. "Exploration of the Flora of Thailand." In K. Larsen and L. B. Holm-Nielsen, eds., *Tropical Botany,* pp. 125–33. London: Academic Press.
Li, H.-L., T. S. Liu, T.-C. Huang, T. Koyama, and C. E. DeVol, eds. 1975–1979. *Flora of Taiwan,* 6 vols. Taipei: Epoch Publishing Co.
Madulid, D. A. 1982. "Plants in Peril." *Filipinas Journal of Science and Culture* 3:8–16.

Merrill, E. D. 1926. *Enumeration of Philippine Flowering Plants,* 4:69. Manila: Bureau of Printing.

Myers, N. 1984. *The Primary Source: Tropical Forests and Our Future,* pp. 363–64. New York: Norton.

Perdue, R. E. Jr. 1976. "Procurement of Plant Materials for Antitumor Screening." *Cancer Treatment Reports* 60 (6):987–98.

Podzorski, A. C. 1985. *The Palawan Botanical Expedition—Final Report,* pp. 1–35 (plus tables, photographs, and contour maps). Stenciled report. Landskrona: Hilleshog Forestry AG.

Prance, G. T. 1977. "Floristic Inventory of the Tropics: Where Do We Stand?" *Annals of the Missouri Botanical Garden* 64:659–84.

Schweitzer, J., F. G. Handley, J. Edwards, W. F. Harris, M. R. Grever, S. A. Schepartz, G. M. Cragg, K. Snader, and A. Bhat. 1991. "Commentary." *Journal of the National Cancer Institute* 83:1294–98.

Smitinand, T. 1987. Personal communication. Dr. T. Smitinand, Forest Herbarium of the Royal Forest Department, Bangkhen, Bangkok, Thailand.

Smitinand, T. 1989. "Thailand." In D. G. Campbell and H. D. Hammond, eds., *Floristic Inventory of Tropical Countries,* pp. 63–82. New York: The New York Botanical Garden.

Soejarto, D. D. 1989. "Plant Collecting in Palawan." *Field Museum Natural History Bulletin* (May): 24–28.

Soejarto, D. D. and N. R. Farnsworth. 1989. "Tropical Rain Forests: Potential Source of New Drugs?" *Perspectives in Biology and Medicine* 32:244–56.

Stearn, W. T. 1978. "Introduction." In H. Hara, W. T. Stearn and L. H. J. Williams, eds., *An Enumeration of the Flowering Plants of Nepal,* 1:7–13. London: British Museum (Natural History).

Stevens, P. F. 1989. "New Guinea." In D. G. Campbell and H. D. Hammond, eds., *Floristic Inventory of Tropical Countries,* pp. 120–32. New York: The New York Botanical Garden.

van Steenis, C. G. G. J. 1950. "The Delimitation of Malesia and Its Main Plant Geographic Divisions." *Flora Malesiana* I, 1:1xx–1xxv.

van Steenis, C. G. G. J. 1971. "Plant Conservation in Malaysia." *Bull. Jard. Bot. Nat. Belg.* 41:189–202.

Wang, H.-P., S.-C. Chen, and S.-Y. Wang. 1989. "China." In D. G. Campbell and H. D. Hammond, eds., *Floristic Inventory of Tropical Countries,* pp. 36–43. New York: The New York Botanical Garden.

Warsita Mahyar, U., J. S. Burley, C. Gyllenhaal, and D. D. Soejarto. 1991. "Medicinal Plants of Seberida (Riau Province, Sumatra, Indonesia)." *Journal of Ethnopharmacology* 31:217–37.

Whitmore, T. C. 1973. "A New Tree Flora of Malaya." *Pacific Science Association Precongress Conference in Indonesia: Planned Utilization of the Lowland Tropical Forests.* Bogor (Indonesia): Pacific Science Association.

Willis, J. C. and H. K. Airy Shaw. 1980. *A Dictionary of the Flowering Plants and Ferns,* 8th ed. Cambridge, U.K.: Cambridge University Press.

22

Medicinal Plants of Mexico: A Program for Their Scientific Validation

Xavier Lozoya, M.D.

HISTORICALLY, in Mexico, there has been a steady interest in the study of medicinal plants. In the past, however, the investigations related to this field were influenced by a pragmatic schedule that paid little attention to, or clearly ignored the cultural background behind, the popular use of these important natural resources. Frequently, the information about ancestral medicinal uses preserved by the indigenous population was ignored and the traditional medical practices were considered elemental manifestations of "primitive cultures" that had nothing to teach to the ethnocentric representatives of the Western dominant society. On the other hand, during that time, scientific research on the plant properties was usually focused only on the development of new drugs by the isolation of biologically active components for later synthesis and industrialization. This was done with the attitude that considered natural resources as raw materials suitable to be exploited quickly and without strategies for their conservation.

The case of the tuber of *Dioscorea composita* Hemsl., discovered in Mexico and used for obtaining diosgenin for its ultimate chemical transformation to cortisone and other hormones, is a clear example of the economic, social, and political aspects linked to this approach. The plant was exhausted and exploited for almost forty years by national and foreign industries without a policy of conservation of the resource and under conditions that finally produced political and economic conflicts that displaced Mexico from the international market of steroidal hormones. An illustrative example is the case of the psychotropic plants and mushrooms of Mexico that produced in the 1960s a striking increase in studies in American anthropology and pharmacology under peculiar approaches that tried mechanically to transfer the use of these originally Indian ritual elements to a completely different Western culture. This resulted in complex social and political problems that alerted the governments about the risks of a nonrestrictive approach in the study of medicinal plants of indigenous cultures.

During the decade of the 1970s and certainly under the influence of the successful policies followed by China in the study of its traditional medicine, the Western world began to modify its approach in the study of natural resources used by Third World countries for medicinal purposes. The ethnomedicine, ethnopharmacology, and ethnobotanical disciplines represent the new answer given by Western universities to the study of medicinal tropical resources. This position promotes the search for new plant drugs from a perspective that recognizes the basic importance of culture. It investigates the local original uses of these resources and promotes the systematization of the traditional indigenous knowledge as a starting point for the experimental study of the medicinal properties of the plants. During the past decades a great number of ethnobotanical and ethnopharmacological journals and congresses have shown the usefulness of this approach. Together with the appearance of the ethnobotanical strategy, chemical and pharmacological studies of crude plant drugs are being dramatically modified. The changes occurring in chemical and biological technologies have clearly contributed to the creation of new knowledge that, today, proposes the medicinal use of plant extracts, infusions, and the so-called soft herbal remedies (SHR) instead of the classic pharmaceutical chemical drugs. This new attitude and interest in whole-plant remedies is also being reinforced by the shift produced in the industrialized societies where a new philosophy of "return to nature" and the growth of an ecological conscience among the population is now linked to proposals of plant conservation and rational exploitation of the tropical forest.

The Mexican Experience

Our team began its activities in 1975 with the creation of the Mexican Institute for the Study of Medicinal Plants (IMEPLAM). The main characteristic of that initial research group was its multidisciplinary approach to the study of Mexican medicinal plants. Although our position respects the role of this institute in the promotion of a national pharmaceutical industry (to avoid the technological and economic dependence of the country on foreign industries), it was quite naive, owing to the limited experience about the costs and time required for the development of a plant drug. Our basic schedule of multidisciplinary research included the participation of anthropologists, historians, medical doctors, chemists, biologists, pharmacologists, and botanists. The IMEPLAM activities from 1975 to 1980 were particularly focused on the recovery of information about plants through field studies and bibliographic investigations of the historical scientific Mexican literature. These also included the collection and taxonomic classification of the first 1,000 specimens, which allowed us to create the first Medicinal Herbarium of Mexico and the first data bank on ethnobotany of medicinal plants. But, probably, the most important result obtained during that time was the discovery of the cultural context in which medicinal plants are used in Mexico, and this induced our identification with a new project that considered Mexican traditional medicine as the center of our interest. In 1980 the IMEPLAM research team was incorporated into the Mexican Social Security Institute (IMSS), a governmental institution that provides medical care and social security to almost 40 million inhabitants. The creation in that year of the Research Centre in Traditional Medicine and Herbology of IMSS (recently renamed South Biomedical Research Unit) not only illustrates the changes that occurred in our original outlook, now that we were recognizing the importance of the cultural framework in which the use of medicinal plants takes place in Mexico, but also shows the importance that the federal government has given to the studies of the popular knowledge and to the plants that are considered the main therapeutic resource of Mexican traditional medicine.

The purpose of this presentation is to describe our experience during the last ten years at this research center.

Methodology

ETHNOBOTANICAL STUDIES

Our studies on the use of medicinal plants in Mexico reached their highest point in 1983–1985. These were based on two main principles. First, the collection of data about the properties and uses of the plants in traditional medicine must be performed by medical doctors appropriately trained by botanical specialists. Second, the information should be obtained directly from the traditional practitioners (e.g., healers, herbalists, midwives, etc.). In those years we were able to conduct a national survey with the participation of 4,000 young doctors working for the IMSS in rural areas of Mexico with the collaboration of approximately 14,000 traditional practitioners who answered questionnaires prepared in the research center. This approach allowed us to determine the plants most frequently used in the country, their attributed medicinal properties, the methods of drug preparation, and the geographical distribution of the resources. The collection of our herbarium grew to almost 6,000 specimens, and the data bank now includes epidemiological data about the practice of traditional medicine, the most commonly treated diseases, the mechanisms of transmission of information, and other important data that were later used to select the plants to be studied experimentally.

From that perspective the selection of plant candidates to be studied experimentally allowed us to apply several criteria, such as: plants most frequently used (high index of citation), plants easily obtained during the entire year owing to their wide distribution (availability), plants used for the treatment of important diseases according to the IMSS priorities (epidemiological priority), plants with single and constant medicinal use (criteria of specificity), and plants with high indices of efficacy according to the experience of traditional practitioners, etc.

I emphasize that the ethnobotanical data, usually including the required information about the plant, its ecological situation, and adequate classification, need to consider not only medical interpretation (sometimes translations) of the attributed properties and uses but also diagnostic procedures followed in traditional medicine. This work is particularly important in directing further chemical and pharmacological research and is better performed by medical doctors or nurses trained in medical anthropology.

PHARMACOLOGICAL STUDIES

The possibility of performing quantitative pharmacological experiments with whole crude extracts has been widely discussed. The opponents of the idea have argued that modern molecular pharmacology requires the use of pure compounds to be assayed in the animal or in in vitro biological models. Nevertheless, nowadays it is considered that if certain control conditions are followed, a plant extract can be assayed in any biological or animal model, including some of the sophisticated ones (such as cultivation of tumor cells to measure cytotoxicity, for example), at least for preliminary screening studies. Three main advantages result: first, the possibility of exploring the biological activity of a large number of plants in a short time; second, the obtaining of a biological model reactive to the whole extract and used during the chemical fractionation and separation process, allowing the detection of the existence of synergistic mechanisms frequently observed in the study of natural products; and third, designing of modern plant medicinal products closer to the original remedy commonly used by the general population, resulting in scientific validation of the ethnomedical ancestral use.

After the screening studies, the plant extract is submitted to fractionation and isolation of active constituents and to regular pharmacological studies to elucidate the mechanism of action. However, the information obtained at different levels of such an experimental approach allows the study of other parameters with the whole extract, such as standardization of the crude extract and dosage, toxicity and safety of the traditional remedy, studies on degradation of the active constituents, etc. This requires that data be obtained before clinical trials with the herbal remedy are proposed.

PHYTOCHEMICAL STUDIES

The combination of pharmacological and phytochemical studies has been the prevalent methodology in the study of medicinal plants in recent years. The existence of numerous chemical components in a plant extract has always been a challenge for the phytochemist traditionally interested in the isolation of new molecules or devoted to the study of certain groups of compounds. It is important to recognize the value of combined studies between pharmacologists and phytochemists, using modern analytical methods such as high-pressure liquid chromatography (HPLC), nuclear magnetic resonance (NMR), and gas chromatography (GC), which reveal in a short time the constituents of a crude extract. The process of purification of the components is, today, the most difficult and time-consuming task. However, the use of a "monitoring biological model" during the separation process permits the bioassay-guided isolation of active constituents, which simplifies the work. Usually the bioactive plant components are obtained from a whole methanolic or water-methanolic extract prepared by maceration. This procedure has been reported to be the most suitable for initiating the study of a medicinal plant.

In recent years phytochemists have observed that well-known chemical groups of components such as flavonoids, tannins, and other water-soluble substances pose important and interesting biological activities that were not discovered in the past because the main focus was on alkaloids, saponins, and other types of molecules that were relatively easier to isolate from organic nonpolar extracts. Data on many glycosides, pigments, and polar compounds were lost from phytochemical studies not using bioassayed-guided isolation methods. In the past, the common procedure was first to obtain pure compounds from plants and then try to discover a possible biomedical application of the isolated substance. Today this picture is changing fast and the main interest is first to demonstrate the bioactivity of a plant crude extract and then to identify the responsible compound or compounds from the original mixture. According to the literature, in general terms, we are now attributing biological effects to groups of well-known compounds, while the discovery of new plant chemical groups is extremely rare.

CLINICAL STUDIES

Clinical studies remain the most controversial area of study in Western science. According to experience in China, clinical trials performed with plant extracts and infusions not necessarily put through basic animal experiment but popularly used in traditional medicines for centuries represent the fastest and more successful approach in the study of medicinal plants. Certainly, in Western medicine, the direct use of a plant remedy is rarely authorized unless a detailed group of animal pharmacology studies is completed. In our countries the majority of the scientific communities will not allow the clinical investigation of a plant infusion based only on ethnomedical information. A permanent controversy surrounds this issue and probably will require in the future a revision of the classical rules established in the past. The development of SHR in forms such as infusions and other crude preparations coming from traditional medicines and used commonly for oral administration is opening a new category of plant drugs that will require adequate regulations for their clinical study and use. It is important to determine the level of scientific experimentation required in such cases and the position that medical science will assume regarding ethnomedical information.

CONSERVATION

In Mexico the majority of the medicinal plants used are obtained from wild growing species. These plants are not cultivated for medicinal purposes. According to our data, all the medicinal plants are used by Mexicans and sold in markets and stores come from areas of the country where these resources grow wild and are apparently protected by people since they are economically important. However, once a plant is widely promoted as particularly efficient for the treatment of a disease, the resource disappears in a few months of opportunistic collection to take advantage of the economic success, which usually lasts a short time.

That has been the case in the last few years for *Mimosa tenuiflora* Benth., a well-known plant called "tepescohuite," which was promoted worldwide as the "marvelous tree of Mexico" used for the treatment of skin burns. After the publication, on the television networks and in newspapers, of some successful treatments with the bark of the tree in Mexico and elsewhere around the world, the "fever" of the collectors produced a catastrophe in the area where this plant grows. Since the bark was the source of the medicinal product promoted by the media, tons of powdered bark materials were produced and were immediately sold to companies around the world without the establishment of any local conservation policy. Thousands of trees were destroyed to obtain this bark, only to obtain short-term economic advantage induced by the spread of irresponsible information. Several years later, when our experimental studies began to demonstrate the risks involved in the use of this powdered bark, the "tepescohuite fever" was controlled. However, the ecological damage was already produced. We must avoid the recurrence of this type of situation. This episode reveals the extreme importance of information produced in the media about topics on medicinal plants, as well as the serious responsibility involved in the diffusion of scientific studies related to this theme.

23

TRAMIL: A Research Project
on the Medicinal Plant Resources
of the Caribbean

Lionel Robineau and Djaja Doel Soejarto

TRAMIL (an acronym for TRAditional Medicine in the Islands) is an applied research project whose chief aims are (1) to provide scientific rationale to the traditional popular uses of plants for therapy in the Caribbean basin and (2) to undertake a campaign to return the findings to the grass roots peoples in this geographic region in the form of recommendations on the safety of these plants, which may serve as a basis for either discouraging or encouraging the continued use(s) of the plant(s) in question for popular therapy. This project was established in 1982 in Haiti under the sponsorship of the Santo Domingo-based Enda-Caribe (Environment and Development in the Third World—the Caribbean region), the Faculty of Pharmacy and Medicine of Port-au-Prince, the Farmers Association Federation of the Dominican Republic, and the SOE Dispensary of Thomonde of central Haiti. It was the lack of modern health facilities and services and a desire to help facilitate efforts by the village people (who do not have adequate financial resources) in taking charge of their own health problems as much as possible, in Haiti and in the Dominican Republic, that led to the birth of TRAMIL (see also Weniger 1991). The task was then defined as the establishment of guidelines for the identification of what is pure belief, what is truly useful and efficacious, and what is harmful, based on scientific studies to be carried out by a network of collaborators.

TRAMIL has a unique working methodology, consisting of fieldwork (inventory phase), literature search and analysis, and experimental laboratory components.

TRAMIL Methodology

Fieldwork Methods

Information on the uses of plants in therapy by the popular masses in the Caribbean basin region, the so-called grass roots people, is gathered from the field through rigorous survey of a particular population, supplemented by data on the medicinal uses from the literature. When a decision is made that a survey is to be performed, an area of the Caribbean (a Carib population) in a particular country with predominantly traditional Carib cultures is selected for the implementation of the operation. TRAMIL members living in that country are the ones who do the survey.

Before implementation of a field operation, the literature pertaining to the medicinal plant resources of a selected community is reviewed, and then on-site interviews with members of the community is performed. Unlike the traditional ethnobotanical interviews, TRAMIL field interviews are disease oriented. As such, medical doctors play an important role in TRAMIL fieldwork, both in the data-collecting phase (uses of medicinal plants), as well as in the feedback campaign phase to return the scientific findings to the grass roots peoples. For the survey,

TABLE 23.1 *Sample Questionnaire for TRAMIL Survey (First Part)*

Treatments used for: (local name for the problems)

1. Description of the disease:

2. What was used as first treatment the last time the problem occurred?

   Medicinal plant   _____

   Healer   _____

   Medical Officer   _____

   Witch Doctor   _____

3. Description and manner medicine was prepared:

4. How was the medicine taken, in what quantity, and how many times?

5. Where do you find the plants? Yard _____ Outside the home _____

6. Have you ever used this medicine? Yes _____ No _____

7. What were the results of treatment?

8. What are the precautions to be observed during the treatment (side effects and dose)?
   a. For adults:

   b. For children:

TABLE 23.2   *Sample Questionnaire for TRAMIL Survey (Second Part)*

What is the first thing you do when you feel sick?

1. Attend the Health Center
2. Go to a physician
3. Go to a pharmacy
4. Prepare home medicine
5. Go to a healer

Do you prefer a healer (than others)?

1. Yes
2. No

How frequently do you attend the Health Center?

1. Always
2. Frequently
3. Occasionally
4. Never

What transportation do you use when you are sick?

1. On foot
2. On boat
3. On bicycle

What is the average time to reach the Health Center?

(_____ minutes)

Do you understand explanation given by the doctor?

1. Always
2. Sometimes
3. Never

Do you have money to go to a doctor?

1. Yes
2. No

Do you pay for the medicine?

1. Yes
2. Sometimes

Do you use home medicines?

1. Always
2. Sometimes
3. Never

Do you use plants to treat complaints?

1. Yes
2. No

Are they (the plants) easy to obtain?

1. Yes
2. No

Where do you obtain them?

1. Gather
2. Purchase
3. Keep at home
4. Parents

Who taught you?

1. Mother
2. Friends and neighbors
3. Grandparents
4. Healer
5. Father

Adapted from Giron et al. 1991.

a multidisciplinary team is assembled, political and health authorities are contacted for further guidance, and schoolteachers are recruited to help in house-to-house interviews. A questionnaire modeled after the one used in the original field survey in Haiti (Weniger et al. 1986) is used.

The questionnaire has five components: (1) general data on the informant, (2) his/her school attendance, (3) housing and living conditions, (4) accessibility to health services, and (5) utilization of plants for medicinal purposes. A sample of the questionnaire as originally used (Robineau, Gyllenhaal, and Soejarto 1991) is presented in table 23.1. For each country, the form may be modified to be adapted to the local conditions. A modified questionnaire is presented in table 23.2.

When a plant is indicated as used during the survey, follow-up questions concerning the local name(s), part(s) used, specific use, preparation, route of administration, and frequency of administration are asked and the answers recorded. For future reference, one or more voucher herbarium specimens, in case of less well-known plants, are also prepared according to standard botanical practices. Plants scoring 20% or higher for a particular use during the interviews are selected and proposed for inclusion in the TRAMIL list (book).

A full report that describes the overall process, the methodology, and the results (and their analysis) of a TRAMIL field survey is given by Giron et al. (1991).

LITERATURE SEARCH

For each species proposed for inclusion in the TRAMIL list, a literature search (ethnomedical, biological/pharmacological, and chemical) is performed. At this stage the NAPRALERT data base at the PCRPS, College of Pharmacy, University of Illinois at Chicago, is queried for information on these plants, in addition to other independent searches. The literature search focuses on the use of the same plant part from other TRAMIL areas, on the chemistry of the plant especially on that specific part used, and on the pharmacology and toxicity data of the plant, also especially on the same part used. The NAPRALERT data base (see Loub et al. 1985, for details about NAPRALERT) has played a role in the TRAMIL project since 1986, beginning with the TRAMIL-2 workshop in Haiti.

Literature data are then submitted to an analysis during discussions and debates in a workshop (TRAMIL workshop), in which international and multidisciplinary participants meet. Although most of the participants of previous workshops were TRAMIL members, specially invited guests with specific expertise also attended.

TRAMIL WORKSHOP

A TRAMIL workshop lasts five to six days with the participation of thirty to forty-five members, including invited guests. The workshop consists of two sessions: the scientific session (days one to five) and the diffusion session (days five to six). The composition of such a group is truly multidisciplinary and international. For example, during the TRAMIL-4 workshop in Honduras (1989), the scientific session of the workshop was attended by thirty scientists with expertise in biology, botany, ethnobotany, ethnology, medicine (medical doctors), pharmacology, pharmacognosy, and phytochemistry, while the diffusion session (on-site visit to the population) was attended, in addition, by educators, social scientists, politicians, and host health authorities.

In a TRAMIL workshop, which is conducted in a roundtable fashion with multilingual simultaneous translation, everybody must contribute; no one is invited or comes as an observer. In order to accomplish the workshop goal, every participant must come with a set of data, ideas, and/or recommendations to be presented and debated at an appropriate time. TRAMIL workshop sessions are exhausting but challenging and stimulating.

Priority Setting for TRAMIL Plants

The primary goal of a TRAMIL workshop is the setting of priorities for plants proposed for inclusion in the TRAMIL list (book), as well as the review of categories of plants already given priorities, in light of new evidence. Thus, the period between one workshop and the next represents a period of work activities, such as field survey, literature search, and laboratory tests or in-depth pharmacological/toxicological studies. Except for field surveys, the literature search and other types of studies may also be performed by individuals who are nonmembers of TRAMIL.

The results of the workshop and the priorities (or the classification of use) of TRAMIL plants are published as a book, in Spanish, French, and English versions. To date, TRAMIL-1, TRAMIL-2, TRAMIL-3, and TRAMIL-4 books have been printed and circulated.

In the TRAMIL book, the use of a particular plant part is classified either as category TOX (toxic), category INV (experimental data inadequate, further investigation is needed), or category REC (recommended).

TOX category:	Experimental data are available showing that the plant (or part of the plant) is toxic or belonging to a genus or family of known toxicity, especially as used in the manner indicated in the survey; thus its use must be discouraged.
INV category:	Experimental data are not available or are inadequate to classify the plant in either TOX or REC categories; further investigation of the plant (which would eventually permit its classification into the respective category) is needed. If no literature information is available, such an investigation may be assigned during a workshop to a TRAMIL member, who will carry it out in his/her laboratory(ies), or to a nonmember laboratory(ies) whose area of expertise is expected to provide data that may help in solving that particular problem.
REC category:	Experimental data (chemistry, pharmacology, toxicology) are available to indicate that the specific use of a plant part as stated in the survey is supported by these data, and moreover, its use is safe; this category of classification is also given to plants that are well known for their innocuousness, even if the biological activity for the specific intended use remains to be demonstrated (thus, its use may be due to a placebo effect). The continued use(s) of plants under this category is recommended/encouraged.

The TRAMIL-3 book (Cuba workshop, 1988; Weniger and Robineau 1988) lists 88 species of plants, and the TRAMIL-4 book (Honduras workshop, 1989; Robineau, Gyllenhaal, and Soejarto 1991) lists 109 species. In both editions, data for all the species listed are presented in a monographic format and itemized as follows:

- Scientific name (including authority citation and family name; most common and well-established synonyms may be given)
- Common name(s) (in the TRAMIL islands and countries)

- Geographic distribution (general range, worldwide)
- Taxonomic description (primarily the diagnostic features of the plant)
- Uses as found by the TRAMIL surveys (namely, as a result of the field surveys)
- Other uses in the Caribbean area (based on the literature)
- Chemical data (produced by TRAMIL members and as recorded in the literature)
- Biological activity data (produced by TRAMIL members and from the literature)
- Discussion and recommendations (where the setting of priorities of a particular use of a plant into the TOX, INV, and REC categories is dealt with)

In the TRAMIL-4 book (109 species listed; table 23.3), the following uses are classified as TOX:

> *Argemone mexicana* L. (Papaveraceae): for gastralgia, root decoction in mixture, oral
>
> *Cameraria latifolia* L. (Apocynaceae): for bad blood, leaf decoction or macerate, either oral or as a bath
>
> *Crescentia cujete* L. (Bignoniaceae): for urethritis, pulp aqueous macerate, oral
>
> *Datura stramonium* L. (Solanaceae): any use by pregnant women of any part of the plant; caution to possible poisoning
>
> *Hippeastrum vittatum* Herb. (Amaryllidaceae): for asthma, juice of bulb, oral; for hypertension, leaf decoction, oral
>
> *Jatropha curcas* L. (Euphorbiaceae): for stomach aches, leaf decoction (in mixture) with salt, oral; for asthma, juice of plant, oral; for hepatic complaints, leaf decoction, oral
>
> *Lantana camara* L. (Verbenaceae): for respiratory ailments, infusion of aerial part, oral
>
> *Momordica charantia* L. (Cucurbitaceae): any internal use of the fruit
>
> *Nerium oleander* L. (Apocynaceae): internal use of any part
>
> *Passiflora suberosa* L. (Passifloraceae): internal use of the leaves (in any form) for bucal candidiasis, bad blood, anorexia
>
> *Polygala penaea* L. (Polygalaceae): for urethritis, aqueous leaf macerate, aqueous root macerate, oral
>
> *Pouteria sapota* (Jacq.) H. E. Moore & Stearn (Sapotaceae): for asthma, crushed seeds, oral
>
> *Ricinus communis* L. (Euphorbiaceae): internal use of the seeds or home-extracted seed oil
>
> *Senna occidentalis* (L.) Link (Caesalpiniaceae): internal use of a drink prepared from the seed
>
> *Trichilia hirta* L. (Meliaceae): for respiratory ailments, leaf decoction with salt, oral

The majority of the 109 species receive either an INV category or a REC category.

What is the final goal of the TRAMIL project? Its final goal is the publication of a plant-based pharmacopoeia of the Caribbean region. When will it be accomplished? At this point in time, two future workshops are projected. One, in November 1992, in Guadeloupe (TRAMIL-6 workshop), the other in San Andres Is-

TABLE 23.3 *Plant Species Listed in TRAMIL-4*

Abelmoschus moschatus (L.) Moench (Malvaceae)
Acalypha alopecuroidea Jacq. (Euphorbiaceae)
Allium sativum L. (Liliaceae)
Ambrosia paniculata L.C. Rich. var. *cumanensis* (HBK.) O. E. Schult. (Asteraceae)
Anethum graveolens L. (Apiaceae)
Annona muricata L. (Annonaceae)
Annona reticulata L. (Annonaceae)
Anredera leptostachys (Moq.) Steenis (Basellaceae)
Argemone mexicana L. (Papaveraceae)
Beta vulgaris L. (Chenopodiaceae)
Bixa orellana L. (Bixaceae)
Cajanus cajan Millsp. (Fabaceae)
Cameraria latifolia L. (Apocynaceae)
Canavalia ensiformis (Jacq.) DC. (Fabaceae)
Capsicum frutescens L. (Solanaceae)
Carica papaya L. (Cariacaceae)
Catalpa longissima (Jacq.) Dum.-Cours (Bignoniaceae)
Chamissoa altissima (Jacq.) HBK. (Amaranthaceae)
Chenopodium ambrosioides L. (Chenopodiaceae)
Chiococca alba (L.) Hitchc. (Rubiaceae)
Cinnamomum verum J. S. Presl (Lauraceae)
Cissampelos pareira L. (Menispermaceae)
Cissus verticillata L. (Vitaceae)
Citrus aurantifolia (Christm.) Swingle (Rutaceae)
Citrus aurantium L. (Rutaceae)
Citrus limetta Risso (Rutaceae)
Citrus sinensis (L.) Osbeck (Rutaceae)
Cocos nucifera L. (Arecaceae)
Coffea arabica L. (Rubiaceae)
Commelina elegans HBK. (Commelinaceae)
Cornutia pyramidata L. (Verbenaceae)
Crescentia cujete L. (Bignoniaceae)
Cucurbita moschata (Duchesne) Poir. (Cucurbitaceae)
Curcuma longa L. (Zingiberaceae)
Cymbopogon citratus (DC.) Stapf (Poaceae)
Datura stramonium L. (Solanaceae)
Dioscorea bulbifera L. (Dioscoreaceae)
Eleocharis interstincta (Vahl) Roem. & Schult. (Cyperaceae)
Eryngium foetidum L. (Apiaceae)
Eucalyptus species (Myrtaceae)
Eupatorium odoratum L. (Asteraceae)
Eupatorium triplinerve Vahl (Asteraceae)
Foeniculum vulgare Mill. (Apiaceae)
Gnaphalium viscosum HBK. (Asteraceae)
Gossypium barbadense L. (Malvaceae)
Guazuma ulmifolia Lam. (Sterculiaceae)
Haematoxylon campechianum L. (Caesalpiniaceae)
Hamelia patens Jacq. (Rubiaceae)
Hippeastrum vittatum Herb. (Amaryllidaceae)
Jatropha curcas L. (Euphorbiaceae)
Jatropha gossypifolia L. (Euphorbiaceae)
Justicia pectoralis Jacq. (Acanthaceae)
Kalanchoe gastonis-bonnieri Raym-Hamet & Perrier (Crassulaceae)
Kalanchoe pinnata (Lam.) Pers. (Crassulaceae)
Lantana camara L. (Verbenaceae)

Leonotis nepetifolia (L.) R.Br. (Lamiaceae)
Lepianthes peltata (L.) Raf. (Piperaceae)
Lycopersicon esculentum Mill. (Solanaceae)
Mangifera indica L. (Anacardiaceae)
Manihot esculenta Crantz (Euphorbiaceae)
Matricaria chamomilla L. (Asteraceae)
Mentha × *piperita* L. var. *citrata* (Ehrh.) Brig. (Lamiaceae)
Mentha × *piperita* L. (Lamiaceae)
Momordica charantia L. (Cucurbitaceae)
Moringa oleifera Lam. (Moringaceae)
Musa × *paradisiaca* L. (Musaceae)
Myristica fragrans Houtt. (Myristicaceae)
Narvalina domingensis Cass. (Asteraceae)
Nerium oleander L. (Apocynaceae)
Nicotiana tabacum L. (Solanaceae)
Ocimum basilicum L. (Lamiaceae)
Ocimum gratissimum L. (Lamiaceae)
Passiflora suberosa L. (Passifloraceae)
Pavonia spinifex (L.) Cav. (Malvaceae)
Peperomia pellucida (L.) HBK. (Piperaceae)
Persea americana Mill. (Lauraceae)
Petiveria alliacea L. (Phytolaccaceae)
Phyllanthus niruri L. (Euphorbiaceae)
Pimenta dioica (L.) Merr. (Myrtaceae)
Pimenta ozua (Urb. & Ekm.) Burret (Myrtaceae)
Pimenta racemosa (Mill.) J. W. Moore var. *racemosa* (Myrtaceae)
Plantago major L. (Plantaginaceae)
Pluchea carolinensis (Jacq.) G. Don (Asteraceae)
Polygala penaea L. (Polygalaceae)
Pouteria sapota (Jacq.) H. E. Moore & Stearn (Sapotaceae)
Prosopis juliflora (Sw.) DC. (Mimosaceae)
Pseudelephantopus spicatus (Juss.) Gleason (Asteraceae)
Psidium guajava L. (Myrtaceae)
Rhoeo spathacea (Sw.) Stearn (Commelinaceae)
Ricinus communis L. (Euphorbiaceae)
Rollinia mucosa (Jacq.) Baill. (Annonaceae)
Saccharum officinarum L. (Poaceae)
Sauvagesia erecta L. (Ochnaceae)
Senna alexandrina P. Miller (Caesalpiniaceae)
Senna occidentalis (L.) Link (Caesalpiniaceae)
Sida rhombifolia L. (Malvaceae)
Simarouba glauca DC. (Simaroubaceae)
Solanum tuberosum L. (Solanaceae)
Spermacoce assurgens Ruiz & Pavon (Rubiaceae)
Spondias purpurea L. (Anacardiaceae)
Stachytarpheta jamaicensis (L.) Vahl (Verbenaceae)
Syzygium aromaticum (L.) Merr. & Perry (Myrtaceae)
Tamarindus indica L. (Caesalpiniaceae)
Tanacetum parthenium (L.) Sch.-Bip. (Asteraceae)
Terminalia catappa L. (Combretaceae)
Trichilia hirta L. (Meliaceae)
Vetiveria zizanioides (L.) Nash ex Small (Poaceae)
Zea mays L. (Poaceae)
Zingiber officinale Roscoe (Zingiberaceae)

lands (Colombia), in February 1995. In addition, popular books and pamphlets are being published addressed to the general population, educating them on the value and dangers of their herbal medicine, thus fulfilling the goal of the project, namely, returning the findings to the "grass roots" peoples.

TRAMIL has accomplished its goal of documenting the medicinal uses of plants of the Caribbean basin. It has also accomplished its goal of evaluating these uses, in particular as regard the safety of such uses, and proposing a classification of TOX, INV, or REC for a particular use. The group feels, however, that they do not have the necessary authority to recommend or not to recommend the use of TRAMIL plants directly to the people. This is the sole responsibility of each individual health authority (Ministry of Health) of each country to implement the recommendations formulated during the TRAMIL workshops and contained in the TRAMIL books. A committee that will serve as a liaison between TRAMIL and the Ministry of Health of each country is being formed.

Because of the high cost of pharmaceutical drugs in the Caribbean, the implementation of TRAMIL's recommendations will permit the unprivileged populations of this region to have a safe alternative to primary health care through the use of medicinal plants for therapy, a popular tradition that has been in practice in the region for more than 400 years, whose origin dates back to the African, Amerindian, and European beliefs (Goldwater 1983). In view of the high degree of similarities between the floras of the different islands and countries of the Caribbean basin (Liogier 1976), TRAMIL findings may certainly be applicable to the entire region.

A large number of the 109 species of flowering plants listed in the current edition of the TRAMIL-4 book (Robineau, Gyllenhaal, and Soejarto 1991; table 22.3) comprises plants originated from tropical forest areas. At a time when a great deal of interest has been expressed concerning the use and the conservation of tropical forest biodiversity, TRAMIL provides an example of our efforts in the optimization of the use of tropical forest medicinal plant resources in primary health care.

Finally, TRAMIL efforts have contributed to the preservation of knowledge on the value of indigenous plants for primary health care, a knowledge accumulated from generation to generation, which at present is in danger because its successful transmission from the old to the younger generation is not always assured.

ACKNOWLEDGMENTS

The authors wish to express their thanks to all members of the TRAMIL organization, who have performed field surveys and who have participated in and contributed to the TRAMIL workshops and who have, eventually, made possible the publication of TRAMIL books. The financial supports of the following agencies are hereby acknowledged: ACCT (Agencia de Cooperacion Cultural y Tecnica), CCFD (Comite Catolico con-tra el Hambre y para el Desarollo), DEVNOG (French Ministry for Foreign Affairs), GTZ (German Society for Technical Cooperation), OAS (Organization of American States), and UNESCO-Mab (UNESCO Man and the Biosphere program). Thanks are also expressed to private foundations, academic institutions, and to governmental agencies in Haiti, the Dominican Republic, Cuba, Honduras, and Guatemala, who have provided supports in the realization of TRAMIL workshops.

REFERENCES

Giron, L. M., V. Freire, A. Alonzo, and A. Caceres. 1991. "Ethnobotanical Survey of the Medicinal Flora Used by the Caribs of Guatemala." *Journal of Ethnopharmacology* 34:173–87.

Goldwater, C. 1983. "La medecine traditionelle en Amerique Latine." In *Medecines Traditionelles et Couverture de soins en Sante*, pp. 37–50. Geneva: OMS.

Liogier, A. 1976. "La flora de la Espanola: Analisis, origen probable." In *Anuario de la Academia de Ciencias de la Republica Dominicana* 2:24. Santo Domingo, Republica Dominicana.

Loub, W., N. R. Farnsworth, D. D. Soejarto, and M. L. Quinn. 1985. "NAPRALERT: Computer Handling of Natural Product Research Data." *Journal of Chemical Information and Computer Science* 25:99–103.

Robineau, L., C. Gyllenhaal, and D. D. Soejarto, eds. 1991. *Towards a Caribbean Pharmacopoeia: TRAMIL 4 Workshop, Tela, Honduras, November 1989.* Santo Domingo: ENDA-CARIBE and National Autonomous University of Honduras.

Weniger, B. 1991. "Interest and Limitation of a Global Ethnopharmacological Survey." *Journal of Ethnopharmacology* 32:37–41.

Weniger, B. and L. Robineau. 1988. *Elementos para una farmacopea Caribena. Seminario TRAMIL 3, La Habana, Cuba, Noviembre 1988.* Santo Domingo: ENDA-CARIBE (Dominican Republic) and Ministerio de Salud Publica, La Habana (Cuba) (Spanish version).

Weniger, B., M. Rouzier, R. Daguilh, D. Henrys, J. H. Henrys and R. Anton. 1986. "La medecine populaire dans le plateau central d'Haiti. 2. Inventaire ethnopharmacologique." *Journal of Ethnopharmacology* 17:13–30.

24

Ethnopharmacological Studies and Biological Conservation in Belize

Michael J. Balick, Rosita Arvigo, Gregory Shropshire, and Robert Mendelsohn

IN the last few decades, the discipline of ethnobotany has undergone great evolution in its methodology and focus, as well as its application. Traditionally, ethnobotanical studies were carried out by systematic botanists, whose goal was to produce lists of useful plants of a particular tribe or region. Most of these studies were presented in encyclopedic form. Ethnobotanical inventory is still very important, because such a small fraction of the total information that exists on the utility of plants has been cataloged. In the last few decades, however, the interdisciplinary approach has become more important in ethnobotanical research, involving the close collaboration of botanists, pharmacologists, anthropologists, chemists, nutritionists, economists, conservationists, policymakers, ecologists, and those in many other fields.

One result of this new approach has been the application of ethnobotany to public policy questions, for example, in the areas of health and ecosystem conservation. Ethnopharmacological studies initiated by Dr. Paul Alan Cox and colleagues in Samoa have resulted in the conservation of significant areas of endangered Samoan rain forest. Ethnobotanical studies in Madagascar, coordinated by Dr. Nat Quansah, take place in forest reserves and seek to establish a sustainable dynamic between the people's use of the area and the biological integrity of the protected ecosystems. This paper will discuss our current efforts in Belize, Central America, involving both ethnobotanical inventory and tropical forest conservation.

The Belize Ethnobotany Project

The Belize Ethnobotany Project (BEP) was initiated in 1988, as a collaborative endeavor between the Ix Chel Tropical Research Foundation and the Belize Center for Environmental Studies, both Belizean nongovernmental organizations, and the Institute of Economic Botany of The New York Botanical Garden. The main goal of the project has been to conduct an inventory of the ethnobotanical diversity of Belize, a country with significant tracts of intact forest. The project has made dozens of expeditions to various locales and has collected some 3,660 plant specimens as of early 1994. The specimens have been deposited at the Belize College of Agriculture and Forestry Department Herbaria, as well The New York Botanical Garden and U.S. National Herbarium. A data base has been established at The New York Botanical Garden with planned distribution to several computer facilities within Belize. The BEP involves gathering of traditional knowledge provided by more than two dozen colleagues who are traditional healers of Mopan, Yucatec, Kekchi Maya, Ladino, Garifuna, Creole, East Indian, and Mennonite decent.

Through a contract with the U.S. National Cancer Institute (NCI), the project has provided some 2,600 bulk plant samples to the NCI for screening in their human cancer and HIV Developmental Therapeutics Program (DTP). Samples, each weighing approximately 500 grams, have been collected and dried at low heat and shipped to the NCI's testing facilities in Frederick, Maryland. While NCI scientists have expressed interest in some of the species collected to date, more nearly comprehensive studies have not identified a particular plant with a novel compound for advanced development in the DTP. In the future, however, as more and more of the species are put through the two HIV screens and forty human cancer screens, we expect that greater interest in some of the species will be shown.

Valuation Studies

A great deal of attention has been given recently to the value of nontimber forest products in the tropical forest. One method of ascertaining this value is to inventory a clearly defined area and estimate the economic value of the species found there. Peters, Gentry, and Mendelsohn (1989) were the first to elucidate the commercial value of nontimber forest products found within a hectare of forest in the Peruvian Amazon. This study did not include medicinal plants in their inventory, and at the suggestion of the authors, this aspect was evaluated in Belize. From two separate plots, a thirty- and fifty-year-old forest respectively, a total biomass of 308.6 and 1,433.6 kilograms (dry weight) of medicines whose value could be judged by local market forces was collected. Local herbal pharmacists and healers purchase and process medicinal plants from herb gatherers and small farmers at an average price of U.S. $2.80/kilogram. Multiplying the quantity of medicine found per hectare above by this price suggests that harvesting the medicinal plants from a hectare would yield the collector between $864 and $4,014 of gross revenue. Subtracting the costs required to harvest, process, and ship the plants, the net revenue from clearing a hectare was calculated to be $564 and $3,054 on each of the two plots. Details of the study can be found in the original article (Balick and Mendelsohn 1992). The lists of plants and their uses are presented in tables 24.1 and 24.2.

TABLE 24.1   *Medicinal Plants Harvested from a Thirty-Year-Old Valley Forest Plot (No. 1) in Cayo, Belize*

Common Name	Scientific Name	Use[a]
Bejuco verde	*Agonandra racemosa* (DC.) Standl.	Sedative, laxative, "gastritis," analgesic
Calawalla	*Phlebodium decumanum* (Willd.) J. Smith	Ulcers, pain, "gastritis," chronic indigestion, high blood pressure, "cancer"
China root	*Smilax lanceolata* L.	Blood tonic, fatigue, "anemia," acid stomach, rheumatism, skin conditions
Cocolmeca	*Dioscorea* sp.	Urinary tract ailments, bladder infection, stoppage of urine, kidney sluggishness and malfunction, mucus loosener in coughs and colds, febrifuge, blood tonic
Contribo	*Aristolochia trilobata* L.	Flu, colds, constipation, fevers, stomach ache, indigestion, "gastritis," parasites

[a]Uses listed are based on disease concepts recognized in Belize, primarily of Maya origin, that may or may not have equivalent states in Western medicine. For example, kidney sluggishness is not a condition commonly recognized by Western-trained physicians but is a common complaint among people in this region.

TABLE 24.2.   *Medicinal Plants Harvested from a Fifty-Year-Old Ridge Forest Plot (No. 2) in Cayo, Belize*

Common Name	Scientific Name	Use[a]
Negrito	*Simarouba glauca* DC.	Dysentery & diarrhea, dysmenorrhea, skin conditions, stomach and bowel tonic
Gumbolimbo	*Bursera simaruba* (L.) Sarg.	Antipruritic, stomach cramps, kidney infections, diuretic
China root	*Smilax lanceolata* L.	Blood tonic, fatigue, "anemia," acid stomach, rheumatism, skin conditions
Cocolmeca	*Dioscorea* sp.	Urinary tract ailments, bladder infection, stoppage of urine, kidney sluggishness and malfunction, mucus loosener in coughs and colds, febrifuge, blood tonic

[a]See note for table 24.1.

Not enough information is available to understand the life cycles and regeneration time needed for each species, and therefore, we cannot comment on the frequency and extent of collection involved in sustainable harvest. However, assuming the current age of the forest in each plot as a rotation length, we calculated an estimate of the present value of harvesting plants sustainably into the future by using the standard Faustman formula: $V = R/(1 - e^{-rt})$, where R is the net revenue from a single harvest and r is the real interest rate; t is the length of the rotation in years. Given a thirty-year rotation in plot 1, this suggests that the present value of medicine is $726 per hectare. Making a similar calculation for plot 2, with a fifty-year rotation, yielded a present value of $3,327 per hectare. These calculations assume a 5% interest rate.

These estimates of the value of using tropical forests for the harvest of medicinal plants compared favorably with alternative land uses in the region such as milpa (corn, bean, and squash cultivation) in Guatemalan rain forest, which yielded $288 per hectare. We also identified commercial products such as allspice, copal, chicle, and construction materials in the plots that could be harvested and added to their total value. Thus, this study suggested that protection of at least some areas of rain forest as extractive reserves for medicinal plants appears to be economically justified. It seems that a periodic harvest strategy is a realistic and sustainable method of utilizing the forest. On the basis of our evaluation of the forest similar to the second plot analyzed, it would appear that one could harvest and clear one hectare per year indefinitely, assuming that all the species found in each plot would regenerate at similar rates. More than likely, however, some species, such as *Bursera simaruba,* would become more dominant in the ecosystem while others, such as *Dioscorea,* could become rare.

The analysis used in this study is based on current market data. The estimates of the worth of the forest could change based on local market forces. For example, if knowledge about tropical herbal medicines becomes even more widespread and their collection increases, prices for specific medicines would fall. Similarly, if more consumers become aware of the potential of some of these medicines or if the cost of commercially produced pharmaceuticals becomes too great, demand for herbal medicines could increase, substantially driving up prices. Finally, destruction of the tropical forest habitats of many of these important plants would increase their scarcity, driving up local prices. This scenario has already been observed in Belize with some species. It seems that the value of tropical forest for the harvest of nontimber forest products will increase relative to other land uses over time, as these forests become more scarce.

The Link Between Medicinal Plants, Drug Development, and Conservation

An often-stated assumption is that the discovery of a new plant drug will undoubtedly help in conservation efforts, especially in rain forest regions. This notion is based on the profit potential and economic impact, as well as on the feeling that governments and people will somehow impose a greater value on a resource if it can produce a product with a multinational market. Table 24.3 is a summary of the distribution of value and potential of medicinal plants to support conservation efforts, viewed from three levels or perspectives: regional traditional medicine, the international herbal industry, and the international pharmaceutical industry. Within each level the distribution of economic benefits varies greatly. In traditional medical systems the economic benefits accrue to professional collectors who sell the plants to traditional healers, or to the healers themselves. The local and international herbal industries produce value for a broad range of people and

TABLE 24.3.   *The Economic Value and Conservation Potential of Plant Medicines*

Sector	Distribution of Economic Benefit	Market Value	Pitfalls	Conservation Potential
International pharmaceutical industry	Upper end of economic system	High—in the billions	• Overharvest • Synthesis (if no provision for benefits included) • Plantations established outside area discovered	Low → high
National and international herbal industry	Full spectrum of economic system	High—in the billions	• Overharvest • Plantations established outside area discovered	Low → high
Regional traditional medicine	Lower end of economic system	High—in the billions	• Overharvest (sustainability)	Low → high

institutions, including collectors, wholesalers, and brokers, as well as companies that produce and sell herbal formulations. Proportionally, the bulk of the economic value in the international pharmaceutical industry is to be found in the upper end of the economic stratum, at the corporate level, as well as to those involved in wholesale and retail sales.

A comparison of the market value of these products reveals an interesting point—that the value of traditional medical products, which are used by billions of people around the world, comprises billions of dollars each year. Whether or not it is comparable to the $80–90 million of global retail sales of pharmaceutical products has not been calculated, to the best of our knowledge. It can, however, be argued that commerce in traditional plant medicines, consisting primarily of local activity such as previously described, comprises a significant economic force. If it is assumed that 3 billion people use traditional plants for their primary health care, and each person utilizes $2.50–$5.00 worth annually (whether harvested, bartered, or purchased), then the annual value of these plants could be in the range $7.5–$15 billion, a sum that is significant and comparable to the two other sectors of the global pharmacopoeia. It is roughly estimated that the international herbal industry is about ten times the size of the U.S. herbal industry, which is about 1.3 billion dollars annually (M. Blumenthal, personal communication).

Those who promote the linkage between conservation and the search for new pharmaceutical products often fail to point out that the time frame from collection of a plant in the forest to its sale on the pharmacist's shelves is eight to twelve years and that programs initiated today must be viewed as having long-term benefits, at best. An exception to this are agreements such as between Merck, Sharp and Dohme and INBio, the National Biodiversity Institute of Costa Rica. This agreement provides a substantial ''up front'' payment from Merck for infrastructure development at INBio and for the national parks system in Costa Rica and will, it is hoped, be a model for such North/South collaborations in the future. In traditional medicine and the herbal industry, the yields are immediate and the economic impact to the individual, community, and region can be quite significant.

The potential for strengthening conservation efforts ranges from low to high, depending on whether or not the extraction of the resource can be sustainably managed over the long term or is simply exploited for short-term benefits by collectors and an industry that has little interest in ensuring a reliable supply into the future. Conservation potential is minimal if the end products are derived from synthetic processes or from plantations developed outside the original area of collection. To address this issue, the National Cancer Institute's Developmental Therapeutics Program seeks to ensure that the primary country of origin of the plant will have the first opportunity to produce the plant, if commercially valuable products should arise as a result of their program (G. Cragg, personal communication).

Finally, table 24.3 summarizes the pitfalls inherent to each level, including overharvest, synthesis with no provision for benefits, land tenure issues, and, as previously mentioned, plantations established outside the range of the species. In any attempt to plan for the maximum conservation potential of a discovery, these pitfalls must be kept in mind.

Further, harvest itself is not without pitfalls. One of the primary concerns about extraction is sustainability. A case in point is the extraction of a drug used in the treatment of glaucoma, pilocarpine. The source of pilocarpine is several species of trees in the genus *Pilocarpus* that occur naturally in the northeast Brazil: *P. pinnatifolius, P. microphylla,* and *P. jaborandi.* Leaves have been harvested from the trees for many decades, usually under subcontract from chemical companies. Limited attempts at sustainable management were undertaken in the 1980s, but for the most part, harvest continued in a destructive fashion. Extinction—at the population level in many areas—has been the fate of these plants. Finally, over the last few years, cultivated plantations of *Pilocarpus* species have been developed, which will reduce the value of the remaining wild stands, as well as eliminate any incentive there was for conserving them.

Development of a Forest-Based Traditional Medicine Industry

One of the primary dilemmas in development of a program of extraction of non-timber forest products (NTFPs) has been the long history of overcollecting of the resources, with a resultant decline in these resources, as well as the export of raw materials to centers and countries far from their origin. Rattan is a classic example of this overexploitation, with people in producing countries who are closest to the resource receiving the smallest percentage of the profits involved in its production into high-quality furniture. At least three locally developed brands of commercialized traditional medicine are now being marketed in Belize. These brands include "Agapi," "Rainforest Remedies," and "Triple Moon," and are all entrepreneurial ventures. A key difference in these types of endeavors is that the "value-added" component of the product is added in the country and region of origin of the raw material. As these particular product brands develop, and as new brands and products appear based on the success of the original endeavors, greater demand for ingredients from rain forest species will result. This could potentially contribute to preservation of tropical forest ecosystems, if people carefully manage the production or extraction of the plant species that are primary ingredients in these unrelated products. In addition, it is expected that small farmers will cultivate some of the native species, for sale to both local herbalists and for commerce. To address this latter possibility, the Belize Ethnobotany Project has been working with the Belize College of Agriculture (BCA), Central Farms, in learning how to propagate and grow more than two dozen different plants currently utilized in traditional medicine in Belize. Mr. Hugh O'Brien, professor of horticulture at BCA, has coordinated this effort, which has included the following genera: *Achras, Aristolochia, Brosimum, Bursera, Cedrela, Croton, Jatropha, Myroxylon, Neurolaena, Piscidia, Psidium, Senna, Simarouba, Smilax, Stachytarpheta,* and *Swietenia.*

An Ethnobiomedical Forest Reserve

In June 1993 the government of Belize designated a 6,000-acre parcel of tropical forest as a government forest reserve, for the purpose of providing a source of native plants used locally in traditional medicine. This forest is rich in medicinally important plant species, as well as serving as a wildlife corridor joining nearby conservation reserves. As this forest reserve is developed, programs in traditional medicine, scientific research, and ecological tourism should create a synergistic effect to translate into economic return for the surrounding community, as well as provide an interface where scientists and traditional healers can work together to develop state-of-the-art management strategies for the sustainable extraction of important plant products.

A unique feature of this reserve is that it has been designated specifically for the extraction of medicinal plants used locally as part of the primary health care network. Accordingly, we propose to call this type of extractive reserve an "ethnobiomedical forest reserve," a term intended to convey a sense of the interaction among people, plants, animals, and the health care system in the region.

It will be many years before this first ethnobiomedical forest reserve can be considered successful. A great deal of work must go into developing the management plan and finding the financial and human resources to implement it. Land use pressures surrounding the reserve, specifically logging and agriculture, as well as sociological and political factors, could endanger the long-term existence of the reserve. However, in Belize there is a great deal of optimism about this reserve, in view of its innovative nature, and much support for it at the grass roots level.

What began as a simple ethnobotanical inventory in the late 1980s has evolved into a complex, multidisciplinary, and interinstitutional program aimed at better understanding the relationship between plant and people in Belize. Some of the initial results beyond ethnobotanical inventory include: refinement of the valuation methodology for the study of traditional medicines; development of nursery protocol for valuable native plants species; progress toward creation of an encyclopedia of the useful plants in the region, as well as of several major publications on the ethnobotany and floristics of the country; development of a teaching curriculum based on the appreciation and use of native plant species; the establishment of a program of pharmacological investigation linking a U.S. governmental agency with a network of traditional healers; and the establishment of a protected forest reserve. The BEP is planned to last through 1997 and perhaps branch out in other directions along the way. The BEP has shown that ethnopharmacological investigation and ethnobotanical surveys can lead directly to the conservation of valuable ecosystems and contribute, it is hoped, to their maintenance over the long term. One of the great priorities in ecosystem conservation today is developing economically sustainable strategies for maintaining such reserves over the long term (measured in hundreds of years) long after initial enthusiasm as well as philanthropic support have subsided.

ACKNOWLEDGMENTS

Gratitude is expressed to the multitude of individuals who have collaborated in the Belize Ethnobotany Project. The following organizations have provided support to the project: The U.S. National Cancer Institute; The U.S. Agency for International Development; The Metropolitan Life Insurance Foundation; The Overbrook Foundation; The Edward John Noble Foundation; The Rex Foundation; The Rockefeller Foundation; The John and Catherine T. MacArthur Foundation; The Nathan Cummings Foundation; The Gildea Foundation; as well as The Philecology Trust, through the establishment of Philecology Curatorship of Economic Botany at The New York Botanical Garden.

REFERENCES

Balick, M. J. and R. O. Mendelsohn. 1992. "Assessing the Economic Value of Traditional Medicines from Tropical Rain Forests." *Conservation Biology* 6 (1):128–30.
Peters, C. P., A. H. Gentry, and R. O. Mendelsohn. 1989. "Valuation of an Amazonian Rain Forest." *Nature* 339:656–66.

25

Tropical Medicinal Plant Conservation and Development Projects: The Case of the Costa Rican National Institute of Biodiversity (INBio)

Ana Sittenfeld

COSTA RICA is a small, developing, peaceful democratic nation in the Central American isthmus. Never a militaristic country, Costa Rica abolished its army in 1949, showing the world that disarmament and a political system based on peaceful coexistence are viable. The social and political stability and the lack of military expenditures allowed the dedication of an important component of its national budget to health and education. In the last decade, the number of students at the main state universities comprised more than 2% of the country's inhabitants.

The biological wealth of the country has been recognized since the 1800s. Viewed as repositories of biological diversity, Costa Rica's forests are among the world's most species-rich ecosystems. Costa Rica is home to about 4% of the total number of species of organisms on earth. However, outside the 27% of the country's protected wildlands where approximately a half-million species reside, there is substantial environmental deterioration. It is imperative that our conserved wildlands become a highly productive sector of our society. We must use them without destroying them. In fact it is likely that in them, there is even greater potential for future economic and intellectual value than in the more traditional agricultural lands.

A presidential decree issued in June 1989 appointed a planning commission of representatives from different national institutions to formulate a National Biodiversity Institute. The commission finished its task in August, recommending the creation of a private, nonprofit public-interest organization with strong ties to the government but having the flexible organization and freedom to operate characteristic of the private sector. In October 1989, using a remodeled tractor warehouse, the Instituto Nacional de Biodiversidad, or more simply INBio, opened its doors as part of Costa Rica's conservation program. Recently approved legislation for the promotion of scientific and technological development agreements with governmental institutions entitle the organization's activities to be of public interest. INBio also receives funding from the private sector, foundations, bilateral agencies, and research agreements. The board of directors and general assembly have representatives from different branches of Costa Rican society who are users of biodiversity or are responsible for its management. The INBio has its own buildings in the outskirts of San José, and new physical facilities are being added to house the rapidly growing needs of the institution.

Costa Rica's conservation program is based on the premise that permanent preservation of biodiversity will be attained only by its intellectual and economic integration with society. Persistence of biodiversity depends on the benefits obtained from it. In other words: use it or lose it.

Costa Rica's conservation program consists of three consecutive overlapping steps, each of which is necessary for biodiversity conservation, but not sufficient alone: The first is to save samples of this biodiversity through the establishment of a system of protected wildlands. The second is to know what that biodiversity is, and where it is located in these wildlands, and the third is to put this biodiversity to sustainable work for society. The first step was attained in Costa Rica through the establishment of a system of conservation areas (SINAC) that comprise nearly 27% of the country. Building on the experience of nearly twenty years of conservation efforts, eighty-five parks and reserves are now incorporated into eight regional conservation areas. This regional and decentralized system involves the neighboring rural communities in the protection, administration, and management of these wildlands. This step of in situ preservation has been very costly in time and money and has required much energy and dedication by motivated individuals, the government, and nongovernmental organizations, with considerable international support.

To bring about the second and third steps of "knowing" and "using," Costa Rica established INBio. Effective conservation of biodiversity is impossible without knowing the identity and geographical distribution of the estimated 500,000 species of plants, animals, and microorganisms present in Costa Rica. To carry out the basic national biodiversity inventory, INBio is training "parataxonomists," laypeople of rural extraction, with basic elementary education, intelligence, and strong desire and motivation to participate in a new and intellectually challenging job. The group is trained to fulfill the goal of figuring out what is in the conserved wildlands. Perceiving their new job as an intellectual promotion, the parataxonomists rapidly become local authorities in biodiversity and are agents of social extension of their work in their own communities. They disseminate their knowledge and information to relatives, neighbors, colleagues, and local schools, as well as gather specimens and data for INBio. Any international visitor who can communicate with them finds them to be truly sponges for biological information. Data from the work of the first group indicate that fifteen parataxonomists generate well in excess of 50,000 prepared specimens per month, and the inventory collections at INBio at present contain more than two and a half million specimens.

The information and specimens gathered by the parataxonomists enter INBio, where Costa Rican curators, working together with international scientists, initiate the taxonomic organization of the specimens. Information on the identity, distribution, natural history, and other characteristics relevant to known or potential uses of the organisms also enters and accumulates in a user-friendly format. Typical users range from students of all ages to scientists. This information is used for intellectual stimulation and by government officers in the planning, environment, and development sectors for the management of natural resources. Commercial users can be numerous and include companies interested in natural products for medical, industrial, or agrochemical purposes, genetic materials for biotechnology, or natural history information for ecotourism.

The functions of the biodiversity inventory are not directed at fulfilling conservation needs per se but rather serve as a major tool in making biodiversity pay for itself, becoming a useful instrument for social and economic development of the country. It is possible to link wealth to the sustained use of living natural resources. However, living natural resources do not become economic assets until the knowledge and means of using them become available. At the same time, knowledge creates economic resources. We expect, therefore, a dramatic increase of revenues from this source in the future. The obtained profits will be used directly to cover Conservation Area management costs and indirectly in the creation of alternatives that will favor the improvement of Costa Rican society and the economy, at the same time diminishing the pressure for land and timber in the conserved areas.

As part of this development process, a widespread screening of Costa Rican biodiversity for chemical and biotechnological activity has been initiated. In this context, a chemical-prospecting project devoted to the discovery of new products to be used in medicine, agriculture, and industry is being carried out with the participation of universities and research organizations and the involvement of pharmaceutical and other industries. Initial support has come from the MacArthur Foundation. A specific long-range aim of the project is to engender financial revenue through the commercialization of chemical discoveries, linking chemical prospecting to conservation of biodiversity and economical development. Any revenues will be used specifically to meet Conservation Area management costs and to continue developing the process.

The basic scheme of the chemical prospecting project depends on the relations among three sectors: science and technology, industry, and Costa Rica's biodiversity. The ongoing project offers steady support to INBio and the Conservation Areas in its functions as a broker, making available highly diverse biotic resources to the academic and commercial communities, while at the same time obtaining economic revenue without destroying the capital. The knowledge of the identity and whereabouts of living organisms becomes as important as the experience of knowing the characteristics and needs of the potential users of biodiversity. The major components of the chemical prospecting project are as follows:

1. Development of relational data bases containing information of three kinds:

   a. The biodiversity inventory: At present, different data bases available in IN-Bio contain information about almost all the mammals and birds, a listing of more than 8,000 plant species with their respective information on taxonomy, specific location, habitats, and phenology. A considerable number of entries also include information on species' traditional and ethnobotanical uses as well as biological leads. While 10,000 insect species have been already identified, at least 50% of the insects collected to date have not been described before.

   b. Information on uses obtained from relevant literature.

   c. Information from screening procedures, purification and industrialization processes, contractual arrangements, market opportunities, business development strategies, follow-up of proposed legislation, lobbying advice to government agencies, etc.

2. Establishment of relations with research organizations and universities that provide strong links with the national and international academic community. At present this includes contracts with Cornell University and with Strathclyde Institute for Drug Research (SIDR) in Scotland, research collaborations with the National Cancer Institute (NCI), and agreements with the main local universities—the University of Costa Rica and the National University.

3. Increase of local scientific capacities to become part of the process of discovering drugs and other biodiversity-derived chemicals, by supporting collaborative projects with investigators from Costa Rican universities and training them through all four steps listed here. The chemical prospecting project, using funds awarded by a grant from the MacArthur Foundation to INBio and Cornell University, is supporting five projects at local Costa Rican universities at a cost of more than $300,000. The projects were selected on the basis of their scientific merit, the confidence in the responsible investigator, and the possibilities for commercialization. A graduate thesis in the area of natural products is also being supported. The general structure of each project includes a group of investigators in charge of bioassays and a group of chemists in charge of making chemical extracts of selected organisms, bioassay-directed fractionation, and chemical characterization.

   The first stage in each of these projects includes the production of chemical extracts and the development and adaptation of various bioassays, where the natural raw material, usually in the form of chemical extracts of increasing polarity, is tested for biological activity. This first stage is carried out at different laboratories at the University of Costa Rica. The screening processes are directed to the identification of active compounds for: malaria, *Toxoplasma gondii, Eimeria* sp., inhibition of phospholipases A_2, coagulant and anticoagulant activities, anti-herpes simplex virus (HSV), bovine leukemia virus (BLV), bovine immunodeficiency virus (BIV), and activity against soil nematodes affecting crops of tomatoes and bananas (table 25.1).

The second stage includes the isolation, purification, and identification of the active molecules that show biological activity, and may be developed at the local universities. Cornell University and SIDR will participate. Special agreements regarding the intellectual property rights between universities and INBio have been signed or are in process.

4. Establishment of agreements and contracts with the industrial and commercial sector and development of adequate mechanisms to transfer the benefits obtained to biodiversity conservation efforts. These benefits are as follows:

   a. Funds up front in a sufficient amount to both run the actual sampling process and train and finance local capacities and foster the development of homegrown biologists, biodiversity prospectors, chemists, and biotechnologists.
   b. Designation of a significant percentage of the total budget as a direct contribution to the national system of Conservation Areas.
   c. Royalties on any profits derived from the commercialization of Costa Rican materials.
   d. Initiation of the process of gradually moving the payroll and other costs of drug research and development from the United States or other industrialized countries to Costa Rica as a biodiversity-rich source country.
   e. Incentives for the development of local human resources that now have a real opportunity for using their products and information.
   f. Serious in-country justification for saving wildlands because they are viewed as living data banks and truly renewable resources.
   g. Development of the necessary legal mechanisms to guarantee the adequate management and distribution of all the obtained benefits.

In a recent publication, Dr. Thomas Eisner at Cornell University stressed that "Systematic screening for uses, by developed and developing countries working together, could pay off for both while aiding conservation efforts of biodiversity." Under this philosophy, in September 1991, INBio signed an agreement with Merck, Sharp and Dohme, Inc., giving the firm rights to search for interesting compounds in a limited number of species for a fixed period. In return, and as part of the two-year renewable agreement, Merck will pay INBio $1,135,000 for research funding and start-up expenses, as well as royalties on the sale of any products that Merck ultimately develops from any INBio sample. Part of the research funding will pass directly to the Costa Rican system

TABLE 25.1   *Local Projects at Costa Rican Universities Supported by the Chemical-Prospecting Program*

Inhibition of Activity	Research Center	Main Investigator	University
Plasmodium, Taxoplasma	Parasitology Faculty of Microbiology	Misael Chinchilla, Ph.D.	University of Costa Rica
Eimeria	Chemistry Dept.	Mariano Barrios	National University
HSV, BIV, HIV	Cell and Molecular Biology Research Center	José Bonilla, Ph.D.	University of Costa Rica
	Virology Department	Libia Herrero, Ph.D.	University of Costa Rica
	Lab of Cell and Molecular Structure	M. A. Gonda, Ph.D.	National Cancer Institute
	Chemistry School	Giselle Tamayo, Ph.D.	University of Costa Rica
Soil nematodes	Nematology Laboratory, Faculty of Agronomy,	Róger López, Ph.D.	University of Costa Rica
	Natural Products Research Center	Oscar Castro, Ph.D.	University of Costa Rica
Phospholipases, A_2 coagulant, anticoagulant	Institute Clodomiro Picado	José M Gutiérrez, Ph.D.	University of Costa Rica
	Chemistry Dept.	Oscar Castro, Ph.D.	National University
Fungi	Chemistry School	Giselle Tamayo, Ph.D.	University of Costa Rica
	Chemistry Dept.	Jon Clardy, Ph.D.	Cornell University

of Conservation Areas. In addition, Merck will aid in the training of Costa Rican scientists in chemical prospecting. INBio has made a subcontract with the University of Costa Rica to perform the chemical extraction process.

5. The process of transferring the obtained benefits to the conservation of biodiversity must include an adequate legal framework in order to guarantee its correct uses. This aspect requires agreements with government entities as well as advice and lobbying at the National Assembly.

   The economic value of species information and the effectiveness of the INBio model in capturing and transferring the economic value of Costa Rican biodiversity will be studied by the London Environmental Economics Centre. More recently, a research proposal was presented to the Rockefeller Foundation and is aimed at helping INBio's business development strategies. This includes an analysis of INBio's present organization in terms of both its strengths and weaknesses, an industry study of market opportunities, and the development and implementation of a business plan.

Biodiversity information is no different from all the other kinds of information provided in the marketplace and can be used sustainably to advance conservation efforts. Fair partnerships between tropical and temperate countries together with research on biodiversity's nondestructive uses are essential for use of conserved wildlands by tropical societies. INBio is an example of a global pilot project and a major Costa Rican mechanism to preserve and use biodiversity. It establishes a new framework for the game, a new and sustainable way to take advantage of heretofore unexplored tropical wealth and build on the human resources of a developing country.

26

FENAMAD's Program in Traditional Medicine: An Integrated Approach to Health Care in the Peruvian Amazon

Miguel N. Alexiades and Didier Lacaze D.

INDIGENOUS peoples throughout the Amazon face considerable difficulties in defining their roles within the context of rapid regional social and ecological change. Contact with the dominant society has led to decimation of their original populations, loss of traditional territories, and widespread erosion of their cultural and biological resource base, ultimately leading to an impoverishment of living conditions while undermining their right to self-determination.

The deterioration of living conditions among tribal societies following acculturation is well documented by medical and anthropological literature (Ciba Foundation Symposium 1977; Dricot-D'Ans and Dricot 1978; McElroy and Townsend 1989; Wirsing 1985). This paper briefly documents the integral link between health and culture change among the indigenous population of the Madre de Dios region in Amazonian Peru, illustrating how current health problems are inextricably linked to the social, cultural, and ecological consequences of colonization and development. The approach utilized by the health program of the regional indigenous federation (FENAMAD) to improve living conditions is discussed within this wider context of health.

The FENAMAD (Federación de Comunidades Nativas del Río Madre de Dios y Afluentes) is the regional federation of native communities in Madre de Dios. Representing all native communities in the department, it deals with issues such as land rights, education, health, and development. The FENAMAD was created in 1982, and it is run by a board representing different ethnic groups and communities, elected by delegates from all communities during the annual general assembly.

AMETRA 2001: *Application of Traditional Medicine*

AMETRA, an acronym for "Aplicación de Medicina Tradicional" (Application of Traditional Medicine), began as a health project among the Shipibo-Conibo ethnic group of the Ucayali region, Peru, in 1982. The project, run in close collaboration with the regional indigenous federation (FECONAU), aimed to improve health conditions in Shipibo-Conibo communities by encouraging the use of medicinal plants, combined with basic aspects of primary health care (Arévalo and Hansson 1985; Follér 1989). A parallel project, known as AMETRA 2001, was set up by the FENAMAD in 1985 in the neighboring region of Madre de Dios (figure 26.1.). AMETRA's general objectives may be summarized as follows (AMETRA 1987):

- To stimulate the official recognition of the importance and value of traditional medicine, as practiced within the cultural context of each ethnic group, in promoting health among the indigenous population

FIGURE 26.1 Location map of the departments of Ucayali and Madre de Dios, Peru.

- To encourage the use of locally available, effective herbal remedies to treat the most common ailments
- To encourage the combined use of adequate herbal and Western medicines, discouraging obsolete or dangerous treatments in both categories of health care
- To promote the conservation and sustained use of natural resources, stressing the importance of the intimate relationship between people and the surrounding forest

In Madre de Dios, AMETRA 2001 expanded its range of activities to include a number of projects dealing with such health-related issues as culture change, nutrition, resource management, and community organization (AMETRA 1987). During the period between 1987 to 1991 AMETRA 2001 trained FENAMAD personnel in logistical, technical, and administrative aspects of running the various projects. As a result, in 1991 the FENAMAD undertook full responsibility for all AMETRA 2001's projects, renaming the program as "programa de medicina tradicional" (traditional medicine program).

FENAMAD'S Traditional Medicine Program: Toward an Integrated Approach to Health

The basic premise behind FENAMAD's approach is that health problems among the Amazonian indigenous and rural population will be effectively tackled only by a decentralized, horizontal health care system that incorporates local expertise and traditional knowledge, optimizing appropriate technology and emphasizing the role of preventive medicine, that is, a program that takes into account the social, political, cultural, and environmental dimensions of health and health care. While this presents an ambitious task for a project with limited financial, technical, and human resources, the solutions that emerge tend to operate at causative rather than symptomatic levels. In this way, health projects can serve as vehicles through which individuals and communities can develop the organizational skills necessary to negotiate their roles within society at large, helping to direct social change in a way that improves rather than worsens living conditions (Behrhorst 1975; Werner 1981).

Health, Development, and Cultural Changes in Madre de Dios

The history of colonization and development of Madre de Dios provides the social and ecological setting to explain many of today's health problems in native communities. The area remained largely isolated from the outside until the rubber boom at the turn of the century (Moore 1990; Rumrill, Dávila, and Barcia 1986). Although short-lived, the rubber boom had a dramatic impact on indigenous people. The combination of epidemics, genocide, and intertribal warfare triggered by rubber tappers combing areas for slave or indentured labor led to the decimation of the native population (Rumrill, Dávila, and Barcia 1986). Today, only six of the twelve ethnic groups native to this part of the Amazon have a population of more than 100 individuals (table 26.1), the total indigenous population having dwindled to approximately 5,000. Epidemics still present a health threat to isolated groups such as the recently contacted Nahua or Yurá, whose population is estimated to have declined by about 60% since 1984, as a result of several epidemic outbreaks (Wahl 1990).

Ethnic groups such as the Piro, Shipibo-Conibo, and Quichua Runa were brought into the area from other parts of the Amazon during the rubber boom. Many groups indigenous to the area were displaced from their ancestral territories as a result of intertribal war, disease, or enslavement or else resettled in missions and "native communities" (*comunidades nativas*). As a result, indigenous people have lost access to most of their traditional lands.

Whenever land rights exist, they are limited to small, discrete territories referred to as native communities. The size of native communities was not originally determined on the basis of subsistence requirements, on patterns of resource utilization, or on other ecological criteria; rather, a fixed quota was employed, based on up to 10 hectares of land per individual (Bodley 1982). Subsequent laws calling for the allotment of land to native communities based on subsistence needs have been implemented very slowly. Of the thirty-three native communities in Madre de Dios, only fifteen have legal titles, two have titles pending, and sixteen have no titles (Source: FENAMAD/Centro Eori, n.d.).

TABLE 26.1. *Ethnic Groups in Madre de Dios*

Linguistical Family	Ethnic Group	Total Population (1990)	Number of Communities
Arawak	Machiguenga	445	8*
	Piro†	339	4*
	Iñapari	18	1
Harakmbut	Amarakaeri	896	5*
	Arasaeri	83	1
	Pukirieri	72	1
	Toyoeri/Kisamoaeri	41	2*
	Sapiteri	26	1
	Wachipaeri	258	3*
Pano	Amahuaca	78	2*
	Shipibo-Conibo†	244	3*
	Yaminahua	120	2
Quechua	Quichua Runa†	364	2
Tacana	Ese-eja	663	5*
Total		3,647	33

Source: FENAMAD/Centro EORI 1990.
Note: * indicates that at least one community is shared with another ethnic group.
†Piro, Shipibo-Conibo, and Quichua Runa families were relocated from other parts of the Amazon by rubber barons at the turn of the century.

Breaking up traditional territories into smaller, discrete parcels of land permitted colonists to occupy land between native communities, further disrupting traditional subsistence and settlement patterns (AIDESEP 1985). The creation of new laws pertaining to native communities and agrarian development in 1978 and 1980 further compromised access to land and resources by the indigenous population, favoring large-scale colonization and commercial exploitation of natural resources (AIDESEP 1985).

Following a series of gold rushes in Madre de Dios beginning in 1930, a road was completed in 1965, linking Madre de Dios to the Andean region. This road and the improvement of air transportation have opened the department to large-scale colonization. Gold mining continues to dominate the regional economy, attracting thousands of laborers from poverty-stricken and politically unstable Andean provinces. There has also been a dramatic increase in the number of agricultural migrants from the Andes. Gold miners and colonists are principal acculturating forces, competing with indigenous people for land and resources and exacerbating the problem of environmental degradation.

Inadequate access to land and natural resources condemns people to resource degradation, malnutrition, poor health, and increased dependency on the outside (Bodley and Benson 1979; Chirif, Garcia, and Smith 1991). Indeed, land rights are still considered by indigenous people to be the basic issue in their struggle for self-determination and a viable future (AIDESEP 1985; Chirif, Garcia, and Smith 1991).

Changes in settlement patterns and social organization among the indigenous population of Madre de Dios have had profound impacts on health. Seminomadic lifestyles and low population densities typical of many Amazonian tribal groups, for example, helped prevent overexploitation of local biological resources, while limiting the build-up of parasites and pathogens around settlements (Polunin 1977). Creation of permanent settlements around missions, schools, and "native communities" has often led to an increase in respiratory and contact infections, together with feco-orally transmitted diseases and parasites (Kroeger 1980). This occurs particularly when difficulties arise in adopting adequate sanitary responses to such changes, including the use of shoes or latrines. Creation of permanent settlements and local overcrowding have also contributed to exhaustion of local biological resources, thereby affecting nutrition and increasing dependency on the outside.

Access to "new" technology such as steel axes, chain saws, guns, and fishing nets has considerably increased the ability of individuals to extract natural resources and modify the environment. In order to obtain desirable manufactured goods such as clothes, tools, guns, or medicines, indigenous people have to market timber and other important subsistence natural resources. As depletion of natural resources increases, so does the dependence on purchased goods, thereby worsening the vicious circle of environmental degradation, poverty, and poor health.

Increased dependency on the market economy also leads to shifts in agricul-

tural practices, which in turn often have nutritional and environmental consequences. Traditional agricultural systems, which tend to maximize production of
a wide variety of nutritious crops while minimizing environmental degradation,
are often replaced by commercially viable monocultures that may have a lower
nutritional return and eventually limit soil productivity (Behrens 1989; Meggers
1973). In Madre de Dios, the shift to commercially viable monocultures and cattle
ranching has been encouraged with loans from the Agrarian Bank and through
other economic incentives. Cattle raising has also been subsidized and encouraged
by development agencies and the Agrarian Bank, as a form of integrating indigenous people into the market economy. In other cases, traditional foodstuffs not
considered acceptable by the dominant society and stigmatized as "Indian food"
have been replaced with nutritionally poor alternatives such as refined carbohydrates.

Incorporation of native people into the market economy as laborers, in gold
mining and logging operations, for example, has direct consequences on health
and nutrition. Subsistence activities are often compromised, leading to dependency on expensive, often nutritionally poor foods. Increased purchasing ability
does not necessarily equate with improved living conditions. The wealthier gold-
mining native communities in Madre de Dios, for example, have some of the worst
health problems. Integration into the capitalist economy, based on individual ac-
cumulation of wealth and the nuclearization of the family, erodes traditional systems of reciprocity. These systems of exchange ensured equitable distribution of
resources, minimized the individual work load, maximized overall protein availability, and strengthened social bonds within the community.

Incorporation of new beliefs and cultural practices has also had a marked impact on the health and nutritional status of acculturating communities. The decline
of breast feeding in favor of bottled milk is a common trend in many communities
throughout the tropics, with multiple negative consequences upon health and
nutrition of infants (Jellife 1962). Suppression of contraception, abortion, and in-
fanticide as a result of acculturation, for example, can lead to increased natality
and decreased weaning periods, exposing infants to contaminated or less nutritious foods at an earlier age. This in turn results in increased infant malnutrition
and morbidity (Neel 1977; Wirsing 1985).

Cultural change has affected ecological relationships in many other ways. Extractive activities are often regulated in traditional Amazonian societies by a religious system that emphasizes close dependency on the environment, penalizing
ecological abuse (Reichel-Dolmatoff 1971, 1976; Von Hildebrand 1983). Shamans
have often played an important role in regulating social and ecological relations,
acting as agents to prevent as well as to cure disease (Cárdenas 1989; Lobo-
Guerrero and Herrera 1983). Indigenous medicine, including shamanism and the
use of medicinal plants, has often been discredited and even repressed by missionaries and the state. This, together with the rapid process of acculturation, has

led to a decline in the number of healers and in the usage and knowledge of medicinal plants.

Though much of the department still remains undeveloped, there are plans for extensive cattle raising and agriculture (Reyes 1989). There is also a proposed project to build a road through Madre de Dios, linking Brazil to the Pacific coast. Given past experience in other parts of the Amazon with similar development models (Bodley 1982, 1988; Davis 1977) and current conflicts between the native population and colonists, these activities may further jeopardize the ability of indigenous communities to accommodate to change.

Today, most of the indigenous population in Madre de Dios lives in communities influenced to varying degrees by the regional and national economy and culture. While some of the more remote communities retain important elements of traditional social organization and technology, maintaining a high degree of self-sufficiency, those closer to the regional capital have been largely absorbed into the regional market economy. Most communities are in an intermediate position, practicing subsistence agriculture, supplemented with hunting, fishing, and small-scale marketing of surplus agricultural produce and forest products.

Health Conditions in Native Communities

A preliminary survey conducted among native communities in the western section of the department by AMETRA 2001 (Cueva 1990) reports rates of mortality of 300 per 1,000 live births for children up to five years old. More than half of this mortality occurs among infants (up to twelve months old), the two most important causes being digestive disorders, mainly diarrhea and dysentery, and acute respiratory infections. Most of the deaths associated with diarrheic disorders occur as a result of dehydration. These preliminary results correspond with data obtained in other areas of the Peruvian Amazon (Eichenberger 1966; Grupo DAM 1978; Hewett and Duggan 1986).

The prevalence of high infestation rates with intestinal parasites among acculturating Indians in the Amazon is widely documented (Hansson et al. 1986; Lawrence et al. 1980). An analysis of stools in two native communities in Madre de Dios revealed levels of infestation with helminthic parasites of close to 100% among the censused population (Cueva and Ojeda 1988). Most of the samples included at least two of the three most common helminths: *Ascaris lumbricoides, Trichuris trichiura,* and *Ancylostoma* sp. *Strongyloides stercoralis* is also fairly common, and *Taenia* sp. is occasionally reported. High levels of helminthic infestation are correlated with anemia, malnutrition, gastrointestinal disorders, and lower resistance to other diseases (Blumenthal and Schultz 1976; Hansson et al. 1986; Layrisse et al. 1967; Stephenson 1980; Tripathy et al. 1971). Preliminary indices of child malnutrition, based on weight and height, vary between 26% and 57% for six censused native communities within and around Manu National Park (Cueva 1990).

Skin disorders, including micosis, ascariosis, and miasis, are generally the third most important cause of morbidity after acute respiratory infections and gastro-intestinal disorders (Cueva 1990). Otitis media is also common, particularly among children. Other fairly common ailments include rheumatism, malaria, snake bites, conjunctivitis, abscesses, and fractures. Medical authorities believe that tuberculosis is becoming much more prevalent in the whole region (Oporto, personal communication), as in the rest of the country, though statistics are not available. Yellow fever is endemic in the area and several outbreaks have occurred in the past. Venereal diseases appear also to be on the increase though no data for native communities exist. Leishmaniasis is relatively rare among the native population but relatively frequent among the immigrant population in some areas.

The Status of Indigenous and "Western" Medical Systems

Although it is beyond the scope of this paper to review the role of indigenous and Western medical health care delivery systems in Madre de Dios, and despite the variations between ethnic groups and communities, we would like to point out some general observations. First, although many indigenous concepts of disease and healing are still widespread (Cueva 1990; Peluso, in preparation), the number of "curanderos," or healers, and other specialized practitioners in indigenous medicine in the region is dwindling. Many communities no longer have a healer, while those living are usually more than fifty years old and have no apprentices. There also appears to be a decline in the usage of and dependence on medicinal plants among groups in which this practice was once common. Many attribute this to the loss of knowledge within the community, as older, knowledgeable people die and the oral knowledge is not transmitted. Religious and educational institutions have often played a role in discrediting the value and status of indigenous knowledge and culture, thus discouraging its transmission to younger generations. In some cases, medicinal plants have become more difficult to obtain owing to ex-cessive extraction for supplying city markets or owing to conversion of forest into agricultural land. In other cases pharmaceutical prescriptions are often preferred because they are easier to use, act faster, or have a higher status value.

At the same time, access to "Western" health care is often inadequate. In 1992 only two communities had health posts tended by government-trained health workers (*sanitarios*). Most communities live days away from the nearest medical post or hospital, and at times transportation is logistically or financially impossible. Medical outreach to communities is largely restricted to government vaccination campaigns or to small-scale efforts by charity organizations or missionaries. Although the government has trained village health workers (*promotores de salud*), their effectiveness is severely curtailed by their limited access to medicines. We have witnessed creative alternatives for empty communal medicine cabinets, ranging from tool boxes to rat-proof storage units for community soccer team shoes.

Even when medicines are available, individuals often do not have the financial resources to purchase them. In January 1992, a single treatment for helminthic parasites, one of the cheapest medicines, was costing the equivalent of 1.50 to 2.00 U.S. dollars. Since most families have five or more children, just to medicate a family once would cost about $10, a considerable amount given the facts that the minimum wage in Peru is $40 a month and that most of the rural population earns considerably less. The limited access to medicines and Western health care in general is compounded by Peru's current financial crisis, which has resulted in a national shortage of medicines, increased prices, and budgetary constraints on what was already an inadequate infrastructure.

As a result, acculturating native communities often find themselves caught between an undervalued and rapidly disintegrating indigenous medical system on the one hand and a financially and logistically inaccessible "Western" medical system on the other. Within this context AMETRA 2001 aims to encourage the reassessment of indigenous medicine and facilitate the access to primary health care, thereby increasing self-reliance among the native population.

FENAMAD'S Traditional Medicine Program and Primary Health Care

FENAMAD's primary health care program aims to increase the ability of native communities to identify and respond to their own health problems effectively, emphasizing the value of indigenous medical resources and facilitating access to appropriate technology. Activities include community education campaigns, training of health workers, recording of the ethnobotanical lore, and promotion of the cultivation of medicinal plants. Health workers are assisted and encouraged to identify the most serious health problems in their communities. Efforts have been made to record basic health-related concepts and practices within each ethnic group, in order to evaluate the potential cultural responses to particular health problems (FENAMAD and AMETRA 1990).

Health workers received initial basic training during one- to two-week-long workshops held twice a year in different communities during the period 1985–1989 (figure 26.2). Subjects covered included diagnosis and treatment of common gastrointestinal and respiratory disorders, skin ailments, eye infections, fever, rheumatism, common dental problems, as well as first aid treatment of acute injuries such as cuts, burns, hemorrhages, and snakebite. Practical sessions included preparation of oral rehydration serums and herbal remedies, application of intramuscular injections, and fracture immobilization (figure 26.3). Workshops were attended by healers from different ethnic groups, as well as by a state nurse or physician.

FIGURE 26.2 A Matsigenka woman discusses medicinal plants in an AMETRA 2001 primary health care workshop. *Photo: D. Lacaze.*

FIGURE 26.3 A Shipibo-Conibo healer, or "curandero," (left) demonstrates the preparation of *Pothomorphe* sp. (Piperaceae) to Matsigenka and Huachipaeri health workers during an AMETRA 2001 workshop.   *Photo: M. Alexiades.*

Upon returning to their communities, health workers were encouraged to disseminate their knowledge to the rest of the community, promoting the use and cultivation of medicinal plants, the use of latrines, and community participation in health-related activities. Health workers were also encouraged to work closely with any traditional practitioners in the community as well as the state nurse. Further on-site assistance is provided to health workers during periodic visits to their communities by FENAMAD personnel.

Three years of experience with workshops and follow-up trips have revealed some of the limitations of a "health worker" type of approach to a primary health care program. Creating a network of trained community health workers has been the approach used by many rural health care projects (Belongia 1988; CAAAP 1985; Hewett and Duggan 1986) and still forms the essence of the state rural health program.

The success of a program based on health workers depends largely on the ease with which such a system can be integrated into the community's social organization, as well as on the health worker's status and organizational and communication skills. Most of the health workers chosen by native communities in Madre de Dios are young men, probably because of their greater literacy and because they often have fewer family and social commitments. In many cases, however, young males do not master the social or political skills of their elders. Education in missionary or state-sponsored schools has often helped to create a sense of psychological alienation and even rejection of traditional cultural norms, hindering communication between generations. This is especially the case in Madre de Dios, where most teachers come from urban settings. Problems of communication between health workers and the community are exacerbated when community organization is poor or internal feuds exist between clans or families, a prevalent situation in acculturating native communities. Finally, the role of men in healing among many groups in Madre de Dios appears to have been more restricted to the realm of shamanism and psychomagical curing. Child rearing, basic health care, and the cultivation of many medicinal plants have been and still remain largely female concerns among many indigenous and rural societies (Buenaventura-Posso and Brown 1989; Cárdenas 1989; McClain 1989). At the same time, however, the social construction of gender roles within acculturating communities has hindered women from being elected as health workers, ignoring their critical role in health care (Peluso, in preparation).

In view of the above-mentioned factors, FENAMAD's program in traditional medicine has been incorporating other approaches complementary to training of health workers. Greater attention is currently given to community education and especially to women (AMETRA 2001 1990; FENAMAD 1990). Given the large area covered, the different ethnic groups involved, and the limited resources available, the health program was divided into two sectors, where two different approaches were used. In the western section of the department corresponding to the area around the Manu Biosphere Reserve, an interdisciplinary team was created composed of a healer, a physician, and an anthropologist. This team conducted a preliminary evaluation of health conditions in the area and elaborated a proposal for a health program (Cueva 1990; Helberg 1989, 1990). In the southern sector of the department, three communities were assigned priority for a pilot community education program involving regular visits and follow-ups.

Greatest priority is given in the program to the treatment of intestinal parasites and diarrheal diseases, for these are the principal causes of morbidity and mortality, especially among children. Priority is also given to the use of the latex of *Ficus insipida* Willd. as an anthelminthic, owing to its proven effectiveness (Hansson et al. 1986) and abundant distribution. Communities are encouraged to use this anthelminthic during regular campaigns where the whole community is treated simultaneously (figure 26.4). The latex of green papaya fruits (*Carica papaya* L.) and the juice of the leaves of *Chenopodium ambrosoides* L. are recommended as alternatives, especially for individual use. For diarrheal diseases, the use of plant-based rehydration drinks is emphasized, with *Psidium guajaba, Anacardium occidentale,* and *Musa* spp. All these plants are well known and easily cultivated. For most other ailments, priority is given to herbal treatments, though the complementary use of medicinal plants and "Western" drugs is recommended in many

FIGURE 26.4 An Amahuaca health care worker prepares an anthelminthic with the latex of *Ficus insipida* Willd. (Moraceae).   *Photo: M. Alexiades.*

cases when the latter offer distinct medical advantages. Communities are alerted about harmful medicines, often banned in their countries of origin, and about the dangers associated with misuse of certain medications, such as antibiotics—both widespread problems in many Third World countries (Melrose 1982).

By promoting the exchange of ethnobotanical knowledge between groups, FENAMAD hopes to increase the number of options available to communities and individuals for treatment of ailments. This exchange is encouraged in workshops and community events, particularly during group walks in the surrounding forest or fields. The uses of more than 100 medicinal plants were discussed in six workshops between 1986 and 1988.

Some ethnomedical systems appear to rely more heavily on medicinal plants than others, and different groups often have different or conflicting beliefs on the use or preparation of medicinal plants. Within this context, FENAMAD's policy has been to encourage the reevaluation of each group's ethnomedical system, presenting other approaches and medicinal plants as alternatives that may or may not be incorporated by the community.

Aside from providing basic training in primary health care and herbalism, community workshops also serve as an effective platform to discuss other issues related to health, including nutrition, sanitation, community organization, and the implications of the loss of indigenous knowledge.

Rather than attempt to implement a standard solution for all communities through the use of an idealized formula, the health workshops and follow-up trips aim to stimulate an interest and a degree of confidence in the indigenous medicine within each ethnic group or community. In this way the program hopes to initiate a self-perpetuating process or dialogue, whereby the community mobilizes its resources and those of the FENAMAD in a way best suited to its particular perception, needs, or problems.

Collaboration Between Medical Systems

The past two decades have seen an increased awareness of and interest in the role of traditional medicine in primary health care (Bannerman 1983; Farnsworth et al. 1985; WHO 1978). Since its creation, AMETRA 2001 and thereafter FENAMAD's traditional medicine program have attempted to serve as a bridge between indigenous and Western health care systems, encouraging a policy of mutual respect and collaboration. This policy has been substantiated by the involvement of medical doctors in AMETRA 2001's primary health care program and through collaboration with local and regional health authorities (AMETRA 2001 1986, 1990). Most health workshops have been attended by a government health practitioner.

AMETRA 2001 has also supported and collaborated with the government in its national vaccination campaigns, as well as its programs for control of tuberculosis, acute respiratory diseases, and diarrheal disorders. In two communities with state medical posts, the communal medicinal plant garden was been built next to it. Although most desirable, this arrangement is often difficult to implement or maintain, for government health workers are usually foreign to the region or to indigenous culture and remain in the communities only for a few years.

AMETRA 2001 has also collaborated with health and research institutions in conducting clinical trials to assess the medical efficacy of key medicinal plants. Medicinal plants studied to date include the latex of *Ficus insipida* Willd. as an anthelminthic and the resin of *Copaifera reticulata* Ducke for the treatment of cutaneous leishmaniasis and as an antiinflamatory (Arroyo, Veliz Rodriguez, and Hansson Raquette 1985). Although clinical trials are considered to be an important component in the promotion of medicinal plants, they are not considered an essential prerequisite for several reasons. First, the effectiveness of medicinal plants often cannot be studied out of the cultural and psychomagical context surrounding its use (Elisabetsky 1986). Second, screening for biologically active components sometimes does not take into account complex interactions between different components of the plant and its admixes (van der Hoogte and Roersch 1985). Finally, chemical analysis and clinical trials depend on human, technical, and financial resources that are often beyond the scope of nonindustrialized countries or their institutions.

Since 1990 FENAMAD has participated in a number of forums and dialogues with the regional government in which the following petitions have been discussed (FENAMAD 1990):

- Official recognition of the indigenous medical systems of Amazonian groups, designating "Western" medicine as complementary
- Recognition that health problems among the indigenous population have to be addressed separately from those of other populations, the unique social and cultural reality of each ethnic group being taken into account
- Collaboration with indigenous organizations in the planning and implementation of health policies, emphasizing training of indigenous staff and the transfer of technology to native peoples
- Implementation of projects designed to assess the socioeconomic, nutritional, and health status among native communities and to assure that such projects integrate indigenous knowledge and patterns of resource management

Although a number of preliminary agreements have been formalized between the departmental health authorities (UDES) and FENAMAD-AMETRA 2001, these have been insufficient to reach the desired degree of collaboration. Among the multiple political, organizational, and ideological obstacles that may hamper an effective policy of mutual collaboration we would like to mention a few. One of the first lies in attempting to juxtapose a vertically oriented, centralized organization with a horizontal, decentralized one. This translates into enormous practical difficulties when one is trying to organize joint actions and collaborate in the transfer of knowledge and technology. Often, initiatives by individuals within the state organization are hampered by the rigidity and complexity of a large bureaucracy. The problem is aggravated by the fact that most positions in the hospital and medical posts are held for only a few years, and this makes it hard to establish continuity in negotiations and establish a long-term dialogue.

A further difficulty in promoting an effective collaborative interaction between medical systems stems from the need to develop a common language of understanding between cultural systems with conflicting concepts of disease causation and health. The use of oral rehydration drinks in cases of diarrhea, for example, conflicts with the oft-held indigenous view that in some cases, drinking liquids worsens the condition. An attempt to introduce new habits or concepts without an adequate understanding of the indigenous concepts of disease causation and cure, and of the material bases behind them, may limit the cultural efficacy of the approach (Crandon 1986; Coreil and Mull 1988; Wellin 1955), hampering the relationship between medical systems and their long-term "integration." At the same time, Western practitioners often have difficulties in accommodating concepts and techniques that clash with a scientific worldview. Anthropologists have an important role to play in this sense, creating an adequate bridge of understanding between both cultures and a sound base for an approach based on mutual respect.

In many communities in Madre de Dios, medical pluralism seems to prevail, where both systems are used to a certain extent simultaneously or sequentially

(Bennett 1988). This tendency has been repeatedly observed in other areas of rural Latin America (Kroeger and Ruiz 1988). Thus a patient may first resort to a pharmaceutical drug prescribed by kinfolks, the state health worker, or a pharmacist. If this fails, the patient may resort to a physician and then to a healer, or vice versa. The tendency to use "Western" medications to treat the symptoms and "traditional" medicine to treat the cause of the disease has been reported among several rural populations in the tropics (Colson 1971; Gonzalez 1966; Hamnett and Connell 1981). This would appear to indicate that a suitable environment often exists for facilitating the reconciliation and cooperation between medical systems. FENAMAD's role in this context appears to be to facilitate the process whereby individuals can choose and have access to both medical systems, in a way that optimizes the overall medical and cultural efficacy of health care.

Construction of a Community Health and Research Center

Since 1987, the native communities of Madre de Dios have been participating in the construction of a complex of traditionally designed houses, named *Centro Ñape* after an ancestral Ese-eja healer, or *eyámitekua* (figure 26.5). The center (as it will be herein referred to) was managed by AMETRA 2001 until 1991, when FENAMAD

FIGURE 26.5 Centro Ñape, a community health and research center along the Tambopata River, Madre de Dios, Peru.   *Photo: M. Alexiades.*

assumed full responsibility for its administration. The center lies within the territory of an Ese-eja community, where each year a different household serves as its caretaker, and is surrounded by 2,000 hectares of primary forest set aside by the host community for the project. Aside from serving as a community and health center, it aims to serve as a model for community development, integrating indigenous knowledge with appropriate technology in a number of health, nutrition, and resource management projects. Most importantly, the center aims to serve as a vehicle for training and for the transfer of technology to native communities.

CULTIVATION OF MEDICINAL PLANTS

Approximately 100 species of medicinal plants are currently being cultivated, some of which are processed to make powders, ointments, and other extracts (AMETRA 2001 1988a; Eláez 1989). Medicinal plants and their derivatives are used to treat patients at the center and distributed to health workers in native communities. The technique used to make plant-based extracts is simple and cheap, enabling its transfer to native communities. Aside from the direct health benefits incurred from the production of herbal remedies, these may eventually become an economically viable activity for native communities who wish to exploit regional or national markets for medicinal plants or their derivatives. The center also serves as a nursery for medicinal plants, distributing seedlings to health workers and communities, thereby encouraging the cultivation of medicinal plants throughout the department.

CENTRO ÑAPE AS A HEALTH CENTER

Healers treat patients both at the center and during visits to different communities. To date, around 700 patients suffering a wide range of conditions have been treated at the center by seven different healers from different ethnic groups who visit it for periods ranging from days to months (figure 26.6). Aside from providing important health care, the presence of healers encourages the transmission of knowledge to younger generations. So far two healers, both from communities with no healers, have received apprenticeships. The center also hosts workshops and meetings designed to bring together indigenous health practitioners, including bone setters (*hueseros*) and midwives (*parteras*). In this way, the center hopes to serve as a catalyst, promoting the reintroduction of indigenous health care delivery systems in native communities.

HEALTH AND CONSERVATION

The notion of health among indigenous cultures relates to a state of equilibrium between the individual, the community, and the natural and supernatural forces

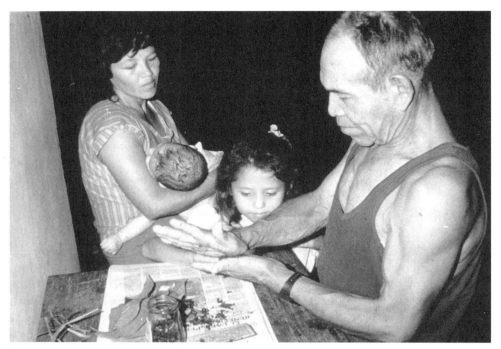

FIGURE 26.6 A Shipibo-Conibo healer prepares a remedy for a skin infection with the leaves of *Hamelia axillaris* Jacq. (Rubiaceae).   *Photo: M. Alexiades.*

of the environment. The role of the center in healing is reinforced by its location in an area of spiritual and magical significance to the Ese-eja. The community hosting the center set aside 2,000 ha. of primary forest for the project, banning the use of guns, the use of chain saws, and the practice of slash-and-burn agriculture (AMETRA 2001 1988b). In this way the center incorporates the elements of a "sacred space" (Olortegui 1988), a concept common to many ethnic groups and whose potential extends into preventive medicine and resource management (Wright, Houseal, and De Leon 1985).

Workers at the center have initiated a number of projects aimed at assessing the distribution of forest resources in the surrounding area and the possibilities for their sustainable use. A survey of the abundance and distribution of three important medicinal tree species (*Ficus insipida, Ficus* sp., and *Copaifera reticulata*) is being carried out, based on the initial work of Phillips (1990) with *F. insipida.*

Reforestation with ethnobotanically important tree species has been started in degraded areas and riparian forest around the center and will be extended into other areas of the community. Species chosen so far include the ones mentioned above, in addition to the palms *Bactris gasipaes* HBK, *Jessenia bataua* (Mart.) Burr., *Euterpe precatoria* Mart., and *Iriartea deltoidea* R. & P. Despite their enormous value as sources of foods, medicines, and building materials (Balick 1984), the populations of these species have been declining through excessive exploitation and lack of cultivation.

Located next to a large unit of conservation, the 1.5-million-ha. Tambopata-Candamo Reserved Zone, the center serves as a model for the participation of native people in resource management and conservation, both through the application of their knowledge and as custodians of forest resources.

Ethnobotany and Community Development

Since 1985, the ethnobotanical lore of several native communities has been compiled in a data base, currently being computerized. Information stored in the data base is fed back to native communities through health courses and other means, such as manuals for health workers on the use of medicinal plants (Lacaze and Alexiades 1995). Ethnobotanical data are gathered by FENAMAD during visits to communities and in health workshops. A trained native collector prepares herbarium specimens that are subsequently distributed to The New York Botanical Garden and the Museo de Historia Natural "Javier Prado" (Lima, Perú) for identification.

Ethnobotanical research techniques have also been used to conduct a quantitative survey of the forest resources in the area of primary forest around the center. The project, carried out in collaboration with The New York Botanical Garden Institute of Economic Botany, used informants from different ethnic groups to assess the subsistence value of all trees in two belt transects totalling 1.1 hectares (Alexiades 1989). The study aims to serve as a first step in evaluating the value and distribution of forest resources in the area, before development of a management plan for their sustainable use. Similar projects in other parts of the Amazon have yielded surprisingly high percentages of useful species (Balée 1987; Boom 1987), illustrating the importance of tropical forests to local peoples and the potential of ethnobotanical knowledge in resource evaluation and conservation (Prance et al. 1987). The results of the Tambopata ethnobotanical project will be presented separately (Alexiades, in preparation).

During the initial stages of fieldwork, an Ese-eja from the host community received training on basic aspects of ethnobotanical research, allowing FENAMAD to continue the project in the future. Duplicates of all botanical collections are kept in the center's herbarium, to be used in educational programs and in the identification of useful plants.

Training in Grass Roots Organization

The ability of a community to deal with its health problems is directly correlated with the degree of community organization and the effectiveness with which it can mobilize its human resources. To this end, the center is open to workshops and meetings encouraging the discussion of common problems and providing orientation on community organization. Recent meetings have aimed to gather women representatives from different communities to discuss their specific problems and facilitate their organization in health.

The health problems affecting the native population in Madre de Dios mirror the social and ecological problems associated with the process of colonization and culture change. Thus initiatives to improve health and living conditions in native communities have to be integrated with current attempts by the indigenous population to retain access to their cultural and biological resources, while resisting marginalization. By dealing simultaneously with land rights, community organization, conservation of natural resources, and health and education, the efforts of FENAMAD are complementary and mutually reinforcing. This integrated approach may be particularly valuable in addressing health and environmental issues at a causative level, initiating a self-sustaining process of change through which native people can attain the skills and degree of empowerment necessary to define and articulate their role in a rapidly changing world. We believe that the general principles and modus operandi encompassed by the FENAMAD's initiative serves as a useful prototype for grass roots community development among forest peoples throughout the tropics and is particularly relevant given current concerns over the loss of tropical forests and cultures.

The views expressed by the authors in this paper are the result of several years of work in collaboration with AMETRA 2001–FENAMAD as administrative and scientific consultants respectively. Although we have tried to present an accurate and objective portrait of the health situation and the work of AMETRA 2001–FENAMAD up to 1990, there is a certain amount of interpretation based on our personal experiences for which we are fully responsible. Similarly, we are responsible for any errors that arise as a result of these interpretations.

ACKNOWLEDGMENTS

On behalf of FENAMAD, we would like to thank all those individuals and organizations that have provided the necessary financial and logistic support. We are particularly grateful to the Anglo Peruvian Society, the Antich family, Bioresources Ltd., Camilo Diaz, Centro EORI, CORDEMAD, Dirección General Forestal y Fauna, Dirección General de Parques Nacionales, Earthlife Foundation, Edward John Noble Foundation, Environmental Tithing Trust, Friends of the Earth-UK, Friends of the Earth-US, Fundación Peruana para la Conservación de la Naturaleza, Dr. Conrad Gorinsky, Dr. Max Gunther, Help the Aged, Joseph and Colette Herk, Movement pour la Cooperation Internationale, Museo de Historia Natural "Javier Prado," Oxfam-US, Parque Nacional del Manu, Partners in Health, Peruvian Safaris S.A., Dr. Ghillean Prance, Rainforest Alliance, Frederick and Jeaninne Roels, Soutien AMETRA 2001–Pérou, Tambopata Reserve Society, Terres des Hommes, The Body Shop, The New York Botanical Garden, Ugo Ugolotti, Unidad Departamental de Salud-Madre de Dios, US-AMETRA Support Group, Vicariato Apostólico de Madre de Dios—especially the Mission at Shintuya, World Wildlife Fund-UK, and World Wildlife Fund-US.

We are most grateful to Libbet Crandon-Malammud, Wil de Jong, Thomas Moore, Christine Padoch, and Daniela Peluso for their constructive suggestions and comments on an earlier version of this article.

REFERENCES

AIDESEP. 1985. "Indigenous People of the Peruvian Amazon: Land, Natural Resources, and the Definition of Indigenous Peoples." *IWGIA Newsletter* 41:17–41.

Alexiades, M. 1989. "Tambopata Ethnobotanical Survey, Madre de Dios, Peru: Preliminary Report." Unpublished manuscript. New York: The New York Botanical Garden.

AMETRA 2001. 1986. "El rol de la medicina tradicional en la atención primaria de salud: Ante-proyecto de convenio entre AMETRA 2001 y la unidad departamental de salud (UDES) de Madre de Dios." Manuscript. Puerto Maldonado, Peru: AMETRA 2001.

AMETRA 2001. 1987. "Escritura de constitución de asociación AMETRA 2001." Unpublished manuscript. Puerto Maldonado, Peru: Asociación AMETRA 2001.

AMETRA 2001. 1988a. "Creación de un huerto medicinal y elaboración de remedios vegetales en el centro etnobiologico "Ñape." Manuscript. Puerto Maldonado, Peru: Asociación AMETRA 2001.

AMETRA 2001. 1988b. "Asociación AMETRA 2001: Primera asamblea general ordinaria, 20–21 febrero de 1988." Manuscript. Puerto Maldonado, Peru: Asociación AMETRA 2001.

AMETRA 2001. 1990. "INFORME: III asamblea general ordinaria. Enero 1990." Manuscript. Puerto Maldonado, Peru: Asociación AMETRA 2001.

Arévalo V., G. and A. Hansson. 1985. "Algunos aspectos de la medicina tradicional en el Ucayali (Proyecto "AMETRA")." Serie Amazonia: Shipibo-Conibo, 2. Lima, Peru: Instituto indigenista Peruano.

Arroyo P., M., G. Veliz Rodriguez, and A. Hansson Raquette. 1985. "Tratamiento de la helmintiasis intestinal con el látex de ojé (*Ficus glabrata* HBK)—estudio en comunidades de la Amazonía Peruana (Selva Baja)." In L. M. Saravia C. and R. Sueiro Cabredo, eds., *Experiencias de desarrolo popular en el campo de la medicina tradicional y moderna,* pp. 43–71. Serie experiencias de desarrollo popular no. 3. Lima, Peru: Centro Amazónico de antropología y aplicación práctica (CAAAP), centro de estudios y promoción del desarrollo (DESCO).

Balée, W. 1987. "A etnobotânica quantitativa dos índios Tembé (Rio Gurupi, Pará)." Boletim do Museu Paraense Emílio Goeldi, *Botânica* 3 (1):29–50.

Balick, M. J. 1984. "Ethnobotany of Palms in the Neotropics." *Advances in Economic Botany* 1:9–23.

Bannerman, R. H. 1983. "The Role of Traditional Medicine in Primary Health Care." In R. H. Bannerman, J. Burton, and C. Wen-Chieh, eds., *Traditional Medicine in Health Coverage: A Reader for Health Administrators and Practitioners,* pp. 318–27. Geneva: World Health Organization.

Behrens, C. A. 1989. "The Scientific Basis for Shipibo Soil Classification and Land Use: Changes in Soil-Plant Associations with Cash Cropping." *American Anthropologist* 91:83–100.

Behrhorst, C. 1975. "The Chimaltenango Development Project in Guatemala." In K. W. Newell, ed., *Health by the People,* pp. 30–52. Geneva: World Health Organization.

Belongia, E. 1988. "The FUNCOL Program for Primary Health Care, Colombia." *Cultural Survival Quarterly* 12 (1):19–25.

Bennett, B. 1988. "Interactions Among Systems of Traditional Medicine in the Peruvian Amazon." Paper presented at the 86th annual meeting of the American Anthropological Association, Phoenix, Arizona.

Blumenthal, D. S. and M. G. Schultz. 1976. "Effects of *Ascaris* Infection on Nutritional Status in Children." *The American Journal of Tropical Medicine and Hygiene* 25 (5):682–90.

Bodley, J. H. 1982. *Victims of Progress*, 2d ed. Palo Alto: Mayfield.

Bodley, J. H., ed., 1988. *Tribal Peoples and Development Issues. A Global Overview.* Mountain View, Calif.: Mayfield.

Bodley, J. H. and F. C. Benson. 1979. *Cultural Ecology of Amazonian Palms*. Reports of Investigations no. 56. Pullman, Wash.: Laboratory of Anthropology, Washington State University (June).

Boom, B. M. 1987. "Ethnobotany of the Chácobo Indians, Beni, Bolivia." *Advances in Economic Botany* 4:1–68.

Buenaventura-Posso, E. and S. E. Brown. 1989. "Forced Transition from Egalitarianism to Male Dominance: The Bari of Colombia." In M. Etienne and E. Leacock, eds., *Women and Colonization: Anthropological Perspectives,* pp. 109–33. New York: J. F. Bergin.

CAAAP. 1985. "Experiencias de trabajo de salud en las zonas marginales de la Selva Baja." In L. M. Saravia C. and R. Sueiro Cabredo, eds., *Experiencias de desarrollo popular en el campo de la medicina tradicional y moderna,* pp. 131–64. Serie experiencias de desarrollo popular no. 3. Lima, Peru: Centro Amazónico de antropología y aplicación práctica (CAAAP), centro de estudios y promoción del desarrollo (DESCO).

Cárdenas, Timoteo C. 1989. *Los unaya y su mundo.* Lima, Peru: Instituto indigenista Peruano (IIP), centro amazónico de antropología y aplicación práctica (CAAAP).

Chirif T., A., P. Garcia H., and R. C. Smith. 1991. *El indigena y su territorio son uno solo. Estrategias para la defensa de los pueblos y territorios indígenas en la cuenca Amazónica.* Lima, Peru: OXFAM América/COICA.

Ciba Foundation Symposium. 1977. *Health and Disease in Tribal Societies.* Ciba Foundation Symposium 49 (new series). Amsterdam: Elsevier/Excerpta Medica/North Holland.

Colson, A. C. 1971. "The Differential Use of Medical Resources in Developing Countries." *Journal of Health and Social Behavior* 12:226–37.

Coreil, J. and J. D. Mull, eds. 1988. "Anthropological Studies of Diarrheal Illness." Special issue of *Social Science and Medicine* 27 (1):87–96.

Crandon, L. 1986. "The Political Economy of Medical Dialogue in Rural Highland Bolivia." *American Ethnologist* 13 (3):463–76.

Cueva M., N. 1990. "Un acercamiento a la situación de salud en la provincia de Manu— Departamento de Madre de Dios (Manu: Un gran reto en la selva)." Manuscript. Puerto Maldonado, Peru: Asociación AMETRA 2001.

Cueva M., N. and L. Ojeda U. 1988. "Apuntes sobre una 'Campaña de Oje' en la comunidad nativa Shintuya-Rio Alto Madre de Dios." In "AMETRA 2001 III asamblea general ordinaria. Enero 1990," pp. 17–22. Manuscript. Puerto Maldonado, Peru: Asociación AMETRA 2001.

Davis, S. H. 1977. *Victims of the Miracle: Development and the Indians of Brasil.* New York: Cambridge University Press.

Dricot-D'Ans, Ch. and J. M. Dricot. 1978. "Influence de l'acculturation sur la situation nutritionnelle en Amazonie Peruvienne." *Annales de la Societé Belge de Medicine Tropicale* 58:39–48.

Eichenberger, R. W. 1966. "Una filosofía de salud pública para la tribus Amazónicas." *América Indígena* 26 (2):119–41.

Eláez R., J. 1989. "Proyecto de investigación y elaboración de medicamentos tradicionales." Manuscript. Puerto Maldonado, Peru: Asociación AMETRA 2001.

Elisabetsky, E. 1986. "New Directions in Ethnopharmacology." *Journal of Ethnobiology* 6 (1):121–28.

Farnsworth, N. R., O. Akerle, A. S. Bingel, D. D. Soejarto, and Z. Guo. 1985. "Medicinal Plants in Therapy." *Bulletin of the World Health Organization* 63 (6):965–81.

FENAMAD. 1990. "Propuesta del projecto de mujeres nativas del Rio Madre de Dios y afluentes." Manuscript. Puerto Maldonado, Peru: Federación de comunidades nativas del Rio Madre de Dios y sus afluentes.

FENAMAD and AMETRA 2001. 1990. "Politica de salud en la población indigena de la cuenca del Rio Madre de Dios y afluentes." Manuscript. Puerto Maldonado, Peru: Federación de comunidades nativas del Rio Madre de Dios y sus afluentes, Asociación AMETRA 2001.

FENAMAD/Centro Eori, n.d. "Información y censo de comunidades nativas del ambito de la 'federación nativa del Río Madre de Dios y afluentes'—FENAMAD." Unpublished table, Puerto Maldonado, Perú: FENAMAD/Centro EORI.

Follér, M-L. 1989. "A New Approach to Community Health." *Social Science and Medicine* 28 (8):811–18.

Gonzalez, N. S. 1966. "Health Behavior in Cross-Cultural Perspective: A Guatemalan Example." *Human Organization* 25 (2):122–25.

Grupo DAM. 1978. "Diagnóstico provisional para el sector salud Rio Cenepa." In A. Chirif, ed., *Salud y etnicidad,* pp. 49–74. Lima, Peru: Centro de investigación y promoción Amazónica (CIPA).

Hamnett, M. P. and J. Connell. 1981. "Diagnosis and Cure: The Resort to Traditional and Modern Medical Practitioners in the North Solomons, Papua New Guinea." *Social Science and Medicine* 15B:489–98.

Hansson, A., G. Veliz, C. Naquira, M. Amren, M. Arroyo, and G. Arevalo. 1986. "Preclinical and Clinical Studies with the Latex from *Ficus glabrata* HBK, a Traditional Intestinal Anthelminthic in the Amazonian Area." *Journal of Ethnopharmacology* 17:105–38.

Helberg C., H. 1989. "A Health Project for the Manu National Park. September 1989." Manuscript. Puerto Maldonado, Peru: Asociación AMETRA 2001.

Helberg, H. 1990. "Proyecto de salud AMETRA 2001 en la reserva de la biosfera del Manu. Informe anual 1990." Manuscript. Puerto Maldonado, Peru: Asociación AMETRA 2001.

Hewett, N. C. and F. E. Duggan. 1986. "A Primary Health Care Project in the Amazonian Jungle of Northern Peru." *British Medical Journal* 293:805–7.

Jellife, D. B. 1962. "Culture, Social Change and Infant Feeding. Current Trends in Tropical Regions." *American Journal of Clinical Nutrition* 10:19–45.

Kroeger, A. 1980. "Housing and Health in the Process of Cultural Adaptation: A Case Study Among Jungle and Highland Natives of Ecuador." *Journal of Tropical Medicine and Hygiene* 83:53–69.

Kroeger, A. and W. Ruiz C., eds. 1988. *Conceptos y tratamientos populares de algunas enfermedades en Latinoamerica,* pp. 13–19. Cusco, Peru: Centro de Medicina Andina.

Lacaze, D. and M. Alexiades. 1995. "Salud para todos: Plantas medicinales y salud indígena en la cuenca del Río Madre de Dios, Peru." Un manual práctico. Cusco, Perú: Centro de estudios rurales Andinos "Bartolomé de las Casas"/FENAMAD.

Lawrence, D. N., J. V. Neel, S. H. Abadie, L. L. Moore, L. J. Adams, G. R. Healy, and I. G. Kagan. 1980. "Epidemiologic Studies Among Amerindian Populations of Amazonia III. Intestinal Parasitoses in Newly Contacted and Acculturating Villages." *American Journal of Tropical Medicine and Hygiene* 29 (4):530–37.

Layrisse, M., L. Aparcedo, C. Martínez-Torres, and M. Roche. 1967. "Blood Loss Due to Infection with *Trichuris trichuria*." *American Journal of Tropical Medicine and Hygiene* 16 (5):613–19.

Lobo-Guerrero, M. and X. Herrera. 1983. "Shamanismo: Irracionalidad o coherencia? In FUNCOL, eds., *Medicina, shamanismo y botánica.* Bogotá, Colombia: FUNCOL.

McClain, C. S., ed. 1989. *Women as Healers: Cross-Cultural Perspectives.* New Brunswick, N. J.: Rutgers University Press.

McElroy, A. and P. K. Townsend eds. 1989. "Health Repercussions of Culture Contact." In *Medical Anthropology in Ecological Prespecive*, 2d ed., pp. 326–73. Boulder: Westview Press.

Meggers, B. J. 1973. "Some Problems of Cultural Adaptation in Amazonia, with Emphasis on the Pre-European Period." In B. J. Meggers, E. S. Ayensu, and W. D. Ducksworth, eds., *Tropical Forest Ecosystems. A Comparative Review*. Washington, D.C.: Smithsonian Institution Press.

Melrose, D. 1982. *Bitter Pills. Medicines and the Third World Poor*. Oxford: OXFAM.

Moore, T. R. 1990. "Toward Effective Popular Conservation in Madre de Dios: A Proposal for a Comprehensive Socio-Economic Analysis of the Tambopata-Candamo Reserve in Tropical Southeastern Peru." Manuscript. Puerto Maldonado, Peru: Centro Eori de investigación y promoción regional.

Neel, J. V. 1977. "Health and Disease in Unacculturated Amerindian Populations." In Ciba Foundation Symposium 1977 *Health and Disease in Tribal Societies*. Ciba Foundation Symposium 49 (new series). Amsterdam: Elsevier/Excerpta Medica/North Holland.

Olortegui del C., T. 1988. "Centro etnobiologico AMETRA 2001, departamento de Madre de Dios, Provincia Tambopata, Peru. memoria descriptiva." Manuscript. Puerto Maldonado. Asociación AMETRA 2001.

Phillips, O. 1990. "*Ficus insipida* (Moraceae): Ethnobotany and Ecology of an Amazonian Anthelminthic." *Economic Botany* 44 (4):534–36.

Polunin, I. V. 1977. "Some Characteristics of Tribal Peoples." In Ciba Foundation Symposium *Health and Disease in Tribal Societies*. Ciba Foundation Symposium 49 (new series). Amsterdam: Elsevier/Excerpta Medica/North Holland.

Prance, G. T., W. Balée, B. Boom, and R. L. Carneiro. 1987. "Quantitative Ethnobotany and the Case for Conservation in Amazonia." *Conservation Biology* 1 (4):296–310.

Reichel-Dolmatoff, G. 1971. *Amazonian Cosmos. The Sexual and Religious Symbolism of the Tukano Indians*, Chicago: The University of Chicago Press.

Reichel-Dolmatoff, G. 1976. "Cosmology as Ecological Analysis: A View from the Rainforest." *Man* 11:307–18.

Reyes, F. 1989. "Tala que arrasa." *Caretas* (junio 10):54–56.

Rumrill, R., C. Dávila H., and F. Barcia G. 1986. *Madre de Dios. El Peru desconocido*. Puerto Maldonado, Peru: CORDEMAD.

Saravia, L. M. and R. Sueiro C. 1985. "Experiencias de desarrollo popular en el campo de la medicina tradicional y moderna." Serie experiencias de desarrollo popular no. 3. Lima, Peru: CAAAP/DESCO.

Stephenson, L. S. 1980. "The Contribution of *Ascaris lumbricoides* to Malnutrition in Children." *Parasitology* 81 (1):221–33.

Temple, I. 1978. "Informe medico sobre una comunidad Amuesha." In A. Chrif, ed., *salud y etnicidad*, pp. 113–28. Lima, Peru: Centro de investigación y promoción Amazónica (CIPA).

Tripathy, K., F. González, H. Lotero, and O. Bolaños. 1971. "Effects of *Ascaris* Infection on Human Nutrition." *The American Journal of Tropical Medicine and Hygiene* 20 (2):212–18.

Van der Hoogte, L. and C. Roersch. 1985. "Prespectivas de la medicina Andina." In L. M. Saravia C. and R. Sueiro Cabredo, eds., *Experiencias de desarrollo popular en el campo de la medicina tradicional y moderna*, pp. 99–128. Serie experiencias de desarollo popular no. 3. Lima, Peru: Centro Amazónico de antropología y aplicación práctica (CAAAP), centro de estudios y promoción del desarrollo (DESCO).

Von Hildebrand, M. 1983. "Cosmovisión y el concepto de enfermedad entre los Ufaina." In FUNCOL, eds., *Medicina, shamanismo y botánica*. Bogotá, Colombia: FUNCOL.

Wahl, L. 1990. "El Manu, los nahua y sepahua frente a la madera: Ideología y producción." *Perú Indígena* 12 (28):145–70.

Wellin, E. 1955. "Water Boiling in a Peruvian Town." In B. D. Paul, ed., *Health, Culture, and Community; Case Studies of Public Reactions to Health Programs,* pp. 61–103. New York: Russel Sage Foundation.

Werner, D. 1981. "The Village Health Worker: Lackey or Liberator?" *World Health Forum* 2 (1):46–68.

Wirsing, R. L. 1985. "The Health of Traditional Societies and the Effects of Acculturation." *Current Anthropology* 26 (3):303–22.

World Health Organization (WHO). 1978. "The Promotion and Development of Traditional Medicine. Report of a WHO Meeting." *WHO Technical Report Series* 622:7–41.

Wright, R. M., B. Houseal, and C. De Leon. 1985. "Kuna Yala: Indigenous Biosphere Reserve in the Making?" *Parks* 10 (3):25–27.

27

Environment, Society, and Disease: The Response of Phytotherapy to Disease Among the Warao Indians of the Orinoco Delta

Werner Wilbert

The Habitat

The Orinoco Delta is the traditional habitat of the Warao Indians. It lies within the newly formed state of Delta Amacuro in northeastern Venezuela between lat. 8°20'–10°N and long. 60°30'–62°30'W. The region extends over an area of 22,500 km² and is flanked by the Cordillera de la Costa to the west and northwest and the Sierra Imataca of the Guiana Shield formation to the south. As it forms the mouth of the Orinoco River, it eventually receives the black-and-white waters of the entire Orinoco Basin, a watershed encompassing about 1,100,000 km².

The average distance between its apex at Barrancas to the coastline is approximately 200 km (J. Wilbert 1980); maximum elevation above sea level does not exceed 10 m, and the overall slope is less than 0.06% (Vásquez and Wilbert 1992). The top soils have been classified as principally entisols near the apical area and histosols towards the ocean (Comerma 1979). The substrate of the flood plain is composed of marine sediments.

Far from being a uniform environment, the subtle local and regional differences in topography, fluvial and marine dynamics, and climate converge to create region-specific conditions that directly affect biodiversity and consequently the demographic distribution of the Warao in the area.

Hydrographically the territory is fed by nine major distributaries: Manamo, Pedernales, Tucupita, Cocuina, Macareo, Araguao, Araguaito, Sacupana, and Merejina. The Río Grande branch discharges 84% of the total Orinoco waters to the Atlantic Ocean (Vásquez and Wilbert 1992). An "interlacing" effect created by an elaborate network of lesser canals divides the zone into two fluvial subsystems:

(1) the Manamo, Pedernales, Tucupita, Cocuina, and the Macareo subsystem, which drains the counties of Pedernales and Tucupita; and (2) the Araguao, Araguaito, Sacupana, Merejina, and the Río Grande subsystem, which drains the county of Antonio Díaz. As a result, the region configurates into a fluvial labyrinth with islands of various dimensions supporting gallery forests, savannas, and temporary as well as permanent lakes (Heinen 1983; J. Wilbert 1980).

The fluvial, fluviomarine, and marine dynamics impose an additional conceptual criterion that, between the apex and the ocean, allows for the further division of the delta into three subregions: (1) Upper, (2) Middle, and (3) Lower. These same regions have also been labeled prelittoral, intermediate, and littoral zones, respectively (J. Wilbert 1980).

The Upper Delta is situated between 5 and 10 m above sea level. Although somewhat influenced by the diurnal pulsing of the tides (60 cm), the most dramatic hydraulic phenomenon in this prelittoral region is the annual flooding of the Orinoco mainstem with fluctuations of approximately 9 vertical meters.

The Upper Delta is characterized by gallery forests and savannas that originally supported large numbers of Cecropia, Ceiba, and Inga. However, the environmental situation changed dramatically during the Colonial era, when extensive areas were cleared for cacao and coffee plantations. Today much of the region is exploited for the grazing of livestock and for small-scale agriculture.

Owing to a lack of desirable natural resources, the Warao never settled in the Upper Delta on a permanent basis. Today, however, one can find here a considerable number of indigenous settlements that were established under mission and Criole influence. The livelihood of these villagers is based on wage labor in agriculture, livestock ranching, and commercial fishing.

The mean elevation of the Middle Delta is between 1.5 m and 2.5 m above sea level. Although somewhat affected by the annual floods produced by the Orinoco River, this intermediate region is influenced most by the diurnal pulsing of the tides, which accounts for fluctuations of approximately 90 cm. Although instruments have measured traces of salinity at Barrancas (Vásquez, personal communication), they usually go unnoticed in this area for most of the year except in critical dry seasons when entire crops are destroyed as far inland as 60 km from the coast.

The most pronounced flora in this region includes such economically vital palms as temiche (*Manicaria saccifera* Gaertn.), several species of manaca (*Euterpe*) and moriche (*Mauritia flexuosa* Lf.), as well as members of the Araceae, *Oneocarpus, Hymenaea courbaril, Bombacopsis, Acrodicilidium,* and the Leguminosae (J. Wilbert 1980; W. Wilbert 1986).

The Lower Delta forms a coastal belt extending inland up to 10 km and 30 km. Owing to the negligible elevation of <1.5 m above sea level, the terrain is perpetually water-saturated. The predominant littoral vegetation is the red mangrove (*Rhizophora* sp.). The growth dynamics of these forests are crucial for the survival of the Warao, for as the inland side of the mangrove forest dies off, it is replaced with the aforementioned palmetum as well as with other species of economic and therapeutic value to the Indians.

The understanding of the hydrological influence in the delta is further confounded by precipitation, which creates localized flood conditions, especially in the morichals. The deltaic climate is tropical monzonic in type. Annual precipitation ranges between 2,000 mm near the apical region, to 3,400 mm along the coast. The relative humidity fluctuates between 60% and 80%, and the trade winds keep the mean annual ambient temperature around 26°C (Vásquez and Wilbert 1992). The most intense rains fall from May to October, leaving a relatively dry season from November to April.

The Middle and Lower Delta regions form the most propitious environments for the Warao. In fact, some 75% of the total population of 20,000 individuals inhabit this area. Microhabitats created by unique insular configurations play an important role in the resource exploitation practiced by the Indians. The "typical" deltaic island tends to have the shape of a lipped saucer. From the low-lying riparian rim, subject to tidal flooding, the surface rises to form a firm-soil levee system, several hundred meters wide, which borders an interior depression of wet savanna with extensive groves of *Mauritia flexuosa*. Although the role of river-savanna-river percolation is not clear, it is certain that precipitation is the principal source of water in these depressed intrainsular areas. During the dry season the water is reduced to smaller ponds and lakes, leaving the soil fairly hard and as easily traversable as that of the levees.

Warao Society

Despite the steady influx of Criole settlers from Venezuela, Guyana, and Trinidad who, with few exceptions, tend to settle in the Upper Delta, the Warao continue to be the principal inhabitants of the Middle and Lower Delta.

Little is known about the time of arrival of their ancestors in the delta. A culture-specific archaeological record is unavailable, owing largely to a perishable material culture that lacks pottery and stone artifacts. However, the oral tradition, linguistic affiliation, modes of subsistence, and general river-sea orientedness of the Warao suggest a littoral lifestyle of great antiquity and different from that of the Amazonian floodplain tradition that is found among populations of Arawakan and Cariban affiliation in regions adjacent to the delta.

Warao traditional history places their ancestors around the mouth of the Orinoco River some 5,000 to 7,000 years ago. Their oral literature recounts events that coincide with geological conditions of the Upper Pleistocene, "a time when the mainland was still connected with, or at least in close proximity to, the island of Trinidad" (J. Wilbert 1979).

Linguistically Waraoan is not related to the predominant language phyla of Greater Guiana. In addition, the tribal autodenomination, *wa* = "canoe" + *arao* = "people"; their seminomadic lifestyle; the importance of fishing and sago recovering; and their general sea-orientedness including seaworthy canoes and a capability of star navigation further support the supposition that the Warao represent an ancient littoral tradition of South America (J. Wilbert 1972, 1979; Greenberg 1987).

With few exceptions, subtribal communities are organized into local bands of 50–100 individuals. Four or five bands constitute a subtribe, that is, the largest socioeconomic division an individual feels related to. Despite the fact that all Indians who speak the language are regarded as Warao, the concept of a "tribe" is not recognized. Consequently, a political infrastructure that permits decision making on a tribal level is equally lacking.

The material culture, though well adapted, is technologically less sophisticated than that of neighboring tribes. It includes: knives, machetes, axes, palm-fiber hammocks, several types of baskets, dugout canoes, bows and arrows, harpoons, spears with wooden or metal tips, and fishing tackle consisting of buoys, metal hooks, and nylon lines. The houses are pile constructions now situated along river banks.

The Warao consider sago of *Mauritia flexuosa* and fish as their "preferred food." However, habitat-specific technologies enable the Indians to exploit extensive nutritional resources from a wide variety of microhabitats, including savannas, levees, and riparian and littoral (maritime) environments. On the island savannas, the moriche palm (*Mauritia flexuosa*) produces an abundance of carbohydrates and edible fruit throughout most of the year and, indirectly, a considerable store of protein in the form of palm borer larvae. Within this habitat the Warao also developed a specific technology for the exploitation of a variety of savanna fishes such as armored catfishes and trahiras (Verónica Ponte, personal communication).

Nowadays, most Warao feel unrestricted in hunting deer, tapir, peccary, and monkey, which predominate in the levee and riparian zones. Traditionally, however, such game was avoided as "people of the forest with blood like humans." Instead, earlier generations concentrated on hunting reptiles (caiman, iguana, turtle), rodents (acure, agouti, capybara), and birds (duck, toucan, turkey).

The Warao obtain fish, their principal source of protein, from the rivers and lakes. The preferred species are morocoto, cachama of the piranha family, and catfish. In the Lower Delta two species of marine crab (blue and red) offer a rich additional source of seasonal protein.

Since the 1920s, the various Warao subtribes have begun to adopt a sedentary lifestyle of horticulturalists, cultivating taro (ocumo) and, to a lesser extent, plantains and bananas. In the Upper Delta agriculture is dedicated to maize and manioc (yuca).

Warao Disease Experience

Warao-related nosogeography is hard to ascertain in concrete epidemiological terms. Owing to the lack of reliable population figures before the 1950s, it is difficult to determine whether the tribal population increased or decreased as a result of colonial contact. According to Murdock (1980), New World hunter/gatherer settlements were small and widely separated. Social and geographical barriers greatly impeded intercommunication between local groups, hampering the spread and maintenance of infectious disease agents. Although this early demographic situation appears to have been quite similar to the one encountered in more recent historic times, available evidence suggests that the isolation of local groups was less than hermetic: (1) sporadic contacts with tribes of Cariban and Arawakan affiliation did occur; (2) Warao cosmogony and geography embrace the island of Trinidad where up to the 1950s, Warao navigators traded with local Indians and non-Indians; and (3) Warao shipwrights provided fishermen from Margarita Island with canoes until most recent times.

Throughout colonial times the Warao actively mingled with Old World populations in areas adjacent to the Orinoco Delta. These populations were composed of Europeans from Spain, England, Holland, and France who subsequently introduced slaves and indentured laborers from Africa, India, China, and Indonesia. Little European expansion actually took place within the delta itself, which offered little in terms of economic resources. Instead the territory became the gateway to the Orinoco Basin for many expeditions that set out in search of El Dorado, the fabled city of gold. The first permanent non-Indian foothold within the region was established by Capuchin missionaries as recently as the 1920s.

Apart from pertaining to the human condition, disease has been the determining element in the pandemic genocide that claimed 99% of the American Indians. Most of the aboriginal inhabitants of Venezuela, Trinidad, and Guyana befell a similar fate. No specific European documentation is available for the Orinoco Delta before the 1930s. But a summary of events in surrounding areas can shed some light on the epidemiological impact that was occasioned by the meeting of the two worlds.

Venezuela (Orinoco Basin).   In 1580 smallpox, believed to have been introduced by a Portuguese expedition, spread like wildfire throughout northern Venezuela. As Morey (1979) points out, "the bodies were encountered by the dozens in villages, roads and in the forest." In 1625 epidemics of influenza, pneumonia, and pleurisy were reported in the area that today is Venezuelan territory. In 1675 malaria and tick-borne relapsing fevers invaded the Orinoco floodplain (Morey 1979). In 1737 an epidemic of bubonic plague persisted for an entire year, and in 1746 a pertussis epidemic swept the Middle Orinoco, followed by malaria in 1800.

Trinidad.   Communicable diseases reported for the period 1777–1900 include cholera, hemorrhagic malarial fevers, leprosy, malaria, malignant comatose fevers, measles, smallpox, typhoid, and yellow fever (Anthony 1975; Arraiz 1954; Brown 1977; Newson 1977; Weller 1968).

Guiana.   In the 1840s, roughly coinciding with the arrival, between 1834 and 1841, of thousands of immigrants from Malta, West Africa, Madeira, Bombay,

Calcutta, and Madras, there were reported outbreaks of cholera, influenza, intermittent fevers, malaria, pleurisy, and smallpox (Daly 1975; Dwarka 1950; Menezes 1979; Rodney 1981). The historic involvement of the Warao in the Guyanese epidemiological disaster was active as well as passive.

In 1768 the governor of Spanish Guayana, Don Manuel Centurión Guerrero, relocated 1,170 Warao in the newly founded town of Angostura, later to be known as Ciudad Bolívar, where they came into contact with settlers of European descent and with Indians of the Upper and Middle Orinoco (Lodares 1930). In 1817 the displaced Warao of Angostura escaped, some returning to the delta and others to Dutch Guiana, where they worked as shipwrights and occasional plantation workers in close proximity to Carib Indians and populations of Eurasian and African origins (Menezes 1979). The refugee Warao also reestablished contact with their delta kinsfolk and, like the traders with Trinidad, were responsible for disease exposure and transmission among the diverse foreign populations of the Guianas and their relatively isolated kinsfolk of the Orinoco Delta (J. Wilbert 1981, 1983).

Surprisingly, there is no indication that the Warao suffered the catastrophic losses experienced by their immediate indigenous neighbors. Localized epidemics are known, however, to have occurred, and Warao oral tradition reveals a familiarity with these plagues.

Quality of Ethnoepidemiological Data

Translating the Warao disease experience into Western epidemiological terminology presents definitional, conceptual, and operational problems. The differential diagnosis employed by the tribe is confounded by the presence of mimicking diseases, such as the paralysis caused by polio and tuberculosis, and further complicated by the tendency to ascribe symptoms of particular diseases to separate ailments. In addition, a significant portion of the data required for analysis led to the consideration of rather "unorthodox" sources, such as folklore and religion. But it would have been grossly ethnocentric to ignore the fact that the logic behind the medical praxis of a tribal health care delivery system operates within a specific social, cultural, and religious context. As such the enculturative factors that develop a native theory of illness become integral components of the therapeutic praxis itself and are indispensable as definitional indicators of the local perception of health, disease, and therapy.

Warao Ethnopathology

According to Warao ethnopathology, diseases are classified according to their etiological agents, be they supernatural or natural. The latter are covert categories labeled by the author. However, in-depth field research has shown that the diseases ascribed to these categories are not confounded by Warao health practitioners.

Supernatural disease is generally attributed to spirit aggression and object intrusion owing either to the volition of the deities or to sorcery. A general distribution of this class of disease is set forth in table 27.1.

Exotic supernatural diseases have been identified as those that were introduced to the Warao in colonial times (J. Wilbert 1983; W. Wilbert 1986). The supernatural masters or owners of these diseases are believed by the Indians to be autochthonous. In traditional medical lore they are said to have lived among the Warao in anthropomorphic disguise, looking like regular tribesmen. Characteristically, these impersonators were chronically ill with a particular disease, when a shaman identified and subsequently expelled them from the ancestral village, condemning them to live beyond the limits of the Warao "world" (Trinidad, Sierra de Imataca, etc.). The data suggest that these "spirits" may have been the initial disease victims who were ostracized by the affected communities for fear of contamination.

Endemic supernatural diseases result from three different sources:

1. Supreme ancestral spirits (*kanobotuma*), who take revenge for taboo transgressions of various kinds. These diseases, effected through spirit aggression, may present clinical symptoms similar to those described for natural diseases. However, they are accompanied by severe psychosomatic symptoms such as depression, incapacity of decision making, apathy toward family members and/or fellow villagers, and these require a shaman's diagnosis.
2. Malevolent shamans or shamans protecting subtribal territories from invaders (including other Warao) cause disease through object intrusion. They implant and conceal an object such as a dart or a stone or the soul of an animal in the victim's body to confound the shamanic diagnostic procedure. A second method of sorcery seeks to asphyxiate the victim by means of a magic noose of tobacco smoke. Not surprisingly, the associated symptomatology may be asthmatic. In all such cases, fear that the disease may be of supernatural origin intensifies the pathology.
3. Bush spirits are the only disease-causing agents that are physically seen by their victims and cause short (rarely longer than one day) but acute episodes of psychological disturbance.

The "natural disease" category is not totally exclusive. Generally the pathogens of this group are described as inert fetid gases found in reservoirs of organic decomposition. Air, water, and fomites serve as inorganic vectors and modes of transportation to the at-risk groups. Access to the body is gained by the portholes of nose and mouth or by the direct penetration of cutaneous membranes. In the body the noxious gas affects particular organs and/or body regions (head, thorax, abdomen), triggering pathogenesis and corresponding clinical symptoms.

This particular category of disease is primarily symptom-oriented. It recognizes febrile, respiratory, gastrointestinal, dermatological, and gynecological/obstetrical disorders as well as a subclass of incidental conditions—such as wounds var-

TABLE 27.1 *Covert Warao Classification of Supernatural Disease*

Exotic	Endemic
Ancestral spirits: spirit aggression	Ancestral spirits: spirit aggression
Cholera	Celestial
Dengue fever	Acute depression
Leprosy	Acute pain
Malaria	Sudden death
Measles	Bush spirits: aggression or possession
Pertussis	Terrestrial (hebu)
Poliomeylitis	acute, short-lived hysteria
Pulmonary tuberculosis	Shamans
Yellow fever	Object intrusion
	Acute pain
	Asphyxiation

iously caused by animals, insects, or sharp objects—and inflammations of the ears, eyes, liver, urinary tract, and muscles (W. Wilbert 1986).

Part of the natural disease category overlaps with the supernatural category because certain diseases call for the application of the protocol of natural disease therapy to alleviate symptoms of supernatural disease. In no case, however, is this expected to effect a total cure. Table 27.2 lists the natural disease classification and those categories that demonstrate supernatural overlap (S.O.)

Warao Health Care Delivery

The diagnosis of disease is often an elaborate process involving various shamans with distinct specialties and the phytotherapist. Supernatural diseases of whatever origin are treated mainly by three kinds of shamans who function as intermediaries between the Supernaturals and humankind.

The *bahanarotu* is a white shaman who derives his power from the Tobacco Spirit residing east of the zenith. This spirit is an avian god who, together with his companions, produces acute health crises and sudden death. The white shaman carries in his chest two of the Tobacco Spirit's cohorts as tutelary spirits who can exit through his arms like darts to cause illness. The shaman propitiates the Supernaturals with tobacco smoke. The highest ranking white shaman is the "Keeper of the Wooden Mannequin," a manifestation of the Tobacco Spirit, which the shaman can send out to produce epidemic outbreaks. The white shaman's practice relates to disease of this kind as a potential intermediary and healer.

The *hoarotu* is the black shaman who is aligned with the cardinal god of the underworld in the west. He carries two of the god's sons in his chest who, in turn, remind him of his initiatory promise to provide the cannibalistic deity and his court with human sacrifices through sorcery. If the shaman should fail in his obligations, the Supernaturals of sunset would destroy mankind and come to an end themselves. "Human sacrifice," through sorcery, is indispensable for the per-

TABLE 27.2 *Covert Warao Classification of Natural Disease*

Febrile	Respiratory (S.O.)	Dermatological (S.O.)
Fever	Pertussis	Leprosy
Fever w/cough	Pulmonary T.B.	
Fever w/diarrhea		Gynecological/obstetrical
Fever w/headache	Gastrointestinal	Umbilical infection
	Diarrhea	Postpartum hemorrhaging
Febrile (S.O.)	Diarrhea w/stomach ache	Fetal positioning
Varicella	Diarrhea w/vomiting	Excessive menstrual flows
Measles	Dysentery	
Poliomeylitis	Vomiting	Various
Malaria	Stomach ache	Anuria
	Parasites	Conjunctivitis
Respiratory		Ear inflammation
Sore throat	Dermatological	Muscle fatigue
Cough	Skin sores	Toothache
	Buccal sores	
	Abscess	
	Mites	
	Hammock mites	

sistence of the band and periodically the dark shaman is obliged to use his magic sling and darts to "kill" a person of a neighboring band. The patron deity of black shamans expresses his gratitude by bestowing on his servant the power to cure all disease accompanied by loss of blood, including dysentery, which represents a major scourge to human life in the delta.

The *wishiratu* is the priest-shaman who derives his power from the gods of the north, the east, or the south. From the time of his initiation, the priest-shaman carries in his body six sons of any one of these cardinal gods who serve as his tutelary spirits. They remind him throughout life of the vows taken during his initiatory encounter with the deity to periodically supply the gods and their entourage with tobacco smoke and moriche sago. Both commodities are difficult to obtain in the desired quantities and require a substantial effort on the part of the entire band. In return, the gods refrain from killing the children and endow the priest-shaman with the power to cure disease. Besides functioning as a curer, the priest-shaman gives psychological counseling and enforces moral standards within his group. The highest ranking priest-shaman is the "Keeper of the Sacred Stone," a manifestation of the patron deity of the subtribal group and the principal source of protection for the shaman's congregation (J. Wilbert 1972).

The *dau yarokotu arotu* is the (female) phytotherapist. Although she is a nonritual curer, she does practice within the general framework of tribal religion. Thus nonritual is not equivalent to secular curing, for the phytotherapist recognizes the fact that the agents of endemic disease are of a metaphysical nature and that her remedies and praxis, like anything else in Warao culture, form part of a religious system. However, the phytotherapist does not undergo shamanic initiation before becoming a healer, and activities such as collecting, preparing, and administering of plant-derived medications are not subject to ritual action.

Diagnostic Procedures

In general, diseases as experienced by the Warao are not season specific. There are, however, tendencies in which the incidence rate increases sufficiently to reach epidemic proportions. Fevers, for example, together with helminths and dermatological and gynecological disorders are nonseasonal while the rates for respiratory and gastrointestinal disease (diarrheas and vomiting) increase during the rainy season.

An individual, once recognized as ill, has two immediate options depending on the geographic location: (1) consult the medical staff of a rural clinic or (2) initiate the traditional diagnostic process. The choice whether to utilize the services of a Western rural clinic is less problematic among the acculturated Warao. However, in more traditional groups there prevails considerable suspicion of the Western doctor who, in the Indian's frame of mind, is but a Criollo-shaman, fully capable (like their own shamans) of causing the very kinds of diseases that are cured. Furthermore, the rural clinic is often located in the territory of a different subtribe, where a sorcerer is likely to attack the traversing party to aggravate or confound the disease condition and cause the patient's death.

The traditional procedure requires that the patient be presented to the three aforementioned shamans. They in turn conduct a diagnosis and confirm or negate that the disease is of their specialty. If all three shamans should come up with a negative diagnosis, the disease is considered to be not of supernatural origin and the patient is referred to the phytotherapist. In case the phytotherapist also fails to identify the ailment, the pathogen is believed to be of exotic origin and Western medical intervention is indicated.

Phytotherapy

As documented over nearly two years of intensive field research the pharmacopoeia of the Warao includes 100 species, 15 of which remain still unidentified (table 27.3). From this pharmacopoeia Warao phytotherapists produce 259 medications of various complexities: simple (one ingredient from one plant per medication); composite (more than one ingredient from a single species); and compound (ingredients from several species). Although distinct levels of competency have been observed among the practitioners, no single practitioner is capable of reproducing the entire repetoire. Rather, the documented pharmacopoeia represents the cumulative knowledge of more than fifty practitioners from distinct sectors of the Upper, Middle, and Lower Delta.

In comparison with other subcontinental regions like the Peruvian Andes (Girault 1984), a pharmacopoeia of 100 species does not appear overimpressive. However, a regional comparison of different biomes is of little statistical significance.

TABLE 27.3 *Warao Botanical Pharmacopoeia and Associated Diseases/Disorders*

Acanthaceae
Justicia secunda Vahl.: muscle fatigue

Anacardiaceae
Mangifera indica L.: cough, diarrhea, diarrhea/vomiting, fever, muscle fatigue, trauma/swelling
Spondias mombin L.: cough, diarrhea, dysentery, diarrhea/vomiting, pulmonary tuberculosis, stomach ache, varicella, wounds in general
Cf. *Tapirira guianensis* Aubl.: measles

Annonaceae
Annona aff. montana Mact.: cough
Annona sp.: fever, pulmonary tuberculosis

Araceae
Anthurium 2: snakebite (venomous)
Colocasia esculenta (L.) Schott: Wasp sting
Montrichardia aborescens (L.) Schott: conjunctivitis, measles, wasp sting
Philodendron: scorpion sting

Bignoniaceae
Tabebuia insignis var *insignis* (Miq.) Sandu.: dysentery, diarrhea, scorpion sting
Unidentified species (Yaroko ebura): conjunctivitis

Bixaceae
Bixa orellana L.: anuria, measles

Bombaceae
Ceiba pentandra Gaertn.: diarrhea, teething pain, toothache
Pachira aquatica Aubl.: cough, fever/headache, pertussis

Boraginaceae
cf. *Tournefortia cuspidata* H. B. K.: anuria

Bromeliaceae
Bromelia plumieri (E. Morr.) L. B. Smith: dysentery, fever

Burseraceae
Protium cf. *guianense* (Aubl.) March.: cough, fever

Combretaceae
Combretum spinosum Bonpl.: muscle fatigue, mites

Commelinaceae
cf. *Commelina nudiflora* L.: diarrhea, measles, skin lesions

Compositae
Clibadium sylvestre L.: skin lesions
Eclipta alba L. Hassk.: diarrhea
Mikania cf. *micrantha, hastata, cirigenta*: cough
Unidentified species (Onoeota): cough, diarrhea, headache

Convolvulaceae
Impomoea batatas Poir: measles

Cucurbitaceae
Cucurbita maxima L.: measles
Fevillea cordifolia L.: stomach ache

Cyperaceae
Torolinium (cyperus) odoratum (L.), Hooper: cough, diarrhea

Dilleniaceae
Tetrecera sp.: cough, fever, sore throat

Gramineae
Coix lacryma-jobi L.: diarrhea, talisman, fever, toothache, vomiting
Paspalum repens Berg.: cough, pertussis

TABLE 27.3 *Continued*

Guttiferae
 Symphonia globulifera L. f.: wounds

Hernandiaceae
 Hernandia sonora L.: fever, cough, pertussis

Humiriaceae
 Sacoglottis amazonica Mart.: cough, pertussis

Labiatae
 Leonotis nepetaefolia (L.) R. Bi.: pertussis
 Mentha cf. *x piperita* L.: diarrhea

Lauraceae
 Ocotea sp.: cough, diarrhea, fever, vomiting
 Unidentified species (Heburu): fever, measles, pertussis, vomiting

Leguminosae
• Caesalpiniaceae
 Macrolobium bifolium (Aubl.) Pers.: menorrhagia, sterilization
• Mimosaceae
 Pentaclethra macroloba (Willd.) Kuntze: diarrhea, dysentery, helminths, wounds
• Papilionaceae
 Dalbergia cf. *monetaria* L. f.: mites
 Desmodium cf. *adscendens* (Sw.) DC.: diarrhea, fever
 Erythrina glauca: cough, fever, fever/skin lesions
 Lonchocarpus cf. *latifolius* Benth.: conjunctivitis, earache, fever/cough malaria
 Machaerium: toothache
 Pterocarpus officinalis Jacq.: buccal sores, diarrhea, dysentery
 Peterocarpus cf. *officinalis* Jacq.: buccal sores, cataract
 Vatairea guianensis Aubl.: mites, skin lesions, vomiting
 Unidentified species (Ero estreya): diarrhea
 Unidentified species (Eroida): buccal sores, cough, dysentery
 Unidentified species (Motana ayari): fever, pertussis
 Unidentified species (Naku ahimarose): snakebite antivenom
 Unidentified species (Osibu aukuarusoru): cough w/fever

Loranthaceae
 Phoradendron: diarrhea/headache, fever/headache/diarrhea
 Unidentified species (Dau daniaru): diarrhea

Malvaceae
 Hibiscus bifurcatus Cav.: pertussis
 Urena sinuata L.: fever, wounds

Meliaceae
 Carapa guianensis Aubl.: abscess, measles
 Cedrela cf. *fissilis* Vell.: wounds

Moraceae
 Cecropia sp.: abscess, cough, pertussis, skin lesions, toothache
 Ficus caballina Sandl.: mites
 Ficus cf. *maxima* P. Miller: mites, helminths, stomach ache

Musaceae
 Musa × *paradisiaca* L.: buccal sores, skin lessions

Myristicaceae
 Virola surinamensis Roland.: buccal sores, caterpillar antivenom, toothache

Myrtaceae
 cf. *Eugenia pseudopsidium* Jacq.: diarrhea, dysentery, vomiting
 Psidium guajava L.: cough, cough/diarrhea, diarrhea, diarrhea/vomiting, measles

(continued)

TABLE 27.3 *Continued*

Onagraceae
Ludwigia cf. *leptocarpa* (Nutt.) Hara.: anuria
Ludwigia cf. *peruviana* Hara.: anuria

Orchidaceae
Epidendrum: conjunctivitis

Palmae
Cocos nucifera L.: burns, diarrhea, earache, fever, measles, mites, vomiting
Desmoncus cf. *polyacanthos* Mart.: buccal sores, toothache
cf. *Euterpe oleraceae* Mart.: cough, diarrhea, dysentery, helminths, measles, menorrhagia, skin lesions, wounds
Jessenia bataua Mart.: cough, pertussis
Manicaria saccifera Gaertn.: cough, diarrhea, fever, headache, muscle fatigue, pertussis, snake antivenom, vomiting
Mauritia flexuosa L. f.: cough, earache, fever, fever/headache, headache, pertussis, postpartum hemorrhaging, sterilization, stomach ache, vomiting, wounds
Unidentified species (Winamoru): cough, pertussis, pulmonary tuberculosis, vomiting

Piperaceae
Peperomia: Liver disorder
Peromia rotundifolia (L.) H. B. K.: cough
Piper coruscans H. B. K.: diarrhea/headache, fever/headache/diarrhea
Pothomorphe peltata (L.) Miq.: diarrhea/headache, headache

Polygonaceae
Coccoloba cf. *marginata* Benth.: pulmonary tuberculosis

Polypodiaceae
Polypodium attenuatum H. B. K.: muscle fatigue
Polypodium aureum L.: pertussis, pulmonary tuberculosis

Rhizophoraceae
Rhizophora mangle L.: diarrhea, dysentery, fever, muscle fatigue, skin lesions, toothache

Rutaceae
Citrus aurantifolium (Christm.) Swingle: diarrhea

Sapindaceae
Paullinia cf. *cururu* L.: diarrhea/stomach ache

Scrophulariaceae
Angelonia salicariaefolia H. & B.: cough
Capraria biflora L.: diarrhea/vomiting, dysentery
Scoparia dulcis L.: cough, diarrhea

Simaroubaceae
Simarouba amara Aubl.: cough

Solanaceae
Solanum americanum Mill.: skin lesions
Solanum stramonifolium Jacq.: toothache

Verbenaceae
Lantana camara L. var. *moritziana* (Otto & Dietr.) Lopez-Palacies: measles

Vitaceae
Cissus sicyoides L.: skin lesions

Zingiberaceae
Costus scaber Rhuiz. & Pavon: conjunctivitis, cough, diarrhea, dysentery, fever, headache, hematuria, morning sickness, pertussis
Renealmia alpinia (Rottb.) Maas.: cough, diarrhea, dysentery, fever, pulmonary tuberculosis, wounds

Unidentified
Daukohi: cough, sterilization
Ero basa: sore throat
Oisaka: cough, fever
Oisakaida: muscle fatigue

More revealing is a comparison of medicinal versus nonmedicinal plants of the same habitat, which gauges the overall intensity with which phytotherapists make use of their environment.

Random 1/4-hectare sampling on primary riparian, secondary riparian, and primary levee forest sites of the Middle Delta demonstrated that an extraordinary percentage of the available flora had been tested or was currently in use. As to be expected, the botanically most diverse sample was from the secondary riparian forest. In total, thirty-nine emicly recognized species were recorded in comparison with nineteen of the primary riparian forest and twenty-eight of the primary levee forest.

From a phytotherapeutic perspective the primary riparian and levee forests produce comparable ratios of medicinal versus nonmedicinal plants. The ratio for the secondary riparian forest was lower owing to increased biodiversity: from the secondary riparian forest phytotherapists employ 49%, from the primary levee forest 68%, and from the primary riparian forest 74% of all plants encountered. This survey of the flora of the Middle Delta reveals a remarkably rich aboriginal pharmacopoeia.

Warao phytotherapy lies in the female domain. Of all medicinal components, 75% are collected by the women and/or their daughters, unaided by men. Furthermore, nearly all medications are prepared by the women. Unwedded girls may accompany any phytotherapist in search of plants because, in most cases, they are either consanguineal or classificatory daughters of the practitioners. Therapeutic information is shared freely among the women although some practitioners become more proficient phytotherapists than others.

Pharmacological Inventory

Usually Warao phytotherapists keep a mental inventory of the therapeutic resources of their surroundings. A majority of the medications require the leaves of trees, which are usually beyond the reach of the individual. Therefore, part of the inventory includes the location not only of mature trees but also of saplings.

In 20% of the recorded cases the phytotherapist relies on her husband or older son to either fell or climb the tree. Since the barks and roots of many of these trees are also of therapeutic value, the decision to fell them requires serious consideration.

Warao phytotherapeutical protocol prescribes that certain plant materials (87%) be collected at dawn when they are considered most potent. The site from which plant components must be selected is specified for almost half of all medications. This includes especially trees and plants of 4–5 meters. Whenever location is important, the eastward side of the species is always favored because it is believed that plant components here are washed clean by the rain and are beneficially fanned by the westerly trade winds. This applies to the gathering of bark, resin, leaves, and fruit. Exempt from these rules are the species that form the forest undergrowth.

The "tools" involved in the processing of the materia medica are an assemblage of fourteen implements, materials, and elements. Some of the tools are produced from local resources while others are trade goods. However, they are not restricted in use to the preparation of medications. Rather, they are considered common household items (table 27.4).

Although of post-Columbian introduction, cast-iron cooking pots have been fully integrated into Warao material culture. Kitchen utensils are identified with the woman in general but in particular with the phytotherapist. Native kettles, dippers, and bottles were made of calabashes (*Cresentia cujete*) and are still extensively used in connection with food and remedy preparation. A woman's cooking pot accompanies her through life and often into the grave. The Warao refer to the pot as "our mother" to indicate that life is made possible through the food and medicine that come from it.

Similarly, the axe of the Warao is referred to as "our father who raises us." The tool is identified with the men who wield it to procure sago, garden products, honey, transportation, and medicinal plant materials. Although women are perfectly capable of using the axe for collecting firewood and other household chores, tree felling for medicinal purposes is a task for males.

The machete is an indispensable tool for men and women alike. Phytotherapists collect most pharmaceutical materials with it. Men keep their personal machetes apart from those of women. This practice is even more strictly observed with knives. Men who smell kitchen odors on their knives would rather throw them into the river than continue using them.

To process medicinal plants, phytotherapists employ the knife rather than the unwieldy machete. Knives are used to cut, rasp, and scrape medicinal material both in the forest and in the kitchen.

Graters used in remedy preparation are usually makeshift devices made from a tin can repeatedly perforated by means of a thick nail. The grater is not an indispensable item; a knife can also be used to replace it.

Most implements fabricated from local natural resources are temporary and discarded after use. The remainder serve a variety of purposes. The pestle is such a tool. Used with a mortar board, it is employed to crush medicinal raw materials and a number of foodstuffs. Many of the medications require straining and filtering. The Warao use flat woven baskets as sieves in the leaching process of sago production. Sieves of this kind can be employed in remedy preparation, but now-

TABLE 27.4 *Processing Implements*

Metal tools:	cast-iron pot, axe, machete knife, and grater
Natural tools:	pestle, mortar board, filter, frond riblets, bast, frond or leaf containers
Heat sources:	fire, sun
Mediums:	water (river, rain, palm fruit)

adays, filters made of imported fabrics are common. From the moriche palm the discardable skewers, strings, and containers are derived.

The most common heat source is fire because a large number of medicinal raw materials require boiling before their administration. The kitchen fire serves as the usual source. For still undetermined reasons, some remedies were explicitly said to be heated by sun radiation. This protocol may represent a relic of prepottery practices when liquids could not be boiled in flammable native containers. But it may also reflect an awareness that boiling diminishes or destroys the effect of active ingredients.

Media used in the preparation of medications include ordinary river water, the water from the infructescence of *Manicaria saccifera,* and the liquid contained in the stem of *Euterpe oleracea.* The former medium is inert; the two latter ones are employed either as uncontaminated media or as medicinal components.

Medication Processing

The processing of raw materials into medications may take up to seven steps and require combinations of up to seven tools, implements, and mediums.

Simple medicaments are most frequently produced. According to the data base approximately 200 such medications are prepared by employing methods ranging from simple (no processing required) to complex, five-step processes.

Composite medicaments, employing more than one ingredient of a single species, number twenty-seven. Preparation techniques range from one- to four-step processing.

Compound medicaments, requiring ingredients from more than one species, number thirty-three. In the preparation of these medications up to six-step sequences are employed, composed of a total of 29 variations.

In processing the materia medica the women who collaborated in tne study were able to prepare 259 remedies by means of 104 different protocols. Of those, 81 require water from the river or from palm fruit. Techniques of this kind require a vessel for mixing and, in many cases, for heating or boiling.

Types of Medication

Warao medications come in the form of fluids, viscous fluids, solids, vapors, and combinations of fluids/nonfluids (table 27.5). Fluid medications comprise 78% percent of the data universe and include all waterlike, nonresinous substances. The solutions, defined as any liquid preparation of one or more soluble chemical substances usually dissolved in water, are the most numerous. In the context of Warao herbalism, they include any liquid end product obtained through soaking, macerating, or boiling of raw materials. Solutions account for 149 medications.

TABLE 27.5 *Physical Consistencies of Medications*

Category	Consistency	Number
Fluid	Processed	22
	Solution	149
	Unprocessed	22
	Water/palatable	10
Viscous	Unprocessed	12
	Processed	4
Nonfluid	Powder	4
	Solid	22
Vapor	Smoke	7
Miscellaneous	Fruit and vine	3
	Processed semisolid and solution	1
	Solution and solid	2
	Unprocessed fluid and solid	1
Total		259

Watery botanical products that require no manipulation by the phytotherapist other than the initial collecting are classified as unprocessed fluids and account for 22 medications. An equal number of remedies are made from processed fluids of plant products. To obtain these fluids the practitioner must manipulate the raw material, usually through heating. Finally the water-palatable category includes 10 preparations. These are medications prepared by carbonization and pulverization of plant materials and the adding of just enough water to suspend the materials.

Prescriptions of Medicaments

The indigenous pharmacopoeia is largely symptom oriented and prescriptions correspond with many of the Western over-the-counter drugs. The primary goal of the phytotherapist is to ease the suffering of the patient and the secondary goal is to effect a cure. Practitioners will continue administering a medication up to four times a day until the symptoms subside.

Prescriptions vary little from disorder to disorder and some therapies are difficult to grasp, for example, the treatment of anuria, cough, and gastrointestinal disorders through ablutions; the treatment of gastrointestinal disorders via the respiratory tract; or the concomitant enteral/parenteral administrations for skin lesions. However, as discussed below, in the context of Warao medical theory, these treatments are quite congruent and to the point.

Warao practitioners administer medicines in thirteen different regimens. The most common schedule of administration is "three times a day." In a total, 128 remedies (49%) are administered in this fashion. This is followed by the "as needed" category, which is applied in 33 prescriptions and involves the patient in the curing process; i.e., the patient is allowed to administer the medication as often as deemed necessary. Some are ointments and salves that are washed off in the river during daily tasks. Others are rehydration treatments in which the patient is asked to drink as much as desired to quench the thirst resulting from the loss of body fluids (diarrhea and some fevers). The "several times a day" category caters to the primary concern of the curer to ease the symptoms and is prescribed in connection with 32 medications. The "one time only" schedule is mainly prescribed for the treatment of cutaneous disorders, amounting to 17 of the 26 medications administered in this fashion.

Pneumatic Theory of Phytotherapy

Therapy according to the Warao pneumatic theory is allopathic. Botanical medications administered as inhalants, ingestants, or ablutants carry remedial odors into the body of the patient via the nose (inhalants), the mouth (ingestants), or the skin (ablutants, salves, or compresses). Once it has obtained access to the body, a therapeutic innoxious and fragrant odor detaches itself from its vehicle of transmission and diffuses throughout the body region permeated by the fetid air. Curing is achieved by the interaction of the two gases and the expulsion of the fetid air through the portholes of the body by the "denser" fragrant air. In the process the odoriferous agent also leaves the body. The fetid gas retreats to the Underworld in the west or it seeks out places such as stagnant water and decaying organic materials where it lingers until the opportunity comes to once more invade a person of "weak" blood. The fragrant gas dissipates into the atmospheric air toward the east. The exit of both gases from the body permits the affected organs and souls that the Warao individual is believed to have to resume their normal function and health is restored.

As a fishing and foraging society the Warao may have occupied stretches of the Middle and Lower Orinoco Delta for thousands of years. Owing to the natural characteristics of the swamp environment, the Old World paid little attention to the region. Instead, the delta was used mainly as a gateway to the Orinoco Basin. This course of events saved the tribe from the scourges of exotic epidemic pestilence that decimated their Arawak and Carib neighbors.

Warao ethnopathology, which is largely symptom oriented, has incorporated many of the known epidemic diseases into the native classification of supernatural disease. The medical lore of the tribe shows great familiarity with these diseases and attributes their origin to autochthonous circumstances and personages. The latter are postulated to be historical and to represent first cases who were ostracized by the Warao and incorporated into the indigenous disease pantheon. In general, all supernatural diseases are attributed to spirit aggression, possession, object intrusion, or sorcery.

Natural diseases are considered endemic by the Warao; i.e., "they have always been." The pathogens are inert fetid gases that contaminate a victim through circumstance related to the patient's age, sex, and "strength of blood." Peculiarly, many of the exotic supernatural diseases are categorized as pertaining to the natural diseases. However, phytotherapy attempts only to alleviate the symptoms and to comfort the patient while shamanic therapy attempts to rid the patient of the ailment.

The diagnostic procedure is long and involved. It requires the shamans to determine whether the disease is of supernatural origin (spirit related). If their diagnosis is negative the patient is referred to a phytotherapist. The praxis of the plant therapist draws on approximately 100 species of plants from which 250 simple, composite, and compound medications are produced through a variety of protocols. Some of the medications require up to seven steps of preparation.

The medication is believed to harbor a therapeutic fragrant odor that upon ingestion displaces the pathogenic fetid odor. In due course the fragrant air too leaves the patient's body and dissipates into the atmosphere. The patient is left in an inodorous state, which, according to Warao beliefs, defines health.

Depending on the relative proximity of a rural clinic, the family of a patient may opt to use Western services. Among the more traditional communities this transfer may present certain dangers if the clinic is situated in the territory of another subtribe that is traditionally believed to be defended by sorcery of a resident shaman.

The phytochemical screening of the plants listed in the pharmacopoeia has only recently begun (Wilbert and Haiek 1991). No definite conclusions concerning their therapeutic value can be offered at this time. Nevertheless, from a practical point of view, it is unreasonable to expect a native pharmacopoeia with an age-old adaptive trajectory in a particular region to retain plant medicaments that do not at least respond to disease on a symptomatological level. From an academic point of view, it falls now to the phytochemists to test the therapeutic qualities of the plant medicaments contained in the pharmacopoeia of the Warao Indians.

REFERENCES

Anthony, M. 1975. *Profile Trinidad: A Historical Survey from the Discovery to 1900.* London: Macmillan Caribbean.
Arraiz, A. 1954. *Historia de Venezuela.* Caracas: Fundación Eugenio Mendoza.
Brown A. W. A. 1977. "Yellow Fever, Dengue, and Dengue Hemmorrhagic Fever." In G. Melvin Howe, ed., *A World Geography of Human Disease*, pp. 42–63. New York: Academic Press.
Comerma, J. 1979. "Suelos: Ordenes y subordenes." *Atlas de Venezuela*, pp. 182–83. Caracas: Ministerio del ambiente y de los recursos naturales renovables.
Daly, V. T. 1975. *A Short History of the Guyanese People.* London: Macmillan Education.
Dwarka, N. 1950. *A History of Indians in Guyana.* London: Published by the author.
Girault, L. 1984. *Kallawaya: Guérisseurs itinérants des Andes. Recherches sur les pratiques médicinales et magiques.* Paris: ORSTOM Publications.

Greenberg, J. H. 1987. *Languages in the Americas.* Stanford: Stanford University Press.

Heinen, H. D. 1983. "Social structure and Mechanisms of Disintegration in Warao Society." ["Estructura social y mecanismos de desintegracion en la sociedad Warao."] *Acta cientifica Venezuela.* Caracas: Asociación Ventzolana para el avance de la ciencia 33 (5):419–23.

Lodares, B. de. 1930. *Los Franciscanos Capuchinos en Venezuela,* vol. 2. Caracas: Empresa Gutenberg.

Menezes, M. N. 1979. *The Amerindians in Guyana, 1803–1873.* London: Frank Cass Publishing.

Morey, R. V. 1979. "A Joyful Harvest of Souls: Disease and the Destruction of the Llanos Indians." *Antropológica* (Caracas) 52:77–108.

Murdock, G. P. 1980. *Theories of Illness: A World Survey.* Pittsburgh: University of Pittsburgh Press.

Newson, L. A. 1977. *Aboriginal and Spanish Colonial Trinidad: A Study in Culture Contact.* San Francisco: Academic Press.

Rodney, Walter. 1981. *A History of the Guyanese Working People: 1881–1905.* London: The Johns Hopkins University Press.

Vásquez, E. and W. Wilbert. 1992 "The Orinoco: Physical, Biological and Cultural Diversity of a Major Tropical Alluvial River." In Peter Calow and Geoffrey E. Petts, eds., *The Rivers Handbook.* England: Blackwell Scientific Publications (1):448–71.

Weller, J. A. 1968. *The East Indian Indenture in Trinidad.* San Juan: University of Puerto Rico.

Wilbert, J. 1972. *Survivors of Eldorado.* New York: Praeger.

Wilbert, J. 1979. "Geography and Telluric Lore of the Orinoco Delta." *Journal of Latin American Lore* 5 (1):129–50.

Wilbert, J. 1980. "The Warao Indians of The Orinoco Delta." In Johannes Wilbert and Miguel Layrisse, eds., *Demographic and Biological Studies of the Warao Indians,* 45:3–12. Los Angeles: UCLA Latin American Center.

Wilbert, J. 1981. "Warao Cosmology and Yekuana Roundhouse Symbolism." *Journal of Latin American Lore* 7 (1):37–72.

Wilbert J. 1983. "Warao Ethnopathology and Exotic Epidemic Disease." *Journal of Ethnopharmacology* 8 (3):357–61.

Wilbert, W. 1986. "Warao Herbal Medicine: A Pneumatic Theory of Illness and Healing." Ph.D. dissertation. University of California, Los Angeles.

Wilbert, W. and G. Haiek. 1991. "Phytochemical Screening of a Warao Pharmacopoeia Employed to Treat Gastrointestinal Disorders." *Journal of Ethnopharmacology* 34:7–11.

28

Medicinal Plant Research in Brazil: Data from Regional and National Meetings

Alba R. M. Souza Brito and Antonio A. Souza Brito

ETHNOPHARMACOLOGICAL investigation in Brazil presents a great challenge. The rich and diverse Brazilian flora has been progressively destroyed and the folk medicine, a rich blend of Indian, African, and European knowledge based on tropical medicinal plants, is now modified by modern culture (Amorozo and Gely 1988). As far as ethnopharmacology is concerned there are five regions (figure 28.1) with an abundance of native plants (Rizzini 1979) that still lack complete chemical and pharmacological studies (Matos 1988).

The first region is the Amazon forest, roughly delimited by latitudes 0° and 12°S and longitudes 48° and 74°W, with an average elevation of 100 m and an area of 3.4 million km². This large and heterogenous territory contains a large number of new undescribed species (Gentry 1982; Schultes, 1979). The loss of botanical resources is astonishing. A large area of more than 1 million hectares (Anderson 1989) of native forest has been burned annually, particularly in southwest Amazon, Rondônia, and Acre States (Setzer 1990). The low population density (less than two inhabitants per km²) allows the existence of places that have been minimally influenced by outside cultures. Some Indian tribes, like the Kayapó (Elisabetsky and Posey 1986), Tiriyó (Calvalcante and Frikel 1973), and Tenharins (Di Stasi et al. 1989), have extensive experience with medicinal plants. The disastrous contact of Indians with other ethnic groups (generally gold miners) has often destroyed the native culture and brought new lethal diseases to unprotected Indians (Elisabetsky 1986). Most of Brazilian ethnopharmacological research is concentrated in that region (Prance 1972; Furtado, Souza, and Van den Berg 1978; Van den Berg 1982; Branch and Silva 1983; Elisabetsky and Setzer 1985).

The second region is the native Mata Atlântica. It extends throughout almost 5,000 km along the coast, on a chain of short mountains (between 200 and 800 m

An earlier version of this article was published in the *Journal of Ethnopharmacology*, vol. 39, no. 1 (May 1993) by Elsevier Scientific Publishers Ltd., Ireland.

☑ AMAZON FOREST   ⊟ CERRADO   ◩ CAATINGA
■ MATA ATLÂNTICA AND COASTAL FOREST
▦ PANTANAL MATOGROSSENSE

FIGURE 28.1 Distribution of main Brazilian botanical resources.

above sea level), reaching less than 100 km away from the Atlantic ocean. The
condensation of sea breezes produces a high rainfall (around 4,000 mm/year) and,
consequently, an exuberant vegetation. Today, the small and poorly protected
forests in the northeast are cut down and used as firewood. A botanically important area located in South Bahia and Espírito Santo States has been almost entirely
destroyed by lumbering in the last twenty years. In the southeast some preserved
areas of native Mata Atlântica have been invaded by tourism and industry. However, ecological groups have succeeded in achieving forest preservation in recent
years. The southern sea fishermen from small villages (*caiçaras*) are the main users

of Mata Atlântica medicinal plants (Born, Diniz, and Rossi 1990). The oral transmission of medicinal plant lore, practiced for generations, does not exist anymore (Simões et al. 1986). Except for limited reserves, the native Mata Atlântica is extinct in the southern region.

The third region, named Cerrado, occupies 1.5 million km² in central-western Brazil, with an elevation range of between 500 and 1,000 m. It is a savanna-like vegetation, usually with scattered trees and a grassy ground layer. Intensive farming and reforestation have destroyed much of the native vegetation. Few reserves were preserved. In spite of the varied and well-known flora (Guimarães Ferri 1975, 1980), few studies (Hirschmann and Arias 1990) have been undertaken on the pharmacological effects of medicinal plants used in this region.

The fourth region is the Caatinga. It covers almost 1 million km² and is the poorest region from a botanical standpoint. Its poor, eroded, and stony soil has an average elevation of 100 m. The plants are affected by long and irregular droughts. Owing to low family income, the use of medicinal plants and self-medication are popular practices in the northeast littoral area. The local *curandeiros* are repositories of a rich verbal transmission of medicinal plant lore. Medicinal herbs consisting of varied plant parts, herbal or animal oils, and *garrafadas* (bottled alcoholic macerate of a blend of dried plants) are sold in stalls at weekly village fairs. Despite the difficulties in tracking and identifying specific useful information, these materials represent an interesting source for ethnopharmacological studies (Braga 1960; Agra 1980). The African lore of medicinal plants is present in the State of Bahia, particularly around Salvador Bay. The African-derived *Umbanda* and *Candomblé* religions use some plants and prayers in healing practices. A preliminary study (Almeida et al. 1990) has attempted an inventory.

The fifth region, the Pantanal, is better known for its fabulous fauna. It is a swamp ecosystem, delimited to the northwest by Paraguay and the southeast by the Miranda River. The south Pantanal extends to Bolívia, Paraguay, and Argentina. Owing to the low elevation (around 100 m) the region is annually flooded by the Paraguay River. The cattle farms are isolated, far from civilized facilities. Despite some river water pollution by pesticides or mercury, it is generally still a preserved area. Ethnobotanical data on this region are scarce (Guarim Neto 1987).

Some perspectives arise from the foregoing analysis:

1. There is an urgent need for collecting, documenting, and saving tropical botanical resources.
2. The actual ethnobotanical knowledge is insufficient to support interdisciplinary research.
3. The official medical system ignores medicinal plant therapy, which, in fact, is a popular practice.
4. Most documented medicinal plant research concerning pharmacological activity is incomplete and restricted to local publications.
5. There is a host of interesting interdisciplinary problems to be studied by local and foreign researchers.

Interest in studying medicinal plants in Brazil is increasing. The Brazilian Foundation of Medicinal Plants, founded in 1986, was established to assist and to be a communication channel for local and foreign researchers. The data base here described and analyzed is one more way to achieve these goals.

Medicinal Plant Research in Brazil

Brazilian medicinal plants have been documented since the last century (Peckolt and Peckolt 1888–1914). Results of research have been presented in annual scientific meetings of the Brazilian Society for the Progress of Science since its foundation in 1949. In the last twenty years, the number of communications on medicinal plants has increased at an annual rate of 8%. In spite of the present difficulties, such as absence of adequate financial support, dimension or size of Brazilian territory, difficulty of botanical identification, and the poor interaction between researchers in Brazil, a growing number of young scientists have become interested in medicinal plants (Anderson 1989). The development of interdisciplinary research projects, in spite of their importance (Malone 1977; Waterman 1990), is a rare practice. Ethnobotanical investigations are restricted to some areas and do not cover the complexity of Brazilian culture and/or flora. The interaction between chemistry and pharmacology of natural products is weak.

The current interest of the pharmaceutical industry is small, while the main research effort has been supported by governmental agencies, such as CNPq (Conselho Nacional de Pesquisas), FINEP (Financiadora de Estudos e Projetos), FAPESP (Fundação de Amparo à Pesquisa no Estado de São Paulo), among others. The use of phytotherapy in the mainstream health service has been introduced into practice only recently in the States of São Paulo (Inoue 1990), Paraná (Perozin 1990), and Pernambuco (Caetano et al. 1990).

In order to avoid repeated studies, the Foundation has provided support for the development of a data base of Brazilian medicinal plant research. The analysis of this data base shows that less than 10% of biologically active extracts have been chemically investigated. On the other hand, the isolation of new compounds from plants without the evaluation of their pharmacological activity is a common practice in Brazil, as elsewhere (Farnsworth and Bingel 1977).

Figure 28.2 presents the geographic distribution of medicinal plant research groups in Brazil. Note that the major research groups are located around São Paulo city, an industrial region far from the most interesting ethnopharmacological regions previously described.

Structure of the Medicinal Plant Data Base

Discussion on the coverage and importance of a natural product data base has been presented by Farnsworth (1984). However, the results of most research on

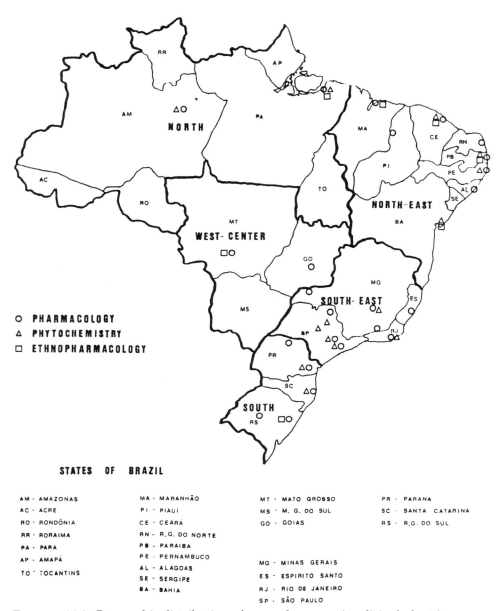

FIGURE 28.2 Geographic distribution of research groups (medicinal plants).

the Brazilian medicinal plants have been presented as communications in Brazilian meetings, in Portuguese, and are limited to local publications. This data base compiled a number of scattered scientific publications but is limited to those that contain pharmacological studies and popular uses. A large number of studies related to the chemistry of Brazilian natural products have been done, but these are beyond the coverage of the data base. Since the practice of submitting abstracts on medicinal plant research to annual scientific meetings has been regularly observed in Brazil since 1949, the period covered by this data base survey starts with that year.

The records, totaling 969 up to 1989, are based on a documented summary of short communications presented in the following Brazilian scientific meetings:

1. Brazilian Society for the Progress of Science (SBPC) (annual meetings), 1949–1989 (41 vols.)
2. Brazilian Symposium on Medicinal Plants, (biannual meetings), 1968–1988 (10 vols.)
3. Brazilian Symposium on Natural Products, 1980–1990 (2 vols.)
4. Brazilian Society of Pharmacology and Experimental Therapeutics (SBFTE) (annual meetings), 1982–1989 (8 vols.)

The following information is coded and entered into the data base: plant species, plant family, plant local name, part of plant used, popular use, type of extract, pharmacological activity, active chemical compound, and reference.

The records contain only plants identified to species. When necessary, the author of a particular paper was requested to complete this information. Activities pointed out by authors were classified following the guidelines set down for this data base (see below). Research results obtained without rigorous scientific methodology or with ambiguous data were not included. Original references are documented in the Foundation's library.

Plants and Plant Families Studied

A total of 402 different plant species (in 969 records, belonging to 286 genera, distributed in 93 families) have been investigated. Except for a few species of *Polypodium* (*Polypodiaceae, Pteridophyta*), all plants belong to the *Angiospermae*. Figure 28.3 shows the families most frequently studied.

Species belonging to two families, *Compositae* (10.2%) and *Leguminosae* (13.9%), comprise almost 25% of the total number studied. Two factors may have been responsible for this phenomenon. First, the popular use has influenced the choice of a plant for study. Furthermore, even in the absence of ethnopharmacological studies, researchers take into account any popular indication to start a particular study (Waterman 1990). Second, these families happen to be most abundantly represented in nature (Joly 1975). As pointed out by Thomson (1981), the popular knowledge of medicinal plants has been developed through trial and error and transmitted verbally from one generation to the next. Therefore, the more abundantly represented the families are, the more widely they are quoted and, consequently, the more frequently they become the subject of pharmacological studies.

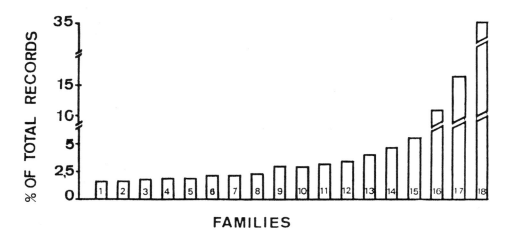

FAMILIES

1 PIPERACEAE	7 ZINGIBERACEAE	13 LABIATAE
2 SOLANACEAE	8 MORACEAE	14 APOCYNACEAE
3 PHYTOLACACEAE	9 CUCURBITACEAE	15 EUPHORBIACEAE
4 LAURACEAE	10 RUBIACEAE	16 COMPOSITAE
5 LILIACEAE	11 VERBENACEAE	17 LEGUMINOSAE
6 GRAMINEAE	12 ANACARDIACEAE	18 OTHERS

FIGURE 28.3 Number of citations per family related to total records.

Among the 402 species studied, 12 have more than 10 citations. Table 28.1 provides information on the botanical and vernacular names and part of the plant used.

Pharmacological Activities Investigated

The total number of pharmacological activities investigated is 106. They may be grouped into 13 main therapeutic classes, encompassing 81.9% of the citations (figure 28.4). The most frequently cited categories are the same ones as those pointed out by Farnsworth and Bingel (1977), namely, antiinflammatory, antimicrobial, analgesic, spasmolytic, central nervous system (CNS) depressor, diuretic, antiulcer, neuromuscular blocker, antitumor, cholinomimetic, hypoglycemic, hypotensive, and toxic.

The antimicrobial activity includes several chemotherapeutic effects (antibacterial, antiprotozoan, antifungal, antiviral), as well as activities against tropical parasitic diseases (schistosomiasis, malaria, chagas, and leishmaniasis). Tranquilizers, sedatives, hypnotics, and anticonvulsants belong to CNS depressor class.

Note that 11.1% of the plants studied have been reported as having toxic effects. This finding raises concern about the popular use and commercial abuse of medicinal plants.

Correlation Between Popular Use and Pharmacological Activity

The belief system of a traditional healer is influenced by psychological and social factors (Malone 1980). The data base has information on thirty-three categories of popular uses of medicinal plants. Its analysis shows that medicinal plants have been largely used for relieving different types of pain; for treatment of snake bites, diabetes, and general inflammatory problems; and as an abortifacient. Important and frequent popular categories of health problems such as cancer, *mal de chagas* (Chagas disease) and *lepra* (leprosy), are rarely treated by traditional healers.

Some facts appear to contribute to the selectiveness of popular use. Medicinal plants are commonly used as a readily available alternative, owing to the lack of official health service in underdeveloped regions. Disease manifestations that are easily identified by the lay person (cough, colds, headache) are more frequently treated by plant-based home-made remedies. Aphrodisiac and abortive plants are

TABLE 28.1   *Plants More Frequently Studied*

Family*	Species	Vernacular Name	Part Used
Anacardiaceae (17)	*Astronium urundeuva* Engl.	Aroeira	Stem bark
Apocynaceae (18)	*Mandevilla velutina* Mart. Wood.	Jalapa	Rhizomes
Compositae (15) (17)	*Achyroclines satureoides* A. D.C. *Stevia rebaudiana* Bert.	Macela Estevia	Flowers Leaves
Crassulaceae (11)	*Kalanchoe brasiliensis* Camb.	Coirama	Leaves
Cucurbitaceae (10)	*Luffa operculata* Cogn.	Buchinha	Fruits
Euphorbiaceae (10)	*Croton zenhtneri* Pax & Hoffm.	Cunhã	Leaves
Leguminosae (15) (11)	*Canavalia ensiformis* A. D.C. *Pterodon polygalaeflorus* Benth.	Feijão Sucupira	Seeds Seeds
Moraceae (10)	*Dorstenia bryoniaeflora* Mart.	Caiapiá	Rhizomes
Phytolaccaceae (16)	*Petiveria alliacea* Linn.	Tipi	Roots
Zingiberaceae (14)	*Alpinia speciosa* Dietr.	Colônia	Rhizomes

*Number of citations in the data base.

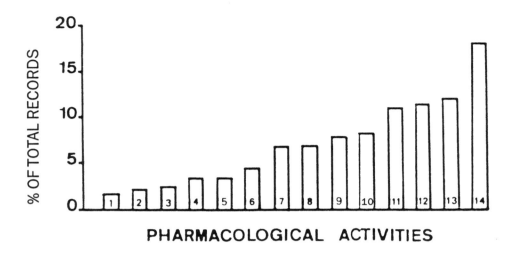

FIGURE 28.4 Number of citations per therapeutic category related to total records.

1 DIURETIC	6 HYPOGLYCEMIC	11 TOXIC
2 ANTIULCER	7 CNS DEPRESSOR	12 ANTIMICROBIAL
3 NEUROMUSCULAR BLOCKER	8 SPASMOLYTIC	13 ANTI-INFLAMMATORY
4 ANTITUMOR	9 HYPOTENSIVE	14 OTHERS
5 CHOLINOMIMETIC	10 ANALGESIC	

TABLE 28.2 *Correlation Between Popular Use and Positive Pharmacological Activity for the Main Therapeutic Categories*

Activity	Number of Popular Use Citations	Number of Positive Investigations	Percentage of Success
Analgesic	59	54	91.5
Antiinflammatory	93	63	67.7
Antimicrobial	116	64	55.2
Antitumor[a]	12	9	75.0
Antiulcer	29	15	51.7
CNS depressor	28	26	92.8
Diuretic	26	8	30.8
Hypoglycemic	54	39	72.2
Hypotensive	56	54	96.4
Spasmogenic[b]	5	5	100.0
Spasmolytic	55	24	43.6
Toxic	34	34	100.0

[a]Also referred to as cancer.
[b]Also referred to as abortive.

also often used, owing to their strong popular appeal, while other disease signs and symptoms, such as those related to cancer, are seldom recognized as such in the traditional health system.

The data indicate that the correlation between popular use and experimental pharmacological activity is high (table 28.2).

Except for diuretics, more than 40% of the alleged popular effects have been confirmed by laboratory investigations. In contrast, several plant infusions for which a diuretic effect has been ascribed usually lead to increased diuresis owing to excessive water intake; they are drunk several times a day. All plants popularly known as toxic (thirty-four species) have had their noxious effects demonstrated experimentally.

Chemical Compounds Isolated from Plants with Pharmacological Activity

A total of ninety-three compounds with one or more pharmacological effects isolated from Brazilian flora are recorded in the data base. It is difficult to define which of them are novel structures or which are potentially useful as new drugs. Table 28.3 shows in alphabetical order the family, species, and active compounds isolated in recent years.

An overview of these data in comparison with popular use leads to some generalizations. Plants rich in essential oils are generally used to treat respiratory diseases; plants rich in tannins have a large number of popular use as antiinflammatory remedies; while plants rich in alkaloids and/or latex are frequently cited as toxic, particularly members of the families *Solanaceae* and *Euphorbiaceae*.

Less than 10% of 402 different species registered in the data base have been subjected to chemical investigation or have had an active pharmacological compound isolated. Sometimes the biological investigation was performed only with crude plant material without further inquiries on the different extracts or without further attempt at the isolation of the active compounds. As pointed out earlier, the poor interaction between chemistry and pharmacology researchers in Brazil is one of the reasons for this failure. Additionally, many research groups have limited their work to the confirmation or negation of the efficacy of popular medicines. Few studies have addressed efforts toward the development of novel drugs.

On the basis of recorded data, it is difficult to establish any correlation between the family of a plant and its pharmacological activity. However, an attempt to correlate major pharmacological activities against plant families studied is presented in table 28.4.

The number of asterisks shows how frequently a therapeutic activity has been found in a specific family. Each asterisk represents fifteen citations for active plants in that therapeutic class.

TABLE 28.3 *Plants with Active Compounds or Class of Compound and Related Pharmacological Effects*

Family and Species	Active Compounds	Effects
Anacardiaceae *Anacardium occidentale* Linn.	Catechin (flavonoid) Tannins	CNS depressor Antiinflammatory, analgesic
Annonaceae *Annona salzmannii* A. DC.	Anonaine (alkaloid)	Antimicrobial
Apocynaceae *Ervatamia coronaria* Stapf.	Indole alkaloid Phenolic acid	Contraceptive CNS depressor
Ervatamia divaricata Burkill.	Voacristine (alkaloid)	CNS stimulant
Geissopermum vellosii Fr. All.	Flavopereirine (alkaloid)	Neuromuscular blocker, anticholinesterase, hypotensive
Mandevilla velutina (Mart.) Wood.	MV 8608 (terpene) MV 8612 (terpene) MV 8612/MV 8613 (terpenes)	Lipoxygenase inhibitor Antiinflammatory Bradykinin antagonist
Tabernaemontana fuchsiaefolia A. DC.	Indole alkaloid	CNS depressor
Arecaceae *Orbignya speciosa* Barb. Rodr.	Steroids	Antiinflammatory
Asteraceae *Eclipta prostrata* Linn.	Wedelo-lactone (coumarin)	Antivenoms
Bignoniaceae *Tabebuia avellanedae* Lorentz	Cycloolivil (lignane)	Antitumor
Boraginaceae *Cordia verbenacea* A. DC.	Artemetin (flavonoid)	Antiinflammatory, antiulcer
Caryocaraceae *Caryocar brasiliense* St. Hil.	Oleanoic acid (fatty acid)	Antitumor
Celastraceae *Catha edulis* Forsk.	Cathinone / cathine (alkaloidal amines)	Anorectic, vasoconstrictor
Chenopodiaceae *Chenopodium ambrosioides* Linn.	Anethole (phenolic ester)	Antiinflammatory
Chloranthaceae *Hedyosmum brasiliense* Mat.	Essential oils (monoterpenes)	Antimicrobial
Compositae *Achyrocline satureioides* Gardn.	Quercetin (flavonol)	Spasmolytic, hypotensive
Arctium lappa Linn. *Bidens bipinnata* Linn.	Onopordopicrin (sesquiterpene) Thymol, B-pinene (monoterpene)	Toxic Spasmolytic, neuromuscular blocker
Eremanthus elaeagnus Sch.	Essential oils (monoterpenes)	Cercaricide
Stevia rebaudiana Helmsl.	Stevioside (diterpenoid)	Hypoglycemic, sweetener
Vanillosmopsis erythropappa Sch.	Essential oils (monoterpenes)	Cercaricide
Cucurbitaceae *Wilbrandia verticillata* Benth. Hook	Cucurbitacin (triterpene)	Cytotoxic, histaminergic, antitumor

TABLE 28.3   *Continued*

Family and Species	Active Compounds	Effects
Eriocaulaceae		
Paepalanthus bromelioides Alv. Silv.	Isocoumarin (coumarin)	Antimicrobial
Euphorbiaceae		
Cnidoscolus phyllacanthus Muell. Arg.	Histamine (amine)	Histaminergic
	5-Hydroxytryptamine (indole group)	Spasmogenic
Cnidoscolus urens Arthur	Histamine (amine)	Histaminergic
	5-Hydroxtryptamine (indole group)	Spasmogenic
Croton campestris St. Hil.	Taspine (alkaloidal amines)	Spasmolytic
Croton sonderianus Muell. Arg.	Diterpenes	Antimicrobial
Croton zenhtneri Pax & Hoffm.	Anethol., estragol (phenolic esters)	Nueromuscular blocker, spasmolytic, local anesthetic
Eurphorbia tirucalli Linn.	Tirucallol (sterol)	Antiinflammatory
Jatropha elliptica Muell. Arg.	Jatrophone (diterpene)	Spasmolytic
Sebastiana schottiana Muell. Arg.	Xanthoxiline (acridine alkaloid)	Antimicrobial
Gentianaceae		
Schultesia guyanensis Malme.	Alkaloids	Cardiotonic
Gramineae		
Cymbopogon citratus Stapf.	Citral, myrcene (monoterpenes)	CNS depressor, analgesic
Labiatae		
Coleus amboinicus Lour.	Quercetin (flavonol)	PAF antagonist
Coleus barbatus Benth.	Forskolin (diterpene)	Glycogenolytic
Hyptis mutabilis Briq.	Essential oils (monoterpenes)	Antiulcer
Hyptis umbrosa Salzm.	Taxodione (diterpene)	Antimicrobial
Mentha longifolia Huds. F. Angl.	Quercetin (flavonol)	PAF antagonist
Peltodon radicans Pohl.	Acylglycoside (phenylpropanoid)	Bronchodilator
Satureja incana Spreng.	Carvacrol, cymene (monoterpenes)	Spasmolytic
Lauraceae		
Ocotea cuprea Mez.	Alpinetin (flavonone)	Antimicrobial, antifungal
Persea americana Mill.	Proantocyanidina (biflavonyl)	CNS depressor, antitumor
Leguminosae		
Acosmium dasycarpum Linn.	Lupeol (triterpene)	CNS depressor, analgesic
Canavalia ensiformis Linn. (A. DC.)	Canatoxin (protein)	Convulsant, toxic, hypoxia, histamine release inhibitor
Cyclolobium claussenii Benth.	Claussequinone (isoflavonoid)	Cytotoxic
Enterolobium ellipticum Benth.	Saponin	Toxic
Hymenaea courbaril L.	Stilbestrol (sterol)	Spasmolytic
Parkinsonia aculeata L.	Flavonoids	CNS depressant

(continued)

TABLE 28.3 *Continued*

Family and Species	Active Compounds	Effects
Pterodon apparicioi Peders.	Epoxygeranyl (monoterpene)	Cercaricide
Pterodon polygalaeflourus Benth.	Furanoditerpene	Antiinflammatory, analgesic, CNS depressant
Pterodon pubescens Benth.	Epoxygeranyl (monoterpene)	Cercaricide
Trifolium subterraneum Linn.	Genistein (isoflavone)	Estrogenic
Loganiaceae *Strychnos trinervis* (Vell.) Mart.	Bisnordihydrotoxiferine Longicaudatine, trinervine (indole alkaloids)	Antidiarrhoea, antimicrobial Calcium release inhibitor Spasmolytic
Malpighiaceae *Lophanthera lactescens* Ducke.	Lophanterine (alkaloid)	Cholinomimetic
Moraceae *Artocarpus integrifolia* Linn.	Jacalin (protein)	Immunological stimulant
Cecropia glaziovii Sneth.	Isovitexin (flavone)	Hypertensive, spasmolytic
Myristicaceae *Virola surinamensis* Warb.	Surinamin, virolin (neolignanes)	Antitumor, cercaricide
Myrtaceae *Syzygium cuminii* Skeels	Pinene, limonene (monoterpenes)	Antimicrobial
Polygonaceae *Polygonum acre* Sieber.	Tannins	Spasmolytic
Rhamnaceae *Ampelozizyphus amazonicus* Ducke.	Saponins	Hypotensive, antimalarial, hemolytic, toxic
Rutaceae *Zanthoxylum rhoifolium* Lam.	Quinovic acid (triterpene)	Antimicrobial
Sapindaceae *Felicium decipiens* Thw.	Saponins	Toxic
Sapotaceae *Bumelia sartorum* Mart.	Bassic acid (triterpene)	Hypoglycemic, antiinflammatory
Scrophulariaceae *Scoparia dulcis* Linn.	Triterpene	Analgesic
Solanaceae *Sessea brasiliensis* Tol.	Alkaloids	Toxic
Solanum paludosum Moric. *Solanum pseudo-quina* St. Hil.	Alkaloids Isosolafloridine (alkaloid)	Neuromuscular blocker CNS stimulant
Sterculiaceae *Theobroma cacao* Linn.	Proanthocyanidin (biflavonyl)	Analgesic
Theobroma leiocarpa Bernoulli	Flavonoids	Antitumor
Verbenaceae *Lippia chamissonis* Dietr.	Essential oils (monoterpenes)	Neuromuscular blocker Spasmolytic, hypotensive
Lippia grata Schau.	Essential oils (monoterpenes)	Spasmolytic
Lippia sidoides Cham.	Thymol (monoterpene)	Spasmolytic, antimicrobial, local anesthetic, sedative

Note: CNS = central nervous system, PAF = platelet-activating factor.

TABLE 28.4   *Correlation Between Pharmacological Activity and Families Frequently Studied*

Family	1	2	3	4	5	6	7	8	9	10	11	12	13	14	15
Anacardiaceae	—	*	*	****	—	—	**	—	—	*	—	—	—	—	**
Apocynaceae	—	*	*	***	*	*	—	—	*	*	—	*	—	—	*
Compositae	—	*	*	*	**	*	—	—	—	*	*	**	*	*	*
Cucurbitaceae	*	—	**	*	**	*	—	—	*	—	*	*	—	—	**
Euphorbiaceae	—	*	*	*	*	**	—	—	*	*	*	*	—	*	—
Gramnineae	—	***	*	*	—	—	—	—	—	*	*	—	—	*	—
Labiatae	—	*	*	—	*	—	*	—	—	**	—	—	—	**	—
Lauraceae	*	—	**	—	***	*	—	—	*	*	*	—	—	*	—
Leguminosae	—	*	*	**	*	*	—	—	*	*	—	*	—	*	**
Liliaceae	—	—	***	—	***	—	—	—	—	—	—	—	—	*	—
Moraceae	—	*	**	*	—	—	—	**	—	*	—	—	—	—	—
Phytolaccaceae	****	*	—	—	—	—	—	—	—	**	—	—	—	—	*
Piperaceae	—	*	*	—	***	—	—	—	—	*	—	*	**	—	—
Rubiaceae	*	**	—	**	*	—	—	—	—	—	—	*	*	*	**
Solanaceae	—	—	**	—	*	—	—	—	*	—	—	**	—	—	**
Verbenaceae	—	*	*	*	*	**	—	—	**	—	—	—	—	—	*
Zingiberaceae	—	—	****	—	—	*	—	—	—	—	**	—	—	*	*

Note: Number of citations: * = up to 15; ** = up to 30; *** = up to 45; **** = up to 60.

Pharmacological activity: 1 = abortive; 2 = analgesic; 3 = antihypertensive; 4 = antiinflammatory; 5 = antimicrobial; 6 = antitumor; 7 = antiulcer; 8 = hallucinogen; 9 = neuromuscular blocker; 10 = CNS depressor; 11 = diuretic; 12 = spasmogenic; 13 = spasmolytic; 14 = hypoglycemic; 15 = toxic.

A large number of uses for native medicinal plants is characteristic of many developing countries; China (Farnsworth 1976; Peigen 1983) may serve as a good example. Developing the medicinal potential of plants into reality requires considerable effort and knowledge of the pharmacology of the local flora.

If we accept Tyler's (1988) optimism, we believe that the most productive period of Brazilian medicinal plant research still lies ahead of us. A number of factors justify this optimism. First, more and more Brazilian research groups are becoming conscious of the importance and diversity of this medicinal plant heritage. The number of new investigators interested in interdisciplinary research on medicinal plants is increasing. Second, in some Brazilian states, governmental projects are introducing the use of phytotherapy into public health services. Third, there is an emerging interest of the local pharmaceutical industries in medicines originating from plants. Fourth, important areas of research, such as ethnopharmacology, will attract more investigators, both local and foreign. The needs for adequate financial support for long enough periods and for well-trained and experienced personnel in the execution of interdisciplinary research projects are challenges at present.

This data base of the Brazilian Foundation of Medicinal Plants could give some hints at new multidisciplinary research. Analysis of data shows the value of searching for medicinal agents from plants based on documented history of folk use.

ACKNOWLEDGMENTS

The authors wish to express their sincere thanks to Professor E. A. Cavalheiro for his keen interest and constant encouragement. Thanks are also due to the Documentation

Research Center of Rhodia/Paulinia for reference facilities, to João Antonio Rodrigues de Moraes (in memoriam), founder of the Brazilian Foundation of Medicinal Plants, and to Mirtes Costa and Isac Almeida Medeiros for indexing the data.

REFERENCES

Agra, M. F. 1980. "Contribuição ao estudo de plantas medicinais de Paraíba." *Ciência e cultura* 33 (suplemento):64–66.

Almeida, M. Z., E. M. R. Prata, R. S. C. Cerqueira, and I. C. S. A. Medrado. 1990. "Levantamento da flora medicinal comercializada em Salvador, BA." *Annals of XI simpósio de plantas medicinais do Brasil.* Comm. 4.60.

Amorozo, M. C. M. and A. Gely. 1988. "Uso de plantas medicinais por caboclos do baixo Amazonas—Barbacena/Pa." *Boletim do Museu Paraense Emílio Goeldi* 4 (1):47–131.

Anderson, A. 1989. "Brazil Walks the Tightrope." *Nature* 342:355–74.

Born, G. C. C., P. S. N. B. Diniz, and L. Rossi. 1990. "Plantas medicinais da estação ecológica Jureia-Itatins, SP." *Annals of XI simpósio de plantas medicinais do Brasil.* Comm. 4.63.

Braga, R. 1960. *Plantas do nordeste, especialmente do Ceará.* Imprensa Oficial, Brasil, 98 pp.

Branch, L. C. and I. M. F. Silva. 1983. "Folk Medicine of "Alter do Chão"/PA—Brasil." *Acta Amazônica* 13 (5/6):737–97.

Caetano, N. P., B. Maia, P. Afiatpour, E. Araújo, and L. M. Rego. 1990. "Projeto de fitoterapia de Olinda/PE—avaliação fitoquímica, microbiológica e farmacológica preliminar do *Acanthospermum hispidum.*" *Annals of XI simpósio de plantas medicinais do Brasil.* Comm. 3.22.

Cavalcante, P. B. and P. Frikel. 1973. "A farmacopeia Tiriyó: estudo étnobotânico." Belém: *Publicações avulsas do Museu Paraense Emílio Goeldi,* no. 24, 157 pp.

Di Stasi, L. C., E. M. G. Santos, C. M. Santos, and C. A. Miruma. 1989. *Plantas medicinais na Amazonia.* Editora da UNESP, Brasil, 194 pp.

Elisabetsky, E. 1986. "New Directions in Ethnopharmacology." *Journal of Ethnobiology* 6 (1):121–28.

Elisabetsky, E. and D. A. Posey. 1986. "Pesquisa etnofarmacológica e recursos naturais no trópico úmido: o caso dos índios Kayapós e suas implições para a ciência médica." *Annals of I simpósio internacional do trópico úmido* 2:85–93. Embrapa CPATU.

Elisabetsky, E. and R. Setzer. 1985. "Caboclo Concepts of Disease, Diagnosis and Therapy: Implications for Ethnopharmacology and Health Systems in Amazonia." In E. P. Parker, ed., *The Amazon Caboclo: Historical and Contemporary Perspectives,* pp. 243–78. Studies in Third World Societies, no. 32. Williamsburg, Va.: College of William and Mary, Department of Anthropology.

Farnsworth, N. R. 1976. "Pharmacy Practice and Pharmaceutical Education in the People's Republic of China." *American Journal of Pharmacology Education* 40:115–21.

Farnsworth, N. R. 1984. "How Can the Well Be Dry When It Is Filled with Water?" *Economic Botany* 38 (1):4–13 (January/March). New York: The New York Botanical Garden.

Farnsworth, N. R. and A. S. Bingel. 1977. "Problems and Prospects of Discovering New Drugs from Higher Plants by Pharmacological Screening." In H. Wagner and P. Wolff, eds., *New Natural Products and Plant Drugs with Pharmacological, Biological or Therapeutical Activity,* pp. 1–22. Berlin: Springer-Verlag, 288 pp.

Furtado, L. G., R. C. Souza, and E. Van den Berg. 1978. "Notas sobre uso terapêutico de plantas pela população cabocla de Marapanim." *Boletim do Museu Paraensi Emílio Goeldi* 70:1–31.

Gentry, A. M. 1982. "Phytogeographic Pattern as Evidence for a Choco Refuge." In G. Prance, ed., *Biological Diversification In the Tropics.* New York: Columbia University Press, 714 pp.

Guarim-Neto, G. 1987. *Plantas utilizadas na medicina popular do estado do Mato Grosso.* CNPq, assessoria editorial, 58 pp.

Guimarães, Ferri, M. 1975. "Contribuição ao conhecimento da ecologia do Cerrado e da Caatinga. Estudo comparativo do balanco de água e de sua vegetação." *Boletim da faculdade de filosofia, ciências e letras* 12:1–170.

Guimarães Ferri, M. 1980. *Vegetação Brasileira,* nova ser 26:51–69. Belo Horizonte: Editora Itatiaia, reconquista do Brasil.

Hirschmann, G. S. and A. R. Arias. 1990. "A Survey of Medicinal Plants of Minas Gerais, Brazil." *Journal of Ethnopharmacology* 29:159–72.

Inoue, A. S. 1990. "Projeto de fitorerapia do estado de São Paulo." *Annals of XI simpósio de plantas medicinais do Brasil.* Comm. 4.69.

Joly, A. B. 1975. *Botânica: introdução à taxonomia vegetal.* Companhia editora nacional, Brasil, 777 pp.

Malone, M. H. 1977. In H. Wagner, P. Wolff, eds., *New Natural Products and Plant Drugs with Pharmacological, Biological or Therapeutical Activity,* 23–53. Berlin: Springer-Verlag.

Malone, M. H. 1980. "Common Problems Encountered in Ethnopharmacological Investigations and How to Solve Them." *Ciência e cultura* 33:19–31.

Matos, F. J. A. 1988. *Introdução á fitoquímica experimental.* Imprensa Universitária da UFC, Brasil, 126 pp.

Peckolt, T. and G. Peckolt. 1914. *História das plantas medicinais e úteis do Brasil.* Typographia Laemmert Brasil, 6 vols.

Peigen, X. 1983. "Recent Developments on Medicinal Plants in China." *Journal of Ethnopharmacology* 7:95–109.

Perozin, M. M. 1990. "Projeto de fitoterapia do SUDS—PR." *XI simpósio de plantas medicinais do Brasil.* Comm. 4.71.

Prance, G. T. 1972. "Ethnobotanical Notes from Amazonian Brazil." *Economic Botany* 26:221–37.

Rizzini, C. T. 1979. *Tratado de fitogeografia do Brasil.* Editora da Universidade de São Paulo, 2 vols., 374 pp.

Schultes, R. E. 1979. "The Amazonia as a Source of New Economic Plants." *Economic Botany* 33 (3):259–66.

Setzer, A. 1990. "Desmate: dados conflitantes." *Ciência hoje* 11 (63):66.

Simöes, C. M. O., L. A. Mentz, E. P. Schenkel, B. E. Irgang, and J. R. Stehmann. 1986. "Plantas da medicina popular do Rio Grande do Sul." Editora da Universidade do Rio Grande do Sul, Brasil, 173 pp.

Thomson, W. A. 1981. *Guia practica ilustrada de las plantas medicinales.* Editorial Blume, Espanha, 220 pp.

Tyler, V. E. 1988. "Medicinal Plant Research: 1953–1987." *Planta Medica.* Stuttgart: Georg Thieme Verlag. 54 (2):95–100 (April).

Van den Berg, E. 1982. *Plantas medicinais na Amazonia: contribuição ao seu conhecimento.* Editora do CNPQ, Brasil, 212 pp.

Waterman, P. G. 1990. "Searching for Bioactive Compounds: Various Strategies." *Journal of Natural Products* 53:13–22.

29

Community Ethnobotany:
Setting Foundations for an Informed Decision
on Trading Rain Forest Resources

Elaine Elisabetsky

THE vast biological diversity of the Brazilian Amazon has been attracting the attention of increasingly larger sectors of society. The potential pharmaceutical wealth of tropical forests, a fact that a few years ago was recognized only by scientists specializing in this region, has become a widely known argument for biodiversity conservation (Reid et al.1993). Accordingly, many attempts have been made to evaluate tropical forests in general or their nontimber products in particular (Balick and Mendelsohn 1992; Peters, Gentry, and Mendelsohn 1989; Tobias and Mendelsohn 1990).

The improvement of well-defined target methods to detect active compounds and the development of technology that allows for screening an enormous number of compounds at previously unimagined speed and low cost (e.g., high-throughput screening systems), make natural products extremely appealing as appropriate and diverse sources of chemical compounds to feed this drug development strategy. The possibilities opened by these systems, along with the development of revolutionary techniques for isolation and elucidation of chemical compounds (Balandrin 1985; Tyler 1986), justify a rekindled interest in natural products by pharmaceutical industries (Cunningham 1993).

Although of undeniable importance and high visibility through the media, the demand for forest products is by no means limited to pharmaceutical products. The current trends in health and fitness appear to be well rooted and support a solid and growing market for natural products in the hygiene and cosmetic areas. Here again the distinct appeal of rain forest products, allied with the awareness of the global environmental crisis and desire of the public to take position through their purchasing choices (Ziffer 1992), offers new opportunities for developing plant-based commercial products.

The idea of marketing rain forest products opens the possibility of putting in place a new model of development in tropical areas, one in which equitable relations result in acceptable benefits to all parties involved, as well as in due respect for the forest products. There is little doubt that many difficulties are bound to arise in dealing with such complex social and environmental matters. Nevertheless, the idea has proven to be successful as judged by Cultural Survival Enterprise's achievements in three years of activity: trading of U.S. $349,000 worth of nontimber forest products imported from tropical areas and sold to seventeen companies that in turn manufacture nineteen different products (Clay 1992). It is to be expected that the success obtained by these so-called rain forest products will open space for many others. Indeed, several companies have ongoing research programs and are actively pursuing contacts with developing countries and local communities.

As a result, we are likely to see communities that up to now were fairly isolated and accustomed to considering their useful flora as an immediate source for their limited needs becoming involved with markets and companies that look at and are prepared to make use of those same resources in an entirely different perspective and scale.

There is little doubt that new models of development for tropical areas in developing countries are sorely needed. Experience has shown that unless people have a direct stake and interest in conserving the environment, even the best-designed conservation projects have to be permanently enforced and supported and are therefore bound to fail (Posey 1992). The marketing of rain forest products has, therefore, raised a fair amount of expectation and interest. I offer here an example of a strategy that aims to allow local communities in the Brazilian Amazon to understand and actively participate in the evolution of this new development model.

Rain Forest Products and Extractive Reserves

Extractive reserves are areas of forest set aside for continuous harvesting of renewable forest products such as rubber, nuts, fruits, fibers, oils, and medicinal plants (Fearnside 1989). In Brazil, extractive reserves are supported by grass roots movements, house some 50,000 people (caboclos, rubber tappers, colonizers) in various places (fourteen reserves, in four states cover more than 3 million hectares) of the Brazilian Amazon, and have gained legal recognition. Extractive reserves are defined by the Brazilian government as "forest areas inhabited by extractive populations granted long-term usufruct rights to forest resources which they collectively manage" (Schwartzman 1989).

Although extraction in the Amazon has historically been associated with resource depletion, environmental degradation, and social disruption, the prospects of extractivism in its contemporary version are far more promising. Extractive reserves have emerged as one of the most promising development strategies for

Amazonia, representing a socially just form of land use that can reconcile economic development and environmental conservation (Allegreti 1990; Anderson 1992).

Extractive communities are therefore an optimal social scenario for implementing the marketing of rain forest products. But, in spite of a long history of extracting forest products in the northern region of Brazil representing 13–20% of the primary economic sector (Homma 1989; Schwartzman 1989), extractive activities are limited to very few species, such as cacao (*Theobroma cacao* L.), latex (*Hevea brasiliensis* M. Arg.), Brazil nuts (*Bertholletia excelsa* Humb.), and several species used as wood.

As noted by Padoch (1992), the limited number of species that generate most of the income to the extractive populations is in sharp contrast to the diversity of products used locally and regionally in various parts of the Amazon (Anderson et al. 1985; Baleé 1986; Milliken et al. 1992). Indeed, extractive reserves can be viewed as repositories of botanical and cultural diversity. Since the majority of plant uses are unknown to outsiders, the value of the knowledge preserved by local specialists cannot be underestimated (Bennett 1992). For instance, Kainer and Dureya (1992) discovered that the women from three extractive reserves located in the State of Acre know the uses and management of as many as 150 different species.

In a meeting called by the National Council of the Rubber Tappers in early 1991, the discussions on development of use strategies of the so-called nontimber forest products were emphasized as having high priority for the communities. The need for inventories became immediately apparent. This demand led to the idea of training members of the community to elicit and organize ethnobotanical data. The main purposes of such a training program could be described as the following: (1) provide extractive communities with the means to collect ethnobotanical information, (2) organize ethnobotanical/ethnopharmacological data, (3) implement a network of field workers to rescue traditional knowledge, and (4) help extractive reserve communities build bridges and negotiate agreements with research and commercial institutions to secure satisfying benefits that are acceptable by all parties involved.

This educational program would also contribute to more general purposes such as discussing the very idea of extractivism and conservation, providing environmental education, giving value to natural resources and associated traditional knowledge, and ultimately contributing to the conservation of Brazilian flora and its culturally based lore.

The Ethnobotanical Manual

For such training, an ethnobotanical manual was developed in very simple language. The manual is intended to be practical and didactic, helping trained personnel to collect data in a systematic and organized form. The manual briefly discusses why we study natural resources, what happens to the information out-side the communities, how this basic information can be useful for developing commercial products, and what benefits and risks are associated with getting in-volved in commercial enterprises.

A standard collection form that includes data on the collector, the informant, the plant, and the plant use(s) (with details of utility, means of preparation, and consumption) guides the text of the manual. The manual also teaches why samples of plants have to be collected and how to collect and store them. The association with researchers is justified and recommended. The courses will teach the person-nel chosen by the communities to work with the collection form and to deal with the practicalities regarding plant samples.

Although this manual was written in Portuguese and focuses on a target pop-ulation of Brazilian extractive communities, the interest shown by nongovernment organizations and researchers from different countries led us to believe that it would be useful to have it translated and published in this volume (see appendix). In so doing, we hope that it can be adapted for other places and peoples, being useful to promote the idea of modern extractivism as a means to implement so-cially and environmentally responsible models of development.

Brazil is a gene-rich country, host to 24% of known primate species, between 10 and 15 million species of insects, and 22% of the world's higher plant species. The debate over how these resources should be protected and who should do so has intensified over the last few years, due to a growing awareness of the links among sustainable utilization of natural resources, conservation of biodiversity, and ec-onomic development. This debate becomes of concrete importance if one considers that, although the Amazon basin is still host to the largest tract of intact tropical forest left in the world, economic growth has been associated with deforestation that transforms species-rich forest into degraded areas or, at best, impoverished secondary forests. This picture highlights the need for establishing new economic activities as the basis for development.

It has been repeatedly pointed out that the development of markets for new plant-based drugs and other products does not necessarily imply conservation. Increasing demand on species that are endemic may actually lead to an unsus-tainable harvest and local extinction of plant populations. Development of new markets must, therefore, be accompanied by rigorous ecological studies of plant habitat, abundance, growth requirements, regeneration, and production/yield. If any degree of conservation is to be expected, local populations must be educated on the value of the resource as well as the value of sustainable management. This is especially true in areas where local communities are pressed and oppressed by poverty.

This paper reports on and discusses an educational program that was generated by the need to increase our knowledge of plant resources that can be successfully explored, in both ecological and economic perspectives, by extractive reserve com-munities. One of its principal tools, namely an ethnobotanical manual, is here offered as a starting point for those interested in implementing similar strategies. Teaching community members about the methods and usefulness of ethnobotanical collection is one approach to enrolling local populations in the overall research effort.

Ethical, economical, and legal considerations seem to have become an unavoidable matter of concern to the scientific community involved with natural products research and development. Whereas it is becoming obvious that the question of intellectual property rights is central to the debate concerning genetic resources utilization, the very concept of information as a tradable resource is foreign to many traditional communities. Communities can nevertheless learn what NGOs and research institutions have long known: organized information, identified species, associated ethnobotanical lore on resource uses, processing, and management can be regarded as value added to the "wild," "raw" genetic material. And, there are precedents that show that companies are willing to pay for this added value. Therefore, permitting and encouraging communities to trade organized information might be a useful adjunct to IPR mechanisms that are already in place.

Extractive communities, represented by the National Council of Rubber Tappers and the Union of the Forest Peoples, have great trust and hope in the future of sustainable development based on nontimber forest products. Cooperation and partnerships are now actively sought. The overall result of such a strategy might be ultimately dependent on how well informed the parties involved in these enterprises are. Only by having a comprehensive view of the social, economic, and environmental consequences of such endeavors can communities come to a decision on the long-term costs and benefits of such activities. Bioprospecting allied to conservation will have to be developed in multiple models as diverse as the consortia of socioeconomic-ecological aspects associated with each resource. Ethnobotanical research with Brazilian extractive communities can be regarded as one such model.

ACKNOWLEDGMENTS

The manual was produced with support from the "Periwinkle Project" of the Rain Forest Alliance. Support was made possible through a donation from TOM's of Maine, Inc.

REFERENCES

Allegreti, M. H. 1990. "Extractive Reserves: An Alternative for Reconciling Development and Environmental Conservation in Amazonia." In A. B. Anderson, ed., *Alternatives to Deforestation: Step Toward Sustainable Use of the Amazon Rain Forest*, p. 252–62, New York: Columbia University Press.

Anderson, A. B. 1992. "Land-Use Strategies for Successful Extractive Economies in Amazonia." In D. C. Nepstad and S. Schwartzman, ed., *Non-Timber Products from Tropical Forests; Evaluation of a Conservation and Development Strategy*, pp. 67–77, *Advances in Economic Botany*, vol. 9, New York: New York Botanical Garden.

Anderson, A. B., A. Gely, J. Strudwick, G. L. Sobel, and M. G. C. Pinto. 1985. "Um sistema agroflorestal na várzea do estuário Amazônico (Ilhas das Onças, Município de Barcarena, Estado do Pará)." *Acta Amazônica,* 15 (1–2) (supl.):195–224.

Balandrin, M. F., J. F. Klocke, E. S. Wurtele, and W. H. Bollinger. 1985. "Natural Plant Chemicals: Sources of Industrial and Medicinal Materials." *Science* 228:1154–60.

Baleé, W. 1986. "Análise preliminar de inventário florestal e a etnobotânica Kaapor (Maranhão)." *Boletim do Museu Paraense Emílio Goeldi* 2 (2):141–67.

Balick, M. J. and R. Mendelsohn. 1992. "Assessing the Economic Value of Traditional Medicines from Tropical Rainforests." *Conservation Biology* 6 (1):128–30.

Bennett, B. C. 1992. "Plants and People of the Amazonian Rainforests: The Role of Ethnobotany in Sustainable Development." *BioScience* 42 (8):599–607.

Clay, J. 1992. "Some General Principles and Strategies for Developing Markets in North America and Europe for Nontimber Forest Products." In M. Plotkin and L. Famolare, eds., *Sustainable Harvest and Marketing of Rain Forest Products,* pp. 302–9. Washington, D.C.: Conservation International, Island Press.

Cunningham, A. B. 1993. *Ethics, Ethnobiological Research, and Biodiversity.* Gland, Switzerland: WWF International Publications.

Fearnside, P. M. 1989. "Extractive Reserves in Brazilian Amazonia—An Opportunity to Maintain Tropical Forest Under Sustainable Use." *BioScience* 39 (6):387–93.

Homma, A. K. O. 1989. *A extração de recursos naturais renováveis: O caso do extrativismo vegetal na Amazônia.* Minas Gerais, Brazil: Universidade Federal de Viçosa.

Kainer, K. A. and M. L. Duryea. 1992. "Tapping Women's Knowledge: Plant Resource Use in Extractive Reserves, Acre, Brazil." *Economic Botany* 46 (4):408–25.

Milliken, W., R. P. Miller, S. R. Pollard, and E. V. Wandelli. 1992. *The Ethnobotany of the Waimiri Atroari Indians of Brazil.* In D. V. Field and J. A. Ratter, eds., Kew: Royal Botanic Gardens. 146 pp.

Padoch, C. 1992. "Marketing of Non-Timber Forest Products in Western Amazonia: General Observation and Research Priorities." In D. C. Nepstad and S. Schwartzman, eds., *Non-Timber Products from Tropical Forests; Evaluation of a Conservation and Development Strategy,* pp. 43–50. *Advances in Economic Botany,* vol. 9. New York: New York Botanical Garden.

Peters, C. P., A. H. Gentry, and R. O. Mendelsohn. 1989. "Valuation of an Amazonian Rainforest." *Nature* 339:655–56.

Posey, D. A. 1992. "Traditional Knowledge, Conservation and the Rain Forest Harvest." In M. Plotkin and L. Famolare, eds., *Sustainable Harvest and Marketing of Rain Forest Products,* pp. 46–50. Washington, D.C.: Conservation International, Island Press.

Reid, W. V., S. A. Laird, C. A. Meyer, R. Gómez, A. Sittenfeld, D. H. Janzen, M. C. Gollin, and C. Juma, eds. 1993. "A New Lease on Life." In *Biodiversity Prospecting: Using Genetic Resources for Sustainable Development,* pp. 1–52. Washington, D.C.: World Resources Institute.

Schwartzman, S. 1989. "Extractive Reserve: The Rubber Tappers' Strategy for Sustainable Use of the Amazonian Rain Forest." In J. O. Browder, ed., *Fragile Lands of Latin America: Strategies for Sustainable Development,* pp. 150–65, Boulder, Colo.: Westview Press.

Tobias, D. and R. Mendelsohn. 1990. "The Value of Recreation in a Tropical Rainforest Reserve." *Ambio* 20:91–93.

Tyler, V. E. 1986. "Plant Drugs in the Twenty-First Century." *Economic Botany* 40:93–103.

Ziffer, K. 1992. "The Tagua Initiative: Building the Market for a Rain Forest Product." In M. Plotkin and L. Famolare, eds., *Sustainable Harvest and Marketing of Rain Forest Products,* pp. 274–79. Washington, D.C.: Conservation International, Island Press.

Appendix:
Manual for Plant Collections

Elaine Elisabetsky, Rachel Trajber, and Lin Chao Ming

Why Research Natural Products?

The people in communities that live very close to the forest, savannah, river, ocean, *várzea*, or *igapó* know that in each of these places there are plants, animals, soil, or water that can be useful or dangerous. All these comprise the *natural resources* used by the communities.

In this manual we talk more about plants. Some we eat, others we use for medicines, and from others we make *paneiros*,[1] *tipitis*,[1] *cavacos*,[1] walls for our homes, and many other things. The knowledge of these plant uses is part of a tradition that has passed from generation to generation, from mother to daughter, from grandfather to grandson, from neighbor to neighbor. And all of it stays stored in peoples' heads.

Local people know something and think that everyone else also knows it. But, for example, by traveling just a bit we find that many people have never even heard of *copaiba*.[2] This manual was prepared to teach communities how to collect, document, and organize the information about their natural resources. This activity is important in order to have more control over traditional knowledge and to decide which use to give to the natural treasures of their homeland.

Each locality has different resources. Each person lives differently and has individual knowledge. Often the knowledge of resource use discovered by one person can be used by another. Each person's knowledge of the resource may have other uses and values to other people. For example, an oil used for lamps in the forest can be used for machines in the city; the plant's perfume becomes part of a shampoo, a fruit is made into ice cream, a nut becomes a cookie.

Because each natural resource can be used in various ways and by various communities, it can also be produced in greater quantities to be sold or exchanged among communities. This idea can be good for the forest communities because as more products are collected, processed, and commercialized, more income sources can be developed for the community.

Other advantages accrue to a community knowing and administering its own resources. If one resource produces less or its sales diminish, others are available to take its place and help sustain the community. Another advantage is that the type of work used to produce the various products allows more family members—elders, women, and children—to participate and help according to their strength, time, and manner. In addition, cultivating various plants helps protect the local soil.

Who Studies Natural Resources?

Lately many researchers and scientists have been writing in notebooks, measuring, photographing, recording conversations, filming, collecting plants, and asking how to use a leaf or how to make a bath or a tea. One part of this research is to obtain information on plants of a region that can be used as medicine, perfume, food, or fiber or for other uses that industries may want to buy.

Scientists and researchers are of many types, and each one studies different subjects. The study of the community's knowledge of its natural resources is called *ethnobiology* (*ethno* = people, *biology* = study of live beings). The study of the knowledge of useful plants is called *ethnobotany* (*ethno* = people, *botany* = study of plants). There is also the field of *economic botany*, which studies plants that can be cultivated and commercialized.

Much of the research can be carried out by the community itself. This manual teaches how to collect ethnobotanical information, because those who have organized information can negotiate. The knowledge belongs to the community and the community should decide what to do with it. This manual will be useful to the communities that decide to organize their knowledge of useful resources and want to exchange information, as well as to those communities that are willing to commercialize their products.

Even with the community as part of the research, cooperation with scientists and researchers is still important. But this cooperation is different because the community and the researchers participate together in the study. Local people collect material and organize its knowledge, and researchers complete the part of the study that has to be done in laboratories, help in the contacts with companies, and promote the communities' work. Researchers assist in providing technical direction so that the community can have an informed voice in deciding the destiny of its resources.

What Information Must Be Collected?

It is not inconceivable to imagine that in an extractive community various products are collected and commercialized. In the same way that rubber, Brazil nuts, and *guaraná* have turned into large-scale commercial products, other products can become important sources of money and jobs. To find out which plants might become such products, it is necessary to find information, that is, to *research* plants and their uses. The best way to do this is to study the plants in the environment in which they grow. Because it is not always possible for us to study and know the plants, we *collect* a piece of each type of plant.

Ethnobotanical research is done by going from home to home, asking people how plants are used, *collecting plants,* and making a *form* for each one. The plants have to be researched and explained in a way that everyone can understand; this way they turn into *information* and the knowledge can be used by others. This kind of research has special norms and rules that allow the exchange of information. It is a bit like dancing: we listen to the music, follow the rules of dancing, and are able to perform the right steps without stepping on our partner's feet. By following the same rules, even two people who do not speak the same language can dance together. By following the same research rules, information can also be exchanged by different peoples and countries.

Research on plants has many steps, takes a long time to be done, and is very costly. The first and most important step is to collect the plant and find out its purpose. To do that, there is a need for appropriate *material* with which to *collect* and *store* plants, and also a collection form must be completed. Because the plant does not speak, things like its odor, its use, or the way to prepare it must be described. All information must therefore be written on a form.

The form that comes with this manual has spaces for information on four topics: the *collector,* the *person interviewed,* the *collected plant,* and the *use of collected plant.* By following the indications and completing all the information requested in each part, the form itself will direct the research on each plant. The forms will help organize the information.

Collection Form

COLLECTOR

The collector is the person who does the interviews, collects the plants, and writes notes. The name and address of who collected the information must be written down on the form of each plant.

The collection number must be written on the top corner of the first page of each form. Each collector gives a number for each plant collected, starting with number 1. This number helps to organize the collected material, connecting each collected plant to the form that contains the information about that plant. The plant will have the same number that is on the form.

Each form corresponds to a plant. Plants that have more than one use have the same collection number but have a form for each use.

For example, an *açaizeiro*[3] will have only one number. If the person interviewed gives five uses for the plant, this *açaizeiro* will have five forms. One form for the fruit ("*açaí*" wine—used as food), one for the leaf (straw—fiber), one for the "trunk's eye" (palm heart—food), one for the trunk (wood—used in house construction) and one for the root (used as medicine).

If another *açaizeiro* is collected in another place, the plant and the form will have another number. If the person interviewed gives only two uses, this plant will have only two forms.

PERSON INTERVIEWED (INFORMANT)

The person interviewed is the one who gives the information. This person shows the plant and explains the uses written on the form. It is important to know the name of each person who gave the information, the name and nickname by which the person is known, and where the person lives. Maybe one day there will be the need to verify, complete, or improve the information, and knowing who gave it will make it easier to find out.

The birthplace must be given in detail, especially if the person interviewed has been living at the place for a short time. The person may have brought the plant knowledge from somewhere else, where the uses can be different from those in the place where the interview is being done. That is not bad, but it is important to have the information because sometimes there are plants, especially medicinal plants, that look alike but have different uses.

Each profession gives a person a different type of knowledge about the uses for plants. A midwife, for example, knows more about plants that are important for pregnant women and babies. Mothers have knowledge of medicine for aches and more common illnesses and have good recipes for using plants for food. A shaman or healer works with many plant remedies for peoples' diseases, and so on.

COLLECTED PLANT

The name of the plant must be written down. All plants have names, some have more than one, and many times different plants may have the same name. If the plant has more than one name, this can cause confusion, and hence, all names must be written in the form.

That is why we have to collect plants, study them, and give them scientific names. When a scientist studies a plant, it receives one name that becomes unique to it. It is as if it were the baptismal name.

We collect plant *samples.* A sample is a piece taken from a plant, arranged, and dried according to some norms. For each sample to be a perfect representation of the plant, it has to be carefully prepared. Only by observance of these norms can plant samples be preserved and even travel to other places to be studied.

Two samples of each plant must be collected. This way, one always stays in the community, while the other may be sent to other places.

The most simple method of collection requires the following materials:

Black pencil—to complete the form
Sharp scissors—to cut the sample
Newspaper—to separate the samples
Wood press—to push the sample onto the newspaper
Nylon cord—to tie up the press

This material must be with the person at each collection interview. The collector asks the people interviewed for the plants they know and use. Samples of the plants that the people mention must be collected, and the forms must be completed.

Seven steps should be followed in collecting plants:

1. Cut a twig or branch ranging from 30 to 40 cm in size. The branch has to be healthy, should not have been eaten by animals, and should not look sick.
    Collect two samples from the same plant.
    The right way is to collect a *branch with leaves and flowers*. For a scientist who wants to name a plant, the most important thing is the study of the flower. If it does not have flowers, collect what is available along with the leaves; this can be a fruit, seed, or pieces of root. During another season, when the plant has flowers, collect it again to have a complete sample. If the plant is small, it can be collected as a whole, including roots.
    If the part of the plant that is useful for the people is not the branch with leaves and flowers, you may collect this useful part also. For example, if the trunk is used for a medicine, a piece of it can be collected along with the branch with leaves and flowers.
2. Put the branch in the middle of a folded newspaper page. Each sample should be put in a different page.
    If the branch has many leaves, flowers, and fruits, you need to cut some, always leaving a piece of the stem. If the branch is bigger than the page, the plant must be cut or folded very carefully so that it fits perfectly. No part of the plant can be off the newspaper page.
    Turn one or two leaves of the branch upside down. This way both sides of the leaf may be seen or studied after being dried without breaking.
    When a branch is collected, quickly write the collection number on the corner of the form. Write the same number on the newspaper page of each plant sample. This newspaper will always be with the plant. This way, the sample will have the same number as the form.
    Large fruits and tubers may be collected in paper bags or wrapped in newspaper. The same collection number must again be written on the tuber or fruit's paper.
3. Pile up the samples that are inside the newspaper pages. Put the pile between the two wood presses. Tie everything very tightly with the nylon cord. This way, everything stays tied and is easier to carry.

It is important to dry the plants so they will not become molded; otherwise they will rot and the work will be lost. Drying should be done at the end of the collection day. If the samples cannot be dried on the same day, put some alcohol in each one. Then, put the samples with their newspaper in a plastic bag and tie the end well. By doing that, the plant will not rot for a couple of days.

There are a few ways to dry the plants. The easiest method that can be used at home needs the following: cardboard to put between the samples, cut to the size of the folded newspaper; wood or charcoal stove.

4. Undo the press and separate the samples. They should always stay inside the pages.

Make a new pile. This time, put the cardboard after each sample: one cardboard, one sample, one cardboard, one sample, and so on.

Put this pile in between the wood presses and tie it tightly with cords.

5. Hang the pile to dry on top of the wood or charcoal stove. For the sample to dry well, the pile has to be placed on its side. This way, the smoke and heat can pass in between the samples and reach all of them.

The bags with large fruits and tubers have to be dried along with the paper. Do not press them. Be careful, do not put them too close to the fire and burn them!

6. The time that the pile stays hanged to dry varies a lot, depending on the amount of heat and the type of plants. This can take many days. The sample is ready when it is dry. To find out if it is already dried, press a leaf against your finger tips: if it breaks, the sample is ready for storage.

Check each sample of the pile. Separate those that are dried. Put those that are not yet dried back in the pile, close the press, tie them—but not too hard so the plants do not break—and hang them back on top of the oven.

In order not to damage the dry samples, they must be kept in a place protected from humidity and animals. To store them you need the following materials:

Plastic bag—to keep the dried samples
Cord—to tie the bags

7. Put the samples (plant and newspaper page with the collection number) inside the plastic bag. Take the air out of the bag. Tie the end very tightly with cord.

If all this is done correctly, the samples may be conserved for a long time. For the scientists to study, these are as good as live plants.

When the plant is to be used for only one thing, it will get only one form, even when many of its parts go into the preparation. When the plant has more than one use, it will have more than one form. For *each* use make a new form.

The collected and dried sample has no color, odor, or sap. You cannot tell the plant's height or where it came from by looking only at a small, dry branch. The information that cannot be deduced has to be available on the form. Estimate the plant's height and write it down.

It is important to know the type of plant from which the sample was obtained. If it is short with green and soft branches like the *jambu,* call it an herb. If it is a tall plant with a hard trunk, call it a tree. If the plant climbs, hangs, or wraps around another, it is called a vine. In case something is interesting or different, and it is not called for in the form, write it down at the end of the page of the form.

Use of the Collected Plant

Each plant has its use. Some yield oil from the seeds, others are used to make fish poison, some provide a dye from the bark, or others are useful only for their fruit. For that reason, for each plant you must mark the square indicating whether it is used for food, wood, oil, fertilizer, poison, fiber, dye, beauty product, or medicine.

What guides the collection form is the use of the plant. When the plant has more than one use, it will have more than one form. For each use of the same plant, you make a new form, repeating the collection number.

Each part of the plant is different and may or may not serve us. Only the part that is useful must be marked on the form. When the leaf is used, the root may be useful or harmful to us. Sometimes the fruit of a plant may be eaten, but the seeds, if eaten, make a person sick. If it is not marked correctly, we will not know which part to use. When more than one part is used for the same purpose, for instance, a tea that is made including leaves and stems in the recipe, all the parts used must be marked on the form.

It is important to know whether the plant part must be used fresh or whether it may also be used when dried. That information is useful to those who live far from its source—whether they can keep it dried at home. Also, some plants vanish in the summer or in the winter. By knowing that it can also be used dried, we know that it can be collected in quantities to be kept and used at times when it is not actually growing in the earth. When it can be used dried, it is more easily saved in large quantities or transported to other places. In case it can be used both dry and fresh, mark both options in the plant form.

How do you make a food or medicine? The recipe must have information starting with the day of collecting the plant, the quantity to be used, the way of preparing it, and the way to use it.

Sometimes the way of preparing it makes the plant useful or makes it so dangerous that it can even kill; for example, the *tucupí*[4]: fresh it is poisonous; when it is boiled it can be used in the *tacacá,*[5] in the pepper sauce and other foods.

Sometimes a medicine prepared in cold water is potent but when boiled it loses all its strength. Other times it is the other way around: you have to leave the root in boiling sugar for a long time for the syrup to have substance.

It is very important to explain very well how to prepare a natural resource. The elders always say that, in the past, things used to last longer because they were done better. When a recipe is not explained well, the plant is badly prepared and does not work well. We might think the plant has no value, but actually it was not prepared well.

There are many recipes in which one plant is not used alone but is mixed with others. When mixed, the recipe has to have only the names of the other plants, while the collected plant has to be described in detail. For each plant that goes into the mixture and is collected, a new form must be filled out.

1. Food.   The majority of things that we eat are made of plants. Some are grown in the fields, others at *jiraus,* and others are harvested from the forest. There are plants that we do not eat but can feed to livestock (chicken, pig, cow).

2. Wood.   It is important to know for what each type of wood can be used. Some woods only float on the *igarapé* and are used for bridges, some woods are so soft they can be used for toys, and some woods are especially good for building canoes or boats.

3. Oil.   Oils can be used in the kitchen or used as medicines, such as the oils of *Andiroba,*[6] *Copaiba,*[6] or *Carrapicho.*[6] Other oils may light lanterns. There are those that give soap its consistency or that, when put on skin or burnt at home, keep insects away. There are also oils with a perfume or scent that we can make into perfumes, put on the water when washing cloths, or even put on the body and hair as a beauty aid.

4. Fibers.   Fibers can be used to make many things, such as hammocks, roofs, and even sieves or *tipití.* Write down the use of the fiber collected. Some might be useful for furniture or basketry in the cities.

5. Fertilizer.   Many plants can be used to protect or enrich the soil—those are what we call fertilizers. It is necessary to write on the collection form what the use of the particular fertilizer is and when it should be used to improve soil fertility.

6. Poison.   Many poisons are made from plants. The *timbó* itself is poison for fish. The uses of plant poisons must be well discussed in the form. There are plants that keep ants and roaches away or that kill ticks or fleas. You have to find out if the insects are killed or just chased away. It is important to write for which insect it works or whether it is effective against many types. Information is also needed regarding the preparation of the poison. Is it to be just mixed in water? In detergent? In kerosene? Is it to be mixed with flour, making a bait, and placed into the insect nests? In the appropriate space on the plant form you have to write exactly how the poison is prepared.

Is the prepared poison to be put in nests? Or is it to be put on the tracks? In this space you have to write how and in what special situation it is used.

7. Dye.   There are plants that give off dye and can be used to paint fabrics, sieves, and other things. The *urucum,* for example, gives color to food. The color given off by the plant must be indicated.

8. Beauty/hygiene.   Products that are used to take care of and to clean the skin, teeth, or hair are very much in demand by industry. Many plants are used in beauty baths, and at times roots, leaves, and bark go into the mixture that can be transformed into perfume. There are oils that are good to put on the skin to clear out stains, and there are others that are good as sun screen.

9. Medicine.   Many medicines made from plants can be of use to many people. Actually, many medicines in pharmacies are made from plants. But we do not notice this because the medicine industry takes only the plant parts that can cure. Like other natural resources, plants used as medicine can be an important resource if industries are able to utilize the medicinal plants that are known to the communities.

Uses: There are many diseases and each medicine is used for certain ones. There are medicines for aches, fevers, colds, coughs, menstrual cramps, diarrhea, *frieira,*[7] *esipla,*[7] furunculosis, rheumatism, *impinge,*[7] and many other diseases. With a good explanation of the disease that the plant cures, we will be able to pay more attention to the curative strength of the medicine. In this way, studies of the use of traditional knowledge can continue for the community and other people.

A medicine can be useful only when it is prepared properly. The explanation of the method of preparation should read as follows:

- How to collect the plant part
- How much of the plant part that goes into the recipe (a handful? only two leaves?)
- What to do with the part (wash? scrape? shred?)
- What and how much to mix it with? (a glass of hot water? 1 liter of red wine?)
- How much of the mixture to be taken (one spoonful? one cup?)
- How many times a day (once a day? three times a week?)
- For how long (only one day? months? until cured?)

How to prepare: if it is prepared as one of the methods indicated in the form just mark it; if it is a different method you will have to write it down.

WHAT WILL BE DONE WITH THE COLLECTED INFORMATION?

As we already know, after some training with this manual, the communities will be able to collect ethnobotanical information. After plants and forms are collected for a while, a collection of information will be formed that can be lost or in which relocation of certain information is difficult.

For the collection to be more useful, plants collected in the field have to be organized and properly arranged, so that the collection becomes information that can be easily shared by the people of the community itself. It can also be used to exchange with people from other communities, researchers, scientists, companies, and all those involved in transforming resources into commercial products. A *data bank* is a way of organizing information in lists by subject. The collection forms can be arranged in groups of plants according to a given use:

plants used as food
plants used as wood
plants used as oil
plants used as fertilizer
plants used as poison
plants used as fiber
plants used as dye
plants used as beauty products
plants used as medicine

With the information arranged in such groups, people of the community can easily find certain types of information.

The question now is: Through what path must the information pass to bring these benefits?

The collected information can become a product with real benefits for many only if information is organized, tested, negotiated, managed, and commercialized. The *data bank* allows the community to know and better control the use of its resources, to exchange information with other communities or researchers, to complete its knowledge with the study done in the laboratories, and to decide what to cultivate and to negotiate.

For example, if someone has diarrhea, all the plant-based medicines that can be helpful and their preparations are found in the data bank. If neighboring communities have other lists, the collection can be increased and the information exchanged. If the medicine industry is interested in medicines for cough, a list of plants that are useful can be negotiated. If perfume is needed, a list of plants that produce pleasant scents can be bought. Following this, communities can benefit more from their resources.

LABORATORY USE

Another path the natural resource research might take is to combine the information collected at the community with the studies that are done in laboratories. The laboratories can be at universities as well as in industries. At these laboratories, tests are done that can complement the traditional knowledge, for example, to clarify whether a given medicine is effective for all kinds of fevers or only for malaria. Or the laboratory will do some tests to find new uses for a given resource, for example, to see whether the oil used for lanterns at a community can also be used in city machinery.

Negotiation

When a plant that can become a product is found, one of the things to be done is to make a contract between people who will grow and/or collect the plant and the company that makes the product. Contracts are written documents of promise between those most interested in the same business. In a contract, it is decided who makes what and who gets what; who takes responsibility and who receives what benefit. When the contract is signed by both parts, it signifies that the interested parties agree with what was decided.

Management and Commercialization

The peoples from the forest live by the resources that are located in the different types of areas around the community. Besides knowing the uses and dangers associated with each resource, they know of other things like the following:

- the type of place in which each resource exist
- the times when a given resource is more abundant or scarce
- the easiest way to collect each resource
- the correct way of collecting a plant so it will regenerate
- whether the plant can be planted and, if so, where and how
- the best way to prepare the resource for use
- other important aspects that allow for the resources to be beneficial to the community

When we refer to all these ways to deal with a given plant or the place where it exists so that the people can make the best possible use of the resource, we are talking about *resource management.* The kind of management that the communities use for their resources is appropriate to the number of resources the community uses for its own needs. When a given plant becomes a commercial product, the quantity to be collected increases and the management of the resources might have to be different so that the plant will not disappear altogether. The study of the best way to collect plant resources according to the quantity that will be used is part of the studies that are done along with the community.

Products

The commercialization of resources can be done only if it results in benefits for the local people and exploitation of that resource will not lead to the destruction of other resources that are so important for the survival of the community. Natural resources are incredibly important for peoples' lives, and it is because these resources exist in their environment that the people do not have to leave and buy everything they need in the cities. After all, no one wants to exchange one problem for another. What we want is to find solutions for the many problems in such a way that the whole situation gets better.

Since the information about the plants is of particular interest to the pharmaceutical industries and companies that produce beauty products (cosmetics) that are searching for natural materials to develop new products, the community must know its rights and obligations and the conditions for negotiating the information collected and organized. Lawyers, researchers, nongovernment organizations, and other specialists could help communities in these issues, which are extremely complicated.

NOTES

1. Home utensils.
2. Well-known plant-based remedy in the Amazon basin.
3. Well-known palm with a variety of uses.
4. Juice produced when manioc is processed to flour.
5. Typical food.
6. Examples of well-known medicinal oils.
7. Very common skin diseases in the Brazilian Amazon.

Epilogue

Richard Deertrack

I THANK the Rainforest Alliance and The New York Botanical Garden for the invaluable opportunity to write on behalf of my people of Taos Pueblo and to address their deep concern about the preservation of a way of life that is threatened throughout the world. I speak of an ancient heritage that echos from the Kivas, the rivers of old, and the mountains worn with age.

You undertake to approach the Caretakers of the Forest and share in their knowledge and their sacred medicinals. These are the ones that carry the knowledge of the Ancient Ones still among us. They know that what you ask for is not for the Red Man, the Black Man, or for any color of man, but was given by the Life Spirit for the nurturance of all. With this great gift comes a responsibility toward life itself: to know that our relatives, the Green People, are equal in Spirit to Humankind; that they are here for a purpose beyond the needs of the men and women of this Earth.

The Ancient Ones of the forest are not going to understand your curiosity, why you explore what gives breath, movement, and existence to the ones that bring healing. They will not understand your wanting to capture the Spirit of the Green Ones, the same way they grieve at how you must harness the waters, possess the ocean, or desecrate the Earth itself in order to satisfy your needs.

All of us come together and begin to ask, what is a fair exchange for our needs? How do we address such a thing? The lives of all Native Peoples are deeply interwoven with the Earth, the Waters, the Four-Legged Ones, the Winged Ones. These are our friends. We share in their communities, receive and give life so that all may prosper and live upon these lands in the way that was meant by the Great Spirit.

It has always been that if anyone comes to us in need, we ask not what is there for us but give of a free heart. This has left us vulnerable to a people who do not understand that we cannot possess or own the elements of the Earth or those that move freely across its surface. What you must first understand in order to share in a way of respect with those "of the Earth" is that your way of life is in deep conflict with our beliefs. If this issue is not faced with deep sensitivity, you may continue the path of destruction that threatens our ability to survive. This is why my people have sent me to address you. They ask that you sit down with us, open your hearts, and begin to understand who we are as a people. We cannot represent our relatives from the south, but we know as indigenous people of the Earth that what we share as a heritage is something held in common.

Contributors

D. K. Abbiw. Department of Botany, University of Ghana, P.O. Box 55, Legon/ Accra, Ghana.

Miguel N. Alexiades. Institute of Economic Botany, The New York Botanical Garden, Bronx, NY 10458–5126, USA.

Rosita Arvigo. Ix Chel Tropical Research Foundation, San Ignacio Cayo, Belize, Central America.

Peter S. Ashton. Arnold Arboretum, Harvard University, 22 Divinity Avenue, Cambridge, MA 02138, USA.

Bruce A. Aylward. Environmental Economics Program, International Institute for Environment and Development, Apdo 8–3870, San José 1000, Costa Rica.

Michael J. Balick. Institute of Economic Botany, The New York Botanical Garden, Bronx, NY 10458–5126, USA.

Michael R. Boyd. Natural Products Branch, Developmental Therapeutics Program, Division of Cancer Treatment, National Cancer Institute, Frederick Cancer Research and Development Center, Bldg. 1052, Room 109, Frederick, MD 21702–1201, USA.

Alba R. M. Souza Brito. Departamento de Fisiologia e Biofísica, Instituto de Biologia UNICAMP, 13083-970 Campinas, São Paulo, Brazil.

Antonio A. Souza Brito. Departamento de Fisiologia e Biofísica, Instituto de Biologia UNICAMP, 13083-970 Campinas, São Paulo, Brazil.

Lynn H. Caporale. CombiChem, Inc., 11099 North Torrey Pines Road, Suite 200, La Jolla, CA 92037, USA.

Brad K. Carté. SmithKline Beecham Pharmaceuticals, Research and Development, 709 Swedeland Road, P.O. Box 1539, King of Prussia, PA 19406–0939, USA.

Lisa A. Conte. Shaman Pharmaceuticals, Inc., 213 E. Grand Avenue, South San Francisco, CA 94080–4812, USA.

Gordon M. Cragg. Natural Products Branch, Developmental Therapeutics Program, Division of Cancer Treatment, National Cancer Institute, Frederick Cancer Research and Development Center, Bldg. 1052, Room 109, Frederick, MD 21702–1201, USA.

Douglas C. Daly. Institute of Systematic Botany, The New York Botanical Garden, Bronx, NY 10458–5126, USA.

Douglas Davidson. Department of Biology, McMaster University, Hamilton, Ontario, Canada L8S 4K1, Canada.

Richard Deertrack. The Organic Agricultural Project, Blue Corn Trading Company, P.O. Box 951, Taos Pueblo, NM 87571, USA.

James A. Duke. National Germplasm Resources Laboratory, U.S. Department of Agriculture, Beltsville, MD 20705, USA.

B. N. Dhawan. Central Drug Research Institute, Chattar Manzil, Post Box No. 173, Lucknow 226 001, India.

Elaine Elisabetsky. Ethnofarmacologia—UFRGS, Caixa Postal 5072, 90.041 Porto Alegre RS, Brasil.

Rodrigo Gámez. Instituto Nacional de Biodiversidad, Apdo. 22–3100, Santo Domingo, Heredia, Costa Rica.

Michael A. Gollin. Keck, Mahin & Cate, 1201 New York Avenue, NW, Washington, DC 20005–3919, USA.

Charlotte Gyllenhaal. Program for Collaborative Research in the Pharmaceutical Sciences—M/C 877, College of Pharmacy, 833 S. Wood Street, University of Illinois at Chicago, Chicago, IL 60612, USA.

Peter J. Hylands. Laundry Cottage, Yewleigh Lane, Upton-Upon-Seven, Worcestershire, WR8 OQW, United Kingdom.

Maurice M. Iwu. Walter Reed Army Institute of Research, Division of Experimental Therapeutics, Washington, DC 20307–5100, USA.

Daniel Janzen. Department of Biology, University of Pennsylvania, Philadelphia, PA 19107, USA.

Randall K. Johnson. SmithKline Beecham Pharmaceuticals, Research and Development, 709 Swedeland Road, P.O. Box 1539, King of Prussia, PA 19406–0939, USA.

Calestous Juma. African Center for Technology Studies, P.O. Box 45917, Nairobi, Kenya.

Steven R. King. Ethnobotany and Conservation, Shaman Pharmaceuticals, Inc., 213 E. Grand Avenue, South San Francisco, CA 94080–4812, USA.

Jack R. Kloppenburg Jr. Department of Rural Sociology, University of Wisconsin–Madison, 350 Agricultural Hall, 1450 Linden Drive, Madison, WI 53706, USA.

Didier Lacaze D. Consultores SERI, Casilla 524, Cuzco, Peru.

E. Laing. Department of Botany, University of Ghana, P.O. Box 55, Legon/Accra, Ghana.

Sarah A. Laird. Rainforest Alliance, 65 Bleeker Street, New York, NY 10011, USA.

Charles F. Limbach. Natividad Medical Center, P.O. 80008, Salinas, CA 93912, USA.

Xavier Lozoya. Instituto Mexicano del Seguro Social, Centro Medico Nacional Siglo XXI, Coordinacion de Investigación Médica, División de Evaluacion, Av. Cuauhtemoc 330 Col. Doctores, Bloque B Unidad de Congresos. 4º. piso., México, D. F. CP 06725.

James D. McChesney. Research Institute of Pharmaceutical Sciences, School of Pharmacy, The University of Mississippi, University, MS 38677, USA.

Robert Mendelsohn. Yale University, School of Forestry and Environmental Studies, 360 Prospect Street, New Haven, CT 06511, USA.

Lin Chao Ming. Universidade Estadual de São Paulo, Botucatú, Brazil.

Domingos Sávio Nunes. Department of Chemistry, Universidade Federal do Pará, Campus Universitário do Guamá, 66065-360 Belém, PA, Brazil.

G. T. Odamtten. Department of Botany, University of Ghana, P.O. Box 55, Legon/Accra, Ghana.

Peter P. Principe. National Exposure Research Laboratory (MD-80A), U.S. Environmental Protection Agency, Research Triangle Park, NC 27711, USA.

Luc Van Puyvelde. Department of Organic Chemistry, Faculty of Agricultural and Applied Biological Sciences, University of Gent, Coupure Links 653, B-9000 Gent, BELGIUM.

Walter V. Reid. Program in Forest & Biodiversity, World Resources Institute, 1709 New York Avenue, N.W., Washington, DC 20006, USA.

Lionel Robineau. ENDA-CARIBE, Apdo 3370, Santo Domingo, Dominican Republic.

Georg Albers-Schönberg. 43 Scribner Court, Princeton, NJ 08540-6764, USA.

William Rod Sharp. The State University of New Jersey Rutgers, Cook College, New Jersey Agricultural Experiment Station, P.O. Box 231, New Brunswick, NJ 08903–0231, USA.

Gregory Shropshire. Ix Chel Tropical Research Foundation, San Ignacio, Cayo, Belize, Central America.

Ana Sittenfeld. Instituto Nacional de Biodiversidad, Apartado 22–3100, Santo Domingo, Heredia, Costa Rica.

Djaja Doel Soejarto. Program for Collaborative Research in the Pharmaceutical Sciences, College of Pharmacy, University of Illinois at Chicago, 833 S. Wood St., Chicago, IL 60612, USA.

S. H. Sohmer. Botanical Research Institute of Texas, 509 Pecan Street, Fort Worth, TX 76102–4060, USA.

Roy W. Stahlhut. Sun Hill Research Institute, Sam Yang Group, 63-2 Hwaam-dong, Yusung-gu, Taejon 305-348, South Korea.

Rachel Trajber. Imagens Conteúdo e Forma, São Paulo, Botucatú, Brazil.

Varro E. Tyler. Department of Medicinal Chemistry and Pharmacognosy, Purdue University, 1333 Robert E. Heine Pharmacy Building, West Lafayette, IN 47907–1333, USA.

Werner Wilbert. Instituto Caribe de Antropología y Sociología, Fundación La Salle de Ciencias Naturales, Apartado 1930, Caracas, Venezuela 1010-A.

Index